MARKETING:
Volume 2

PEARSON CUSTOM PUBLISHING

MARKETING: Volume 2

Compiled from:

Marketing Management
Fourteenth Edition
by Philip Kotler and Kevin Lane Keller

Marketing Research: An Applied Approach
Third European Edition
by Naresh K. Malhotra and David F. Birks

Innovation Management and New Product Development
Fifth Edition
by Paul Trott

Learning from Case Studies
Second Edition
by Geoff Easton

Marketing Management
Second Edition
by Philip Kotler, Kevin Keller, Mairead Brady, Malcolm Goodman and Torben Hansen

PEARSON

Harlow, England • London • New York • Boston • San Francisco • Toronto • Sydney • Auckland • Singapore • Hong Kong
Tokyo • Seoul • Taipei • New Delhi • Cape Town • Sao Paulo • Mexico City • Madrid • Amsterdam • Munich • Paris • Milan

Pearson Education Limited
Edinburgh Gate
Harlow
Essex CM20 2JE

And associated companies throughout the world

Visit us on the World Wide Web at:
www.pearsoned.co.uk

This Custom Book Edition © Pearson Education Limited 2012

Compiled from:

Marketing Management
Fourteenth Edition
by Philip Kotler and Kevin Lane Keller
ISBN 978 0 273 75336 0
© Pearson Education Limited 2012

Marketing Research: An Applied Approach
Third European Edition
by Naresh K. Malhotra and David F. Birks
ISBN 978 0 273 70689 2
© Pearson Education Limited 2000, 2003, 2006, 2007

Innovation Management and New Product Development
Fifth Edition
by Paul Trott
ISBN 978 0 273 73656 1
© Pearson Professional Limited 1998
© Pearson Education 2002, 2005, 2008, 2012

Learning From Case Studies
Second Edition
by Geoff Easton
ISBN 978 0 13 528688 3
© Prentice Hall Europe 1982, 1992

Marketing Management
Second Edition
by Philip Kotler, Kevin Keller, Mairead Brady, Malcolm Goodman
and Torben Hansen
ISBN 978 0 273 74361 3
© Pearson Education Limited 2009, 2012

ISBN 978 1 78236 469 6

Printed and bound in Great Britain by Clays Ltd, Bungay, Suffolk

Contents

Section 7

Marketing Communication

Managing Mass Communications: Advertising, Sales Promotions, Events and Experiences, and Public Relations

Although there has been an enormous increase in the use of personal communications by marketers in recent years, due to the rapid penetration of the Internet and other factors, the fact remains that mass media, if used correctly, is still an important component of a modern marketing communications program. The old days of "if you build a great ad, they will come," however, are long gone. To generate consumer interest and sales, mass media must often be supplemented and carefully integrated with other communications, as was the case with Procter & Gamble's Old Spice.[1]

 Among the more successful of the 30-second ads estimated to cost over $2.5 million to run during the broadcast of the 2010 Super Bowl was one for Old Spice body wash. Turning a potential negative of being an old brand into a positive of being experienced, Old Spice has made a remarkable transformation in recent years from "your father's aftershave" to a contemporary men's fragrance brand. In a new strategic move, given their important role in the purchase process, the Super Bowl spot targeted women as well as men. The tongue-in-cheek ad featured rugged ex-NFL football player Isaiah Mustafa as "The Man Your Man Could Smell Like." In one seamless take, Mustafa confidently strikes a variety of romantic poses while passing from a shower in a bathroom to standing on a boat to riding a white horse. Uploaded onto YouTube and other social networking sites, the ad was viewed over 10 million additional times. Old Spice's Facebook page included a Web application called "My Perpetual Love," which featured Mustafa offering men the opportunity to be "more like him" by e-mailing and tweeting their sweethearts virtual love notes. For its efforts, the ad agency behind the campaign, Wieden+Kennedy, received a Grand Prix at the Cannes International Ad festival. A follow-up ad in June 2010 showed Mustafa in a new series of "perfect man" activities including baking birthday cakes, building a home with his own hands, swan-diving into a hot tub, and, yes, walking on water.

Although Old Spice clearly has found great success with its ad campaign, other marketers are trying to come to grips with how to best use mass media in the new—and still changing—communication environment.[2] In this chapter, we examine the nature and use of four mass-communication tools—advertising, sales promotion, events and experiences, and public relations and publicity.

Developing and Managing an Advertising Program

Advertising can be a cost-effective way to disseminate messages, whether to build a brand preference or to educate people. Even in today's challenging media environment, good ads can pay off. P&G has also enjoyed double-digit sales gains in recent years from ads touting the efficacy of Olay Definity antiaging skin products and Head & Shoulders Intensive Treatment shampoo.[3]

In developing an advertising program, marketing managers must always start by identifying the target market and buyer motives. Then they can make the five major decisions, known as "the five Ms": *Mission:* What are our advertising objectives? *Money:* How much can we spend and how do we allocate our spending across media types? *Message:* What message should we send? *Media:* What media should we use? *Measurement:* How should we evaluate the results? These decisions are summarized in △ Figure 18.1 and described in the following sections.

Setting the Objectives

The advertising objectives must flow from prior decisions on target market, brand positioning, and the marketing program.

An **advertising objective** (or goal) is a specific communications task and achievement level to be accomplished with a specific audience in a specific period of time:[4]

> *To increase among 30 million homemakers who own automatic washers the number who identify brand X as a low-sudsing detergent, and who are persuaded that it gets clothes cleaner, from 10 percent to 40 percent in one year.*

We can classify advertising objectives according to whether their aim is to inform, persuade, remind, or reinforce. These objectives correspond to different stages in the *hierarchy-of-effects* model discussed in Chapter 17.

- *Informative advertising* aims to create brand awareness and knowledge of new products or new features of existing products.[5] To promote its OnStar in-vehicle safety, security, and information service that uses wireless and GPS satellite technology, GM launched the "Real Stories" campaign in 2002. The award-winning TV, radio, and print ad campaign used actual subscriber stories in their own words and voices to share the importance and benefits of OnStar through life-changing experiences. By 2005, the OnStar brand had reached 100 percent awareness among consumers shopping for a new vehicle.[6]

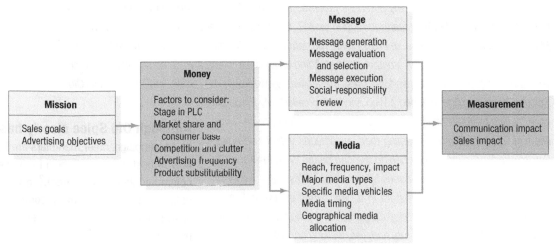

|Fig. 18.1| △

The Five Ms of Advertising

- *Persuasive advertising* aims to create liking, preference, conviction, and purchase of a product or service. Some persuasive advertising uses comparative advertising, which makes an explicit comparison of the attributes of two or more brands. Miller Lite took market share from Bud Lite by pointing out that Bud Lite had higher carbs. Comparative advertising works best when it elicits cognitive and affective motivations simultaneously, and when consumers are processing advertising in a detailed, analytical mode.[7]
- *Reminder advertising* aims to stimulate repeat purchase of products and services. Expensive, four-color Coca-Cola ads in magazines are intended to remind people to purchase Coca-Cola.
- *Reinforcement advertising* aims to convince current purchasers that they made the right choice. Automobile ads often depict satisfied customers enjoying special features of their new car.

The advertising objective should emerge from a thorough analysis of the current marketing situation. If the product class is mature, the company is the market leader, and brand usage is low, the objective is to stimulate more usage. If the product class is new, the company is not the market leader, but the brand is superior to the leader, then the objective is to convince the market of the brand's superiority.

Deciding on the Advertising Budget

How does a company know it's spending the right amount? Although advertising is treated as a current expense, part of it is really an investment in building brand equity and customer loyalty. When a company spends $5 million on capital equipment, it may treat the equipment as a five-year depreciable asset and write off only one-fifth of the cost in the first year. When it spends $5 million on advertising to launch a new product, it must write off the entire cost in the first year, reducing its reported profit, even if the effects will persist for many years to come.

FACTORS AFFECTING BUDGET DECISIONS Here are five specific factors to consider when setting the advertising budget:[8]

1. *Stage in the product life cycle*—New products typically merit large advertising budgets to build awareness and to gain consumer trial. Established brands usually are supported with lower advertising budgets, measured as a ratio to sales.
2. *Market share and consumer base*—High-market-share brands usually require less advertising expenditure as a percentage of sales to maintain share. To build share by increasing market size requires larger expenditures.
3. *Competition and clutter*—In a market with a large number of competitors and high advertising spending, a brand must advertise more heavily to be heard. Even simple clutter from advertisements not directly competitive to the brand creates a need for heavier advertising.
4. *Advertising frequency*—The number of repetitions needed to put the brand's message across to consumers has an obvious impact on the advertising budget.
5. *Product substitutability*—Brands in less-differentiated or commodity-like product classes (beer, soft drinks, banks, and airlines) require heavy advertising to establish a unique image.

ADVERTISING ELASTICITY The predominant response function for advertising is often concave but can be S-shaped. When consumer response is S-shaped, some positive amount of advertising is necessary to generate any sales impact, but sales increases eventually flatten out.[9]

One classic study found that increasing the TV advertising budget had a measurable effect on sales only half the time. The success rate was higher for new products or line extensions than for established brands, and when there were changes in copy or in media strategy (such as an expanded target market). When advertising increased sales, its impact lasted up to two years after peak spending. Moreover, the long-term incremental sales generated were approximately double the incremental sales observed in the first year of an advertising spending increase.[10]

Other studies reinforce these conclusions. In a 2004 IRI study of 23 brands, advertising often didn't increase sales for mature brands or categories in decline. A review of academic research found that advertising elasticities were estimated to be higher for new (.3) than for established products (.1).[11]

Developing the Advertising Campaign

In designing and evaluating an ad campaign, marketers employ both art and science to develop the *message strategy* or positioning of an ad—*what* the ad attempts to convey about the brand—and its *creative strategy*—*how* the ad expresses the brand claims. Advertisers go through three steps: message generation and evaluation, creative development and execution, and social-responsibility review.

MESSAGE GENERATION AND EVALUATION Many of today's automobile ads look similar—a car drives at high speed on a curved mountain road or across a desert. Advertisers are always seeking "the big idea" that connects with consumers rationally and emotionally, sharply distinguishes the brand from competitors, and is broad and flexible enough to translate to different media, markets, and time periods.[12] Fresh insights are important for avoiding using the same appeals and position as others.

Got Milk? After a 20-year decline in milk consumption among Californians, in 1993 milk processors from across the state formed the California Milk Processor Board (CMPB) with one goal in mind: to get people to drink more milk. The ad agency commissioned by the CMPB, Goodby, Silverstein & Partners, developed a novel approach to pitching milk's benefits. Research had shown that most consumers already believed milk was good for them. So the campaign would remind consumers of the inconvenience and annoyance of running out of milk when they went to eat certain foods, which became known as "milk deprivation." The "got milk?" tagline reminded consumers to make sure they had milk in their refrigerators. A year after the launch, sales volume had increased 1.07 percent. In 1995, the "got milk?" campaign was licensed to the National Dairy Board. In 1998, the National Fluid Milk Processor Education Program, which had been using the "milk mustache" campaign since 1994 to boost sales, bought the rights to the "got milk?" tagline. The "got milk?" campaign continues to pay strong dividends by halting the decline in sales of milk in California more than 13 years after its launch.[13]

To learn how the protein in milk helps build muscle, visit bodybymilk.com/albertpujols

Want muscle? **got milk?**

The tagline for California Milk Processor Board's "Got milk?" campaign has also been used as part of the "milk mustache" print ad series, featuring numerous celebrities such as St. Louis Cardinals baseball slugger Albert Pujols.

A good ad normally focuses on one or two core selling propositions. As part of refining the brand positioning, the advertiser should conduct market research to determine which appeal works best with its target audience and then prepare a *creative brief*, typically one or two pages. This is an elaboration of the *positioning statement* and includes considerations such as key message, target audience, communications objectives (to do, to know, to believe), key brand benefits, supports for the brand promise, and media.

How many alternative ad themes should the advertiser create before making a choice? The more ad themes explored, the higher the probability of finding an excellent one. Fortunately, an ad agency's creative department can inexpensively compose many alternative ads in a short time by drawing still and video images from computer files. Marketers can also cut the cost of creative dramatically by using consumers as their creative team, a strategy sometimes called "open source" or "crowdsourcing."[14]

Consumer-Generated Advertising One of the first major marketers to feature consumer-generated ads was Converse, whose award-winning campaign, "Brand Democracy," used films created by consumers in a series of TV and Web ads. Some of the most popular ads during recent Super Bowl broadcasts have been homemade contest winners for Frito-Lay's Doritos tortilla chips. H. J. Heinz ran a "Top This TV Challenge" inviting the public to create the next commercial for its Heinz Ketchup brand and win $57,000. More than 6,000 submissions and more than 10 million online views resulted, and sales rose over 13 percent year over year. In addition to creating ads, consumers can help disseminate advertising. A UK "Life's for Sharing" ad for T-Mobile in which 400 people break into a choreographed dance routine in the Liverpool Street Station was shown exactly once on the *Celebrity Big Brother* television show, but it was watched more than 15 million times online when word about it spread via e-mail messages, blogs, and social networks.

Although entrusting consumers with a brand's marketing effort can be pure genius, it can also be a regrettable failure. When Kraft sought a hip name for a new flavor variety of its iconic Vegemite

T-Mobile's highly entertaining "Life's for Sharing" subway dance became an online viral marketing sensation.

product in Australia, it labeled the first 3 million jars "Name Me" to enlist consumer support. From 48,000 entries, however, the marketer selected one that was thrown in as a joke—iSnack 2.0—and sales plummeted. The company had to pull iSnack jars from the shelves and start from scratch in a more conventional fashion, yielding the new name Cheesybite.[15]

CREATIVE DEVELOPMENT AND EXECUTION The ad's impact depends not only on what it says, but often more important, on *how* it says it. Execution can be decisive. Every advertising medium has advantages and disadvantages. Here, we briefly review television, print, and radio advertising media.

Television Ads Television is generally acknowledged as the most powerful advertising medium and reaches a broad spectrum of consumers at low cost per exposure. TV advertising has two particularly important strengths. First, it can vividly demonstrate product attributes and persuasively explain their corresponding consumer benefits. Second, it can dramatically portray user and usage imagery, brand personality, and other intangibles.

Because of the fleeting nature of the ad, however, and the distracting creative elements often found in it, product-related messages and the brand itself can be overlooked. Moreover, the high volume of nonprogramming material on television creates clutter that makes it easy for consumers to ignore or forget ads. Nevertheless, properly designed and executed TV ads can still be a powerful marketing tool and improve brand equity and affect sales and profits. In the highly competitive insurance category, advertising can help a brand to stand out.[16]

Aflac Aflac, the largest supplier of supplemental insurance, was relatively unknown until a highly creative ad campaign made it one of the most recognized brands in recent history. (Aflac stands for American Family Life Assurance Company.) Created by the Kaplan Thaler ad agency, the lighthearted campaign features an irascible duck incessantly squawking the company's name, "Aflac!" while consumers or celebrities discuss its products. The duck's frustrated bid for attention appealed to consumers. Sales were up 28 percent in the first year the duck aired, and name recognition went from 13 percent to 91 percent. Aflac has stuck with the duck in its advertising, even incorporating it into its corporate logo in 2005. Social media have allowed marketers to further develop the personality of the duck—it has 170,000 Facebook fans and counting! The Aflac duck is not just a U.S. phenomenon. It also stars in Japanese TV ads—with a somewhat brighter disposition—where it has been credited with helping to drive sales in Aflac's biggest market.

Print Ads Print media offer a stark contrast to broadcast media. Because readers consume them at their own pace, magazines and newspapers can provide detailed product information and effectively

Aflac's iconic duck character has been the centerpiece of its brand-building advertising for years.

communicate user and usage imagery. At the same time, the static nature of the visual images in print media makes dynamic presentations or demonstrations difficult, and print media can be fairly passive.

The two main print media—magazines and newspapers—share many advantages and disadvantages. Although newspapers are timely and pervasive, magazines are typically more effective at building user and usage imagery. Newspapers are popular for local—especially retailer—advertising. On an average day, roughly one-half to three-quarters of U.S. adults read a newspaper, although increasingly that is an online version. Print newspaper circulation fell almost 9 percent in 2009.[17] Although advertisers have some flexibility in designing and placing newspaper ads, relatively poor reproduction quality and short shelf life can diminish the ads' impact.

Researchers studying print advertisements report that the *picture, headline,* and *copy* matter in that order. The picture must be strong enough to draw attention. The headline must reinforce the picture and lead the person to read the copy. The copy must be engaging and the brand's name sufficiently prominent. Even then, less than 50 percent of the exposed audience will notice even a really outstanding ad. About 30 percent might recall the headline's main point, about 25 percent register the advertiser's name, and fewer than 10 percent will read most of the body copy. Ordinary ads don't achieve even these results.

Given how consumers process print ads, some clear managerial implications emerge, as summarized in "Marketing Memo: Print Ad Evaluation Criteria." One print ad campaign that successfully carved out a brand image is Absolut vodka.[18]

marketing Memo

Print Ad Evaluation Criteria

In judging the effectiveness of a print ad, in addition to considering the communication strategy (target market, communications objectives, and message and creative strategy), marketers should be able to answer yes to the following questions about the ad's execution:

1. Is the message clear at a glance? Can you quickly tell what the advertisement is all about?
2. Is the benefit in the headline?

3. Does the illustration support the headline?
4. Does the first line of the copy support or explain the headline and illustration?
5. Is the ad easy to read and follow?
6. Is the product easily identified?
7. Is the brand or sponsor clearly identified?

Source: Adapted from Scott C. Purvis and Philip Ward Burton, *Which Ad Pulled Best,* 9th ed. (Lincolnwood, IL: NTC Business Books, 2002).

Absolut Vodka   Vodka is generally viewed as a commodity product, yet the amount of brand preference and loyalty in the vodka market is astonishing and attributed mostly to brand image. When the Swedish brand Absolut entered the U.S. market in 1979, the company sold a disappointing 7,000 cases. By 1991, sales had soared to over 2 million cases. Absolut became the largest-selling imported vodka in the United States, with 65 percent of the market, thanks in large part to its marketing and advertising strategies aimed at sophisticated, upwardly mobile, affluent drinkers. The vodka comes in a distinctive clear bottle that served as the centerpiece of 15,000 ad executions over a 25-year period. The campaign cleverly juxtaposed a punning caption against a stylized image of the bottle—for example, "Absolut Texas" under an image of an oversized bottle, or "Absolut 19th" with a bottle made of a golf green. But feeling that consumers were beginning to tune out the message, in 2007 Absolut introduced a new global campaign that showed what things would be like "In an Absolut World." In this fantasy world, men get pregnant, soap bubbles flow from smokestacks, masterpiece paintings hang in Times Square, protesters and police fight with feather pillows, and perhaps most fantastically of all, the Cubs win the World Series. The revitalized campaign led to a 9 percent increase in case sales before the recession hit in 2008.

Radio Ads   Radio is a pervasive medium: Ninety-three percent of all U.S. citizens age 12 and older listen to the radio daily and for around 20 hours a week on average, numbers that have held steady in recent years. Much radio listening occurs in the car and out of home. As streaming Internet access gains ground, traditional AM/FM radio stations are feeling the pressure and account for less than half of all listening at home.[19]

Perhaps radio's main advantage is flexibility—stations are very targeted, ads are relatively inexpensive to produce and place, and short closings allow for quick response. Radio is a particularly effective medium in the morning; it can also let companies achieve a balance between broad and localized market coverage.

The obvious disadvantages of radio are its lack of visual images and the relatively passive nature of the consumer processing that results. Nevertheless, radio ads can be extremely creative. Some see the lack of visual images as a plus because they feel the clever use of music, sound, and other creative devices can tap into the listener's imagination to create powerfully relevant and liked images. Here is an example:

DFT   Faced with a high rate of motorcycle collisions with cars, the Department of Transport in the United Kingdom (DFT) conducted a research study. Its findings showed that many bike accidents resulted from "unintentional blindness," in which a car driver fails to see a motorcyclist. DFT wanted to increase drivers' awareness of motorcyclists by encouraging them to identify with riders and see them as real people. Radio was the only medium that allowed DFT to bring the campaign to life, with regional voices and copy, mentioning specific places and roads that listeners could identify with. It also allowed DFT to speak to listeners while they were driving. The aims of the advertising campaign were to increase awareness of motorcyclists from 51 percent to 58 percent, and to raise the number of motorists who checked their blind spots from 78 percent to 83 percent. DFT's advertisement won the award for the Best Use of Radio to Drive Awareness from the Radio Advertising Bureau in the United Kingdom.[20]

LEGAL AND SOCIAL ISSUES To break through clutter, some advertisers believe they have to be edgy and push the boundaries of what consumers are used to seeing in advertising. In doing so, marketers must be sure advertising does not overstep social and legal norms[21] or offend the general public, ethnic groups, racial minorities, or special-interest groups.

A substantial body of laws and regulations governs advertising. Under U.S. law, advertisers must not make false claims, such as stating that a product cures something when it does not. They must avoid false demonstrations, such as using sand-covered Plexiglas instead of sandpaper to demonstrate that a razor blade can shave sandpaper. It is illegal in the United States to create ads that have the capacity to deceive, even though no one may actually be deceived. A floor wax advertiser can't say the product gives six months' protection unless it does so under typical conditions, and the maker of a diet bread can't say it has fewer calories simply because its slices are thinner. The challenge is telling the difference between deception and "puffery"—simple exaggerations that are not meant to be believed and that *are* permitted by law.

Splenda versus Equal   Splenda's tagline for its artificial sweetener was "Made from sugar, so it tastes like sugar," with "but it's not sugar" in small writing almost as an afterthought. McNeil Nutritionals, Splenda's manufacturer, does begin production of Splenda with pure cane sugar but burns it off in the manufacturing process. However, Merisant, maker of Equal, claimed that Splenda's advertising confuses consumers who are likely to conclude that a product "made from sugar" is healthier than one made from aspartame, Equal's main ingredient. A document used in court and taken from McNeil's own files notes that consumers' perception of Splenda as "not an artificial sweetener" was one of the biggest triumphs of the company's marketing campaign, which began in 2003. Splenda became the runaway leader in the sugar-substitute category with 60 percent of the market, leaving roughly 14 percent each to Equal (in the blue packets) and Sweet'N Low (pink packets). Although McNeil eventually agreed to settle the lawsuit and pay Merisant an undisclosed but "substantial" award (and change its advertising), it may have been too late for consumers to change their perception of Splenda as something sugary *and* sugar-free.[22]

Sellers in the United States are legally obligated to avoid bait-and-switch advertising that attracts buyers under false pretenses. Suppose a seller advertises a sewing machine at $149. When consumers try to buy the advertised machine, the seller cannot then refuse to sell it, downplay its features, show a faulty one, or promise unreasonable delivery dates in order to switch the buyer to a more expensive machine.[23]

Advertising can play a more positive broader social role. The Ad Council is a nonprofit organization that uses top-notch industry talent to produce and distribute public service announcements for nonprofits and government agencies. From its early origins with "Buy War Bonds" posters, the Ad Council has tackled innumerable pressing social issues through the years. One of its recent efforts featured beloved *Sesame Street* stars Elmo and Gordon exhorting children to wash their hands in the face of the H1N1 flu virus.[24]

Deciding on Media and Measuring Effectiveness

After choosing the message, the advertiser's next task is to choose media to carry it. The steps here are deciding on desired reach, frequency, and impact; choosing among major media types; selecting specific media vehicles; deciding on media timing; and deciding on geographical media allocation. Then the marketer evaluates the results of these decisions.

Deciding on Reach, Frequency, and Impact

Media selection is finding the most cost-effective media to deliver the desired number and type of exposures to the target audience. What do we mean by the desired number of exposures? The advertiser seeks a specified advertising objective and response from the target audience—for example, a target level of product trial. This level depends on, among other things, level of brand awareness. Suppose the rate of product trial increases at a diminishing rate with the level of audience awareness, as shown in △ Figure 18.2(a). If the advertiser seeks a product trial rate of T^*, it will be necessary to achieve a brand awareness level of A^*.

The next task is to find out how many exposures, E^*, will produce a level of audience awareness of A^*. The effect of exposures on audience awareness depends on the exposures' reach, frequency, and impact:

- **Reach (R).** The number of different persons or households exposed to a particular media schedule at least once during a specified time period
- **Frequency (F).** The number of times within the specified time period that an average person or household is exposed to the message
- **Impact (I).** The qualitative value of an exposure through a given medium (thus a food ad will have a higher impact in *Bon Appetit* than in *Fortune* magazine)

Figure 18.2(b) shows the relationship between audience awareness and reach. Audience awareness will be greater, the higher the exposures' reach, frequency, and impact. There are important trade-offs here. Suppose the planner has an advertising budget of $1,000,000 and the cost per thousand exposures of average quality is $5. This means 200,000,000 exposures ($1,000,000 ÷ [$5/1,000]). If the advertiser seeks an average exposure frequency of 10, it can reach 20,000,000 people (200,000,000 ÷ 10) with the given budget. But if the advertiser wants higher-quality media costing $10 per thousand exposures, it will be able to reach only 10,000,000 people unless it is willing to lower the desired exposure frequency.

The relationship between reach, frequency, and impact is captured in the following concepts:

- **Total number of exposures (E).** This is the reach times the average frequency; that is, $E = R \times F$, also called the *gross rating points* (GRP). If a given media schedule reaches 80 percent of homes with an average exposure frequency of 3, the media schedule has a GRP of 240 (80 × 3). If another media schedule has a GRP of 300, it has more weight, but we cannot tell how this weight breaks down into reach and frequency.
- **Weighted number of exposures (WE).** This is the reach times average frequency times average impact, that is $WE = R \times F \times I$.

Reach is most important when launching new products, flanker brands, extensions of well-known brands, or infrequently purchased brands; or when going after an undefined target market. Frequency is most important where there are strong competitors, a complex story to tell, high consumer resistance, or a frequent-purchase cycle.[25]

A key reason for repetition is forgetting. The higher the forgetting rate associated with a brand, product category, or message, the higher the warranted level of repetition. However, advertisers should not coast on a tired ad but insist on fresh executions by their ad agency.[26] GEICO has found advertising success by keeping both its campaigns and their executions fresh.

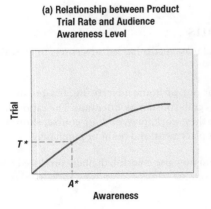

(a) Relationship between Product Trial Rate and Audience Awareness Level

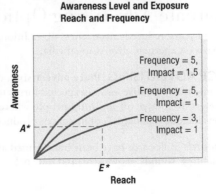

(b) Relationship between Audience Awareness Level and Exposure Reach and Frequency

|Fig. 18.2| △

Relationship Among Trial, Awareness, and the Exposure Function

GEICO   Have the hundreds of millions of dollars GEICO has spent on TV advertising been worth it? Warren Buffet, chairman and CEO of GEICO's parent company Berkshire Hathaway, sure thinks so. He told shareholders he would spend *millions* on GEICO advertising! GEICO has more than quadrupled its revenue over the last decade, from slightly under $3 billion in 1998 to more than $13 billion in 2009—making it the fastest-growing auto insurance company in the United States. The company eschews agents to sell directly to consumers with a basic message, "15 Minutes Could Save You 15% or More on Your Car Insurance." Partnering with The Martin Agency, GEICO has run different award-winning TV campaigns to emphasize different benefits of the brand. Popular TV spots advertising GEICO's claim that its Web site is "So Easy, a Caveman Can Use It" featured offended Neanderthals expressing indignation at the prejudice they face. TV ads featuring the Cockney-speaking Gecko lizard spokes-character reinforce GEICO's brand image as credible and accomplished. A third campaign, themed "Rhetorical Questions," uses cultural icons and touch points to make it seem obvious that GEICO saves customers money by asking self-evident questions such as, "Does Elmer Fudd have trouble with the letter R?" and "Did the Waltons take way too long to say goodnight?" The multiple campaigns complement each other and build on each other's success; the company dominates the TV airwaves with so many varied car insurance messages that any competitors' ads are lost.[27]

Choosing Among Major Media Types

The media planner must know the capacity of the major advertising media types to deliver reach, frequency, and impact. The major advertising media along with their costs, advantages, and limitations are profiled in Table 18.1. Media planners make their choices by considering factors such as target audience media habits, product characteristics, message requirements, and cost.

Saving is easy.

Get a free car insurance quote today.

GEICO.
geico.com

Motorcycle and ATV coverages are underwritten by GEICO Indemnity Company. Homeowners, renters, boat and PWC coverages are written through non-affiliated insurance companies and are secured through the GEICO Insurance Agency, Inc. Some discounts, coverages, payment plans and features are not available in all states or all GEICO companies. Government Employees Insurance Co. • GEICO General Insurance Co. • GEICO Indemnity Co. • GEICO Casualty Co. These companies are subsidiaries of Berkshire Hathaway Inc. GEICO: Washington, DC 20076. GEICO Gecko image © 1999-2010. © 2010 GEICO

One of the most active advertisers around, GEICO employs multiple ad campaigns, including a series featuring the gecko lizard.

Alternate Advertising Options

In recent years, reduced effectiveness of traditional mass media has led advertisers to increase their emphasis on alternate advertising media.

PLACE ADVERTISING **Place advertising**, or out-of-home advertising, is a broad category including many creative and unexpected forms to grab consumers' attention. The rationale is that marketers are better off reaching people where they work, play, and, of course, shop. Popular options include billboards, public spaces, product placement, and point of purchase.

Billboards Billboards have been transformed and now use colorful, digitally produced graphics, backlighting, sounds, movement, and unusual—even 3D—images.[28] In New York, manhole covers

TABLE 18.1 ⬭ Profiles of Major Media Types		
Medium	**Advantages**	**Limitations**
Newspapers	Flexibility; timeliness; good local market coverage; broad acceptance; high believability	Short life; poor reproduction quality; small "pass-along" audience
Television	Combines sight, sound, and motion; appealing to the senses; high attention; high reach	High absolute cost; high clutter; fleeting exposure; less audience selectivity
Direct mail	Audience selectivity; flexibility; no ad competition within the same medium; personalization	Relatively high cost; "junk mail" image
Radio	Mass use; high geographic and demographic selectivity; low cost	Audio presentation only; lower attention than television; nonstandardized rate structures; fleeting exposure
Magazines	High geographic and demographic selectivity; credibility and prestige; high-quality reproduction; long life; good pass-along readership	Long ad purchase lead time; some waste in circulation
Outdoor	Flexibility; high repeat exposure; low cost; low competition	Limited audience selectivity; creative limitations
Yellow Pages	Excellent local coverage; high believability; wide reach; low cost	High competition; long ad purchase lead time; creative limitations
Newsletters	Very high selectivity; full control; interactive opportunities; relative low costs	Costs could run away
Brochures	Flexibility; full control; can dramatize messages	Overproduction could lead to runaway costs
Telephone	Many users; opportunity to give a personal touch	Relative high cost; increasing consumer resistance
Internet	High selectivity; interactive possibilities; relatively low cost	Increasing clutter

have been reimagined as steaming cups of Folgers coffee; in Belgium, eBay posted "Moved to eBay" stickers on empty storefronts; and in Germany, imaginary workers toiling inside vending machines, ATMs, and photo booths were justification for a German job-hunting Web site to proclaim, "Life Is Too Short for the Wrong Job."[29]

New "Eyes On" measurement techniques allow marketers to better understand who actually has seen their outdoor ads.[30] The right billboard can make all the difference. Chang Soda in Bangkok had enough money in its budget for only one digital billboard. To maximize impact, it built a giant bubbling bottle onto the billboard to illustrate the product's carbonation. Subsequent word-of-mouth buzz quintupled bottle sales from 200,000 to 1 million.[31]

A strong creative message can also break through visual clutter. Snickers out-of-home program used billboards and taxi-top signs with puns combining the brand's benefits and key locations, such as "Satisflying" at the airport, "Transfer to the Ate Train" in the subway, and "Snackonomics" on cabs in Wall Street.[32]

Public Spaces Advertisers have been increasingly placing ads in unconventional places such as on movie screens, on airplanes, and in fitness clubs, as well as in classrooms, sports arenas, office and hotel elevators, and other public places.[33] Billboard-type poster ads are showing up everywhere. Transit ads on buses, subways, and commuter trains—around for years—have become a valuable way to reach working women. "Street furniture"—bus shelters, kiosks, and public areas—is another fast-growing option.

Advertisers can buy space in stadiums and arenas and on garbage cans, bicycle racks, parking meters, airport luggage carousels, elevators, gasoline pumps, the bottom of golf cups and swimming pools, airline snack packages, and supermarket produce in the form of tiny labels on apples and bananas. They can even buy space in toilet stalls and above urinals which, according to one

Snickers uses clever taxi-top signs to increase its brand salience.

research study, office workers visit an average of three to four times a day for roughly four minutes per visit.[34]

Product Placement Marketers pay product placement fees of $100,000 to as much as $500,000 so their products will make cameo appearances in movies and on television.[35] Sometimes placements are the result of a larger network advertising deal, but other times they are the work of small product-placement shops that maintain ties with prop masters, set designers, and production executives. Some firms get product placement at no cost by supplying their product to the movie company (Nike does not pay to be in movies but often supplies shoes, jackets, bags, and so on). Increasingly, products and brands are being woven directly into the story.[36]

Staples and *The Office*   When Staples introduced a new $69.99 paper-shredding device called the MailMate in 2006, the company struck a two-episode deal with NBC's popular television program, *The Office*. In the first episode, the character Kevin Malone was given the responsibility of shredding paper with the MailMate; in the second, another character, Dwight Schrute, took a job at Staples. The writers and producers of the show tried to accommodate Staples' marketing objectives for the product as much as possible. To make sure the shredder looked small enough, it sat on Kevin's desk. To emphasize the shredder was sturdy, Kevin shredded not only paper but also his credit card. To emphasize that the shredder was available only at Staples, the episode closed with Kevin shredding lettuce and making it into a salad. When a colleague asked where he got the salad, he replied, "Staples."

Product placement is not immune to criticism as lawmakers increasingly criticize its stealth nature, threatening to force more explicit disclosure of participating advertisers.

Point of Purchase Chapter 16 discussed the importance of shopper marketing and in-store marketing efforts. The appeal of point-of-purchase advertising lies in the fact that in many product categories consumers make the bulk of their final brand decisions in the store, 74 percent according to one study.[37]

There are many ways to communicate with consumers at the **point of purchase** (P-O-P). In-store advertising includes ads on shopping carts, cart straps, aisles, and shelves, as well as promotion options such as in-store demonstrations, live sampling, and instant coupon machines.[38] Some supermarkets are selling floor space for company logos and experimenting with talking shelves. P-O-P radio provides FM-style programming and commercial messages to thousands of food stores and drugstores nationwide. Programming includes a store-selected music format, consumer tips, and commercials. Video screens in some stores allow for TV-type ads to be run.[39]

Walmart SMART Network One of the in-store advertising pioneers, Walmart, replaced its original Walmart TV with its new SMART network in 2008. The new TV network allows Walmart to monitor and control more than 27,000 individual screens in some 2,700 stores nationwide, reaching 160 million viewers every four weeks. Its "triple play" feature permits ads to be shown on a large welcome screen at the entrance of the store, a category screen in departments, and endcap screens on each aisle. Those highly visible endcap viewings are not cheap. Advertisers pay $325,000 for 30-second spots per two-week cycle in the grocery section and $650,000 per four-week run in the health and beauty aid department. Five-second ads running every two minutes for two weeks on the welcome screens cost advertisers $80,000, and 10-second spots running twice every six minutes on the full network cost $50,000 per week. By linking the time when ads were shown and when product sales were made, Walmart can estimate how much ads increase sales by department (from 7 percent in Electronics to 28 percent in Health & Beauty) and by product type (mature items increase by 7 percent, seasonal items by 18 percent).

EVALUATING ALTERNATE MEDIA Ads now can appear virtually anywhere consumers have a few spare minutes or even seconds to notice them. The main advantage of nontraditional media is that they can often reach a very precise and captive audience in a cost-effective manner. The message must be simple and direct. Outdoor advertising, for example, is often called the "15-second sell." It's more effective at enhancing brand awareness or brand image than creating new brand associations.

Unique ad placements designed to break through clutter may also be perceived as invasive and obtrusive, however. Consumer backlash often results when people see ads in traditionally ad-free spaces, such as in schools, on police cruisers, and in doctors' waiting rooms. Nevertheless, perhaps because of its sheer pervasiveness, some consumers seem to be less bothered by nontraditional media now than in the past.

The challenge for nontraditional media is demonstrating its reach and effectiveness through credible, independent research. Consumers must be favorably affected in some way to justify the marketing expenditures. But there will always be room for creative means of placing the brand in front of consumers, as occurred with McDonald's' alternate-reality game called "The Lost Ring."[40] "Marketing Insight: Playing Games with Brands" describes the role of gaming in marketing in general.

McDonald's and The Lost Ring As an official sponsor of the 2008 Beijing Olympics, McDonald's created a multipronged marketing effort. Looking to engage young adults immune to traditional media ploys, McDonald's, its marketing agency AKQA, and game developer Jane McGonigal created a global, multilingual alternate-reality game (ARG) called The Lost Ring. The Web-based game centered around Ariadne, a fictional amnesiac female Olympic athlete from a parallel universe, and united players around the world in an online quest to recover ancient Olympic secrets. Discreetly sponsored by McDonald's, the game began with 50 gaming bloggers receiving enigmatic packages on February 29, 2008 (Leap Day). The packages included an Olympic-themed poster from 1920 and other teasers with a clue to TheLostRing.com. Almost 3 million people in more than 100 countries eventually played the game, which ended August 24, 2008, the last day of the Olympics. The game received the Grand Prize in *Adweek*'s 2008 Buzz Awards.

Marketing Insight

Playing Games with Brands

More than half of U.S. adults age 18 and older play video games, and about one in five play every day or almost every day. Virtually all teens (97 percent) play video games. As many as 40 percent of gamers are women. Women seem to prefer puzzles and collaborative games, whereas men seem more attracted to competitive or simulation games. Given this explosive popularity, many advertisers have decided, "if you can't beat them, join them."

A top-notch "advergame" can cost between $100,000 and $500,000 to develop. The game can be played on the sponsor's corporate homepage, on gaming portals, or even on public locations such as at restaurants. 7-Up, McDonald's, and Porsche have all been featured in games. Honda developed a game that allowed players to choose a Honda and zoom around city streets plastered with Honda logos. In the first three months, 78,000 people played for an average of eight minutes each. The game's cost per thousand (CPM) of $7 compared favorably to a prime-time TV commercial's CPM of $11.65. Marketers collect valuable customer data upon registration and often seek permission to send e-mail. Of game players sponsored by Ford Escape SUV, 54 percent signed up to receive e-mail.

Marketers are also playing starring roles in popular video games. In multiplayer Test Drive Unlimited, players can take a break from the races to go shopping, where they can encounter at least 10 real-world brands such as Lexus and Hawaiian Airlines. Tomb Raider's Lara Craft tools around in a Jeep Commander. Mainstream marketers such as Apple, Procter & Gamble, Toyota, and Visa are all jumping on board. Overall, research suggests that gamers are fine with ads and the way they affect the game experience. One study showed that 70 percent of gamers felt dynamic in-game ads "contributed to realism," "fit the games" in which they served, and looked "cool."

Sources: "In-Game Advertising Research Proves Effectiveness for Brands across Categories and Game Titles," www.microsoft.com, June 3, 2008; Amanda Lenhart, "Video Games: Adults Are Players Too," Pew Internet & American Life Project, www.pewresearch.org, December 7, 2008; "Erika Brown, "Game On!" *Forbes*, July 24, 2006, pp. 84–86; David Radd, "Advergaming: You Got It," *BusinessWeek*, October 11, 2006; Stuart Elliott, "Madison Avenue's Full-Court Pitch to Video Gamers," *New York Times*, October 16, 2005.

Selecting Specific Media Vehicles

The media planner must search for the most cost-effective vehicles within each chosen media type. The advertiser who decides to buy 30 seconds of advertising on network television can pay around $100,000 for a new show, over $300,000 for a popular prime-time show such as *Sunday Night Football, American Idol, Grey's Anatomy,* or *Desperate Housewives,* or over $2.5 million for an event such as the Super Bowl.[41] These choices are critical: The average cost to produce a national 30-second television commercial in 2007 was about $342,000.[42] It can cost as much to run an ad once on network TV as to create and produce the ad to start with!

In making choices, the planner must rely on measurement services that estimate audience size, composition, and media cost. Media planners then calculate the cost per thousand persons reached by a vehicle. A full-page, four-color ad in *Sports Illustrated* cost approximately $350,000 in 2010. If *Sports Illustrated*'s estimated readership was 3.15 million people, the cost of exposing the ad to 1,000 persons is approximately $11.20. The same ad in *Time* cost approximately $500,000, but reached 4.25 million people—at a higher cost-per-thousand of $11.90.

The media planner ranks each magazine by cost per thousand and favors magazines with the lowest cost per thousand for reaching target consumers. The magazines themselves often put together a "reader profile" for their advertisers, describing average readers with respect to age, income, residence, marital status, and leisure activities.

Marketers need to apply several adjustments to the cost-per-thousand measure. First, they should adjust for *audience quality.* For a baby lotion ad, a magazine read by 1 million young mothers has an exposure value of 1 million; if read by 1 million teenagers, it has an exposure value of almost zero. Second, adjust the exposure value for the *audience-attention probability.* Readers of *Vogue* may pay more attention to ads than do readers of *Newsweek.*[43] Third, adjust for the medium's *editorial quality* (prestige and believability). People are more likely to believe a TV or radio ad and to become more positively disposed toward the brand when the ad is placed within a program they like.[44] Fourth, consider *ad placement policies and extra services* (such as regional or occupational editions and lead-time requirements for magazines).

Media planners are using more sophisticated measures of effectiveness and employing them in mathematical models to arrive at the best media mix. Many advertising agencies use software programs to select the initial media and make improvements based on subjective factors.[45]

Deciding on Media Timing and Allocation

In choosing media, the advertiser has both a macroscheduling and a microscheduling decision. The *macroscheduling decision* relates to seasons and the business cycle. Suppose 70 percent of a product's sales occur between June and September. The firm can vary its advertising expenditures to follow the seasonal pattern, to oppose the seasonal pattern, or to be constant throughout the year.

The *microscheduling decision* calls for allocating advertising expenditures within a short period to obtain maximum impact. Suppose the firm decides to buy 30 radio spots in the month of September. △ Figure 18.3 shows several possible patterns. The left side shows that advertising messages for the month can be concentrated ("burst" advertising), dispersed continuously throughout the month, or dispersed intermittently. The top side shows that the advertising messages can be beamed with a level, rising, falling, or alternating frequency.

The chosen pattern should meet the communications objectives set in relationship to the nature of the product, target customers, distribution channels, and other marketing factors. The timing pattern should consider three factors. *Buyer turnover* expresses the rate at which new buyers enter the market; the higher this rate, the more continuous the advertising should be. *Purchase frequency* is the number of times the average buyer buys the product during the period; the higher the purchase frequency, the more continuous the advertising should be. The *forgetting rate* is the rate at which the buyer forgets the brand; the higher the forgetting rate, the more continuous the advertising should be.

In launching a new product, the advertiser must choose among continuity, concentration, flighting, and pulsing.

- **Continuity** means exposures appear evenly throughout a given period. Generally, advertisers use continuous advertising in expanding market situations, with frequently purchased items, and in tightly defined buyer categories.
- **Concentration** calls for spending all the advertising dollars in a single period. This makes sense for products with one selling season or related holiday.
- **Flighting** calls for advertising during a period, followed by a period with no advertising, followed by a second period of advertising activity. It is useful when funding is limited, the purchase cycle is relatively infrequent, or items are seasonal.
- **Pulsing** is continuous advertising at low-weight levels, reinforced periodically by waves of heavier activity. It draws on the strength of continuous advertising and flights to create a compromise scheduling strategy.[46] Those who favor pulsing believe the audience will learn the message more thoroughly, and at a lower cost to the firm.

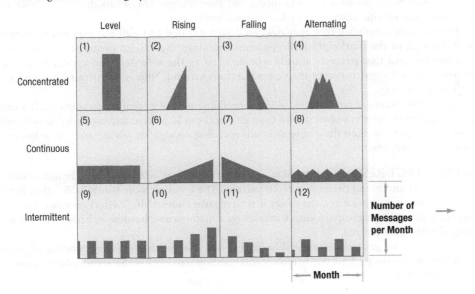

|Fig. 18.3| △

Classification of Advertising Timing Patterns

TABLE 18.2 💿	Advertising Pretest Research Techniques

For Print Ads

Starch and Gallup & Robinson Inc. are two widely used print pretesting services. Test ads are placed in magazines, which are then circulated to consumers. These consumers are contacted later and interviewed. Recall and recognition tests are used to determine advertising effectiveness.

For Broadcast Ads

In-home tests: A video is taken or downloaded into the homes of target consumers, who then view the commercials.

Trailer tests: In a trailer in a shopping center, shoppers are shown the products and given an opportunity to select a series of brands. They then view commercials and are given coupons to be used in the shopping center. Redemption rates indicate commercials' influence on purchase behavior.

Theater tests: Consumers are invited to a theater to view a potential new television series along with some commercials. Before the show begins, consumers indicate preferred brands in different categories; after the viewing, consumers again choose preferred brands. Preference changes measure the commercials' persuasive power.

On-air tests: Respondents are recruited to watch a program on a regular TV channel during the test commercial or are selected based on their having viewed the program. They are asked questions about commercial recall.

A company must decide how to allocate its advertising budget over space as well as over time. The company makes "national buys" when it places ads on national TV networks or in nationally circulated magazines. It makes "spot buys" when it buys TV time in just a few markets or in regional editions of magazines. These markets are called *areas of dominant influence* (ADIs) or *designated marketing areas* (DMAs). The company makes "local buys" when it advertises in local newspapers, radio, or outdoor sites.

Evaluating Advertising Effectiveness

Most advertisers try to measure the communication effect of an ad—that is, its potential impact on awareness, knowledge, or preference. They would also like to measure the ad's sales effect.

COMMUNICATION-EFFECT RESEARCH **Communication-effect research**, called *copy testing*, seeks to determine whether an ad is communicating effectively. Marketers should perform this test both before an ad is put into media and after it is printed or broadcast. 💿 Table 18.2 describes some specific advertising pretest research techniques.

Pretest critics maintain that agencies can design ads that test well but may not necessarily perform well in the marketplace. Proponents maintain that useful diagnostic information can emerge and that pretests should not be used as the sole decision criterion anyway. Widely acknowledged as one of the best advertisers around, Nike is notorious for doing very little ad pretesting.

Many advertisers use posttests to assess the overall impact of a completed campaign. If a company hoped to increase brand awareness from 20 percent to 50 percent and succeeded in increasing it to only 30 percent, then the company is not spending enough, its ads are poor, or it has overlooked some other factor.

SALES-EFFECT RESEARCH What sales are generated by an ad that increases brand awareness by 20 percent and brand preference by 10 percent? The fewer or more controllable other factors such as features and price are, the easier it is to measure advertising's effect on sales. The sales impact is easiest to measure in direct marketing situations and hardest in brand or corporate image-building advertising.

Companies are generally interested in finding out whether they are overspending or underspending on advertising. One way to answer this question is to work with the formulation shown in △ Figure 18.4.

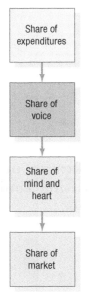

|Fig. 18.4| △

Formula for Measuring Different Stages in the Sales Impact of Advertising

A company's *share of advertising expenditures* produces a *share of voice* (proportion of company advertising of that product to all advertising of that product) that earns a *share of consumers' minds and hearts* and, ultimately, a *share of market.*

Researchers try to measure the sales impact by analyzing historical or experimental data. The *historical approach* correlates past sales to past advertising expenditures using advanced statistical techniques.[47] Other researchers use an *experimental design* to measure advertising's sales impact.

A growing number of researchers are striving to measure the sales effect of advertising expenditures instead of settling for communication-effect measures.[48] Millward Brown International has conducted tracking studies for years to help advertisers decide whether their advertising is benefiting their brand.[49]

Sales Promotion

Sales promotion, a key ingredient in marketing campaigns, consists of a collection of incentive tools, mostly short term, designed to stimulate quicker or greater purchase of particular products or services by consumers or the trade.[50]

Whereas advertising offers a *reason* to buy, sales promotion offers an *incentive*. Sales promotion includes tools for *consumer promotion* (samples, coupons, cash refund offers, prices off, premiums, prizes, patronage rewards, free trials, warranties, tie-in promotions, cross-promotions, point-of-purchase displays, and demonstrations), *trade promotion* (prices off, advertising and display allowances, and free goods), and *business* and *sales force promotion* (trade shows and conventions, contests for sales reps, and specialty advertising).

Objectives

Sales promotion tools vary in their specific objectives. A free sample stimulates consumer trial, whereas a free management-advisory service aims at cementing a long-term relationship with a retailer.

Sellers use incentive-type promotions to attract new triers, to reward loyal customers, and to increase the repurchase rates of occasional users. Sales promotions often attract brand switchers, who are primarily looking for low price, good value, or premiums. If some of them would not have otherwise tried the brand, promotion can yield long-term increases in market share.[51]

Sales promotions in markets of high brand similarity can produce a high sales response in the short run but little permanent gain in brand preference over the longer term. In markets of high brand dissimilarity, they may be able to alter market shares permanently. In addition to brand switching, consumers may engage in stockpiling—purchasing earlier than usual (purchase acceleration) or purchasing extra quantities. But sales may then hit a postpromotion dip.[52]

Advertising versus Promotion

Sales promotion expenditures increased as a percentage of budget expenditure for a number of years, although its growth has recently slowed. Several factors contributed to this growth, particularly in consumer markets. Promotion became more accepted by top management as an effective sales tool, the number of brands increased, competitors used promotions frequently, many brands were seen as similar, consumers became more price-oriented, the trade demanded more deals from manufacturers, and advertising efficiency declined.

But the rapid growth of sales promotion created clutter. Consumers began to tune out promotions: Coupon redemption peaked in 1992 at 7.9 billion coupons redeemed but dropped to 2.6 billion by 2008. Incessant price reductions, coupons, deals, and premiums can also devalue the product in buyers' minds. There is a risk in putting a well-known brand on promotion over 30 percent of the time. Having turned to 0 percent financing, hefty cash rebates, and special lease programs to ignite sales in the soft post-9/11 economy, auto manufacturers have found it difficult to wean consumers from discounts ever since.[53]

Loyal brand buyers tend not to change their buying patterns as a result of competitive promotions. Advertising appears to be more effective at deepening brand loyalty, although we can distinguish added-value promotions from price promotions.[54] Gain's "Love at First Sniff" campaign used direct mail and in-store scented tear-pads and ShelfVision TV to entice consumers to smell the product, resulting in an almost 500 percent increase in shipments over the goal.[55]

Price promotions may not build permanent total-category volume. One study of more than 1,000 promotions concluded that only 16 percent paid off.[56] Small-share competitors may find it advantageous to use sales promotion, because they cannot afford to match the market leaders' large advertising budgets, nor can they obtain shelf space without offering trade allowances or stimulate consumer trial without offering incentives. Dominant brands offer deals less frequently, because most deals subsidize only current users.

The upshot is that many consumer-packaged-goods companies feel forced to use more sales promotion than they wish. They blame heavy use of sales promotion for decreased brand loyalty, increased price sensitivity, brand-quality image dilution, and a focus on short-run marketing planning. One review of promotion effectiveness concluded, "When the strategic disadvantages of promotions are included, that is, losing control to the trade and training consumers to buy only on deal, the case is compelling for a reevaluation of current practices and the incentive systems responsible for this trend."[57]

Major Decisions

In using sales promotion, a company must establish its objectives, select the tools, develop the program, pretest the program, implement and control it, and evaluate the results.

ESTABLISHING OBJECTIVES Sales promotion objectives derive from broader communication objectives, which derive from more basic marketing objectives for the product. For consumers, objectives include encouraging purchase of larger-sized units, building trial among nonusers, and attracting switchers away from competitors' brands. Ideally, promotions with consumers would have short-run sales impact as well as long-run brand equity effects.[58] For retailers, objectives include persuading retailers to carry new items and higher levels of inventory, encouraging off-season buying, encouraging stocking of related items, offsetting competitive promotions, building brand loyalty, and gaining entry into new retail outlets. For the sales force, objectives include encouraging support of a new product or model, encouraging more prospecting, and stimulating off-season sales.[59]

SELECTING CONSUMER PROMOTION TOOLS The promotion planner should take into account the type of market, sales promotion objectives, competitive conditions, and each tool's cost-effectiveness. The main consumer promotion tools are summarized in Table 18.3. *Manufacturer promotions* are, for instance in the auto industry, rebates, gifts to motivate test-drives and purchases, and high-value trade-in credit. *Retailer promotions* include price cuts, feature advertising, retailer coupons, and retailer contests or premiums.[60]

We can also distinguish between sales promotion tools that are *consumer franchise building* and those that are not. The former impart a selling message along with the deal, such as free samples, frequency awards, coupons when they include a selling message, and premiums when they are related to the product. Sales promotion tools that typically are *not* brand building include price-off packs, consumer premiums not related to a product, contests and sweepstakes, consumer refund offers, and trade allowances.

Consumer franchise-building promotions offer the best of both worlds—they build brand equity while moving product. Sampling has gained popularity in recent years—companies such as McDonald's, Dunkin' Donuts, and Starbucks have given away millions of samples of their new products—because consumers like them and they often lead to higher long-term sales for quality products.[61]

Digital coupons eliminate printing costs, reduce paper waste, are easily updatable, and have higher redemption rates. Coupons.com receives almost 5 million unique visitors a month for money-saving deals. Almost 2 million consumers visit CoolSavings.com each month for money-saving coupons and offers from name brands, as well as helpful tips and articles, newsletters, free recipes, sweepstakes, free trials, free samples, and more. Electronic coupons can arrive by cell phone, Twitter, e-mail, or Facebook.[62]

SELECTING TRADE PROMOTION TOOLS Manufacturers use a number of trade promotion tools (see Table 18.4).[63] Manufacturers award money to the trade (1) to persuade the retailer or wholesaler to carry the brand; (2) to persuade the retailer or wholesaler to carry more units than the normal amount; (3) to induce retailers to promote the brand by featuring, display, and price reductions; and (4) to stimulate retailers and their sales clerks to push the product.

The growing power of large retailers has increased their ability to demand trade promotion at the expense of consumer promotion and advertising.[64] The company's sales force and its brand

TABLE 18.3 ⬭	Major Consumer Promotion Tools

Samples: Offer of a free amount of a product or service delivered door to door, sent in the mail, picked up in a store, attached to another product, or featured in an advertising offer.

Coupons: Certificates entitling the bearer to a stated saving on the purchase of a specific product: mailed, enclosed in other products or attached to them, or inserted in magazine and newspaper ads.

Cash Refund Offers (rebates): Provide a price reduction after purchase rather than at the retail shop: Consumer sends a specified "proof of purchase" to the manufacturer who "refunds" part of the purchase price by mail.

Price Packs (cents-off deals): Offers to consumers of savings off the regular price of a product, flagged on the label or package. A *reduced-price pack* is a single package sold at a reduced price (such as two for the price of one). A *banded pack* is two related products banded together (such as a toothbrush and toothpaste).

Premiums (gifts): Merchandise offered at a relatively low cost or free as an incentive to purchase a particular product. A *with-pack premium* accompanies the product inside or on the package. A *free in-the-mail premium* is mailed to consumers who send in a proof of purchase, such as a box top or UPC code. A *self-liquidating premium* is sold below its normal retail price to consumers who request it.

Frequency Programs: Programs providing rewards related to the consumer's frequency and intensity in purchasing the company's products or services.

Prizes (contests, sweepstakes, games): *Prizes* are offers of the chance to win cash, trips, or merchandise as a result of purchasing something. A *contest* calls for consumers to submit an entry to be examined by a panel of judges who will select the best entries. A *sweepstakes* asks consumers to submit their names in a drawing. A *game* presents consumers with something every time they buy—bingo numbers, missing letters—which might help them win a prize.

Patronage Awards: Values in cash or in other forms that are proportional to patronage of a certain vendor or group of vendors.

Free Trials: Inviting prospective purchasers to try the product without cost in the hope that they will buy.

Product Warranties: Explicit or implicit promises by sellers that the product will perform as specified or that the seller will fix it or refund the customer's money during a specified period.

Tie-in Promotions: Two or more brands or companies team up on coupons, refunds, and contests to increase pulling power.

Cross-Promotions: Using one brand to advertise another noncompeting brand.

Point-of-Purchase (P-O-P) Displays and Demonstrations: P-O-P displays and demonstrations take place at the point of purchase or sale.

TABLE 18.4 ⬭	Major Trade Promotion Tools

Price-Off (off-invoice or off-list): A straight discount off the list price on each case purchased during a stated time period.

Allowance: An amount offered in return for the retailer's agreeing to feature the manufacturer's products in some way. An *advertising allowance* compensates retailers for advertising the manufacturer's product. A *display allowance* compensates them for carrying a special product display.

Free Goods: Offers of extra cases of merchandise to intermediaries who buy a certain quantity or who feature a certain flavor or size.

Reflecting changes in consumer behavior, digital coupons such as these, available at Coupons.com, have grown in importance.

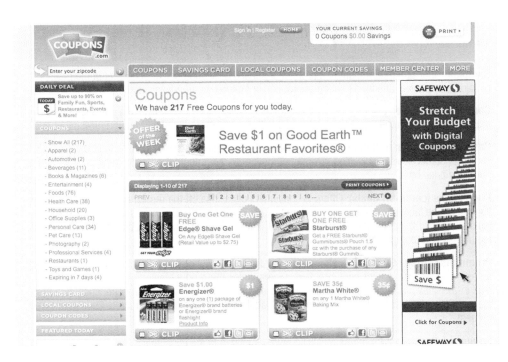

managers are often at odds over trade promotion. The sales force says local retailers will not keep the company's products on the shelf unless they receive more trade promotion money, whereas brand managers want to spend their limited funds on consumer promotion and advertising.

Manufacturers face several challenges in managing trade promotions. First, they often find it difficult to police retailers to make sure they are doing what they agreed to do. Manufacturers increasingly insist on proof of performance before paying any allowances. Second, some retailers are doing *forward buying*—that is, buying a greater quantity during the deal period than they can immediately sell. Retailers might respond to a 10 percent-off-case allowance by buying a 12-week or longer supply. The manufacturer must then schedule more production than planned and bear the costs of extra work shifts and overtime. Third, some retailers are *diverting*, buying more cases than needed in a region where the manufacturer offers a deal and shipping the surplus to their stores in nondeal regions. Manufacturers handle forward buying and diverting by limiting the amount they will sell at a discount, or by producing and delivering less than the full order in an effort to smooth production.[65]

Ultimately, many manufacturers feel trade promotion has become a nightmare. It contains layers of deals, is complex to administer, and often leads to lost revenues.

SELECTING BUSINESS AND SALES FORCE PROMOTION TOOLS Companies spend billions of dollars on business and sales force promotion tools (see ▭ Table 18.5) to gather leads, impress and reward customers, and motivate the sales force.[66] They typically develop budgets for tools that remain fairly constant from year to year. For many new businesses that want to make a splash to a targeted audience, especially in the B2B world, trade shows are an important tool, but the cost per contact is the highest of all communication options.

DEVELOPING THE PROGRAM In planning sales promotion programs, marketers are increasingly blending several media into a total campaign concept, such as the following award-winning promotion.[67]

Oreo Double Stuf Promotion   Winner of the Promotional Marketing Association's Super Reggie award for best integrated marketing program of 2008, Kraft's Oreo Double Stuf Racing League promotion cleverly capitalized on the images of professional athlete siblings. In its teaser launch ad, NFL star quarterback brothers Peyton and Eli

TABLE 18.5	Major Business and Sales Force Promotion Tools

Trade Shows and Conventions: Industry associations organize annual trade shows and conventions. Trade shows are an $11.5 billion business, and business marketers may spend as much as 35 percent of their annual promotion budget on trade shows. Trade show attendance can range from a few thousand people to over 70,000 for large shows held by the restaurant or hotel-motel industries. The International Consumer Electronics Show is one of the largest trade shows in the world with more than 200,000 attendees in 2009. Participating vendors expect several benefits, including generating new sales leads, maintaining customer contacts, introducing new products, meeting new customers, selling more to present customers, and educating customers with publications, videos, and other audiovisual materials.

Sales Contests: A sales contest aims at inducing the sales force or dealers to increase their sales results over a stated period, with prizes (money, trips, gifts, or points) going to those who succeed.

Specialty Advertising: Specialty advertising consists of useful, low-cost items bearing the company's name and address, and sometimes an advertising message that salespeople give to prospects and customers. Common items are ballpoint pens, calendars, key chains, flashlights, tote bags, and memo pads.

Manning announced they were officially becoming two-sport competitors. A follow-up ad with the brothers revealed that the classic "split and lick" ritual with Oreo cookies was becoming a professional sport. The Mannings encouraged the public to join the league and to enter a sweepstakes that would award 10 winners a three-day trip to New Orleans to take part in a Double Stuf Lick Race (DSLR) competition and compete for a $10,000 prize. Kraft promoted the DSLR sweepstakes by placing the image of the Mannings on 15 million Oreo packages and setting up in-store and point-of-purchase displays. An instant-win game on the Web site gave visitors a chance to earn one of 2,000 DSLR "training kits," including a cooler, two glasses, and a branded jersey. Professional tennis star sisters Serena and Venus Williams later appeared in a second round of ads, challenging the Mannings to cookie-licking supremacy in what was billed as the "ultimate sibling rivalry."

In deciding to use a particular incentive, marketers must first determine its *size*. A certain minimum is necessary if the promotion is to succeed. Second, the marketing manager must establish *conditions* for participation. Incentives might be offered to everyone or to select groups. Third, the marketer must decide on the *duration* of the promotion. Fourth, the marketer must choose a *distribution vehicle*. A 15-cents-off coupon can be distributed in the product package, in stores, by mail, online, or in advertising. Fifth, the marketing manager must establish the *timing* of promotion, and finally, the *total sales promotion budget*. The cost of a particular promotion consists of the administrative cost (printing, mailing, and promoting the deal) and the incentive cost (cost of premium or cents-off, including redemption costs), multiplied by the expected number of units sold. The cost of a coupon deal would recognize that only a fraction of consumers will redeem the coupons.

IMPLEMENTING AND EVALUATING THE PROGRAM Marketing managers must prepare implementation and control plans that cover lead time and sell-in time for each individual promotion. *Lead time* is the time necessary to prepare the program prior to launching it.[68] *Sell-in time* begins with the promotional launch and ends when approximately 95 percent of the deal merchandise is in the hands of consumers.

Manufacturers can evaluate the program using sales data, consumer surveys, and experiments. Sales (scanner) data helps analyze the types of people who took advantage of the promotion, what they bought before the promotion, and how they behaved later toward the brand and other brands. Sales promotions work best when they attract competitors' customers who then switch. *Consumer surveys* can uncover how many consumers recall the promotion, what they thought of it, how many took advantage of it, and how the promotion affected subsequent brand-choice behavior.[69] *Experiments* vary such attributes as incentive value, duration, and distribution media. For example, coupons can be sent to half the households in a consumer panel. Scanner data can track whether the coupons led more people to buy the product and when.

Additional costs beyond the cost of specific promotions include the risk that promotions might decrease long-run brand loyalty. Second, promotions can be more expensive than they appear. Some are inevitably distributed to the wrong consumers. Third are the costs of special production runs, extra sales force effort, and handling requirements. Finally, certain promotions irritate retailers, who may demand extra trade allowances or refuse to cooperate.

Events and Experiences

The IEG Sponsorship Report projected that $17.1 billion would be spent on sponsorships in North America during 2010, with 68 percent going to sports; another 10 percent to entertainment tours and attractions; 5 percent to festivals, fairs, and annual events; 5 percent to the arts; 3 percent to associations and membership organizations; and 9 percent to cause marketing.[70] Becoming part of a personally relevant moment in consumers' lives through events and experiences can broaden and deepen a company or brand's relationship with the target market.

Daily encounters with brands may also affect consumers' brand attitudes and beliefs. *Atmospheres* are "packaged environments" that create or reinforce leanings toward product purchase. Law offices decorated with Oriental rugs and oak furniture communicate "stability" and "success."[71] A five-star hotel will use elegant chandeliers, marble columns, and other tangible signs of luxury. Many firms are creating on-site and off-site product and brand experiences. There is Everything Coca-Cola in Las Vegas and M&M World in Times Square in New York.[72]

Many firms are creating their own events and experiences to create consumer and media interest and involvement. To showcase its international reach and upgrades in seating, food, and beverage, Delta Airlines created a temporary SKY360 pop-up retail lounge on West 57th Street in Manhattan. The lounge featured samples of wine and food items from chef Todd English to eat and drink, comfortable leather seats found in coach to sit in, and the seat-back entertainment system to listen to.[73] Given its central business location for the media industry, Manhattan is the site of many events and experiences.[74]

GE Profile To promote its new GE Profile Frontload Washer and Dryer with SmartDispense Technology—designed to optimize the amount of detergent used in any one wash—GE used traditional online and mass media. To create even more buzz, the firm hung 800 feet of jeans and shirts on a massive clothesline in Times Square to represent the six months' worth of washing the new machines could typically handle before needing more detergent. On one of the traffic islands were 20-foot-high inflatable versions of the new washer/dryer. A live celebrity auction to benefit the nonprofit Clothes Off Our Back Foundation was hosted by television mom Alison Sweeney. A small army of 20 representatives handing out product-related goodies (such as bottles of water and coloring books shaped like the appliance's door) added to the spectacle. GE also ran an online promotion. All these efforts combined to attract 150,000 entrants to a washer/dryer giveaway contest.

A major Times Square event to support the launch of a new line of GE Profile washers and dryers was part of an extensive integrated marketing communications program.

Events Objectives

Marketers report a number of reasons to sponsor events:

1. *To identify with a particular target market or lifestyle*—Customers can be targeted geographically, demographically, psychographically, or behaviorally according to events. Old Spice sponsors college sports and motor sports—including a 10-year deal with driver Tony Stewart's entries in the Nextel Cup and Busch Series—to highlight product relevance and sample among its target audience of 16- to 24-year-old males.[75]

2. *To increase salience of company or product name*—Sponsorship often offers sustained exposure to a brand, a necessary condition to reinforce brand salience. Top-of-mind awareness for World Cup soccer sponsors such as Emirates, Hyundai, Kia, and Sony benefited from the repeated brand and ad exposure over the one month–long tournament.

3. *To create or reinforce perceptions of key brand image associations*—Events themselves have associations that help to create or reinforce brand associations.[76] To toughen its image and appeal to America's heartland, Toyota Tundra elected to sponsor B.A.S.S. fishing tournaments and a Brooks & Dunn country music tour.

4. *To enhance corporate image*—Sponsorship can improve perceptions that the company is likable and prestigious. Although Visa views its long-standing Olympic sponsorship as a means of enhancing international brand awareness and increasing usage and volume, it also engenders patriotic goodwill and taps into the emotional Olympic spirit.[77]

5. *To create experiences and evoke feelings*—The feelings engendered by an exciting or rewarding event may indirectly link to the brand. Audi models featured prominently in the 2010 blockbuster *Iron Man 2*, including main character Tony Stark's personal R8 Spyder, the A8, Q5 and Q7 SUVs, and A3 hatchback. Backed by a month-long marketing blitz, surveys revealed that positive word of mouth doubled for the brand.[78]

6. *To express commitment to the community or on social issues*—Cause-related marketing sponsors nonprofit organizations and charities. Firms such as Timberland, Stonyfield Farms, Home Depot, Starbucks, American Express, and Tom's of Maine have made cause-related marketing an important cornerstone of their marketing programs.

7. *To entertain key clients or reward key employees*—Many events include lavish hospitality tents and other special services or activities only for sponsors and their guests. These perks engender goodwill and establish valuable business contacts. From an employee perspective, events can also build participation and morale or serve as an incentive. BB&T Corp., a major banking and financial services player in the South and Southeast United States, used its NASCAR Busch Series sponsorship to entertain business customers and its minor league baseball sponsorship to generate excitement among employees.[79]

8. *To permit merchandising or promotional opportunities*—Many marketers tie contests or sweepstakes, in-store merchandising, direct response, or other marketing activities with an event. Ford, Coca-Cola, and AT&T Mobility have all used their sponsorship of the hit TV show *American Idol* in this way.

Despite these potential advantages, the result of an event can still be unpredictable and beyond the sponsor's control. Although many consumers will credit sponsors for providing the financial assistance to make an event possible, some may resent the commercialization of events.

Major Sponsorship Decisions

Making sponsorships successful requires choosing the appropriate events, designing the optimal sponsorship program, and measuring the effects of sponsorship.[80]

CHOOSING EVENTS Because of the number of opportunities and their huge cost, many marketers are becoming more selective about choosing sponsorship events.

The event must meet the marketing objectives and communication strategy defined for the brand. The audience must match the target market. The event must have sufficient awareness, possess the desired image, and be capable of creating the desired effects. Consumers must make favorable attributions for the sponsor's engagement. An ideal event is also unique but not encumbered with many sponsors, lends itself to ancillary marketing activities, and reflects or enhances the sponsor's brand or corporate image.[81]

DESIGNING SPONSORSHIP PROGRAMS Many marketers believe the marketing program accompanying an event sponsorship ultimately determines its success. At least two to three times the amount of the sponsorship expenditure should be spent on related marketing activities.

Event creation is a particularly important skill in publicizing fund-raising drives for nonprofit organizations. Fund-raisers have developed a large repertoire of special events, including anniversary celebrations, art exhibits, auctions, benefit evenings, book sales, cake sales, contests, dances, dinners, fairs, fashion shows, phonathons, rummage sales, tours, and walkathons.

More firms are now using their names to sponsor arenas, stadiums, and other venues that hold events. Billions of dollars have been spent over the past decade for naming rights to major North American sports facilities. But as with any sponsorship, the most important consideration is the additional marketing activities.[82]

MEASURING SPONSORSHIP ACTIVITIES It's a challenge to measure the success of events. The *supply-side* measurement method focuses on potential exposure to the brand by assessing the extent of media coverage, and the *demand-side* method focuses on exposure reported by consumers. "Marketing Memo: Measuring High Performance Sponsorship Programs" offers some guidelines critical to issues of sponsorship measurement from industry experts IEG.

Supply-side methods approximate the amount of time or space devoted to media coverage of an event, for example, the number of seconds the brand is clearly visible on a television screen or the column inches of press clippings that mention it. These potential "impressions" translate into a value equivalent to the dollar cost of actually advertising in the particular media vehicle. Some industry consultants have estimated that 30 seconds of TV logo exposure during a televised event can be worth 6 percent, 10 percent, or as much as 25 percent of a 30-second TV ad spot.

Although supply-side exposure methods provide quantifiable measures, equating media coverage with advertising exposure ignores the content of the respective communications. The advertiser uses media space and time to communicate a strategically designed message. Media coverage and telecasts only expose the brand and don't necessarily embellish its meaning in any direct way. Although some public relations professionals maintain that positive editorial coverage can be worth 5 to 10 times the equivalent advertising value, sponsorship rarely provides such favorable treatment.[83]

The **demand-side method** identifies the effect sponsorship has on consumers' brand knowledge. Marketers can survey event spectators to measure recall of the event as well as resulting attitudes and intentions toward the sponsor.

Creating Experiences

A large part of local, grassroots marketing is experiential marketing, which not only communicates features and benefits but also connects a product or service with unique and interesting experiences. "The idea is not to sell something, but to demonstrate how a brand can enrich a customer's life."[84]

marketing
Memo

Measuring High Performance Sponsorship Programs

1. *Measure outcomes, not outputs.* Focus on what a sponsorship actually produced rather than what a sponsor got or did—rather than focus on 5,000 people sampled at an event, how many of those people would be classified as members of the target market and what is the likely conversion rate between their trial and future behaviors?

2. *Define and benchmark objectives on the front end.* Specific objectives help to identify what measures should be tracked. An objective of motivating the sales force and distributors suggests different measures than one of building brand image and key brand benefits. Contrast measures in terms of sponsorship effects and what might have happened if the sponsorship had not occurred.

3. *Measure return for each objective against prorated share of rights and activation fees.* Rank and rate objectives by importance and allocate the total sponsorship budget against each of those objectives.

4. *Measure behavior.* Conduct a thorough sales analysis to identify shifts in marketplace behavior as a result of the sponsorship.

5. *Apply the assumptions and ratios used by other departments within the company.* Applying statistical methods used by other departments makes it easier to gain acceptance for any sponsorship analysis.

6. *Research the emotional identities of customers and measure the results of emotional connections.* In what ways does a sponsorship psychologically affect consumers and facilitate and deepen long-term loyalty relationships?

7. *Identify group norms.* How strong of a community exists around the sponsored event or participants? Are their formal groups that share interests that will be impacted by the sponsorship?

8. *Include cost savings in ROI calculations.* Contrast expenses that a firm has typically incurred in the past achieving a particular objective from those expenses allocated to achieve the objective as part of the sponsorship.

9. *Slice the data.* Sponsorship affects market segments differently. Breaking down a target market into smaller segments can better identify sponsorship effects.

10. *Capture normative data.* Develop a core set of evaluation criteria that can be applied across all different sponsorship programs.

Source: "Measuring High Performance Sponsorship Programs," IEG Executive Brief, IEG Sponsorship Consulting, www.sponsorship.com, 2009.

Consumers seem to appreciate that. In one survey, four of five respondents found participating in a live event was more engaging than all other forms of communication. The vast majority also felt experiential marketing gave them more information than other forms of communication and would make them more likely to tell others about participating in the event and to be receptive to other marketing for the brand.[85]

Companies can even create a strong image by inviting prospects and customers to visit their headquarters and factories. Ben & Jerry's, Boeing, Crayola, and Hershey's all sponsor excellent company tours that draw millions of visitors a year. Companies such as Hallmark, Kohler, and Beiersdorf (makers of NIVEA) have built corporate museums at or near their headquarters that display their history and the drama of producing and marketing their products.

Crayola brings colorful fun to its company tours and visits.

Public Relations

Not only must the company relate constructively to customers, suppliers, and dealers, it must also relate to a large number of interested publics. A **public** is any group that has an actual or potential interest in or impact on a company's ability to achieve its objectives. **Public relations (PR)** includes a variety of programs to promote or protect a company's image or individual products.

The wise company takes concrete steps to manage successful relationships with its key publics. Most companies have a public relations department that monitors the attitudes of the organization's publics and distributes information and communications to build goodwill. The best PR departments counsel top management to adopt positive programs and eliminate questionable practices so negative publicity doesn't arise in the first place. They perform the following five functions:

1. *Press relations*—Presenting news and information about the organization in the most positive light
2. *Product publicity*—Sponsoring efforts to publicize specific products
3. *Corporate communications*—Promoting understanding of the organization through internal and external communications
4. *Lobbying*—Dealing with legislators and government officials to promote or defeat legislation and regulation
5. *Counseling*—Advising management about public issues, and company positions and image during good times and bad

Marketing Public Relations

Many companies are turning to **marketing public relations (MPR)** to support corporate or product promotion and image making. MPR, like financial PR and community PR, serves a special constituency, the marketing department.

The old name for MPR was **publicity**, the task of securing editorial space—as opposed to paid space—in print and broadcast media to promote or "hype" a product, service, idea, place, person, or organization. MPR goes beyond simple publicity and plays an important role in the following tasks:

- *Launching new products.* The amazing commercial success of toys such as LeapFrog, Beanie Babies, and even the latest kids' craze, Silly Bandz, owes a great deal to strong publicity.
- *Repositioning a mature product.* In a classic PR case study, New York City had extremely bad press in the 1970s until the "I Love New York" campaign.
- *Building interest in a product category.* Companies and trade associations have used MPR to rebuild interest in declining commodities such as eggs, milk, beef, and potatoes and to expand consumption of such products as tea, pork, and orange juice.
- *Influencing specific target groups.* McDonald's sponsors special neighborhood events in Latino and African American communities to build goodwill.

- *Defending products that have encountered public problems.* PR professionals must be adept at managing crises, such as those weathered by such well-established brands as Tylenol, Toyota, and BP in 2010.
- *Building the corporate image in a way that reflects favorably on its products.* Steve Jobs's heavily anticipated Macworld keynote speeches have helped to create an innovative, iconoclastic image for Apple Corporation.

As the power of mass advertising weakens, marketing managers are turning to MPR to build awareness and brand knowledge for both new and established products. MPR is also effective in blanketing local communities and reaching specific groups and can be more cost-effective than advertising. Nevertheless, it must be planned jointly with advertising.[86]

Clearly, creative public relations can affect public awareness at a fraction of the cost of advertising. The company doesn't pay for media space or time but only for a staff to develop and circulate the stories and manage certain events. An interesting story picked up by the media can be worth millions of dollars in equivalent advertising. Some experts say consumers are five times more likely to be influenced by editorial copy than by advertising. The following is an example of an award-winning PR campaign.[87]

Man Lives in IKEA
IKEA showed that a highly successful marketing campaign does not have to cost a lot of money if PR is properly employed. With its PR firm Ketchum, the company created the clever "Man Lives in IKEA" PR campaign. Using a budget of only $13,500, IKEA allowed comedian Mark Malkoff to live in an apartment in the Paramus, New Jersey, store from January 7 to 12, 2007, during which time he was allowed 24-hour access to film anything and everything. The campaign's goals included increasing sales, boosting traffic to IKEA-USA.com, and promoting two key brand messages: "IKEA has everything you need to live and make a home" and "Home is the most important place in the world." Ketchum and IKEA secured interviews with store executives and planned the week's schedule, which included a good-bye party featuring singer Lisa Loeb. Malkoff's team documented his interactions, including with security guards and customers relaxing in his "home," and posted 25 videos during the week. MarkLivesInIKEA.com received more than 15 million hits, and home-related IKEA blog coverage rose 356 percent from January 2007 to January 2008. IKEA calculated that the effort generated more than 382 million positive media impressions. Coverage highlights included the AP, *Today*, *Good Morning America*, and CNN. Sales at the Paramus store were up 5.5 percent compared to January 2007, while traffic to the IKEA Web site was up 6.8 percent.

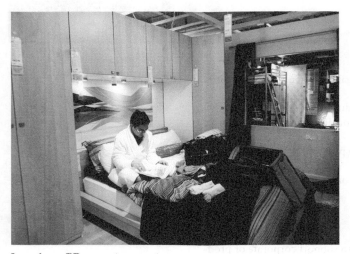

In a clever PR campaign to reinforce its "everything for the home" brand message, a man lived in an IKEA store for almost a week, which many people heard about through the film crew following him for a short documentary on his Web site: http://www.marklivesinikea.com.

Major Decisions in Marketing PR

In considering when and how to use MPR, management must establish the marketing objectives, choose the PR messages and vehicles, implement the plan carefully, and evaluate the results. The main tools of MPR are described in Table 18.6.

ESTABLISHING OBJECTIVES MPR can build *awareness* by placing stories in the media to bring attention to a product, service, person, organization, or idea. It can build *credibility* by communicating the message in an editorial context. It can help boost sales force and dealer *enthusiasm* with stories about a new product before it is launched. It can hold down *promotion cost* because MPR costs less than direct-mail and media advertising.

Whereas PR practitioners reach their target publics through the mass media, MPR is increasingly borrowing the techniques and technology of direct-response marketing to reach target audience members one-on-one.

CHOOSING MESSAGES AND VEHICLES Suppose a relatively unknown college wants more visibility. The MPR practitioner will search for stories. Are any faculty members working on unusual projects? Are any new and unusual courses being taught? Are any interesting events taking place on campus? If there are no interesting stories, the MPR practitioner should propose newsworthy events the college could sponsor. Here the challenge is to create meaningful news.

TABLE 18.6	Major Tools in Marketing PR

Publications: Companies rely extensively on published materials to reach and influence their target markets. These include annual reports, brochures, articles, company newsletters and magazines, and audiovisual materials.

Events: Companies can draw attention to new products or other company activities by arranging and publicizing special events such as news conferences, seminars, outings, trade shows, exhibits, contests and competitions, and anniversaries that will reach the target publics.

Sponsorships: Companies can promote their brands and corporate name by sponsoring and publicizing sports and cultural events and highly regarded causes.

News: One of the major tasks of PR professionals is to find or create favorable news about the company, its products, and its people and to get the media to accept press releases and attend press conferences.

Speeches: Increasingly, company executives must field questions from the media or give talks at trade associations or sales meetings, and these appearances can build the company's image.

Public Service Activities: Companies can build goodwill by contributing money and time to good causes.

Identity Media: Companies need a visual identity that the public immediately recognizes. The visual identity is carried by company logos, stationery, brochures, signs, business forms, business cards, buildings, uniforms, and dress codes.

PR ideas include hosting major academic conventions, inviting expert or celebrity speakers, and developing news conferences.

Each event and activity is an opportunity to develop a multitude of stories directed at different audiences. A good PR campaign will engage the public from a variety of angles, as did this award-winning Dreyer's Ice Cream campaign.[88]

Dreyer's Ice Cream In *PRWeek*'s Campaign of the Year in 2010, Dreyer's Ice Cream teamed up with PR firm Ketchum to launch a campaign to turn the tough economic environment into a positive. Taking advantage of the 80th anniversary of its introduction of the Rocky Road flavor—designed to cheer people up during the Great Depression—Dreyer's launched a celebratory limited edition "Red, White & No More Blues!" flavor. The ice cream combined rich, creamy vanilla ice cream with swirls of real strawberry and blueberry. The ensuing "A Taste of Recovery" campaign was designed to reinforce the feel-good aspects of the brand. A Monster.com-posted contest asked contestants to submit videos explaining a personal dream they would fulfill if they earned $100,000 for scooping ice cream. The contest drew over 85,000 online visits and more than 14,000 entries. A media blitz greeting the winner helped to contribute to the 46 million media impressions the campaign enjoyed. Despite tough economic times, sales of Dreyer's Slow Churned Limited Editions ice cream increased over 25 percent from the previous year.

A brand anniversary is a great opportunity to celebrate what is good about a brand, as Dreyer's did via its special-edition ice cream.

IMPLEMENTING THE PLAN AND EVALUATING RESULTS MPR's contribution to the bottom line is difficult to measure, because it is used along with other promotional tools.

The easiest measure of MPR effectiveness is the number of *exposures* carried by the media. Publicists supply the client with a clippings book showing all the media that carried news about the product and a summary statement such as the following:

Media coverage included 3,500 column inches of news and photographs in 350 publications with a combined circulation of 79.4 million; 2,500 minutes of air time on

290 radio stations and an estimated audience of 65 million; and 660 minutes of air time on 160 television stations with an estimated audience of 91 million. If this time and space had been purchased at advertising rates, it would have amounted to $1,047,000.[89]

This measure is not very satisfying because it contains no indication of how many people actually read, heard, or recalled the message and what they thought afterward; nor does it contain information about the net audience reached, because publications overlap in readership. It also ignores the effects of electronic media. Publicity's goal is reach, not frequency, so it would be more useful to know the number of unduplicated exposures across all media types.

A better measure is the *change in product awareness, comprehension, or attitude* resulting from the MPR campaign (after allowing for the effect of other promotional tools). For example, how many people recall hearing the news item? How many told others about it (a measure of word of mouth)? How many changed their minds after hearing it?

Summary

1. Advertising is any paid form of nonpersonal presentation and promotion of ideas, goods, or services by an identified sponsor. Advertisers include not only business firms but also charitable, nonprofit, and government agencies.

2. Developing an advertising program is a five-step process: (1) Set advertising objectives, (2) establish a budget, (3) choose the advertising message and creative strategy, (4) decide on the media, and (5) evaluate communication and sales effects.

3. Sales promotion consists of mostly short-term incentive tools, designed to stimulate quicker or greater purchase of particular products or services by consumers or the trade.

4. In using sales promotion, a company must establish its objectives, select the tools, develop the program, pretest the program, implement and control it, and evaluate the results.

5. Events and experiences are a means to become part of special and more personally relevant moments in consumers' lives. Events can broaden and deepen the sponsor's relationship with its target market, but only if managed properly.

6. Public relations (PR) includes a variety of programs designed to promote or protect a company's image or its individual products. Marketing public relations (MPR), to support the marketing department in corporate or product promotion and image making, can affect public awareness at a fraction of the cost of advertising and is often much more credible. The main tools of PR are publications, events, news, community affairs, identification media, lobbying, and social responsibility.

Applications

Marketing Debate
Should Marketers Test Advertising?

Advertising creatives have long lamented ad pretesting. They believe it inhibits their creative process and results in too much sameness in commercials. Marketers, on the other hand, believe pretesting provides necessary checks and balances to ensure the ad campaign will connect with consumers and be well received in the marketplace.

Take a position: Ad pretesting in often an unnecessary waste of marketing dollars *versus* Ad pretesting provides an important diagnostic for marketers as to the likely success of an ad campaign.

Marketing Discussion
Television Advertising

What are some of your favorite TV ads? Why? How effective are the message and creative strategies? How are they creating consumer preference and loyalty and building brand equity?

Marketing Excellence

>>Coca-Cola

When it comes to mass marketing, perhaps no one does it better than Coca-Cola. Coke is the most popular and best-selling soft drink in history. With an annual marketing budget of nearly $3 billion and annual sales exceeding $30 billion, the brand tops the Interbrand ranking year after year. Today, Coca-Cola holds a current brand value of $68 billion and reaches consumers in over 200 countries, making it the best-known product in the world. In fact, Coca-Cola is such a global phenomenon that its name is the second-most understood word in the world (after *okay*).

The history of Coke's success is astonishing. The drink was invented in 1886 by Dr. John S. Pemberton, who mixed a syrup of his own invention with carbonated water to cure headaches. The company's first president later turned the product into a pop culture phenomenon by introducing it to pharmacists and consumers around the world and handing out clocks, posters, and other paraphernalia with the Coca-Cola logo.

Coca-Cola believed early on that to gain worldwide acceptance, the brand needed to connect emotionally and socially with the masses, and the product needed to be "within arm's-length of desire." So the company focused on gaining extensive distribution and worked hard at making the product loved by all. In World War II, it declared that "every man in uniform gets a bottle of Coca-Cola for 5 cents, wherever he is, and whatever it costs the company." This strategy helped introduce the soft drink to people around the world as well as connect with them positively in a time of turmoil.

Why is Coca-Cola so much bigger than any other competitor? What Coke does better than everyone else is create highly current, uplifting global campaigns that translate well into different countries, languages, and cultures. Coke's advertising over the years has primarily focused on the product's ability to quench thirst and the brand's magical ability to connect people no matter who they are or how they live. Andy Warhol said it best, "A Coke is a Coke and no amount of money can get you a better Coke than the one the bum on the corner is drinking."

One of Coca-Cola's most memorable and successful commercials was called "Hilltop" and featured the song, "I'd like to buy the world a Coke." Launched in 1971, the ad featured young adults from all over the world sharing a happy, harmonious moment and common bond (drinking a Coke) on a hillside in Italy. The commercial touched so many consumers emotionally and so effectively showed the worldwide appeal of Coke that the song became a top ten hit single later that year.

Coca-Cola's television commercials still touch upon the message of universal connection over a Coke, often in a lighthearted tone to appeal to a young audience. In one spot, a group of young adults sit around a campfire, playing the guitar, laughing, smiling, and passing around a bottle of Coke. The bottle reaches a slimy, one-eyed alien who joins in on the fun, takes a sip from the bottle, and passes it along. When the next drinker wipes off the slime in disgust, the music stops suddenly and the group stares at him in disappointment. The man hesitantly hands the bottle back to the alien to get re-slimed and then drinks from it, and the music and the party continue in perfect harmony.

Coca-Cola's mass communications strategy has evolved over the years and today mixes a wide range of media including television, radio, print, online, in-store, digital, billboard, public relations, events, paraphernalia, and even its own museum. The company's target audience and reach are so massive that choosing the right media and marketing message is critical. Coca-Cola uses big events to hit huge audiences; it has sponsored the Olympics since 1928 and advertises during the Super Bowl. Red Coke cups are placed front and center during top-rated television shows like *American Idol*, and the company spends over $1 billion a year on sports sponsorships such as NASCAR and the World Cup. Coca-Cola's global campaigns must also be relevant on a local scale. In China, for example, Coca-Cola has given its regional managers control over its advertising so they can include appropriate cultural messages.

The delicate balance between Coca-Cola's local and global marketing is crucial because, as one Coca-Cola executive explained, "Creating effective marketing at a local level in the absence of global scale can lead to huge inefficiencies." In 2006, for example, Coca-Cola ran two campaigns during the FIFA World Cup as well as several local campaigns. In 2010, the company ran a single campaign during the same event in over 100 markets. Executives at Coca-Cola estimated that the latter, more global strategy saved the company over $45 million in efficiencies.

Despite its unprecedented success over the years, Coke is not perfect. In 1985, in perhaps the worst product launch ever, Coca-Cola introduced New Coke—a sweeter concoction of the original secret formula. Consumers instantly rejected it and sales plummeted. Three months later, Coca-Cola retracted New Coke and relaunched the original formula under the name Coca-Cola Classic, to the delight of customers everywhere. Then-CEO Roberto Goizueta stated, "The simple fact is that all the time and money and skill poured into consumer research on the new Coca-Cola could not measure or reveal the deep and abiding emotional attachment to original Coca-Cola felt by so many people."

Coca-Cola's success at marketing a product on such a global, massive scale is unique. No other product is so universally available, universally accepted, and universally loved. As the company continues to grow, it seeks out new ways to better connect with even more individuals.

Referring to itself as a "Happiness Factory," it is optimistic that it will succeed.

Questions

1. What does Coca-Cola stand for? Is it the same for everyone? Explain.

2. Coca-Cola has successfully marketed to billions of people around the world. Why is it so successful?

3. Can Pepsi or any other company ever surpass Coca-Cola? Why or why not? What are Coca-Cola's greatest risks?

Sources: Natalie Zmuda, "Coca-Cola Lays Out Its Vision for the Future at 2010 Meeting." *Advertising Age*, November 22, 2009; Natalie Zmuda, "Coke's 'Open Happiness' Keeps It Simple for Global Audience," *Advertising Age*, January 21, 2009; John Greenwald, "Will Teens Buy It?" *Time*, June 24, 2001; "Coca-Cola Still Viewed as Most Valuable Brand." *USA Today*, September 18, 2009; Edward Rothstein, "Ingredients: Carbonated Water, High-Fructose Corniness . . ." *New York Times*, July 30, 2007; Brad Cook, "Coca-Cola: A Classic," *Brandchannel*, December 2, 2002; Coca-Cola, *Annual Report*.

Marketing Excellence

>>Gillette

Gillette knows men. Not only does the company understand what products men desire for their grooming needs, it also knows how to market to men all around the world. Since the invention of the safety razor by King C. Gillette in 1901, Gillette has had a number of breakthrough product innovations. These include the first twin-blade shaving system in 1971 named the Trac II, a razor with a pivoting head in 1977 called the Atra, and the first razor with spring-mounted twin blades in 1989 dubbed the Sensor. In 1998, Gillette introduced the first triple-blade system, Mach3, which became a billion-dollar brand surpassed only by the 2006 launch of the "best

shave on the planet"—the six-bladed Fusion, with five blades in the front for regular shaving and one in the back for trimming.

Today, Gillette holds a commanding lead in the shaving and razor business with a 70 percent global market share and $7.5 billion in annual sales. Six hundred million men use a Gillette product every day, and the Fusion razor accounts for 45 percent of the men's razors sold in the United States. Gillette's mass appeal is a result of several factors, including extensive consumer research, quality product innovations, and successful mass communications.

While Gillette's product launches have improved male grooming, it's the company's impressive marketing knowledge and campaigns that have helped it reach this international level of success. Traditionally, Gillette uses one global marketing message rather than individual targeted messages for each country or region. This message is backed by a wide spectrum of advertising support, including athletic sponsorships, television campaigns, in-store promotions, print ads, online advertising, and direct marketing.

Gillette's most recent global marketing effort, "The Moment," launched in 2009, is an extension of its well-recognized campaign, "The Best a Man Can Get." The campaign features everyday men as well as the Gillette Champions—baseball star Derek Jeter, tennis champion Roger Federer, and soccer great Thierry Henry—experiencing moments of doubt and Gillette's grooming products helping them gain confidence. The campaign was designed to help Gillette expand beyond razors and shaving and increase sales of its entire line of grooming products. The massive marketing effort launched around the globe and included television, print, online, and point-of-sale advertising.

Another crucial element in Gillette's marketing strategy is sports marketing. Gillette's natural fit with baseball and tradition has helped the company connect emotionally with its core audience, and its sponsorship with Major League Baseball dates to 1939. Tim Brosnan, EVP for Major League Baseball, explained, "Gillette is a sports marketing pioneer that paved the way for modern day sports sponsorship and endorsements." Gillette ads have featured baseball heroes such as Hank Aaron, Mickey Mantle, and Honus Wagner from as early as 1910.

Gillette also has ties to football. The company sponsors Gillette Stadium, home of the New England Patriots, and is a corporate sponsor of the NFL, making four of its products, Gillette, Old Spice, Head & Shoulders, and Febreze, "Official Locker Room Products of the NFL." Gillette's partnership includes sweepstakes to win NFL game tickets, Web site promotions, and ties to the NFL, such as the presence of some NFL players in its commercials. Gillette also sponsors several NASCAR races and drivers and the UK Tri-Nations rugby tournament. It even created a Zamboni at the Boston Bruins game that looked like a huge Fusion razor shaving the ice.

While sports marketing is a critical element of Gillette's marketing strategy, the brand aims to reach all men and therefore aligns itself with musicians, video games, and movies—in one James Bond film, *Goldfinger*, a Gillette razor contained a homing device.

When Procter & Gamble acquired Gillette in 2005 for $57 billion (a record five times sales), it aimed for more than sales and profit. P&G, an expert on marketing to women, wanted to learn about marketing to men on a global scale, and no one tops Gillette.

Questions

1. Gillette has successfully convinced the world that "more is better" in terms of number of blades and other razor features. Why has that worked in the past? What's next?

2. Some of Gillette's spokespeople such as Tiger Woods have run into controversy after becoming endorsers for the brand. Does this hurt Gillette's brand equity or marketing message? Explain.

3. Can Gillette ever become as successful at marketing to women? Why or why not?

Sources: Gillette press release, "Gillette Launches New Global Brand Marketing Campaign," July 1, 2009; Major League Baseball press release, "Major League Baseball Announces Extension of Historic Sponsorship with Gillette Dating Back to 1939," April 16, 2009; Gillette, *2009 Annual Report*; Jeremy Mullman and Rich Thomaselli, "Why Tiger Is Still the Best Gillette Can Get," *Advertising Age*, December 7, 2009; Louise Story, "Procter and Gillette Learn from Each Other's Marketing Ways," *New York Times*, April 12, 2007; Dan Beucke, "A Blade Too Far," *BusinessWeek*, August 14, 2006; Jenn Abelson, "And Then There Were Five," *Boston Globe*, September 15, 2005; Jack Neff, "Six-Blade Blitz," *Advertising Age*, September 19, 2005, pp. 3, 53; Editorial, "Gillette Spends Smart on Fusion," *Advertising Age*, September 26, 2005, p. 24.

Chapter 19

Managing Personal Communications: Direct and Interactive Marketing, Word of Mouth, and Personal Selling

In the face of the Internet revolution, marketing communications today increasingly occur as a kind of personal dialogue between the company and its customers. Companies must ask not only "How should we reach our customers?" but also "How should our customers reach us?" and "How can our customers reach each other?" New technologies have encouraged companies to move from mass communication to more targeted, two-way communications. Consumers now play a much more participatory role in the marketing process. Consider how Pepsi has engaged the consumer in its marketing communications.[1]

For the first time in 23 years, PepsiCo chose not to advertise any of its soft drink brands during the biggest U.S. media event, the Super Bowl. Instead, it launched its ambitious Pepsi Refresh Project. With a tagline "Every Pepsi Refreshes the World," Pepsi earmarked $20 million for the program to fund ideas from anyone, anywhere, anytime to make a difference in six areas: health, arts and culture, food and shelter, the planet, neighborhoods, and education. Ideas are submitted at refresheverything.com and voted online by the general public. A significant presence on Facebook, Twitter, and other social networks is a key aspect to the program. The first grant recipients received funding for a variety of different projects, including building a community playground, providing care packages and comfort items for troops in the field or recovering from wounds at home, and conducting financial literacy sessions for teens. Pepsi also allocated an additional $1.3 million in the summer of 2010 to support communities in the Gulf of Mexico region affected by the catastrophic oil spill.

Marketers are trying to figure out the right way to be part of the consumer conversation. Personalizing communications and creating dialogues by saying and doing the right thing to the right person at the right time is critical for marketing effectiveness. In this chapter, we consider how companies personalize their marketing communications to have more impact. We begin by evaluating direct and interactive marketing, then move to word-of-mouth marketing, and finish by considering personal selling and the sales force.

Direct Marketing

Today, many marketers build long-term relationships with customers.[2] They send birthday cards, information materials, or small premiums. Airlines, hotels, and other businesses adopt frequency reward programs and club programs.[3] **Direct marketing** is the use of consumer-direct (CD) channels to reach and deliver goods and services to customers without using marketing middlemen.

Direct marketers can use a number of channels to reach individual prospects and customers: direct mail, catalog marketing, telemarketing, interactive TV, kiosks, Web sites, and mobile devices. They often seek a measurable response, typically a customer order, through **direct-order marketing**. Direct marketing has been a fast-growing avenue for serving customers, partly in response to the high and increasing costs of reaching business markets through a sales force. Sales produced through traditional direct marketing channels (catalogs, direct mail, and telemarketing) have been growing rapidly, along with direct-mail sales, which include sales to the consumer market, B2B, and fund-raising by charitable institutions.

Direct marketing has been outpacing U.S. retail sales. It accounted for almost 53 percent of total advertising spending in 2009, and companies spent more than $149 billion on direct marketing per year, accounting for 8.3 percent of GDP.[4]

The Benefits of Direct Marketing

Market demassification has resulted in an ever-increasing number of market niches. Consumers short of time and tired of traffic and parking headaches appreciate toll-free phone numbers, always-open Web sites, next-day delivery, and direct marketers' commitment to customer service. In addition, many chain stores have dropped slower-moving specialty items, creating an opportunity for direct marketers to promote these to interested buyers instead.

Sellers benefit from demassification as well. Direct marketers can buy a mailing list containing the names of almost any group: left-handed people, overweight people, millionaires. They can customize and personalize messages and build a continuous relationship with each customer. New parents will receive periodic mailings describing new clothes, toys, and other goods as their child grows.

Direct marketing can reach prospects at the moment they want a solicitation and therefore be noticed by more highly interested prospects. It lets marketers test alternative media and messages to find the most cost-effective approach. Direct marketing also makes the direct marketer's offer and strategy less visible to competitors. Finally, direct marketers can measure responses to their campaigns to decide which have been the most profitable. One successful direct marketer is L.L.Bean.[5]

L.L.Bean   L.L.Bean's founder Leon Leonwood (L.L.) Bean returned from a Maine hunting trip in 1911 with cold, damp feet and a revolutionary idea. His Maine Hunting Shoe stitched leather uppers to workmen's rubber boots to create a comfortable, functional boot. To a mailing list of hunters, Bean sent a three-page flyer describing the benefits of the new product and backing it with a complete guarantee. The shoe, however, did not meet with initial success. Of his first 100 orders, 90 were returned when the tops and bottoms separated. True to his word, Bean refunded the purchase price and the problem was fixed. L.L.Bean quickly became known as a trusted source for reliable outdoor equipment and expert advice. The L.L.Bean guarantee of 100 percent satisfaction is still at the core of the company's business, as is the original L.L. Bean's Golden Rule, "Sell good merchandise at a reasonable profit, treat your customers like human beings, and they will always come back for more." Today, L.L.Bean is a $1.4 billion company. In 2009, it produced 49 different catalogs and received 11 million customer contacts. The company's Web site is among the top-rated e-commerce sites, and its growing number of retail stores and outlets retain the company's legendary customer service.

Direct marketing must be integrated with other communications and channel activities.[6] Direct marketing companies such as Eddie Bauer, Lands' End, and the Franklin Mint made fortunes building their brands in the direct marketing mail-order and phone-order business and then opened retail stores. They cross-promote their stores, catalogs, and Web sites, for example, by putting their Web addresses on their shopping bags.

Successful direct marketers view a customer interaction as an opportunity to up-sell, cross-sell, or just deepen a relationship. These marketers make sure they know enough about each customer to customize and personalize offers and messages and develop a plan for lifetime marketing to each valuable customer, based on their knowledge of life events and transitions. They also carefully

L.L.Bean has a decades-long legacy of fully satisfying customer needs—guaranteed!

orchestrate each element of their campaigns. Here is an example of an award-winning campaign that did just that.[7]

New Zealand Yellow Pages One of the Direct Marketing Association's top ECHO award winners in 2009 was New Zealand's Yellow Pages Group. With a theme of "Job Done," the group recruited a young woman to be the focus of the campaign and gave her the task of building a restaurant 40 feet above the ground in a redwood tree, using only help found via the Yellow Pages. A TV ad, billboard, and online media launched the campaign, and a Web site provided updates. Access to the striking pod-shaped structure Treehouse was provided by an elevated treetop walkway. The restaurant actually operated from December 2008 to February 2009 as part of the campaign. Highly popular, the campaign was credited with increasing the use of Yellow Pages by 11 percent to record levels.

We next consider some of the key issues that characterize different direct marketing channels.

To dramatically demonstrate the utility of its product, the New Zealand Yellow Pages engaged a designer to build a tree-top restaurant using only help hired through the Yellow Pages.

Direct Mail

Direct-mail marketing means sending an offer, announcement, reminder, or other item to an individual consumer. Using highly selective mailing lists, direct marketers send out millions of mail pieces each year—letters, flyers, foldouts, and other "salespeople with wings." Some direct marketers mail multimedia DVDs to prospects and customers.

Direct mail is a popular medium because it permits target market selectivity, can be personalized, is flexible, and allows early testing and response measurement. Although the cost per thousand is higher than for mass media, the people reached are much better prospects. The success of direct mail, however, has also become its liability—so many marketers are sending out direct-mail pieces that mailboxes are becoming stuffed, leading some consumers to disregard the blizzard of solicitations they receive.

In constructing an effective direct-mail campaign, direct marketers must choose their objectives, target markets and prospects, offer elements, means of testing the campaign, and measures of campaign success.

OBJECTIVES Most direct marketers aim to receive an order from prospects and judge a campaign's success by the response rate. An order-response rate of 2 percent to 4 percent is normally considered good, although this number varies with product category, price, and the nature of the offering.[8] Direct mail can also produce prospect leads, strengthen customer relationships, inform and educate customers, remind customers of offers, and reinforce recent customer purchase decisions.

TARGET MARKETS AND PROSPECTS Most direct marketers apply the RFM (*recency, frequency, monetary amount*) formula to select customers according to how much time has passed since their last purchase, how many times they have purchased, and how much they have spent since becoming a customer. Suppose the company is offering a leather jacket. It might make this offer to the most attractive customers—those who made their last purchase between 30 and 60 days ago, who make three to six purchases a year, and who have spent at least $100 since becoming customers. Points are established for varying RFM levels; the more points, the more attractive the customer.[9]

Marketers also identify prospects on the basis of age, sex, income, education, previous mail-order purchases, and occasion. College freshmen will buy laptop computers, backpacks, and compact refrigerators; newlyweds look for housing, furniture, appliances, and bank loans. Another useful variable is consumer lifestyle or "passions" such as electronics, cooking, and the outdoors.

Dun & Bradstreet provides a wealth of data for B2B direct marketing. Here the prospect is often not an individual but a group or committee of both decision makers and decision influencers. Each member needs to be treated differently, and the timing, frequency, nature, and format of contact must reflect the member's status and role.

The company's best prospects are customers who have bought its products in the past. The direct marketer can also buy lists of names from list brokers, but these lists often have problems, including name duplication, incomplete data, and obsolete addresses. Better lists include overlays of demographic and psychographic information. Direct marketers typically buy and test a sample before buying more names from the same list. They can build their own lists by advertising a promotional offer and collecting responses.

OFFER ELEMENTS The offer strategy has five elements—the *product,* the *offer,* the *medium,* the *distribution method,* and the *creative strategy*.[10] Fortunately, all can be tested. The direct-mail marketer also must choose five components of the mailing itself: the outside envelope, sales letter, circular, reply form, and reply envelope. A common direct marketing strategy is to follow up direct mail with an e-mail.

TESTING ELEMENTS One of the great advantages of direct marketing is the ability to test, under real marketplace conditions, different elements of an offer strategy, such as products, product features, copy platform, mailer type, envelope, prices, or mailing lists.

Response rates typically understate a campaign's long-term impact. Suppose only 2 percent of the recipients who receive a direct-mail piece advertising Samsonite luggage place an order. A much larger percentage became aware of the product (direct mail has high readership), and some percentage may have formed an intention to buy at a later date (either by mail or at a retail outlet). Some may mention Samsonite luggage to others as a result of the direct-mail piece. To better estimate a promotion's impact, some companies measure the impact of direct marketing on awareness, intention to buy, and word of mouth.

MEASURING CAMPAIGN SUCCESS: LIFETIME VALUE By adding up the planned campaign costs, the direct marketer can determine the needed break-even response rate. This rate must be net of returned merchandise and bad debts. A specific campaign may fail to break even in the short run but can still be profitable in the long run if customer lifetime value is factored in (see Chapter 5) by calculating the average customer longevity, average customer annual expenditure, and average gross margin, minus the average cost of customer acquisition and maintenance (discounted for the opportunity cost of money).[11]

Catalog Marketing

In catalog marketing, companies may send full-line merchandise catalogs, specialty consumer catalogs, and business catalogs, usually in print form but also as DVDs or online. In 2009, three of the top B-to-C catalog sellers were Dell ($51 billion), Staples ($8.9 billion), and CDW ($8.1 billion). Three top B-to-B catalog sellers were Thermo Scientific lab and research supplies ($10.5 billion), Henry Schien dental, medical, and vet supplies ($6.4 billion), and WESCO International electrical and industry maintenance supplies ($6.1 billion). Thousands of small businesses also issue specialty catalogs.[12] Many direct marketers find combining catalogs and Web sites an effective way to sell.

Catalogs are a huge business—the Internet and catalog retailing industry includes 16,000 companies with combined annual revenue of $235 billion.[13] The success of a catalog business depends on managing customer lists carefully to avoid duplication or bad debts, controlling inventory, offering good-quality merchandise so returns are low, and projecting a distinctive image. Some companies add literary or information features, send swatches of materials, operate a special online or telephone hotline to answer questions, send gifts to their best customers, and donate a percentage of profits to good causes. Putting their entire catalog online also provides business marketers with better access to global consumers than ever before, saving printing and mailing costs.

Telemarketing

Telemarketing is the use of the telephone and call centers to attract prospects, sell to existing customers, and provide service by taking orders and answering questions. It helps companies increase revenue, reduce selling costs, and improve customer satisfaction. Companies use call centers for *inbound telemarketing*—receiving calls from customers—and *outbound telemarketing*—initiating calls to prospects and customers.

Although outbound telemarketing historically has been a major direct marketing tool, its potentially intrusive nature led the Federal Trade Commission to establish a National Do Not Call Registry in 2003. About 191 million consumers who did not want telemarketing calls at home were registered by 2009. Because only political organizations, charities, telephone surveyors, or companies with existing relationships with consumers are exempt, consumer telemarketing has lost much of its effectiveness.[14]

Business-to-business telemarketing is increasing, however. Raleigh Bicycles used telemarketing to reduce the personal selling costs of contacting its dealers. In the first year, sales force travel costs dropped 50 percent and sales in a single quarter went up 34 percent. As it improves with the use of videophones, telemarketing will increasingly replace, though never eliminate, more expensive field sales calls.

Other Media for Direct-Response Marketing

Direct marketers use all the major media. Newspapers and magazines carry ads offering books, clothing, appliances, vacations, and other goods and services that individuals can order via toll-free numbers. Radio ads present offers 24 hours a day. Some companies prepare 30- and 60-minute *infomercials* to combine the sell of television commercials with the draw of information and entertainment. Infomercials promote products that are complicated or technologically advanced, or that require a great deal of explanation (Carnival Cruises, Mercedes, Universal Studios, and even Monster.com). At-home shopping channels are dedicated to selling goods and services on a toll-free number or via the Web for delivery within 48 hours.

Public and Ethical Issues in Direct Marketing

Direct marketers and their customers usually enjoy mutually rewarding relationships. Occasionally, however, a darker side emerges:

- *Irritation.* Many people don't like hard-sell, direct marketing solicitations.
- *Unfairness.* Some direct marketers take advantage of impulsive or less sophisticated buyers or prey on the vulnerable, especially the elderly.[15]
- *Deception and fraud.* Some direct marketers design mailers and write copy intended to mislead or exaggerate product size, performance claims, or the "retail price." The Federal Trade Commission receives thousands of complaints each year about fraudulent investment scams and phony charities.
- *Invasion of privacy.* It seems that almost every time consumers order products by mail or telephone, apply for a credit card, or take out a magazine subscription, their names, addresses, and purchasing behavior may be added to several company databases. Critics worry that marketers may know too much about consumers' lives, and that they may use this knowledge to take unfair advantage.

People in the direct marketing industry know that, left unattended, such problems will lead to increasingly negative consumer attitudes, lower response rates, and calls for greater state and federal regulation. Most direct marketers want the same thing consumers want: honest and well-designed marketing offers targeted only to those who appreciate hearing about them.

Interactive Marketing

The newest and fastest-growing channels for communicating and selling directly to customers are electronic.[16] The Internet provides marketers and consumers with opportunities for much greater *interaction* and *individualization.* Soon few marketing programs will be considered complete without a meaningful online component.

Advantages and Disadvantages of Interactive Marketing

The variety of online communication options means companies can send tailored messages that engage consumers by reflecting their special interests and behavior. The Internet is also highly accountable and its effects can be easily traced by noting how many unique visitors or "UVs" click on a page or ad, how long they spend with it, and where they go afterward.[17]

Marketers can build or tap into online communities, inviting participation from consumers and creating a long-term marketing asset in the process. The Web offers the advantage of *contextual placement,* buying ads on sites related to the marketer's offerings. Marketers can also place advertising based on keywords from search engines, to reach people when they've actually started the buying process.

Using the Web also has disadvantages. Consumers can effectively screen out most messages. Marketers may think their ads are more effective than they are if bogus clicks are generated by software-powered Web sites.[18] Advertisers also lose some control over their online messages, which can be hacked or vandalized.

But many feel the pros outweigh the cons, and the Web is attracting marketers of all kinds. Beauty pioneer Estée Lauder, who said she relied on three means of communication to build her multimillion-dollar cosmetics business—"telephone, telegraph, and tell a woman"—would now have to add the Web, where the company's official site describes new and old products, announces special offers and promotions, and helps customers locate stores where they can buy Estée Lauder products.[19]

Marketers must go where the customers are, and increasingly that's online. U.S. consumers go to the Web over 25 percent of the time they spend with all media (see △ Figure 19.1). Customers

Online	4:13
TV and video	3:17
Music and radio	1:26
Mobile phone	1:18
Landline phone	0:36
Gaming	0:36
Reading	0:24

|Fig. 19.1| △

Average Time Spent per Day with Select Media According to US Consumers, 2009 (hrs:mins)

Source: Yankee Group, "2009 Advertising Forecast Update: Less TV, More Internet," April 6, 2010. Copyright 1997-2010. Yankee Group. All rights reserved.

define the rules of engagement, however, and insulate themselves with the help of agents and intermediaries if they so choose. Customers define what information they need, what offerings they're interested in, and what they're willing to pay.[20]

Online advertising continues to gain on traditional media. Total Internet ad spending is estimated to have grown to $26 billion in 2009 from $24 billion in 2008; TV advertising was estimated to have dropped to $41 billion in 2009 from $52 billion in 2008. Helping fuel online growth is the emergence of rich media ads that combine animation, video, and sound with interactive features.[21] Consider what Burger King has done online.

Burger King   "If you have a global brand promise, 'Have It Your Way,'" said Russ Klein, Burger King's former president for global marketing, strategy, and innovation, "it's about putting the customer in charge," even if they say "bad things" about the brand. In competing against McDonald's, with its family-friendly image, "it's more important for us to be provocative than pleasant," added Klein, especially when appealing to a market of mainly teenage boys. Burger King's brash ad campaigns—featuring its creepy bobble-head king and talking chicken—have appeared on YouTube and MySpace, so the company can take advantage of "social connectivity" as consumers react to the ads. Burger King encourages customers to build online communities around their favorite company icons and products. To celebrate the 50th anniversary of its popular Whopper hamburger, the company took over a Burger King restaurant in Las Vegas for a day and told people the Whopper had been permanently removed from the menu. Customers' outraged reactions were filmed as part of an award-winning campaign dubbed "Whopper Freakout," which served as the basis of TV ads and online videos. Over 5 million consumers watched an 8-minute streaming video, another 14 million watched it or the TV spots on YouTube, and millions more heard or read about it via PR or word of mouth.[22]

Interactive Marketing Communication Options

A company chooses which forms of interactive marketing will be most cost-effective in achieving communication and sales objectives.[23] Some of the main categories, discussed next, are: (1) Web sites, (2) search ads, (3) display ads, and (4) e-mails. After summarizing some developments in mobile marketing, we'll describe social media and word-of-mouth effects.

WEB SITES Companies must design Web sites that embody or express their purpose, history, products, and vision and that are attractive on first viewing and interesting enough to encourage repeat visits.[24] Jeffrey Rayport and Bernard Jaworski propose that effective sites feature seven design

Vividly demonstrating its customers' loyalty, Burger King's online "Whopper Freakout" videos became a viral hit.

|Fig. 19.2| △

Seven Key Design
Elements of an
Effective Web Site

Source: Jeffrey F. Rayport and Bernard J. Jaworski,
e-commerce (New York: McGraw-Hill, 2001), p. 116.

- *Context.* Layout and design
- *Content.* Text, pictures, sound, and video the site contains
- *Community.* How the site enables user-to-user communication
- *Customization.* Site's ability to tailor itself to different users or to allow users to personalize the site
- *Communication.* How the site enables site-to-user, user-to-site, or two-way communication
- *Connection.* Degree that the site is linked to other sites
- *Commerce.* Site's capabilities to enable commercial transactions

elements they call the 7Cs (see △ Figure 19.2):[25] To encourage repeat visits, companies must pay special attention to context and content factors and embrace another "C"—constant change.[26]

Visitors will judge a site's performance on ease of use and physical attractiveness.[27] *Ease of use* means: (1) The site downloads quickly, (2) the first page is easy to understand, and (3) it is easy to navigate to other pages that open quickly. *Physical attractiveness* is assured when: (1) Individual pages are clean and not crammed with content, (2) typefaces and font sizes are very readable, and (3) the site makes good use of color (and sound).

Firms such as comScore and Nielsen Online track where consumers go online through page views, unique visitors, length of visit, and so on.[28] Companies must also be sensitive to online security and privacy-protection issues.[29]

Besides their Web sites, companies may employ **microsites,** individual Web pages or clusters of pages that function as supplements to a primary site. They're particularly relevant for companies selling low-interest products. People rarely visit an insurance company's Web site, but the company can create a microsite on used-car sites that offers advice for buyers of used cars and at the same time a good insurance deal.

SEARCH ADS A hot growth area in interactive marketing is **paid search** or **pay-per-click ads,** which now account for roughly half of all online ad spending.[30] Thirty-five percent of all searches are reportedly for products or services.

In paid search, marketers bid in a continuous auction on search terms that serve as a proxy for the consumer's product or consumption interests. When a consumer searches for any of the words with Google, Yahoo!, or Bing, the marketer's ad may appear above or next to the results, depending on the amount the company bids and an algorithm the search engines use to determine an ad's relevance to a particular search.[31]

Advertisers pay only if people click on the links, but marketers believe consumers who have already expressed interest by engaging in search are prime prospects. Average click-through is about 2 percent, much more than for comparable online ads. The cost per click depends on how high the link is ranked and the popularity of the keyword. The ever-increasing popularity of paid search has increased competition among keyword bidders, significantly raising search prices and putting a premium on choosing the best possible keywords, bidding on them strategically, and monitoring the results for effectiveness and efficiency.

Search engine optimization has become a crucial part of marketing given the large amount of money being spent by marketers on search. A number of guidelines have been suggested for more effective search ads.[32] Broader search terms are useful for general brand building; more specific ones—for example, specifying a particular product model or service—are useful for generating and converting sales leads. Search terms need to be spotlighted on the appropriate pages so search engines can easily identify them. Multiple keywords are usually needed for any one product, but each keyword must be bid for according to its likely return on revenue. It also helps to have popular sites link back to the site. Data can be collected to track the effects of paid search.

DISPLAY ADS **Display ads** or **banner ads** are small, rectangular boxes containing text and perhaps a picture that companies pay to place on relevant Web sites.[33] The larger the audience, the higher the cost. Some banners are accepted on a barter basis. In the early days of the Internet, viewers clicked on 2 percent to 3 percent of the banner ads they saw, but that percentage quickly plummeted to as little as 0.25 percent and advertisers began to explore other forms of communication.

Given that Internet users spend only 5 percent of their time online actually searching for information, display ads still hold great promise compared to popular search ads. But ads need to be more attention-getting and influential, better targeted, and more closely tracked.[34]

Interstitials are advertisements, often with video or animation, which pop up between changes on a Web site. For example, ads for Johnson & Johnson's Tylenol headache reliever would pop up on brokers' Web sites whenever the stock market fell by 100 points or more. Because consumers find pop-up ads intrusive and distracting, many use software to block them.

A popular vehicle for advertising is *podcasts*, digital media files created for playback on portable MP3 players, laptops, or PCs. Sponsors pay roughly $25 per thousand listeners to run a 15- or 30-second audio ad at the beginning of the podcast. Although these rates are higher than for popular radio shows, podcasts are able to reach very specific market segments, and their popularity has grown.[35]

E-MAIL E-mail allows marketers to inform and communicate with customers at a fraction of the cost of a "d-mail," or direct mail, campaign. Consumers are besieged by e-mails, though, and many employ spam filters. Some firms are asking consumers to say whether and when they would like to receive emails. FTD, the flower retailer, allows customers to choose whether to receive e-mail reminders to send flowers for virtually any holiday as well as specific birthdays and anniversaries.[36]

E-mails must be timely, targeted, and relevant. For example, the United Way of Massachusetts Bay and Merrimack Valley used video-embedded e-mails to increase sign-ups for their events and to cut costs. Videos were made one minute in length when testing revealed that two minutes was too long but 30 seconds was too short.[37] "Marketing Memo: How to Maximize the Marketing Value of E-mails" provides some important guidelines for productive e-mail campaigns.

MOBILE MARKETING With cell phones' ubiquitous nature and marketers' ability to personalize messages based on demographics and other consumer behavior characteristics (see Chapter 15), the appeal of mobile marketing as a communication tool is obvious.[38]

With over 4.1 billion mobile subscribers in the world in 2009—there are more than twice as many mobile phones in the world as personal computers—cell phones represent a major opportunity for advertisers to reach consumers on the "third screen" (TV and the computer are first and second). Some firms are moving fast into m-space. One mobile pioneer in the banking industry is Bank of America.[39]

 **marketing Memo**   **How to Maximize the Marketing Value of E-mails**

- *Give the customer a reason to respond.* Offer powerful incentives for reading e-mail pitches and online ads, such as trivia games, scavenger hunts, and instant-win sweepstakes.

- *Personalize the content of your e-mails.* Customers who agree to receive IBM's weekly iSource newsletter select "the news they choose" from topics on an interest profile.

- *Offer something the customer can't get via direct mail.* Because e-mail campaigns can be carried out quickly, they can offer time-sensitive information. Travelocity sends frequent e-mails pitching last-minute cheap airfares, and Club Med pitches unsold vacation packages at a discount.

- *Make it easy for customers to "unsubscribe."* Online customers demand a positive exit experience. Dissatisfied customers leaving on a sour note are more likely to spread the displeasure to others.

- *Combine with other communications such as social media.* Southwest Airlines found the highest number of reservations occur after an e-mail campaign followed by a social media campaign. Papa John's was able to add 45,000 fans to its Facebook page through an e-mail campaign inviting customers to participate in a "March Madness" NCAA basketball tournament contest.

To increase the effectiveness of e-mails, some researchers are employing "heat mapping," by which they can measure what people read on a computer screen by using cameras attached to a computer that track eye movements. One study showed that clickable graphic icons and buttons that linked to more details of a marketing offer increased click-through rates by 60 percent over links that used just an Internet address.

Sources: Richard Westlund, "Success Stories in eMail Marketing," *Adweek Special Advertising Section to Adweek, Brandweek, and Mediaweek,* February 16, 2010; Suzanne Vranica, "Marketers Give E-mail Another Look," *Wall Street Journal,* July 17, 2006; Seth Godin, *Permission Marketing: Turning Strangers into Friends and Friends into Customers* (New York: Simon & Schuster, 1999).

Bank of America Bank of America is using mobile as a communication channel and a means to provide banking solutions for the many ways its customers lead their lives. More than 2 million of its 59 million customers use mobile banking applications, which the bank credits as a significant drawing card given that 8 percent to 10 percent of these mobile users are new customers. Initially targeting a younger group of users between 18 and 30 years old—with special emphasis on college students—the bank's mobile banking services increasingly appeal to other groups such as older, higher-income users. Its smart-phone apps and traditional browser-based solutions have been praised for clean navigation, ease of use, and reach. The branch and ATM locator, for instance, is used by one in eight mobile customers. Mobile marketing is integrated all through the bank's marketing efforts: The Web site provides demos and tours of its mobile services; the TV campaigns stress the benefits of its mobile banking. With one click on a mobile banner ad, smart-phone users can download the free Bank of America app or just learn more about its mobile banking services.

- *Mobile marketing options.* Mobile ad spending was almost $1 billion worldwide in 2009, most of which went into SMS text messages and simple display ads. With the increased capabilities of smart phones, however, mobile ads can be more than just a display medium using static "mini-billboards."[40]

  Much recent interest has been generated in mobile apps—"bite-sized" software programs that can be loaded on to smart phones. In a short period of time, thousands were introduced by companies large and small. VW chose to launch its GTI in the United States with an iPhone app, receiving 2 million downloads in three weeks. In Europe, it launched the VW Tiguan with a mobile app as well as text messages and an interstitial Web site.[41]

  Smart phones also allow loyalty programs with which customers can track their visits and purchases at a merchant and receive rewards.[42] By tracking the location of receptive customers who opt in to receive communications, retailers can send them location-specific promotions when they are in proximity to shops or outlets. Sonic Corp. used GPS data and proximity to cell towers in Atlanta to identify when those customers who had signed up for company communications were near one of roughly 50 Sonic restaurants in the area. When that was the case, Sonic sent customers a text message with a discount offer or an ad to entice them to visit the restaurant.[43]

  With traditional coupon redemption rates declining for years, the ability of cell phones to permit more relevant and timely offers to consumers at or near the point of purchase has piqued the interest of many marketers. These new coupons can take all forms; digital in-store signs can now dispense them to smart phones.[44]

- *Developing mobile marketing programs.* Even with newer generation smart phones, the Web experience can be very different for users given smaller screen sizes, longer downloads, and the lack of some software capabilities (such as Adobe Flash Player on iPhones). Marketers would be wise to design simple, clear, and "clean" sites, paying even greater attention than usual to user experience and navigation.[45]

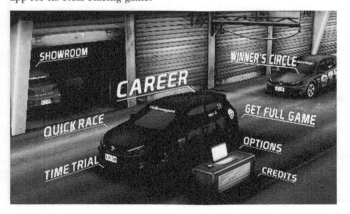

VW launched its GTI model in the United States with an iPhone app for its Real Racing game.

U.S. marketers can learn much about mobile marketing by looking overseas. In developed Asian markets such as Hong Kong, Japan, Singapore, and South Korea, mobile marketing is fast becoming a central component of customer experiences.[46] In developing markets, high cell phone penetration also makes mobile marketing attractive. A pioneer in China, Coca-Cola created a national campaign asking Beijing residents to send text messages guessing the high temperature in the city every day for just over a month, for a chance to win a one-year supply of Coke products. The campaign attracted more than 4 million messages over the course of 35 days.[47]

Although a growing population segment uses mobile phones for everything from entertainment to banking, different people have different attitudes and experiences with mobile technology. "Marketing Memo: Segmenting Tech Users" profiles the role of mobile Internet access in several groups' digital lifestyles.

Segmenting Tech Users

Group Name	% of Adults	What You Need to Know About Them	Key Demographic Facts
Motivated by Mobility (39%)			
Digital Collaborators	8%	With the most tech assets, Digital Collaborators use them to work with and share their creations with others. They are enthusiastic about how ICTs help them connect with others and confident in how to manage digital devices and information.	Mostly male (56%), late 30s, well-educated, and well-off.
Ambivalent Networkers	7%	Ambivalent Networkers have folded mobile devices into how they run their social lives, whether through texting or social networking tools online. They also rely on ICTs for entertainment. But they also express worries about connectivity; some find that mobile devices are intrusive and many think it is good to take a break from online use.	Primarily male (60%), they are young (late 20s) and ethnically diverse.
Media Movers	7%	Media Movers have a wide range of online and mobile habits, and they are bound to find or create an information nugget, such as a digital photo, and pass it on. These social exchanges are central to this group's use of ICTs. Cyberspace, as a path to personal productivity or an outlet for creativity, is less important.	Males (56%) in their mid-30s, many with children and in middle income range.
Roving Nodes	9%	Roving Nodes are active managers of their social and work lives using their mobile device. They get the most out of basic applications with their assets such as e-mail or texting and find them great for arranging the logistics of their lives and enhancing personal productivity.	Mostly women (56%), in their late 30s, well educated and well-off.
Mobile Newbies	8%	This group rates low on tech assets, but its members really like their cell phones. Mobile Newbies, many of whom acquired a cell in the past year, like how the device helps them be more available to others. They would be hard pressed to give up the cell phone.	Mainly women (55%), about age 50, lower educational and income levels.
Stationary Media Majority (61%)			
Desktop Veterans	13%	This group of older, veteran online users is content to use a high-speed connection and a desktop computer to explore the Internet and stay in touch with friends, placing their cell phone and mobile applications in the background.	Mainly men (55%), in their mid 40s, well-educated and well-off economically.
Drifting Surfers	14%	Many have the requisite tech assets, such as broadband or a cell phone, but Drifting Surfers are infrequent online users. When they use technology, it is for basic information gathering. It wouldn't bother the typical Drifting Surfer to give up the Internet or a cell phone.	Majority women (56%), in their early 40s, middle income, and average education levels.
Information Encumbered	10%	Most people in this group suffer from information overload and think taking time off from the Internet is a good thing. The Information Encumbered are firmly rooted in old media to get information.	Two-thirds men, in their early 50s, average education, lower-middle income.
Tech Indifferent	10%	Members of this group are not heavy Internet users and although most have cell phones, they don't like their intrusiveness. The Indifferent could easily do without modern gadgets and services.	Mainly women (55%), in their late 50s, low-income and education levels.
Off the Network	14%	Members of this group have neither cell phones nor online access, and tend to be older and low-income. But a few have experience with ICTs; some used to have online access and as many as one in five used to have a cell phone.	Low-income senior women, high share of African Americans.

Source: "The Mobile Difference—Tech User Types," Pew Internet & American Life Project, March 31, 2009, www.pewinternet.org/Infographics/The-Mobile-Difference—Tech-User-Types.aspx.

Word of Mouth

Consumers use *word of mouth* to talk about dozens of brands each day, from media and entertainment products such as movies, TV shows, and publications to food products, travel services, and retail stores.[48]

Companies are acutely aware of the power of word of mouth. Hush Puppies shoes, Krispy Kreme doughnuts, the blockbuster movie *The Passion of the Christ*, and, more recently, Crocs shoes have been built through strong word of mouth, as were companies such as The Body Shop, Palm, Red Bull, Starbucks, and Amazon.com.

Positive word of mouth sometimes happens organically with little advertising, but it can also be managed and facilitated.[49] It is particularly effective for smaller businesses, with whom customers may feel a more personal relationship. Many small businesses are investing in various forms of social media at the expense of newspapers, radio, and Yellow Pages to get the word out. Southern Jewelz, started by a recent college grad, found sales doubling over six months after it began to actively use Facebook, Twitter, and e-commerce software.[50]

With the growth of social media, as Chapter 17 noted, marketers sometimes distinguish paid media from earned or free media. Although different points of view prevail, *paid media* results from press coverage of company-generated advertising, publicity, or other promotional efforts. *Earned media*—sometimes called *free media*—is all the PR benefits a firm receives without having directly paid for anything—all the news stories, blogs, social network conversations that deal with a brand. Earned media isn't literally free—the company has to invest in products, services, and their marketing to some degree to get people to pay attention and write and talk about them, but the expenses are not devoted to eliciting a media response.

We first consider how social media promotes the flow of word of mouth before delving into more detail on how word of mouth is formed and travels. To start our discussion, consider some of the different ways Intuit uses social media.[51]

Intuit   Always a marketing pioneer in the software industry, Intuit has received much recognition for its extensive social media programs. Intuit adopted a narrowcasting approach with its QuickBooks Live Community, which serves the small business market: It is available only to customers who buy QuickBooks 2009 on a PC or a Mac and is a place where customers can trade tips and ask questions, 70 percent of which are answered by other QuickBooks customers. One accountant has posted 5,600 answers on the site. The community also provides Intuit with useful product feedback. Intuit has run TurboTax contests to encourage product placement in Facebook, MySpace, and Twitter. Users with the most "original and unique" status updates related to TurboTax receive prizes. Intuit's "Love a Local Business" program awards $1,000 grants to local businesses based on the community's online votes. A variety of other social networking events help Intuit interact with small businesses. As one social media expert at the company said: "Social media is one of the key trends driving our business . . . It's about fast connections with customers and building an on-going relationship."

Social Media

Social media are a means for consumers to share text, images, audio, and video information with each other and with companies and vice versa. Social media allow marketers to establish a public voice and presence on the Web and reinforce other communication activities. Because of their day-to-day immediacy, they can also encourage companies to stay innovative and relevant.

There are three main platforms for social media: (1) online communities and forums, (2) bloggers (individuals and networks such as Sugar and Gawker), and (3) social networks (like Facebook, Twitter, and YouTube).

ONLINE COMMUNITIES AND FORUMS Online communities and forums come in all shapes and sizes. Many are created by consumers or groups of consumers with no commercial interests or company affiliations. Others are sponsored by companies whose members communicate with the company and with each other through postings, instant messaging, and chat discussions about special interests related to the company's products and brands. These online communities and forums can be a valuable resource for companies and provide multiple functions by both collecting and conveying key information.

A technology marketing pioneer, Intuit created a strong online brand community for its QuickBooks software product.

A key for success of online communities is to create individual and group activities that help form bonds among community members. The Idea Center at Kodak Gallery is an online community for exchanging ideas about how to use Kodak products to create personalized gifts and other creative products using digital photos. Kodak has found that peer-to-peer recommendations within the community led to more frequent, larger purchases.[52] Apple hosts a large number of discussion groups organized by product lines and also by consumer versus professional use. These groups are customers' primary source of product information after warranties expire.

Information flow in online communities and forums is two-way and can provide companies with useful, hard-to-get customer information and insights. When GlaxoSmithKline prepared to launch its first weight-loss drug, Alli, it sponsored a weight-loss community. The firm felt the feedback it gained was more valuable than what it could have received from traditional focus groups. Research has shown, however, that firms should avoid too much democratization of innovation. Groundbreaking ideas can be replaced by lowest-common-denominator solutions.[53]

BLOGS *Blogs*, regularly updated online journals or diaries, have become an important outlet for word of mouth. There are millions in existence and they vary widely, some personal for close friends and families, others designed to reach and influence a vast audience. One obvious appeal of blogs is bringing together people with common interests. Blog networks such as Gawker Media offer marketers a portfolio of choices. Online celebrity gossip blog PopSugar has spawned a family of breezy blogs on fashion (FabSugar), beauty (BellaSugar), and romance and culture (TrèsSugar), attracting women aged 18 to 49.[54]

Corporations are creating their own blogs and carefully monitoring those of others.[55] Blog search engines provide up-to-the-minute analysis of millions of blogs to find out what's on people's minds.[56] Popular blogs are creating influential opinion leaders. At the TreeHugger site, a team of bloggers tracks green consumer products for 3.5 million unique visitors per month, offering video and reference guides and an average of 35 daily posts.[57]

Because many consumers examine product information and reviews contained in blogs, the Federal Trade Commission has also taken steps to require bloggers to disclose their relationship with marketers whose products they endorse. At the other extreme, some consumers use blogs and videos as a means of retribution and revenge on companies for bad service and faulty products. Dell's customer-service shortcomings were splashed all over the Internet through a series of "Dell Hell" postings. AOL took some heat when a frustrated customer recorded and broadcast online a service representative's emphatic resistance to canceling his service. Comcast was embarrassed when a video surfaced of one of its technicians sleeping on a customer's couch.[58]

The TreeHugger Web site tracks blogs and Internet activity with respect to green products.

SOCIAL NETWORKS Social networks have become an important force in both business-to-consumer and business-to-business marketing.[59] Major ones include Facebook, which is the world's biggest; MySpace, which concentrates on music and entertainment; LinkedIn, which targets career-minded professionals; and Twitter, which allows members to network via 140-character messages or "tweets." Different networks offer different benefits to firms. For example, Twitter can be an early warning system that permits rapid response, whereas Facebook allows deeper dives to engage consumers in more meaningful ways.[60]

Marketers are still learning how to best tap into social networks and their huge, well-defined audiences. Given networks' noncommercial nature—users are generally there looking to connect with others—attracting attention and persuading are more challenging. Also, given that users generate their own content, ads may find themselves appearing beside inappropriate or even offensive content.[61]

Advertising is only one avenue, however. Like any individual, companies can also join the social groups and actively participate. Having a Facebook page has become a virtual prerequisite for many companies. Twitter can benefit even the smallest firm. To create interest in its products and the events it hosted, small San Francisco bakery Mission Pie began to send tweet alerts, quickly gaining 1,000 followers and a sizable up-tick in business. "Follow Me on Twitter" signs are appearing on doors and windows of more small shops.[62]

And although major social networks offer the most exposure, niche networks provide a more targeted market that may be more likely to spread the brand message, as with CafeMom.[63]

CafeMom Started in 2006 by parent company CMI Marketing, CafeMom has 6.7 million unique visitors per month on Cafemom.com and 18 million on boutique ad network CafeMom plus. Visitors participate in dozens of different forums for moms. When the site started a forum for discussing developmentally appropriate play activities, toymaker Playskool sent toy kits to over 5,000 members and encouraged them to share their experiences with each other, resulting in 11,600 posts at Playskool Preschool Playgroup. "The great thing is you get direct feedback from actual moms," says the director of media at Hasbro, Playskool's parent company. This kind of feedback can be invaluable in the product-development process as well. The site's sweet spot is young, middle-class women with kids who love the opportunity to make friends and seek support, spending an average of 44 minutes a day on the site.

USING SOCIAL MEDIA Social media allow consumers to become engaged with a brand at perhaps a deeper and broader level than ever before. Marketers should do everything they can to encourage willing consumers to engage productively. But as useful as they may be, social media can never become the sole source of marketing communications.

Embracing social media, harnessing word of mouth, and creating buzz requires companies to take the good with the bad. Look what happened to the marketers of Motrin at Johnson & Johnson.[64]

Motrin When marketers at J&J decided to run a slightly tongue-in-cheek online Web video for Motrin implying that young mothers carrying their babies everywhere in slings and chest packs as a means of bonding—or perhaps just to be trendy—were inadvertently risking back pain, they had no idea the pain they would in fact experience. After the ad ran online for several weeks without notice, a few vocal mothers took offense on Twitter on a Friday night, creating a weekend firestorm that stretched all over the Web. On the following Monday, marketers for Motrin quickly took to e-mail to personally apologize and replaced the video with a broader message of apology. Then they were criticized for caving in to pressure and overreacting.

The negative online response to Motrin's new ad posed a significant social media challenge to the brand.

The Motrin example shows the power and speed of social media, but also the challenges they pose to companies. The reality, however, is that whether a company chooses to engage in social media or not, the Internet will always permit scrutiny, criticism, and even "cheap shots" from consumers and organizations. By using social media and the Web in a constructive, thoughtful way, firms at least have a means to create a strong online presence and better offer credible alternative points of view if such events occur.[65]

Buzz and Viral Marketing

Some marketers highlight two particular forms of word of mouth—buzz and viral marketing.[66] *Buzz marketing* generates excitement, creates publicity, and conveys new relevant brand-related information through unexpected or even outrageous means.[67] *Viral marketing* is another form of word of mouth, or "word of mouse," that encourages consumers to pass along company-developed products and services or audio, video, or written information to others online.[68]

With user-generated content sites such as YouTube, MySpace Video, and Google Video, consumers and advertisers can upload ads and videos to be shared virally by millions of people. Online videos can be cost-effective—costing $50,000 to $200,000—and marketers can take more freedoms with them.

Blendtec

Utah-based Blendtec used to be known primarily for its commercial blenders and food mills. The company wasn't really familiar to the general public until it launched a hilarious series of "Will It Blend?" online videos to promote some of its commercial products for home use. The videos feature founder and CEO Tom Dickson wearing a white lab coat and pulverizing objects ranging from golf balls and pens to beer bottles, all in a genial but deadpan manner. The genius of the videos (www.willitblend.com) is that they tie into current events. As soon as the iPhone was launched with huge media fanfare, Blendtec aired a video in which Dickson smiled and said, "I love my iPhone. It does everything. But will it blend?" After the blender crushed the iPhone to bits, Dickson lifted the lid on the small pile of black dust and said simply, "iSmoke." The clip drew more than 3.5 million downloads on YouTube. Dickson has appeared on the *Today* and other network television shows and has had a cameo in a Weezer video. One of the few items *not* to blend: A crowbar![69]

Blendtec's classic "Will It Blend?" online videos created significant brand equity for a brand that was previously fairly unknown.

Outrageousness is a two-edged sword. The Blendtec Web site clearly puts its comic videos in the "*Don't* try this at home" category and another set showing how to grind up vegetables for soup, for instance, in the "*Do* try this at home" category.

Contrary to popular opinion, products don't have to be outrageous or edgy to generate buzz. Companies can help to create buzz; and media or advertising are not always necessary for buzz to occur.[70] Some agencies have been created solely to help clients create buzz. P&G has 225,000 teens enlisted in Tremor and 600,000 mothers enrolled in Vocalpoint. Both groups are built on the premise that certain individuals want to learn about products, receive samples and coupons, share their opinions with companies, and, of course, talk up their experiences with others. P&G chooses well-connected people—the Vocalpoint moms have big social networks and generally speak to 25 to 30 other women during the day, compared to an average of 5 for other moms—and their messages carry a strong reason to share product information with a friend.[71] BzzAgent is another buzz-building firm.[72]

BzzAgent

Boston-based BzzAgent has assembled an international word-of-mouth media network powered by 600,000 demographically diverse—but essentially ordinary—people who volunteer to talk up any of the clients' products they deem worth promoting. The company pairs consumers with products, information, and digital tools to activate widespread opinion-sharing throughout its own social media site, called BzzScapes, and within each member's personal social circles. BzzAgent believes this unique combination of people and platform accelerates measurable word of mouth and fosters sustained brand advocacy. BzzAgent participants have spread their own personal views and opinions to nearly 100 million friends and family. Each time an agent completes an activity, he or she is expected to file a report describing the nature of the buzz and its effectiveness. The company claims the buzz is honest because the process requires just enough work that few agents enroll solely for freebies, and agents don't talk up products they don't like. Agents are also supposed to disclose they're connected to BzzAgent. The company has completed hundreds of projects, working with clients such as Levi's Dockers, Anheuser-Busch, Cadbury-Schweppes, V Guide, Bacardi, Dunkin' Donuts, Silk, Tropicana Pure, Mrs. Dash, and the publishers of *Freakonomics* and *Eats, Shoots and Leaves*, both bestsellers.

Buzz and viral marketing both try to create a splash in the marketplace to showcase a brand and its noteworthy features. Some believe these influences are driven more by the rules of entertainment than the rules of selling. Consider these examples: Quicksilver puts out surfing videos and surf-culture books for teens, Johnson & Johnson and Pampers both have popular Web sites with parenting advice for babies; Walmart places videos with money-saving tips on YouTube; Grey Goose vodka has an entire entertainment division; Mountain Dew has a record label; and Hasbro is joining forces with Discovery to create a TV channel.[73] Ultimately, however, the success of any viral or buzz campaign depends on the willingness of consumers to talk to other consumers.[74]

Opinion Leaders

Communication researchers propose a social-structure view of interpersonal communication.[75] They see society as consisting of *cliques*, small groups whose members interact frequently. Clique members are similar, and their closeness facilitates effective communication but also insulates the clique from new ideas. The challenge is to create more openness so cliques exchange information with others in society. This openness is helped along by people who function as liaisons and connect two or more cliques without belonging to either, and by *bridges*, people who belong to one clique and are linked to a person in another.

Best-selling author Malcolm Gladwell claims three factors work to ignite public interest in an idea.[76] According to the first, "The Law of the Few," three types of people help to spread an idea like an epidemic. First are *Mavens*, people knowledgeable about big and small things. Second are *Connectors*, people who know and communicate with a great number of other people. Third are *Salesmen*, who possess natural persuasive power. Any idea that catches the interest of Mavens, Connectors, and Salesmen is likely to be broadcast far and wide. The second factor is "Stickiness." An idea must be expressed so that it motivates people to act. Otherwise, "The Law of the Few" will not lead to a self-sustaining epidemic. Finally, the third factor, "The Power of Context," controls whether those spreading an idea are able to organize groups and communities around it.

Not everyone agrees with Gladwell's ideas.[77] One team of viral marketing experts caution that although influencers or "alphas" start trends, they are often too introspective and socially alienated to spread them. They advise marketers to cultivate "bees," hyperdevoted customers who are not just satisfied knowing about the next trend but live to spread the word.[78] More firms are in fact finding ways to actively engage their passionate brand evangelists. LEGO's Ambassador Program targets its most enthusiastic followers for brainstorming and feedback.[79]

Companies can stimulate personal influence channels to work on their behalf. "Marketing Memo: How to Start a Buzz Fire" describes some techniques. Companies can also trace online activity to identify more influential users who may function as opinion leaders.[80]

Consumers can resent personal communications if unsolicited. Some word-of-mouth tactics walk a fine line between acceptable and unethical. One controversial tactic, sometimes called *shill marketing* or *stealth marketing*, pays people to anonymously promote a product or service in public places without disclosing their financial relationship to the sponsoring firm. To launch its T681 mobile camera phone, Sony Ericsson hired actors dressed as tourists to approach people at tourist locations and ask to have their photo taken. Handing over the mobile phone created an opportunity to discuss its merits, but many found the deception distasteful.[81] Heineken took another tack and turned an admittedly deceptive stunt into a huge PR win.[82]

How to Start a Buzz Fire

Although many word-of-mouth effects are beyond marketers' control, certain steps improve the likelihood of starting a positive buzz.

- *Identify influential individuals and companies and devote extra effort to them.* In technology, influencers might be large corporate customers, industry analysts and journalists, selected policy makers, and a sampling of early adopters.

- *Supply key people with product samples.* When two pediatricians launched MD Moms to market baby skin care products, they liberally sampled the product to physicians and mothers hoping for mentions on Internet message boards and parenting Web sites. The strategy worked—the company hit year one distribution goals by the end of the first month.

- *Work through community influentials such as local disk jockeys, class presidents, and presidents of women's organizations.* Ford's prelaunch "Fiesta Movement" campaign invited 100 handpicked young adults or "millennials" to live with the Fiesta car for six months. People were chosen based on their online experience with blogging and social friends and a video they submitted about their desire for adventure. After six months, the campaign had 4.3 million YouTube views, over 500,000 Flickr views, over 3 million Twitter impressions, and 50,000 potential customers, 97 percent of whom didn't already own a Ford.[83]

- *Develop word-of-mouth referral channels to build business.* Professionals will often encourage clients to recommend their services.

Weight Watchers found that word-of-mouth referrals from someone in the program had a huge impact on business.

- *Provide compelling information that customers want to pass along.* Companies shouldn't communicate with customers in terms better suited for a press release. Make it easy and desirable for a customer to borrow elements from an e-mail message or blog. Information should be original and useful. Originality increases the amount of word of mouth, but usefulness determines whether it will be positive or negative.

Ford Fiesta used 100 young adult consumers to provide an online, real-life preview of its new car.

Sources: Matthew Dolan, "Ford Takes Online Gamble with New Fiesta," *Wall Street Journal*, April 8, 2009; Sarit Moldovan, Jacob Goldenberg, and Amitava Chattopadhyay, "What Drives Word of Mouth? The Roles of Product Originality and Usefulness," *MSI Report No. 06-111* (Cambridge, MA: Marketing Science Institute, 2006); Karen J. Bannan, "Online Chat Is a Grapevine That Yields Precious Fruit," *New York Times*, December 25, 2006; John Batelle, "The Net of Influence," *Business 2.0* (March 2004): 70; Ann Meyer, "Word-of-Mouth Marketing Speaks Well for Small Business," *Chicago Tribune*, July 28, 2003; Malcolm Macalister Hall, "Selling by Stealth," *Business Life* (November 2001), pp. 51–55.

Heineken   Nothing may be more important to young European adult males than soccer—which they call football. Heineken took advantage of that fact to stage a fake classical musical concert at the same time as a crucial Real Madrid versus AC Milan match, enlisting girlfriends, bosses, and professors as accomplices in the hoax. Over 1,000 passionate AC Milan fans reluctantly showed up at the theater with their companions for the performance. As the string quarter began to play and the soccer fans squirmed, words on a screen behind the musicians slowly revealed clues about the nature of the prank and then showed the game in all its big-screen glory. Over 1.5 million people watched the audience reactions on live SkySport TV, and the Heineken site devoted to the event received 5 million visitors. Subsequent PR and word of mouth made it a worldwide phenomenon.

Measuring the Effects of Word of Mouth[84]

Research and consulting firm Keller Fay notes that although 80 percent of word of mouth occurs offline, many marketers concentrate on online effects given the ease of tracking them through advertising, PR, or digital agencies.[85] Gatorade created a "Mission Control Center"—set up like a broadcast television control room—to monitor the brand on social networks around the clock.

Through demographic information or proxies and cookies, firms can monitor when customers blog, comment, post, share, link, upload, friend, stream, write on a wall, or update a profile. With these tracking tools it is possible, for example, to sell movie advertisers "1 million American women between the ages of 14 and 24 who had uploaded, blogged, rated, shared, or commented on entertainment in the previous 24 hours."[86]

DuPont employs measures of online word of mouth such as campaign scale (how far it reached), speed (how fast it spread), share of voice in that space, share of voice in that speed, whether it achieved positive lift in sentiment, whether the message was understood, whether it was relevant, whether it had sustainability (and was not a one-shot deal), and how far it moved from its source.

Other researchers focus more on characterizing the source of word of mouth. For example, one group is looking to evaluate blogs according to three dimensions: relevance, sentiment, and authority.[87]

Designing the Sales Force

The original and oldest form of direct marketing is the field sales call. To locate prospects, develop them into customers, and grow the business, most industrial companies rely heavily on a professional sales force or hire manufacturers' representatives and agents. Many consumer companies such as Allstate, Amway, Avon, Mary Kay, Merrill Lynch, and Tupperware use a direct-selling force.

U.S. firms spend over a trillion dollars annually on sales forces and sales force materials—more than on any other promotional method. Over 10 percent of the total workforce work full time in sales occupations, both nonprofit and for profit.[88] Hospitals and museums, for example, use fund-raisers to contact donors and solicit donations. For many firms, sales force performance is critical.[89]

SoBe   John Bello, founder of SoBe nutritionally enhanced teas and juices, has given much credit to his sales force for the brand's successful ascent. Bello claims that the superior quality and consistent sales effort from the 150 salespeople the company had at its peak was directed toward one simple goal: "SoBe won in the street because our salespeople were there more often and in greater numbers than the competition, and they were more motivated by far." SoBe's sales force operated at every level of the distribution chain: At the distributor level, steady communication gave SoBe disproportionate focus relative to the other brands; at the trade level, with companies such as 7-Eleven, Costco, and Safeway, most senior salespeople had strong personal relationships; and at the individual store level, the SoBe team was always at work setting and restocking shelves, cutting in product, and putting up point-of-sale displays. According to Bello, bottom-line success in any entrepreneurial endeavor depends on sales execution.

An essential ingredient to SoBe's initial beverage market success was a highly motivated and skilled sales force.

Although no one debates the importance of the sales force in marketing programs, companies are sensitive to the high and rising costs of maintaining one, including salaries, commissions, bonuses, travel expenses, and benefits. Not surprisingly, companies are trying to increase sales force productivity through better selection, training, supervision, motivation, and compensation.[90]

The term *sales representative* covers six positions, ranging from the least to the most creative types of selling:[91]

1. *Deliverer*—A salesperson whose major task is the delivery of a product (water, fuel, oil).
2. *Order taker*—An inside order taker (standing behind the counter) or outside order taker (calling on the supermarket manager).
3. *Missionary*—A salesperson not permitted to take an order but expected rather to build goodwill or educate the actual or potential user (the medical "detailer" representing an ethical pharmaceutical house).
4. *Technician*—A salesperson with a high level of technical knowledge (the engineering salesperson who is primarily a consultant to client companies).
5. *Demand creator*—A salesperson who relies on creative methods for selling tangible products (vacuum cleaners, cleaning brushes, household products) or intangibles (insurance, advertising services, or education).
6. *Solution vendor*—A salesperson whose expertise is solving a customer's problem, often with a system of the company's products and services (for example, computer and communications systems).

|Fig. 19.3| △

Designing a Sales Force

|Fig. 19.4| △

A Hypothetical (Dysfunctional) Sales Marketing Exchange

Source: Based on a talk by Scott Sanderude and Jeff Standish, "Work Together, Win Together: Resolving Misconceptions between Sales and Marketing," talk given at Marketing Science Institute's *Marketing, Sales, and Customers* conference, December 7, 2005.

Salespeople are the company's personal link to its customers. In designing the sales force, the company must develop sales force objectives, strategy, structure, size, and compensation (see △ Figure 19.3).

Sales Force Objectives and Strategy

The days when all the sales force did was "sell, sell, and sell" are long gone. Sales reps need to know how to diagnose a customer's problem and propose a solution that can help improve the customer's profitability.

Companies need to define specific sales force objectives. For example, a company might want its sales representatives to spend 80 percent of their time with current customers and 20 percent with prospects, and 85 percent of their time on established products and 15 percent on new products. Regardless of the selling context, salespeople perform one or more specific tasks:

- *Prospecting.* Searching for prospects or leads
- *Targeting.* Deciding how to allocate their time among prospects and customers
- *Communicating.* Communicating information about the company's products and services
- *Selling.* Approaching, presenting, answering questions, overcoming objections, and closing sales
- *Servicing.* Providing various services to the customers—consulting on problems, rendering technical assistance, arranging financing, expediting delivery
- *Information gathering.* Conducting market research and doing intelligence work
- *Allocating.* Deciding which customers will get scarce products during product shortages

To manage costs, most companies are choosing a *leveraged sales force* that focuses reps on selling the company's more complex and customized products to large accounts and uses inside salespeople and Web ordering for low-end selling. Salespeople handle fewer accounts and are rewarded for key account growth; lead generation, proposal writing, order fulfillment, and postsale support are turned over to others. This is far different from expecting salespeople to sell to every possible account, the common weakness of geographically based sales forces.[92]

Companies must deploy sales forces strategically so they call on the right customers at the right time in the right way, acting as "account managers" who arrange fruitful contact between people in the buying and selling organizations. Selling increasingly calls for teamwork and the support of others, such as *top management,* especially when national accounts or major sales are at stake; *technical people,* who supply information and service before, during, and after product purchase; *customer service representatives,* who provide installation, maintenance, and other services; and *office staff,* consisting of sales analysts, order expediters, and assistants.[93]

To maintain a market focus, salespeople should know how to analyze sales data, measure market potential, gather market intelligence, and develop marketing strategies and plans. Especially at the higher levels of sales management, they need analytical marketing skills. Marketers believe sales forces are more effective in the long run if they understand and appreciate marketing as well as selling. Too often marketing and sales are in conflict: the sales force complains marketing isn't generating enough leads and marketers complain the sales force isn't converting them (see △ Figure 19.4). Improved collaboration and communication between these two can increase revenues and profits.[94]

Sales: I need leads, but marketing never sends me any good leads. How am I supposed to get new business with no good leads?

Marketing: We deliver tons of leads and they just sit in the system. Why won't sales call on any of them?

Sales: I have nothing new to sell. What is marketing doing? Why can't they figure out what customers want before they give it to us? Why don't they give me anything that's easy to sell?

Marketing: Why won't sales get out and sell my new programs? How do they expect customers to place orders without sales contacts?

Sales: My people spend too much time on administration and paperwork. I need them out selling.

Marketing: We need information to get new ideas. How long does it take to type in a few words? Don't they know their own customers?

Sales: How am I going to hit my number? Marketing is a waste of time. I'd rather have more sales reps.

Marketing: How am I going to hit my number? Sales won't help and I don't have enough people to do it myself.

Once the company chooses its strategy, it can use a direct or a contractual sales force. A **direct (company) sales force** consists of full- or part-time paid employees who work exclusively for the company. Inside sales personnel conduct business from the office using the telephone and receive visits from prospective buyers, and field sales personnel travel and visit customers. A **contractual sales force** consists of manufacturers' reps, sales agents, and brokers, who earn a commission based on sales.

Sales Force Structure

The sales force strategy also has implications for its structure. A company that sells one product line to one end-using industry with customers in many locations would use a territorial structure. A company that sells many products to many types of customers might need a product or market structure. Some companies need a more complex structure. Motorola, for example, manages four types of sales forces: (1) a strategic market sales force composed of technical, applications, and quality engineers and service personnel assigned to major accounts; (2) a geographic sales force calling on thousands of customers in different territories; (3) a distributor sales force calling on and coaching Motorola distributors; and (4) an inside sales force doing telemarketing and taking orders via phone and fax.

Established companies need to revise their sales force structures as market and economic conditions change. SAS, seller of business intelligence software, reorganized its sales force into industry-specific groups such as banks, brokerages, and insurers and saw revenue soar by 14 percent.[95] "Marketing Insight: Major Account Management" discusses a specialized form of sales force structure.

Major Account Management

Marketers typically single out for attention major accounts (also called key accounts, national accounts, global accounts, or house accounts). These are important customers with multiple divisions in many locations who use uniform pricing and coordinated service for all divisions. A major account manager (MAM) usually reports to the national sales manager and supervises field reps calling on customer plants within their territories. The average company manages about 75 key accounts. If a company has several such accounts, it's likely to organize a major account management division, in which the average MAM handles nine accounts.

Large accounts are often handled by a strategic account management team with cross-functional members who integrate new-product development, technical support, supply chain, marketing activities, and multiple communication channels to cover all aspects of the relationship. Procter & Gamble has a strategic account management team of 300 staffers to work with Walmart in its Bentonville, Arkansas, headquarters, with more stationed at Walmart headquarters in Europe, Asia, and Latin America. P&G has credited this relationship with saving the company billions of dollars.

Major account management is growing. As buyer concentration increases through mergers and acquisitions, fewer buyers are accounting for a larger share of sales. Many are centralizing their purchases of certain items, gaining more bargaining power. And as products become more complex, more groups in the buyer's organization participate in the purchase process. The typical salesperson might not have the skill, authority, or coverage to sell effectively to the large buyer.

In selecting major accounts, companies look for those that purchase a high volume (especially of more profitable products), purchase centrally, require a high level of service in several geographic locations, may be price sensitive, and want a long-term partnership. Major account managers act as the single point of contact, develop and grow customer business, understand customer decision processes, identify added-value opportunities, provide competitive intelligence, negotiate sales, and orchestrate customer service.

Many major accounts look for added value more than a price advantage. They appreciate having a single point of dedicated contact; single billing; special warranties; EDI links; priority shipping; early information releases; customized products; and efficient maintenance, repair, and upgraded service. And there's the value of goodwill. Personal relationships with people who value the major account's business and have a vested interest in its success are compelling reasons for remaining a loyal customer.

Sources: Noel Capon, Dave Potter, and Fred Schindler, *Managing Global Accounts: Nine Critical Factors for a World-Class Program*, 2nd ed. (Bronxville, NY: Wessex Press, 2008); Peter Cheverton, *Global Account Management: A Complete Action Kit of Tools and Techniques for Managing Key Global Customers* (London, UK: Kogan Page, 2008); Malcolm McDonald and Diana Woodburn, *Key Account Management: The Definitive Guide*, 2nd ed. (Oxford, UK: Butterworth-Heinemann, 2007); Jack Neff, "Bentonville or Bust," *Advertising Age*, February 24, 2003. More information can be obtained from SAMA (Strategic Account Management Association) and the *Journal of Selling and Major Account Management*.

Sales Force Size

Sales representatives are one of the company's most productive and expensive assets. Increasing their number increases both sales and costs. Once the company establishes the number of customers it wants to reach, it can use a *workload approach* to establish sales force size. This method has five steps:

1. Group customers into size classes according to annual sales volume.
2. Establish desirable call frequencies (number of calls on an account per year) for each customer class.
3. Multiply the number of accounts in each size class by the corresponding call frequency to arrive at the total workload for the country, in sales calls per year.
4. Determine the average number of calls a sales representative can make per year.
5. Divide the total annual calls required by the average annual calls made by a sales representative, to arrive at the number of sales representatives needed.

Suppose the company estimates it has 1,000 A accounts and 2,000 B accounts. A accounts require 36 calls a year, and B accounts require 12, so the company needs a sales force that can make 60,000 sales calls (36,000 + 24,000) a year. If the average full-time rep can make 1,000 calls a year, the company needs 60.

Sales Force Compensation

To attract top-quality reps, the company must develop an attractive compensation package. Sales reps want income regularity, extra reward for above-average performance, and fair pay for experience and longevity. Management wants control, economy, and simplicity. Some of these objectives will conflict. No wonder compensation plans exhibit a tremendous variety from industry to industry and even within the same industry.

The company must quantify four components of sales force compensation. The *fixed amount,* a salary, satisfies the need for income stability. The *variable amount,* whether commissions, bonus, or profit sharing, serves to stimulate and reward effort. *Expense allowances* enable sales reps to meet the expenses of travel and entertaining. *Benefits,* such as paid vacations, sickness or accident benefits, pensions, and life insurance, provide security and job satisfaction.

Fixed compensation is common in jobs with a high ratio of nonselling to selling duties, and jobs where the selling task is technically complex and requires teamwork. Variable compensation works best where sales are cyclical or depend on individual initiative. Fixed and variable compensation give rise to three basic types of compensation plans—straight salary, straight commission, and combination salary and commission. One survey revealed that over half of sales reps receive 40 percent or more of their compensation in variable pay.[96]

Straight-salary plans provide a secure income, encourage reps to complete nonselling activities, and reduce incentive to overstock customers. For the firm, these plans represent administrative simplicity and lower turnover. Straight-commission plans attract higher performers, provide more motivation, require less supervision, and control selling costs. On the negative side, they emphasize getting the sale over building the relationship. Combination plans feature the benefits of both plans while limiting their disadvantages.

Plans that combine fixed and variable pay link the variable portion to a wide variety of strategic goals. One current trend deemphasizes sales volume in favor of gross profitability, customer satisfaction, and customer retention. Other companies reward reps partly on sales team or even company-wide performance, motivating them to work together for the common good.

Managing the Sales Force

Various policies and procedures guide the firm in recruiting, selecting, training, supervising, motivating, and evaluating sales representatives to manage its sales force (see △ Figure 19.5).

Recruiting and Selecting Representatives

At the heart of any successful sales force is a means of selecting effective representatives. One survey revealed that the top 25 percent of the sales force brought in over 52 percent of the sales. It's a great

|Fig. 19.5| △

Managing the Sales Force

waste to hire the wrong people. The average annual turnover rate of sales reps for all industries is almost 20 percent. Sales force turnover leads to lost sales, the expense of finding and training replacements, and often pressure on existing salespeople to pick up the slack.[97]

After management develops its selection criteria, it must recruit. The human resources department solicits names from current sales representatives, uses employment agencies, places job ads, and contacts college students. Selection procedures can vary from a single informal interview to prolonged testing and interviewing.

Studies have shown little relationship between sales performance on one hand, and background and experience variables, current status, lifestyle, attitude, personality, and skills on the other. More effective predictors have been composite tests and assessment centers that simulate the working environment so applicants are assessed in an environment similar to the one in which they would work.[98] Although scores from formal tests are only one element in a set that includes personal characteristics, references, past employment history, and interviewer reactions, they have been weighted quite heavily by companies such as IBM, Prudential, and Procter & Gamble. Gillette claims tests have reduced turnover and scores correlated well with the progress of new reps.

Training and Supervising Sales Representatives

Today's customers expect salespeople to have deep product knowledge, add ideas to improve operations, and be efficient and reliable. These demands have required companies to make a much greater investment in sales training.

New reps may spend a few weeks to several months in training. The median training period is 28 weeks in industrial-products companies, 12 in service companies, and 4 in consumer-products companies. Training time varies with the complexity of the selling task and the type of recruit. For all sales, new hire "ramp up" to full effectiveness is taking longer than ever, with 27 percent taking 3 to 6 months, 38 percent taking 6 to 12 months, and 28 percent needing 12 months or more.

New methods of training are continually emerging, such as the use of audio- and videotapes, CDs and CD-ROMs, programmed learning, distance learning, and films. Some firms use role playing and sensitivity or empathy training to help reps identify with customers' situations and motives.

Reps paid mostly on commission generally receive less supervision. Those who are salaried and must cover definite accounts are likely to receive substantial supervision. With multilevel selling, such as Avon, Sara Lee, Virgin, and others use, independent distributors are also in charge of their own sales force selling company products. These independent contractors or reps are paid a commission not only on their own sales but also on the sales of people they recruit and train.[99]

Sales Rep Productivity

How many calls should a company make on a particular account each year? Some research suggests today's sales reps spend too much time selling to smaller, less profitable accounts instead of focusing on larger, more profitable accounts.[100]

NORMS FOR PROSPECT CALLS Left to their own devices, many reps will spend most of their time with current customers, who are known quantities. Reps can depend on them for some business, whereas a prospect might never deliver any. Companies therefore often specify how much time reps should spend prospecting for new accounts. Spector Freight wants its sales representatives to spend 25 percent of their time prospecting and stop after three unsuccessful calls. Some companies rely on a missionary sales force to open new accounts.

USING SALES TIME EFFICIENTLY The best sales reps manage their time efficiently. *Time-and-duty analysis* helps reps understand how they spend their time and how they might increase their productivity. In the course of a day, sales reps spend time planning, traveling, waiting, selling, and doing administrative tasks (report writing and billing; attending sales meetings; and talking to others in the company about production, delivery, billing, and sales performance). It's no wonder face-to-face selling accounts for as little as 29 percent of total working time![101]

Companies constantly try to improve sales force productivity.[102] To cut costs, reduce time demands on their outside sales force, and leverage computer and telecommunications innovations, many have increased the size and responsibilities of their inside sales force.

Inside salespeople are of three types: *Technical support people* provide technical information and answers to customers' questions. *Sales assistants* provide clerical backup for outside salespersons, call ahead to confirm appointments, run credit checks, follow up on deliveries, and answer customers' business-related questions. *Telemarketers* use the phone to find new leads, qualify them, and sell to them. Telemarketers can call up to 50 customers a day, compared to 4 for an outside salesperson.

The inside sales force frees outside reps to spend more time selling to major accounts, identifying and converting new major prospects, placing electronic ordering systems in customers' facilities, and obtaining more blanket orders and systems contracts. Inside salespeople spend more time checking inventory, following up orders, and phoning smaller accounts. Outside sales reps are paid largely on an incentive-compensation basis, and inside reps on a salary or salary-plus-bonus pay.

SALES TECHNOLOGY The salesperson today has truly gone electronic. Not only is sales and inventory information transferred much faster, but specific computer-based decision support systems have been created for sales managers and sales representatives. Using laptop computers, salespeople can access valuable product and customer information. With a few keystrokes, salespeople can prime themselves on backgrounds of clients; call up prewritten sales letters; transmit orders and resolve customer-service issues on the spot; and send samples, pamphlets, brochures, and other materials to clients.

One of the most valuable electronic tools for the sales rep is the company Web site, and one of its most useful applications is as a prospecting tool. Company Web sites can help define the firm's relationships with individual accounts and identify those whose business warrants a personal sales call. They provide an introduction to self-identified potential customers and might even receive the initial order. For more complex transactions, the site provides a way for the buyer to contact the seller. Selling over the Internet supports relationship marketing by solving problems that do not require live intervention and thus allows more time for issues best addressed face-to-face.

Motivating Sales Representatives

The majority of sales representatives require encouragement and special incentives, especially those in the field who encounter daily challenges.[103] Most marketers believe that the higher the salesperson's motivation, the greater the effort and the resulting performance, rewards, and satisfaction—all of which in turn further increase motivation.

INTRINSIC VERSUS EXTRINSIC REWARDS Marketers reinforce intrinsic and extrinsic rewards of all types. One research study found the reward with the highest value was pay, followed by promotion, personal growth, and sense of accomplishment.[104] Least valued were liking and respect, security, and recognition. In other words, salespeople are highly motivated by pay and the chance to get ahead and satisfy their intrinsic needs, and may be less motivated by compliments and security. Some firms use sales contests to increase sales effort.[105]

SALES QUOTAS Many companies set annual sales quotas, developed from the annual marketing plan, on dollar sales, unit volume, margin, selling effort or activity, or product type. Compensation is often tied to degree of quota fulfillment. The company first prepares a sales forecast that becomes the basis for planning production, workforce size, and financial requirements. Management then establishes quotas for regions and territories, which typically add up to more than the sales forecast to encourage managers and salespeople to perform at their best. Even if they fail to make their quotas, the company nevertheless may reach its sales forecast.

Each area sales manager divides the area's quota among its reps. Sometimes a rep's quotas are set high, to spur extra effort, or more modestly, to build confidence. One general view is that a salesperson's quota should be at least equal to last year's sales, plus some fraction of the difference between territory sales potential and last year's sales. The more favorably the salesperson reacts to pressure, the higher the fraction should be.

Conventional wisdom is that profits are maximized by sales reps focusing on the more important products and more profitable products. Reps are unlikely to achieve their quotas for established products when the company is launching several new products at the same time. The company will need to expand its sales force for new-product launches.

Setting sales quotas can create problems. If the company underestimates and the sales reps easily achieve their quotas, it has overpaid them. If it overestimates sales potential, the salespeople will find it very hard to reach their quotas and be frustrated or quit. Another downside is that quotas can drive reps to get as much business as possible—often ignoring the service side of the business. The company gains short-term results at the cost of long-term customer satisfaction. For these reasons, some companies are dropping quotas. Even hard-driving Oracle has changed its approach to sales compensation.

Oracle Finding sales flagging and customers griping, Oracle, the second-largest software company in the world, decided to overhaul its sales department and practices. Its rapidly expanding capabilities, with diverse applications such as human resources, supply chain, and CRM, meant one rep could no longer be responsible for selling all Oracle products to certain customers. Reorganization let reps specialize in a few particular products. To tone down the sales force's reputation as overly aggressive, Oracle changed the commission structure from a range of 2 percent to 12 percent to a flat 4 percent to 6 percent and adopted guidelines on how to "play nice" with channels, independent software vendors (ISVs), resellers, integrators, and value-added resellers (VARs). The six principles instructed sales staff to identify and work with partners in accounts and respect their positions and the value they add, in order to address partner feedback that Oracle should be more predictable and reliable.[106]

Evaluating Sales Representatives

We have been describing the *feed-forward* aspects of sales supervision—how management communicates what the sales reps should be doing and motivates them to do it. But good feed-forward requires good *feedback,* which means getting regular information from reps to evaluate performance.

SOURCES OF INFORMATION The most important source of information about reps is sales reports. Additional information comes through personal observation, salesperson self-reports, customer letters and complaints, customer surveys, and conversations with other reps.

Sales reports are divided between *activity plans* and *write-ups of activity results.* The best example of the former is the salesperson's work plan, which reps submit a week or month in advance to describe intended calls and routing. This report forces sales reps to plan and schedule their activities and inform management of their whereabouts. It provides a basis for comparing their plans and accomplishments or their ability to "plan their work and work their plan."

Many companies require representatives to develop an annual territory-marketing plan in which they outline their program for developing new accounts and increasing business from existing accounts. Sales managers study these plans, make suggestions, and use them to develop sales quotas. Sales reps write up completed activities on *call reports.* Sales representatives also submit expense reports, new-business reports, lost-business reports, and reports on local business and economic conditions.

These reports provide raw data from which sales managers can extract key indicators of sales performance: (1) average number of sales calls per salesperson per day, (2) average sales call time per contact, (3) average revenue per sales call, (4) average cost per sales call, (5) entertainment cost per sales call, (6) percentage of orders per hundred sales calls, (7) number of new customers per period, (8) number of lost customers per period, and (9) sales force cost as a percentage of total sales.

FORMAL EVALUATION The sales force's reports along with other observations supply the raw materials for evaluation. One type of evaluation compares current to past performance. An example is shown in ▭ Table 19.1.

The sales manager can learn many things about a rep from this table. Total sales increased every year (line 3). This does not necessarily mean he is doing a better job. The product breakdown shows he has been able to push the sales of product B further than the sales of product A (lines 1 and 2). According to his quotas for the two products (lines 4 and 5), his increasing product B sales could be at the expense of product A sales. According to gross profits (lines 6 and 7), the company earns more selling A than B. The rep might be pushing the higher-volume, lower-margin product at the expense of the more profitable product. Although the rep increased total sales by $1,100 between 2009 and 2010 (line 3), gross profits on total sales actually decreased by $580 (line 8).

Sales expense (line 9) shows a steady increase, although total expense as a percentage of total sales seems to be under control (line 10). The upward trend in total dollar expense does not seem to be explained by any increase in the number of calls (line 11), although it might be related to success in

TABLE 19.1 ▭ Form for Evaluating Sales Representative's Performance				
Territory: Midland Sales Representative: John Smith	2007	2008	2009	2010
1. Net sales product A	$251,300	$253,200	$270,000	$263,100
2. Net sales product B	423,200	439,200	553,900	561,900
3. Net sales total	674,500	692,400	823,900	825,000
4. Percent of quota product A	95.6	92.0	88.0	84.7
5. Percent of quota product B	120.4	122.3	134.9	130.8
6. Gross profits product A	$50,260	$50,640	$54,000	$52,620
7. Gross profits product B	42,320	43,920	55,390	56,190
8. Gross profits total	92,580	94,560	109,390	108,810
9. Sales expense	$10,200	$11,100	$11,600	$13,200
10. Sales expense to total sales (%)	1.5	1.6	1.4	1.6
11. Number of calls	1,675	1,700	1,680	1,660
12. Cost per call	$6.09	$6.53	$6.90	$7.95
13. Average number of customers	320	24	328	334
14. Number of new customers	13	14	15	20
15. Number of lost customers	8	10	11	14
16. Average sales per customer	$2,108	$2,137	$2,512	$2,470
17. Average gross profit per customer	$289	$292	$334	$326

acquiring new customers (line 14). Perhaps in prospecting for new customers, this rep is neglecting present customers, as indicated by an upward trend in the annual number of lost accounts (line 15).

The last two lines show the level and trend in sales and gross profits per customer. These figures become more meaningful when compared with overall company averages. If this rep's average gross profit per customer is lower than the company's average, he could be concentrating on the wrong customers or not spending enough time with each customer. A review of annual number of calls (line 11) shows he might be making fewer annual calls than the average salesperson. If distances in the territory are similar to those in other territories, the rep might not be putting in a full workday, is poor at sales planning and routing, or is spending too much time with certain accounts.

Even if effective in producing sales, the rep may not rate high with customers. Success may come because competitors' salespeople are inferior, the rep's product is better, or new customers are always found to replace those who dislike the rep. Managers can glean customer opinions of the salesperson, product, and service by mail questionnaires or telephone calls. Sales reps can analyze the success or failure of a sales call and how they would improve the odds on subsequent calls. Their performance could be related to internal factors (effort, ability, and strategy) and/or external factors (task and luck).[107]

Principles of Personal Selling

Personal selling is an ancient art. Effective salespeople today have more than instinct, however. Companies now spend hundreds of millions of dollars each year to train them in methods of analysis and customer management and to transform them from passive order takers into active order getters. Reps are taught the SPIN method to build long-term relationships, with questions such as:[108]

1. *Situation questions*— These ask about facts or explore the buyer's present situation. For example, "What system are you using to invoice your customers?"
2. *Problem questions*— These deal with problems, difficulties, and dissatisfactions the buyer is experiencing. For example, "What parts of the system create errors?"
3. *Implication questions*— These ask about the consequences or effects of a buyer's problems, difficulties, or dissatisfactions. For example, "How does this problem affect your people's productivity?"
4. *Need-payoff questions*— These ask about the value or usefulness of a proposed solution. For example, "How much would you save if our company could help reduce errors by 80 percent?"

Most sales training programs agree on the major steps in any effective sales process. We show these steps in △ Figure 19.6 and discuss their application to industrial selling next.[109]

The Six Steps

PROSPECTING AND QUALIFYING The first step in selling is to identify and qualify prospects. More companies are taking responsibility for finding and qualifying leads so salespeople can use their expensive time doing what they can do best: selling. Companies qualify the leads by contacting them by mail or phone to assess their level of interest and financial capacity. "Hot" prospects are turned over to the field sales force and "warm" prospects to the telemarketing unit for follow-up. Even then, it takes about four calls on a prospect to consummate a business transaction.

PREAPPROACH The salesperson needs to learn as much as possible about the prospect company (what it needs, who takes part in the purchase decision) and its buyers (personal characteristics and buying styles). How is the purchasing process conducted at the company? How is purchasing structured? Many purchasing departments in larger companies have been elevated into strategic supply departments with more professional practices. Centralized purchasing may put a premium on having larger suppliers able to meet all the company's needs. At the same time, some companies are also decentralizing purchasing for smaller items such as coffeemakers, office supplies, and other inexpensive necessities.

The sales rep must thoroughly understand the purchasing process in terms of "who, when, where, how, and why" in order to set call objectives: to qualify the prospect, gather information, or make an immediate sale. Another task is to choose the best contact approach—a personal visit, a phone call, or a letter. The right approach is crucial given that it has become harder and harder for sales reps to get into the offices of purchasing agents, physicians, and other possible time-starved and Internet-enabled customers. Finally, the salesperson should plan an overall sales strategy for the account.

PRESENTATION AND DEMONSTRATION The salesperson tells the product "story" to the buyer, using a *features*, *advantages*, *benefits*, and *value* (FABV) approach. Features describe physical characteristics of a market offering, such as chip processing speeds or memory capacity. Advantages describe why the features provide an advantage to the customer. Benefits describe the economic, technical, service, and social pluses delivered by the offering. Value describes the offering's worth (often in monetary terms). Salespeople often spend too much time on product features (a product orientation) and not enough time stressing benefits and value (a customer orientation). The pitch to a prospective client must be highly relevant, engaging, and compelling—there is always another company waiting to take that business.[110]

OVERCOMING OBJECTIONS Customers typically pose objections. *Psychological resistance* includes resistance to interference, preference for established supply sources or brands, apathy, reluctance to give up something, unpleasant associations created by the sales rep, predetermined ideas, dislike of making decisions, and neurotic attitude toward money. *Logical resistance* might be objections to the price, delivery schedule, or product or company characteristics.

To handle these objections, the salesperson maintains a positive approach, asks the buyer to clarify the objection, questions in such a way that the buyer answers his own objection, denies the validity of the objection, or turns it into a reason for buying. Although price is the most frequently negotiated issue—especially in an economic recession—others include contract completion time; quality of goods and services offered; purchase volume; responsibility for financing, risk taking, promotion, and title; and product safety.

Salespeople sometimes give in too easily when customers demand a discount. One company recognized this problem when sales revenues went up 25 percent but profit remained flat. The company decided to retrain its salespeople to "sell the price," rather than "sell through price." Salespeople were given richer information about each customer's sales history and behavior. They received training to recognize value-adding opportunities rather than price-cutting opportunities. As a result, the company's sales revenues climbed and so did its margins.[111]

CLOSING Closing signs from the buyer include physical actions, statements or comments, and questions. Reps can ask for the order, recapitulate the points of agreement, offer to help write up the order, ask whether the buyer wants A or B, get the buyer to make minor choices such as color or size, or indicate what the buyer will lose by not placing the order now. The salesperson might offer specific inducements to close, such as an additional service, an extra quantity, or a token gift.

Prospecting and qualifying

Preapproach

Presentation and demonstration

Overcoming objections

Closing

Follow-up and maintenance

|Fig. 19.6| △

Major Steps in Effective Selling

If the client still isn't budging, perhaps the salesperson is not interacting with the right executive—a more senior person may have the necessary authority. The salesperson also may need to find other ways to reinforce the value of the offering and how it alleviates financial or other pressures the client faces.[112]

FOLLOW-UP AND MAINTENANCE Follow-up and maintenance are necessary to ensure customer satisfaction and repeat business. Immediately after closing, the salesperson should cement any necessary details about delivery time, purchase terms, and other matters important to the customer. The salesperson should schedule a follow-up call after delivery to ensure proper installation, instruction, and servicing and to detect any problems, assure the buyer of the salesperson's interest, and reduce any cognitive dissonance. The salesperson should develop a maintenance and growth plan for the account.

Relationship Marketing

The principles of personal selling and negotiation are largely transaction-oriented because their purpose is to close a specific sale. But in many cases the company seeks not an immediate sale but rather a long-term supplier–customer relationship. Today's customers prefer suppliers who can sell and deliver a coordinated set of products and services to many locations, who can quickly solve problems in different locations, and who can work closely with customer teams to improve products and processes.

Salespeople working with key customers must do more than call only when they think customers might be ready to place orders. They should call or visit at other times and make useful suggestions about the business. They should monitor key accounts, know customers' problems, and be ready to serve them in a number of ways, adapting and responding to different customer needs or situations.[113]

Relationship marketing is not effective in all situations. But when it is the right strategy and is properly implemented, the organization will focus as much on managing its customers as on managing its products.

Summary

1. Direct marketing is an interactive marketing system that uses one or more media to effect a measurable response or transaction at any location. Direct marketing, especially electronic marketing, is showing explosive growth.

2. Direct marketers plan campaigns by deciding on objectives, target markets and prospects, offers, and prices. Next, they test and establish measures to determine the campaign's success.

3. Major channels for direct marketing include face-to-face selling, direct mail, catalog marketing, telemarketing, interactive TV, kiosks, Web sites, and mobile devices.

4. Interactive marketing provides marketers with opportunities for much greater interaction and individualization through well-designed and executed Web sites, search ads, display ads, and e-mails. Mobile marketing is another growing form of interactive marketing that relies on text messages, software apps, and ads.

5. Word-of-mouth marketing finds ways to engage customers so they choose to talk with others about products, services, and brands. Increasingly, word of mouth is being driven by social media in the form of online communities and forums, blogs, and social networks such as Facebook, Twitter, and YouTube.

6. Two notable forms of word-of-mouth marketing are buzz marketing, which seeks to get people talking about a brand by ensuring that a product or service or how it is marketed is out of the ordinary, and viral marketing, which encourages people to exchange online information related to a product or service.

7. Salespeople serve as a company's link to its customers. The sales rep *is* the company to many of its customers, and it is the rep who brings back to the company much-needed information about the customer.

8. Designing the sales force requires choosing objectives, strategy, structure, size, and compensation. Objectives may include prospecting, targeting, communicating, selling, servicing, information gathering, and allocating. Determining strategy requires choosing the most effective mix of selling approaches. Choosing the sales force structure entails dividing territories by geography, product, or market (or some combination of these). To estimate how large the sales force needs to be, the firm estimates the total workload and how many sales hours (and hence salespeople) will be needed. Compensating the sales force entails determining what types of salaries, commissions, bonuses, expense accounts, and benefits to give, and how much weight customer satisfaction should have in determining total compensation.

9. There are five steps in managing the sales force: (1) recruiting and selecting sales representatives; (2) training the representatives in sales techniques and in the company's products, policies, and customer-satisfaction orientation; (3) supervising the sales force and helping

reps to use their time efficiently; (4) motivating the sales force and balancing quotas, monetary rewards, and supplementary motivators; (5) evaluating individual and group sales performance.

10. Effective salespeople are trained in the methods of analysis and customer management, as well as the art of sales professionalism. No single approach works best in all circumstances, but most trainers agree that selling is a six-step process: prospecting and qualifying customers, preapproach, presentation and demonstration, overcoming objections, closing, and follow-up and maintenance.

Applications

Marketing Debate
Are Great Salespeople Born or Made?

One debate in sales is about the impact of training versus selection in developing an effective sales force. Some observers maintain the best salespeople are born that way and are effective due to their personalities and interpersonal skills developed over a lifetime. Others contend that application of leading-edge sales techniques can make virtually anyone a sales star.

Take a position: The key to developing an effective sales force is selection *versus* The key to developing an effective sales force is training.

Marketing Discussion
Corporate Web Sites

Pick a company and go to its corporate Web site. How would you evaluate the Web site? How well does it score on the 7Cs of design elements: context, content, community, customization, communication, connection, and commerce?

Marketing Excellence

>>Facebook

Facebook has brought a whole new level of personal marketing to the world of business. The social networking Web site fulfills people's desire to communicate and interact with each other and uses that power to help other companies target very specific audiences with personalized messages.

Facebook was founded in 2004 by Mark Zuckerberg, who was a student at Harvard University at the time and created the first version of the Web site in his dorm room. Zuckerberg recalled, "I just thought that being able to have access to different people's profiles would be interesting. Obviously, there's no way you can get access to that stuff unless people are throwing up profiles, so I wanted to make an application that would allow people to do that, to share as much information as they wanted while having control over what they put up." From the beginning, Facebook has kept its profiles and navigation tools relatively simple in order to unify the look and feel for each individual. Within the first 24 hours the Facebook Web site was up, between 1,200 and 1,500 Harvard students had registered and become part of the Facebook community. Within the first month, half the campus had registered.

Initially, Facebook's Web site could only be viewed and used by Harvard students. The early momentum was tremendous, though, and Facebook soon expanded to include students throughout the Ivy League and other colleges. The initial decision to keep Facebook exclusive to college students was critical to its early success. It gave the social Web site a sense of privacy, unity, and exclusivity that social media competitors like MySpace did not offer. Eventually, in 2006, Facebook opened up to everyone.

Today, Facebook is the most popular social networking Web site in the world, with over 500 million active users. The site allows users to create personal profiles with information such as their hometowns, work, educational background, favorite things, and religious affiliation. It encourages them to extend their network by adding other users as friends, and many people try to see how many "friends" they can accumulate. To interact with Facebook friends, users can send messages; "poke" each other; upload and view albums, photos, games, and videos; and "tag" or label people in their photos. They can post comments on friends' "walls" and create status updates viewable to everyone. In summary, Facebook is fulfilling its mission to "give people the power to share and make the world more open and connected."

Facebook has become a critical marketing component for just about any brand for several reasons. First, companies, sports teams, musicians, and politicians can create Facebook pages—a place to communicate to and with their fans. Facebook pages offer groups and brands a way to personally interact, build awareness, communicate, and offer information to anyone who takes an interest. Companies use Facebook to introduce new products, launch videos and promotions, upload images, communicate to consumers, listen to feedback, and create an overall personal look and feel. Even politicians from around the world—from the United States to the Philippines—use Facebook to push their campaigns and communicate with supporters on a local, personalized basis.

Facebook also offers targeted advertising opportunities. Banner ads—the company's major source of income—can target individuals by demographic or keywords based on the specific information they have placed in their profiles. adidas, for example, uses Facebook to promote specific labels within the company, target consumers regionally, and give the brand a personal touch. The head of adidas's digital marketing group explained, "Wherever our fans are, we're going to use Facebook to speak to them and we're going to try to speak to them in a locally relevant way."

Facebook's growth and influence have been incredible. In one survey, college students named Facebook the second most popular thing in their undergraduate world, tied only with beer. And Facebook is not used only by undergrads. Of the 150+ million users in the United States, 29 percent are aged 35 to 54, while 25 percent are aged 18 to 24. Overall, women represent the fast-growing segment. Facebook also tends to have a more upscale, educated, desirable demographic than competitive social networks, and therefore it charges more for its advertising ads.

In 2010, Facebook surpassed Google as the top Web site in the world based on unique visitors per month and also ranked number one for number of pages viewed per month. Facebook has become an important part of consumers' everyday lives and therefore a critical component in personal marketing strategies.

Questions

1. Why is Facebook unique in the world of personal marketing?

2. Is Facebook just a passing fad or is it here to stay? What are the company's greatest strengths and risks?

3. Discuss the recent privacy issues that challenged Facebook. Will privacy restrictions limit its ability to offer personal marketing opportunities?

Sources: John Cassidy, "Me Media," *New Yorker,* May 15, 2006; "Survey: College Kids Like iPods Better Than Beer," *Associated Press,* June 8, 2006; Peter Corbett, "Facebook Demographics and Statistics Report 2010," I Strategy Labs, www.istrategylabs.com; Brian Womack, "Facebook Sees Fourfold Jump in Number of Advertisers Since 2009," *BusinessWeek,* June 2, 2010; Kermit Pattison, "How to Market Your Business with Facebook," *New York Times,* November 11, 2009; Facebook, www.facebook.com.

Marketing Excellence

>>Oxford University

In the past, universities had to mail out bulky printed prospectuses to prospective students who had expressed an interest in their courses. Universities around the world are now using Web-based marketing communications to enable interaction with their prospective and current students and to provide information for their local, national, and international communities.

According to the Times Higher Education World University rankings 2010, Oxford University is ranked sixth among the world's top 200 universities. With its 800-year history, iconic buildings, and famous alumni from around the world, Oxford University enjoys an international reputation for excellence in teaching and research. Sir Tim Berners-Lee, inventor of the World Wide Web, is a former student of the University.

The university's Web site has a distinctive blue background to reflect its logo and corporate color. A single photograph showing an image of university life appears at the top of the page and is changed regularly to reflect current news. The homepage has a clear, uncluttered structure, and it is divided into eight sections with drop-down menus targeted at specific audiences. The university attracts students from 138 countries, so the admissions section provides links to information about undergraduate and postgraduate courses and additional information for international students. Prospectuses are available online or can be downloaded in PDF format. An admissions icon provides a link to direct contact details for visitors who want further information to meet their personal requirements

Prospective students can access information about the university using a variety of media. A link to the *Wall of 100 Faces* feature uses video technology to show short films of current students discussing their experiences of studying at Oxford. Users can customize the video wall feature by clicking the *Only Show Me* option; for example, the films featuring interviews only with international students can be specifically selected for viewing.

The Web site also hosts links to other media such as podcasts, video-sharing Web sites, and social network-ing. Through *i-Tunes U*, the university makes available to a wide range of audiences material including podcasts about the university's applications process and lectures on subjects such as the works of William Shakespeare,

tropical medicine, and philosophy. Oxford University has its own education channel on YouTube, which provides access to filmed lectures and admissions information. Potential, present, and past students can also access short, instant updates on the latest news by following the university on Twitter, and Oxford also has a Facebook page.

Web-based marketing communications enable Oxford University to provide direct information for a range of audiences, to establish a dialogue with interested parties, and to build long-term relationships. In the increasingly competitive world of higher education, the ability to communicate directly with worldwide audiences is an important part of a university's marketing strategy.

Questions

1. With reference to the 7Cs model, discuss why the Oxford University Web site is an example of effective design.

2. What are the advantages and disadvantages of using social networking as part of a university marketing strategy?

3. How can Web-based communications help universities build long-term relationships with their students?

Sources: *Oxford University*, www.ox.ac.uk; *Times Higher Education*, www.timeshighereducation.co.uk; *YouTube*, www.youtube.com.

Section 8

Market Intelligence, Innovation and New Product Development

8a

Market Research

1

Introduction to marketing research

Marketing researchers support decision-makers by collecting, analysing and interpreting information needed to identify and solve marketing problems.

Objectives

After reading this chapter, you should be able to:

1 understand the nature and scope of marketing research and its role in supporting the design and implementation of successful marketing decisions;

2 describe a conceptual framework for conducting marketing research as well as the steps of the marketing research process;

3 distinguish between problem identification and problem-solving marketing research;

4 appreciate the relative importance of marketing research in countries throughout the world;

5 understand the types and roles of research suppliers, including internal and external, full-service and limited-service suppliers;

6 understand why some marketers may be sceptical of the value of marketing research;

7 appreciate the demands for marketing researchers to supplement their technical research skills with managerial skills;

8 appreciate the complexities involved in international marketing research;

9 understand the basis of ethical aspects of marketing research and the responsibilities that marketing research stakeholders have to them-selves, each other and to the research project;

10 appreciate the potential opportunities and threats of the Internet to marketing researchers.

| STAGE 1 Problem definition | STAGE 2 Research approach developed | STAGE 3 Research design developed | STAGE 4 Fieldwork or data collection | STAGE 5 Data preparation and analysis | STAGE 6 Report preparation and presentation |

Overview

Marketing research comprises one of the most important and fascinating facets of marketing. In this chapter, we describe the nature and scope of marketing research, emphasising its role of supporting marketing decision making, and provide several real-life examples to illustrate the basic concepts of marketing research. We give a formal definition of marketing research and show how this links to a six-stage description of the marketing research process. This description is extended to illustrate many of the interconnected activities in the marketing research process. We then subdivide marketing research into two areas: problem identification and problem-solving research. The extent and growth rates of marketing research expenditure throughout the world are then presented followed by an overview of marketing research suppliers and services.

There are many successful marketing decisions that have been founded upon sound marketing research: however marketing research does not replace decision making. The limitations of marketing research are established and these lead on to the growing demands upon the marketing research industry to produce research findings that are actionable and relevant to marketing decision makers. Many individual examples will be presented to illustrate the managerial challenges of making marketing research actionable and relevant, but beyond these individual examples we showcase the exciting work of Sports Marketing Surveys. This independent marketing research agency has specialised in the sponsorship and sports industry over the past 20 years. The sports industry and many sponsorship deals are often multi-country in their reach and activity, and to meet these challenges Sports Marketing Surveys has the capability of working and reporting on a worldwide basis, in over 200 countries for events such as the Olympic Games and the Football World Cup. Work from four projects conducted by Sports Marketing Surveys will be used as running examples throughout this book.

The topic of international marketing research is introduced. International marketing research will be discussed systematically in subsequent chapters and will be tackled in a dedicated chapter.

The ethical aspects of marketing research and the responsibilities that marketing research stakeholders have to themselves, to each other and to the research project are presented and developed in more detail throughout the text.

Finally, a general introduction to the use of the Internet in the marketing research industry is made. Specific issues relating to the impact of the Internet and computers will be developed throughout the text.

What does marketing research encompass?

The term 'marketing research' is broad in meaning. This breadth will be explored and illustrated throughout this chapter. What will become apparent is that it is related to supporting marketing decision making in many ways. The following example illustrates the variety of marketing research techniques used at Royal Ahold and the role of marketing research in supporting decision-makers.

Example **Listening to the customer – research at Royal Ahold[1]**

Royal Ahold is a world supermarket leader. In the Netherlands Ahold operates six chains with over 1,750 outlets, including the flagship Albert Heijn supermarkets. Worldwide, Ahold serves 20 million customers weekly in 3,400 stores in 17 countries across the USA, Central and Western Europe, Latin America and Asia. Customer orientation is at the top of the fundamental principles of the company. Its credo is that the customer comes first: 'However big we become, however international, it is ultimately the customer who determines our success.'

The following list summarises the ways that Royal Ahold 'listens' to its customers to maintain its customer orientation and continued success:

- Produces economic analyses and forecasts. It does this by gathering secondary data and intelligence that give it an understanding of retail developments, competitive threats and market changes.
- Uses and contributes to audit data from A.C. Nielsen to obtain global data about developments in their markets.
- Sees its stores as a major 'market research laboratory' to study customers. It knows when they come in, how often and what they buy. Fundamental to these observations is the use of scanner systems and loyalty cards.
- Uses focus groups as a major source of information about how customers and noncustomers feel. It insists that management teams watch and listen to these discussions.
- Uses observation approaches to watch how customers behave in store, using protocol tapes (where people think aloud about the purchases they are making).
- Selects some researchers to supply raw data, where it performs its own analyses and interpretations, whilst in other projects it uses specialised strategic input from researchers to provide added value.
- Shares its best practices and know-how. It has an electronic market research platform where researchers discuss their projects and any problems they have. For example, if a successful approach has been used in the Netherlands, they can consider using it in the USA.
- Circulates a digest to the Corporate Executive Board and management teams all over the world. *Market Research Findings* is issued twice a year, giving details of important papers, articles and reports on retail research from inside or outside the Ahold company.

Bert L. J. van der Herberg, Vice President Market Research, summarises the role of market researchers at Royal Ahold:

Researchers are backroom consultants. I see the market researcher as a philosopher who can take a critical view of the internal and external world. The researcher can act as 'the serious fool' to the court. The Board takes on our ideas and our language, but the market researcher is not the spokesman for the company. They are listeners and interpreters.[1]

The use of a variety of techniques is vital to support a variety of key marketing decisions. The following two examples from Philips and the Nordea Bank illustrate how integral marketing research can be to sound decision making.

Example **Research is integral to marketing at Philips[2]**

A few years ago, Philips Consumer Electronics determined that the market for traditional personal audio was diminishing. Its researchers looked into what the key needs and drivers of teenagers were and came up with concepts such as adaptability, choice flexibility, sharing experiences and spontaneity. They selected a few of these as a basis for their designers to start developing products. They also meticulously identified the value proposition they wanted to offer with new products coming out of the designer pipeline. Subsequently, when a product was presented during the trial phase, Philips let the researchers determine, through qualitative research, what the consumer saw as the primary benefits and concerns of the product. Philips wanted to identify exactly why it would make a product, for whom it would make it and how it would be differentiated from other products. After Philips had decided to go to market with these products (a series of very small portable MP3 players/cameras that fit on a key ring), it again turned to its researchers to test the advertising campaign that was developed for the product.

Example ### Nordea: a new brand in the making[3]

Nordea is a leading bank in the Nordic region with around 1,200 branch offices and some 11 million clients of which 3.9 million are e-customers. It was created around 2000 through a series of mergers between Nordbanken in Sweden, Merita Bank in Finland, Unibank in Denmark and Christiana Bank og Kreditkasse in Norway. Before the merger, each original bank conducted ongoing customer and employee satisfaction surveys, including monitoring its reputation and image. At the time of the merger there was a solid basis to continue these surveys. Since branding of the new name was central to creating Nordea, concurrent with the satisfaction surveys, specific surveys were needed to support the brand building process.

This consisted of five phases:

1 **Establishing common core values**: surveys were instituted to ensure the basis to launch the new brand, for instance a comprehensive laddering survey to form the basis of Nordea's positioning strategy.
2 **Choosing a new name**: the name studies took several months to complete and substantial resources were committed to test associations with potential candidates including 'Nordea'.
3 **Ensuring name awareness**: on launching the Nordea name, a frequent and detailed name awareness tracking was initiated. As awareness grew, the tracking was phased out and eventually focused exclusively on the quality of the awareness.
4 **Positioning the brand**: the initial purpose of the brand positioning survey was to create a common understanding of the original banks' positioning and to identify the position towards which the brand should move based on the company's business strategy. As the survey had to reflect feelings and values in four different languages when employees did not even 'speak the same language', linguistic pitfalls had to be taken into account.
5 **Building reputation**: as a company turn-around process was initiated at the time, the focus shifted towards the bank's corporate reputation. This was measured by Reputation Excellence, a syndicated Nordic survey marketed by Danish MarkedsConsult. Nordea took an active role in designing the survey when launched in 2003. The survey was based on 15,000 CATI interviews in the Nordic countries carried out by Nordic Norstat.

These examples illustrate only a few of the methods used to conduct marketing research, which may range from highly structured surveys with large samples to in-depth interviews with small samples; from the collection and analysis of readily available data to the generation of 'new' data; from direct interaction with consumers to the distant observation of consumers. These examples illustrate a few of the applications of marketing research in supporting decision-makers. This book will introduce you to the full complement of marketing research techniques. These examples also illustrate the crucial role played by marketing research in designing and implementing successful marketing plans.[4] This book will also introduce you to a broad range of marketing applications supported by marketing research.

The role of marketing research can be better understood in light of the basic marketing paradigm depicted in Figure 1.1. The emphasis in marketing, as illustrated in the Royal Ahold example above, is on the identification and satisfaction of customer needs. To

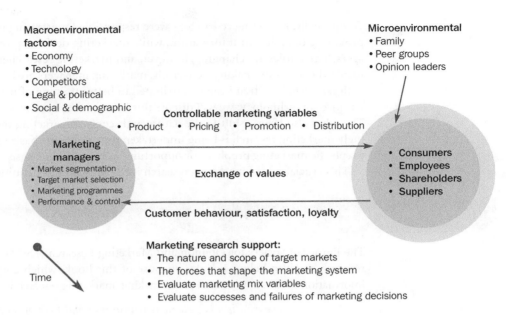

**Figure 1.1
The role of marketing research within the marketing system**

determine customer needs and to implement marketing strategies and plans aimed at satisfying those needs, marketing managers need information about customers, competitors and other forces in the marketplace. In recent years, many factors have increased the need for more accurate and timely information. As firms have become national and international in scope, the need for information on larger, and more distant, markets has increased. As consumers have become more affluent, discerning and sophisticated, marketing managers need better information on how they will respond to new products and other marketing offerings. As competition has become more intense, managers need information on the effectiveness of their marketing tools. As the environment is changing more rapidly, marketing managers need more timely information to cope with the impact of changes.[5]

Marketers make decisions about what they see as potential opportunities and problems, i.e. a process of identifying issues. They go on to devise the most effective ways to realise these opportunities and overcome problems they have identified. They do this based on a 'vision' of the distinct characteristics of the target markets and customer groups. From this 'vision' they develop, implement and control marketing programmes. This 'vision' of markets and subsequent marketing decisions may be complicated by the interactive effects of an array of environmental forces that shape the nature and scope of target markets. These forces also affect the marketers' ability to satisfy their chosen target markets.

Within this framework of decision making, marketing research helps the marketing manager link the marketing variables with their environment and customer groups. It helps remove some of the uncertainty by providing relevant information about marketing variables, environment and consumers.

The role of the marketing researcher in supporting the marketing decision-maker can therefore be summarised as helping to:

- describe the nature and scope of customer groups;
- understand the nature of forces that shape customer groups;
- understand the nature of forces that shape the marketer's ability to satisfy targeted customer groups;
- test individual and interactive marketing mix variables;
- monitor and reflect upon past successes and failures in marketing decisions.

Traditionally, marketing researchers were responsible for assessing information needs and providing the relevant information, while marketing decisions were made by the managers. These roles are changing, however, and marketing researchers are becoming more involved in decision making; conversely, marketing managers are becoming more involved with research. This trend can be attributed to better training of marketing managers and advances in technology; we will discuss this in more detail towards the end of this chapter. There has also been a shift in the nature and scope of marketing research, where increasingly marketing research is being undertaken on an ongoing basis rather than in response to specific marketing problems or opportunities on an ad hoc basis.[6]

This crucial role of marketing research is recognised in its definition.

Definition of marketing research

The European Society for Opinion and Marketing Research (ESOMAR) defines marketing research as given below. For the purpose of this book, which emphasises the need for information in the support of decision making, marketing research is defined as:

> **Marketing research** *is a key element within the total field of marketing information. It links the consumer, customer and public to the marketer through information which is used to identify and define marketing opportunities and problems; to generate, refine and evaluate marketing actions; and to improve understanding of marketing as a process and of the ways in which specific marketing activities can be made more effective.*

Marketing research
A key element within the total field of marketing information. It links the consumer, customer and public to the marketer through information which is used to identify and define marketing opportunities and problems; to generate, refine and evaluate marketing actions; and to improve understanding of marketing as a process and of the ways in which specific marketing activities can be made more effective.

Several aspects of this definition are noteworthy. First, it reinforces the notion of basing marketing decisions upon a strong understanding of target customers. It stresses the role of 'linking' the marketer to the consumer, customer and public to help improve the whole process of marketing decision making.

ESOMAR further qualifies its definition of marketing research by stating:

> *Marketing research specifies the information required to address these issues* [of linking the consumer, customer and public to the marketer]; *designs the method for collecting information; manages and implements the data collection process; analyses the results; and communicates the findings and their implications.*

Marketing research process
A set of six steps which define the tasks to be accomplished in conducting a marketing research study. These include problem definition, developing an approach to the problem, research design formulation, fieldwork, data preparation and analysis, and report generation and presentation.

The above qualification of the definition of marketing research encapsulates the **marketing research process**. The process is founded upon an understanding of the marketing decision(s) needing support. From this understanding, research aims and objectives are defined. To fulfil defined aims and objectives, an approach to conducting the research is established. Next, relevant information sources are identified and a range of data collection methods are evaluated for their appropriateness, forming a research design. The data are collected using the most appropriate method; they are analysed and interpreted, and inferences are drawn. Finally, the findings, implications and recommendations are provided in a format that allows the information to be used for marketing decision making and to be acted upon directly.

Marketing research should aim to be objective. It attempts to provide accurate information in an impartial manner. Although research is always influenced by the researcher's research philosophy, it should be free from the personal or political biases of the researcher or decision-makers. Research motivated by personal or political gain involves a breach of professional standards. Such research is deliberately biased to result in predetermined findings. The motto of every researcher should be 'Find it and tell it like it is.' Second, it is worth noting the term 'total field of information'. This recognises that marketing decisions are not exclusively supported by marketing research. There are other

Source: © Alamy

means of information support for marketers from management consultants, raw data providers such as call centres, direct marketing, database marketing and telebusinesses.[7] These alternative forms of support are now competing with a 'traditional' view of marketing research. The methods of these competitors may not be administered with the same scientific rigour and/or ethical standards applied in the marketing research industry. Nonetheless, many marketing decision-makers are increasingly using these other sources which collectively are changing the nature of skills demanded in marketing researchers. These demands will be discussed in more detail later in this chapter.

The marketing research process

The marketing research process consists of six broad stages. Each of these stages is developed in more detail in subsequent chapters; thus, the discussion here is brief. The process illustrated in Figure 1.2 is of the marketing research seen in simple stages. Figure 1.3 takes the process a stage further to show the many iterations and connections between stages. This section will explain the stages and illustrate the connections between the stages.

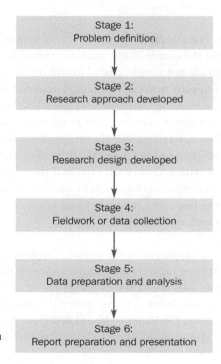

Figure 1.2
Simple description of the marketing research process

Stage 1:
Problem definition

Stage 2:
Research approach developed

Stage 3:
Research design developed

Stage 4:
Fieldwork or data collection

Stage 5:
Data preparation and analysis

Stage 6:
Report preparation and presentation

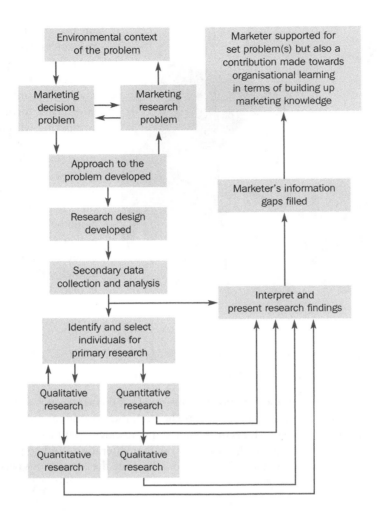

**Figure 1.3
The marketing
research process,
detailing iterations
between stages**

Step 1: problem definition. The logical starting point in wishing to support the decision-maker is trying to understand the nature of the marketing problem that requires research support. Marketing problems are not simple 'givens', as will be discussed in Chapter 2, and the symptoms and causes of a problem are not as neatly presented as they may be in a case study such as those found in marketing textbooks. In Figure 1.3, the first three stages show the iterations between *environmental context of the problem, marketing decision problem and marketing research problem*. Understanding the environmental context of the problem has distinct stages that will be discussed in Chapter 2. It involves discussion with decision-makers, in-depth interviews with industry experts, and the collection and analysis of readily available published information (from both inside and outside the firm). Once the problem has been precisely defined, the researcher can move on to designing and conducting the research process with confidence.

Step 2: development of an approach to the problem. The development of an approach to the problem involves identifying factors that influence research design. A key element of this step involves the selection, adaptation and development of an appropriate theoretical framework to underpin a research design. Understanding the interrelated characteristics of the nature of target respondents, the issues to be elicited from them and the context in which this will happen rely upon 'sound' theory. 'Sound' theory helps the researcher to decide 'what should be measured or understood' and 'how best to encapsulate and communicate the measurements or understandings'. In deciding what should be either measured or encapsulated, the researcher also develops a broad appreciation of how the data collected will be analysed. The issues involved in developing an approach are tackled in more detail in Chapter 2.

Step 3: research design developed. A research design is a framework or blueprint for conducting a marketing research project. It details the procedures necessary for obtaining the required information. Its purpose is to establish a study design that will either test the hypotheses of interest or determine possible answers to set research questions, and ultimately provide the information needed for decision making. Conducting any exploratory techniques, precisely defining variables to be measured, and designing appropriate scales to measure variables can also be part of the research design. The issue of how the data should be obtained from the respondents (e.g. by conducting a survey or an experiment) must be addressed. These steps are discussed in detail in Chapters 3 to 13.

Step 4: fieldwork or data collection. In Figure 1.2, this stage could be simplified to 'collecting the required data'. In Figure 1.3, a whole array of relationships between stages of data collection is shown, starting at *Secondary data collection and analysis* through to *Quantitative research* or *Qualitative research*. The process starts with a more thorough collection and analysis of secondary data sources. Secondary data are data collected for some other purpose than the problem at hand. They may be held within the organis-ation as databases that detail the nature and frequency of customer purchases, through to surveys that may have been completed some time ago that may be accessed through libraries, CD-ROMs or the Internet. Going through this stage avoids replication of work and gives guidance in sampling plans and in deciding what to measure or encapsulate using quantitative or qualitative techniques. Secondary data collection and analysis may complete the research process, i.e. sufficient information may exist to interpret and report findings to a point whereby the information gaps that the decision-maker has are filled. Secondary data forms a vital foundation and essential focus to primary data collection.

In Figure 1.3, the stage of *Identify and select individuals for primary research* covers sampling issues for both quantitative and qualitative studies. This stage may include the selection of individuals for in-depth qualitative research. In qualitative research, issues of 'representativeness' are less important than the quality of individuals targeted for investigation and the quality of response elicited. However, as can be seen from the line leading up from *Qualitative research* to *Identify and select individuals for primary research*, the qualitative research process may help in the identification and classification of individuals who may be targeted using more formal sampling methods. These sampling methods are covered in detail in Chapters 14 and 15.

Beyond the issues of identifying and selecting individuals, the options available for primary data collection vary considerably. A stage of *Qualitative research* alone may be sufficient to support the decision-maker, as indeed could a stage of *Quantitative research*. The following example illustrates the use of qualitative observation to support marketing decision making. This example mirrors one of the research techniques used by Royal Ahold (presented at the start of this chapter), helping it to build up a 'picture' of its customers. As a technique in its own right, it does not necessarily have to be followed by a survey or quantitative work to confirm the observations. This technique will be developed under the heading 'Ethnographic research' in Chapter 6.

Example	**Supermarket Sweep**[8]

Video camera analysis can be used to gain vital information about the way in which supermarket consumers spend their money. People behave in certain ways within the supermarket environment, according to store design specialist company ID Magasin. Patterns of consumer behaviour can be used to maximise profits. Store managers who work on store design without video footage are sometimes wrong about their conclusions. Consumers, for example, often ignore the products placed on shelves at eye level, despite popular belief to the contrary.

The research problem may require a stage of qualitative and quantitative research to run concurrently, perhaps measuring and encapsulating different characteristics of the problem under investigation.

A stage of qualitative research could be used to precede a stage of quantitative research. For example, a series of focus groups may help to generate a series of statements or expectations that are subsequently tested out in a survey to a representative sample. Conversely, a survey may be conducted and, upon analysis, there may be clear statistically significant differences between two distinct target markets. A series of qualitative in-depth interviews may follow to allow a more full exploration and understanding of the reasons for the differences between the two groups.

Step 5: data preparation and analysis. Data preparation includes the editing, coding, transcription and verification of data. In Figure 1.3, this stage is not drawn out as a distinct stage in its own right, but is seen as integral to the stages of *Secondary data collection and analysis* through to *Quantitative research* or *Qualitative research*. The process of data preparation and analysis is essentially the same for both quantitative and qualitative techniques, for data collected from both secondary and primary sources. Considerations of data analysis do not occur after data have been collected; such considerations are an integral part of the development of an approach, the development of a research design, and the implementation of individual quantitative or qualitative methods. If the data to be collected are qualitative, the analysis process can occur as the data are being collected, well before all observations or interviews have been completed. An integral part of qualitative data preparation and analysis requires researchers to reflect upon their own learning and the ways they may interpret what they see and hear. These issues will be developed in Chapters 6 to 9.

If the data to be analysed are quantitative, each questionnaire or observation form is inspected or edited and, if necessary, corrected. Number or letter codes are assigned to represent each response to each question in the questionnaire. The data from the questionnaires are transcribed or keypunched into a proprietary data analysis package. Verification ensures that the data from the original questionnaires have been accurately transcribed, whereas data analysis gives meaning to the data that have been collected. Univariate techniques are used for analysing data when there is a single measurement of each element or unit in the sample; if there are several measurements of each element, each variable is analysed in isolation (see Chapter 18). On the other hand, multivariate techniques are used for analysing data when there are two or more measurements of each element and the variables are analysed simultaneously (see Chapters 18 to 24).

Step 6: report preparation and presentation. The entire project should be documented in a written report that addresses the specific research questions identified, describes the approach, research design, data collection and data analysis procedures adopted, and presents the results and major findings. Research findings should be presented in a comprehensible format so that they can be readily used in the decision-making process. In addition, an oral presentation to management should be made using tables, figures and graphs to enhance clarity and impact. This process is encapsulated in Figure 1.3 with the reminder that the marketer's information gaps are filled and that the marketer is supported for the set problem, but also a contribution is made towards organisational learning in terms of building up marketing knowledge (see Chapter 25).

A classification of marketing research

The ESOMAR definition encapsulates two key reasons for undertaking marketing research: (1) to identify opportunities and problems, and (2) to generate and refine marketing actions. This distinction serves as a basis for classifying marketing research into problem identification research and problem-solving research, as shown in Figure 1.4. Linking this classification to the basic marketing paradigm in Figure 1.1, problem identification research can be linked to: the description of the nature and scope of customer groups, understanding the nature of forces that shape customer groups, and understanding the nature of forces that shape the marketer's ability to satisfy targeted customer groups. Problem-solving research can be linked to: test individual and interactive marketing mix variables, and to monitor and reflect upon past successes and failures in marketing decisions.

Problem identification research
Research undertaken to help identify problems that are not necessarily apparent on the surface, yet exist or are likely to arise in the future.

Problem identification research is undertaken to help identify problems that are, perhaps, not apparent on the surface and yet exist or are likely to arise in the future. Examples of problem identification research include market potential, market share, brand or company image, market characteristics, sales analysis, short-range forecasting, long-range forecasting and business trends research. Research of this type provides information about the marketing environment and helps diagnose a problem. For example, a declining market potential indicates that the firm is likely to have a problem achieving its growth targets. Similarly, a problem exists if the market potential is increasing but the firm is losing market share. The recognition of economic, social or cultural trends, such as changes in consumer behaviour, may point to underlying problems or opportunities.

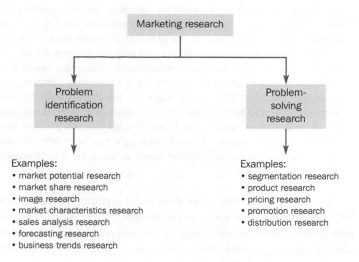

Figure 1.4
A classification of marketing research

Example ### Beer research shows overspill[9]

The proliferation of new brands in Europe's booming beer market could result in shorter product lifecycles and, ultimately, destroy brand loyalty. The report 'Western European Beer' reveals that the industry is in danger of an overspill of brands, with the number of brands available exceeding demand. As a result, consumers are likely to fall back on 'tried and tested brands', normally owned by large manufacturers, at the expense of lesser known brands, which are likely to fall by the wayside.

The example above presents either a problem or an opportunity for beer manufacturers, depending largely upon whether their brand is 'tried and tested' or not. The research could be classified as 'business trends research' or even 'market potential research'. It could be followed by individual beer manufacturers conducting their own 'image research' to reveal the extent to which their brand(s) are perceived as being 'tried and tested'.

Problem-solving research
Research undertaken to help solve specific marketing problems.

Once a problem or opportunity has been identified, **problem-solving research** may be undertaken to help develop a solution. The findings of problem-solving research are used to support decisions that tackle specific marketing problems. Problem-solving research linked to problem identification research is illustrated by the following example of developing a new cereal at Kellogg's.

Example ### Crunchy Nut Red adds colour to Kellogg's sales[10]

In 2001, Kellogg's was faced with the challenge of reviving low cereal sales. Through problem identification research, it was able to identify the problem, and through problem-solving research, to develop several solutions to increase the sales of cereals.

To identify the problem, Kellogg's researchers interviewed decision-makers within the company, interviewed industry experts, conducted analyses of available secondary data, conducted some qualitative research and surveyed consumers about their perceptions and preferences for cereals. Several important problems were identified:

- Current products were being targeted at children.
- Bagels and muffins were becoming more favoured breakfast foods.
- High prices were turning consumers to generic brands.
- Quick breakfast foods that required liitle or no preparation were becoming more popular.

These issues helped Kellogg's to define the problem: Kellogg's was not being creative in introducing new products to meet the needs of adult consumers. Based on this definition, Kellogg's introduced new flavours that were more suited to the adult palette but were not tasteless varieties of the past. For example, it introduced Crunchy Nut Red. This new cereal included cranberry pieces, almonds and yogurt-flavoured flakes. The new cereal was supported by a national television advertising campaign, major in-store promotions, and 2 million specially produced sachets for a nationwide sampling campaign. Kellogg's partnered with the 2002 US Olympic team and the 2002 Winter Olympic Games. The company distributed Olympic themed packages, products and promotional offers as a way to welcome the Olympic Games back to the USA. Through creative problem identification research followed by problem-solving research, Kellogg's has seen not only an increase in sales, but also an increase in consumption of cereal at times other than breakfast.

This example illustrates how the careful crafting of problem identification research can help to develop a clear focus to problem-solving research. The outcome was research that supported marketing decisions in many ways. A problem-solving perspective enabled Kellogg's management to focus on issues of product development and an integrated promotions campaign. Table 1.1 shows the different types of issues that can be addressed using problem-solving research.

Table 1.1 Examples of problem-solving research

Segmentation research	Determine basis of segmentation
	Establish market potential and responsiveness for various segments
	Select target markets and create lifestyle profiles: demography, media, and product image characteristics
Product research	Test concept
	Determine optimal product design
	Package tests
	Product modification
	Brand positioning and repositioning
	Test marketing
Pricing research	Importance of price in brand selection
	Pricing policies
	Product line pricing
	Price elasticity of demand
	Initiating and responding to price changes
Promotions research	Optimal promotional budget
	Optimal promotion mix
	Copy decisions
	Creative advertising testing
	Evaluation of advertising effectiveness
Distribution research	Attitudes of channel members
	Intensity of wholesale and retail coverage
	Channel margins
	Retail and wholesale locations

Problem identification research and problem-solving research go hand in hand as seen in the Kellogg's case, and a given marketing research project may combine both types of research. A marketing research project for a European beer manufacturer that sees its market share diminish may determine through image research that its brand is perceived in a most positive manner. This may indicate that the brand should be extended into other types of beer or even into clothes and fashion accessories. Appropriate target markets may be selected, with detailed profiles of potential customers and an associated media and product image. These decisions can clearly be supported with problem-solving research. Whether the focus is upon problem identification or problem-solving research, it is vital that the process of marketing research is conducted in a systemic and rigorous manner.

The global marketing research industry

With the rising demand for managerial skills in marketing researchers, we turn our attention to the relative rates of demand for marketing research and industry growth rates across the globe. To monitor rates of expenditure and growth, we follow the annual ESOMAR Global Market Research Industry Study (**www.esomar.nl**), with summaries and commentary from the magazine *Research World*.

The figures presented are estimates of all the work conducted within individual countries, by research agencies. Not included in the data is marketing research undertaken by non-profit research institutes, governments, universities or advertising agencies using their own resources. The data also do not include the internal supply of marketing research, i.e. the costs of a marketing research function located within a firm. In addition, not included are costs incurred by the more sophisticated users of marketing research who integrate the data and analyses of their operational databases to understand customers and support marketing decision making. Though these estimates are static, may quickly go out of date and only tell part of the story of supporting marketing decision making, they are a vital means to illustrate developments in the marketing research industry.

The total global expenditure on marketing research in 2004 amounted to €17,415 million. Where this money was spent is illustrated in Table 1.2 which lists the top 20 countries with the highest marketing research spend per capita. Though it is clear to see that the USA as a country spent the most on marketing research, on a per capita basis a different story emerges. Five European countries spent more than the USA, with the UK spending €32.18 on marketing research for every citizen, with Sweden second at €27.96 and France at €24.70. The top 20 is dominated by countries with mature marketing research industries and with relatively high price levels for their research services.

In countries with marketing research industries that are relatively young, though the overall turnover and per capita rates may be low, the potential for growth may be immense. This is not the case in many developed economies: for example, in 2003, of the EU15 countries[12] the UK, Germany, the Netherlands, Sweden, Belgium, Denmark and Ireland had negative growth rates, with the Netherlands and Belgium continuing this decline in 2004. These negative growth rates increased the competitive intensity in marketing research suppliers and exacerbate the demand for managerial skills from marketing researchers. Marketing research in Europe is far from in decline as illustrated by the healthy growth rates of the new EU member states and other non-EU European countries.

Table 1.2 Top 20 countries with highest MR spend per capita, 2004[11]

Country	Turnover (€m)	Population (million)	Spend per capita (€ per capita)
1 UK	1,901	59.07	32.18
2 Sweden	248	8.87	27.96
3 France	1,478	59.84	24.70
4 Switzerland	147	7.17	20.50
5 Germany	1,677	82.41	20.35
6 USA	5,892	291.04	20.24
7 Finland	103	5.20	19.81
8 Denmark	101	5.35	18.88
9 Australia	367	19.54	18.78
10 Norway	78	4.51	17.29
11 New Zealand	65	3.85	16.88
12 Netherlands	271	16.07	16.86
13 Ireland	63	3.91	16.11
14 Canada	430	31.27	13.75
15 Belgium	131	10.30	12.72
16 Austria	87	8.16	10.65
17 Italy	540	57.48	9.39
18 Spain	382	41.16	9.28
19 Singapore	36	4.18	8.61
20 Japan	1,042	127.48	8.17

When set in a global context, Table 1.3 shows that Central and South America have the highest regional growth rates for marketing research expenditure in the world. This table presents the turnover, growth rates and market share for all regions of the world. It also shows that Europe as a whole has the largest share of the global market for marketing research at 44.93%.

Though Table 1.3 presents the relative expenditure, growth rates and shares on a regional basis, it masks the individual countries where marketing research is growing at the greatest rates. Table 1.4 ranks the countries with a real growth rate over 10%. Countries with healthy economic growth show the highest growth levels in marketing research. This table shows the increased demand for and expenditure in the booming Central and Latin America, where several countries like Venezuela, Argentina and Mexico have emerged from recession and are displaying high growth rates for marketing research. Examples of marketing research conducted in these emerging and fast-growing economies will be used throughout the text in the sections of International Marketing Research.

Table 1.3 Turnover, growth rates and market share per region, 2003–2004[13]

Region	Turnover 2003, (€m)	Growth rate (unadjusted for inflation) (%)	Real growth rate (adjusted for inflation) (%)	Share of global market, 2003 (%)
EU15	7,150	5.2	3.0	41.06
New member states	242	10.5	6.0	1.39
Other Europe	433	10.7	6.1	2.48
Total Europe	**7,825**	**5.6**	**3.2**	**44.93**
North America	6,361	9.5	6.7	36.53
Central & South America	672	14.8	8.2	3.86
Asia Pacific	2,319	6.5	5.2	13.32
Middle East & Africa	238	8.6	6.3	1.37
Total World	**17,415**	**7.5**	**5.0**	

Table 1.4 Countries with growth rate expectations over 10% for 2005[14]

Region	Expected growth rate, 2005
Venezuela	30
Argentina	25
Russian Fed.	25
Ukraine	20
Poland	19
Turkey	17
Kenya	15
Lithuania	15
Mexico	15
Singapore	12.5
Brazil	10
Cyprus	10

External suppliers
Outside marketing research companies hired to supply marketing research services.

The bases for the estimates in Tables 1.2 to 1.4 emerge from external marketing research suppliers or agencies. **External suppliers** are outside firms hired to supply marketing research data. These external suppliers collectively comprise the 'marketing research industry'. They range from small (one or a few persons) operations to very large global corporations. We now examine the nature of services that may be supplied by external suppliers. As illustrated in Figure 1.5, external suppliers can be classified as full-service or limited-service suppliers.

Full-service suppliers
Companies that offer the full range of marketing research activities.

Full-service suppliers offer the entire range of marketing research services: for example, defining a problem, developing a research design, conducting focus group interviews, designing questionnaires, sampling, collecting, analysing and interpreting data, and presenting reports. They may also address the marketing implications of the information they present, i.e. have the management skills to interpret and communicate the impact of their research findings at the highest levels. They may also manage customer database analyses, being able to integrate the management and analyses databases with the management and analyses of conventional marketing research techniques.

Syndicated services
Companies that collect and sell common pools of data designed to serve information needs shared by a number of clients.

The services provided by these suppliers can be further broken down into syndicated services, standardised services and customised services (see Figure 1.5).

Syndicated services collect information that they provide to subscribers. Surveys, diary panels, scanners and audits are the main means by which these data are collected.

Standardised services
Companies that use standardised procedures to provide marketing research to various clients.

Standardised services are research studies conducted for different clients but in a standard way. For example, procedures for measuring advertising effectiveness have been standardised so that the results can be compared across studies and evaluative norms can be established.

Customised services
Companies that tailor research procedures to best meet the needs of each client.

Customised services offer a variety of marketing research services specifically designed to suit a client's particular needs. Each marketing research project is treated uniquely.

Internet services
Companies which specialise in the use of the Internet to collect, analyse and distribute marketing research information.

Internet services offer a combination or variety of secondary data and intelligence gathering, survey or qualitative interviewing, and the analysis and publication of research findings, all through the Internet.

Limited-service suppliers
Companies that specialise in one or a few phases of a marketing research project.

Limited-service suppliers specialise in one or a few phases of a marketing research project. Services offered by such suppliers are classified as field services, coding and data entry, analytical services, data analysis and branded products.

Field services
Companies whose primary service offering is their expertise in collecting data for research projects.

Field services collect data through mail, personal interviews or telephone interviews, and firms that specialise in interviewing are called field service organisations. These

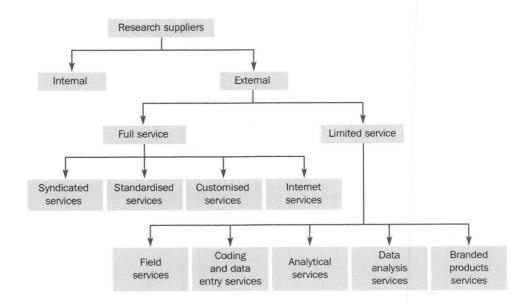

Figure 1.5 Marketing research suppliers

organisations may range from small proprietary organisations that operate locally to large multinationals. Some organisations maintain extensive interviewing facilities across the country for interviewing shoppers. Many offer qualitative data collection services such as focus group interviewing (discussed in detail in Chapter 7).

Coding and data entry services include editing completed questionnaires, developing a coding scheme and transcribing the data for input into a computer.

Analytical services include designing and pretesting questionnaires, determining the best means of collecting data, and designing sampling plans, as well as other aspects of the research design. Some complex marketing research projects require knowledge of sophisticated procedures, including specialised experimental designs (discussed in Chapter 10) and analytical techniques such as conjoint analysis and multidimensional scaling (discussed in Chapter 24). This kind of expertise can be obtained from firms and consultants specialising in analytical services.

Data analysis services are offered by firms, also known as tab houses, that specialise in computer analysis of quantitative data such as those obtained in large surveys. Initially, most data analysis firms supplied only tabulations (frequency counts) and cross-tabulations (frequency counts that describe two or more variables simultaneously). Now, many firms offer sophisticated data analysis using advanced statistical techniques. With the proliferation of microcomputers and software, many firms now have the capability to analyse their own data, but data analysis firms with expert statisticians are still in demand.

Branded marketing research products and services are specialised data collection and analysis procedures developed to address specific types of marketing research problems. These procedures may be patented, given brand names, and marketed like any other branded product. *Microscope* by Retail Marketing (In-Store) Services is an example of a branded product. It is a test marketing package for new product development that supplies cost-effective measurements of new product performance.

Coding and data entry services
Companies whose primary service offering is their expertise in converting completed surveys or interviews into a usable database for conducting statistical analysis.

Analytical services
Companies that provide guidance in the development of research design.

Data analysis services
Firms whose primary service is to conduct statistical analyses of quantitative data.

Branded marketing research products
Specialised data collection and analysis procedures developed to address specific types of marketing research problems.

The limitations of marketing research

It must be recognised that using researchers, even if they follow the marketing research process to the letter, does not guarantee that a marketing decision supported by that research will be successful. The act of decision making and conducting marketing research are distinctive activities and there are examples where the vital link between these activities has resulted in failure. In the following example, the entrepreneur Sahar Hashemi makes the case for marketing research, but not for the use of external suppliers as discussed above. Following her points, we then move on to the arguments and examples of the limitations of marketing research.

Example ### The birth of an idea[15]

Sahar Hashemi, co-founder of the coffee chain Coffee Republic, believes marketing research to be tremendously important. 'You shouldn't ever start a business without it. Of course you have to make gut instinct decisions but they should be informed by market research, like educated guesses.' However, Sahar believes in the importance of doing marketing research yourself. 'Why would you give research to an agency to do?' she asks. 'You have to become a real expert in the area you want to work in. You have to get your head around these things.' Sahar believes that a slick research agency might give you a glossy report packed with facts and figures, but if you do the work yourself you'll gain more insight. She also thinks that better ideas can grow out of research – facts and figures mixing with inspired thought to create what she calls 'fertile ground in which to cultivate new ideas'.

If decision-makers have gaps in their knowledge, if they perceive risk and uncertainty in their decision making and cannot find support at hand within their organisation, they can gain support from marketing research. However, many marketers can recount cases where the use of marketing research has resulted in failure or where decisions based upon gut feeling or intuition have proved to be successful. Such cases present a challenge to marketing researchers, especially in light of the competition faced by the industry from alternative information sources. Reflecting upon such cases should remind marketing researchers to maintain a focus of offering real and valuable support to decision-makers. Understanding what real and valuable support means should underpin the whole array of creative data collection and analysis procedures available to the marketing researcher. The following example starts this reflection process with a case that is very close to home!

Example   ### What's this marketing research then, Dave?

James Birks founded and successfully ran a kiln construction company for over 40 years. He designed, built and maintained kilns for some of the most demanding porcelain and ceramics manufacturers worldwide, including Wedgwood, Royal Doulton and Spode. At retirement age he sold his company as a going concern – a very wealthy man.

James was presented with a copy of the first edition of this text by his nephew, David Birks. He was very pleased with the present but was intrigued by the title and asked 'What's this marketing research then, Dave?' He certainly had a clear idea of what marketing meant to his business and what was involved in being a successful marketer in his industry, but the notion of researching marketing activities was alien to him.

The intriguing aspect of this question is that James Birks had run a successful business on an international basis for over 40 years without the need to be aware of or to use marketing research. Had he used marketing research, could he have been even more successful, or would it have been a wasted investment? Could he have been practising marketing research 'activities' in a very informal manner to support marketing decisions? In his business-to-business marketing situation, he knew his customers and competitors well, and knew what shaped their demands. This knowledge he acquired on a day-to-day basis, nurturing a curiosity about opportunities and how to realise them – without resorting to support from formal ad hoc marketing research. The example of James Birks shows that decision-makers do not rely solely upon marketing research, and in certain circumstances can survive and perform well without it.

Another view to reflect upon is the damning comment from Anita Roddick of The Body Shop, who said that 'market research is like looking in the rear view mirror of a speeding car'.[16] This may be a valid point if one sees the relationship of marketing and marketing research from the perspective illustrated by the respected research practitioner, Wendy Gordon:[17]

Traditional marketers delegate responsibility to the processes of marketing research. They believe that you can ask people what they want and need in the future and then deliver it to them. It is a fallacy. Marketing research removes people from experiencing reality, where the signs of change bubble up in unexpected places. Sitting in comfort behind a one-way mirror, listening to a debrief from researchers describing the world 'out there' or reading statistical reports on markets and the 'aggregate consumer' is not real, it is sanitised and second-hand.

Given the above criticisms, it is a fair point to acknowledge that there are cases where the use of marketing research has resulted in poor decision making or even failure. Ultimately, this examination should lead to a stronger justification of what ensures strong and valuable marketing research support. It may be a painful path to tread but this journey has to be made!

There are two areas of misconception of the role of marketing research:[18]

1 *Marketing research does not make decisions.* The role of marketing research is not to make decisions. Rather, research replaces hunches, impressions or a total lack of knowledge with pertinent information.
2 *Marketing research does not guarantee success.* Research, at best, can improve the odds of making a correct decision. Anyone who expects to eliminate the possibility of failure by doing research is both unrealistic and likely to be disappointed. The real value of research can be seen over a long period where increasing the percentage of good decisions should be manifested in improved bottom-line performance and in the occasional revelation that arises from research.

The last point shows the long-term benefits of conducting marketing research, i.e. that the results of a study may help decision-makers with an immediate problem, but by building their knowledge they can also have long-term benefits.

A great proportion of marketing research money has been spent on developing and testing new products. Questions have been posed that examine the role marketing research plays in poor success rates of new products across a wide range of industries.[19] Clearly, marketing research cannot be blamed for every failure, and the following two reasons may explain why decision-makers can make poor decisions when sound research has been conducted:

1 *Blind optimism/disbelief in research.* Many patently bad products have been launched because marketing management did not believe research findings.
2 *Political pressures.* Given how many personal reputations may be at stake in the lengthy and costly process of new product development, there may be political pressures to launch a 'borderline' case.

The following example illustrates where research was used in new product development but the designer and entrepreneur chose to ignore the findings, and ultimately achieved immense levels of success.

Example   ### Doing a Dyson[20]

Just 23 months after its launch in the UK, the Dyson bagless vacuum cleaner became the country's best seller, overtaking sales of Hoover, Electrolux, Panasonic, Miele and all other vacuum cleaners. The Dyson clear bin was given a resounding thumbs-down in marketing research. People said they did not like the dirt being visible in the bin in case their neighbours saw how much dirt had been picked up in their homes. Some retailers said they would not want to have dust on display in demonstration machines. Yet, the dust was there because they began using Dyson display machines to clean their shops. Dyson felt compelled to launch its vacuum cleaner with a clear bin, believing that it is important to see when it is full. Moreover, what better way was there to show stockists, sales staff and customers proof of its increased efficiency than to see the dirt being collected?

How would consumers react to a new vacuum cleaner with totally radical styling, revolutionary internal engineering and a price tag almost twice that of the current brand leader? The public's response proved immediately that innovative products do sell, even at a premium price. However, marketing research did not point to this product having the potential to be a success. James Dyson argued that 'marketing research will only tell you what has happened. No research can tell you what is going to happen.'

This is a theme that James Dyson has reiterated over the years. In an interview in 2006, giving tips to would-be inventors and entrepreneurs, he said:

you can't go out and do marketing research to try and solve these problems about what to do next because usually, or very often, you're doing the opposite of what marketing research would tell you. You can't base a new project two years ahead on current market trends and what users are thinking at the moment. That sounds very arrogant. But it isn't arrogance. You can't go and ask your customers to be your inventors. That's your job.

Other researchers offer reasons why decision-makers may reject research findings. These go beyond the confines of developing and testing new products. Examples of these reasons include:

- *Invalidity of research methods.* If the decision-maker suspects the accuracy or appropriateness of the methods for the problem faced, lack of confidence would lead to a rejection of findings.
- *Faulty communication.* This would lead to the findings being difficult to comprehend or utilise, or being unconvincing.
- *Irrelevance.* The decision-maker may see the findings as irrelevant to the perceived marketing problem.

If decision-makers reject research findings, and have been taken to task as a consequence, they can easily support their stance. They could question the time taken to conduct research (and the possible consequences of delays in decision making), and the cost required (not only in paying for marketing research projects but also in managerial effort). They could point to the few reliable methods of evaluating the return on investment in marketing research. They may also question the amount of support that can be given by a researcher who may have little understanding of the context and environment in which the decisions are made.

Collectively, the examples in this section illustrate that out of the array of research and information support approaches, there is no one guaranteed approach, research design or technique that can create the perfect means to support decision-makers. Given the vast array of marketing decisions and styles of marketing decision-maker, the hallmark of marketing decision making is creativity. Creativity in decision making can be supported well by accurate and relevant information. Generating accurate and relevant information is also a creative act. The diagnosis of problems, the measurement of consumers and the interpretation of those measurements are all creative acts, not a set system. The following PlayStation example illustrates the task of researching creative images, using a creative research design. It shows how the marketing researcher 'stepped back' and devised a creative solution to encapsulate the impact of the film being used in the advert.

| **Example** | **Marketing research supports PlayStation advertising[21]** |

Trevor Beattie, Creative Director of the ad agency TBWA (**www.tbwa-europe.com**), describes that the 'The Third Place' campaign for PlayStation2 was about 'the experience'. He wanted to create imagery that would live with people long after the commercial break had finished. Neil Hourston, TBWA London Head of Planning, described the creative intention: 'Our desired response on the creative brief was "excited fear",' he says. 'If we were going to be true to that then in the research we were looking for an idea that made people both excited and a little bit worried.'

London agency Firefish was given the job of researching how to develop what turned out to be an odd bit of 60 seconds. 'The finished ad was an incredibly surreal David Lynch piece of film. It was utterly random and bizarre and quite dark and incredibly original,' recalls Jem Fawcus, Co-founder and Director of Firefish:

We made a conscious decision not to begin trying to research anything like the finished film. We took a huge step back and just researched the idea of The Third Place: what do you think of the idea of The Third Place? What would it be like? Does it strike a chord with people? Is it something that could be used to support PlayStation2's new positioning? If we had gone in and said, 'We got a really weird film by David Lynch, and its got a duck and a man dressed up in bandages in it, and its all in black and white, and its got strange music,' it would have absolutely bombed. No one would have understood what we were talking about.

Whether or not PlayStation2 gamers, or anyone else for that matter, understood what David Lynch was on about does not matter. It got consumers excited about the arrival of the new video game experience. 'We used research for that properly, which was for development,' says Neil. 'We gave Jem some executional elements rather than the whole thing. We asked him to work with the respondents to see whether it had the potential in bits to create the response that we were looking for.'

If decision-makers complain that research is misleading or is only telling them what they already know, the marketing researcher may argue that the fault lies with managers who pose the wrong questions or problem in the first place. If one takes the narrow view that the decision-maker poses the questions and the researcher finds the answers, there may be some validity in such an argument. It does not hold if one considers that the decision-maker and the researcher have a joint commitment to solve problems. In this joint commitment they have quite distinct but complementary creative skills that they can bring together to understand what problem they should be researching, how they conduct the research and how they interpret their findings.

Can marketing researchers survive in an age of increasing competition from other information providers? How can the industry fend off the challenge from the armies of consultants and other information suppliers? To achieve this, the industry has to offer clients insights rather than just data analysis. The marketing researcher's input must be seen to benefit the bottom line. Initiatives that bring clients and researchers closer together are needed – initiatives that educate buyers that marketing research has as much if not more to offer than very expensive consultancy firms.[22]

The future – the growing demand for managerial skills in marketing researchers

Over the past few years, a debate has emerged about the value of marketing research and consultancy in supporting marketing decisions.[23] Many marketing researchers are feeling the pressure to move away from a position of being seen as mere data collectors and data analysts towards becoming providers of strategic marketing intelligence. One of the drivers behind this change is that data collection is seen by many marketers as a 'commodity' with comparatively low added value. An example of this pressure on marketing researchers emerges from Denmark, which is home to a number of high-quality research organisations. In Denmark the industry is faced with concerns about commoditisation. 'Many research buyers now see marketing research as a commodity' explains Erik Liljeberg of the Association of Market Research Institutes in Denmark.[24] 'They think that if you go to one research agency or another it won't make much of a difference. If an agency will not give you a discount, then you try someone else who will.' In Germany, ADM (Arbeitskreis Deutscher Markt), the association of private market and social research agencies, reports a development from straightforward marketing research 'data supply' to information-based consultancy. It describes the growing competition from research providers outside the traditional marketing research industry, with advertising and media agencies, business consultants and academic research institutions entering the arena.[25]

Many marketing research agencies have concluded that in the long term, information will become a commodity, and that it therefore now makes sound business sense to extend their offer beyond the provision of professionally collected data. These agencies are seeking to provide value-added services, around their skills of being able to interpret data, and relate this precisely to business decision-making processes.[26] Professor Frank Wimmer, board member at the German agency GfK, believes that a seat at the decision-maker's table is what most career-driven marketing researchers desire. 'To have a genuine impact on company policy, rather than being restricted to a role as a numbers-supplier.'[27] He contends that marketing research should develop into a more decision-making, management-orientated direction. That way, the researcher will be taken seriously by businesses, and no longer be looked upon as a 'number cruncher'. In the following two examples, we see this development illustrated by the perspectives of the Premier Automotive Group of Ford and Phillip Morris International in their need to work with marketing researchers with managerial skills.

Example | ### Luxury cars – a key role for research[28]

Ford is a multi-faceted company, with different divisions facing their own particular challenges. At the Premier Automotive Group – its collection of European luxury brands comprising Jaguar, Volvo, Aston Martin and Land Rover – it's a matter of predicting which of its vehicles will be important in an evermore congested market. The ability of the Premier Automotive Group, as elsewhere in the Ford empire, to get closer to the hearts and minds of its consumers has been enhanced by changes to the marketing research function within the company. Instead of being specialists in one particular methodology or another, they are being transformed into consultants who will have a more holistic view of the business. 'Marketing researchers have always had a tendency to be backroom people', says their Marketing Research Manager, Simon Wilson. 'There is a much greater need nowadays for communication of research and this can only be achieved effectively if you are say, front of house.' This change in attitude has meant a certain amount of retraining, and even recruiting internally and externally, but Wilson is convinced that investment in this area will be well worth it. It should mean that, in time, most of his staff would be capable of looking at the big picture.

Example | ### What do clients want from research?[29]

Richard Henchoz, Director Marketing Planning Services with responsibility for marketing research for Africa and the Middle East and Duty Free at Phillip Morris International, expects that clients increasingly want and ask for actionable insights from researchers, the kind of insights that include an answer to the question: 'What would you do if you were in my place?' Henchoz believes researchers must be able to provide this kind of strategic information. Richard, a Swiss national based at Phillip Morris International's headquarters in Lausanne, puts into perspective concerns about the feared loss of relevance of the research function:

> *I have been in research for about 20 years now and the call for more creativity has been going on for a long time. In the 1980s, when working as a researcher for Proctor & Gamble, I already aspired to move on from just executing research projects to a role in which I could be more creative, by making concrete recommendations to decision-makers. To me, it seemed an almost natural inclination for a researcher. And yes, clients will indeed require far more creativity and business intelligence from providers and international researchers. We are definitely working towards this goal at Phillip Morris.*

The emerging generation of marketing researchers will be expected to continue to master the skill of borrowing and adapting tried and tested techniques from the social sciences. The challenges of writing engaging questionnaires, drawing meaningful samples, and making sense of data will still have to be met. Increasingly, marketing decision-makers demand a far more integrated approach to analysing often contradictory and imperfect sources of evidence; there is a mounting need for the capacity to work in an eclectic and holistic way with qualitative and quantitative data. Increasingly, marketing researchers have to analyse multiple and often imperfect datasets. To do this, they need new holistic analytic frameworks to be able to make sense of the data and to present this to decision-makers in a coherent, confident and effective manner.[30]

John Forsyth, Partner of McKinsey and Company and Director of the firm's global Customer Insights Practice, believes that adding new skills to the current set of capabilities of marketing researchers is crucial. Describing some of the lingering shortcomings of research professionals, he points out that marketing researchers in many cases still tend to focus on their own processes instead of client's needs:

> Senior decision-makers don't want a 15 page explanation of why a specific tool and technique has been used. They want researchers to tell them what they should do. Marketing researchers should provide actionable consumer insights that can be used to improve the decision-making process for key executives. This requires a twist in researchers' approach. Interacting with senior management is different from dealing with management at the mid-level, then you really need to understand the business issue, you need to know how to communicate with them and understand how they make decisions. Marketing researchers should be more comfortable with them and understand how they take decisions.[31]

The marketing research industry is seeing a broad differentiation between types of marketing research companies and marketing researchers. One type is the marketing researcher who becomes 'techniques focused', driven by the demands of marketers and buyers who view marketing research as a commodity. The alternative is the marketing researcher driven by the demands described by Richard Henchoz of Phillip Morris International in his search for researchers with more creativity and strategic marketing intelligence. Moving towards a business model that is driven by marketing researchers offering strategic marketing intelligence means that researchers and the marketing research industry of the future will be required to:[32]

- **Think conceptually** – by recruiting a new generation of 'conceptual' thinkers, i.e. researchers who feel comfortable working with higher order business concepts and talking the language of senior decision-makers. These individuals must understand the relationship between information and key business concepts. They must go beyond their technical and skill-based knowledge and offer strategic and tactical advice for business advantage based on detailed consumer and market knowledge.
- **Communicate in the way that those who commission research think** – by knowing how to communicate in the way senior people think, i.e. researchers presenting findings as a compelling narrative, not as disparate blocks of information.
- **Interpret findings in terms of the whole picture** – by thinking holistically about 'evidence', i.e. researchers with the skills to work in a 'holistic' way with all available customer evidence, recognising the need to interpret often imperfect marketing information. They must draw knowledge from a host of different sources including qualitative and quantitative techniques, a variety of forms of observation, customer relationship management systems, financial and customer profile information. These individuals will have to draw heavily upon the use of analytical models that represent the way customers think and behave.
- **Integrate findings with others that support marketing decision-makers** – by working in a multi-disciplinary way with related marketing services companies, with researchers working alongside branding and design and other marketing specialisms to gain a wider market understanding. This makes sure that everything is tailored to business solutions and is not just the result of rigid prescriptive research designs. This bottom-up, multi-disciplinary approach provides flexibility and differentiates 'strategic marketing

intelligence' from the 'top-down' approach of full-blown management consultants. This will also mean the cultivating of a more creative environment with a more 'hands-off' management style rather than a prescriptive techniques-driven approach.

Supporting decision-makers in sports marketing

Focus on   Sports Marketing Surveys

Sports Marketing Surveys quality research for management action

In most chapters of the text, examples will be presented based upon work conducted by the marketing research agency **Sports Marketing Surveys**. Four of its projects have been selected to illustrate how marketing research is managed in practice. Elements of these commercially sensitive projects will be chosen to show how the Agency managed the challenges of conducting actionable marketing research. The four chosen projects are:

Racetrack 2003 – a syndicated study to measure the attitudes and opinions of and profile the Formula 1 fan across eight countries worldwide.

Nestea – sponsorship evaluation in *Water, Wind and Waves* in Hungary and Germany, and Beach Volleyball in Italy, Germany and Sweden.

Flora London Marathon 2004 – TV media analysis, public awareness tracking and target market research.

Rugby Football League – evaluation of the core values of the sport and a deeper understanding of its target audience.

Sports Marketing Surveys (**www.sportsmarketingsurveys.com**) is a full-service independent marketing research agency that has specialised in the sponsorship and sports industry over the past 20 years. The sports industry and many sponsorships are often multi-country in their reach and activity. Sports Marketing Surveys has responded to this by having the capability of working and reporting on a worldwide basis in over 200 countries for events such as the Olympic Games and the Football World Cup. Its head office is in Surrey in the UK with global offices in: **Europe** – Belgium, France, Greece, Italy, Netherlands, Spain, Turkey: the **Americas** – Brazil, USA; **Australasia** – Australia; **Asia** – Japan, Korea, Singapore.

The sectors in which it specialises include: **sponsorship** (exposure and evaluation, effectiveness and event research), **sports goods** (sports equipment and footwear companies, e.g. golf, tennis and snow sports), **sports leisure and tourism** (supporting sports federations, venues and local governments).

The services they offer include: **media research** (covering TV, press, Internet and radio), **marketing research** (on an ad hoc or syndicated basis), **publications** (reports covering, e.g. European sports fans, profile of the European golfer and motorsport fans), **selection and valuation** (analytical model to select appropriate sponsorship and a tool to value the sponsorship investment) and **consultancy** (combining all the knowledge bases within the company and helping clients to use multiple sources in areas such as matching the understanding of potential markets and the strategic plans to maximise that potential).

International marketing research

With the spread of marketing and research skills has come a noticeable decline in a 'national research culture'. There was a time when each country had a stubbornly distinctive approach to research, making it extremely difficult to get a consistent research design across markets. Most people are aware now that there are different, equally legitimate, ways to approach research problems and that no one school of thought has absolute authority for all types of problem. This greater flexibility has made multi-country coordinated projects much more feasible – not easier, as they represent intellectually, logistically and diplomatically the most demanding of problems.

Conducting international marketing research is much more complex than conducting domestic marketing research. All research of this kind will be discussed and illustrated in individual chapters as individual techniques are developed and in greater detail in Chapter 26. The marketing, government, legal, economic, structural, socio-cultural and informational environments prevailing in target international markets, and the characteristics of target consumers that are being studied, influence the manner in which the marketing research process should be performed. Examples of these environmental factors and their impact on the marketing research process are illustrated in detail in subsequent chapters. The following example illustrates the problems and challenges faced by researchers in the European context.

Example	### Crossing borders[33]

What is this thing called Europe? Despite binding influences like a single currency, Europe's national marketing research markets have distinct cultural, cost and quality characteristics. For example, German marketing research still feels the effects of reunification, while Spanish agencies are trying to leverage Spain's historical links with Latin America to capture a slice of the coordination market there.

For research buyers and users, the diversity of Europe is very real, and the trickiest part of their remit is to get comparable data systems across the different country markets. Andrew Grant, European Research Director at Ford, says: 'From our perspective, actually getting to a single methodology, a single questionnaire, a single data collection method and a single set of attributes that means the same thing across markets is a hugely difficult part of what we do.'

Europe may be moving towards becoming a single market, but from a research cost perspective it is still far from being a level playing field. In the absence of tax and social cost harmonisation across Europe, countries like France and Sweden are two of the region's most expensive places to conduct research. The euro will have an increasingly positive effect, agencies say, for those countries that participate. 'It makes contracting and financing easier,' says Klaus Wübbenhorst, Chief Executive of German-based group GfK. 'The euro won't mean that prices in all European countries will be the same, you have to take into account different levels of productivity and efficiency. But it makes pricing more transparent between countries.'

Against a background of centralisation, standardisation and increasing cooperation, Europe's researchers believe that the region's defining diversity will survive. 'The fact that we're multicultural means that we have great creative potential,' says Meril James of GIA.

Ethics in marketing research

Marketing research often involves contact with the respondents and the wider public, usually by way of data collection, dissemination of the research findings, and marketing activities such as advertising campaigns based on these findings. Thus, there is the potential to abuse or misuse marketing research by taking advantage of these people. If respondents feel that they or their views are being abused or misrepresented, they either will not take part in future studies or may do so without honesty or full engagement in the issues being researched. They may also lobby politicians to protect them from what they see as intrusions into their privacy and liberties. In short, unethical research practices can severely impair the quality of the research process, undermine the validity of research findings and ultimately inflict serious damage upon the body of professional marketing researchers. If respondents cannot distinguish between genuine marketing research and unethical telemarketing or direct marketing where surveys are used to gain access to respondents to deliver a sales pitch or to generate sales, there can be severe repercussions for the marketing research industry through legislation designed to protect the privacy of citizens. The marketing research industry in Europe and the USA has got to a point where it has had to defend the quality of its practices.

The Alliance for Research, based in Brussels, was established in May 2002 as the first representative and lobbying body with a prime objective to improve understanding of the value and distinctive characteristics of marketing research among European parliamentarians and officials at the European Commission. The Alliance was initially funded by ESOMAR and from its inception it has been closely liaising with equivalent organisations in the USA for global alignment on legislative issues. The concern of such bodies was based on their assessment that parliamentarians, in both Europe and the USA (CASRO, Council of American Survey Research Organisations, and CMOR, Council for Marketing and Opinion Research), were very eager to protect citizens' privacy, especially against intrusive actions by telemarketers or direct marketers. Protection against intrusive actions tended to be afforded through legislation that also hurt the freedom to conduct research. In many cases, legislators were not aware of the differences between telemarketing and direct marketing on the one hand and marketing and opinion research on the other. Often they just did not realise that banning unsolicited phone calls across the board would infringe upon the ability to collect through social research some of the information they themselves needed as input for formulating their policies.[34] The Alliance for Research monitors all potentially damaging EU legislation and has been engaged in a dialogue with the EU data protection authorities. The Alliance is stepping up efforts to work in partnership with the authorities and to replace 'self-regulation' by 'co-regulation'. In the USA, the achievements of CASRO and CMOR include a ban by the federal authorities on selling or fundraising under the guise of research.[35]

Beyond support for the Alliance for Research, ESOMAR have been proactive in a review and reform of the entire framework of marketing research codes and guidelines. In the Quo Vadis project, initiated by ESOMAR in 2003, experts from the USA, Japan and Europe met for a workshop in Amsterdam in July 2003 to discuss the latest developments in the industry and their impact upon the quality of marketing research. They recognised the effect of a shift in focus of marketing research from data collection towards organisational decision making and agreed that current codes and guidelines had not kept up with this development. The experts pointed out that a concise list of codes would be a tool for self-regulation and support international convergence: 'A good ethical basis helps minimise legal restrictions.' They agreed and presented eight principles that would encapsulate to the outside world the scientific aim and character of marketing research as well as its special responsibility towards respondents, clients and the public.

The eight principles that have now been incorporated into the ESOMAR code of conduct are:[36]

1 Marketing researchers will conform to all relevant national and international laws.
2 Marketing researchers will behave ethically and will not do anything which might damage the reputation of marketing research.

3 Marketing researchers will take special care when carrying out research among children and other vulnerable groups of the population.

4 Respondents' cooperation is voluntary and must be based on adequate, and not misleading, information about the general purpose and nature of the project when their agreement to participate is being obtained and all such statements must be honoured.

5 The rights of respondents as private individuals will be respected by marketing researchers and they will not be harmed or disadvantaged as the result of cooperating in a marketing research project.

6 Marketing researchers will never allow personal data they collect in a marketing research project to be used for any purpose other than marketing research.

7 Marketing researchers will ensure that projects and activities are designed, carried out, reported and documented accurately, transparently, objectively and to appropriate quality.

8 Marketing researchers will conform to the accepted principles of fair competition.

The basic principles of the ESOMAR code of conduct and the full array of ESOMAR codes of conduct can be viewed at: **www.esomar.nl/codes_and_guidelines.html**.

ESOMAR distinguishes marketing research from other competitive forms of data gathering, primarily through the issue of the anonymity of respondents. It stresses that in marketing research the identity of the provider of information is not disclosed. It makes a clear distinction between marketing research and database marketing where the names and addresses of the people contacted are to be used for individual selling, promotional, fundraising or other non-research purposes. The distinction between marketing research and the database as a research tool is ultimately not so clear. There is a growing amount of support given to marketing decision-makers from database analyses that are not 'respondent specific'. It is possible to perform database analyses with the same level of professional standards as is applied in the marketing research industry.

There are many instances where database analyses can add clarity and focus to marketing research activities. For example, since the start of 1995 the highly respected marketing research agency Taylor Nelson AGB has been building the European Toiletries & Cosmetics Database (ETCD). Some 14,000 usage diaries of personal care products are collected each year, across the UK, France, Germany, Italy and Spain. Given the huge impact that database analyses are having upon marketing decision making, these issues will be developed more fully in Chapter 5. In the meantime, the maxim stated by ESOMAR of preserving the anonymity of respondents is vital for the continuing support of respondents and the ultimate health of the marketing research industry.

Internet and computer applications

As the applications of the Internet in research first became apparent, there was no real consensus within the marketing research industry of just what its impact would be. Many predicted that the Internet would ultimately replace all other methods of data collection, whilst others argued that it would just add another means to measure, understand or observe respondents.[37] In 2004, online research methods accounted for an estimated 11% of global research turnover. This is still some way behind telephone (20%) and face-to-face (31%). However, the actual usage, the amount of projects that use the Internet compared with other techniques, is likely to be much higher because the low-cost nature of the Internet keeps its revenue contributions down. The Internet

→

may not have gained such popularity had it not been for its low-cost characteristics and the ever-increasing cost and time pressures on research agencies. As an example, online access panels are seen as faster and more cost efficient than other methods of research. According to the ESOMAR 2005 Prices Study, for a tracking study they are on average 60% cheaper than face-to-face interviewing.[38]

Many argue that the growth of online research will be driven by new research clients, who see that they can enjoy the benefits of marketing research at a level they could not previously afford. The downside of the low costs of the technique is that the barriers to entry to the marketing research industry have been lowered. Effectively, anyone can establish a business with online survey software, a data analysis package and a basic understanding of research, undertaking surveys, customer satisfaction studies, and so on. This may have profound effects upon the quality and ethical standards of marketing research.

Given the importance of the Internet and developing technologies to the marketing research process and industry, key issues and debates in this subject will be continually addressed. Throughout this book we show how the stages of the marketing research process are facilitated by the Internet and other developing technologies and software. On the Companion Website to this text, demonstration versions of marketing research software will illustrate the use of computing technology in the process of questionnaire design, data entry, data analysis and reporting, and the application of geodemographic information systems.

Summary

Marketing research provides support to marketing decision-makers by helping to describe the nature and scope of customer groups, understand the nature of forces that shape the needs of customer groups and the marketer's ability to satisfy those groups, test individual and interactive controllable marketing variables, and monitor and reflect upon past successes and failures in marketing decisions. The overall purpose of marketing research is to assess information needs and provide the relevant information in a systematic and objective manner to improve marketing decision making. The marketing research process consists of six broad steps that must be followed creatively and systematically. The process involves problem definition, research approach development, research design formulation, fieldwork or data collection, data preparation and analysis, and report preparation and presentation. Within these six broad steps are many iterations and routes that can be taken, reflecting the reality of marketing research in practice. Marketing research may be classified into problem identification research and problem-solving research. In general terms, problem identification uncovers the potential that may be exploited in markets, problem-solving uncovers the means to realize that potential.

The major developed economies, especially in Europe and the USA, are the biggest users of marketing research on a per capita and total expenditure basis. The growth rates for the marketing research industries in these economies are low, the major growth occurring in countries like Chile, China and Bulgaria. Marketing research may be conducted internally (by internal suppliers) or may be purchased from external suppliers. Full-service suppliers provide the entire range of marketing research services, from problem definition to report preparation and presentation. They may also manage customer database analyses, being able to integrate the management and analyses databases with the management and analyses of conventional marketing research techniques. Limited-service suppliers specialise in one or a few phases of the marketing research project. Services offered by these suppliers can be classified as field services, coding and data entry, data analysis, analytical services or branded products.

Marketing research is not a panacea for all marketing problems. There are examples where marketing research has not adequately supported decision-makers. Many of the problems that arise from poor marketing research derive from poor communications between decision-makers and researchers. In order to resolve these problems, there are growing demands upon the marketing research industry to produce research findings that are more actionable and relevant to marketing decision-makers. As well as having the technical skills to conduct research in a professional and ethical manner, marketing researchers are increasingly expected to have the ability to interpret their findings in a manner that is relevant to decision-makers.

International marketing research can be much more complex than domestic research because the researcher must consider the environments prevailing in the international markets being researched. Research is founded upon the willing cooperation, of the public and of business organisations. Ethical marketing research practices nurture that cooperation, allowing a more professional approach and more accurate research information. Marketing research makes extensive use of the great opportunities afforded by the Internet. There are also many competitive threats to the marketing research industry that have been exacerbated by the Internet.

Questions

1 Describe the task of marketing research.

2 What decisions are made by marketing managers? How does marketing research help in supporting these decisions?

3 What do you see as the major challenges for marketing researchers that emerge from the ESOMAR definition of marketing research?

4 What problems are associated with using consumer databases in marketing research?

5 How may the sound practice of problem identification research enhance the sound practice of problem-solving research?

6 What challenges exist in trying to quantify the size and growth of the marketing research industry on a global basis?

7 Explain one way to classify marketing research suppliers and services.

8 Describe the steps in the simple marketing research process.

9 Explain why there may be the need for iterations between stages of the marketing research process.

10 What arguments can be used by sceptics of marketing research?

11 What management skills are increasingly being demanded from marketing researchers?

12 What arguments would you use to defend investment in marketing research?

13 What factors fuel the growth of international marketing research?

14 Discuss the ethical issues in marketing research that relate to (a) the client, (b) the supplier, and (c) the respondent.

15 Summarise the nature of threats and opportunities that the Internet offers the marketing researcher.

Exercises

1 Visit the website of Taylor Nelson Sofres **www.tns-global.com**. Examine the nature of the Research Services and the Business Solutions it offers. How do you see these fitting together and what is the impact of this fit upon the career opportunities the company advertises?

2 Visit the website of the Market Research Society, **www.mrs.org.uk**. Work through the array of publications and support it gives to its members. Specifically examine and register for **www.research-live.com/** and examine the published code of conduct. Compare the MRS code of conduct with that available on the ESOMAR website, **www.esomar.org**. Are there any differences in their respective approaches to maintaining professional standards in the marketing research industry?

3 Visit the website **www.trendwatching.com** and register for trend-watching updates if you wish. Critically evaluate the worth of trend watching for the marketing researcher.

4 From national or international newspapers, track down stories of successful entrepreneurial ventures. Evaluate the extent to which marketing research is attributed to their success and/or an awareness of their market(s).

5 In a small group discuss the following issues: 'What is the ideal educational background for someone seeking a career in marketing research?' and 'Is it possible to enforce ethical standards within the marketing research industry?'

Video Case Exercise: Burke Inc.

Burke describes marketing research as 'an important and dynamic component of modern business'. How are other means of supporting the marketing decision-maker affecting the importance and dynamism of marketing research?

video case

download from
www.pearsoned.co.uk/
malhotra_euro

Notes

1 Vangelder, P., 'Listening to the customer – research at Royal Ahold', *ESOMAR Newsbrief* 4 (April 1999), 14–15.

2 Johansen, T. and Herlin, K., 'Banner advertising – more than clicks', *Admap* (October 2001), 15–17.

3 Jensen, N.M. and Wegloop, P., 'Nordea: a new brand in the making', *Research World*, (January 2005), 34.

4 For the strategic role of marketing research, see Jarratt, D. and Fayed, R., 'The impact of market and organizational challenges on marketing strategy decision making', *Journal of Business Research* 51 (January 2001), 61–72; Higgins, L.F., 'Applying principles of creativity management to marketing research efforts in high-technology markets', *Industrial Marketing Management* 28 (3) (May 1999), 305–317; Zabriskie, N.B. and Huellmantel, A.B., 'Marketing research as a strategic tool', *Long-Range Planning* 27 (February 1994), 107–118.

5 For relationships between information processing, marketing decisions and performance, see Glazer, R. and Weiss, A.M., 'Marketing in turbulent environments: decision process and the time-sensitivity of information', *Journal of Marketing Research* 30 (November 1993), 509–521.

6 Samuels, J., 'Research methodologies', *Research World* (November 2003), 20–21.

7 Savage, M., 'Downstream danger', *Research* (May 2000), 25–27.

8 Anon., 'Supermarket sweep', *The Grocer* (13 July 1996), 28.

9 Anon., 'Beer research shows overspill', *Marketing* (9 October 1997), 6.

10 Anon, 'Kellogg's brings Olympic spirit to America's breakfast table', PR Newswire (6 December 2001); 'Anon, Kellogg's Crunchy Nuts gets ready for adult breakfast', *Grocer* 224 (7524) (October 6 2001), 53.

11 Vonk, T., 'ESOMAR Annual Study on the Market Research Industry 2003', *Research World* (September 2004), 28–33.

12 The 15 EU member countries in 2003.

13 ESOMAR – *Industry study on 2004*, 8.

14 ESOMAR – *Industry study on 2004*, 15.

15 Tarran, B., 'The birth of an idea', *Research* (August 2003), 23.

16 Lury, G., 'Market research cannot cover for the "vision thing"', *Marketing* (9 November 2000), 34.

17 Gordon, W., 'Be creative to innovate', *Research* (January 2000), 23.

18 Lehmann, D.R., *Market Research and Analysis*, 3rd edn (Homewood, IL: Irwin, 1994), 14.

19 Sampson, P. and Standen, P., 'Predicting sales volume and market shares', in *New Product Development Research Contributions to Strategy Formulation, Idea Generation and Screening Product, Product Testing and Final Marketing*, ESOMAR (November 1983).

20 Muranka, T. and Rootes, N., *Doing a Dyson* (Dyson Appliances, 1996), 22; Mesure, S., 'A day in the life of James Dyson', *Independent* (27 May 2006), 55.

21 Escobales, R., 'A little less conversation', *Research*, (January 2004), 18.

22 Chervi, B. and Savage, M., 'Innovate to survive', *Research* (October 1999), 16.

23 Havermans, J., 'A seat at the boardroom table', *Research World* (January 2004), 16.

24 Wilson, V., 'Worldwide: Denmark', *Research* (August 2005), 28.

25 Heeg, R., 'Back on the path of growth', *Research World* (April 2005), 19.

26 Van Hamersveld, M. and Smith, D., 'From data collection to decision support (3)' *Research World* (December 2003), 19.

27 Heeg, R., 'A career in market research is a hard sell', *Research World* (September 2004), 11.

28 Miles, L., 'Luxury cars – a key role for research', *Research World* (January 2004), 14.

29 Havermnans, J., 'What do clients want from research?', *Research World* (March 2005), 10.

30 Van Hamersveld, M. and Smith, D., 'From data collection to decision support (2)', (November 2003), 18.

31 Havermans, J., 'Revive apprenticeship in research', *Research World* (September 2004), 14.

32 Van Hamersveld, M. and Smith, D., 'From data collection to decision support (3)', *Research World* (December 2003), 20.

33 McElhatton, N., 'Crossing borders', *Research, Guide to Europe* (May 2000), 4–5.

34 Havermans, J., 'Look out post for research', *Research World* (November 2004), 30.

35 Havermans, J., 'Market research leaders agree on next steps in industry effort', *Research World* (February 2005), 8.

36 Havermans, J., 'New international MR practice in 8 principles', *Research World* (May 2004), 20–21.

37 Tarran, B., 'Worldwide global', *Research* (November 2005), 27.

38 Ibid.

4

Secondary data collection and analysis

The act of sourcing, evaluating and analysing secondary data can realise great insights for decision-makers. It is also vital to successful problem diagnosis, sample planning and collection of primary data.

Objectives

After reading this chapter, you should be able to:

1 define the nature and scope of secondary data and distinguish secondary data from primary data;

2 analyse the advantages and disadvantages of secondary data and their uses in the various steps of the marketing research process;

3 evaluate secondary data using the criteria of specifications, error, currency, objectives, nature and dependability;

4 describe in detail the different sources of secondary data, focusing upon external sources in the form of published materials and syndicated services;

5 discuss in detail the syndicated sources of secondary data, including household and consumer data obtained via surveys, mail diary panels and electronic scanner services, as well as institutional data related to retailers, wholesalers and industrial or service firms;

6 explain the need to use multiple sources of secondary data and describe single-source data;

7 identify and evaluate the sources of secondary data useful in international marketing research;

8 understand the ethical issues involved in the use of secondary data.

STAGE 1 Problem definition	STAGE 2 Research approach developed	STAGE 3 Research design developed	STAGE 4 Fieldwork or data collection	STAGE 5 Data preparation and analysis	STAGE 6 Report preparation and presentation

Overview

The collection and analysis of secondary data help to define the marketing research problem and develop an approach. In addition, before collecting primary data, the researcher should locate and analyse relevant secondary data. Thus, secondary data can be an essential component of a successful research design. Secondary data can help in sample designs and in the details of primary research methods. In some projects, research may be largely confined to the analysis of secondary data because some marketing problems may be resolved using only secondary data. Given the huge explosion of secondary data sources available, sufficient data may be accessed to solve a particular marketing research problem.

This chapter discusses the distinction between primary data, secondary data and marketing intelligence. The advantages and disadvantages of secondary data are considered, and criteria for evaluating secondary data are presented, along with a classification of secondary data. Internal secondary data are described and major sources of external secondary data, such as published materials, online and offline databases, and syndicated services, are also discussed. Useful sources of secondary data in international marketing research are discussed. Several ethical issues that arise in the use of secondary data are also identified.

To begin with, we present an example that illustrates the nature of secondary data, how it may be evaluated, and its relationship to primary data collection.

Example Flying high on secondary data[1]

Money magazine published the results of a study conducted to uncover the airline characteristics that consumers consider most important. In order of importance, these characteristics were safety, price, baggage handling, on-time performance, customer service, ease of reservations and ticketing, comfort, frequent flyer schemes and food.

If Air France was considering conducting a marketing research study to identify characteristics of its service that should be improved, this article might be a useful source of secondary data. Before using the data, Air France should evaluate them according to several criteria.

First, the research design used to collect the data should be examined. This *Money* magazine article includes a section that details the research design used in the study. *Money* used a face-to-face survey of 1,017 'frequent flyers'. The results of the survey had a margin of error of 3%. Air France would have to decide whether 'frequent flyers' in the USA could be generalised to the population it wishes to understand, whether 1,017 was a sufficient sample size for its purposes and whether a margin of error of 3% was acceptable. In addition, Air France should evaluate what type of response or non-response errors may have occurred in the data collection or analysis process.

The currency of the data and objective of the study would be important to Air France in deciding whether to utilise this article as a source of secondary data. Air France would also need to look at the nature and dependability of the data. For example, it would need to examine how the nine choice criteria were defined. If the criterion price was measured in terms of fare per kilometre, is this a meaningful and acceptable definition to decision-makers at Air France? With regard to dependability, Air France would need to evaluate the reputation of *Money* magazine and of ICR, the research company hired by *Money* to undertake the survey. It would also need to recognise the fact that *Money* used secondary data in its study; how dependable are the sources it used?

The *Money* magazine article might be useful as a starting place for a marketing research project for Air France. It could be helpful in formulating the nature of decision-making problems and associated research objectives. There may be limitations in regard to reliability, dependability or even how generalisable it may be to Air France's target consumers. Many lessons and ideas may be generated from this article that may lead to other secondary data sources and in the design of a well-focused primary data collection.

Defining primary data, secondary data and marketing intelligence

Primary data
Data originated by the researcher specifically to address the research problem.

Primary data are data originated by a researcher for the specific purpose of addressing the problem at hand. They are individually tailored for the decision-makers of organisations that pay for well-focused and exclusive support. Compared with readily available data from a variety of sources, this exclusivity can mean higher costs and a longer time frame in collecting and analysing the data.

Secondary data
Data collected for some purpose other than the problem at hand.

Secondary data are data that have already been collected for purposes other than the problem at hand. At face value this definition seems straightforward, especially when contrasted to the definition of primary data. However, many researchers confuse the term, or quite rightly see some overlap with marketing intelligence.

Marketing intelligence
Qualified observations of events and developments in the marketing environment.

Marketing intelligence can be defined as 'qualified observations of events and developments in the marketing environment'. The use of the word 'observations' is presented in a wide sense to include a variety of types of data, broadly concerned with 'environmental scanning'.[2] In essence, though, marketing intelligence is based upon data that in many instances have been collected for purposes other than the problem at hand. To clarify this overlap in definitions, Table 4.1 compares secondary data with marketing intelligence through a variety of characteristics.

Table 4.1 A comparison of secondary data and marketing intelligence[3]

Characteristic	Secondary data	Marketing intelligence
Structure	Specifications and research design tend to be apparent	Can be poorly structured; no universal conventions of reporting
Availability	Tend to have regular updates	Irregular availability
Sources	Generated in-house and from organisations with research prowess	Generated in-house and from unofficial sources
Data type	Tend to be quantitative; many issues need qualitative interpretation	Tends to be qualitative; many issues difficult to quantify
Source credibility	Tend to be from reputable and trustworthy research sources of credibility	Questionable credibility; can be generated from a broad spectrum
Terms of reference	Tend to have clear definitions of what is being measured	Ambiguous definitions; difficult to compare over different studies
Analysis	Mostly conventional quantitative techniques	Opinion based, interpretative
Ethics	In-company data gathering may be covered by Data Protection Acts; externally generated data may be covered by research codes of conduct, e.g. ESOMAR	Some techniques may be seen as industrial espionage – though there is an ethical code produced by the Society of Competitive Intelligence Professionals

Note in these comparisons the repeated use of the word 'tend'. The boundaries between the two are not absolutely rigid. Consider the example at the start of this chapter, an article published in *Money* magazine. The journalist may have collected, analysed and presented quantitative data to support the qualitative interpretation of the future developments of a market. The data used and presented may come from credible sources and be correctly analysed, but what about the choice of data to support the journalist's argument? Other sources of data that may contradict this view may be ignored. The data presented can be seen as a secondary data source and interpreted in its own right by a researcher. The interpretation and argument of the journalist can be seen as intelligence and have some credibility. In its entirety, such an article has elements of both secondary data and marketing intelligence, and it may be impossible to pull them apart as mutually exclusive components.

As will become apparent in this chapter, there are clear criteria for evaluating the accuracy of secondary data, which tend to be of a quantitative nature. Marketing intelligence is more difficult to evaluate but this does not mean that it has less value to decision-makers or researchers. Certain marketing phenomena cannot be formally measured: researchers may not be able to gain access to conduct research, or the rapid unfolding of events means that it is impracticable to conduct research. The following example illustrates the importance of intelligence to many companies.

Example   **Behind enemy lines[4]**

Robin Kirkby, Director of European Consulting for intelligence specialist Fuld & Company, says there are three principal factors driving investment in intelligence:

The Internet, globalisation and higher expectations from customers are all putting companies under more pressure to differentiate themselves from the competition. It's frustrating that intelligence gets associated with spying; it's actually a highly ethical activity, focused on underlying competitive dynamics and planning future change.

According to research by The Futures Group (TFG), 60% of companies have an organised system for collecting competitive intelligence, while 82% of companies with revenues over €10 billion make systematic use of it. TFG ranked the leading eight users of competitor intelligence as:

1   Microsoft
2   Motorola
3   IBM
4   Procter & Gamble
5= General Electric
5= Hewlett-Packard
7= Coca-Cola
7= Intel

Shadow team
A small cross-functional boundary-spanning group that learns everything about a competitive unit.

Many major organisations invest huge amounts in the hardware and software needed for a systematic approach to gathering intelligence, some even engaging in the use of 'shadow teams'. A **shadow team** is a small cross-functional boundary-spanning group that learns everything about a competitive unit. A competitive unit can be a competitor, product line, supply chain or prospective partner in a strategic alliance. The objective of a shadow team is to learn everything possible about its target through published data, personnel and network connection, and organisation knowledge or hearsay. It brings together knowledge from across an organisation, so that it can think, reason and react like the competitive unit.[5] Competitive intelligence will be discussed in more detail in the context of business-to-business marketing research in Chapter 27.

Such widespread use of intelligence in major organisations means it has a role to play in supporting decision-makers, but it has many limitations, which are apparent in Table 4.1. In the development of better founded information support, credible support can come from the creative collection and evaluation of secondary data. This requires researchers to connect and validate different data sources, ultimately leading to decision-maker support in its own right and support of more focused primary data collection. As this chapter and Chapter 5 unfold, examples of different types of secondary data will emerge and the applications of secondary data will become apparent.

Advantages and uses of secondary data

Secondary data offer several advantages over primary data. Secondary data are easily accessible, relatively inexpensive and quickly obtained. Some secondary data, such as those provided by the National Censuses, are available on topics where it would not be feasible for a firm to collect primary data. Although it is rare for secondary data to provide all the answers to a non-routine research problem, such data can be useful in a variety of ways.[6] Secondary data can help you to:

1 Diagnose the research problem.
2 Develop an approach to the problem.
3 Develop a sampling plan.
4 Formulate an appropriate research design (e.g., by identifying the key variables to measure or understand).
5 Answer certain research questions and test some hypotheses.
6 Interpret primary data with more insight.
7 Validate qualitative research findings.

Given these advantages and uses of secondary data, we state the following general rule:

Examination of available secondary data is a prerequisite to the collection of primary data. Start with secondary data. Proceed to primary data only when the secondary data sources have been exhausted or yield marginal returns.

The rich dividends obtained by following this rule are illustrated in the example at the start of this chapter. It shows that the collection and analysis of even one relevant secondary data source can provide valuable insights. The decision-maker and researcher can use the ideas generated in secondary data as a very strong foundation to primary data design and collection. However, the researcher should be cautious in using secondary data, because they have some limitations and disadvantages.

Disadvantages of secondary data

Because secondary data have been collected for purposes other than the problem at hand, their usefulness to the current problem may be limited in several important ways, including relevance and accuracy. The objectives, nature and methods used to collect the secondary data may not be appropriate to the present situation. Also, secondary data may be lacking in accuracy or may not be completely current or dependable. Before using secondary data, it is important to evaluate them according to a series of factors.[7] These factors are discussed in more detail in the following section.

Criteria for evaluating secondary data

The quality of secondary data should be routinely evaluated, using the criteria presented in Table 4.2 and the discussion in the following sections.[8]

Specifications and research design

The specifications or the research design used to collect the data should be critically examined to identify possible sources of bias. Such design considerations include size and nature of the sample, response rate and quality, questionnaire design and administration, procedures used for fieldwork, and data analysis and reporting procedures. These checks provide information on the reliability and validity (these concepts will be further developed in Chapter 13) of the data and help determine whether they can be generalised to the problem at hand. The reliability and validity can be further ascertained by an examination of the error, currency, objectives, nature and dependability associated with the secondary data.

Error and accuracy

The researcher must determine whether the data are accurate enough for the purposes of the present study. Secondary data can have a number of sources of error or inaccuracy, including errors in the approach, research design, sampling, data collection, analysis, and

Table 4.2 Criteria for evaluating secondary data

Criteria	Issues	Remarks
Specifications and research design	• Data collection method • Response rate • Population definition • Sampling method • Sample size • Questionnaire design • Fieldwork • Data analysis	Data should be reliable, valid and generalisable to the problem at hand
Error and accuracy	Examine errors in: • Approach • Research design • Sampling • Data collection • Data analysis • Reporting	Assess accuracy by comparing data from different sources
Currency	Time lag between collection and publication. Frequency of updates	Census data are periodically updated by syndicated firms
Objective	Why the data were collected	The objective will determine the relevance of data
Nature	• Definition of key variables • Units of measurement • Categories used • Relationships examined	Reconfigure the data to increase their usefulness, if possible
Dependability	Source: • Expertise • Credibility • Reputation • Trustworthiness	Preference should be afforded to an original rather than an acquired source

reporting stages of the project. Moreover, it is difficult to evaluate the accuracy of secondary data because the researcher did not participate in the research. One approach is to find multiple sources of data if possible, and compare them using standard statistical procedures.

| *Example* | Number crunch[9] |

In December 1997, the Audit Bureau of Circulations (ABC) met UK newspaper publishers and major media buyers from the Institute of Practitioners in Advertising. The meeting aimed to thrash out a formula that could restore ABC's credibility in measuring newspaper readship which forms the basis of negotiation for advertising rates.

Most observers agreed that ABC's troubles were a direct result of squabbling between media owners. As newspaper circulations continued to slide, they fought to hold on to market share through price cuts, promotions and enhanced editorial packages. This has introduced an unprecedented volatility into their sales figures. Not content with trumpeting their own gains, some newspapers have sought to show up the deficiencies in their rivals' sales figures.

Figures under fire

The argument is best understood through an example of what was at stake. The October 1997 ABC figure for *The Times* was 814,899. This was a monthly circulation average which, prior to the dispute, would have been the only official benchmark that agencies used as a negotiating point between newspapers and advertisers (though they turn to data from the National Readership Survey and the Target Group Index to argue their case). At the heart of the dispute was what that monthly figure comprised. For example, were all the issues sold at the full price or were some given away cheaply as part of a subscription or promotional offer? Were any sold or given in bulk to an airliner or retailer, and if so how many? What about papers sold to Ireland or Spain? Were they included in the total, and if so how could that be justified as a piece of credible advertising data?

Another hot issue was the reliability of the monthly figure. Advertisers were dissatisfied with a number that they believe fails to reflect the reality of what they were buying. Director of Press Buying at The Media Centre, Tim Armes, says:

we'd like to know what each paper sells daily and we'd like to know week to week fluctuations. The papers all boast about Saturday but keep quiet about Tuesday and Thursday. If one day is dramatically higher than the average, you don't have to be a brain surgeon to realise the others are lower.

As this example indicates, the accuracy of secondary data can vary: What is being measured? What rules apply to those measurements? What happens if there are rapid changes in what is being measured? With different researchers potentially measuring the 'same' phenomena, data obtained from different sources may not agree. In these cases, the researcher should verify the accuracy of secondary data by conducting pilot studies or by other exploratory work that verifies the analytical framework used to arrive at certain figures. Often, by judicious questioning of those involved in compiling the figures, this can be done without much expense or effort.

Currency: when the data were collected

Secondary data may not be current and the time lag between data collection and publication may be long, as is the case with much census data which may take up to two years from collection to publication. Moreover, the data may not be updated frequently enough for the purpose of the problem at hand. Decision-makers require current data; therefore, the value of secondary data is diminished as they become dated. For instance, although the Census of Population data are comprehensive, they may not be applicable to major cities in which the population has changed rapidly during the last two years.

Objective: the purpose for which the data were collected

Data are invariably collected with some objective in mind, and a fundamental question to ask is why the data were collected in the first place. The objective for collecting data will ultimately determine the purpose for which that information is relevant and useful. Data collected with a specific objective in mind may not be appropriate in another situation. In the example at the start of this chapter, the sample surveyed by *Money* magazine was made up of 'frequent flyers'. The objective of the study was 'to uncover the airline characteristics consumers consider most important'. Air France, however, may wish to target 'business class' flyers and 'to uncover perceptions related to trade-offs made in customer service–price–safety'. Even though there may be identical questions used in both studies, the target respondents may be different, the rationale for the study presented to respondents will be different, and ultimately the 'state of mind' respondents may be in when they come to comparable questions will be different. The *Money* survey was conducted for entirely different objectives from those Air France has for its study. The findings from the *Money* survey may not directly support decision making at Air France, though they may help to define who Air France should talk to and what questions it should put to them.

Nature: the content of the data

The nature, or content, of the data should be examined with special attention to the definition of key variables, the units of measurement, the categories used and the relationships examined. If the key variables have not been defined or are defined in a manner inconsistent with the researcher's definition, then the usefulness of the data is limited. Consider, for example, secondary data on consumer preferences for TV programmes. To use this information, it is important to know how preference for programmes was defined. Was it defined in terms of the programme watched most often, the one considered most needed, most enjoyable, most informative, or the programme of greatest service to the community?

Likewise, secondary data may be measured in units that may not be appropriate for the current problem. For example, income may be measured by individual, family, household or spending unit and could be gross or net after taxes and deductions. Income may be classified into categories that are different from research needs. If the researcher is interested in high-income consumers with gross annual household incomes of over €120,000, secondary data with income categories of less than €20,000, €20,001–€50,000, €50,001–€75,000 and more than €75,000 will not be of use. Determining the measurement of variables such as income may be a complex task, requiring the wording of the definition of income to be precise. Finally, the relationships examined should be taken into account in evaluating the nature of data. If, for example, actual behaviour is of interest, then data inferring behaviour from self-reported attitudinal information may have limited usefulness. Sometimes it is possible to reconfigure the available data – for example, to convert the units of measurement – so that the resulting data are more useful to the problem at hand.

Dependability: how dependable are the data?

An overall indication of the dependability of data may be obtained by examining the expertise, credibility, reputation and trustworthiness of the source. This information can be obtained by checking with others who have used the information provided by the source. Data published to promote sales, to advance specific interests, or to carry on propaganda should be viewed with suspicion. The same may be said of data published anonymously or in a form that attempts to hide the details of the data collection research design and process. It is also pertinent to examine whether the secondary data came from an original source, one that generated the data, or an acquired source, one that procured the data from an original source and published it in a different context. Generally, secondary data should be secured from an original rather than an acquired source. There are at least two reasons for this rule: first, an original source is the one that specifies the details of the data collection research design; and, second, an original source is likely to be more accurate and complete than a surrogate source.

Classification of secondary data

Internal data
Data available within the organisation for whom the research is being conducted.

Figure 4.1 presents a classification of secondary data. Secondary data may be classified as either internal or external. **Internal data** are those generated within the organisation for which the research is being conducted. An example of this source of data for any marketing decision-maker and marketing researcher is the corporate sales ledger at individual transaction level. Analyses of who is buying and the different ways that these customers may be classified or segmented, what they bought, how frequently and the monetary value of their purchases, can give a basic level of understanding customer buying behaviour. With a number of years of transaction data, the lifestages of customer segments can be better understood and how customers have reacted to an array of marketing activities. One of the main problems that marketing researchers face with accessing and analysing transaction data is 'corporate territorialism', i.e. the attitude that each department should only be concerned with the operational data it needs for the business to run on a day-to-day basis. Given that the marketing department in many companies is still not expected to need access to data beyond that needed to execute direct mail campaigns, analysing transactional data may well be a major internal political challenge.[10] Given the importance of this element of marketing decision support, secondary data generated from internal sources will be examined in more detail in Chapter 5.

External data
Data that originate outside the organisation.

External data, on the other hand, are those generated by sources outside the organisation. These data may exist in the form of published material, online databases, or information made available by syndicated services. Externally generated secondary data may be more difficult to access, more expensive and more difficult to evaluate for accuracy, in comparison with internal secondary data. These factors mean that, before collecting external secondary data, it is vital to gather, analyse and interpret any readily available internal secondary data and intelligence.

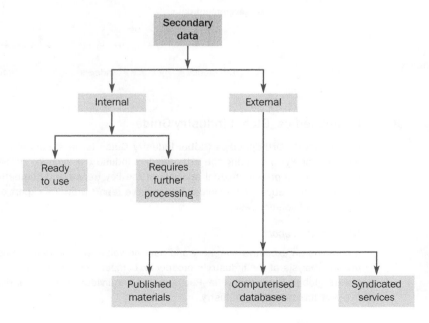

Figure 4.1
A classification of secondary data

Published external secondary sources

Sources of published external secondary data include local authorities, regional and national governments, the EU, non-profit organisations (e.g. Chambers of Commerce), trade associations and professional organisations, commercial publishers, investment brokerage firms and professional marketing research firms.[11] In fact, such a quantity of data is available that the researcher can be overwhelmed. Therefore, it is important to classify published sources (see Figure 4.2). Published external sources may be broadly classified as general business data or government data. General business sources comprise guides, directories, indexes and statistical data. Government sources may be broadly categorised as census data and other publications. These data types are discussed further with specific sources used as examples.

General business sources

Businesses publish a lot of information in the form of books, periodicals, journals, newspapers, magazines, reports and trade literature. This information can be located by using guides, directories and indexes. Sources are also available to identify statistical data.

Guides. Guides are an excellent source of standard or recurring information. A guide may help identify other important sources of directories, trade associations and trade publications. Guides are one of the first sources a researcher should consult. The following example illustrates the Global Industry Guide for Orthopaedics (**www.bioportfolio.com**).

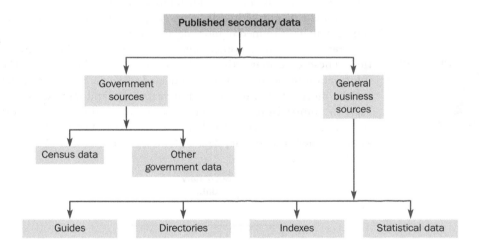

Figure 4.2
A classification of published secondary sources

Example   **Orthopaedics: Global Industry Guide**

Datamonitor's Orthopaedics Global Industry Guide is an essential resource for top-level data and analysis covering the orthopaedics industry. It includes detailed data on market size and segmentation, textual analysis of the key trends and competitive landscape, and profiles of the leading companies. This incisive report provides expert analysis on a global, regional and country basis.

Scope of the report

It contains an executive summary and data on value, volume and segmentation. It provides textual analysis of the industry's prospects, competitive landscape and leading companies; covers global, European, Asia–Pacific and 11 individual country markets; and includes a five-year forecast of the industry.

Highlights

Detailed information is included on market size, measured by both value and volume. Market shares are covered by manufacturer and by brand, including private label. Distribution channels are also analysed. Published December 2004, 162 pages, PDF. Price: $995.00 (€780).

Directories. Directories are helpful for identifying individuals or organisations that collect specific data. An example of a directory that you can examine on the Internet is the Central and Eastern European Business Directory. This interactive site provides current information on businesses and organisations in 24 Central and Eastern European countries (**www.ceebd.co.uk**). Another example is Europages, a reference business directory in Europe that classifies 500,000 companies in 30 European countries. Again, this can be accessed through the Internet and is available in English, French, German, Italian and Spanish versions (**www.europages.com**). Other directories worth exploring include **www.bizeurope.com**.

Indexes. It is possible to locate information on a particular topic in several different publications by using an index and abstracts. Indexes and abstracts, therefore, can increase the efficiency of the search process. Several indexes and abstracts are available for both academic and business sources. Examples of newspaper indexes include the *Financial Times Index* (**www.ft.com**), *Le Monde Index* (**www.le-monde.fr**) and the Japanese Business News online, *The Nikkei Weekly* (**www.nikkei.co.jp**). These indexes allow researchers to identify sources of particular topics, industries and individuals.

An example of a marketing index is the *Marketing Surveys Index* published by Euromonitor (**www.euromonitor.com**). This is a most comprehensive and up-to-date directory of business research on European and world markets. The index contains details of published research reports, a brief summary of its contents, a keyword index to the markets and products covered, and bibliographic details of the report.

A most valuable directory for marketing researchers is the *Directory of Research Organisations* published by ESOMAR (**www.esomar.com**). Finally, a particularly useful abstract source for marketing researchers is the *Market Research Abstracts* published by the Market Research Society in the UK (**www.warc.com**). Major European and American journals that relate to marketing research are reviewed and an abstract of each article is presented. The abstract is published twice a year. It is divided into sections that cover survey techniques; statistics, models and forecasting; attitude and behaviour research; psychographics, personality and social psychology; advertising and media research; applications of research; industrial market research; market research and general applications; and new product development. Such an abstract allows the researcher to identify and evaluate quickly the worth of journal papers that are relevant to the particular study.

Non-government statistical data. Published statistical data are of great interest to researchers. Graphic and statistical analyses can be performed on these data to draw important insights. Examples of non-governmental statistical data include trade associations such as the Swedish Tourism Trade Association (**www.sverigeturism.se**). The Swedish Information 'Smorgasbord' is a large single source of information in English on Sweden, Swedish provinces, nature, culture, lifestyle, society and industry. Another example is Euromonitor (**www.euromonitor.com**), which publishes monthly market research journals covering subjects under the headings of Market Research Europe, Market Research GB, Market Research International and Retail Monitor International.

The United Nations provides an example of an organisation with a Statistics Division that provides a wide range of statistical outputs on a global basis (**www.unstats. un.org/unsd**). The

Statistics Division produces printed publications of statistics and statistical methods in the fields of international merchandise trade, national accounts, demography and population, social indicators, gender, industry, energy, environment, human settlements and disability. The Statistics Division also produces general statistical compendiums including the *Statistical Yearbook* and *World Statistics Pocketbook*. Many of its databases in these fields are available as electronic publications in the form of CD-ROM and on the Internet.

Government sources

European governments and the EU also produce large amounts of secondary data. Each European country has its own statistical office which produces lists of the publications available (and the costs involved). Examples of national statistical offices include the Centraal Bureau voor de Statistiek Nederlands (**www.cbs.nl**), Danmarks Statistik (**www.dst.dk**), the Federal Statistical Office of Germany (**www.destatis.de**), the French Institut National de la Statistique et des Études Economiques (**www.insee.fr**) and the British Office for National Statistics (**www.statistics.gov.uk**). All of these offices have Internet links that allow you to examine quickly the array of publications that they produce. Their publications may be divided into census data and other publications.

Census data. Most European countries produce either catalogues or newsletters that describe the array of census publications available and the plans for any forthcoming census. In the UK, for example, *Census News* (**www.statistics.gov.uk/census**) is a newsletter that contains the latest information about the 2007 and 2011 Censuses and previous censuses and is available four to six times a year. Census Marketing in Britain can supply unpublished data from the 1961, 1971, 1981, 1991, 2001 Censuses in the form of Small Area Statistics (SAS). SAS are available for standard census areas within England and Wales, such as counties, local government districts, London boroughs, wards, civil parishes and enumeration districts. Maps can also be purchased to complement the data.

Census data can be kept in electronic format, allowing them to be analysed and presented in a variety of formats at a detailed geographical level. Given the long periods between the national Censuses and the amount of change that can occur in these periods, other data sources are used to maintain an up-to-date picture of specific regions.

As well as general population censuses, national statistical offices produce an array of industrial censuses. These may include industrial production, housing, construction, agriculture, restaurants and hotels, and financial services, e.g. **www.statistics.gov.uk/statbase/mainmenu.asp**.

Other government publications. In addition to the census, national statistical offices collect and publish a great deal of statistical data. Examining the Department of Statistics and Research in Cyprus as an example (**www.mof.gov.cy**), major industrial categories such as agriculture, construction, retailing and tourism are classified, with a whole array of available statistics. More generally, demographic, health, household income and expenditure, and labour statistical reports are also available.

Examples of reports from the British Office for National Statistics include *Social Trends*. *Social Trends* draws together social and economic data from a wide range of government departments and other organisations to provide a comprehensive guide to British society today, and how it has been changing. In 2005 *Social Trends* celebrated 35 years of social reporting. The 2005 edition featured an overview chapter that highlights some of the major changes in society since *Social Trends* was first published. The UK has an ageing population, and growth in the minority ethnic population has resulted in a more diverse society. Household income has risen over the past 35 years, although income inequality has widened. Life expectancy has also increased but so have the number of years that the population can expect to live in poor health or with a disability. Technology has transformed many lives and dependence on the car is greater than ever.

In the EU, statistics are collected and published by the Statistical Office of the European Community (SOEC) in a series called Eurostat (**www.europa.eu**) (**www.epp.eurostat. cec.eu.int**). Tables normally contain figures for individual member states of the EU plus totals for all countries. Eurostat divides its publications into themes, which are:

- *Theme 1* – General and regional statistics
- *Theme 2* – Economy and finance
- *Theme 3* – Population and social conditions
- *Theme 4* – Industry trade and services
- *Theme 5* – Agriculture and fisheries
- *Theme 6* – External trade
- *Theme 7* – Transport
- *Theme 8* – Environment and energy
- *Theme 9* – Science and technology.

It also produces general titles which include *Eurostat Yearbook* (annual), *Basic Statistics* (annual), *Europe in Figures* (annual), *Key Figures* (monthly) and *Eurostatistics* (monthly).

To examine any of the national statistics offices in Europe and Global Regions, visit the excellent Central Statistics Office Ireland website **www.cso.ie/links/** and follow the country links. There are also links to many other important organisations with relevant statistics such as the European Central Bank and the International Monetary Fund.

Computerised databases

Most published information is also available in the form of computerised databases. Computerised databases contain information that has been made available in computer-readable form for electronic distribution. From the 1980s to today, the number of databases, as well as the vendors providing these services, has grown enormously.[12] Computerised databases offer a number of advantages over printed data, including:[13]

1 The data are current and up to date, as publishers and data compilers are now using computers as the primary production technology.
2 The search process is more comprehensive, quicker and simpler. Online vendors provide ready access to hundreds of databases. Moreover, this information can be accessed instantaneously, and the search process is simplified as the vendors provide uniform search protocols and commands for accessing the database.
3 The cost of accessing these is relatively low, because of the accuracy of searching for the right data, and the speed of location and transfer of data.
4 It is convenient to access these data using a personal computer fitted with an appropriate communication device, such as a modem or a communication network.

While computerised database information can be helpful, it is vast and can be confusing. Thus a classification of computerised databases is helpful.

Classification of computerised databases

Computerised databases may be classified as online, Internet or offline as shown in Figure 4.3. Online databases consist of a central data bank that is accessed with a computer (or dumb terminal) via a telecommunications network. Internet databases can be accessed, searched and analysed on the Internet. It is also possible to download data from the Internet and store it in the computer or on an auxiliary storage device.[14] Offline databases

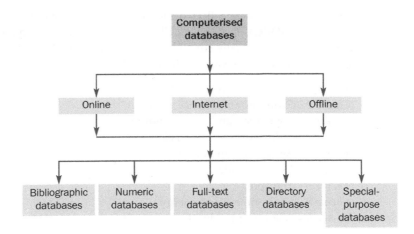

**Figure 4.3
A classification of
computerised
databases**

Online databases
Databases, stored in
computers, that require a
telecommunications network
to access.

Internet databases
Databases that can be
accessed, searched and
analysed on the Internet. It is
also possible to download
data from the Internet and
store it on the computer or
an auxiliary device.

Offline databases
Databases that are available
on CD-ROM.

Bibliographic databases
Databases composed of
citations to articles in
journals, magazines,
newspapers, marketing
research studies, technical
reports, government
documents, and the like.
They often provide
summaries or abstracts of
the material cited.

Numeric databases
Databases containing
numerical and statistical
information that may be
important sources of
secondary data.

Full-text databases
Databases that contain the
complete text of secondary
source documents
comprising the database.

Directory databases
Databases that provide
information on individuals,
organisations and services.

**Special-purpose
databases**
Databases that contain
information of a specific
nature, e.g. data on a
specialised industry.

make the information available on CD-ROM. Thus, offline databases can be accessed at the user's location without the use of an external telecommunications network.[15]

Online, Internet and **offline databases** may be further classified as bibliographic, numeric, full text, directory or special-purpose databases. **Bibliographic databases** are composed of citations to articles in journals, magazines, newspapers, marketing research studies, technical reports, government documents and the like.[16] They often provide summaries or abstracts of the material cited. The earlier example of *Market Research Abstracts* (**www.imriresearch.com**) is an example of a bibliographic database. Another example is the *Aslib Index to Theses* (**www.theses.com**); this bibliographic database lists theses at masters and doctoral level and research degrees, including abstracts from the UK and Ireland.

Numeric databases contain numerical and statistical information. For example, some numeric databases provide time series data about the economy and specific industries. The earlier examples of census-based numeric databases using data over a series of censuses provide an example of a numeric database.

Full-text databases contain the complete text of the sources of the database. Examples include *World Advertising Research Center WARC* (**www.warc.com**), *FT Intelligence* (**www.ft.chadwyck.co.uk**) and *Infotrac Searchbank* (accessed through academic library links). WARC is a supplier of intelligence to the global marketing, advertising, media and research communities. *Searchbank* has over 100 full-text journals on subjects including business, economics, current affairs and new technologies. It includes a spectrum of journals from professional trade publications through to refereed academic journals. *FT Intelligence*, which includes *Europe Intelligence Wire*, was developed to offer access to a range of key sources of accurate and unbiased financial, economic and political news. It is possible to search on specific countries, sectors and publications based upon over 150 daily and weekly newspapers and business magazines from the UK and Europe.

Directory databases provide information on individuals, organisations and services. *European Interactive Directories* (**www.euroyellowpages.com**) is an example of a directory that has channels based upon EU community activities, country channels and thematic channels such as suppliers, wholesalers and shopping centres. Another example worth examining is the *ESOMAR directory* (**www.esomar.nl**) which provides details of member organisations throughout the world as well as many other publications of value to marketing researchers based in Europe.

Finally, there are **special-purpose databases**. For example, the *Non-Governmental Organisation NGO directory* (**www.rec.org/REC/Databases/databases.html**) helps to track down information about environmental organisations working in Central and Eastern Europe. It has contact information for over 2,700 organisations from over 15 Central and Eastern European countries.

In addition, virtually all libraries of major universities maintain special-purpose databases of research activities that reflect the distinct specialisms of that university. Beyond the internally generated, special-purpose databases, university libraries and reference libraries maintain computerised databases with instructions relating to what may be accessed and how it may be accessed. Another library source worth examining for computerised sources is the European Commission's 'Libraries' site (**www.europa.eu.int**). The site, which is multi-lingual, is distributed by the EUROPA server. EUROPA is the portal site of the EU. It provides up-to-date coverage of European affairs and essential information on European integration. Users can access websites of each of the EU institutions.

Syndicated sources of secondary data

Syndicated sources (services)
Information services offered by marketing research organisations that provide information from a common database to different firms that subscribe to their services.

In addition to published data or data available in the form of computerised databases, syndicated sources constitute the other major source of external secondary data. **Syndicated sources**, also referred to as **syndicated services**, are companies that collect and sell common pools of data designed to serve information needs shared by a number of clients. These data are not collected with a focus on a specific marketing problem, but the data and reports supplied to client companies can be personalised to fit specific needs. For example, reports could be organised based on the clients' sales territories or product lines. Using syndicated services is frequently less expensive than commissioning tailored primary data collection. Figure 4.4 presents a classification of syndicated sources. Syndicated sources can be classified based on the unit of measurement (house-

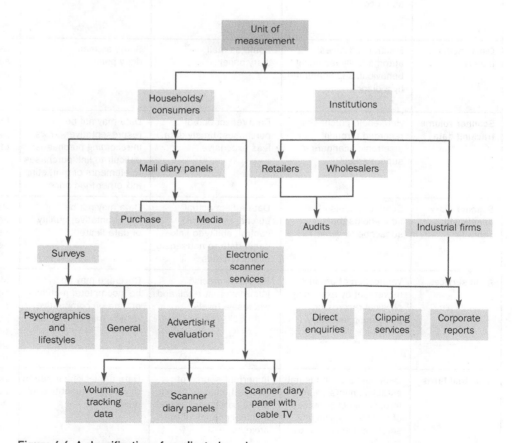

Figure 4.4 A classification of syndicated services

holds and consumers or institutions). Household and consumer data may be obtained from surveys, diary panels or electronic scanner services. Information obtained through surveys consists of values and lifestyles, advertising evaluation, or general information related to preferences, purchase, consumption and other aspects of behaviour. Diary panels emphasise information on purchases or media consumption. Electronic scanner services might provide scanner data only, scanner data linked to diary panels, or scanner data linked to diary panels and (cable) TV. When institutions are the unit of measurement, the data may be obtained from retailers, wholesalers or industrial firms. An overview of the various syndicated sources is given in Table 4.3. Each of these sources will be discussed.

Table 4.3 Overview of syndicated services

Type	Characteristics	Advantages	Disadvantages	Uses
Surveys	Surveys conducted at regular intervals	Most flexible way of obtaining data; information on underlying motives	Interviewer errors; respondent errors	Market segmentation, advertising theme selection and advertising advertising effectiveness
Mail diary panels	Households provide specific information regularly over an extended period of time; respondents asked to record specific behaviour as it occurs	Recorded purchase behaviour can be linked to the demographic/ psychographic characteristics	Lack of representativeness; response bias; maturation	Forecasting sales, market share and trends; establishing consumer profiles, brand loyalty and switching; evaluating test markets, advertising and distribution
Diary media panels	Electronic devices automatically recording behaviour, supplemented by a diary	Same as mail diary panel	Same as mail diary panel	Establishing advertising selecting media programme or air time; establishing viewer profiles
Scanner volume tracking data	Household purchases recorded through electronic scanners in supermarkets	Data reflect actual purchases; timely data, less expensive	Data may not be respresentative; errors in recording purchases; difficult to link purchases to elements of marketing mix other than price	Price tracking, modelling effectiveness of in-store modelling
Scanner diary panels with cable TV	Scanner panels of households that subscribe to cable TV	Data reflect actual purchases; sample control; ability to link panel data to household characteristics	Data may not be representative; quality of data limited	Promotional mix analyses, copy testing, new product testing, positioning
Audit services	Verification of product movement by examining physical records or performing inventory analysis	Relatively precise information at retail and wholesale levels	Coverage may be be incomplete; matching of data on competitive activity may be difficult	Measurement of consumer sales and market share; competitive activity; analysing distribution patterns; tracking of new products
Industrial firms	Data banks on industrial establishments created through direct enquiries of companies, clipping services and corporate reports	Important source of information in industrial firms; particularly useful in initial phases of the projects	Data are lacking in terms of content, quantity and quality	Determining market potential by geographic area, defining sales territories, allocating advertising budget

Syndicated data from households

Surveys

Surveys
Interviews with a large number of people using a questionnaire.

Various syndicated services regularly conduct **surveys** and **omnibus surveys**. In general, these surveys involve interviews with a large number of respondents using a pre-designed questionnaire. The distinction of the omnibus survey is that it targets particular types of respondents such as those in certain geographic locations, e.g. Luxembourg residents, or consumers of particular types of products, e.g. business air travellers. The following example illustrates just one of many omnibus surveys conducted by Taylor Nelson Sofres Omnibus Services (**www.tns-global.com**) and the nature of interpretation that can emerge from an omnibus survey.

Example   **Children are savvy consumers who increasingly understand the role of marketing**[17]

Anita Emery, Group Director of TNS Omnibus Services, argues that children also have a strong influence on the buying decisions of their peers or family members. Despite children showing high recognition and awareness of advertising campaigns, TNS's children's omnibus research with youngsters aged 10–19 shows that only 8% say 'you can trust everything you read or hear in an ad'. Even among 10 year olds, just 16% agreed with this statement, a relatively cynical attitude normally associated with much older consumers. Marketers cannot underestimate the influence children have on consumer decisions and the impact that advertising campaigns have on children's appeal and appreciation of brands and products.

Omnibus survey
A distinctive form of survey that serves the needs of a syndicate group. The omnibus survey targets particular types of respondents such as those in specific locations, e.g. Luxembourg residents, or customers of particular types of product, e.g. business air travellers. With that target group of respondents, a core set of questions can be asked with other questions added as syndicate members wish.

Psychographics
Quantified profiles of individuals based upon lifestyle characteristics.

Lifestyles
Distinctive patterns of living described by the activities people engage in, the interests they have, and the opinions they hold of themselves and the world around them.

With a defined target group of respondents, a core set of questions can be asked with other questions added as syndicate members wish. Other syndicate members can 'jump on the omnibus' and buy the answers to all the questionnaire responses or to specific questions of their choice. Surveys and omnibus surveys may be broadly classified based on their content as psychographics and lifestyles, advertising evaluation, or general surveys.

Psychographics and lifestyles. **Psychographics** refer to the psychological profiles of individuals and to psychologically based measures of lifestyle. **Lifestyles** refer to the distinctive modes of living of a society or some of its segments. Together, these measures are generally referred to as activities, interests and opinions. A good example of a marketing research agency that works upon the measurement and marketing applications of psychographics and lifestyles can be found at **www.espconsultancy.co.uk**.

Advertising evaluation. The purpose of advertising evaluation surveys is to assess the effectiveness of advertising using print and broadcast media. TV commercials are evaluated using either the recruited audience method or the in-home viewing method. In the former method, respondents are recruited and brought to a central viewing facility, such as a theatre or mobile viewing laboratory. The respondents view the commercials and provide data regarding knowledge, attitudes and preferences related to the product being advertised and the commercial itself. In the in-home viewing method, consumers evaluate commercials at home in their normal viewing environment. New commercials can be pretested at the network level or in local markets. A survey of viewers is then conducted to assess the effectiveness of the commercials. The following example illustrates the importance of advertising evaluation, how qualitative research helps in the development of advertisements and quantitative research measures their performance.

Example | **Gut or numbers? Pretesting ads[18]**

Larry Friedman, Global Director of Brand and Advertising Research at TNS, confirms that testing advertising has grown faster than other forms of research over the past few years. 'Everyone is trying to build a connection between their brands and consumers and trying to understand how advertising contributes to that,' he explains. Research to pretest advert can be qualitative (focus groups and one-to-one interviews; the moderator elicits general discussion about the advert) or quantitative (interviewees answer specific questions that aim to measure their responses to the advert). Qualitative research tends to be used in early stages of an advert's production, with groups of consumers discussing concepts before anything is created. Then an animatic, a moving storyboard, is often drawn up, and this is researched quantitatively. Millward Brown is the market leader in ad testing (**www.imsl.ie**). Millward Brown's quantitative 'Link' tests are used across the industry. Link measures three areas of ad performance: communication, branded memorability and consumer response. Branded memorability is measured as an AI (Awareness Indicator) number, which is made up of scores for branding, enjoyment and engagement. Link now incorporates a facility for measuring the following emotional responses: surprised, excited, attracted, proud, inspired, confident, contented, affectionate, hatred, repelled, annoyed, inadequate, disappointed, guilty, unimpressed, sad.

The following example illustrates one element of the media research work that is conducted by Sports Marketing Surveys. It describes the techniques for media exposure analysis. Visit the agency's website at **www.sportsmarketingsurveys.com** to see the nature of, and how it manages, media evaluation, media coverage and compliance monitoring.

Focus on | **Sports Marketing Surveys**

Media exposure analysis

TV exposure

The majority of sports sponsorships are focused on the opportunity of exposure through TV. Media exposure is recorded if the sighting is at least 1 second in duration and the brand/logo is clearly readable. This is monitored using Sports Marketing Surveys' leading-edge TV monitoring systems: FREDI (Freeze Frame Enhanced Digital Imaging) and Magellan (automated image recognition).

Press exposure

In the UK, national newspapers, mostly with a large sports section, are read by four out of five adults every week and sponsor mentions and logos can return notable media values. In other markets there are one or more daily papers devoted to sport. Sports Marketing Surveys undertakes press analysis in a number of countries on a regular basis. Sports Marketing Surveys has access to national, regional and specialist publications through specialist press agencies, which are monitored for brand exposure. Brand exposure is recorded if all letters of a sponsor' s name appear in full and the brand/logo is clearly readable, with a method comparable with TV.

Radio exposure

Sports coverage is considerable on national and regional radio stations and commentators and presenters alike offer verbal mentions for event and team sponsors. Sports Marketing Surveys monitors sponsor mentions on national, regional and specialist sports stations. Since verbal mentions carry more impact than visual exposure, each mention is offered the equivalent of 10 seconds of exposure.

Internet exposure

The Internet is now proving to be a major source of information to sports fans and a value can be placed on the exposure of sponsor logos. Sports Marketing Surveys can monitor brand exposure across the Web using specialist web-search agencies or in-house searches for selected sites.

General surveys. Surveys are also conducted for a variety of other purposes, including examination of purchase and consumption behaviour. Because a variety of data can be obtained, survey data have numerous uses. They can be used for market segmentation, as with psychographic and lifestyle data, and for establishing consumer profiles. Surveys are also useful for determining product image, measurement and positioning, and conducting price perception analysis. Other notable uses include advertising theme selection and evaluation of advertising effectiveness.

Purchase and media panels

About a quarter of all research budgets is spent on panels in their various formats, the largest investors in this format in Europe being Switzerland at 41%, Germany 35% and the Netherlands 31%.[19] Panels were discussed in Chapter 3 in the context of longitudinal research designs. Panels are samples of respondents who provide specified information at regular intervals over an extended period of time. These respondents may be organisations, households or individuals, although household diary panels are most common. The distinguishing feature of panels is that the respondents record specific behaviours as they occur. Previously, behaviour was recorded in a diary, and the diary returned to the research organisation every one to four weeks. Panel diaries have been gradually replaced by electronic diaries. Now, most of the panels are online and the behaviour is recorded electronically, either entered online by the respondents or recorded automatically by electronic devices as illustrated by the following example.

Example	### The battle for media measurement[20]

Audience measurement for radio has traditionally used weekly diaries, where respondents record their own listening habits. However, this method is completely reliant on the memory of respondents, and has often led to excessive claims for stations or programmes they listen to regularly and to reduced claims for those they listen to less frequently. Passive measurement of radio usage is being developed through the following methods.

The Personal People Meter (PPM)

A small pager-type device is worn by respondents throughout the day. This inserts an inaudible code into a broadcast transmission at the radio station. The codes are then downloaded to a central computer. PPM is used in Belgium, Canada, Norway and Singapore.

The Media Monitor

This samples sounds to which respondents are exposed using an audio matching pager-type device. It can collect other information such as the location of respondents and active or passive listening. The technology is still being tested. There are plans to start a multimedia survey in Italy in 2006.

→

The Media Watch

The unit is built into a wristwatch and is designed to record exposure to radio, TV, cinema, posters as well as readership. It is currently used in Switzerland, Liechtenstein and the UK with testing in Denmark, France, Germany, the Netherlands, Sweden and Tokyo. Recent formal tests were less than satisfactory as the watch identified fewer listening occasions compared with other methods.

The Mobile Phone

This works on an encoded signal basis using mobile phone technology to capture and transmit the encoded signal for analysis. This is being tested in the UK. Interest is strongest in South America and the larger markets in Europe, and Commercial Radio Australia is working with the manufacturer.

Media panels
A data gathering technique composed of samples of respondents whose TV viewing behaviour is automatically recorded by electronic devices, supplementing the purchase information recorded in a diary.

In diary media panels, electronic devices automatically record viewing behaviour, thus supplementing a diary. Diary **media panels** yield information helpful for establishing advertising rates by radio and TV networks, selecting appropriate programming, and profiling viewer or listener subgroups. Advertisers, media planners and buyers find panel information particularly useful. Another media vehicle that competes heavily for advertising budgets is the Internet. The following example illustrates how A.C. Nielsen use media panels to understand Internet usage.

Example   The Nielsen way[21]

The Nielsen/NetRatings (**www.netratings.com**) approach to monitoring consumer behaviour online is to employ panels of randomly selected consumers to form a representative subset of the total online population. The panel's behaviour is used to provide estimates of behaviour in the population as a whole. Panellists install unobtrusive tracking software on their PCs that records everything they do, providing continual information on their behaviour. This allows comparison of all the sites that appear in the research and provides data that can be tested against 13 different panels established in other countries. People are the focus of this research: who they are, how they behave online, and how their behaviour changes over time, by country and demographic profile. This ability to link visits to sites to an individual and hence to track usage behaviour within a session and across many sessions is unique to panel-based research. It provides a complete picture of the Internet landscape, allowing key players to understand not only their performance, but also that of their competitors.

Purchase panels
A data gathering technique in which respondents record their purchases in a diary.

Purchase panels provide information useful for forecasting sales, estimating market shares, assessing brand loyalty and brand-switching behaviour, establishing profiles of specific user groups, measuring promotional effectiveness, and conducting controlled store tests.

Compared with sample surveys (see Chapter 10), diary panels offer certain distinct advantages.[22] Panels can provide longitudinal data (data can be obtained from the same respondents repeatedly). People who are willing to serve on panels may provide more and higher quality data than sample respondents. In diary purchase panels, information is recorded at the time of purchase, eliminating recall errors.[23] Information recorded by electronic devices is accurate because it eliminates recall errors.

Source: © George Disano/CORBIS

The disadvantages of diary panels include lack of representativeness, maturation and response biases. They may under-represent certain groups such as minorities and those with low education levels. This problem is further compounded by refusal to respond and attrition of panel members. Over time, maturation sets in, and the panel members must be replaced. Response biases may occur, since simply being on the panel may alter behaviour. Because purchase or media data are entered by hand, recording errors are also possible (see Chapter 3).

Electronic scanner services

The following example illustrates the nature and scope of electronic scanner services as undertaken by A.C. Nielsen, which conducts consumer panel services in 18 countries around the world.

Example

A.C. Nielsen – the business economist at work[24]

Most of A.C. Nielsen's revenue comes from selling information on *fast-moving consumer goods* (FMCG). This information is compiled either from scanner data obtained from thousands of supermarkets, pharmacists and department stores, or from a 40,000-household panel who electronically record every aspect of every goods purchase they made using that item's bar code.

Panel members go beyond their standard forms of analysing and presenting existing data to more creative interpretations that attempt to tell the marketer something he or she does not know. Often, creativity is valued more than sophisticated econometric techniques, as illustrated in the following two examples.

Inventory and sales data are available on food store retail sales, so an inventory–sales ratio can be calculated. This ratio had been increasing for several years up to 1992 when it began to shrink. Yet it is generally accepted that the size of the average new store is increasing, implying the need for additional inventories relative to sales. Coincidentally, more sophisticated inventory management techniques have become especially prevalent in food stores in recent years. Apparently, the ratio is being driven more by improved inventory management than by the opening of new, larger stores. A discrete cause and effect cannot be proven, but a linkage between the ratio and better inventory control mechanisms is highly probable.

Consumer spending patterns in Asia are very difficult to analyse, given the paucity of data available and the lack of data comparability across countries or spending components. By calculating consumer spending on food as a share of total consumer spending, and then ordering the results by per capita GDP, a relationship becomes obvious. Poorer countries spend proportionately more of their resources on food, around 50%. For middle-income countries, this ratio slides from around 40% to 20%, and then holds steady near 20% for the developed economies. The implication is that, as a country obtains a middle-income status, because of this declining ratio, food sales will not grow as fast as other categories of consumer spending.

Scanner data
Data obtained by passing merchandise over a laser scanner that reads the UPC from the packages.

Volume tracking data
Scanner data that provide information on purchases by brand, size, price and flavour or formulation.

Scanner diary panels
Scanner data where panel members are identified by an ID card, allowing information about each panel member's purchases to be stored with respect to the individual shopper.

Scanner diary panels with cable TV
The combination of a scanner diary panel with manipulations of the advertising that is being broadcast by cable TV companies.

Although information provided by surveys and diary panels is useful, electronic scanner services are becoming increasingly popular. The role of scanned data as a foundation to developing sophisticated consumer databases is developed in Chapter 5. In this chapter we examine scanned data as a distinct source of syndicated data. **Scanner data** reflect some of the latest technological developments in the marketing research industry. They are collected by passing merchandise over a laser scanner that optically reads the bar-coded description (Universal Product Code, or UPC) printed on the merchandise. This code is then linked to the current price held in the computer memory and used to prepare a sales slip. Information printed on the sales slip includes descriptions as well as prices of all items purchased. Checkout scanners, now used in many retail stores, are revolutionising packaged goods marketing research.

Three types of scanner data are available: **volume tracking data, scanner diary panels** and **scanner diary panels with cable TV**. Volume tracking data provide information on purchases by brand, size, price and flavour or formulation, based on sales data collected from the checkout scanner. This information is collected nationally from a sample of supermarkets with electronic scanners. In scanner diary panels, each household member is given an ID card that looks like a credit card. Panel members present the ID card at the checkout counter each time they shop. The checker keys in the ID numbers and each item of that customer's order. The information is stored by day of week and time of day.[25]

Scanner diary panels with cable TV combine diary panels with new technologies growing out of the cable TV industry. Households on these panels subscribe to one of the cable or TV systems in their market. By means of a cable TV 'split', the researcher targets different commercials into the homes of the panel members. For example, half the households may see test commercial A during the 6 p.m. newscast while the other half see test commercial B. These panels allow researchers to conduct fairly controlled experiments in a relatively natural environment.[26]

Scanner data are useful for a variety of purposes.[27] National volume tracking data can be used for tracking sales, prices and distribution, for modelling, and for analysing early warning signals. Scanner diary panels with cable TV can be used for testing new products, repositioning products, analysing promotional mixes, and making advertising decisions, including budget, copy and media, and pricing. These panels provide marketing researchers with a unique controlled environment for the manipulation of marketing variables. The following example gives a basic description of GfK's BEHAVIORSCAN.

Example

GfK BEHAVIORSCAN: Europe's first experimental test market using targetable TV

GfK's household panel is demographically, nationally representative. It helps to answer important questions such as: How successful will a new product be? Who are the purchasers of a new product? How well does TV advertising drive sales? Which level of media spending is optimal? Which TV ad copy is more successful at increasing sales? GfK cooperates with all relevant outlets and all test stores utilise scanners. GfK personnel handle all elements associated with the test, and execute promotions, price changes, handle product stocking and check the test stores daily to ensure 100% distribution and no out-of-stocks. Their three European test markets are:

1 **Hassloch, Germany:** *3,000 households* with GfK ID card, 2,000 households with targetable TV and 1,000 control households, *TV Broadcasters:* ARD, ZDF, Kabel 1, Pro7, Sat.1, RTL, RTL2, VOX, Super RTL, *Print:* Hörzu (with split-panel), daily newspapers, supplements.
2 **Angers, France:** *4,000 households* with GfK ID card, *11 partner stores, TV broadcasters:* 14 channels; TF1, France 2, France 3, Canal+, France 5, M6, Paris Première, Série Club,

LCI, Eurosport, TMC Monte Carlo, MCM, Canal J, RTL9, *Print*: Femme Actuelle or Télé Loisirs (with split-panel), *Radio*: 10 channels: Alouette, Chérie FM, Europe 1, Europe 2, MFM, Nostagie, RFM, NRJ, RTL, RTL2, *Postering, Cinema, Internet.*

3 **Le Mans, France:** *4,000 households* with GfK ID card, *9 partner stores, TV broadcasters:* 14 channels; TF1, France 2, France 3, Canal+, France 5, M6, Paris Première, Série Club, LCI, Eurosport, TMC Monte Carlo, MCM, Canal J, RTL9, *Postering, Cinema, Internet.*

Scanner data have an obvious advantage over surveys and diary panels: they reflect purchasing behaviour that is not subject to interviewing, recording, memory or expert biases. The record of purchases obtained by scanners is complete and unbiased by price sensitivity, because the panellist is not required to be particularly conscious of price levels and changes. Another advantage is that in-store variables such as pricing, promotions and displays are part of the dataset. The data are also likely to be current and can be obtained quickly. Finally, scanner panels with cable TV provide a highly controlled testing environment.

The quality of scanner data may be limited by several factors. Not all products may be scanned. For example, to avoid lifting a heavy item, a sales assistant may use the register to ring it up. If an item does not scan on the first try, the assistant may key in the price and ignore the bar code. Sometimes a consumer purchases many flavours of the same item, but the assistant scans only one package and then rings in the number of purchases. Thus, the transaction is inaccurately recorded. Although scanner data provide behavioural and sales information, they do not provide information on underlying attitudes and preferences and the reasons for specific choices.

Syndicated data from institutions

Retailer and wholesaler audits

As Figure 4.4 shows, syndicated data are available from retailers and wholesalers as well as industrial firms (see the example of the work of German marketing research company GfK at **www.gfkms.com** which conducts retail and wholesale audits in the following sectors: automotive aftermarket, consumer electronics/brown goods, do-it-yourself, entertainment, furniture, gardening, imaging photo, information technology, lighting products, luggage, major domestic appliances/white goods, office equipment, optics, small domestic appliances, stationery, telecommunication, wristwatches).

Audit
A data collection process derived from physical records or performing inventory analysis. Data are collected personally by the researcher, or by representatives of the researcher, and are based on counts usually of physical objects rather than people.

The most popular means of obtaining data from retailers and wholesalers is an audit. An **audit** is a formal examination and verification of product movement carried out by examining physical records or analysing inventory. Retailers and wholesalers who participate in the audit receive basic reports and cash payments from the audit service. Audit data focus on the products or services sold through the outlets or the characteristics of the outlets themselves.

Example | **Retail auditing for retailing information**[28]

In the USA in 1933, A.C. Nielsen pioneered food and drug indices to measure and understand the performance and dynamics of product sales. The Retail Measurement Service of A.C. Nielsen uses store audit data on product movement, market share, distribution, price and other market-sensitive information in over 80 countries across six continents. Using in-store scanning of product codes and store visits by auditors, sample and census information is gathered across the food, household, health and beauty, durables, confectionery and beverage industries.

Retail audit data can be useful to consumer product firms. For example, if Colgate-Palmolive is contemplating the introduction of a new toothpaste brand, a retail audit can help determine the size of the total market and distribution of sales by type of outlet and by different regions.

Wholesale audit services, the counterpart of retail audits, monitor warehouse withdrawals. Participating operators, which include supermarket chains, wholesalers and frozen-food warehouses, typically account for over 80% of the volume in the area.

The uses of retail and wholesale audit data include:

- determining the size of the total market and the distribution of sales by type of outlet, region or city;
- assessing brand shares and competitive activity;
- identifying shelf space allocation and inventory problems;
- analysing distribution problems;
- developing sales potentials and forecasts;
- developing and monitoring promotional allocations based on sales volume.

Audits provide relatively accurate information on the movement of many different products at the wholesale and retail levels. Furthermore, this information can be broken down by a number of important variables, such as brand, type of outlet and size of market. Audits have limited coverage, however; not all markets or operators are included. In addition, audit information may not be timely or current, particularly compared with scanner data. Typically, there is a two-month gap between the completion of the audit cycle and the publication of reports. Another disadvantage is that, unlike scanner data, audit data cannot be linked to consumer characteristics. In fact, there may even be a problem in relating audit data to advertising expenditures and other marketing efforts. Some of these limitations are overcome in computerised audit panels.

Industrial firms

These provide syndicated data about industrial firms, businesses and other institutions. Syndicated data are collected by making direct enquiries to organisations, from clipping services (see an example at **www.romeike.com**) to the analysis of corporate reports (see example of corporate analysis of the telecoms market at www.insight-corp.com). Dunn & Bradstreet's International Business Locator (**www.dnb.com**) provides access to over 28 million public/private companies in over 200 countries. After finding a business, the Locator will provide key business data including full address information, line of business details, business size (sales, net worth, employees), names of key principals, and identification of this location's headquarters, domestic parent company and/or global parent company.

Industrial firm information is useful for sales management decisions, including identifying prospects, defining territories, setting quotas, and measuring market potential by geographic areas. It can also aid in advertising decisions such as targeting prospects, allocating advertising budgets, selecting media, and measuring advertising effectiveness. This kind of information is useful for segmenting the market and for designing custom products and services for important segments.

International marketing research

A wide variety of secondary data are available for international marketing research.[29] The problem is not a lack of data but the potential overabundance of information. The international marketing researcher has to work through an array of potential sources to find accurate, up-to-date and relevant information. Evaluation of secondary data is even more critical for international than for domestic projects. Different sources report different values for a given statistic, such as the GDP, because of differences in the way the unit is defined. Measurement units may not be equivalent across countries. In France, for example, some workers are still paid a 13-monthly salary each year as an automatic bonus, resulting in a measurement construct that is different from those in other countries.[30] The accuracy of secondary data may also vary from country to country. Data from highly industrialised countries in Europe are likely to be more accurate than those from developing nations. Business and income statistics are affected by the taxation structure and the extent of tax evasion. Population censuses may vary in frequency and year in which the data are collected. In the UK, for example, the census is conducted every 10 years, whereas in the People's Republic of China there was a 29-year gap between the censuses of 1953 and 1982. This situation, however, is changing quickly. Several syndicated firms are developing huge sources of international secondary data, as illustrated in the following example.

Example

Los Medios y Mercados de Latinoamerica (LMML)[31]

Started in 1994 by Roper Audits & Surveys Worldwide (**www.roperasw.com**), *Los Medios y Mercados de Latinoamerica* (The Markets and Media of Latin America) is the largest multinational survey of media and consumer habits that is conducted in Latin America to provide managers with important information for their marketing strategies. The study, which is repeated every year, aims at tracking the development of media and consumer habits in Latin America.

A recent multinational survey was conducted in 18 Latin American countries, including Argentina, Brazil, Colombia, Mexico and Venezuela. It sampled 6,634 respondents between the ages of 12 and 64. Its probability sample, representing urban as well as rural Latin America, can be projected to 280 million people or 79 million households.

The research design for this survey involved two steps. First, the personal interview technique was used to measure the variety of media, including newspapers, multinational and local magazines, TV and radio. Then a 25-page self-administered booklet was passed to the respondents to measure their product consumption and usage in over 100 categories and 800 brands. Demographic data gathered about the respondents included country/region, age, sex, employment status, occupation, education, household size, annual household income, car ownership, household goods owned and services taken. Subscribing companies can easily use these data, as the survey results are provided in a set of 14 printed volumes, and also in computer database formats including an SPSS format.

Ethics in marketing research

Possible ethical dilemmas exist when using internal or external secondary data. Some ethical issues that are pertinent include:

- The unnecessary and expensive collection of primary data when the problem can be addressed based on secondary data alone.
- Cutting corners through the use of only secondary data when primary data are needed.
- The use of secondary data that are not applicable.

- The use of secondary data that have been gathered through morally questionable means.
- Compromising the anonymity of customer details held on databases.

As was discussed in Chapter 2, the unnecessary collection of expensive primary data when the research problem can be addressed using only secondary data is unethical. In this case, the researcher is using a more expensive method that is less appropriate. Similarly, the exclusive reliance on secondary data when the research problem requires primary data collection could raise ethical concerns. This is particularly true if the researcher is charging a fixed fee for the project and the research design was not specified in advance. Here again, the researcher's profit goes up, but at the expense of the client.

The researcher is ethically obliged to ensure the relevance and usefulness of secondary data to the problem at hand. The secondary data should be evaluated by the criteria discussed earlier in this chapter. Only data judged to be appropriate should be used.

Internet and computer applications

The World Wide Web as an online source of secondary data

The World Wide Web is a vital source of secondary data and intelligence for the marketing researcher. Given the global nature of the technology, the Internet is a vital tool for the international marketing researcher. One can go directly to the websites of traditional suppliers of secondary data from government or business sources. Many of those sites also have inside search engines that sort data from the supplier's internal database. Information on the Web is of great value as generally it is current, though care must be taken to note when web pages have been updated. It should be noted that not all secondary data on the Web is free. The Web may reveal the existence of data on a particular subject or industry, but remember the costs involved in conducting quality research. Hence the Web may be used to give an awareness and a 'taste' of secondary data but it does not necessarily mean 'free' data.

Internal secondary data

Large organisations have intranets, which greatly facilitate the search for access to secondary data. The Coca-Cola Company (**www.cocacola.com**), for example, has developed powerful intranet applications that enable Coca-Cola managers worldwide to search for past and present research studies and a wide variety of marketing-related information on the basis of keywords. Once located, the information can be accessed online. Even sensitive and restricted information can be accessed by obtaining permission electronically. Visit **www.intranets.com** for a fuller description of intranet technology, evaluations of software and an interactive tour.

External secondary data

As we have illustrated throughout this chapter, information can be obtained by visiting various business-related sites that provide sales leads and mailing lists, business profiles and credit ratings. Various newspapers, magazines and journals can be accessed on the Web with excellent indexing facilities to locate particular subjects, companies and individuals. Government data for the European Community and for individual countries through to regional and city councils can be accessed via the Web, though the quality and quantity of data available through government sources can vary enormously.

Online and syndicated sources of information

A substantial amount of face-to-face and telephone research in Europe has been replaced by the cheaper option of online panel research in recent years through many Western European countries.[32] With European data protection laws, other EU rules such as the Distance Selling Directive and falling response rates, many commentators predict more growth for online panels. It is worth examining the approaches used and case histories of online panel research at **www.him.uk.com**, **www.greenfieldonline.com**, **www.lightspeedresearch.com** and **www.intelliquest.com**.

For syndicated sources of information one can visit the home pages of the various marketing research companies and providers of syndicated information. The A.C. Nielsen home page at **www.acnielsen.com** is a good example. This site provides links to various manufacturers and to various countries such as the UK, Canada and Spain. Other good sources of syndicated data include Mintel, which can be reached at **www.mintel.co.uk**, Euromonitor at **www.euromonitor.com** and Taylor Nelson Sofres at **www.tnsofres.com** (it is worth working through the great array of marketing research products they offer).

International secondary data

The Internet has emerged as the most extensive source of secondary information. The utility of the Internet for the marketing researcher is further enhanced by the easy accessibility and retrieval of information and the ability to cross-validate information from a variety of sources. Most of the Internet links highlighted in this chapter allow for secondary data to be gathered from countries all over the world. Whilst necessarily we have a focus on European matters, it is well worth visiting **www.quirks.com**. This website is a most thorough source for information on marketing research, including case studies of successful research projects and a comprehensive list of directories.

Summary

In contrast to primary data, which originate with the researcher for the specific purpose of the problem at hand, secondary data and intelligence are data originally collected for other purposes. Secondary data can be obtained quickly and are relatively inexpensive. They have limitations, and should be carefully evaluated to determine their appropriateness for the problem at hand. The evaluation criteria consist of specifications, error, currency, objectivity, nature and dependability.

A wealth of information exists in the organisation for which the research is being conducted. This information constitutes internal secondary data. External data are generated by sources outside the organisation. These data exist in the form of published (printed) material, online and offline databases, or information made available by syndicated services. Published external sources may be broadly classified as general business data or government data. General business sources comprise guides, directories, indexes and statistical data. Government sources may be broadly categorised as census data and other data. Computerised databases may be online or offline. Both online and offline databases may be further classified as bibliographic, numeric, full-text, directory or specialised databases.

Syndicated sources are companies that collect and sell common pools of data designed to serve a number of clients. Syndicated sources can be classified based on the unit of measurement (households and consumers or institutions). Household and consumer data may be obtained via surveys, diary purchase or media panels, or electronic scanner services. When institutions are the unit of measurement, the data may be obtained from retailers, wholesalers or industrial units. It is desirable to combine information obtained from different secondary sources.

Several specialised sources of secondary data are useful for conducting international marketing research. The evaluation of secondary data becomes even more critical, however, because the usefulness and accuracy of these data can vary widely. Ethical dilemmas that can arise include the unnecessary collection of primary data, the use of only secondary data when primary data are needed, the use of secondary data that are not applicable, and the use of secondary data that have been gathered through morally questionable means.

Questions

1 What are the differences between primary data, secondary data and marketing intelligence?

2 What are the relative advantages and disadvantages of secondary data?

3 At what stages of the marketing research process can secondary data be used?

4 Why is it important to locate and analyse secondary data before progressing to primary data?

5 How may secondary data be used to validate qualitative research findings?

6 What is the difference between internal and external secondary data?

7 How can intranet technology help in the location and dissemination of secondary data?

8 By what criteria may secondary data be evaluated?

9 What criteria would you look for when examining the design and specifications of secondary data? Why is it important to examine these criteria?

10 To what extent should you use a secondary data source if you cannot see any explicit objectives attached to that research?

11 If you had two sources of secondary data for a project, the first being dependable but out of date, the second not dependable but up to date, which would you prefer?

12 Evaluate the desirability of using multiple sources of secondary data and intelligence.

13 List and describe the main types of syndicated sources of secondary data.

14 Explain what an online panel is, giving examples of different types of panel. What are the advantages and disadvantages of online panels?

15 What is an audit? Describe the uses, advantages and disadvantages of audits.

Exercises

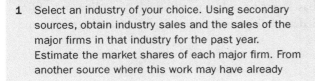

1 Select an industry of your choice. Using secondary sources, obtain industry sales and the sales of the major firms in that industry for the past year.
Estimate the market shares of each major firm. From another source where this work may have already been completed, e.g. Mintel, compare and contrast the estimates:
a To what extent do they agree?
b If there are differences in the estimates, what may account for these differences?

2 Select an industry of your choice. Write a report on the potential growth in that industry and the factors that are driving that growth. Use both secondary data and intelligence sources to build your case.

3 You are a brand manager for Proctor & Gamble, in charge of a shampoo brand. How would you use the information available from a store audit? Ask another student to play the role of marketing director. What case would you make to the marketing director about the value of investing in store audit information related to shampoos?

4 Visit the Central Statistics Office Ireland website (**www.cso.ie/links/**) and follow a link to the national

statistics office in a country of your choice. Write a report about the secondary data available from this office that would be useful to a national housing developer for the purpose of formulating its marketing strategy

5 In a small group discuss the following issues: 'What is the significance and limitations of government census data for marketing researchers?' and 'Given the growing array of alternative data sources that describe characteristics of individuals and households in a country, would it be a disaster for marketing researchers if formal government censuses were scrapped?'

Notes

1 Keating, P., 'The best airlines to fly today', *Money* (November 1997), 118–128.

2 Rothberg, H.N. and Erickson, G.S., *From knowledge to intelligence: creating competitive advantage in the next economy*, (Burlington MA: Butterworth-Heinemann, 2005); Aguilar, F.J., *Scanning the Business Environment* (London: Macmillan, 1967).

3 Adapted from Brownlie, D., 'Environmental scanning', in Baker, M.J., *The Marketing Book*, 3rd edn (Oxford: Butterworth–Heinemann), 158.

4 Curtis, J., 'Behind enemy lines', *Marketing* (24 May 2001), 28–29.

5 Rothberg, H.N. and Erickson, G.S., *From knowledge to intelligence: creating competitive advantage in the next economy* (Burlington MA: Butterworth-Heinemann, 2005), 21.

6 For applications of secondary data, see Kotabe, M., 'Using Euromonitor database in international marketing research', *Journal of the Academy of Marketing Science* 30 (2) (Spring 2002), 172; Bottomley, P.A. and Holden, S.J.S., 'Do we really know how consumers evaluate brand extensions? Empirical generalizations based on secondary analysis of eight studies', *Journal of Marketing Research* 38 (4) (November 2001) 494–500.

7 Jacob, H., *Using Published Data: Errors and Remedies* (Beverly Hills, CA: Sage, 1984).

8 Stewart, D.W., *Secondary Research: Information Sources and Methods* (Beverly Hills, CA: Sage, 1984), 23–33.

9 Fry, A., 'Number crunch', *Marketing* (4 December 1997), 29.

10 Lawson, J., 'Buying behaviour', *Database Marketing* (October 2004), 35–38.

11 Fries, J.R., 'Library support for industrial marketing research', *Industrial Marketing Management* 11 (February 1982), 47–51.

12 Schwartz, E., 'Dawn of a new database', *InfoWorld* 24 (11) (18 March, 2002), 32.

13 Post, C., 'Marketing data marts help companies stay ahead of the curve and in front of the competition', *Direct Marketing* 59 (April 1997), 37–40.

14 Tucker, D.M., 'Technology: online database set to debut this summer', *Business Press* (18 March 2002), 8; Notess, G.R., 'Searching the hidden Internet', *Database* 20 (June/July 1997), 37–40.

15 Quint, B., 'Assume the position, take the consequences', *Information Today* 13 (June 1996), 11–13.

16 Tenopir, C., 'Links and bibliographic databases', *Library Journal* 126 (4) (1 March 2001), 34–35; Notess, G.R., 'The Internet as an on-line service: bibliographic databases on the net', *Database* 19 (August/September 1996), 92–95.

17 Kilby, N., 'Trends insight', *Marketing Week* (21 July 2005), 33.

18 Murphy, C., 'Gut or numbers?', *Marketing* (15th June 2005), 31.

19 ESOMAR, 'Industry Study on 2004', Esomar World Research Report (2005), 27.

20 Mareck, M., 'The battle for media measurement', *Research World* (July/August 2005), 24–25.

21 Green, L., 'We know what you're looking at', *Research* (November 2004), 16.

22 Eunkyu, L., Hu, M.Y. and Toh, R.S., 'Are consumer survey results distorted? Systematic impact of behavioural frequency and duration on survey response errors', *Journal of Marketing Research* 37 (1) (February 2000), 125–133; Parfitt, J.H. and Collins, B.J.K., 'Use of consumer panels for brand share predictions', *Journal of the Market Research Society* 38 (4) (October 1996), 341–367; Ramaswamy, V. and Desarbo, W.S., 'SCULPTURE: a new methodology for deriving and analyzing hierarchical product-market structures from panel data', *Journal of Marketing Research* 27 (November 1990), 418–427

23 Clancy, K.J., 'Brand confusion', *Harvard Business Review* 80 (3) (March 2002), 22; Sudman, S., *On the Accuracy of Recording of Consumer Panels II*, Learning Manual (New York: Neal-Schumen, 1981).

24 Handler, D., 'The business economist at work: linking economics to market research: A.C. Nielsen', *Business Economics* 31 (October 1996), 51.

25 Andrew, R.L. and Srinivasan, T.C., 'Studying consideration effects in empirical choice models using scanner panel data', *Journal of Marketing Research* 32 (February 1995), 30–41; Bucklin, R.E., Gupta, S. and Han, S., 'A brand's eye view of response segmentation in consumer brand choice behaviour', *Journal of Marketing Research* 32 (February 1995), 66–74.

26 It is possible to combine store-level scanner data with scanner panel data to do an integrated analysis. See, for example, Russell, G.J. and Kamakura, W.A., 'Understanding brand competition using micro and macro scanner data', *Journal of Marketing Research* 31 (May 1994), 289–303.

27 Examples of scanner data applications include Lemon, K.W. and Nowlis, S.M., 'Developing synergies between promotions and brands in different price-quality tiers', *Journal of Marketing Research* 39 (2) (May 2002), 171–185; Chintagunta, P.K., 'Investigating category pricing behaviour at a retail chain', *Journal of Marketing Research* 39 (2) (May 2002), 141–154.

28 Based on information obtained from the suppliers.

29 For an example of international marketing research based on secondary data see Luk, S.T.K., 'The use of secondary information published by the PRC Government', *Journal of the Market Research Society* 41 (3) (3rd Quarter 1999), 355–365.

30 Chisnall, P.M., 'Marketing research: state of the art perspectives', *Journal of the Market Research Society* 44 (1) (1st Quarter 2002), 122–125.

31 Rydholm, J., 'A united effort', *Quirk's Marketing Research Review* (October 1996).

32 ESOMAR, 'Industry study on 2004', Esomar World Research Report (2005), 6.

8b

Innovation and New
Product
Development

Chapter 1
Innovation management:
an introduction

Introduction

Innovation is one of those words that suddenly seem to be all around us. Firms care about their ability to innovate, on which their future allegedly depends (Christensen and Raynor, 2003), and many management consultants are busy persuading companies about how they can help them improve their innovation performance. Politicians care about innovation too, how to design policies that stimulate innovation has become a hot topic at various levels of government. The European Commission, for instance, has made innovation policy a central element in its attempt to invigorate the European economy (see Chapter 2). A large literature has emerged, particularly in recent years, on various aspect of innovation and many new research units focusing on innovation have been formed (Fagerberg and Verspagen, 2009).

There is extensive scope for examining the way innovation is managed within organisations. Most of us are well aware that good technology can help companies achieve competitive advantage and long-term financial success. But there is an abundance of exciting new technology in the world and it is the transformation of this technology into products that is of particular concern to organisations. There are numerous factors to be considered by the organisation, but what are these factors and how do they affect the process of innovation? This book will explain how and why most of the most significant inventions of the past two centuries have not come from flashes of for-profit inspiration, but from communal, multilayered endeavour – one idea being built on another until a breakthrough is reached (Johnson, 2010). The Apple case study at the end of this chapter helps illustrates Apple's rise and fall over the past twenty years.

Chapter contents

Learning objectives

When you have completed this chapter you will be able to:

- recognise the importance of innovation;
- explain the meaning and nature of innovation management;
- provide an introduction to a management approach to innovation;
- appreciate the complex nature of the management of innovation within organisations;
- describe the changing views of innovation over time;
- recognise the role of key individuals within the process; and
- recognise the need to view innovation as a management process.

The importance of innovation

Corporations must be able to adapt and evolve if they wish to survive. Businesses operate with the knowledge that their competitors will inevitably come to the market with a product that changes the basis of competition. The ability to change and adapt is essential to survival. But can firms manage innovation? The answer is certainly yes as Bill Gates confirmed in 2008:

> *The share price is not something we control. We control innovation, sales and profits.*
> (Rushe and Waples, 2008)

Today, the idea of innovation is widely accepted. It has become part of our culture – so much so that it verges on becoming a cliché. But even though the term is now embedded in our language, to what extent do we fully understand the concept? Moreover, to what extent is this understanding shared? A scientist's view of innovation may be very different from that of an accountant in the same organisation.

The Apple Inc. story in Illustration 1.1 puts into context the subject of innovation and new product development. In this case Apple's launch of a new product in the mobile phone market will help Apple generate increases in revenue and grow the firm. Innovation is at the heart of many companies' activities. But to what extent is this true of all businesses? And why are some businesses more innovative than others?

Illustration 1.1

Apple launches iPad

FT

With his customary flourish, Steve Jobs unveiled Apple's widely anticipated touch-screen tablet computer, dubbed the iPad, on Wednesday. Arriving with few new content deals despite months of heavy hype, the half-inch thick gadget, which looks like a giant iPhone, met with mixed reviews. But Apple's co-founder and chief executive called it a 'revolutionary product' that would fill the gap between smartphones and laptop computers. Mr Jobs said the iPad would have a wide range of uses, from e-mailing and internet browsing to viewing videos and reading e-books.

'If there's going to be a third category it has to be better at these tasks, otherwise it has no reason for being', said Mr Jobs. The Apple chief is still looking thin after a fight with cancer.

Challenging the big mobile technology companies, Mr Jobs said Apple's total revenues from mobile gear – including its iPod and iPhone lines – now exceeded those of Nokia. 'We're a mobile company. That's what we do', he said.

Source: Getty Images/Bloomberg

The new iBooks store and electronic reading functions 'stand on the shoulders' of Amazon's Kindle, Mr Jobs said, offering titles from a handful of publishers to start, including HarperCollins and Penguin.

Source: Waters, R. and Menn, J. (2010) Jobs unveils 'revolutionary' Apple iPad, Ft.com, 27 January. Reprinted with permission.

What is meant by innovation? And can it be managed? These are questions that will be addressed in this book.

'. . . not to innovate is to die', wrote Christopher Freeman (1982) in his famous study of the economics of innovation. Certainly companies that have established themselves as technical and market leaders have shown an ability to develop successful new products. In virtually every industry, from aerospace to pharmaceuticals and from motor cars to computers, the dominant companies have demonstrated an ability to innovate (*see* Table 1.1). Furthermore, in *Business Week*'s 2006 survey of the world's most innovative companies these same firms are delivering impressive growth and/or return to their shareholders (*see* Table 1.2).

Table 1.1 **Market leaders in 2011**

Industry	Market leaders	Innovative new products and services
Cell phones	Nokia	Design and new features
Internet-related industries	eBay; Google	New services
Pharmaceuticals	Pfizer; GlaxoSmithKline	Impotence; ulcer treatment drug
Motor cars	Toyota; BMW	Car design and associated product developments
Computers and software development	Intel; IBM and Microsoft; SAP	Computer chip technology, computer hardware improvements and software development

Table 1.2 **World's most innovative companies**

2009 Rank	Company	Revenue growth 2006–09 %	Margin growth 2006–09 %
1	Apple	30	29
2	Google	31	2
3	Microsoft	10	–4
4	IBM	2	11
5	Toyota	–11	n/a
6	Amazon	29	6
7	LG	16	707
8	BYD	42	–1
9	General Electric	–1	–25
10	Sony	–5	n/a
11	Samsung	17	–9
12	Intel	0	12
13	Ford	–12	n/a
14	Research in Motion	75	–6
15	Volkswagen	0	14
16	Hewlett-Packard	8	9
17	Tata	Private	Private
18	BMW	0	n/a
19	Coca-Cola	9	1
20	Nintendo	22	3

Source: *Business Week*, 25 February 2010.

Table 1.3 **Nineteenth-century economic development fuelled by technological innovations**

Innovation	Innovator	Date
Steam engine	James Watt	1770–80
Iron boat	Isambard Kingdom Brunel	1820–45
Locomotive	George Stephenson	1829
Electromagnetic induction dynamo	Michael Faraday	1830–40
Electric light bulb	Thomas Edison and Joseph Swan	1879–90

A brief analysis of economic history, especially in the United Kingdom, will show that industrial technological innovation has led to substantial economic benefits for the innovating *company* and the innovating *country*. Indeed, the industrial revolution of the nineteenth century was fuelled by technological innovations (*see* Table 1.3). Technological innovations have also been an important component in the progress of human societies. Anyone who has visited the towns of Bath, Leamington and Colchester will be very aware of how the Romans contributed to the advancement of human societies. The introduction over 2,000 years ago of sewers, roads and elementary heating systems is credited to these early invaders of Britain.

Pause for thought

Not all firms develop innovative new products, but they still seem to survive. Do they thrive?

The study of innovation

Innovation has long been argued to be the engine of growth. It is important to note that it can also provide growth almost regardless of the condition of the larger economy. Innovation has been a topic for discussion and debate for hundreds of years. Nineteenth-century economic historians observed that the acceleration in economic growth was the result of technological progress. However, little effort was directed towards understanding *how* changes in technology contributed to this growth.

Schumpeter (1934, 1939, 1942) was among the first economists to emphasise the importance of *new products* as stimuli to economic growth. He argued that the competition posed by new products was far more important than marginal changes in the *prices* of existing products. For example, economies are more likely to experience growth due to the development of products such as new computer software or new pharmaceutical drugs than to reductions in prices of existing products such as telephones or motor cars. Indeed, early observations suggested that economic development does not occur in any regular manner, but seemed to occur in 'bursts' or waves of activity, thereby indicating the important influence of external factors on economic development.

This macro view of innovation as cyclical can be traced back to the mid-nineteenth century. It was Marx who first suggested that innovations could be associated with waves of economic growth. Since then others such as Schumpeter (1934, 1939), Kondratieff (1935/51), and Abernathy and Utterback (1978) have argued the long-wave theory of innovation. Kondratieff was unfortunately imprisoned by Stalin for his views on economic growth theories, because they conflicted with those of Marx. Marx suggested that capitalist economies would eventually decline, whereas Kondratieff argued that they would experience waves of growth and decline. Abernathy and Utterback (1978) contended that at the birth of any industrial sector there is radical product innovation which is then followed by radical innovation in production processes, followed, in turn, by widespread incremental innovation. This view was once popular and seemed to reflect the life cycles of many industries. It has, however, failed to offer any understanding of *how* to achieve innovative success.

After the Second World War economists began to take an even greater interest in the causes of economic growth (Harrod, 1949; Domar, 1946). One of the most important influences on innovation seemed to be industrial research and development. After all, during the war, military research and development (R&D) had produced significant technological advances and innovations, including radar, aerospace and new weapons. A period of rapid growth in expenditure by countries on R&D was to follow, exemplified by US President Kennedy's 1960 speech outlining his vision of getting a man on the moon before the end of the decade. But economists soon found

Illustration 1.2

A review of the history of economic growth

The classical economists of the eighteenth and nineteenth centuries believed that technological change and capital accumulation were the engines of growth. This belief was based on the conclusion that productivity growth causes population growth, which in turn causes productivity to fall. Today's theory of population growth is very different from these early attempts at understanding economic growth. It argues that rising incomes slow the population growth because they increase the rate of opportunity cost of having children. Hence, as technology advances, productivity and incomes grow.

The Austrian economist, Joseph Schumpeter, was the founder of modern growth theory and is regarded as one of the world's greatest economists. In the 1930s he was the first to realise that the development and diffusion of new technologies by profit-seeking entrepreneurs formed the source of economic progress. One important insight arising from Schumpeter's ideas is that innovation can be seen as *creative destruction* waves that restructure the whole market in favour of those who grasp discontinuities faster. In his own words *'the problem that is usually visualized is how capitalism administers existing structures, whereas the relevant problem is how it creates and destroy them'*.

Robert Solow, who was a student of Schumpeter, advanced his professor's theories in the 1950s and won the Nobel Prize for economic science. Paul Romer has developed these theories further and is responsible for the modern theory of economic growth, sometimes called neo-Schumpeterian economic growth theory, which argues that sustained economic growth arises from competition among firms. Firms try to increase their profits by devoting resources to creating new products and developing new ways of making existing products. It is this economic theory that underpins most innovation management and new product development theories.

Source: Adapted from M. Parkin *et al.* (2008) *Economics*, 7th edn, Addison-Wesley, Harlow.

that there was no *direct* correlation between R&D spending and national rates of economic growth. It was clear that the linkages were more complex than first thought (this issue is explored more fully in Chapter 8).

There was a need to understand *how* science and technology affected the economic system. The neo-classical economics approach had not offered any explanations. A series of studies of innovation were undertaken in the 1950s which concentrated on the internal characteristics of the innovation process within the economy. A feature of these studies was that they adopted a cross-discipline approach, incorporating economics, organisational behaviour and business and management. The studies looked at:

- the generation of new knowledge;
- the application of this knowledge in the development of products and processes;
- the commercial exploitation of these products and services in terms of financial income generation.

In particular, these studies revealed that firms behaved differently (*see* Simon, 1957; Woodward, 1965; Carter and Williams, 1957). This led to the development of a new theoretical framework that attempted to understand how firms managed the above, and why some firms appeared to be more successful than others. Later studies in the 1960s were to confirm these initial findings and uncover significant differences in organisational characteristics (Myers and Marquis, 1969; Burns and Stalker, 1961; Cyert and March, 1963). Hence, the new framework placed more emphasis on the firm and its internal activities than had previously been the case. The firm and how it used its resources was now seen as the key influence on innovation.

Neo-classical economics is a theory of economic growth that explains how savings, investments and growth respond to population growth and technological change. The rate of technological change influences the rate of economic growth, but economic growth does not influence technological change. Rather, technological change is determined by chance. Thus population growth and technological change are exogenous. Also, neo-classical economic theory tends to concentrate on industry or economy-wide performance. It tends to ignore differences among firms in the same line of business. Any differences are assumed to reflect differences in the market environments that the organisations face. That is, differences are not achieved through choice but reflect differences in the situations in which firms operate. In contrast, research within business management and strategy focuses on these differences and the decisions that have led to them. Furthermore, the activities that take place within the firm that enable one firm seemingly to perform better than another, given the same economic and market conditions, has been the focus of much research effort since the 1960s.

The Schumpeterian view sees firms as different – it is the way a firm manages its resources over time and develops capabilities that influences its innovation performance. The varying emphasis placed by different disciplines on explaining how innovation occurs is brought together in the framework in Figure 1.1. This overview of the innovation process includes an economic perspective, a business management strategy perspective and organisational behaviour which attempts to look at the internal activities. It also recognises that firms form relationships with other firms and trade, compete and cooperate with each other. It further recognises that the activities of individuals within the firm also affect the process of innovation.

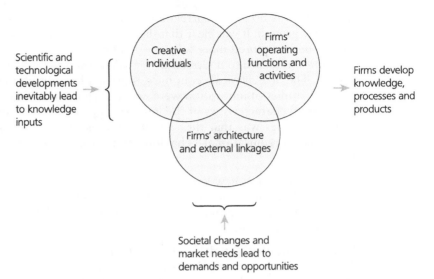

Figure 1.1 **Overview of the innovation process**

Each firm's unique organisational architecture represents the way it has constructed itself over time. This comprises its internal design, including its functions and the relationships it has built up with suppliers, competitors, customers, etc. This framework recognises that these will have a considerable impact on a firm's innovative performance. So too will the way it manages its individual functions and its employees or individuals. These are separately identified within the framework as being influential in the innovation process.

Recent and contemporary studies

As the twentieth century drew to a close there was probably as much debate and argument concerning innovation and what contributes to innovative performance as a hundred years ago. This debate has, nonetheless, progressed our understanding of the area of innovation management. It was Schumpeter who argued that modern firms equipped with R&D laboratories have become the central innovative actors. Since his work others have contributed to the debate (Chandler, 1962; Nelson and Winter, 1982; Cohen and Levinthal, 1990; Prahalad and Hamel, 1990; Pavitt, 1990; Patel and Pavitt, 2000). This emerging Schumpeterian or evolutionary theory of dynamic firm capabilities is having a significant impact on the study of business and management today. Success in the future, as in the past, will surely lie in the ability to acquire and utilise knowledge and apply this to the development of new products. Uncovering how to do this remains one of today's most pressing management problems.

The importance of uncovering and satisfying the needs of customers is the important role played by marketing and these activities feed into the new product development process. Recent studies by Hamel and Prahalad (1994) and Christensen (2003) suggest that listening to your customer may actually stifle technological innovation and be detrimental to long-term business success. Ironically, to be successful in industries characterised by technological change, firms may be required to pursue innovations that are not demanded by their current customers. Christensen (2003) distinguishes between 'disruptive innovations' and 'sustaining innovations' (radical or incremental innovations). Sustaining innovations appealed to existing customers, since they provided improvements to established products. For example, the introduction of new computer software usually provides improvements for existing customers in terms of added features. Disruptive innovations tend to provide improvements greater than those demanded. For example, while the introduction of 3.5-inch disk drives to replace 5.25-inch drives provided an enormous improvement in performance, it also created problems for users who were familiar with the previous format. These disruptive innovations also tended to create new markets, which eventually captured the existing market (*see* Discontinuous innovations, later in this chapter for more on this).

The need to view innovation in an organisational context

During the early part of the nineteenth century manufacturing firms were largely family oriented and concentrated their resources on one activity. For example, one firm would produce steel from iron ore, another would roll this into sheet steel for use by, say, a manufacturer of cooking utensils. These would then be delivered to shops for sale. Towards the latter part of the century these small enterprises were gradually replaced by large firms that would perform a much wider variety of activities. The expansion in manufacturing activities was simultaneously matched by an expansion in administrative activities. This represented the beginnings of the development of the diversified functional enterprise. The world expansion in trade during the early part of the twentieth century saw the quest for new markets by developing a wide range of new products (Chandler, 1962).

Unfortunately, many of the studies of innovation have treated it as an artefact that is somehow detached from knowledge and skills and not embedded in know-how. This inevitably leads to a simplified understanding, if not a misunderstanding, of what constitutes innovation. This section shows why innovation needs to be viewed in the context of organisations and as a process within organisations.

The diagram in Figure 1.1 shows how a number of different disciplines contribute to our understanding of the innovation process. It is important to note that firms do not operate in a vacuum. They trade with each other, they work together in some areas and compete in others. Hence, the role of other firms is a major factor in understanding innovation. As discussed earlier, economics clearly has an important role to play. So too does organisational behaviour as we try to understand what activities are necessary to ensure success. Studies of management will also make a significant contribution to specific areas such as marketing, R&D, manufacturing operations and competition.

As has been suggested, in previous centuries it was easier in many ways to mobilise the resources necessary to develop and commercialise a product, largely because the resources required were, in comparison, minimal. Today, however, the resources required, in terms of knowledge, skills, money and market experience, mean that significant innovations are synonymous with organisations. Indeed, it is worthy of note that more recent innovations and scientific developments, such as significant discoveries like mobile phones or computer software and hardware developments,

Table 1.4 **Twentieth-century technological innovations**

Date	New product	Responsible organisation
1930s	Polythene	ICI
1945	Ballpoint pen	Reynolds International Pen Company
1950s	Manufacturing process: float glass	Pilkington
1970/80s	Ulcer treatment drug: Zantac	GlaxoSmithKline
1970/80s	Photocopying	Xerox
1980s	Personal computer	Apple Computer
1980/90s	Computer operating system: Windows 95	Microsoft
1995	Impotence drug: Viagra	Pfizer
2000s	Cell phones	Motorola/Nokia
2005	MP3 players	Creative; Apple

are associated with organisations rather than individuals (*see* Table 1.4). Moreover, the increasing depth of our understanding of science inhibits the breadth of scientific study. In the early part of the twentieth century, for example, the German chemical company Bayer was regarded as a world leader in chemistry. Now it is almost impossible for a single chemical companies to be scientific leaders in all areas of chemistry. The large companies have specialised in particular areas. This is true of many other industries. Even university departments are having to concentrate their resources on particular areas of science. They are no longer able to offer teaching and research in all fields. In addition, the creation, development and commercial success of new ideas require a great deal of input from a variety of specialist sources and often vast amounts of money. Hence, today's innovations are associated with groups of people or companies. Innovation is invariably a team game. This will be explored more fully in Chapters 3, 6 and 15.

Pause for thought

If two different firms, similar in size, operating in the same industry spend the same on R&D, will their level of innovation be the same?

Individuals in the innovation process

Figure 1.1 identifies individuals as a key component of the innovation process. Within organisations it is individuals who define problems, have ideas and perform creative linkages and associations that lead to inventions. Moreover, within organisations it is individuals in the role of managers who decide what activities should be undertaken, the amount of resources to be deployed and how they should be carried out. This has led to the development of so-called key individuals in the innovation process such as inventor, entrepreneur, business sponsor, etc. These are discussed in detail in Chapter 3.

Problems of definition and vocabulary

While there are many arguments and debates in virtually all fields of management, it seems that this is particularly the case in innovation management. Very often these centre on semantics. This is especially so when innovation is viewed as a single event. When viewed as a *process*, however, the differences are less substantive. At the heart of this book is the thesis that innovation needs to be viewed as a process. If one accepts that inventions are new discoveries, new ways of doing things, and that products are the eventual outputs from the inventions, that process from new discovery to eventual product is the innovation process. A useful analogy would be education, where qualifications are the formal outputs of the education process. Education, like innovation, is not and cannot be viewed as an event (Linton, 2009).

Arguments become stale when we attempt to define terms such as new, creativity or discovery. It often results in a game of semantics. First, what is new to one company may be 'old hat' to another. Second, how does one judge success in terms of commercial gain or scientific achievement? Are they both not valid and justified goals in themselves? Third, it is context dependent – what is viewed as a success today may be viewed as a failure in the future. We need to try to understand how to encourage innovation in order that we may help to develop more successful new products (this point is explored in Chapters 11 and 12).

Entrepreneurship

Illustration 1.3 shows the remarkable entrepreneurial skills of an eight-year-old boy. This has been the traditional view of entrepreneurship; that entrepreneurs often seem

Illustration 1.3

Penny apples – selling them thrice over

In his autobiography the Irish entrepreneur Billy Cullen (2003) tells the story of how, as an eight-year-old boy, he demonstrated sharp entrepreneurial skills. In a poverty stricken area of Dublin young Billy would buy wooden crates of apples for a shilling and then sell the apples on a Saturday afternoon to the hundreds of local people who would flock to watch their local football team play. This provided Billy with a healthy profit of a shilling if he could sell all the apples. But, his entrepreneurial skills did not stop there. He would then take the wooden apple boxes to the football ground and sell them for a penny to people at the back of the crowds so that they could stand on the box for a better view. And

Source: Pearson Education Ltd/Westend 61

finally, when the match had finished Billy would collect up the wooden boxes, break them up and sell them in bundles for firewood.

Paypal entrepreneur nets $1.3 billion in sale to eBay

Elon Musk (born 28 June 1971) is a South African-American engineer, entrepreneur and philanthropist. He is best known for co-founding PayPal. He is currently the CEO and Product Architect of Tesla Motors, and has degrees in business and physics from the University of Pennsylvania. In March 1999, Musk co-founded X.com, an online financial services and email payment company. One year later, X.com merged with Confinity, originally a company formed to transfer money between Palm Pilots. The new combined entity focused on email payments through the PayPal domain, acquired as part of Confinity.

In February 2001, X.com changed its legal name to PayPal. In October 2002, PayPal was acquired by eBay for US$1.5 billion in stock.

Musk decided to invest some of his fortune in Tesla Motors, of which he is a co-founder, chairman of the board and the sole product architect. First investing in April 2004, he led several rounds of financing, and became CEO in October 2008. Tesla Motors built an electric sports car, the Tesla Roadster, and plans to produce a more economical four-door electric vehicle. Musk is responsible for a business strategy that aims to deliver affordable electric vehicles to mass-market consumers.

---

to have innate talents. In the United States the subject of innovation management is often covered in terms of 'entrepreneurship'. Indeed, it has been taught for many years and there are many courses available for students in US business schools on this topic. In a study of past and future research on the subject of entrepreneurship, Howard Stevenson, who did so much to establish entrepreneurship as a discipline at Harvard Business School and was Director of the Arthur Rock Centre for entrepreneurship there, defines entrepreneurship as:

> the pursuit of opportunity beyond the resources you currently control.
> (Stevenson and Amabile, 1999)

It is the analysis of the role of the individual entrepreneur that distinguishes the study of entrepreneurship from that of innovation management. Furthermore, it is starting small businesses and growing them into large and successful businesses that was the traditional focus of attention of those studying entrepreneurship. This has been changing over the past ten years especially across Europe. Where there is now considerable emphasis especially within the technical universities on trying to understand how entrepreneurship and innovation can help create the new technology intensive businesses of tomorrow. Moreover it is the recognition of the entrepreneur's desire to change things that is so important within innovation. We will see later that the role of an entrepreneur is central to innovation management. Illustration 1.4 shows how a serial entrepreneur has driven innovation and new product development in several industries.

Design

The definition of design with regard to business seems to be widening ever further and encompassing almost all aspects of business (*see* the Design Council, www.Designcouncil.com). For many people design is about developing or creating something; hence we are into semantics regarding how this differs from innovation. Hargadon and Douglas (2001: 476) suggest design is concerned with the emergent arrangement of concrete details that embody a new idea. A key question, however, is how design relates to research and development. Indeed, it seems that in most cases the word *design* and the word *development* mean the same thing. Traditionally design referred to the development of drawings, plans and sketches. Indeed, most dictionary definitions continue with this view today and refer to a designer as a 'draughtsman who makes plans for manufacturers or prepares drawings for clothing or stage productions' (*Oxford English Dictionary*, 2005). In the aerospace industry engineers and designers would have previously worked closely together for many years, developing drawings for an aircraft. Today the process is dominated by computer software programmes that facilitate all aspects of the activity; hence the product development activities and the environments in which design occurs have changed considerably. Figure 1.2 shows, along the horizontal axis, the wide spectrum of activities that design encompasses from clothing design to design within electronics. The vertical axis shows how the areas of design feed into outputs from choice of colour to cost effectiveness; all of which are considered in the development of a product. The position taken by this book is to view design as an applied activity within research and development, and to recognise that in certain industries, like clothing for example, design is the main component in product development. In other industries, however, such as pharmaceuticals, design forms only a small part of the product development activity.

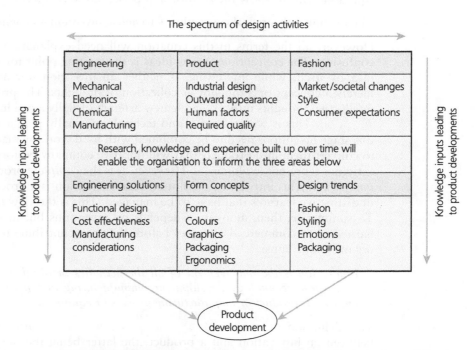

Figure 1.2 **The interaction between development activities and design environment**

Innovation and invention

Many people confuse these terms. Indeed, if you were to ask people for an explanation you would collect a diverse range of definitions. It is true that innovation is the first cousin of invention, but they are not identical twins that can be interchanged. Hence, it is important to establish clear meanings for them.

Innovation itself is a very broad concept that can be understood in a variety of ways. One of the more comprehensive definitions is offered by Myers and Marquis (1969):

> *Innovation is not a single action but a total process of interrelated sub processes. It is not just the conception of a new idea, nor the invention of a new device, nor the development of a new market. The process is all these things acting in an integrated fashion.*

It is important to clarify the use of the term 'new' in the context of innovation. Rogers and Shoemaker (1972) do this eloquently:

> *It matters little, as far as human behaviour is concerned, whether or not an idea is 'objectively' new as measured by the lapse of time since its first use or discovery. . . . If the idea seems new and different to the individual, it is an innovation.*
>
> [emphasis added]

Most writers, including those above, distinguish innovation from invention by suggesting that innovation is concerned with the *commercial and practical application* of ideas or inventions. Invention, then, is the conception of the idea, whereas innovation is the subsequent translation of the invention into the economy. The following simple equation helps to show the relationship between the two terms:

Innovation = theoretical conception + technical invention + commercial exploitation

However, all the terms in this equation will need explanation in order to avoid confusion. The *conception* of new ideas is the starting point for innovation. A new idea by itself, while interesting, is neither an invention nor an innovation; it is merely a concept or a thought or collection of thoughts. The process of converting intellectual thoughts into a tangible new artefact (usually a product or process) is an invention. This is where science and technology usually play a significant role. At this stage inventions need to be combined with hard work by many different people to convert them into products that will improve company performance. These later activities represent *exploitation*. However, it is the *complete* process that represents *innovation*. This introduces the notion that innovation is a process with a number of distinctive features that have to be managed. This is the view taken by this book. To summarise, then, innovation depends on inventions but inventions need to be harnessed to commercial activities before they can contribute to the growth of an organisation. Thus:

> *Innovation is the management of all the activities involved in the process of idea generation, technology development, manufacturing and marketing of a new (or improved) product or manufacturing process or equipment.*

This definition of innovation as a management process also offers a distinction between an innovation and a product, the latter being the output of innovation. Illustration 1.5 should help to clarify the differences.

Illustration 1.5

An example of an invention

Scientists and development engineers at a household cleaning products company had been working for many months on developing a new lavatory cleaning product. They had developed a liquid that when sprayed into the toilet pan, on contact with water, would fizz and sparkle. The effect was to give the impression of a tough, active cleaning product. The company applied for a patent and further developments and market research were planned.

However, initial results both from technical and market specialists led to the abandonment of the project. The preliminary market feedback suggested a fear of such a product on the part of consumers. This was because the fizz and sparkle looked too dramatic and frightening. Furthermore, additional technical research revealed a short shelf-life for the mixture. This is a clear example of an invention that did not progress beyond the organisation to a commercial product.

It is necessary at this point to cross-reference these discussions with the practical realities of managing a business today. The senior vice-president for research and development at 3M, one of the most highly respected and innovative organisations, recently defined innovation as:

Creativity: the thinking of novel and appropriate ideas. Innovation: the successful implementation of those ideas within an organisation.

Successful and unsuccessful innovations

There is often a great deal of confusion surrounding innovations that are not commercially successful. A famous example would be the Kodak Disc Camera or the Sinclair C5. This was a small, electrically driven tricycle or car. Unfortunately for Clive Sinclair, the individual behind the development of the product, it was not commercially successful. Commercial failure, however, does not relegate an innovation to an invention. Using the definition established above, the fact that the product progressed from the drawing board into the marketplace makes it an innovation – albeit an unsuccessful one.

Pause for thought

Apple's iPhone looks set to be as successful as the iPod, but Apple has experienced similar success before with its Apple Mac computer and eventually lost out to Microsoft. Will history repeat itself?

Different types of innovation

Industrial innovation not only includes major (radical) innovations but also minor (incremental) technological advances. Indeed, the definition offered above suggests that successful commercialisation of the innovation may involve considerably wider organisational changes. For example, the introduction of a radical, technological innovation, such as digital cameras by Kodak and Fuji, invariably results in substantial internal organisational changes. In this case substantial changes occurred with the manufacturing, marketing and sales functions. Both of these firms decided to concentrate on the rapidly developing digital photography market. Yet both Fuji and Kodak were the market leaders in supplying traditional 35mm film cartridges. Their market share of the actual camera market was less significant. Such strategic decisions forced changes on all areas of the business. For example, in Kodak's case the manufacturing function underwent substantial changes as it began to substantially cut production of 35mm film cartridges. Opportunities existed for manufacturing in producing digital cameras and their associated equipment. Similarly, the marketing function had to employ extra sales staff to educate and reassure retail outlets that the new technology would not cannibalise their film-processing business. While many people would begin to print photographs from their PCs at home, many others would continue to want their digital camera film processed into physical photographs. For both Fuji and Kodak the new technology has completely changed the photographic industry. Both firms have seen their revenues fall from film cartridge sales, but Kodak and Fuji are now market leaders in digital cameras whereas before they were not.

Hence, technological innovation can be accompanied by additional managerial and organisational changes, often referred to as innovations. This presents a far more blurred picture and begins to widen the definition of innovation to include virtually any organisational or managerial change. Table 1.5 shows a typology of innovations.

Innovation was defined earlier in this section as the application of knowledge. It is this notion that lies at the heart of all types of innovation, be they product, process or service. It is also worthy of note that many studies have suggested that product innovations are soon followed by process innovations in what they describe as an industry innovation cycle (*see* Chapter 6). Furthermore, it is common to associate innovation with physical change, but many changes introduced within organisations involve very little physical change. Rather, it is the activities performed

Table 1.5 **A typology of innovations**

Type of innovation	Example
Product innovation	The development of a new or improved product
Process innovation	The development of a new manufacturing process such as Pilkington's float glass process
Organisational innovation	A new venture division; a new internal communication system; introduction of a new accounting procedure
Management innovation	TQM (total quality management) systems; BPR (business process re-engineering); introduction of SAPR3*
Production innovation	Quality circles; just-in-time (JIT) manufacturing system; new production planning software, e.g. MRP II; new inspection system
Commercial/marketing innovation	New financing arrangements; new sales approach, e.g. direct marketing
Service innovation	Internet-based financial services

Note: SAP is a German software firm and R3 is an enterprise resource planning (ERP) product.

by individuals that change. A good example of this is the adoption of so-called Japanese management techniques by automobile manufacturers in Europe and the United States.

It is necessary to stress at the outset that this book concentrates on the management of product innovation. This does not imply that the list of innovations above are less significant; this focus has been chosen to ensure clarity and to facilitate the study of innovation.

Technology and science

We also need to consider the role played by *science and technology* in innovation. The continual fascination with science and technology at the end of the nineteenth century and subsequent growth in university teaching and research have led to the development of many new strands of science. The proliferation of scientific journals over the past 30 years demonstrates the rapidly evolving nature of science and technology. The scientific literature seems to double in quantity every five years (Rothwell and Zegveld, 1985).

Science can be defined as systematic and formulated knowledge. There are clearly significant differences between science and technology. Technology is often seen as being the application of science and has been defined in many ways (Lefever, 1992).

Illustration 1.6

The young world rising

Three forces are shaping the twenty-first century: youth, entrepreneurship and ICT. Young entrepreneurs around the world are blending new technologies and next-generation thinking, building radically new kinds of organisations adapted to a flat and crowded world. Rob Salkowitz *illustrates* the new centres of entrepreneurial innovation on five continents. He identifies an exciting new trend in global business and introduces us to a fresh young cast of entrepreneurs whose ideas are literally changing the world.

The Boston Consulting Group (BCG) confirms that the information-technology revolution continues apace. It calculates that there are already about 610 million internet users in the BRICI countries (Brazil, Russia, India, China and Indonesia). BCG predicts that this number will nearly double by 2015. And in one respect many consumers in emerging markets are leapfrogging over their western peers. They are much more likely to access the internet via mobile devices (which are ubiquitous in the emerging world) rather than PCs. That gives local entrepreneurs an advantage, says Rob Salkowitz, the author of *The Young World Rising*. Whereas western companies are hampered by legacy systems and legacy mindsets, they can build their companies around the coming technology. One of the most popular films in America at the moment is *The Social Network*, about a group of young Harvard students who founded one of the world's fastest-growing companies, Facebook. The next Facebook is increasingly likely to be founded in India or Indonesia rather than middle-aged America or doddery old Europe.

Sources: *The Economist* (2010) Schumpeter: The other demographic dividend, 7 October © The Economist Newspaper Limited London 2010; Salkowitz, R. (2010) *The Young World Rising*, John Wiley and Sons, New Jersey.

It is important to remember that technology is not an accident of nature. It is the product of deliberate action by human beings. The following definition is suggested:

Technology is knowledge applied to products or production processes.

No definition is perfect and the above is no exception. It does, however, provide a good starting point from which to view technology with respect to innovation. It is important to note that technology, like education, cannot be purchased off the shelf like a can of tomatoes. It is embedded in knowledge and skills.

In a lecture given to the Royal Society in 1992 the former chairman of Sony, Akio Morita, suggested that, unlike engineers, scientists are held in high esteem. This, he suggested, is because science provides us with information which was previously unknown. Yet technology comes from employing and *manipulating science* into concepts, processes and devices. These, in turn, can be used to make our life or work more efficient, convenient and powerful. Hence, it is technology, as an *outgrowth of science*, that fuels the industrial engine. And it is *engineers* and not scientists who make technology happen. In Japan, he argued, you will notice that almost every major manufacturer is run by an engineer or technologist. However, in the United Kingdom, some manufacturing companies are led by chief executive officers (CEOs) who do not understand the technology that goes into their own products. Indeed, many UK corporations are headed by chartered accountants. With the greatest respect to accountants, their central concerns are statistics and figures of *past* performance. How can an accountant reach out and grab the future if he or she is always looking at *last* quarter's results (Morita, 1992)?

The above represents the personal views of an influential senior figure within industry. There are many leading industrialists, economists and politicians who would concur (Hutton, 1995). But there are equally many who would profoundly disagree. The debate on improving economic innovative performance is one of the most important in the field of political economics. This debate should also include 'The young world rising' (*see* Illustration 1.6).

Innovation in action

Put your waste to work

Ahmed Khan was so concerned about the amount of plastic waste his company was producing he decided to do something about it.

Discarded plastic bottles and bags are a major problem in India. Discarded bags have even clogged underground drainage systems which means that roads are more prone to cracking and washing away in monsoon rains. Khan and his brother decided to turn the problem into the solution – roads made with recycled plastic.

Their company, Bangalore-based KK Plastic Waste Management, mixes waste plastic with asphalt into a product they call 'polymerised bitumen'. This is used to build roads that last longer than traditional ones. The surface also offers less resistance to tyres and so improves fuel efficiency.

So far the Khans have helped build 1,600 kilometres of 'plastic' roads around Bangalore and shown how, with a bit of ingenuity, environmental benefits can mean economic gains.

Source: 100 Thoughts (2010) HSBC, London.

Popular views of innovation

Science, technology and innovation have received a great deal of popular media coverage over the years, from Hollywood and Disney movies to best-selling novels (*see* Figure 1.3). This is probably because science and technology can help turn vivid imaginings into a possibility. The end result, however, is a simplified image of scientific discoveries and innovations. It usually consists of a lone professor, with a mass of white hair, working away in his garage and stumbling, by accident, on a major new discovery. Through extensive trial and error, usually accompanied by dramatic experiments, this is eventually developed into an amazing invention. This is best demonstrated in the blockbuster movie *Back to the Future*. Christopher Lloyd plays the eccentric scientist and Michael J. Fox his young, willing accomplice. Together they are involved in an exciting journey that enables Fox to travel back in time and influence the future.

Cartoons have also contributed to a misleading image of the innovation process. Here, the inventor, usually an eccentric scientist, is portrayed with a glowing lightbulb above his head, as a flash of inspiration results in a new scientific discovery. We have all seen and laughed at these funny cartoons.

This humorous and popular view of inventions and innovations has been reinforced over the years and continues to occur in the popular press. Many industrialists and academics have argued that this simple view of a complex phenomenon has caused immense harm to the understanding of science and technology.

Figure 1.3 **The popular view of science**

Models of innovation

Traditional arguments about innovation have centred on two schools of thought. On the one hand, the social deterministic school argued that innovations were the result of a combination of external social factors and influences, such as demographic changes, economic influences and cultural changes. The argument was that *when* the conditions were 'right' innovations would occur. On the other hand, the individualistic school argued that innovations were the result of unique individual talents and such innovators are born. Closely linked to the individualistic theory is the important role played by serendipity; more on this later.

Over the past ten years the literature on what 'drives' innovation has tended to divide into two schools of thought: the market-based view and the resource-based view. The market-based view argues that market conditions provide the context which facilitate or constrain the extent of firm innovation activity (Slater and Narver, 1994; Porter, 1980, 1985). The key issue here, of course, is the ability of firms to recognise opportunities in the marketplace. Cohen and Levinthal (1990) and Trott (1998) would argue that few firms have the ability to scan and search their environments effectively.

The resource-based view of innovation considers that a market-driven orientation does not provide a secure foundation for formulating innovation strategies for markets which are dynamic and volatile; rather a firm's own resources provide a much more stable context in which to develop its innovation activity and shape its markets in accordance to its own view (Penrose, 1959; Wernerfelt, 1984; Wernerfelt, 1995; Grant, 1996; Prahalad and Hamel, 1990; Conner and Prahalad, 1996; Eisenhardt and Martin, 2000). The resource-based view of innovation focuses on the firm and its resources, capabilities and skills. It argues that when firms have resources that are valuable, rare and not easily copied they can achieve a sustainable competitive advantage – frequently in the form of innovative new products. Chapter 6 offers a more detailed overview of the resource-based theory of the firm.

Serendipity

Many studies of historical cases of innovation have highlighted the importance of the unexpected discovery. The role of serendipity or luck is offered as an explanation. As we have seen, this view is also reinforced in the popular media. It is, after all, everyone's dream that they will accidentally uncover a major new invention leading to fame and fortune.

On closer inspection of these historical cases, serendipity is rare indeed. After all, in order to recognise the significance of an advance one would need to have some prior knowledge in that area. Most discoveries are the result of people who have had a fascination with a particular area of science or technology and it is following extended efforts on their part that advances are made. Discoveries may not be expected, but in the words of Louis Pasteur, 'chance favours the prepared mind'.

Linear models

It was US economists after the Second World War who championed the linear model of science and innovation. Since then, largely because of its simplicity, this model has taken a firm grip on people's views on how innovation occurs. Indeed, it dominated science and industrial policy for 40 years. It was only in the 1980s that management schools around the world began seriously to challenge the sequential linear process. The recognition that innovation occurs through the interaction of the

Creation of new knowledge, dominated by universities and large science-based organisations

Technology development, dominated by organisations

Consumers express their needs and wants through the consumption of products

Science and technology base

Technological developments

Needs of the market

Figure 1.4 **Conceptual framework of innovation**

science base (dominated by universities and industry), technological development (dominated by industry) and the needs of the market was a significant step forward (*see* Figure 1.4). The explanation of the interaction of these activities forms the basis of models of innovation today. Students may also wish to note that there is even a British Standard (BS7000), which sets out a design-centred model of the process (BSI, 2008).

There is, of course, a great deal of debate and disagreement about precisely what activities influence innovation and, more importantly, the internal processes that affect a company's ability to innovate. Nonetheless, there is broad agreement that it is the linkages between these key components that will produce successful innovation. Importantly, the devil is in the detail. From a European perspective an area that requires particular attention is the linkage between the science base and technological development. The European Union (EU) believes that European universities have not established effective links with industry, whereas in the United States universities have been working closely with industry for many years.

As explained above, the innovation process has traditionally been viewed as a sequence of separable stages or activities. There are two basic variations of this model for product innovation. First, and most crudely, there is the technology-driven model (often referred to as 'technology push') where it is assumed that scientists make unexpected discoveries, technologists apply them to develop product ideas and engineers and designers turn them into prototypes for testing. It is left to manufacturing to devise ways of producing the products efficiently. Finally, marketing and sales will promote the product to the potential consumer. In this model the marketplace was a passive recipient for the fruits of R&D. This technology-push model dominated industrial policy after the Second World War (*see* Figure 1.5). While this model of innovation can be applied to a few cases, most notably the

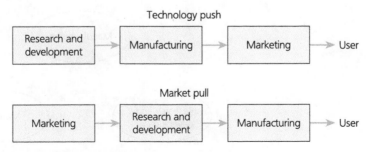

Technology push

| Research and development | → | Manufacturing | → | Marketing | → User |

Market pull

| Marketing | → | Research and development | → | Manufacturing | → User |

Figure 1.5 **Linear models of innovation**

pharmaceutical industry, it is not applicable in many other instances; in particular where the innovation process follows a different route.

It was not until the 1970s that new studies of actual innovations suggested that the role of the marketplace was influential in the innovation process (von Hippel, 1978). This led to the second linear model, the 'market-pull' model of innovation. The customer need-driven model emphasises the role of marketing as an initiator of new ideas resulting from close interactions with customers. These, in turn, are conveyed to R&D for design and engineering and then to manufacturing for production. In fast-moving consumer goods industries the role of the market and the customer remains powerful and very influential. The managing director of McCain Foods argues that knowing your customer is crucial to turning innovation into profits:

> It's only by understanding what the customer wants that we can identify the innovative opportunities. Then we see if there's technology that we can bring to bear on the opportunities that exist. Being innovative is relatively easy – the hard part is ensuring your ideas become commercially viable.   (Murray, 2003)

Simultaneous coupling model

Whether innovations are stimulated by technology, customer need, manufacturing or a host of other factors, including competition, misses the point. The models above concentrate on what is driving the downstream efforts rather than on *how* innovations occur (Galbraith, 1982). The linear model is only able to offer an explanation of *where* the initial stimulus for innovation was born, that is, where the trigger for the idea or need was initiated. The simultaneous coupling model shown in Figure 1.6 suggests that it is the result of the simultaneous coupling of the knowledge within all three functions that will foster innovation. Furthermore, the point of commencement for innovation is not known in advance.

Architectural innovation

Henderson and Clark (1990) divide technological knowledge along two new dimensions: *knowledge of the components* and knowledge of the linkage between them, which they called *architectural knowledge*. The result is four possible types of innovation: incremental, modular, radical and architectural innovation. Essentially they distinguish between the components of a product and the ways they are integrated

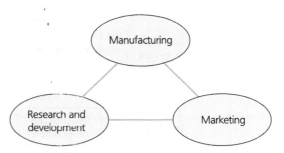

Figure 1.6 **The simultaneous coupling model**

into the system, that is, the product 'architecture', which they define as innovations that change the architecture of a product without changing its components. Prior to the Henderson and Clark model the radical/incremental dimension suggests that incumbents will be in a better position if the innovation is incremental since they can use existing knowledge and resources to leverage the whole process. New entrants, on the other hand, will have a large advantage if the innovation is radical because they will not need to change their knowledge background. Furthermore incumbents struggle to deal with radical innovation both because they operate under a 'managerial mindset' constraint and because strategically they have less of an incentive to invest in the innovation if it will cannibalise their existing products.

Kodak illustrates this well. The company dominated the photography market over many years, and throughout this extended period all the incremental innovations solidified its leadership. As soon as the market experienced a radical innovation – the entrance of digital technology – Kodak struggled to defend its position against the new entrants. The new technology required different knowledge, resources and mindsets. This pattern of innovation is typical in mature industries. This concept is explored further in Chapter 6.

Interactive model

The interactive model develops this idea further (*see* Figure 1.7) and links together the technology-push and market-pull models. It emphasises that innovations occur as the result of the interaction of the marketplace, the science base and the organisation's capabilities. Like the coupling model, there is no explicit starting point. The use of information flows is used to explain how innovations transpire and that they can arise from a wide variety of points.

While still oversimplified, this is a more comprehensive representation of the innovation process. It can be regarded as a logically sequential, though not necessarily continuous, process that can be divided into a series of functionally distinct but interacting and interdependent stages (Rothwell and Zegveld, 1985). The overall innovation process can be thought of as a complex set of communication paths over which knowledge is transferred. These paths include internal and external linkages. The

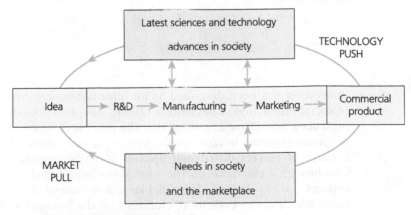

Figure 1.7 **Interactive model of innovation**

Source: Adapted from R. Rothwell and W. Zegveld (1985) *Reindustrialisation and Technology*, Longman, London.

innovation process outlined in Figure 1.7 represents the organisation's capabilities and its linkages with both the marketplace and the science base. Organisations that are able to manage this process effectively will be successful at innovation.

At the centre of the model are the organisational functions of R&D, engineering and design, manufacturing and marketing and sales. While at first this may appear to be a linear model, the flow of communication is not necessarily linear. There is provision for feedback. Also, linkages with the science base and the marketplace occur between all functions, not just with R&D or marketing. For example, as often happens, it may be the manufacturing function which initiates a design improvement that leads to the introduction of either a different material or the eventual development by R&D of a new material. Finally, the generation of ideas is shown to be dependent on inputs from three basic components (as outlined in Figure 1.4): organisation capabilities; the needs of the marketplace; the science and technology base.

Innovation life cycle and dominant designs

The launch of an innovative new product into the market is usually only the beginning of technology progress. At the industry level, the introduction of a new technology will cause a reaction: competitors will respond to this new product, hence technological progress depends on factors other than those internal to the firm. We need to consider the role of the competition. Product innovation, process innovation, competitive environment and organisational structure all interact and are closely linked together. Abernathy and Utterback (1978) argued there were three different phases in an innovation's life cycle: fluid, transitional and specific. This concept will be discussed in detail in Chapter 6, but at this stage we need only to recognise that one can consider innovation in the form of a life cycle that begins with a major technological change and product innovation. This is followed by the emergence of competition and process innovations (manufacturing improvements). As the life cycle proceeds a dominant design usually emerges prior to standardisation and an emphasis on lowering cost. This model can be applied to many consumer product innovations over the past 20–30 years, such as VCRs, CD players and mobile phones.

Open innovation and the need to share and exchange knowledge (network models)

Innovation has been described as an information–creation process that arises out of social interaction. Chesbrough (2003), adopting a business strategy perspective, presents a persuasive argument that the process of innovation has shifted from one of closed systems, internal to the firm, to a new mode of open systems involving a range of players distributed up and down the supply chain. Significantly, it is Chesbrough's emphasis on the new knowledge-based economy that informs the concept open innovation. In particular it is the use of cheap and instant information flows which places even more emphasis on the linkages and relationships of firms. It is from these linkages and the supply chain in particular that firms have to ensure that they have the capability to fully capture and utilise ideas.

Furthermore, the product innovation literature, in applying the open innovation paradigm, has been debating the strengths and limitations of so-called 'user toolkits' which seem to ratchet up further this drive to externalise the firm's capabilities to capture innovation opportunities (von Hippel, 2005).

Authors such as Thomke (2003), Schrange (2000) and Dodgson *et al.* (2005) have emphasised the importance of learning through experimentation. This is similar to Nonaka's work in the early 1990s which emphasised the importance of learning by doing in the 'knowledge creating company' (Nonaka, 1991). However, Dodgson *et al.* argue that there are significant changes occurring at all levels of the innovation process, forcing us to reconceptualise the process with emphasis placed on the three areas that have experienced most significant change through the introduction and use of new technologies. These are: technologies that facilitate creativity, technologies that facilitate communication and technologies that facilitate manufacturing. For example, they argue that information and communication technologies have changed the way individuals, groups and communities interact. Mobile phones, email and websites are obvious examples of how people interact and information flows in a huge osmosis process through the boundaries of the firm. When this is coupled with changes in manufacturing and operations technologies, enabling rapid prototyping and flexible manufacturing at low costs, the process of innovation seems to be undergoing considerable change (Dodgson *et al.*, 2005; Chesbrough, 2003; Schrange, 2000). Models of innovation need to take account of these new technologies which allow immediate and extensive interaction with many collaborators throughout the process from conception to commercialisation.

Table 1.6 summarises the historical development of the dominant models of the industrial innovation process.

Table 1.6 **The chronological development of models of innovation**

Date	Model	Characteristics
1950/60s	Technology-push	Simple linear sequential process; emphasis on R&D; the market is a recipient of the fruits of R&D
1970s	Market-pull	Simple linear sequential process; emphasis on marketing; the market is the source for directing R&D; R&D has a reactive role
1970s	Dominant design	Abbernathy and Utterback (1978) illustrate that an innovation system goes through three stages before a dominant design emerges
1980s	Coupling model	Emphasis on integrating R&D and marketing
1980/90s	Interactive model	Combinations of push and pull
1990	Architectural innovation	Recognition of the role of firm embedded knowledge in influencing innovation
1990s	Network model	Emphasis on knowledge accumulation and external linkages
2000s	Open innovation	Chesbrough's (2003) emphasis on further externalisation of the innovation process in terms of linkages with knowledge inputs and collaboration to exploit knowledge outputs

Discontinuous innovation – step changes

Occasionally something happens in an industry which causes a disruption – the rules of the game change. This has happened in many different industries: for example, telephone banking and internet banking have caused huge changes for the banking industry. Likewise, the switch from photographic film to digital film changed the landscape in that industry. And the music industry is still grappling with the impact of downloading as the dominant way to consume music. These changes are seen as not continuous, that is discontinuous: the change is very significant (see Figure 1.8). Sometimes this is referred to as disruptive innovation. Schumpeter referred to this concept as creative destruction.

The term disruptive innovation as we know it today first appeared in *The Innovator's Dilemma*. In this book, Clayton Christensen investigated why some innovations that were radical in nature reinforced the incumbent's position in a certain industry, contrary to what previous models (for instance the Henderson–Clark model) would predict. More specifically he analysed extensively the disk drive industry because it represented the most dynamic, technologically discontinuous and complex industry one could find in the economy. Figure 1.8 shows how a disruptive innovation creates a step change in performance.

This very same pattern of disruption can be observed with video rental services, department stores and newspapers. The appearance of online news services, web portals and other media platforms such as blogs and wikis clearly represent a disruptive innovation for the traditional newspaper industry. Will the likes of *The Times*, the *Guardian* and the *New York Times* be able to survive such disruption? For many years newspapers embraced the web and provided content online, but sales of newspapers continued to decline. A key question for the industry is: *What indispensable roles can we play in the lives of the consumers we want to serve?*

Other examples of disruptive innovations are:

- steamships (which disrupted sailing ships);
- music downloads (which disrupted CDs); and
- internet shopping (which disrupted high street retailing).

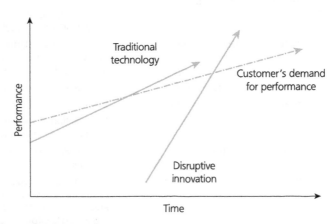

Figure 1.8 **Disruptive innovations**

Discontinuity can also come about by reframing the way we think about an industry. Table 14.3 shows a wide range of new services that also created new business models. This includes online gambling and low cost airlines. What these examples – and many others – have in common is that they represent the challenge of discontinuous innovation. How do incumbent firms cope with these dramatic shifts in technology, service and/or the business model.

What many firms would also like to know is how they can become the disruptor or radical innovator. In a study of radical innovation in the highly innovative motorsport industry Delbridge and Mariotti (2009) found that successful innovators:

- engage in wide exploratory innovation search activities, looking beyond their own knowledge base and domain of expertise;
- identify the advantages offered by new combinations of existing knowledge, through the application of technologies and materials initially developed elsewhere;
- often partner with 'unusual' firms, beyond the usual sphere of collaboration;
- engage with partner companies to establish a close working relationship;
- promote lateral thinking within an existing web of partners.

Innovation as a management process

> *The fact is coming up with an idea is the least important part of creating something great. The execution and delivery are what's key.*
>
> (Sergey Brin, Co-founder of Google, quoted in the *Guardian* (2009)).

The statement by Sergey Brin, Co-founder of Google, confirms that we need to view innovation as a management process. The preceding sections have revealed that innovation is not a singular event, but a series of activities that are linked in some way to the others. This may be described as a process and involves:

1 a response to either a need or an opportunity that is context dependent;
2 a creative effort that if successful results in the introduction of novelty;
3 the need for further changes.

Usually, in trying to capture this complex process, the simplification has led to misunderstandings. The simple linear model of innovation can be applied to only a few innovations and is more applicable to certain industries than others. The pharmaceutical industry characterises much of the technology-push model. Other industries, like the food industry, are better represented by the market-pull model. For most industries and organisations innovations are the result of a mixture of the two. Managers working within these organisations have the difficult task of trying to manage this complex process.

A framework for the management of innovation

Industrial innovation and new product development have evolved considerably from their early beginnings outlined above. We have seen that innovation is extremely complex and involves the effective management of a variety of different activities. It is precisely how the process is managed that needs to be examined. Over the past

Table 1.7 **Explanations for innovative capability**

Innovative firm	Explanation for innovative capability
Apple	Innovative chief executive
Google	Scientific freedom for employees
Samsung	Speed of product development
Procter & Gamble	Utilisation of external sources of technology
IBM	Share patents with collaborators
BMW	Design
Starbucks	In-depth understanding of customers and their cultures
Toyota	Close cooperation with suppliers

Table 1.8 **Studies of innovation management**

	Study	Date	Focus
1	Carter and Williams	1957	Industry and technical progress
2	Project Hindsight – TRACES (Isenson)	1968	Historical reviews of US government-funded defence industry
3	Wealth from knowledge (Langrish et al.)	1972	Queens Awards for technical innovation
4	Project SAPPHO (Rothwell et al.)	1974	Success and failure factors in chemical industry
5	Minnesota Studies (Van de Ven)	1989	14 case studies of innovations
6	Rothwell	1992	25-year review of studies
7	Sources of innovation (Wheelwright and Clark)	1992	Different levels of user involvement
8	MIT studies (Utterback)	1994	5 major industry-level cases
9	Project NEWPROD (Cooper)	1994	Longitudinal survey of success and failure in new products
10	Radical innovation (Leifer et al.)	2000	Review of mature businesses
11	TU Delft study (van der Panne et al.)	2003	Literature review of success and failure factors

50 years there have been numerous studies of innovation attempting to understand not only the ingredients necessary for it to occur but also what levels of ingredients are required and in what order. Furthermore, a study by the Boston Consulting Group reported in *Business Week* (2006) of over 1,000 senior managers revealed further explanations as to what makes some firms more innovative than others. The key findings from this survey are captured in Table 1.7. While these headline-grabbing bullet points are interesting, they do not show us what firms have to do to become excellent in design (BMW) or to improve cooperation with suppliers (Toyota). Table 1.8 captures some of the key studies that have influenced our understanding.

This chapter so far has helped to illustrate the complex nature of innovation management and also identified some of the limitations of the various models and schools of thought. Specifically, these are:

- Variations on linear thinking continue to dominate models of innovation. Actually, most innovation models show innovation paths, representing a stage-gate type of activity, controlling the progress from idea to market introduction, rather than giving insight into the dynamics of actual innovation processes.
- Science is viewed primarily as technology orientated (physical sciences) and R&D is closely linked to manufacturing, causing insufficient attention to be paid to the behavioural sciences. As a consequence, service innovation is hardly addressed.
- The complex interactions between new technological capabilities and emerging societal needs are a vital part of the innovation process, but they are underexposed in current models.
- The role of the entrepreneur (individual or team) is not captured.
- Current innovation models are not embedded within the strategic thinking of the firm; they remain isolated entities.

Innovation needs to be viewed as a management process. We need to recognise that change is at the heart of it. And that change is caused by decisions that people make. The framework in Figure 1.9 attempts to capture the iterative nature of the network processes in innovation and represents this in the form of an endless innovation circle with interconnected cycles. This circular concept helps to show how the firm gathers information over time, how it uses technical *and* societal knowledge, and how it develops an attractive proposition. This is achieved through developing linkages and partnerships with those having the necessary capabilities ('open innovation'). In addition, the entrepreneur is positioned at the centre.

The framework in Figure 1.9 is referred to as the the 'cyclic innovation model' (CIM) (Berkhout *et al.*, 2010); a cross-disciplinary view of change processes (and their interactions) as they take place in an open innovation arena. Behavioural sciences and

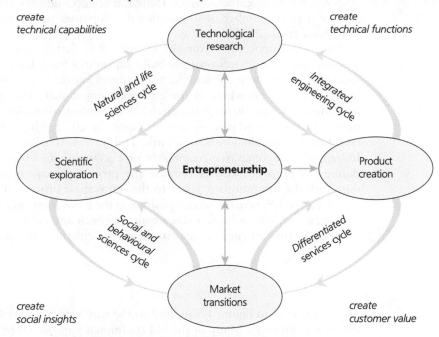

Figure 1.9 The innovation circle with interconnected cycles
Source: Berkhout *et al.* (2010).

engineering as well as natural sciences and markets are brought together in a coherent system of processes with four principal nodes that function as roundabouts. The combination of the involved changes leads to a wealth of business opportunities. Here, entrepreneurship plays a central role by making use of those opportunities. The message is that without the drive of entrepreneurs there is no innovation, and without innovation there is no new business. Figure 1.9 shows that the combination of change and entrepreneurship is the basis of new business.

Adopting this approach to the management of innovation should help firms as processes should not be forced into simple one-way pipelines, but rather be organised by interconnected cycles with feedforward and feedback connections: from linear to non-linear thinking. In that way, a dynamic network environment is created in which the social and behavioural sciences are linked to engineering, and where the natural and life sciences connect with market goals (Berkhout, 2000). This is what is captured in the proposed innovation framework. Supported by today's powerful communication technology, serial process management along a linear path is replaced by parallel networking along a largely self-organising circle. Vital decisions in innovation do not occur in the gates of a staged project management pipeline, but do occur on the innovation shop floor itself; or in the nodes of the cyclic networks. In my experience young people like to work in such an environment. Moreover, according to Salkowitz (2010), young entrepreneurs around the world are blending new technologies and next-generation thinking, building radically new kinds of organisations adapted to a flat and crowded world (*see* Illustration 1.6).

The cyclic innovation model is the result of a combination of analysis of theory and practical evidence, based on many years of experience within industries that work with scientists to develop valuable new products and services. Furthermore, evidence has been gathered from Delphi, a science-industry consortium which consists of a large number of international companies within the field of geo-energy (Berkhout *et al.*, 2010).

The most important feature of Figure 1.9 is that the model architecture is not a chain but a *circle*: innovations build on innovations. Ideas create new concepts, successes create new challenges, and failures create new insights. Note that new ideas may start anywhere in the circle, causing a wave that propagates clockwise and anti-clockwise through the circle. In an innovative society businesses are transparent and the speed of propagation along the circle is high, resulting in minimum travel time along the innovation path. Today, time is a crucial factor in innovation. Indeed, when it comes to managing the process within the firm the stage-gate approach dominates practice. This is because the project management advantages tend to outweigh the limitations it poses to the innovation process. This can be illustrated within Figure 1.9; here the central position in the innovation circle is frequently occupied by a manager, who adopts a stage-gate approach and culture, rather than an entrepreneur; having an entrepreneur in the centre enhances the innovation process.

New skills

The framework in Figure 1.9 underpins the way managers need to view the management of innovation. Many of the old traditional approaches to management need to change and new approaches need to be adopted. Increasingly, managers and those who work for them are no longer in the same location. Gone are the days when managers could supervise the hour-to-hour work of individuals. Often complex management relationships need to be developed because organisations are trying to produce complex products and services and do so across geographic boundaries. Cross-functional and cross-border task forces often need to be created. And managers have to manage without authority. In these circumstances, individual managers need to work with and influence people who are not their subordinates and over whom they have no formal authority. Frequently this means leadership must be shared across the team members. An important part of getting work done without authority is having an extensive network of relationships. In today's complex and virtual organisations, managers need information and support from a wide range of individuals. To summarise then, new skills are required in the following areas:

- virtual management;
- managing without authority;
- shared leadership;
- building extensive networks.

Pause for thought

Surely all innovations start with an idea and end with a product; so does that not make it a linear process?

Innovation and new product development

Such thinking is similarly captured in the framework outlined in Figure 1.9. It stresses the importance of interaction and communication within and between functions and with the external environment. This networking structure allows lateral communication, helping managers and their staff unleash creativity. This framework emphasises the importance of informal and formal networking across all functions (Pittaway *et al.*, 2004).

This introduces a tension between the need for diversity, on the one hand, in order to generate novel linkages and associations, and the need for commonality, on the other, to facilitate effective internal communication.

The purpose of this book is to illustrate the interconnections of the subjects of innovation management and new product development. Indeed, some may argue they are two sides of the same coin. By directly linking together these two significant areas of management the clear connections and overlaps between the subjects can be more fully explored and understood.

It is hoped that this framework will help to provide readers with a visual reminder of how one can view the innovation process that needs to be managed by firms. The industry and products and services will determine the precise requirements necessary. It is a dynamic process and the framework tries to emphasise this. It is also a complex process and this helps to simplify it to enable further study. Very often product innovation is viewed from a purely marketing perspective with little, if any, consideration of the R&D function and the difficulties of managing science and technology. Likewise, many manufacturing and technology approaches to product innovation have previously not taken sufficient notice of the needs of the customer. Into this mix we must not forget the role played by the entrepreneur in visioning the future.

The success of the iPod and iPhone raises the licensing question for Apple . . . again

Introduction

This case study explores the rise of the Apple Corporation. The Apple iPod is one of the most successful new product launches of recent years, transforming the way the public listens to music, with huge ramifications for major record labels. More than 100 million iPod's have been sold since its launch in November 2001. Mobile phones have long been regarded as the most credible challenger to MP3 players and iPods. The launch of digital download services via mobile phones illustrates the dramatic speed of convergence between the telecoms and media industries, which has ushered in a new era of growth for smart phones. Users are willing to pay more for additional services and many analysts predict that mobile phone handsets will eventually emerge as the dominant technology of the age, combining personal organisers, digital music players and games consoles in a single device. Indeed, Microsoft founder Bill Gates predicted that mobile phones would supersede the iPod as the favoured way of listening to digital music. Apple has responded to this challenge by launching the iPhone, but will this be enough. Apple faces tough competition from not only Microsoft, but also Blackberry, Google and Nokia.

Apple and the iPod

For those not yet fully plugged into digital music listening, MP3 is an acronym for MPEG layer 3, which is a compressed audio format. A compression ratio of up to 12 to 1 compression is possible, which produces high sound quality. Layer 3 is one of three coding schemes (layer 1, layer 2 and layer 3) for the compression of audio signals. It reduces the amount of data required to represent audio, yet still sound like a faithful reproduction of the original uncompressed audio to most listeners. It was invented by a team of German engineers of the Fraunhofer Society, and it became an ISO/IEC standard in 1991. This format of compression facilitates the transfer of audio files via the internet and storage in portable players, such as the iPod, and digital audio servers.

The remarkable success of the iPod music player has propelled Apple back into the FT100 ranking of global companies. This marks a return of the technology company to the ranks of the world's top companies after falling out of the list in 2001. Its shares have risen dramatically in the past two years, valuing the company at $220 billion (£150 billion), finally surpassing its great rival Microsoft in 2010. Apple, founded (in 1975) 35 years ago by Steven Jobs, who is now chief executive, has seen its fortunes ebb and flow. Mr Jobs has achieved a transformation since his return to the company in 1997 after leaving some 10 years earlier following a dispute with John Sculley, who was then chief executive (Coggan, 2005).

Historically Apple is a computer company and its core customer base today is only about 10 million active users; in a world of 400 million Windows users. Apple has always understood that its core franchise was very closely connected to the core computer franchise. Consumer electronics products, for example, are sold through different channels and they have different product life cycles. Making the transition has been extremely hard. What made the iPod transition easier is that the iPod began as a PC peripheral, even though it is ultimately a consumer electronics product. Eventually, Apple recognised that the iPod could not be limited to the Mac and it

Source: A. Harrison/Pearson Education Ltd

had to become a PC peripheral as well. The move into the PC market enabled Apple to access a much broader market than its core customer base. Indeed sales of the iPod started sluggishly as sales were directed initially towards a relatively small audience of Macintosh users, and even when a PC version of the iPod was released, its FireWire-only design limited its appeal to mainstream PC users.

Apple's iTune Music Store website

Apple's success with its iPod is helped by its iTune Music Store website (www.Apple.com/itunes), which offers consumers the ability to digitise all their CDs as well as download new music at 79p per song. This site has sold over 6 billion songs since its launch in April 2003, bringing considerable revenue to Apple (Schonfeld, 2009). However, downloads from the iTunes Music Store will only play on Apple's iPods (Webb, 2007). The site is universally regarded as being simple and fun; it also offers a legal way to add music to your library. To import songs into iTunes, you simply insert a CD into your computer and click 'Import CD'. iTunes also compresses and stores music in AAC – a format that builds upon state-of-the-art audio technology from Dolby Labs. It also offers users the ability to select different audio formats. iTunes lets you convert music to MP3 at high bit-rate at no extra charge. Using AAC or MP3, you can store more than 100 songs in the same amount of space as a single CD. iTunes also supports the Apple Lossless format, which gives you CD-quality audio in about half the storage space.

The rise and fall and rise of Apple

Apple computers began in 1977 when Steven Wozniak and Steven Jobs designed and offered the Apple I to the personal computer field. It was designed over a period of years, and was only built in printed circuit-board form. It debuted in April 1976 at the Homebrew Computer Club in Palo Alto, but few took it seriously. Continual product improvements and wider technological developments including micro-processor improvements led to the launch of the Apple Macintosh personal computer in 1984.

The Macintosh computer was different because it used a mouse driven operating system; all other PCs used the keyboard driven system known as MS DOS (Microsoft disc operating system). Early in the 1980s Microsoft licensed its operating system to all PC manufacturers, but Apple decided against this approach, opting instead to stay in control of its system. The 1980s was a period of dramatic growth for personal computers as virtually every office and home began to buy into the PC world. Slowly Microsoft became the market leader, not because its technology was better, but largely because its system became the dominant standard. As people bought PCs, so with it they would buy the operating system: MS Windows; hence it became the de-facto dominant standard. The Apple operating system was only available if you bought an Apple PC. Consequently Apple's market share plummeted. This was also the time when Steven Jobs quit Apple after disagreements with other members of the board. Interestingly in 1986 Steven Jobs became involved in another new venture, Pixar Animation Studios (see Illustration 1.7). By the mid-1990s Apple had grown to a $12 billion company, twice the size of Microsoft; but Microsoft was powering ahead on the back of the launch of Windows and it would soon become the colossus firm it is today (Schofield, 2005; 2009).

In 1993 Apple launched the Newton, its first completely new product in many years. Indeed, it represented Apple's entry into (and perhaps creation of) an entirely new market: personal digital assistants (PDAs). The PDA market was barely present when the Newton was released, but other companies were working on similar devices. The Newton Message Pad featured a variety of personal-organisation applications, such as an address book, a calendar and notes, along with communications capabilities such as faxing and email. It featured a pen-based

Illustration 1.7

Pixar Animation Studios

Pixar Animation Studios eventually became the Academy Award winning computer animation pioneer. The northern California studio has created six of the most successful and beloved animated films of all time: *Toy Story* (1995); *A Bug's Life* (1998); *Toy Story 2* (1999); *Monsters, Inc.* (2001); *Finding Nemo* (2003); and *The Incredibles* (2004). Pixar's six films have earned more than $3 billion at the worldwide box office to date. *Toy Story 3* is launched in 2010.

interface, which used a word-based, trainable handwriting recognition engine. Unfortunately this engine had been developed by a third party, and was notoriously difficult to use and was partly responsible for the product's failure.

In the mid-1990s Apple's future in the computer technology industry looked bleak, with a diversified product portfolio and a low market share within the PC market of only 3 per cent. It was also building a portfolio of product failures including the Apple Pipin (a games consol). Many were therefore surprised when Steven Jobs returned to the company as chief executive in 1997. He quickly set about culling many product lines and much of its operations and decided to focus on only a few products including the new looking iMac. This coincided with the economic boom in the late 1990s and allowed Apple to generate cash very quickly. This provided revenue for the development of the iPod, which was launched in 2003 (*see* Figure 1.10).

iPod dominates MP3 market, but competition is fierce

Since 2003 the spectacular growth of Apple's iconic digital music player sent the company's share price soaring. The challenge for Apple, however, is how to maintain the success of the iPod, especially with its indirect impact on sales of its PCs: most notably the iMac and its Notebook range of portable PCs, including the Mac Air laptop. Apple could continue to cut prices, but this would mean smaller margins. The launch of the iPhone, to capitalise on the convergence

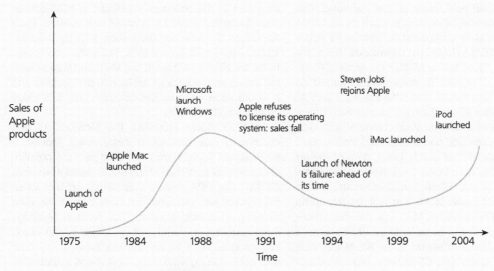

Figure 1.10 **The rise and fall and rise of Apple**

of technologies between mobibe phones and media, has helped boost growth of the firm. In actual fact Apple began fighting the competition in the MP3 market by cutting prices and improving the product. In 2005 it launched lower-priced versions of its best selling iPod digital music player, the Shuffle, with significantly improved battery performance, plus an ultra thin iPod Nano. Later came the iPod Touch with its impressive touch screen interface (the precursor to the iPhone). However, at the same time a potential big threat in the form of Sony Electronics announced a new, low-price, high-performance digital music player under its Walkman brand. Since October 2001, when Apple first launched its iPod, it has slowly reduced the price and improved the performance of the product. The design and styling have significantly contributed to Apple's success with its 50 per cent market share for MP3 players. Competitors including Dell, Creative Technologies and Rio have launched many rival players, most cheaper and offering better battery performance. Yet it seems the iPod has an iconic status that is proving difficult to attack.

iPod patent battles

Despite the success of the iPod and iPhone Apple continues to fend off challenges to the propriety of its technology. In August 2005 Creative Technology, the Singapore maker of the Zen digital music player, suggested it was considering a legal battle with several digital music manufactures including Apple Computer, alleging that the US company's popular iPod and iPod mini music players use Creative's recently patented technology. Creative was one of the first companies to market digital music players in 2000, but the company's devices have been overshadowed by Apple's popular iPod product line.

Apple has extensive experience of fighting patent infringement cases and understands that such legal battles can take many years to settle. Its own battle with Microsoft over infringement of its operating system technology was eventually settled after eight years without a satisfactory outcome. It may be better for Creative to seek royalties from Apple, as patent cases can drag out for many years and are highly unpredictable.

More recently Apple has been fighting Nokia in a battle over mobile phone technologies. Nokia is suing Apple for violations of 10 patents it holds on several wireless technologies. The patents in question, Nokia says, are fundamental to making devices like the iPhone compatible with certain wireless network standards on which the iPhone operates around the world, as well as wireless LAN technologies, which means Wi-Fi and UMTS. Apple countersued Nokia in January 2010, claiming that Nokia phones infringe on 13 Apple patents. Nokia responded by asking that the countersuit be dismissed. Experts have suggested Nokia is probably seeking royalty payments from iPhone (and now iPad) sales, rather than a full injunction. This would afford Nokia a 1–2 per cent cut from each sale.

The rise of Apple as a lifestyle brand

'iMac', 'iPod', 'iPhone', 'iPad' have all been very successful products for Apple. The impact has been more than simply sales and profits. At the centre of Apple's recent success is the emergence of Apple as a lifestyle brand rather than as a technology company. Apple is very keen, for instance, to reinforce its California heritage (the person credited with designing the iPod is Johnathan Ive, a graduate from Newcastle Polytechnic and now Apple's vice president for design). Every iPod comes with the words 'Designed in California'. Also, it may have been a subtle move, but remaining friendly – not just user-friendly but friendly, as opposed to the unfriendly giant Microsoft – may be helping to increase the brand's appeal. It may be that people at last have become tired of Microsoft and efficiency and effectiveness and now are searching for something different. If Apple can capitalise on the success of the iPod and iPhone and translate this into increased market share of the PC market, this will truly signify a dramatic turnaround for the firm in the PC industry.

To reinforce the idea of a lifestyle brand one need look no further than the huge increase in accessories for the iPod. It seems cool-conscious iPod buyers cannot get enough of carrying cases, adaptors, microphones or software; these accessories give consumers the edge as they take their iPods on the road, into classrooms and on to the street. Indeed, the road provides a big growth opportunity for Apple and the iPod. The challenge for Apple is whether it can establish the iPod in the in-car entertainment market by becoming the product of choice for those wishing to move effortlessly from *'home-to-car-to-sidewalk'* without any interruptions to listening, simply by plugging and unplugging your digital music player.

Apps

App is short for application software. iPhone apps are applications for the Apple iPhone. Most iPhone apps are meant for the newer iPhone 3G model and will also work on the most recent versions of the iPod Touch. Free or purchased Apps can be downloaded from the iTunes music store to an iPhone or iPod Touch. When the new app is downloaded, it will place an icon on the screen of an iPhone or iPod Touch, so you can access the app directly by touching the icon on the screen. Accessing applications this way eliminates the step of having to use the web browser. There are thousands of apps for the iPhone and iPod Touch. Categories of apps include Business, Games, Entertainment, Sports, Education, Medical, Fitness, News, Travel, Photography, etc. There are both paid and free app categories.

In March 2010 Apple launched its iPad. This is essentially a combination of a smartphone and a laptop. Many analysts and commentators argued that the product offered nothing new and that it was too big as a phone and too small as a laptop. Yet, two months after its launch Apple announced that sales of its iPad had reached 2 million units. The touchscreen tablet has been more successful than experts predicted. This may partly reflect the power of the Apple brand and its successful new product launch strategy.

The licensing question returns to haunt Apple

Since Apple launched the iPod in 2001 and the iPhone in 2007, doubters have said it was only a matter of time before Microsoft, Nokia or Google developed a cheaper industry-standard music player that would relegate Apple to the fringes of the market; just like Microsoft did with Windows. Few forget how Apple's refusal to license its technology contributed to its demise in the personal computer market and critics say the company appears determined to make the same mistake again. A key issue for Apple is whether it can sustain the huge premiums that it earns with the iPod and iPhone when Dell, Google, Nokia and others begin entering the market with much lower priced product offerings. Also, Apple is running into the same challenge as it experienced with the Mac of selling a proprietary solution. That is, music on the iPod cannot play on non-Apple devices.

Essentially, just like the mid-1980s, there is a standards war; just as there was between VHS and Betamax. There is a proprietary standard with iTunes, and there will be alternative standards pushed by Microsoft, Real Networks, and others. One can still detect an Apple orientated approach to growth rather than one driven by absolute growth. For example, iTunes, was initially available only on the Mac. This was meant to drive Macintosh sales, and then six or nine months later Apple would bring out a Windows version. The problem is that it gave competitors six to nine months to bring out Window's products, which creates a more competitive environment. Some analysts argue that if Apple had really been thinking in terms of breaking away from Apple users and its heritage, it would have started out on Windows and come to Macintosh later like everybody else in the world. But, critics argue that is not the way Apple thinks.

There are clearly advantages when developing a new product to target the 400 million market and then target the total Apple user and ex-user market of 25 million. But there are also advantages of doing it the Apple way.

If Apple does not open itself up and make sure that it becomes the dominant standard, it could end up becoming again the niche product, which makes it a little bit less attractive for users. Apple may be able to learn from Sony's experiences, for although Sony lost the VCR industry standards battle it did win huge market shares with its Walkman. Sony drove the Walkman into a mass audience by drastically bringing down the price. Apple may be able to do this successfully with the iPod, but it has never been very good at very high volume manufacturing at very low costs. However, it may be that the iPod is becoming the dominant platform in MP3 players just as Microsoft managed with its Windows operating system. It is less clear though that the iPhone is equally becoming the dominant standard in the smartphone market.

The key issue here is whether Apple can do what Microsoft did in the 1980s and 1990s and get people to pay it large amounts of cash via licensing. Apple could license its technology to other manufacturers as Microsoft did with its DOS and later Windows operating systems. Every mobile phone or MP3 player that is sold would potentially result in a licensing fee to Apple, in the same way as Microsoft receives a royalty for every PC, laptop, notebook and netbook that is sold with Windows installed. This could be a serious windfall. Apple would have to change strategy and decide to license its iPod/iPhone technology to the 'masses' and undo its hardware exclusivity. If Apple adopted this approach it is likely that it would make up the money in its walled garden of iTunes and applications and Apple would really become the Microsoft of the next decade. However, this looks unlikely.

More significantly, new smart phones are emerging based on the Google open source Android operating system. Worryingly for Apple, in terms of technical performance, these look superior. Moreover, some of these products are much cheaper than the iPhone. For example, Blackberry and its RIM technology are gaining market share from Apple, and Blackberries are three times cheaper! If one peers into the future, and recognising what we know from past experience, creativity is likely to emerge from the open source Android operating system, particularly as its use becomes more widespread. For Apple it may be that in seeking control it may be stifling creativity and innovation.

Troubles ahead?

The inexorable shift from separate devices to a single handheld device appears to be gathering momentum (see Figure 1.11). In particular third-generation (3G) smartphones offer the capability to download high-speed data over the airwaves including television pictures. Not surprisingly, Google, Blackberry, Nokia and others are entering the market with smartphones. Apple's iPod sales have grown every year since its 2001 launch. But during 2009 Apple sold fewer iPods than the previous year. This marks the first time that iPod sales have dropped year-over-year. Sales of the iPod have been replaced by sales of the iPhone and iPod touch, which look as if they may be the future of the iPod product line. Apple expects sales of its traditional MP3 players to decline over time as it cannibalises sales for the iPod touch and the iPhone. Nonetheless, the products still perform a useful function as an introduction to the iPod line for first-time buyers.

An area of criticism levelled against Apple Inc. that has also received considerable media coverage is the issue of excessive secrecy and obsessive control exerted by Apple on its suppliers. One of these suppliers is Foxconn, the world's biggest contract maker of IT goods including the iPhone. It is far less well known than the brands it assembles, but it is one of Taiwan's largest companies. Reuters news agency reported in 2010 that Apple goes to 'extreme lengths' to protect even the smallest details of its new products under development (Pomfret and Soh, 2010). At Foxconn's assembly plant in Longhua, South China, workers swipe security cards at the gate and guards check the occupants of each vehicle with fingerprint recognition scanners. It resembles a fortress – so much for open innovation! Many of Apple's finished gadgets, from iPods to iPads, are assembled at industrial compounds like the one in Longhua. Some of Apples's tactics seem like they have emerged from a James Bond film: information is assiduously

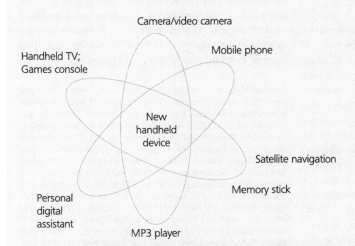

Figure 1.11 **The future handheld device will probably incorporate many separate devices**

guarded and handed out only on a need-to-know basis; employees suspected of leaks may be invest-igated by the contractor; and the company makes it clear that it will not hesitate to sue if secrets are spilled. To try to control information, Apple will give contract manufacturers different products, just to try them out. That way, the source of any leaks becomes immediately obvious.

Apple's obsession with secrecy is the stuff of legend in Silicon Valley. Over the years, it has fired executives over leaks and sued bloggers to stop trade secrets from being exposed. Apple also helps keep its components out of the mainstream by insist-ing on custom designs rather than off-the-shelf parts – a practice that leaves many suppliers frustrated. Not surprisingly, landing a contract with Apple will always include a confidentiality clause. And they usually come with stiff penalties in the event that a breach is discovered. Such agreements often come on top of unannounced checks by Apple officials to maintain standards. However, the difficulty lies in proving the source of a leak. In the absence of solid evidence, the most Apple can do is to switch suppliers once the contract runs out. At times all of this secrecy seems to run out of control. In a case that made global headlines, a Foxconn employee in China was believed to have jumped to his death after being interrogated by his employer. According to local press reports, he was under suspicion of taking an iPhone prototype – to which he had access – out of the factory (Watts, 2010).

Conclusions

The success of the Apple iPod, and to a lesser extent the iPhone, has been remarkable by any measure. It has surprised Apple's competitors but, moreover, it has surprised market analysts and investors, who had largely believed Apple was a niche player in the com-puter world. To be successful in the mainstream mass market is unusual for Apple. Many people recognise the Apple brand, but far fewer buy its products. Profit margins are small for its range of PCs and laptops; this is why it is difficult for Apple to produce any revenue from the iMac despite its success. Indeed, it is the iPod that has delivered the cash for Apple.

Apple has been here before, 20 years ago in fact. The success of the Apple Mac in 1984 delivered piles of cash for Apple and a rising market share of the growing PC market, yet it was Microsoft that emerged the winner largely because it licensed its operating system to all PC manufacturers, whereas Apple decided against this approach, opting instead to stay in control of its system. Microsoft has gone on to be the dominant software company in the world.

In 2010 Apple's iPod/iPod Touch is the leading digital music player, but should it license its success-ful technology? There are certainly lots of mobile phone handset manufacturers that would like to incorporate iPod/iPhone technology into their prod-ucts. And there are many electronic companies such as Sony, Sharp, Cannon and others that would be able to develop digital music players using iPod tech-nology. It may be that Apple feels the technology, in this case the software, is an integral part of the physical product and that to separate the aesthetics of the music player/phone from the software would damage the brand, leading to a commoditisation of the digital music player market and an overall decline in the iPod and iPhone. Furthermore, margins are relatively good for Apple and licensing the technology would surely mean increased competition and reduced margins.

Apple, once best known for its Macintosh com-puters, and now known for its iPod, iPhone and its iTune online Music Store is as last making up for its lack of market gains in the highly competitive PC market. It is necessary to remind students of busi-ness that ultimately this is about money and Apple was twice the size of Microsoft in 1992 and since then has largely failed to deliver growth for its share-holders. It is only in the past few years that Apple has started to repay investors, reaching an equivalent market value of Microsoft in 2010. Fortunes change quickly in technology intensive industries, but they change even quicker in the world of fashion.

Sources: Coggan, P. (2005) iPod's popularity fires Apple back into FT500 ranks, *Financial Times*, 11 June; Durman, P. (2005) A second bite of Apple, *Sunday Times*, Business, 25 September, p. 5; Inman, P. (2005) Fraudsters use iPods to steal company information, *Guardian*, 14 June; Morrison, S. (2005) Wall St wants Apple to raise iPod volume, FT.com, 12 July; Schofield, J. (2005) Microsoft gets creative to stave off its midlife crisis, *Technology Guardian*, 29 September, p. 9; Webb, A. (2007) The end of the road for DRM, *Technology Guardian*, 8 February, p. 10; Pomfret, J. and Soh, K. (2010) For Apple suppliers loose lips can sink con-tracts, Reuters, 17 February; Watts, J. (2010) iPhone factory offers pay rises and suicide nets as fears grow over spate of deaths, *Guardian*, 29 May, p. 30; Schonfeld, E. (2009) iTunes Sells 6 Billion Songs, And Other Fun Stats, from The Philnote, Techcrunch, http://techcrunch.com, 6 January.

Questions

1 Explain how the iPod is helping Apple achieve increased sales of its range of Mac personal computers.

2 What are the potential benefits and limitations of licensing the iPod software to other MP3 manufacturers?

3 With sales of the iPod falling and Apple facing fierce competition from all quarters such as Sony, Dell and other electronics firms as well as mobile phone makers who are incorporating MP3 players into their devices, can the iPod survive?

4 If Open Innovation has been so successful for Procter & Gamble and others, why is Apple not adopting this model of innovation?

5 Can Apple continue to be successful in the long term by adopting a 'BMW strategy' (BMW strategy is to target high-premium segments) for its iPod, iPhone and iPad?

6 What are the advantages and disadvantages of the Apple approach to launching a new product at Apple users first and then the larger Microsoft Windows user audience second?

7 Discuss whether Apple's demands for secrecy from its suppliers may have gone too far.

Chapter summary

This initial chapter has sought to introduce the subject of innovation management and place it in context with the theory of economic growth. One can quickly become ensnarled in stale academic debates of semantics if innovation is viewed as a single event, hence the importance of viewing it as a process. The chapter has also stressed the importance of understanding how firms manage innovation and how this can be better achieved by adopting a management perspective.

The level of understanding of the subject of innovation has improved significantly over the past half century and during that time a variety of models of innovation have emerged. The strengths and weaknesses of these were examined and a conceptual framework was presented that stressed the linkages and overlaps between internal departments and external organisations.

Discussion questions

1 Explain why it is necessary to view innovation as a management process.

2 What is wrong with the popular view of innovation in which eccentric scientists develop new products?

3 How does an 'Open Innovation' approach help firms?

4 What is the difference between an unsuccessful innovation and an invention?

5 To what extent do you agree with the controversial view presented by the chairman of Sony?

6 Show how the three forces shaping the twenty-first century, according to Salkowitz (2010) – youth, entrepreneurship and ICT – are captured in the cyclical model of innovation.

7 Explain Sergey Brin's (co-founder of Google) comment that coming up with an idea is easy, but innovation is difficult.

Key words and phrases

Economic growth *6*

Organisational architecture *9*

Entrepreneurship *9*

Invention *15*

Innovation as a management process *15*

Models of innovation *20*

Resource-based theory of the firm *21*

Open innovation *25*

Discontinuous innovation *27*

References

Abernathy, W.J. and Utterback, J. (1978) 'Patterns of industrial innovation', in Tushman, M.L. and Moore, W.L. *Readings in the Management of Innovation*, HarperCollins, New York, 97–108.

Berkhout, A.J. (2000) *The Dynamic Role of Knowledge in Innovation. An Integrated Framework of Cyclic Networks for the Assessment of Technological Change and Sustainable Growth*, Delft University Press, Delft, The Netherlands, 2000.

Berkhout, A.J., Hartmann, D. and Trott, P. (2010) Connecting technological capabilities with market needs using a cyclic innovation model, *R&D Management*, Vol. 40, No. 5, 474–90.

BSI (2008) *Design Management Systems*, Guides to Managing Innovation, British Standards Institute, London.

Burns, T. and Stalker, G.M. (1961) *The Management of Innovation*, Tavistock, London.

Business Week (2006) The world's most innovative firms, 24 April.

Carter, C.F. and Williams, B.R. (1957) The characteristics of technically progressive firms, *Journal of Industrial Economics*, March, 87–104.

Chandler, A.D. (1962) *Strategy and Structure: Chapters in the History of American Industrial Enterprise*, MIT Press, Cambridge, MA.

Chesbrough, H. (2003) *Open Innovation: The new imperative for creating and profiting from technology*, Harvard Business School Press, Boston, MA.

Christensen, C.M. (2003) *The Innovator's Dilemma: When New Technologies Cause Great Firms to Fail*, 3rd edn, HBS Press, Cambridge, MA.

Christensen, C. M. and Raynor, M.E. (2003) *Six Keys to Creating New-Growth Businesses*, Harvard Business School Press, Boston, MA.

Cohen, W.M. and Levinthal, D.A. (1990) A new perspective on learning and innovation, *Administrative Science Quarterly*, Vol. 35, No. 1, 128–52.

Conner, K.R. and Prahalad, C.K. (1996) A resource-based theory of the firm: knowledge versus opportunism, *Organisation Science*, Vol. 7, No. 5, 477–501.

Cooper, R. (1994) Third generation new product processes, *Journal of Product Innovation Management*, Vol. 11, No. 1, 3–14.

Cullen, B. (2003) *It's a long way from penny apples*, Coronet, London.

Cyert, R.M. and March, J.G. (1963) *A Behavioural Theory of the Firm*, Prentice-Hall, Englewood Cliffs, NJ.

Delbridge, R. and Mariotti, F. (2009) *Reaching for radical innovation: How motorsport companies harness network diversity for discontinuous innovation*, Advanced Institute of Management Research (AIM), London.

Dodgson, M., Gann, D. and Salter, A. (2005) *Think, Play, Do*, Oxford University Press, Oxford.

Domar, D. (1946) Capital expansion, rate of growth and employment, *Econometra*, Vol. 14, 137–47.

Eisenhardt, K.M. and Martin, J.A. (2000) 'The knowledge-based economy: from the economics of knowledge to the learning economy', in Foray, D. and Lundvall, B.-A. (eds) *Employment and Growth in the Knowledge-Based Economy*, OECD, Paris.

Fagerberg, J. and Verspagen, B. (2009) Innovation studies – The emerging structure of a new scientific field, *Research Policy*, Vol. 38, No. 2, 218–33.

Freeman, C. (1982) *The Economics of Industrial Innovation*, 2nd edn, Frances Pinter, London.

Galbraith, J.R. (1982) Designing the innovative organisation, *Organisational Dynamics*, Winter, 3–24.

Grant, R.M. (1996) Towards a knowledge-based theory of the firm, *Strategic Management Journal*, Summer Special Issue, Vol. 17, 109–22.

Guardian (2009) Interview with Technology Guardian, 18 June, p. 1.

Hamel, G. and Prahalad, C.K. (1994) Competing for the future, *Harvard Business Review*, Vol. 72, No. 4, 122–8.

Hargadon, A. and Douglas, Y. (2001) When innovations meet institutions: Edison and the design of the electric light, *Administrative Science Quarterly*, Vol. 46, 476–501.

Harrod, R.F. (1949) An essay in dynamic theory, *Economic Journal*, Vol. 49, No. 1, 277–93.

Henderson, R. and Clark, K. (1990) Architectural innovation: the reconfiguration of existing product and the failure of established firms, *Administrative Science Quarterly*, Vol. 35, 9–30.

Hutton, W. (1995) *The State We're In*, Jonathan Cape, London.

Isenson, R. (1968) 'Technology in retrospect and critical events in science' (Project Traces), Illinois Institute of Technology/National Science Foundation, Chicago, IL.

Kondratieff, N.D. (1935/51) 'The long waves in economic life', *Review of Economic Statistics*, Vol. 17, 6–105 (1935), reprinted in Haberler, G. (ed.) *Readings in Business Cycle Theory*, Richard D. Irwin, Homewood, IL (1951).

Langrish, J., Gibbons, M., Evans, W.G. and Jevons, F.R. (1972) *Wealth from Knowledge*, Macmillan, London.

Lefever, D.B. (1992) 'Technology transfer and the role of intermediaries', PhD thesis, INTA, Cranfield Institute of Technology.

Leifer, R., Colarelli O'Connor, G. and Peters, L.S. (2000) *Radical Innovation*, Harvard Business School Press, Boston, MA.

Linton, J. (2009) De-babelizing the language of innovation, *Technovation*, Vol. 29, No. 11, 729–37.

Morita, A. (1992) 'S' does not equal 'T' and 'T' does not equal 'I', paper presented at the Royal Society, February 1992.

Murray, S. (2003) 'Innovation: A British talent for ingenuity and application', www.ft.com, 22 April.

Myers, S. and Marquis, D.G. (1969) 'Successful industrial innovation: a study of factors underlying innovation in selected firms', National Science Foundation, NSF 69–17, Washington, DC.

Nelson, R.R. and Winter, S. (1982) *An Evolutionary Theory of Economic Change*, Harvard University Press, Boston, MA.

Nonaka, I. (1991) The knowledge creating company, *Harvard Business Review*, November–December, 96–104.

Oxford English Dictionary (2005) Oxford University Press, London.

Patel, P. and Pavitt, K. (2000) 'How technological competencies help define the core (not the boundaries) of the firm', in Dosi, G., Nelson, R. and Winter, S.G. (eds) *The Nature and Dynamics of Organisational Capabilities*, Oxford University Press, Oxford, 313–33.

Pavitt, K. (1990) What we know about the strategic management of technology, *California Management Review*, Vol. 32, No. 3, 17–26.

Penrose, E.T. (1959) *The Theory of the Growth of the Firm*, Wiley, New York.

Pittaway, L., Robertson, M., Munir, K., Denyer, D. and Neely, A. (2004) Networking and innovation: a systematic review of the evidence, *International Journal of Management Reviews*, Vol. 5/6, Nos 3 and 4, 137–68.

Porter, M.E. (1980) *Competitive Strategy*, The Free Press, New York.

Porter, M.E. (1985) *Competitive Strategy*, Harvard University Press, Boston, MA.

Prahalad, C.K. and Hamel, G. (1990) The core competence of the corporation, *Harvard Business Review*, Vol. 68, No. 3, 79–91.

Rogers, E. and Shoemaker, R. (1972) *Communications of Innovations*, Free Press, New York.

Rothwell, R. (1992) Successful industrial innovation: critical factors for the 1990s, *R&D Management*, Vol. 22, No. 3, 221–39.

Rothwell, R. and Zegveld, W. (1985) *Reindustrialisation and Technology*, Longman, London.

Rothwell, R., Freeman, C., Horlsey, A., Jervis, V.T.P., Robertson, A.B. and Townsend, J. (1974) SAPPHO updated: Project SAPPHO phase II, *Research Policy*, Vol. 3, 258–91.

Salkowitz, R. (2010) *Young World Rising: How youth technology and entrepreneurship are changing the world from the bottom up*, John Wiley & Sons, NJ.

Schrange, M. (2000) *Serious Play – How the world's best companies stimulate to innovate*, Harvard Business School Press, Boston, MA.

Schumpeter, J.A. (1934) *The Theory of Economic Development*, Harvard University Press, Boston, MA.

Schumpeter, J.A. (1939) *Business Cycles*, McGraw-Hill, New York.

Schumpeter, J.A. (1942) *Capitalism, Socialism and Democracy*, Allen & Unwin, London.

Simon, H. (1957) *Administrative Behaviour*, Free Press, New York.

Slater, S.F. and Narver, J. (1994) Does competitive environment moderate the market orientation performance relationship? *Journal of Marketing*, Vol. 58 (January), 46–55.

Stevenson, H.H. and Amabile, T.M. (1999) 'Entrepreneurial Management: In Pursuit of Opportunity', in McCraw, T.K. and Cruikshank, J.L. (eds) *The Intellectual Venture Capitalist: John H. McArthur and the Work of the Harvard Business School, 1980–1995*, Harvard Business School Press, Boston, MA.

Thomke, S.H. (2003) *Experimentation Matters: Unlocking the potential of new technologies for innovation*, Harvard Business School Press, Boston, MA.

Trott, P. (1998) Growing businesses by generating genuine business opportunities, *Journal of Applied Management Studies*, Vol. 7, No. 4, 211–22.

Utterback, J. (1994) *Mastering the Dynamics of Innovation*, Harvard Business School Press, Boston, MA.

Van de Ven, A.H. (1989) *The Innovation Journey*, Oxford University Press, New York.

van der Panne, G. van Beers, C. and Kleinknecht, A. (2003) Success and failure of innovation: A review of the literature, *International Journal of Innovation Management*, Vol. 7, No. 3, 309–38.

von Hippel, E. (1978) Users as innovators, *Technology Review*, Vol. 80, No. 3, 30–4.

von Hippel, E. (2005) *Democratizing Innovation*, MIT Press, Cambridge, MA.

Wernerfelt, B. (1984) A resource based view of the firm, *Strategic Management Journal*, Vol. 5, No. 2, 171–80.

Wernerfelt, B. (1995) The resource-based view of the firm: ten years after, *Strategic Management Journal*, Vol. 16, No. 3, 171–4.

Wheelwright, S. and Clark, K. (1992) *Revolutionising Product Development*, The Free Press, New York.

Woodward, J. (1965) *Industrial Organisation: Theory and Practice*, 2nd edn, Oxford University Press, Oxford.

Further reading

For a more detailed review of the innovation management literature, the following develop many of the issues raised in this chapter:

Adams, R., Bessant, J. and Phelps, R. (2006) Innovation management measurement: A review, *International Journal of Management Reviews*, Vol. 8, No. 1, 21–47.

Berkhout, A.J., Hartmann, D. and Trott, P. (2010) Connecting technological capabilities with market needs using a cyclic innovation model, *R&D Management*, Vol. 40, No. 5, 474–90.

Evans, H. (2005) The Eureka Myth, *Harvard Business Review*, 83, June, 18–20.

Linton, J. (2009) De-babelizing the language of innovation, *Technovation*, Vol. 29, No. 11, 729–37.

Salkowitz, R. *Young World Rising: How youth technology and entrepreneurship are changing the world from the bottom up*, John Wiley & Sons, NJ.

Shavinina, L.V. (ed.) (2003) *The International Handbook on Innovation*, Elsevier, Oxford.

Tidd, J., Bessant, J. and Pavitt, K. (2009) *Managing Innovation*, 4th edn, John Wiley & Sons, Chichester.

Chapter 2
Economics and market adoption

Introduction

This chapter explores the wider context in which the process of innovation occurs and also explores how national governments can help firms. The national systems of innovation have for many years been exploring what factors influence a nation's ability to undertake innovation. The United States, in particular, is frequently cited as a good example of a nation where the necessary conditions for innovation to flourish are in place. This includes both tangible and intangible features, including, on the one hand, economic, social and political institutions and, on the other, the way in which knowledge evolves over time through developing interactions and networks. This chapter examines how these influence innovation.

The role of the market within the wider context of innovation is ever-present; hence this chapter explores this key challenge within innovation. The relationship between new technology and the market is examined within the diffusion of innovations and market adoption.

The case study at the end of this chapter tells the story of how three university students had an idea for a folding shipping container and went about building a business. One of the key problems they faced was how to get the industry to adopt a new container.

Chapter contents

Learning objectives

When you have completed this chapter you will be able to:

- understand the wider context of innovation and the key influences;

- recognise that innovation cannot be separated from its local and national context and from political and social processes;

- understand that the role of national states considerably influences innovation;

- identify the structures and activities that the state uses to facilitate innovation;

- recognise the role marketing plays in the early stages of product innovation;

- explain how market vision helps the innovation process; and

- understand how the pattern of consumption influences the likely success or failure of a new product.

Innovation in its wider context

According to many, the process of innovation is the main engine of (continued) economic growth. As far back as 1943 Joseph Schumpeter (in what is known as Schumpeterian theory) emphasised that:

the fundamental impulse that sets and keeps the capitalist engine in motion comes from the new consumers' goods, the new methods of production or transportation, the new markets, the new forces of industrial organisation that capitalist enterprise creates.

(1943: 10)

However, such potential to create new products, processes, markets or organisations are path-dependent in the sense that there are certain nations and locations which seem to have acquired that capability over time, for innovation relies upon the accumulation and development of a wide variety of relevant knowledge (Dicken, 1998).

The view that much needs to be in place for innovation to occur and that there is a significant role for the state is confirmed by Alfred Marshall, whose ideas were responsible for the rebuilding of Europe after the Second World War. He commented on both the tangible and intangible aspects of the Industrial Revolution and suggested that 'the secrets of Industry are in the air'. Marshall (cited in Dicken, 1998: 20) recognised a number of characteristics that influenced innovation:

- the institutional set-up;
- the relationship between the entrepreneurs and financiers;
- society's perception of new developments;
- the openness to science and technology;
- networks between scientific and academic communities and business circles;
- the productive forces and financial institutions;
- the growing liberal–individualist economic paradigm;
- the role played by the state in accommodating and promoting capitalistic changes and preparing the framework for the development of capitalism.

The process of innovation has so far been treated as an organisational issue. We have seen, and will continue to see over the course of the book, that within the organisation, management of the innovation process is an extremely demanding discipline, for converting a basic discovery into a commercial product, process or service is a long-term, high-risk, complex, interactive and non-linear sequence. However, the capability of organisations in initiating and sustaining innovation is to a great extent determined by the wider local and national context within which they operate. This is essentially why 'innovation within' requires a favourable 'context outside'. That is, economic and social conditions will play a major role in whether the organisations or corporate actors will take the risk and establish the longer-term vision that innovation is key to competitiveness, survival and sustained growth. To get a better understanding of this, it is necessary to 'look out of the window' at the business environment in which economic actors strive to get an upper hand in the marketplace in a mix of competition and cooperation through network, market and hierarchical relations. This notion is reinforced by the interactions between the organisation and the external environment, which is emphasised in Figure 1.7.

Much can be learned from glancing at recent history. The development of science and technology in the West opened a wide gap between the so-called industrialised nations and their followers, 'late-industrialisers'. Late-industrialisers refer to countries with no or limited indigenous technology development capacity. Some states, including Japan and some east Asian countries, have managed to close that gap with strategies that focus mainly on industrialisation. In these countries, economic growth was achieved through imitation by diffusion of technology, development of new technology and efforts to develop their own capacities. So the cycle that began with imitation was later turned into a creative and broader basis upon which economic transformation could be achieved. This transformation required continual efforts by entrepreneurs and businesses and a collaborative framework promoted by the state. However, to reach maturity in today's economy, i.e. to be able to create high-value-added and knowledge-based products and services, would appear to be a gigantic task for the states and societies of the latecomers. Apart from its regulatory and redistribution functions, the state must play a significant role through strategic intervention into infrastructure development and technological capacity formation as well as into human capital formation.

This wider view of the economic environment is referred to as *integral economics*, where the economic processes are viewed in their social and political entirety. As pointed out by Dicken (1998: 50), 'technology is a social process which is socially and institutionally embedded'. In this context, it would be useful to remind ourselves that innovation cannot be separated from its local and national (as well as global) contexts and from political and social processes, let alone main economic trends.

Given the nature of 'the game', however, there is always the risk that entrepreneurs and businesses may only focus on high-return opportunities in the short term, marginalise strategic and innovative perspective and ignore the long-term implications of such behaviour (as will be seen in Chapter 14). Economies dominated by this type of philosophy will have serious difficulties in moving beyond commercial activities (that is, in current popular business discourse, 'moving boxes'). This so called 'short-termism' has characterised the economy of Turkey which, despite its strategic geographic position, has failed to develop significantly. In this context, we find that the businesses themselves and the business philosophy were progressively created by the Republican state within a modernist approach only to observe that the so-called entrepreneurs opted to become rich rather than entrepreneurs. So, the act of 'business-making' was only undertaken on the surface; and policy changes such as liberalisation only led the entrepreneurs and businesses to seek their ends in the short run with no calculated risk-taking in business. Thus, business in Turkey developed its own weakness by becoming dependent on the weaknesses of the Turkish state, e.g. using high and growing budget deficits as a money-making opportunity. In this chapter, we will try to highlight why the situation for economies such as the Turkish economy remain unchanged, while some societies and economies enjoyed sustained growth over several decades and have become powerful players in the global economy.

Pause for thought

For Schumpeter, the idea of being entrepreneurial was not simply buying something cheap and selling it for a quick profit. It was bound up with new products and new methods of production; by implication it was long term rather than short term in nature. Is our understanding of entrepreneurship different now?

The role of the state and national 'systems' of innovation

To support our understanding of the process of innovation within the capitalist enterprise we must also grasp a basic understanding of the way the economy inter-relates with global and regional economies on local and national levels. Not only do national economies tend to be dominated by a form of economic organisation (e.g. the *Chaebol* in South Korea or *Keiretsu* in Japan), it is also the case that the relationship between state and business differs radically from one national space to the other. Such interrelationships in society generate a business environment with a unique business value system, attitude and ethic. Historically, this difference created advantages and disadvantages for business organisation across a range of activities, the most important of which may be perceived as the process of innovation. This would seem to be the case given the crucial role played by innovation in the history of capitalism.

The answer to the question of whether there is a role for the state in the process of innovation has been addressed in different contexts (e.g. Porter, 1990; Afuah, 2003). The literature on the subject has attracted attention to the following points, where state action may be necessary:

1 *The 'public' nature of knowledge that underpins innovation.* This refers to the role that can be played by the government in the process of idea generation and its subsidisation and distribution. This way, economic actors may be stimulated to work on new ideas, alongside state organisations, and may endeavour to convert such ideas into marketable goods or services. For instance, by granting intellectual property rights to producers of knowledge and by establishing the necessary legal infrastructure to support those rights, the state may promote knowledge generation.

2 *The uncertainty that often hinders the process of innovation.* Macroeconomic, technological or market uncertainties may hinder innovation. When the companies are risk-averse in investing funds in innovation projects, then the state may promote such activities through subsidising, providing tax advantages and supporting firms to join R&D projects. Forming a stable economic environment, where funds could be extended by the banking system to productive firms, also creates a favourable long-term perspective, for one of the first preconditions of strategy making is economic stability. Thus, expectations of low inflation, low interest rates and stable growth will encourage firms to invest in entrepreneurial activity (particularly given that other areas, e.g. portfolio investments, are less profitable to invest in).

3 *The need for certain kinds of complementary assets.* Provision of electricity, roads and water has historically assisted industrial development; recently, the establishment of communication systems (e.g. communication superhighways), legal infrastructure and the formation of industrial districts have been issues where state action has led to favourable outcomes with tangible and intangible conditions created for enterprises.

4 *The need for cooperation and governance, resulting from the nature of certain technologies.* For the development of possible networks, which will enhance and promote the diffusion of new technologies and innovations, the state may set the vision and enhance the possibilities for better communication and joint decision making. In the United Kingdom the government is providing funds (through

education and promotion) to encourage households to switch from analogue television signal to a digital television signal. Such action helps countries/society to upgrade from one old established technology to a newer improved technology.

5 *Politics*. Lastly, in terms of politics, national states still have a key role in foreseeing and contributing to international and regional standards of business making within the system of 'national states' and in creating consent and cohesion in the national arena among domestic forces. Such standards are increasingly becoming environmental, safety and human rights standards in industrial or business activities. The German government has an impressive record of being at the forefront of introducing legislation in automobile safety and environmental recycling which has contributed to Germany becoming a world leader in these two industries.

How national states can facilitate innovation

Figure 2.1 highlights the possible roles that can be played by national states. It takes Porter's industry attractiveness framework and develops the role the state can play in relation to innovation. It underlines a firm's relationship with the buyers, factor conditions (e.g. labour, capital, raw materials), related and supporting industries (e.g. technology providers, input providers, etc.) and other institutions that help facilitate strategic orientation and innovative capabilities. These will determine to a great extent the firm's opportunities – notwithstanding the fact that its inner strengths, i.e. its strategy-making capabilities and structural features, will clearly affect this potential.

As a financier of R&D and major purchaser, the state has a significant impact on strategic direction towards critical industries and encouraging entrepreneurial spirit. For instance, in 1995, the United States committed to a budget for R&D spending of $71.4 billion, which was spent on defence, health, space, general science, energy,

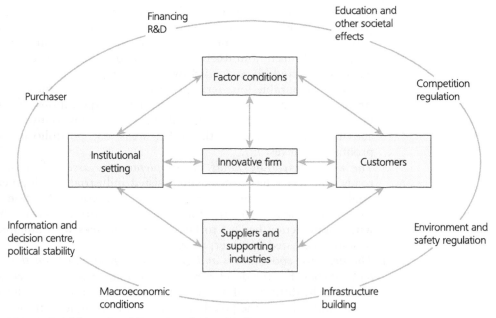

Figure 2.1 **The role of the state in innovation**

transportation, environment and agriculture. Most of the funds went to industrial research laboratories, universities, non-profit laboratories and federally funded research R&D centres. There are also indirect ways of financing R&D, such as tax exemptions, subsidies, loan guarantees, export credits and forms of protection. For example, Boeing paid no taxes between 1970 and 1984, and also received a tax refund amounting to $285 million (Afuah, 2003). As a major purchaser, the state will also reduce uncertainty and create favourable cash flows for firms by its willingness to pay higher (monopolistic) prices for early models.

Through education, information dissemination, governance and other societal actions, the state can impact upon the way the society perceives discoveries and adapts new technologies at the same time as creating cohesion in the society and making strategic interventions to promote, for instance, the formation of a highly qualified workforce. Interdependency between state and society may create a favourable national culture which welcomes scientific development, and removes the potential for conflict between leading sectors and traditional sectors, economic interests and social forces and cultural traditions and new trends. By incubating a form of unity between state and society, the state may set in motion an overall vision and dynamic in the society and for the industry.

Regulation of competition is another critical area for the reproduction/expansion of the capitalist system, as the state can promote the system by preventing monopolies that can result in under-innovation and by protecting the society against possible abuse by companies. Microsoft's very high profile antitrust case with the European Union (EU) is a good illustration (*see* Illustration 2.1). A summary of the complex way in which the state can impact upon the behaviour of capitalist firms and how they manage their economic and social relationships is shown in Figure 2.1.

Fostering innovation in the United States and Japan

Although local characteristics also play a very significant role in the innovation process, the overall tendencies of nations and nation states are linked to success on a very local level. While some states, such as Japan, provided extensive support and subsidies to promote industrial innovation, others, such as the United States, have aimed to create positive effects in the economy by letting the market achieve the most efficient allocation of resources with minimal possible intervention. The so-called Chicago School paradigm for promoting competitiveness and innovation, which created a belief in the free market to maximise innovation and productivity (Rosenthal, 1993), has, for more than two decades, been the dominant perspective in the United States. At this instance, we can cite the impact on the industry of public R&D with such expected transformative effects as provided by the internet's later commercial application, initially a military project initiated by the state. In fact, the United States is leading the way in performing half of the world's basic research, making most of the seminal discoveries, thanks to the trillion-dollar investment in US universities and government laboratories.

In the case of more interventionist states, incentives were provided either as direct support (e.g. subsidies, location provision, etc.) or in the form of 'governance', assuming a coordinating and leading role in the management of innovation projects. In this instance governance refers to the efforts at creating cohesion and complementarity, which are directed to the realisation of a joint objective that is deemed to be mutually beneficial to the various parties involved. A good example of the latter was the role played by the Japanese state in bringing universities, state organisations (primarily the Ministry of International Trade and Industry (MITI)), sector organisations and business enterprises together for research on the development of the Trinitron television (a technology that dominated home electronics for more than two decades) with financial support attached. Although the Japanese model has come under severe criticism, particularly by Porter *et al.* (2000), as a result of the recent economic slowdown, the weaknesses mainly attributed to the lack of concern for strategy in Japanese companies and being stuck in between two competitive strategies of cost and quality, as well as low profitability, the success of the model has been long acknowledged (*see*, for instance, Johnson, 1982; Hart, 1992; Castells, 1992). In the case of innovation, governance requires the establishment of a proper framework for the smooth flow of knowledge between universities, state institutions, private sector organisations and corporations until the end result takes some form of a marketable commodity. In this framework, while some economies are better placed with innovation capabilities, some are at a disadvantage because of their characteristics.

Illustration 2.1

Brussels threatens Microsoft with further antitrust fines

Microsoft was yesterday dealt a serious setback in its long-running antitrust battle with the European Commission, when Brussels threatened to impose yet another massive fine on the US software group for failing to comply with a landmark competition ruling handed down almost three years ago.

Europe's top antitrust regulator yesterday issued a new set of charges against Microsoft, a step that is likely to result in another ruling and a new fine against the group. Since the Commission opened its probe against the world's largest software maker more than eight years ago, Microsoft has been fined close to €780 million (£526 million) for abusing its dominant market position and failing to respect the regulator's ruling.

The Commission refused to comment on the size of any new fine that could arise from yesterday's charges. However, Brussels could – in the worst-case scenario for Microsoft – hit the group with a penalty in excess of €800 million. The Commission accused Microsoft of demanding excessive royalties from companies wishing to license technical information about its Windows operating system. The order to make such information available to rivals formed a key plank of the Commission's March 2004 ruling against the group.

The Commission stressed that Microsoft was the first group to be accused of ignoring a European Union antitrust ruling. 'This is a company which apparently does not like to have to conform with antitrust decisions', said the spokesman for Neelie Kroes, the EU competition commissioner. Brad Smith, Microsoft's general counsel, rejected the Commission's allegations. He said Microsoft's proposed pricing scheme would be 30 per cent cheaper than comparable licensing fees.

Under the terms of the 2004 ruling, Microsoft has to make available 'interoperability' information to other software makers so that rivals can design server software that functions smoothly with Windows-driven computers and servers. The Commission said yesterday it had found 'no significant innovation in the interoperability information'. It also claimed that companies were being asked to give Microsoft 35 per cent of the net operating profits they made by selling products designed with the help of the licence.

The original 2004 ruling is under appeal in front of an EU court, which is expected to issue its ruling in the next six months.

Source: Tobias Buck, *Financial Times*, 2 March 2007. Reprinted with permission.

The concept of 'developmental states' is used to show the way in which some states achieved a major transformation of the economy and society. At the other end of the spectrum there are the 'predatory states', which capture most of the funds in the economy and reallocate them in the form of rents to a small group of the population, thus impeding the growth potential in the state (Evans, 1989). This development was found in particular to be a major characteristic of some east Asian states, especially the so-called Tigers of Korea, Taiwan, Singapore and Hong Kong (Castells, 1992). Although such states were not immune to corruption, fraud and other forms of inefficiency, they brought about major changes in the economy, particularly in upgrading the potential of the industry from imitation towards innovation and technology development, which is by no means an easy task.

Pause for thought

Is it true that in a developed market economy the role of the state is a minor one? Why is it *not* surprising that many consumer products such as in-car satellite navigational guidance, mobile telephones and computers have their origins in defence research?

The right business environment is key to innovation

Schumpeter preached technology as the engine of growth but also noted that to invest in technology there had to be spare resources and long time-horizons. So the business environment must give the 'right' signals to the business units for them to invest in such operations. In this regard, not only does macroeconomic stability play a significant role but also the availability of quick (short-term) returns and opportunistic trends needs to be suppressed so that the money can flow into basic research and R&D. Likewise, the approach of business would differ if it faced strong (external or internal) competition. A protected domestic market more often than not amounts to signalling to business units that they should seek monopolistic or oligopolistic returns by not making enough investment into new product development or even product improvement.

The next chapter explores the organisational characteristics that need to be in place for innovation to occur. From the preceding discussion one can already begin to see what these characteristics might be.

Waves of innovation and growth: historical overview

When we investigate the history of capitalist development, there is a pattern of economic growth. The work of Kondratieff and Schumpeter has been influential in identifying the major stages of this development. The five waves, or growth cycles, are identified in Figure 2.2. This highlights that technological developments and innovations have a strong spatial dimension; however, leadership in one wave is not necessarily maintained in the succeeding waves. So one can observe shifts in the

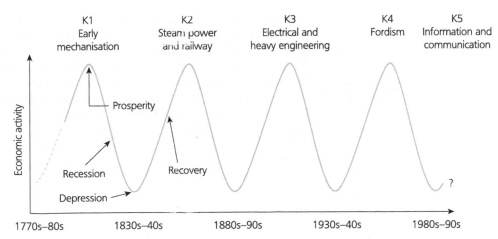

Figure 2.2 **Kondratieff waves of growth and their main features**

geography of innovation through time. The leaders of the first wave were Britain, France and Belgium. The second wave brought new players into the game, namely the United States and Germany. Wave three saw the strengthening of the positions of the United States and Germany. In wave four, Japan and Sweden joined the technology and innovation race. More recently, in wave five, Taiwan and South Korea are becoming key players in the global economy.

In these Kondratieff waves, the capitalist economy grew on the basis of major innovations in product, process and organisation with accompanying shifts in the social arena. Kuhn's theory on the nature of scientific revolutions has been justified: each wave comes to an end due to its major shortcomings and the successive wave fundamentally restructures and improves those weaknesses. Each major phase of innovation produced a 'star' industry or industry branch, which seemed to affect the way the economy was organised. The leap forward provided by such industry(ies) resulted in a major transformation of the economy and economic relations – given that other factors such as demand, finance, industrial and social conditions were favourable. Products, processes and organisations created by technological development became universal and cheaply available to a vast population, which, in turn, created the economic shift. These Kondratieff waves took place in the order of early mechanisation, steam power and railways, electrical and heavy engineering, 'Fordism' (i.e. use of mass-production methods), and information and communication. The last of these waves is currently underway with what is now termed the information revolution. Almost every day we are presented with a number of 'new' ways in which we can do business, search for information, communicate and socialise with other people or carry out our bank operations. This means that the new developments deeply affect not only economic relations but also our private (home and relations) and work (public) spheres.

In the very first Kondratieff wave, the rise of the factory and mechanisation in textiles was only part of the story. The need to produce in greater quantities to start serving the growing overseas markets with the improved transport methods now available was complemented by the abundance of finance with the money flowing in from the colonies, particularly the United States. Universally and cheaply available input (i.e. cotton), improving nationwide transport infrastructure (with rising

Table 2.1 Characteristics of the five waves of growth

	Wave 1	Wave 2	Wave 3	Wave 4	Wave 5
Main branches	Textiles Textile machinery Iron working Water power Pottery	Steam engines Steamships Machine tools Iron and steel Railway equipment	Electrical engineering Electrical machinery Cable and wire Heavy engineering Steel ships Heavy chemicals	Automobiles Trucks/tractors/ planes Consumer durables Process plant Synthetic materials Petrochemicals	Computers Electronic capital goods Telecommunications Robotics Information services
Universal and cheap key factors	Cotton	Coal, iron	Steel; electricity	Oil; plastics	Gas; oil; microelectronics
Infrastructure	Trunk canals Turnpike roads	Railways Shipping	Electricity supply and distribution	Highways; airports/ airlines	Digital networks; satellites
Limitations of previous technoeconomic paradigm; solutions	Limitations of scale, process control and mechanisation in 'putting out' system; solutions offered through mechanisation and factory organisation towards productivity and profitability	Limitations of water power: inflexibility of location, scale of production, reliability; solutions offered through steam engine and transport system	Limitations of iron as an engineering material (strength, durability, precision, etc.) overcome by steel and alloys; limitations of steam engine overcome by unit and group electrical machinery, power tools, permitting layout improvement and capital saving; standardisation	Limitations of batch production overcome by flow processes and assembly line; full standardisation and replaceability of components and materials; universal availability and cheapening of mass consumption goods	Inflexibility of dedicated assembly line and process plant overcome by flexible manufacturing systems, networking and economies of scope; electronic control systems and networking provide for necessitated flexibility
Organisation of firms	Individual entrepreneurs and small firms (<100 employees); partnership between technical innovators and financial circles	Small firms dominate but large firms and large markets emerge; limited liability and joint stock companies emerge	Emergence of giant firms, cartels, trusts, mergers; regulation of or state ownership of natural monopolies; concentration of finance and banking capital; emergence of middle management	Oligopolistic competition; TNCs; 'arm's-length' subcontracting or vertical integration; bureaucratic control and bureaucratisation	Networks of large and small firms based increasingly on computers; trust-based networks with close cooperation in technology, quality control, training and production planning (e.g. JIT)
Geographical focus	Britain, France, Belgium	Britain, France, Belgium, Germany, United States	Germany, United States, Britain, France, Belgium, The Netherlands, Switzerland	United States, Germany, other EU, Japan, Switzerland, other EFTA, Canada, Australia	Japan, United States, Canada, Germany, Sweden, other EU and EFTA, Taiwan, Korea

Note: EFTA, European Free Trade Association; JIT, just-in-time; TNC, transnational corporation.

Source: Reproduced and adapted from P. Dicken (1998) *Global Shift: Transforming the World Economy*, Paul Chapman, London (a Sage Publications company); C. Freeman and L. Soete (1997) *The Economics of Industrial Innovation*, 3rd edn, Pinter, London (Cengage Learning Services Ltd).

investment in canals and roads by landlords), the advent of the so-called adventurers (now widely recognised as entrepreneurs), pools of labour available for employment in some local markets, the growing education infrastructure, the role played by academic and scientific societies and the attitude of the state towards manufacturing interests were the other complementary factors affecting change (Freeman and Soete, 1997).

With the decline of the previous techno-economic paradigm, the next one starts to take shape with features that offer solutions to the weaknesses of the earlier phase. As Marx foresaw, capitalism has always found a way of reproducing itself with changes in the way factors of production were organised. For instance, the organisational characteristics have changed from the first through to the fifth wave, and the early emphasis on individual entrepreneurs has given way to small firms, then to the monopolists, oligopolists and cartels of the third wave, centralised TNCs (transnational corporations) of the fourth wave and, finally, to the so-called 'network' type, flexible organisations of the information age (*see* Table 2.1 for an overview of the waves of growth).

Pause for thought

The Kondratieff theory suggests that networks constitute a key organisational attribute to the current wave of economic growth. Does this mean it is not possible for a firm to be innovative on its own?

Fostering innovation in 'late-industrialising' countries

We have already noted that there is no guarantee for continued technological leadership. The geography of innovation has shown regional, national or local variations in time. One proof in this regard has been the case of south-east Asia. Although the late developers followed more or less similar paths towards industrialisation, some managed significant achievements, particularly in the attitude of the private sector to innovation and technology development (for example, Taiwan, Malaysia and Korea). Almost all latecomers started with the exports of basic commodities, and through the application of a mix of policies in different periods, they aimed for industrialisation. When innovation is considered, the focus of entrepreneurs and businesses was initially on imitative production (so-called 'reverse engineering') in relatively unsophisticated industries. More recently Hobday *et al.* (2004) have illustrated that Korean firms have adopted a policy of 'copy and develop', which has taken them to the technological frontier in industries from automotive to telecommunications. When the business environment became conducive to business activity, after initial capital accumulation in key industries, then an upward move was observed along the ladder of industrialisation. In many countries such a transformation required an envisioning state, actively interfering with the functioning of the private enterprise system. In some cases, it set 'the prices wrong' deliberately (Amsden, 1989) to protect and promote infant industries; in others, it created enterprises itself in order to compensate for the lack of private initiative in the economy (Toprak, 1995).

Although there are significant differences between the cases of Latin American countries and their south Asian counterparts, their paths of industrialisation also bear similarities. Initially, all were exporters of raw materials and importers of higher-technology products. In achieving the transformation, the move from simple technology sectors towards higher-value-added and heavy industries seems to be the key to their successes. This was achieved with the complementary use of (inward-looking) import-substituting industrialisation (ISI) and (outward-looking) export-oriented (EOI) economic policies. The main difference in south Asian economies, which, in retrospect, seems to be their main advantage, was that after the initial phase of ISI, they opened up to international competition through an EOI regime in contrast particularly to Latin American countries and Turkey. Turkey had a set of problems that were established over a long period of time, which led to a weak business system. This was partly due to the nation building and 'Turkification' of the economy during the twentieth century. This resulted in the Turkish business system becoming state dependent. Thus trying to create a business class from scratch during the 1970s and 80s had its costs: entrepreneurs and businesses, which are expected to invest their accumulation into business activities along the value chain were after easy and quick returns ('petty entrepreneurship') or invested their accumulation into luxury goods. In a favourable environment, such accumulation could have meant the deepening of the economy. However, the case of Turkey proved that without a proper legal and institutional framework, and a social code, established business values and ethic, the outcome turned out to be a sluggish business system.

Pause for thought

In order to compete much emphasis is placed on the need to cut costs and improve efficiency. Why would an emphasis on efficiency alone be bad for businesses and economic growth in general?

Innovation within the 25 EU states

In a response to increased competition and globalisation the European Council argued for increased and enhanced efforts to improve the EU's performance in innovation. In March 2000 in the picturesque city of Lisbon the EU set itself the goal of becoming the most competitive and dynamic knowledge-based economy in the world within the next decade. Fine words one may say, but precisely how does one set about achieving this laudable goal? A strategy was developed and presented in Stockholm in March 2001. The strategy was to build on the economic convergence that had been developed over the past 10 years within the EU single market and to coordinate an 'open method' of developing policies for creating new skills, knowledge and innovation. To support this approach the European Commission stated that there was a need for an assessment of how member countries were performing in the area of innovation. The idea of a 'Scoreboard' was launched to indicate the performance of member states. This would be conducted every year as a way of assessing the performance of member countries. It is essentially a bench-marking exercise where the European Union can assess its performance against other countries, most notably Japan and the United States. The Scoreboard also analyses Bulgaria, Romania, Turkey, Iceland and Switzerland.

This is an extremely ambitious project to try to assess innovative ability. There have been many studies over the past two decades that have tried to identify the factors necessary for innovation to occur (*see* Table 1.8), and while many factors have been identified several of these are necessary but not sufficient in themselves. Moreover, some governments have attempted to develop 'innovation toolkits' and 'scorecards' to try to help firms in their own countries to become more innovative (for example, the UK Department of Trade and Industry). Most of these have not been successful. This ambitious project by the European Union is full of limitations and is generally regarded as oversimplistic. This is largely because the economic conditions of the member countries are so very different and all have a wide variety of strengths and weaknesses. Nonetheless, in order to assess where the European Union should target help and the precise type of help required by each member it is necessary to analyse the innovative performance of countries. The latest European Innovation Survey was conducted in 2009 (EIS, 2010). Figure 2.3, shows a map of

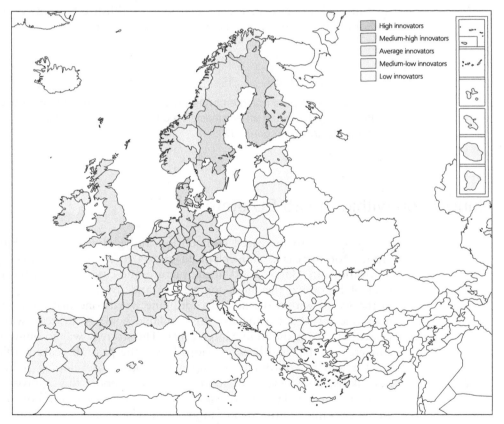

Figure 2.3 **The EU showing five performance groups, ranging from the highest to lowest overall performers**

Table 2.2 **Four different groups**

Group	Growth rate (%)	Growth leaders	Moderate growers	Slow growers
Innovation leaders	1.5	Switzerland (CH)	Finland (FI), Germany (DE)	Denmark (DK), Sweden (SE), United Kingdom (UK)
Innovation followers	2.7	Cyprus (CY), Estonia (EE)	Iceland (IS), Slovenia (SI)	Austria (AT), Belgium (BE), France (FR), Ireland (IE), Luxembourg (LU), Netherlands (NL)
Moderate innovators	3.3	Czech Republic (CZ), Greece (GR), Malta (MT), Portugal (PT)	Hungary (HU), Lithuania (LT), Poland (PL), Slovakia (SK)	Italy (IT), Norway (NO), Spain (ES)
Catching-up countries	5.5	Bulgaria (BG), Romania (RO)	Latvia (LV)	Turkey (TR), Croatia (HR)

the European Union indicating five performance groups, ranging from the highest to the lowest overall performers. Table 2.2 illustrates how the EIS (2010) divides the countries into four key groups.

Improving the innovation performance of the EU

All the elements in the Scoreboard are necessary but not sufficient in themselves to ensure that innovation occurs. For example, in this chapter we have seen the example of Turkey, a late-industrialising country on the edge of Europe, a country with a population of 60 million, already a member of the North Atlantic Treaty Organisation (NATO) and a prospective member of the European Union. Turkey is a good example of a late-industrialising economy. Sitting on the edge of Europe and bestriding two continents, Turkey should be in a position to develop a successful economy. However, in Turkey there seems to be a missing link in terms of the innovative intention and capabilities of enterprises. Turkey needs to put in place many of the things detailed in the Scoreboard. This would surely help to develop enterprise in the country, but it will not convert Turkey into a Germany or Finland overnight.

By identifying, comparing and disseminating best practices in financing and technology transfer, Europe can improve its innovation performance. One area that needs particular attention is the overall perception of the entrepreneur. The image of the entrepreneur needs to have greater value, as in the United States where the drive to try to market new products, with the in-built risk of failure, is seen much more positively than in Europe.

The Scoreboard may be helpful to governmental policymakers in deciding where to invest substantial sums of money. However, this chapter and Chapter 1 have emphasised that firms behave differently given similar circumstances and that some firms appeared to be more successful than others. Given this, the Scoreboard's practical help is likely to be extremely limited.

The times they are a changing: how frugal innovation is providing a future path for firms in emerging markets

The emerging world, long a source of cheap labour, now rivals the rich countries for business innovation. Developing countries are becoming hotbeds of business innovation in much the same way as Japan did from the 1950s onwards. They are coming up with new products and services that are dramatically cheaper than their western equivalents: $3,000 cars, $300 computers and $30 mobile phones that provide nationwide services for just 2 cents a minute. They are reinventing systems of production and distribution, and they are experimenting with entirely new business models.

The United Nations World Investment Report calculates that there are now around 21,500 multinationals based in the emerging world. The best of these, such as India's Bharat Forge (forging), China's BYD (batteries) and Brazil's Embraer (jet aircraft), are as good as anybody in the world. The number of companies from Brazil, India, China or Russia on the Financial Times 500 list more than quadrupled in 2006–08.

Furthermore, the world's biggest multinationals are becoming increasingly happy to do their research and development in emerging markets. Companies in the Fortune 500 list have 98 R&D facilities in China and 63 in India. And the opportunities are equally impressive. The potential market is huge. Populations are already much higher than in the developed world and growing much faster.

This combination is producing an exciting cocktail of creativity. Because so many consumers are poor, companies have to go for volume. And because piracy is so commonplace, they also have to keep upgrading their products. Again the similarities with Japan in the 1950s are striking.

The very nature of innovation is having to be rethought. Most people in the West equate it with technological breakthroughs, embodied in revolutionary new products that are taken up by the elites and eventually trickle down to the masses. But many of the most important innovations consist of incremental improvements to products and processes aimed at the middle or bottom of the income pyramid. The emerging world has already surpassed the West in areas such as mobile money (using mobile phones to make payments).

In Chennai, India, Tata Consultancy Services (TCS) has developed a low-tech water filter. It uses rice husks (which is one of the country's most common waste products) to purify water. It can provide a family with an abundant supply of bacteria free water for about $24. Tata is planning to produce 1 million of the devices over the next year. Frugal innovation is more than simply cutting costs. Nokia's cheapest handsets come equipped with flashlights (because of frequent power cuts), multiple phone books (because they often have different users), rubberised key pads and menus in several languages.

Finally, the developing world's most innovative business model may be the application of mass-production techniques to sophisticated services. Extending Henry Ford's manufacturing revolution to heart and eye surgery is truly innovative.

Innovation and the market

We have explored the reasons why some state contexts are more conducive to deeper levels of entrepreneurial activity and innovation, while some others promote 'petty entrepreneurialism' with short-term, accumulation-ridden intentions. This chapter has also tried to explain how some nations achieved a strong transformation from basic industries and joined the vanguard of technology development. In that respect, it was suggested that although knowledge accumulation is a socially and spatially focused process, geographical shifts have occurred throughout history when 'state–societal arrangements' were conducive and there may be possible openings for late-developing nations in the future. This, however, is by no means a simple process.

Chapter 1 emphasised the inclusion of commercialisation within the process of innovation. It is this part of the innovation process that proves so extremely difficult for many firms. There have been many exciting scientific advances such as Alexander Flemming's discovery of penicillin (1928) and Crick and Watson's discovery of DNA (1953), but in both cases it was over 20 years later that commercial products emerged from the science and technology: antibiotics in the first case and numerous genetic advances including genetic fingerprinting in the second. Commercialising technology and new products in particular, then, is one of the key challenges within innovation. We now turn our attention to this process and in particular the diffusion of innovations and market adoption.

Innovation and market vision

We all respond differently to different types of innovations and in different ways. It is because of this that the role of marketing is so valuable to firms developing new products and services. For example, in the context of disruptive innovations which require a greater change in existing patterns of behaviour and thinking, consumers would perceive a higher level of risk and uncertainty in their adoption decisions relative to continuous innovations that depend on established behavioural patterns and perceptions. Take internet banking as an example: this is a type of service that necessitates changes in perceptions and the established patterns of behaviour and requires the formation of new consumption practices. Indeed, the underlying internet technology itself is a disruptive innovation. Yet herein lies the problem: highly innovative products have an inherent high degree of uncertainty about exactly how an emerging technology may be formulated into a usable product and what the final product application will be. Market vision, or the ability to look into the future and picture products and services that will be successful is a fundamental requirement for those firms wishing to engage in innovation. It involves assessing ones own technological capability and present or future market needs and visioning a market offering that people will want to buy. While this may sound simple it lies at the heart of the innovation process and focuses our attention on the need to examine not only the market but the way the new product offering is used or consumed.

Innovative new products and consumption patterns

Consumption pattern refers to the degree of change required in the thinking and behaviour of the consumer in using the product. Products involving consumption pattern changes such as internet banking or MP3 players can require customers to alter their thinking and habits and this may affect their willingness to embrace a new product. A product can be familiar or novel in the way it requires users to interact

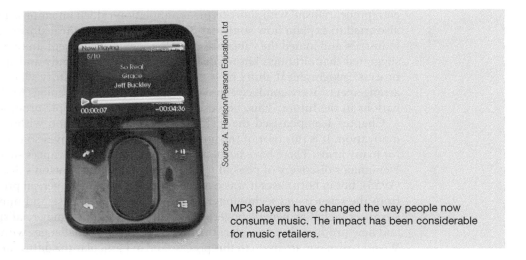

MP3 players have changed the way people now consume music. The impact has been considerable for music retailers.

with it. The nature of the change involved with respect to this aspect of a new product can play a significant role in product evaluation and adoption (Veryzer, 2003). It is this dimension that Apple Inc. has so successfully addressed in its MP3 player, the iPod. Apple was not the first to develop an MP3 player. Indeed, five years after launch its capabilities are still fewer than its rivals (for example, in 2006 it did not have an FM radio). Yet, in terms of ease of use it is considerably ahead of its nearest rival. In considering highly innovative products it is crucial to take the customer's view and experience of the product into account. A technology focused approach to innovation that does not consider the customer's perspective would surely result in a product that is at odds with the market's perception of it. Even though technology is the means for enabling an innovation, new products are more than simply bundles of technology. As Apple has demonstrated with its iPod. Innovative new products must deliver benefits and be used by people who can enjoy them and the advantages that they can bring about.

This introduces another variable that needs to be considered by the firm developing innovative products. In addition to new technology within the product and product capabilities the firm must also consider how these will affect consumption of the product. Figure 2.4 illustrates the relationship between these three key variables

Figure 2.4 **Three critical dimensions of change-of-technology intensive products**

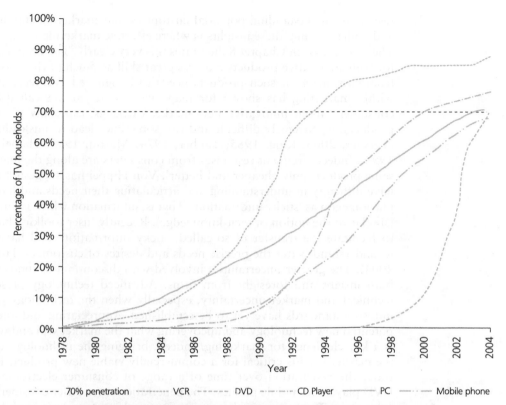

Figure 2.5 **Penetration of consumer electronics, 1978–2004**

that the firm needs to consider as it develops new product ideas. Sometimes, while the technology has been proven and the capabilities of the product demonstrated to be superior to existing products, if the extent of change in the pattern of consumption by the consumer is too great, the product may yet fail or take a long time to succeed. A good example of this would be the failed Apple Newton (personal digital assistant) or even the personal computer which, as Figure 2.5 illustrates, took over 20 years to achieve a 70 per cent market penetration rate.

Pause for thought

If consumers are unwilling to embrace new products that impose a high degree of change in the consumption pattern for consumers, does this mean that firms should only introduce products that are similar to existing products?

Marketing insights to facilitate innovation

Marketing can provide the necessary information and knowledge required by the firm to ensure the successful development of innovative new products and the successful acceptance and diffusion of new products. In both cases it is usually the insights with respect to understanding potential customers that marketing supplies. Uncovering and understanding these insights is where effective marketing is extremely valuable. The Viagra case in Chapter 8 illustrates this very clearly. The deep insights necessary for truly innovative products requires great skill as much of the information gained from customers for such products needs to be ignored (Veryzer, 2003). Research within marketing has shown for many years that gaining valuable insight from consumers about innovative new market offerings, especially discontinuous new products, is extremely difficult and can sometimes lead to misleading information (Veryzer, 2003; King, 1985; Tauber, 1974; Martin, 1995; Hamel and Prahalad, 1994). Indeed, frequent responses from consumers are along the lines of 'I want the same product, only cheaper and better'. Von Hippel has suggested that consumers have difficulty in understanding and articulating their needs and has described this phenomenon as 'sticky information'. That is, information which is difficult to transfer (similar to the notion of tacit knowledge). Recently 'user toolkits' have been shown to facilitate the transfer of so-called 'sticky information' and have enabled firms to understand better the precise needs and desires of customers (Franke and Piller, 2004). The greater uncertainties involved with discontinuous innovations demands both insight and foresight from firms. Advanced technology presents significant technical and market uncertainty, especially when the technology is emerging and industry standards have yet to be established. Appreciating and understanding the potential new technology and uncovering what the market will and will not embrace is a key challenge for marketing. Indeed, bridging the technology uncertainty and the market need is critical for a commercially viable new product. Figure 2.5 illustrates the penetration over time of a range of consumer electronic products from DVD players to mobile phones. The penetration rates differ considerably with some achieving a 70 per cent market penetration within a few years, such as DVD players, whereas PCs took over 20 years.

Highly innovative or discontinuous new products are particularly demanding in terms of early timely information if they are to avoid being harshly judged later by the market. Whether this information and knowledge is provided by marketing personnel or by R&D scientists and engineers does not matter, but its input into the new product development process is essential. The product development team need to determine (Leifer et al., 2000: 81):

- What are the potential applications of a technology as a product?
- Which application(s) should be pursued first?
- What benefits can the proposed product offer to potential customers?
- What is the potential market size and is this sufficient?

Beyond consumer concerns that are relevant to the development and marketing of innovative products are more 'macro' influences that can affect adoption and thus need to be considered. The substitution of one technology for another is an obvious concern (the case study in Chapter 6 discusses this in more detail with regard to screw-caps replacing cork). Along with this, the issue of product complementarity, or when there is a positive interrelationship between products (e.g. a computer printer and a computer), can also be important with respect to product adoption. Thus, in addition to displacing products, new technological innovations often modify or complement existing products that may still be diffusing throughout a given market. This has significant implications for market planning decisions for both products since their diffusion processes are interlinked (Norton and Bass, 1987, 1992; Dekimpe *et al.*, 2000). In such cases, e.g. new electric motor vehicles, the following need to be carefully considered:

- whether there is a positive interdependence between a new product and existing products;
- whether the old technology will be fully replaced by a newer product;
- how the size of the old technology's installed base will affect the speed of diffusion of the new product or product generation.

Innovation in action

A $900 shop

Looking to build a new office or shop? How about adopting the ultimate in recycling – a building made out of stacked shipping containers?

It's generally too expensive to ship an empty container back to its point of origin so there are thousands of them sitting in docks around the world. They are strong, stackable and cost as little as $900.

The Dordoy Bazaar in Bishkek, Kyrgyzstan is one of Asia's largest markets. It stretches for more than a kilometre and is almost entirely constructed from empty shipping containers stacked two high.

(See the case study at the end of this chapter for further details on shipping containers.)

Source: 100 Thoughts (2010) HSBC, London.

Lead users

When it comes to technology-intensive products it is so-called 'lead users' that form the basis for much insight into products and also help with the diffusion process. Lead users are those who demand requirements ahead of the market and indeed are often involved themselves in developing product ideas because there is nothing in the market at present to meet their needs. For example, Stephan Wozniak co-founded Apple Computer with Steve Jobs in 1976 and created the Apple I and Apple II computers in the mid-1970s. He was a lead user computer engineer, ahead of the general population. Such lead users can help to co-develop innovations, and are therefore often early adopters of such innovations. The initial research by Eric von Hippel in the 1970s suggested that lead users adopt an average of seven years before typical users. In a recent study Morrison *et al.* (2004) identified a number of characteristics of lead users:

- recognise requirements early;
- expect high level of benefits from the product;
- develop their own innovations and applications;
- perceived to be pioneering and innovative.

Lead users are particularly significant for products that are using technology at the frontiers of development and those within technology-intensive industries such as software, engineering and science.

Innovation diffusion theories

Innovation diffusion theories try to explain how an innovation is diffused in a social system over time; the adoption of an innovation is therefore a part of the wider diffusion process. Such theories tend to be more comprehensive relative to their adoption theory cousins. This is because they investigate the reasons for adoption at the aggregate level. Perceived innovation characteristics theory, which is a part of the innovation diffusion theory of Rogers (1962), is similar to adoption theories such as the theory of reasoned action (TRA), the theory of planned behaviour (TPB) and the technology acceptance model (TAM) as it includes analysis down to the individual level. Yet, diffusion of innovations theories in general includes many more factors such as the influences of psychological or personal features, technology perceptions, communication behaviour and socio-demographic attributes on diffusion or adoption process. It is worth saying at this point that the study of how and why consumers purchase goods and services falls within the arena of consumer buyer behaviour and there are lots of very good textbooks that explore this subject in great detail. The purpose of introducing some of these concepts here is to ensure the reader is aware of the important influence of this body of research on explaining how and why some new product innovations are successful and why others are not.

Everett Rogers is usually credited with introducing the concept of diffusion theory to the business community. Rogers' work was initially undertaken in developing countries where he studied the diffusion of new ideas among communities (Rogers, 1962). He later developed his work and applied it to new product innovations in the market and was able to illustrate different consumer categories on the basis of its relative time of adoption. Rogers (1983) stated that the adopter categorisation in relation to adoption time requires the determination of the number of adopter categories, the percentage of adopters in each category, and a method to define these categories. Rogers' (1962) adopter categorisation is based on a normal distribution curve that shows the adoption of an innovation over time on a frequency basis which takes the form of an 'S' when plotted on a cumulative basis (*see* Figure 2.6). Indeed, the diffusion curve is much related to the concept of the product life cycle, which shows the level of total sales

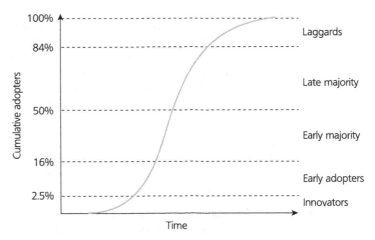

Figure 2.6 **S-curve of cumulative adopters**

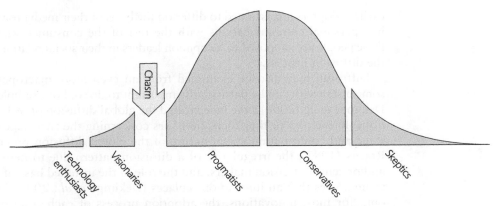

Figure 2.7 Adopter categorisation on the basis of innovativeness
Source: Adapted from Moore, G.A. (1991) *Crossing the Chasm*, Harper Business.

over time. The close relationship between these two concepts would be expected to the extent that sales are proportional to cumulative adoption.

In this model, Rogers (1962) classified different adopter segments in terms of their standard deviation positions from the mean time of adoption of the innovation for the entire market. In this way, he utilised the average and a normal distribution of adopters in order to group them into five categories and obtain the percentage of individuals to be included in each of these categories (*see* Figure 2.7). Rogers stated that innovators comprise the adopter segment which adopts an innovation earlier than the other adopter groups. Innovators are followed by early adopters, early majority, late majority and laggards. In this context, Rogers assumed that these five diverse adopter segments differ on the basis of their demographical features, personality-related characteristics, communication behaviour and social relationships.

Rogers classifies stages in the technology life cycle by the relative percentage of customers who adopt it at each stage (Rogers, 1995). Early on are the innovators and early adopters (who are concerned with the underlying technology and its performance). Then come in succession the early majority pragmatists, the late majority conservatives and lastly the laggards (all of whom are more interested in solutions and convenience). In a contribution to this debate Geoffrey Moore depicts the transition between the early adopters and early majority pragmatists as a chasm that many high-technology companies never successfully cross (*see* Figure 2.7) (Moore, 2004). Moore's contribution to the diffusion debate helped create new approaches for marketing in high-tech industries. His successful book *Crossing the Chasm* has proved popular for helping firms bring cutting-edge products to progressively larger markets. Clayton Christensen prefers to look at the phenomenon of technology take-up from the perspective of the level of performance required by average users (those in the early and late majority categories in Figure 2.7) (Christensen, 1997). He argues that once a technology product meets customers' basic needs they regard it as 'good enough' and no longer care about the underlying technology.

In terms of demographic characteristics, earlier adopters such as innovators and early adopters are presumed to be younger, wealthier and better educated people. When personality-related characteristics are considered, the most distinguishing features of earlier adopters are that they are more eager to take risks and they hold more positive perceptions towards technology in general. Communication behaviours of earlier adopters are assumed to differ on the basis of their media usage behaviour and interpersonal communications with the rest of the consumer segments. Therefore these people are supposed to be opinion leaders in their social relationships throughout the diffusion process.

Diffusion may also be examined from an even more macroperspective, and in some instances it can be particularly important to do so. For example, researchers like Dekimpe *et al.* (2000) have investigated the global diffusion of technological innovations. In their work they focus on issues concerning the two-stage (implementation stage and confirmation stage) nature of the global diffusion process as defined by Rogers (1983), the irregularity of a diffusion pattern due to network externalities and/or central decision makers, and the role of the installed base of older-generation technologies that an innovation replaces (Dekimpe *et al.*, 2000: 51). As they point out, 'for most innovations, the adoption process of each country starts with the implementation stage, which is followed by the confirmation stage'. However, they point out that for technological innovations within-country diffusion might be instantaneous – due to network externalities (e.g. established standards) or central decision makers – and, as such, the confirmation stage for certain countries may have a zero duration. A good example of this is the introduction of digital television within the UK. The UK government, through the BBC, has invested considerable sums of money to educate and inform the population about the advantages of digital television over analogue and to explain that the country will eventually stop transmitting television over analogue signals.

Pause for thought

Given that internet banking has been available for over 10 years, do you think internet banking has crossed the 'chasm'? Is it always just a matter of time and, so long as you are patient, products will always eventually succeed?

Adopting new products and embracing change

Diffusion is essentially consumer willingness to embrace change. But change can be simple and complex. These range from a change in perception to a significant change in required behaviour in order to use the product. For example, dishwasher appliances require a significant shift in the way people behave in the kitchen and their approach to using cutlery and crockery; similarly for MP3 players with regard to storing and collecting music. Consumers' reactions to innovative new products and their willingness to embrace them are also, of course, driven by the benefit they expect to derive from the products. For discontinuous innovations such products, which often involve new technologies, frequently require changes in thinking and behaviour and hence require more from the consumer. Unsurprisingly these products carry a high risk of market failure. When it comes to technology, consumers have a love–hate relationship with it and this is because of the paradoxes of technological products. For example, products such as appliances that are purchased in order to save time often end up wasting time. In their codification of the various paradoxes discussed across the technology literature, Mick and Fournier (1998) present a

Table 2.3 **Paradoxes of technological products**

Paradox	Description	Illustration
Control–chaos	Technology can facilitate order and it can lead to disorder	Telephone answering machine can help record messages but leads to disorder due to uncertainty about whether the message has been received
Freedom–enslavement	Technology can provide independence and it can lead to dependence	The motor car clearly gives independence to the driver but many drivers feel lost without it
New–obsolete	The user is provided with the latest scientific knowledge but this is soon outmoded	Computer games industry
Efficiency–inefficiency	Technology can help reduce effort and time but it can also lead to more effort and time	Increased complexity in VCRs has led to many wasting time in setting recordings
Fulfils needs–creates needs	Technology can help fulfil needs and it can lead to more desires	The internet has satisfied the curiosity of many but has also stimulated many desires
Assimilation–isolation	Technology can facilitate human togetherness and can lead to human separation	Email and chat rooms help communication but in some cases heavy users can become isolated
Engaging–disengaging	Technology can facilitate involvement but it can also lead to disconnection	Advances in mobile phone memory means that many people no longer need or have the skills to discover the telephone number from a telephone directory

Source: Adapted from Mick and Fournier (1998).

typology of paradoxes of technological products. These are captured in Table 2.3. These paradoxes play an important role in shaping consumers' perceptions of innovations as well as determining their willingness to adopt new products.

In addition to the various trade-offs or paradoxes that affect consumers' willingness to embrace innovative products – an aspect of a new product offering that should be considered in the design stage as well as the later product launch stage – consumers develop their own ways of coping with innovations and these can impact diffusion as well. Potential customers may ignore a new technology altogether, delay obtaining the new product, attempt to try an innovative new product without the risk of outright purchase, embrace the product and master it, and so on (Carver *et al.*, 1989; Mick and Fournier, 1998). Furthermore, in evaluating discontinuous new products, there are certain factors that are likely to come into play more than they do for less innovative products. Lack of familiarity, 'irrationality', user-product interaction problems, uncertainty and risk, and accordance or compatibility issues may play a decisive role in customers' evaluations of products in either the development and testing stages or once the product is introduced into a market (Veryzer, 1998a: 144). For example, during the course of one radical innovation development project, managers were struck by how 'irrational' customers were in that they often focused on things that the product development team thought to be unimportant, and test customers ignored aspects of a prototype product that the team had expounded a great deal of effort and money on. Even though this type of 'irrationality' may frustrate product development teams, in the domain of highly innovative products, assumptions must be checked against those who will be the final arbitrators of success (Veryzer, 1998b).

Generally, radical innovations are not easily adopted in the market. Potential adopters experience difficulties to comprehend and evaluate radical innovations due to their newness in terms of technology and benefits offered. Consequently, adoption intentions may remain low. A study by Reinders *et al.* (2010) shows that product bundling enhances the new product's evaluation and adoption intention, although it does not increase comprehension of the radical innovation. Thus offering a radical innovation in a product bundle could be a fruitful strategy for companies that target customers with little or no prior knowledge of the product domain.

Market adoption theories

There is a considerable amount of confusion with regard to adoption and diffusion. This is largely due to differences in definition. Most researchers in the field, however, view adoption of innovations as a process though which individuals pass from awareness to the final decision to adopt or not adopt; whereas diffusion concerns the communication over time within a wider social system. The adoption research is derived mainly from social psychology and focuses on the individual. This includes such models as the theory of reasoned action (TRA), the theory of planned behaviour (TPB) and the technology acceptance model (TAM). The diffusion of innovations theory combines both adoption and the wider societal issues derived from sociology (*see* Yu and Tao, 2009). As previously mentioned, the study of how and why consumers purchase goods and services falls within the arena of consumer buyer behaviour and is beyond the scope of this book.

Case study

How three students built a business that could affect world trade

This case study tells the story of how three MSc students at the Technical University of Delft in The Netherlands had an idea for a folding shipping container and went about building a business. There are many examples of university students starting businesses, but few of these have the potential to revolutionise world trade.

Almost all containers today that you see on ships, trains or on trucks are 20 ft or 40 ft in length. The reason for the massive change in both transportation and the global economy is because of this simplicity of size – a small set of standard sizes that allowed

Source: Pearson Education Ltd/Photodisc

ships, trucks, receiving bays, and all of the related logistical systems to easily adapt to an industry-wide standard. Prior to standardisation there were major inefficiencies in commercial shipping: packaging and crating was inconsistent. But, what about empty containers? Are there ships travelling the world with containers that are empty? If so is this a business opportunity?

Introduction

Jan, Mark and Stephan were studying for their MSc in mechanical engineering at the Technical University of Delft in The Netherlands. They had arrived late for their lecture and had been forced to sit at the front. They had cycled the short distance from their house on the other side of town and would have arrived on time if it had not been for the lifting bridge over the canal, which had to be raised for a large boat carrying steel shipping containers. This incident was to prove significant. For it was during the lecture by a professor of mechanics that the students hit upon the idea of a folding steel container. The professor was explaining that springs can, in theory, be used to lift very heavy weights providing the springs are large enough. We are all aware of the Anglepoise lamp that uses springs to enable the movement of its steel arm and lamp. The same principle can be used to move much larger objects providing one has much larger springs. Initially, the students thought about springs to raise and lower a bridge, but this was soon dismissed. A steel container that could be folded into a small space had many more attractions. The three

students went away to experiment with their idea and conduct calculations on weight, force, stress and strain measurements. Eventually they developed a prototype and modelled it on a computer simulation program. It worked. After much dancing around the computer lab the three then looked at each other as if to say 'now what?' It was a good question. Should they run and get a patent on their idea before someone else steals it? What are the benefits of a folding container? Maybe a folding container already exists? A working computer simulation is a long way from a folding 40 ft steel container. (By way of illustration you can drive a large car into one of these containers.) Would anyone be interested? And how can we make any money out of the idea? Having interesting technology is a long way from a profitable money-making business.

The first thing Jan did was to contact the Port of Rotterdam, which is only 15 km from Delft and is one of the world's busiest container ports (see Table 2.4). Eventually he was able to speak to the Commercial Director of the Port. He explained to Jan that folding and collapsible containers have been around for many years, but they have never really worked. This is primarily because they are expensive to manufacture (usually 10 per cent more than the standard container) and bits get lost, for example the roof from one container sometimes does not fit another container, and the additional equipment required to assemble the containers all adds to the cost. The list of criticisms seemed to be very long. At the end Jan asked what about folding containers that are all

Table 2.4 Busiest container ports

	Port	Country	TEUs* (000s)	% change from 2004
1	Singapore	Singapore	23,192	8.7
2	Hong Kong	China	22,427	2.0
3	Shanghai	China	18,084	24.2
4	Shenzhen	China	16,197	19.0
5	Busan	South Korea	11,843	3.6
6	Kaohsiung	Taiwan (Republic of China)	9,471	0.0
7	**Rotterdam**	**Netherlands**	**9,287**	**12.2**
8	Hamburg	Germany	8,088	15.5
9	Dubai	United Arab Emirates	7,619	18.5
10	Los Angeles	USA	7,485	2.2

*Twenty-foot equivalent units.

in one piece, where the sides can be folded down by hand? The Director laughed and said: 'Yeah, right, like on the Disney channel!' Jan reported back to his friends that potential customers may not believe that they could deliver such a product.

The friends faced a number of difficulties and many uncertainties. They needed advice, after all they were engineers, very clever engineers, but not experts in developing businesses. Fortunately, the university had a business incubator that helped students develop their ideas and create businesses. It would be able to help them with their patent application, but Jan, Mark and Stephan soon realised they did not know simple answers to questions such as: Who would buy it? Who are the customers? How many containers are there in the Netherlands/Europe/world? How much does it cost to make a container? How much does it cost to buy one? It was soon clear that many days of research lay ahead. This would have to be squeezed in between lectures and coursework.

A brief history of shipping containers

The students' research uncovered the following. During the 1960s, 1970s and 1980s the standardisation of shipping containers revolutionised global trade and has dramatically reduced the cost of transporting goods around the world. According to Marc Levinson (2006), author of *The Box: How the Shipping Container Made the World Smaller and the World Economy Bigger*, much of this revolution was down to one man – Malcolm McLean – who challenged the norm and introduced standardised, packaged shipping. More than 50 years ago, Malcom McLean, a North Carolina trucking entrepreneur, originally hatched the idea of using containers to carry cargo. He loaded 58 containers onto his ship, *Ideal X*, in Newark, New Jersey, and once the vessel reached Houston, Texas the uncrated containers were moved directly onto trucks – and reusable rectangular boxes soon became the industry standard. What was new in the USA about McLean's innovation was the idea of using large containers that were never opened in transit between shipper and consignee and that were transferable on an intermodal basis, among trucks, ships and railroad cars.

Now, most students of business will immediately recognise the benefits that can flow from the introduction of a uniform standard. And history is littered with examples of industries struggling to grow until a single uniform standard is adopted, thereby signalling

the end of uncertainty and the start of the adoption of the standard technology. Prior to a standard width gauge, the UK railway industry had two competing gauges and the computer industry has battled for many years over operating systems. The shipping industry was in a similar position with many different types of containers. Packaging and crating products was inconsistent and inefficient. Large numbers of people were employed in ports around the world to break bulk cargo. Frequently separate items had to be handled individually, such as bags of sugar or flour packed next to copper tube. Today, approximately 90 per cent of non-bulk cargo worldwide moves by containers stacked on transport ships. Some 18 million containers make over 200 million trips per year. For the past 10 years, demand for cargo capacity has been growing almost 10 per cent a year.

This background research on the industry proved to be more interesting than the students had first thought and it delivered some exciting findings. Most importantly, that this was a growing industry, it had international firms with large budgets. And they had uncovered the fact that the storage of containers poses a significant problem for the shipping lines that are always on the look out for ways to reduce this cost.

Background: containers

The students now needed to explore in detail the shipping container and how it is used. More research was required and soon they uncovered more useful information. The history of the use of purpose-built containers for trade can be traced back to the 1830s; railroads on several continents were carrying containers that could be transferred to trucks or ships, but these containers were small by today's standards. Originally used for shipping coal on and off barges, 'loose boxes' were used to containerise coal from the late 1780s. By the 1840s, iron boxes were in use as well as wooden ones. The early 1900s saw the adoption of closed container boxes designed for movement between road and rail. Towards the end of the Second World War, the US Army began using specialised containers to speed up the loading and unloading of transport ships. After the US Department of Defense standardised an 8 ft × 8 ft cross-section container in multiples of 10 ft lengths for military use it was rapidly adopted for shipping purposes. These standards were adopted in the United Kingdom for containers and rapidly displaced the older wooden containers in the 1950s.

Table 2.5 Specifications of the three most common types of container

		20′ container		40′ container		45′ high-cube container	
		Imperial	Metric	Imperial	Metric	Imperial	Metric
External dimensions	Length	20′ 0″	6.096 m	40′ 0″	12.192 m	45′ 0″	13.716 m
	Width	8′ 0″	2.438 m	8′ 0″	2.438 m	8′ 0″	2.438 m
	Height	8′ 6″	2.591 m	8′ 6″	2.591 m	9′ 6″	2.896 m
Volume		1,169 ft^3	33.1 m^3	2,385 ft^3	67.5 m^3	3,040 ft^3	86.1 m^3
Maximum gross mass		66,139 lb	30,400 kg	66,139 lb	30,400 kg	66,139 lb	30,400 kg
Empty weight		4,850 lb	2,200 kg	8,380 lb	3,800 kg	10,580 lb	4,800 kg
Net load		61,289 lb	28,200 kg	57,759 lb	26,600 kg	55,559 lb	25,600 kg

Containers, also known as intermodal containers or as ISO containers because the dimensions have been defined by the ISO, are the main type of equipment used in intermodal transport, particularly when one of the modes of transportation is by ship. Containers are 8 ft wide by 8 ft high. Since their introduction, there have been moves to adopt other heights. The most common lengths are 20 ft and 40 ft although other lengths exist. They are made out of steel and can be stacked on top of each other.

Container capacity is often expressed in *twenty-foot equivalent units* (TEU, or sometimes teu). An equivalent unit is a measure of containerised cargo capacity equal to one standard 20 ft (length) × 8 ft (width) container. The use of Imperial measurements to describe container size reflects the fact that the US Department of Defense played a major part in the development of containers. The overwhelming need to have a standard size for containers, in order that they fit all ships, cranes, and trucks, and the length of time that the current container sizes have been in use, makes changing to an even metric size impractical. Table 2.5 shows the weights and dimensions of the three most common types of container worldwide. The weights and dimensions quoted above are averages, different manufactured series of the same type of container may vary slightly in actual size and weight.

Handling containers

On ships, containers are typically stacked up to seven units high. When carried by rail, containers can be loaded on flatcars or in container well cars. When the container ship arrives at the container terminal (port) specialist equipment is required. The transfer from ship to land may be between ships and land vehicles, for example trains or trucks. Maritime container terminals tend to be part of a larger port, whereas inland container terminals tend to be located in or near major cities, with good rail connections to maritime container terminals.

A container crane or gantry crane, is used at container terminals for loading and unloading shipping containers from container ships. Cranes normally transport a single container at once, however some newer cranes have the capability to pick up up to four 20 ft containers at once. Handling equipment is designed with intermodality in mind, assisting with transferring containers between rail, road and sea. These can include:

- Transtainer for transferring containers from sea-going vessels onto either trucks or rail wagons. A transtainer is mounted on rails with a large boom spanning the distance between the ship's cargo hold and the quay, moving parallel to the ship's side.
- Gantry cranes, also known as straddle carriers, are able to straddle rail and road vehicles allowing for quick transfer of containers. A spreader beam moves in several directions allowing accurate positioning of the cargo.
- Reach stackers are fitted with lifting arms as well as spreader beams and lift containers to swap bodies or stack containers on top of each other.

Container shipping companies

Informally known as 'box boats' these vessels carry the majority of the world's manufactured goods. Cargoes like metal ores, coal or wheat are carried in bulk carriers. There are large mainline vessels that ply the deep-sea routes, and then many small 'feeder' ships that supply the large ships at centralised hub ports. Most container ships are propelled by diesel engines, and have crews of between 20 and 40. Container ships now carry up to 15,000 TEU. The world's largest container ship, the M/V *Emma Mærsk* has a capacity of 15,200 containers.

The capacity of a container ship is measured in TEUs, which is the number of standard 20-foot containers a vessel can carry. This not withstanding, most containers used today measure 40 ft (12 m) in length. Above a certain size, container ships do not carry their own loading gear, so loading and unloading can only be done at ports with the necessary cranes. However, smaller ships with capacities of up to 2,900 TEU are often equipped with their own cranes.

The world's oceans can be a scary places in bad weather, hence the transit of containers around the world inevitably carries a considerable risk. And yet, the well-known challenging routes, such as round the Cape Horn, are not where most containers are lost. Most risks are linked to the loading and unloading of containers. The risks involved in these operations affect both the cargo being moved on to or off the ship, as well as the ship itself. Containers, due to their fairly nondescript nature and the sheer number handled in major ports, require complex organisation to ensure they are not lost, stolen or misrouted. In addition, as the containers and the cargo they contain make up the vast majority of the total weight of a cargo ship, the loading and unloading is a delicate balancing act, as it directly affects the whole ships centre of mass. There have been some instances of poorly loaded ships capsizing at port.

It has been estimated that container ships lose over 10,000 containers at sea each year. Most go overboard on the open sea during storms but there are some examples of whole ships being lost with their cargo. When containers are dropped, they immediately become an environmental threat – termed 'marine debris'.

It is not surprising that when the three students visited Rotterdam Container Port to discuss their idea with senior managers from the port, the managers were very enthusiastic about containers and the benefits they deliver. They explained that container cargo could be moved nearly 20 times faster than pre-container break bulk cargo. They also argued that while there were increased fuel costs, due to the extra weight of the containers, labour efficiencies more than compensate. Nonetheless, for certain bulk products this makes containerisation unattractive. On railways the capacity of the container is far from its maximum weight capacity. In some areas (mostly the USA and Canada) containers are double-stacked, but this not usually possible in other countries.

At the end of the meeting the Commercial Director explained to the students that, for their idea to succeed, they would need to receive the necessary certification from agencies such as Lloyds Register or Bureau Veritas. Their approval is required regarding the seaworthiness of any marine equipment. Without such certification no shipping company would be interested in their ideas. There seemed to be many obstacles to their business idea.

Table 2.6 **Biggest shipping container companies**

Top 10 container shipping companies in order of TEU capacity			
Company	TEU capacity	Market share (%)	Number of ships
A.P. Moller-Maersk Group	1,665,272	18.2	549
Mediterranean Shipping Company S.A.	865,890	11.7	376
CMA CGM	507,954	5.6	256
Evergreen Marine Corporation	477,911	5.2	153
Hapag-Lloyd	412,344	4.5	140
China Shipping Container Lines	346,493	3.8	111
American President Lines	331,437	3.6	99
Hanjin-Senator	328,794	3.6	145
COSCO	322,326	3.5	118
NYK Line	302,213	3.3	105

Business opportunity: moving empty containers

Containers are intended to be used constantly, being loaded with a new cargo for a new destination soon after being emptied of the previous cargo. This is not always possible, and in some cases the cost of transporting an empty container to a place where it can be used is considered to be higher than the worth of the used container. This can result in large areas in ports and warehouses being occupied by empty containers left abandoned. The shipping industry spends a great deal of time and money in repositioning empty containers. If trade was balanced, there would be no empty containers. But trade imbalance, especially between Europe and North America with Asia, has resulted in approximately 2.5 million TEUs of empty containers stored in yards around the world with empties comprising 20–23 per cent of the movement of containers around the world. According to research conducted by International Asset Systems, the average container is idle or undergoing repositioning for over 50 per cent of its life span. The research also determined that shipping companies spend $16 billion in repositioning empties. To compensate for these costs, carriers add surcharges, ranging from $100 to $1,000 per TEU, to freight rates.

Folding containers would provide further advantages: for example, they would relieve congestion at ports. Storing empty containers takes up prime real estate. For example, the storage yards around the Port of Jersey, UK, are cluttered with an estimated 100,000 empty containers belonging to leasing companies and an additional 50,000 belonging to ocean carriers. Folding containers would be quicker to load (four at a time), resulting in faster turnaround time for ships. Energy costs would drop as well, as one trailer rather than four would transport empties. Finally, there is also a security feature to the folded container built to ISO standards. Nothing can be smuggled in a collapsed empty. It is estimated that if 75 per cent of empty containers were folded by 2010, the result would be a yearly saving in shipping of 25 million TEUs or 50 per cent of the total volume of empty containers shipped.

Concept to product

The background research had been done. There was genuine interest from potential customers. The students now needed money to build a working scale model of the folding container. They had to

prove to everyone that it would work. Moreover, the concept also had to be compatible with existing equipment for intermodal transport. That is, it would need to be exactly the same size/shape/weight, etc. It would also have to have proper sealing and locking devices, and should interlock with other containers. Computer models were fine to a point, but a physical model was now required, especially if they were going to convince people to invest. With the help of the university and the Incubator the students set about constructing a full working steel model. It was to be a 1/10th scale. So it would be 2 ft long 0.8 ft high. Real working springs would have to be in place. The friends realised immediately that a patent drawing is theory and it did not resemble reality. Numerous fabrication and manufacturing problems had to be overcome. Eventually, after two months of experimenting with steel springs and welding equipment in the workshop a fully working model emerged that required two people to manoeuvre the steel box. More importantly it had taken a considerable amount of time and investment in materials and equipment. When the model was demonstrated to senior figures at the Port of Rotterdam they were very impressed and immediately wanted to see a full size version – a prototype. But, who would pay for a full size prototype? It would be enormous and probably cost thousands of euros to produce.

The three students had made some significant steps forward with their business idea, but they still did not have an order, let alone any sales or cash. Was this to be just a hobby, something they enjoyed but did not generate any cash? Would anyone pay for one of these things? The students needed money to finance the next stage, but as well as being impoverished they were not manufacturers!

→

Decision time

All three students were excited about the possibilities and the huge potential that existed. They would love to start their own business, rather than work for someone else. There were many uncertainties: money, career, what happens if they fail? As if to underline their concerns an open page of the *Financial Times* glared at them and gave them further worries:

Credit crunch hits shipping as trade falls
2009 has seen a considerable slowdown in global trade. It has left the Indian shipping industry high and dry, with the country's idle capacity set to rise from 150,000 TEUs in October 2008 to 750,000. Not surprisingly freight rates for container ships from India have also fallen by almost 80 per cent since summer 2008. The freight rates on the India–UK sector was $1,100 for a 20 ft container and this has come down to $280 to $300, And to ferry a 20 ft container unit to the Gulf is just $90 against $550 in 2007. Globally, things are similar elsewhere. In Singapore, one of the world's busiest ports, some vessels are now being used to store empty containers to save on port rentals. Port-related businesses, such as inland container ports and container freight stations, are also suffering.

The global downturn raised further worries for the friends – maybe this was the wrong time to start a business?

Source: Levinson, M. (2006) *The Box: How the Shipping Container Made the World Smaller and the World Economy Bigger*, Princeton University Press, Princeton.

Questions

1 Would you advise the students to start this business?
2 Who are their customers going to be?
3 Who can they license the technology to?
4 Can they form any partnerships or alliances?
5 How would you enter this market?
6 What aspects of product diffusion will they need to address?
7 Use the CIM (Figure 1.9) to illustrate the innovation process in this case.
8 Is patent protection essential here? If not why not?
9 How can the students help customers adopt the product?
10 Standardisation led to growth in container usage: what will be the effect of this non-standard folding container?

Note: This case has been written as a basis for class discussion rather than to illustrate effective or ineffective managerial or administrative behaviour. It has been prepared from a variety of sources and from observations.

Chapter summary

This chapter has explored the wider context of innovation, in particular the role of the state and the role of the market. It has shown that innovation cannot be separated from political and social processes. This includes both tangible and intangible features, including economic, social and political institutions, and processes and mechanisms that facilitate the flow of knowledge between industries and firms. It has also shown the powerful influence of the market on innovation; in particular the need to consider long time frames when developing technology and innovative new products. Finally, this chapter discussed an aspect of innovation that is frequently overlooked – the pattern of consumption of the new product or new service. It is changes to the way the new product or service is consumed that all too often determines whether it will be a success or not.

Discussion questions

1   Discuss the tangible features that it is necessary for the state to put in place to foster innovation.

2   How can the state encourage entrepreneurs and businesses to invest in longer time horizons?

3   Explain Schumpeter's view of entrepreneurial behaviour and economic growth.

4   Discuss the evidence for the fifth Kondratieff wave of growth.

5   What is meant by a 'weak business system'?

6   How does diffusion differ from adoption?

7   What role should marketing play in the early stages of product innovation?

8   List some of the additional factors that affect the adoption of highly innovative products.

9   Explain how market vision can help the innovation process.

10 How does the pattern of consumption influence the likely success or failure of a new product?

Key words and phrases

Schumpeterian theory *48*

Short-termism *49*

Entrepreneurship *49*

National systems of innovation *50*

Corruption *54*

Kondratieff waves of growth *55*

Business system *58*

Market vision *62*

Lead-user theory *66*

Adoption theory *67*

Diffusion theory *67*

References

Afuah, A. (2003) *Innovation Management: Strategies, Implementation and Profits*, 2nd edn, Oxford University Press, Oxford.

Amsden, A. (1989) *Asia's Next Giant: South Korea and Late Industrialisation*, Oxford University Press, Oxford.

Carver, C.S., Scheier, M.F. and Weintraub, J.K. (1989) Assessing coping strategies: A theoretically based approach, *Journal of Personality and Social Psychology*, Vol. 56, 267–83.

Castells, M. (1992) 'Four Asian Tigers with a dragon head: a comparative analysis of the state, economy, and society in the Asian Pacific Rim', in Appelbaum, R.P. and Henderson, J. (eds) *States and Development: The Asian Pacific Rim*, Oxford University Press, Oxford, 33–70.

Christensen, C.M. (1997) *The Innovator's Dilemma: When new technologies cause great firms to fail*, HBS Press, Cambridge.

Dekimpe, M.G., Parker, P.M. and Sarvary, M. (2000) 'Multimarket and global diffusion', in Mahajan, V., Muller, E. and Wind, Y. (eds) *New-product diffusion models*, Kluwer Academic, Dordrecht, The Netherlands, 49–73.

Dicken, P. (1998) *Global Shift: Transforming the World Economy*, Paul Chapman, London.

European Innovation Scoreboard (EIS) (2010) Pro Inno Europe Paper No. 15, http://www.proinno-europe.eu/metrics.

Evans, P.B. (1989) Predatory, developmental, and other apparatuses: a comparative political economy perspective on the Third World state, *Sociological Forum*, Vol. 4, No. 4, 561–87.

Franke, N. and Piller, F. (2004) Value creation by toolkits for user innovation and design: The case of the watch market, *Journal of Product Innovation Management*, Vol. 21, No. 6, 401–16.

Freeman, C. and Soete, L. (1997) *The Economics of Industrial Innovation*, 3rd edn, Pinter, London.

Hamel, G. and Prahalad, C.K. (1994) Competing for the future, *Harvard Business Review*, Vol. 72, No. 4, 122–8.

Hart, J.A. (1992) *Rival Capitalists: International Competitiveness in the United States, Japan, and Western Europe*, Cornell University Press, London.

Hobday, M., Rush, H. and Bessant, J. (2004) Approaching the innovation frontier in Korea: the transition phase to leadership, *Research Policy*, Vol. 33, No. 10, 1433–57.

Johnson, C. (1982) *MITI and the Japanese Miracle: The Growth of Industrial Policy 1925–75*, Stanford University Press, Stanford, CA.

King, S. (1985) Has marketing failed or was it never really tried?, *Journal of Marketing Management*, Vol. 1, No. 1, 1–19.

Leifer, R., Colarelli O'Connor, G., Peters, L.S., Rice, M. Veryzer, R.W. and McDermott, C.M. (2000) *Radical Innovation*, HBS Press, Boston, MA.

Martin, J. (1995) Ignore your customer, *Fortune*, Vol. 1, No. 8, 121–5.

Mick, D.G. and Fournier, S. (1998) Paradoxes of Technology: Consumer Cognizance, Emotions, and Coping Strategies, *Journal of Consumer Research*, Vol. 25, No. 9, 123–47.

Moore, G.A. (2004) *Crossing the chasm: Marketing and selling technology products to mainstream customers*, 2nd edn, Capstone, Oxford.

Morrison, P.J., Roberts, J. and Midgley, D. (2004) The nature of lead users and measurement of leading edge status, *Research Policy*, Vol. 33, 351–62.

Norton, J.A. and Bass, F.M. (1987) A diffusion theory model of adoption and substitution for successive generations of high technology products, *Management Science*, Vol. 33, No. 9, 1069–86.

Norton, J.A. and Bass, F.M. (1992) Evolution of technological change: The law of capture, *Sloan Management Review*, Vol. 33, No. 2, 66–77.

Porter, M. (1990) *The Competitive Advantage of Nations*, Macmillan, London.

Porter, M., Takeuchi, H. and Sakakibara, M. (2000) *Can Japan Compete?*, Perseus Pub., Cambridge, MA.

Reinders, M.J., Frambach, R.T. and Schoormans, J.P.L. (2010) Using Product Bundling to Facilitate the Adoption Process of Radical Innovations, *Journal of Product Innovation Management*, Vol. 27, 1127–40.

Rogers, E.M. (1962) *Diffusion of innovations*, Free Press, New York.

Rogers, E.M. (1983) *Diffusion of innovations*, 3rd edn, The Free Press, New York.

Rogers, E.M. (1995) *Diffusion of innovations*, 4th edn, The Free Press, New York.

Rosenthal, D.E. (1993) Reevaluating the Chicago School paradigm for promoting innovation and competitiveness, *Canada–United States Law Journal*, Vol. 19, 97–104.

Schumpeter, J. (1943) *Capitalism, Socialism and Democracy*, Allen & Unwin, London.

Tauber, E.M. (1974) Predictive validity in consumer research, *Journal of Advertising Research*, Vol. 15, No. 5, 59–64.

Toprak, Z. (1995) National Economics-National Bourgeoisie: Economy and Society in Turkey 1908–1950 (in Turkish: Milli Iktisat-Milli Burjuvazi: Türkiye'de Ekonomi ve Toplum 1908–1950), Türkiye Toplumsal ve Ekonomik Tarih Vakfı, Istanbul.

van der Panne, G., van Beers, C. and Kleinknecht, A. (2003) Success and failure of innovation: a review of the literature, *International Journal of Innovation Management*, Vol. 7, No. 3, 309–38.

Veryzer, R.W. (1998a) Key factors affecting customer evaluation of discontinuous products, *Journal of Product Innovation Management*, Vol. 15, No. 2, 136–50.

Veryzer, R.W. (1998b) Discontinuous innovation and the new product development process, *Journal of Product Innovation Management*, Vol. 15, No. 4, 304–21.

Veryzer, R. (2003) 'Marketing and the development of innovative products', in Shavinina, L. (ed.) *International Handbook on Innovation*, Pergamon Press, Canada, 43–54.

Yu, C. and Tao, Y. (2009) Understanding business-level innovation technology adoption, *Technovation*, Vol. 29, No. 2, 92–109.

Further reading

For a more detailed review of the role of the state in innovation management, the following develop many of the issues raised in this chapter:

Afuah, A. (2003) *Innovation Management: Strategies, Implementation and Profits*, 2nd edn, Oxford University Press, Oxford.

Freeman, C. and Soete, L. (2009) Developing science, technology and innovation indicators: What we can learn from the past, *Research Policy*, Vol. 38, No. 4, 583–9.

HSBC (2010) 100 thoughts, HSBC, London.

Hobday, M., Rush, H. and Bessant, J. (2004) Approaching the innovation frontier in Korea: The transition phase to leadership, *Research Policy*, Vol. 33, No. 10, 1433–57.

Moore, G.A. (2004) *Crossing the Chasm: Marketing and selling technology products to mainstream customers*, 2nd edn, Capstone, Oxford.

Rogers, E.M. (2003) *Diffusion of Innovations*, 5th edn, Free Press, New York.

Veryzer, R. (2003) 'Marketing and the development of innovative products', in Shavinina, L. (ed.) *The International Handbook on Innovation*, Pergamon Press, Canada.

Chapter 12
New product development

Introduction

Few business activities are heralded for their promise and approached with more justified optimism than the development of new products. Successful new products also have the added benefit of revitalising the organisation. Small wonder then that the concept of new product development (NPD) has received enormous attention in the management literature over the past 20 years. The result is a diverse range of literature from practitioners, management consultants and academics. This chapter explores this literature and examines the various models of NPD that have been put forward. It also explains the importance of NPD as a means of achieving growth.

The case study at the end of this chapter features one of the fastest growing brands in Europe – innocent. Its range of 'smoothies' and other beverages has propelled it into the top flight of brands. The case explores how this start-up firm acquired funding and developed its products.

Chapter contents

Learning objectives

When you have completed this chapter you will be able to:

- examine the relationship between new products and prosperity;
- recognise the range of product development opportunities that can exist;
- recognise that a new product is a multi-dimensional concept;
- identify the different types of models of NPD;
- provide an understanding of the importance of external linkages in the new product development process.

Innovation management and NPD

When one considers a variety of different industries, a decline in product innovations is matched only by a decline in market share. For example, Table 6.2 illustrates that across a wide variety of industries product innovation has led to winning market share and leadership.

This chapter looks at the exciting process of developing new products. Part One of this book has highlighted the importance of innovation and how the effective management of that process can lead to corporate success. To many people new products are the outputs of the innovation process, where the new product development (NPD) process is a subprocess of innovation. Managing innovation concerns the conditions that have to be in place to ensure that the organisation as a whole is given the opportunity to develop new products. The actual development of new products is the process of transforming business opportunities into tangible products.

Innovation in action

Hero Honda – Just4her

When Indian scooter maker Hero Honda introduced a scooter specifically targeted at women, it went beyond a 'feminised product'. To start with, it opened up 22 dedicated women-only scooter 'Just4her' showrooms across the country. With an all-female sales staff, the entire showroom is designed to make women buyers feel more at ease.

The company is working on creating all-women teams of mechanics. It's also introduced the Lady Rider Club, the first of its kind, offering special benefits that include milestone rewards, personal accident insurance and special events for members.

Source: HSBC (2010) 100 Thoughts, HSBC, London.

Source: Corbis/Larry Williams/Larry Williams and Associates

New product development concerns the management of the disciplines involved in the development of new products. These disciplines have developed their own perspectives on the subject of NPD. These are largely based on their experiences of involvement in the process. Hence, production management examines the development of new products from a manufacturing perspective, that is, how can we most effectively manufacture the product in question? Marketing, on the other hand, would take a slightly different perspective and would be concerned with trying to understand the needs of the customer and how the business could best meet these needs. However, producing what the customer wants may or may not be

Figure 12.1 **A variety of perspectives from which to analyse the development of new products**

either possible or profitable. The lack of a common approach to the development of new products is due to this multiple perspective. This is illustrated in Figure 12.1. The variety of views presented on the subject is not a weakness. Indeed, it should be viewed as a strength, for these different perspectives illuminate the areas that are left in the dark by other perspectives.

Usually, competition between companies is assessed using financial measures such as return on capital employed (ROCE), profits and market share. Non-financial measures such as design, innovativeness and technological supremacy may also be used.

Theoretically it is possible for a firm to survive without any significant developments to its products, but such firms are exceptions to the norm. Where long-term success is dependent on the ability to compete with others, this is almost always achieved by ensuring that your company's products are superior to the competition.

Product development as a series of decisions

The existing literature on product development is vast. The Brown and Eisenhardt (1995) review provides a comprehensive overview of the literature, and an illustration of the diversity of the literature, largely adopting an organisational perspective, which is arguably the main focus of the existing new product literature. However, other key perspectives on new product development are evident. The reviews by Finger and Dixon (1989a; 1989b) provide an excellent insight into the engineering design literature. The marketing perspective on new product development is reviewed by Green and Srinivasan (1990) and Mahajan and Wind (1992) and Barczak *et al.*, (2009). Arguably the paper by Krishnan and Uldrich (2001) remains one of very few papers that attempts to pull this wide and vast literature together. This review examines product development as a series of decisions. Within the product development project the authors divide the decisions into four categories: concept development; supply chain design; product design; and production ramp-up/launch.

Focusing on the study of Krishnan and Uldrich (2001), within concept development there are five basic decisions to be made:

1 What are the target values of the product attributes?
2 What will the product concept be?
3 What variants of the product will be offered?
4 What is the product architecture?
5 What will be the overall physical form and industrial design of the product?

Within the decisions surrounding supply chain design Krishnan and Uldrich (2001) argue that the following questions are key:

- Which components will be designed specifically for the product?
- Who will design and produce the product?
- What is the configuration of the physical supply chain?
- What type of process will be used to assemble the product?
- Who will develop and supply the process equipment?

New products and prosperity

The potential rewards of NPD are enormous. One only has to consider the rapid success of companies such as Microsoft and Compaq in the rapidly growing home computer industry. Similar success was achieved by Apple, and prior to this IBM, in the early development of the same industry. This example illustrates an important point, that success in one year does not ensure success in the next. Both Apple and IBM experienced severe difficulties in the 1990s.

Research by Cooper (1999) has suggested that, on average, new products (defined here as those less than five years old) are increasingly taking a larger slice of company sales. For 3M, for example, new products contributed to 30 per cent of sales in 2009, for Johnson & Johnson it was 25 per cent of sales in 2009 and for Du Pont a staggering 39 per cent of sales came from new products. The life cycles of products are becoming increasingly shorter. This is clearly evident in the mobile phone handset business where virtually all of Motorola's and Nokia's sales are from products that are less than three years old.

Considerations when developing an NPD strategy

Chapter 6 outlined many of the activities and factors that organisations need to consider in managing a business in the short and long term. In addition, Chapter 11 highlighted many of the factors that a business needs to consider if it is successfully to manage its products. It should be clear that establishing a direction for a business and the selection of strategies to achieve its goals form an ongoing, evolving process that is frequently subject to change. This is particularly evident at the product strategy level (Figure 12.2 illustrates the main inputs into the decision-making process). The process of product strategy was highlighted in Chapter 11 and is the creative process of recognising genuine business opportunities that the business might be able to exploit. It is commonly referred to as 'opportunity identification'.

Ongoing corporate planning

In large organisations this can be a very formal activity involving strategic planners and senior managers with responsibility for setting the future direction of the business. In smaller organisations this activity may be undertaken by the owner of the business in an informal, even *ad hoc* way. For many businesses it is somewhere in the middle of these two extremes. The effects of any corporate planning may be

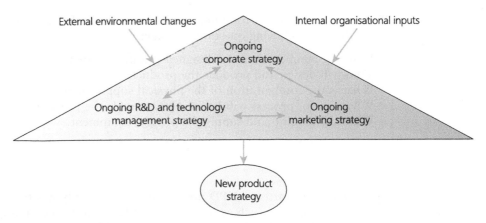

Figure 12.2 **Main inputs into the decision-making process**

important and long term. For example, the decision by a sports footwear manufacturer to exit the tennis market and concentrate on the basketball market due to changing social trends will have a significant impact on the business.

Ongoing market planning

Decisions by market planners may have equally significant effects. For example, the realisation that a competitor is about to launch an improved tennis shoe that offers additional benefits may force the business to establish five new product development projects. Two of these projects may be established to investigate the use of new materials for the sole, one could be used to develop a series of new designs, one could look at alternative fastenings and one could be used to reduce production costs.

Ongoing technology management

In most science- and technology-intensive industries such as the pharmaceutical and computer software industries, this activity is probably more significant than ongoing market planning. Technology awareness is very high. The continual analysis of internal R&D projects and external technology trawling will lead to numerous technical opportunities that need to be considered by the business. Say that a recent review of the patent literature has identified a patent application by one of the company's main competitors. This forces the business to establish a new project to investigate this area to ensure that it is aware of any future developments that may affect its position. This area is explored in more detail in Chapter 9.

Opportunity analysis/serendipity

In addition to the inputs that have been classified above, there are other inputs and opportunities that are often labelled miscellaneous or put down to serendipity (*see* Chapter 1). The vice-president of 3M remarked that 'chaos is a necessary part of an innovative culture. It's been said that 3M's competitors never know what we are going to come up with next. The fact is neither do we.'

NPD as a strategy for growth

The interest expressed by many companies in the subject of developing new products is hardly surprising given that the majority of businesses are intent on growth. Although, as was discussed in Chapter 11, this does not apply to all companies, none the less the development of new products provides an opportunity for growing the business. (It is worth reminding ourselves that new product development is only one of many options available to a business keen on growth.)

One of the clearest ways of identifying the variety of growth options available to a business is using Ansoff's (1965, 1968) directional policy matrix. This well-known matrix, shown in Figure 12.3, combines two of the key variables that enable a business to grow: an increase in market opportunities and an increase in product opportunities. Within this matrix new product development is seen as one of four available options. Each of the four cells considers various combinations of product–market options. Growth can be achieved organically (internal development) or through external acquisition. A criticism of this matrix is that it adopts an environmental perspective that assumes that opportunities for growth exist – they may not. Indeed, often consolidation and retrenchment need to be considered, especially in times of economic downturn. Each of the cells in the matrix is briefly discussed below.

Market penetration

Opportunities are said to exist within a business's existing markets through increasing the volume of sales. Increasing the market share of a business's existing products by exploiting the full range of marketing-mix activities is the common approach adopted by many companies. This may include branding decisions. For example, the cereal manufacturer Kellogg's has increased the usage of its cornflakes product by promoting it as a snack to be consumed at times other than at breakfast.

	Current products	New products
Current markets	1 Market penetration strategy	3 Product development strategy
New markets	2 Market development strategy	4 Diversification strategy

Figure 12.3 **Ansoff matrix**

Source: Adapted from I. Ansoff (1965) *Corporate Strategy*, Penguin, Harmondsworth; (1968) *Toward a Strategy of the Theory of the Firm*, McGraw-Hill, New York.

Market development

Growth opportunities are said to exist for a business's products through making them available to new markets. In this instance the company maintains the security of its existing products but opts to develop and enter new markets. Market development can be achieved by opening up new segments. For example, Mercedes decided to enter the small car market (previously the company had always concentrated on the executive or luxury segment). Similarly, companies may decide to enter new geographic areas through exporting.

Product development

Ansoff proposes that growth opportunities exist through offering new or improved products to existing markets. This is the subject of this chapter and, as will become clear, trying to establish when a product is new is sometimes difficult. None the less, virtually all companies try to ensure that their products are able to compete with the competition by regularly improving and updating their existing products. This is an ongoing activity for most companies.

Diversification

It hardly needs to be said that opportunities for growth exist beyond a business's existing products and markets. The selection of this option, however, would be significant in that the business would move into product areas and markets in which it currently does not operate. The development of the self-adhesive notepads (Post-it) by 3M provided an opportunity for the company to enter the stationery market, a market of which it had little knowledge, with a product that was new to the company and the market.

Many companies try to utilise either their existing technical or commercial knowledge base. For example, Flymo's knowledge of the electric lawnmower market enabled it to diversify into a totally new market. Indeed, the introduction of its Garden-vac product led to the creation of the 'garden-tidy' product market. While this is an example of organic growth, many companies identify diversification opportunities through acquisition. For example, in the United Kingdom some of the privatised electricity companies have purchased significant holdings in privatised water companies. The knowledge base being utilised here is the commercial know-how of the provision of a utility service (former public service).

Additional opportunities for diversified growth exist through forward, backward and horizontal diversification. A manufacturer opening retail outlets is an example of forward integration. Backward integration is involvement in activities which are inputs to the business, for example a manufacturer starting to produce components. Horizontal diversification is buying up competitors.

A range of product development opportunities

A development of Ansoff's directional policy matrix was Johnson and Jones's (1957) matrix for product development strategies (see Figure 12.4). This matrix

Increasing technology newness ⟶

Products objectives	No technological change	Improved technology	New technology To acquire scientific knowledge and production skills new to the company
No market change	Sustain	Reformulation To maintain an optimum balance of cost, quality and availability in the formulae of present products	Replacement To seek new and better ingredients of formulation for present company products in technology not now employed
Strengthened market To exploit more fully the existing markets for the present company's products	Remerchandising To increase sales to consumers of types now served by the company	Improved product To improve present products for greater utility and merchandisability to consumers	Product line extension To broaden the line of products offered to present consumers through new technology
New market To increase the number of types of consumer served by the company	New use To find new classes of consumer that can utilise present company products	Market extension To reach new classes of consumer by modifying present products	Diversification To add to the classes of consumer served by developing new technology knowledge

Increasing market newness (left axis label)

Figure 12.4 New product development strategies

Source: S.C. Johnson and C. Jones (1957) How to organise for new products, *Harvard Business Review*, May–June, Vol. 35, 49–62.

replaces Ansoff's product variable with technology. It builds on Ansoff's matrix by offering further clarification of the range of options open to a company contemplating product decisions. In particular, the use of technology as a variable better illustrates the decisions a company needs to consider. For example, Johnson and Jones distinguish between improving existing technology and acquiring new technology, the latter being far more resource intensive with higher degrees of risk. Ansoff's directional policy matrix made no such distinction. Similarly, the market-newness scale offers a more realistic range of alternatives. Many other matrices have since been developed to try to help firms identify the range of options available (*see* Dolan, 1993).

The range of product development strategies that are open to a company introduces the notion that a new product can take many forms. This is the subject of the next section.

Illustration 12.1

New products crucial to success for Shimano

As a keen cyclist, Yoshizo Shimano knows all about the importance of keeping in touch with his company's products. Mr Shimano is president of Shimano, the world's biggest maker of bicycle components.

Frequently, he borrows a bike from the company's R&D division to keep in touch with what researchers are up to. 'We won't compete with our customers by building complete bikes. But we must keep in mind how our components are going to be used and have a vision of the product that is safe as well as being fun', he says.

Mr Shimano's interest in trying out bicycles containing his company's components underlines how manufacturers must pay increasing importance to bringing out new products. These must either solve a pressing customer problem or come up with an idea that breaks completely new ground within a few years. In either case, manufacturers' strategies on new product development are crucial to their chances of long-term success in a world where competition is becoming steadily tougher.

In 1921 Shozaburo Shimano established Shimano Iron Works and began production of the bicycle freewheel. Today, some 90 years later, Shimano is a world leader in the manufacture and supply of bicycle parts, fishing tackle and rowing equipment. Sales in 2009 were ¥186 billion and profits were ¥20 billion. Shimano Inc. is the world's largest bicycle component manufacturer. Furthermore:

- Shimano has about a 70–80 per cent share of the worldwide bicycle component market;
- bicycle components make up about 78 per cent of sales while fishing tackle makes up the rest of sales;
- operating margin has increased nicely for the past seven years: from 9 per cent in 2001 to 14.8 per cent in 2007;
- operating margin has averaged about 14 per cent for the past eight years;
- Shimano has a strong history of sponsoring some of the best athletes and cycling teams in the world.

Source: Len Holsborg/Alamy Images

Shimano is quoted on the Tokyo stock exchange, with the family retaining a minority stake.

Mr Shimano says Shimano keeps in touch on product development by talking continually to the 400–500 bicycle manufacturers world-wide it supplies. It makes 13 main types of parts – gears, brake systems and drive chains – each of which can come in up to 100 different variants.

In the early 1990s, the company prospered through the development of products, such as specialist gears, that suited the then fashion for rugged, off-road mountain bikes. Now the mountain bike craze has died away, Mr Shimano says the company is increasing its development of products such as automatic gears that will give cyclists, particularly on congested city roads, safer, smoother rides.

'If the cyclist does not have to bother with changing gears, he can concentrate on other aspects of controlling the bike which is likely to lead to safer journeys', says Mr Shimano.

Source: P. Marsh (2002) New products crucial to success, FT.com, 21 May; Shimano.com (2010).

What is a new product?

Attempting to define what is and what is not a new product is not a trivial task, although many students of business management have had much fun arguing over whether the Sony Walkman was indeed a new product or merely existing technology repackaged. Another example that illustrates this point is the product long-life milk, known in the United States as aspectic milk (sold without refrigeration). This product has been consumed for many years in Europe but it is a relatively new concept for most consumers in the United States. Consumers who drink refrigerated milk may be extremely wary of milk sold from a non-refrigerated shelf. Once again, while clearly this product is not absolutely new, it can be seen that it is more useful from a product manager's perspective to adopt a relativistic view.

It is important to note, as was explained in Chapter 11, that a product is a multi-dimensional concept. It can be defined differently and can take many forms. Some dimensions will be tangible product features and others intangible. Does the provision of different packaging for a product constitute a new product? Surely the answer is no – or is it? New packaging coupled with additional marketing effort, especially in terms of marketing communications, can help to reposition a product. This was successfully achieved by GlaxoSmithKline with its beverage product Lucozade. Today this product is known as a sports drink, yet older readers will recall that the product was originally packaged in a distinctive bottle wrapped in yellow cellophane and commonly purchased at pharmacists for sick children. This

Illustration 12.2

The repositioning of BMW's Mini

The Mini is one of the most established and successful product brands in the automotive industry. It has been in existence for over 45 years and had sold over 4 million units before its highly successful relaunch in 2001. The Mini was designed and manufactured in Britain; the car was launched in 1959 by the British Leyland Motor Corporation. The Mini remained under British ownership until 1994 when BMW acquired the Rover Group; though it later sold off much of the group, BMW kept the Mini. In 1999 the Mini celebrated its 40th birthday and *Autocar* named it the car of the century. The Mini itself remained relatively unchanged from its original launch until it was completely withdrawn from production in 2000. A new Mini and Mini Cooper (designed and manufactured by BMW) were launched in 2001. It has been a very successful project with sales growing from 25,000

Source: Mini UK

units in 2001 to over 200,000 units in 2006 (Arlidge, 2006).

Source: Arlidge, J. (2006) Minis maxi challenge, *Sunday Times*, S3 Business, p. 11, 17 September; Simms, C. and Trott, P. (2006) The perceptions of the BMW Mini brand: the importance of historical associations and the development of a model, *Journal of Product & Brand Management*, Vol. 15, No. 4, 228–38.

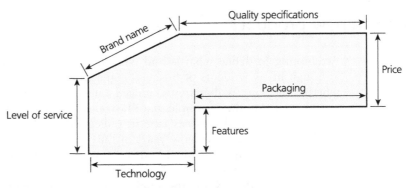

Figure 12.5 **A product is multi-dimensional**

illustrates the difficulty of attempting to offer a single definition for a new product. (Also, *see* the example of BMW's Mini in Illustration 12.2.)

If we accept that a product has many dimensions, then it must follow that it is theoretically possible to label a product 'new' by merely altering one of these dimensions, for example packaging. Figure 12.5 illustrates this point. In addition Corrocher and Zirulia (2010) found that mobile communication operators used pricing tariffs to develop innovative new services. Each dimension is capable of being altered. These alterations create a new dimension and in theory a new product, even if the change is very small. Indeed, Johne and Snelson (1988) suggest that the options for both new and existing product lines centre on altering the variables in the figure. Table 12.1 shows what this means in practice.

Defining a new product

Chapter 1 established a number of definitions to help with the study of this subject and provided a definition of innovation. In addition, it highlighted a quotation by Rogers and Shoemaker (1972) concerning whether or not something is new. It is useful at this juncture to revisit their argument. They stated that while it may be difficult to establish whether a product is actually new as regards the passage of time, so long as it is perceived to be new it *is* new. This is significant because it

Table 12.1 **Different examples of 'newness'**

1 Changing the performance capabilities of the product (for example, a new, improved washing detergent)

2 Changing the application advice for the product (for example, the use of the Persil ball in washing machines)

3 Changing the after-sales service for the product (for example, frequency of service for a motor car)

4 Changing the promoted image of the product (for example, the use of 'green'-image refill packs)

5 Changing the availability of the product (for example, the use of chocolate-vending machines)

6 Changing the price of the product (for example, the newspaper industry has experienced severe price wars)

Source: F.A. Johne and P.A. Snelson (1988) The role of marketing specialists in product development, Proceedings of the 21st Annual Conference of the Marketing Education Group, Huddersfield, Vol. 3, 176–91.

Table 12.2 **A new product has different interpretations of new**

New product A
A snack manufacturer introduces a new, larger pack size for its best-selling savoury snack. Consumer research for the company revealed that a family-size pack would generate additional sales without cannibalising existing sales of the standard-size pack.

New product B
An electronics company introduces a new miniature compact disc player. The company has further developed its existing compact disc product and is now able to offer a much lighter and smaller version.

New product C
A pharmaceutical company introduces a new prescription drug for ulcer treatment. Following eight years of laboratory research and three years of clinical trials, the company has recently received approval from the government's medical authorities to launch its new ulcer drug.

illustrates that newness is a relative term. In the case of a new product it is relative to what preceded the product. Moreover, the overwhelming majority of so-called new products are developments or variations on existing formats. Research in this area suggests that only 10 per cent of new products introduced are new to both the market and the company (Booz, Allen & Hamilton, 1982). New to the company (in this case) means that the firm has not sold this type of product before, but other firms could have. New to the market means that the product has not appeared before in the market. However, the examples in Table 12.2 illustrate the confusion that exists in this area.

The three products in the table are all new in that they did not exist before. However, many would argue, especially technologists, that Product A does not contain any new technology. Similarly, Product B does not contain any new technology although its configuration may be new. Product C contains a new patented chemical formulation, hence this is the only truly new product. Marketers would, however, contend that all three products are new simply because they did not previously exist. Moreover, meeting the needs of the customer and offering products that are wanted is more important than whether a product represents a scientific breakthrough. Such arguments are common to many companies, especially those that have both a strong commercial and technological presence and expertise.

Pause for thought ?

Has the BMW Mini been repositioned? Or is it a new product?

For the student of innovation and new product development, awareness of the debate and the strong feelings that are associated with it is more important than trying to resolve the polemics. Indeed, the long-term commercial success of the company should be the guiding principle on which product decisions are made. However, in some industries, the advancement of knowledge and subsequent scientific breakthroughs can lead to possible product offerings that would help certain sections of the population. Commercial pressures alone would, however, prevent these new products from being offered, as we saw in the tooth whitening case study in Chapter 11. The science and technology perspective should therefore not be dismissed.

Classification of new products

There have been many attempts to classify new products into certain categories. Very often the distinction between one category and another is one of degree and attempting to classify products is subject to judgement. It is worthy of note, however, that only 10 per cent of all new products are truly innovative. These products involve the greatest risk because they are new to both the company and the marketplace. Most new product activity is devoted to improving existing products. At Sony 80 per cent of new product activity is undertaken to modify and improve the company's existing products. The following classification (Booz, Allen & Hamilton, 1982) identifies the commonly accepted categories of new product developments.

New-to-the-world products

These represent a small proportion of all new products introduced. They are the first of their kind and create a new market. They are inventions that usually contain a significant development in technology, such as a new discovery, or manipulate existing technology in a very different way, leading to revolutionary new designs such as Dyson's vacuum cleaner. Other examples include Apple's iPad, 3M's Post-it notes and Guinness's 'in-can' system.

New product lines (new to the firm)

Although not new to the marketplace, these products are new to the particular company. They provide an opportunity for the company to enter an established market for the first time. For example, Alcatel, Samsung and Sony-Ericsson have all entered the mobile phone market to compete with market leaders Nokia and Motorola, originators of the product.

Additions to existing lines (line additions)

This category is a subset of new product lines above. The distinction is that while the company already has a line of products in this market, the product is significantly different from the present product offering but not so different that it is a new line. The distinction between this category and the former is one of degree. For example, Hewlett-Packard's colour ink-jet printer was an addition to its established line of ink-jet printers.

Improvements and revisions to existing products

These new products are replacements of existing products in a firm's product line. For example, Hewlett-Packard's ink-jet printer has received numerous modifications over time and, with each revision, performance and reliability have been improved. Also, manufacturing cost reductions can be introduced, providing increased added value. This classification represents a significant proportion of all new product introductions.

Cost reductions

This category of products may not be viewed as new from a marketing perspective, largely because they offer no new benefits to the consumer other than possibly reduced costs. From the firm's perspective, however, they may be very significant. The ability to offer similar performance while reducing production costs provides enormous added-value potential. Indeed, frequently it is this category of new product that can produce the greatest financial rewards for the firm. Improved manufacturing processes and the use of different materials are key contributing factors. The effect may be to reduce the number of moving parts or use more cost-effective materials (*see* Chapter 4). The difference between this category and the improvement category is simply that a cost reduction may not result in a product improvement.

Repositioning

These new products are essentially the discovery of new applications for existing products. This has as much to do with consumer perception and branding as technical development. This is none the less an important category. Following the medical science discovery that aspirin thins blood, for example, the product has been repositioned from an analgesic to an over the-counter remedy for blood clots and one that may help to prevent strokes and heart attacks.

In practice most of the projects in a firm's portfolio are improvements to products already on the market, additions to existing lines (line extensions), and products new to the firm but already manufactured by competitors (new product lines). Figure 12.6 illustrates the average project portfolio within firms. Here, 70 per cent of new products are improvements, cost reductions and additions to existing lines.

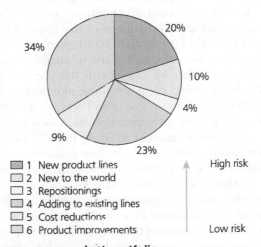

Figure 12.6 **The average new product portfolio**

Source: Adapted from A. Griffin (1997) PDMA research on new product development practices: updating trends and benchmarking best practices, *Journal of Product Innovation Management*, Vol. 14, 429.

Product category

		New	Existing
Brand name	New	New brand	Flanker
	Existing	Brand extension	Line extension

Figure 12.7 **Tauber's growth matrix**

Source: Tauber, E.M. (1981) Brand franchise extension: new product benefits from existing brand names, *Business Horizons*, Vol. 24, No. 2, 36–41.

Repositioning and brand extensions

The concepts of brand extension and repositioning appear as two distinct elements within classifications of new product development. When it comes to brand extension Tauber's (1981) growth matrix categorises a firm's growth opportunities using two different dimensions: product category, and brand name used. The resulting matrix is shown in Figure 12.7. Tauber makes a key distinction between brand extension and line extension. However, as Ambler and Styles (1997) have shown in a survey of the academic literature, each concept has been given a variety of definitions and the terms are used interchangeably (see Ambler and Styles, 1997). For example, Kotler (1991: 556) defines a brand extension strategy as: 'any effort to extend a successful brand name to launch new or modified products or lines'. Whereas Doyle (1994: 159) is more specific: 'a brand extension means using a brand name successfully established for one segment or channel to enter another one in the same broad market'.

Saunders and Jobber's phasing continuity spectrum (Saunders and Jobber, 1994) illustrates the extent of marketing mix effort required for each of the options open to firms considering new product development (*see* Figure 12.8). Product changes are on the horizontal axis and changes to the rest of the marketing mix are on the vertical axis. Product developments are classified according to the extent of change. This ranges from no change in the upper left-hand quadrant to a new innovative product in the bottom right-hand quadrant. Significantly Saunders and Jobber introduce the notion of tangible and intangible repositioning, and these are distinguished from each other by changes to the physical product. Yet, Bingham and Raffield (1995) identified six positioning alternatives for firms: price, technology, product quality, distribution, image and service. It follows, therefore, that any decision by a firm to alter the perceptual position of a brand (that is, reposition it) will demand careful consideration of all of the brand's attributes (Park *et al.*, 2002). Indeed, Bhat and Reddy (1998) argue in their research on brand positioning that brands can be positioned at a symbolic and/or functional level.

Within FMCG industries product and brand development are considered together. Indeed, according to Yakimov and Beverland (2004), who examined eight brand repositioning case studies, successful brand management firms place the brand at the centre of their organisation and strategy, and build integrated strategies to continually support the brand. While this may be understandable for FMCG, where differences in products is frequently limited, the extent to which this is also the case in non-FMCG goods, and technology-intensive industries in particular, is

| | **Product** | | |
	No change	Modified	Technology change
No change	**No change** No change	**Facelift** Appearance	**Inconspicuous substitution** Technology Materials Manufacturing
Modified	**Re-merchandising** Name Promotion Price Distribution Packaging	**Relaunch** Costs Promotion Price Distribution	**Conspicuous substitution** Technology Materials Name Appearance Promotion Price Distribution
New market/ segment	**Intangible repositioning** Name Promotion Price Distribution Target market Competition	**Tangible repositioning** Name Appearance Costs Promotion Price Distribution Target market Competition	**Neo-innovation** Technology Materials Manufacturing Promotion Price Distribution Target market Competition

Marketing (row label spanning the left side)

Figure 12.8 **Saunders and Jobber's phasing continuity spectrum**

Source: Saunders, J. and Jobber, D. (1994) Product replacement: Strategies for simultaneous product deletion and launch, *Journal of Product Innovation Management*, Vol. 11, No. 5, 433–50.

less clear. Within technology-intensive industries, such as personal computers, it could be argued that product specification vis á vis price is a more significant factor for consumers.

New product development as an industry innovation cycle

Abernathy and Utterback (1978) suggested that product innovations are soon followed by process innovations in what they described as an industry innovation cycle (*see* Chapter 1). A similar notion can be applied to the categories of new products. The cycle can be identified in a wide variety of industries. New-to-the-world products (Category 1) are launched by large companies with substantial resources, especially technical or marketing resources. Other large firms react swiftly to the launch of such a product by developing their own versions (Categories 2 and 3). Many small and medium-sized companies participate by developing their own new products to compete with the originating firm's product (Category 4). Substantial success and growth can come to small companies that adopt this strategy. Hewlett-Packard has grown into one of the most successful personal computer manufacturers even though it was not, unlike Apple and IBM, at the forefront of the development of the personal computer. As competition intensifies, companies will compete in the market for profits. The result is determined efforts to reduce costs in order to improve these profits, hence there are many cost reductions (Category 5).

Overview of NPD theories

The early stages of the new product development process are most usually defined as idea generation, idea screening, concept development and concept testing. They represent the formation and development of an idea prior to its taking any physical form. In most industries it is from this point onwards that costs will rise significantly. It is clearly far easier to change a concept than a physical product. The subsequent stages involve adding to the concept as those involved with the development (manufacturing engineers, product designers and marketers) begin to make decisions regarding how best to manufacture the product, what materials to use, possible designs and the potential market's evaluations.

The organisational activities undertaken by the company as it embarks on the actual process of new product development have been represented by numerous different models. These have attempted to capture the key activities involved in the process, from idea to commercialisation of the product. The representation of these tasks has changed significantly over the past 30 years. For example, the pharmaceutical industry is dominated by scientific and technological developments that lead to new drugs; whereas the food industry is dominated by consumer research that leads to many minor product changes. And yet the vast majority of textbooks that tackle this subject present the NPD process as an eight-stage linear model regardless of these major differences (Figure 12.9 shows how the process is frequently presented). Consequently this simple linear model is ingrained in the minds of many people. This is largely because new product development is viewed from a financial perspective where cash outflows precede cash inflows (*see* Figure 12.10). This graph shows the cumulative effect on cash flow through the development phases, from the build-up

Figure 12.9 Commonly presented linear NPD model

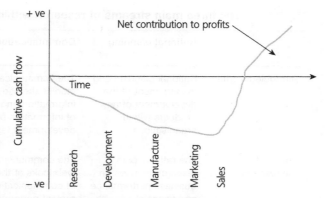

Figure 12.10 **Cash flows and new product development**

of stock and work in progress in the early stages of production, when there is no balancing in-flow of cash from sales, to the phase of profitable sales which brings the cash in-flow.

Virtually all those actually involved with the development of new products dismiss such simple linear models as not being a true representation of reality. More recent research suggests that the process needs to be viewed as a simultaneous and concurrent process with cross-functional interaction (Hart, 1993; Barczak *et al.*, 2009).

For the reasons outlined above, the different perspectives on NPD have produced a wealth of literature on the subject (Brown and Eisenhardt, 1995; Barczak *et al.*, 2009). In addition, the subject has attracted the attention of many business schools and business consultants, all interested in uncovering the secrets of successful product development. Numerous research projects have been undertaken including indepth case studies across many industries and single companies and broad surveys of industries (e.g. Ancona and Caldwell, 1992; Clark and Fujimoto, 1991; Dougherty, 1990; Biemans *et al.*, 2007).

As a result, research on new product development is varied and fragmented, making it extremely difficult to organise for analysis. Brown and Eisenhardt (1995) have tackled this particular problem head on and have produced an excellent review of the literature. In their analysis they identify three main streams of literature, each having its own particular strengths and limitations (*see* Table 12.3). These streams have evolved around key research findings and together they continue to throw light on many dark areas of new product development.

While this is an important development and a useful contribution to our understanding of the subject area, it offers little help for the practising manager on how he or she should organise and manage the new product development process. An analysis of the models that have been developed on the subject of new product development may help to identify some of the activities that need to be managed.

The fuzzy front end

Within the new product development literature the concept of the so-called 'fuzzy front end' is the messy 'getting started' period of new product development processes. It is at the beginning of the process, or 'the front end', where the organisation develops a concept of the product to be developed and decides whether or not to invest resources

Table 12.3 **The three main streams of research within the NPD literature**

	Rational planning	**Communication web**	**Disciplined problem solving**
Aim/objective/title	Rational planning and management of the development of new products within organisations	The communication web studies the use of information and sources of information by product development teams	Disciplined problem solving focuses on how problems encountered during the NPD process were overcome
Focus of the research	The rational plan research focuses on business performance and financial performance of the product	The communication web looks at the effects of communication on project performance	The third stream tries to examine the process and the wide range of actors and activities involved
Seminal research	The work by Myers and Marquis (1969) and SAPPHO studies (Rothwell et al., 1974) was extremely influential in this field	Thomas Allen's (1969, 1977) research into communication patterns in large industrial laboratories dominates this perspective	The work by the Japanese scholars Imai et al. (1985) lies at the heart of this third stream of literature

Source: S.L. Brown and K.M. Eisenhardt (1995) Product development: past research, present findings and future directions, *Academy of Management Review*, Vol. 20, No. 2, 343–78.

in the further development of an idea. It is the phase between first consideration of an opportunity and when it is judged ready to enter the structured development process (Kim and Wilemon, 2002; Koen *et al.*, 2001). It includes all activities from the search for new opportunities through the formation of a germ of an idea to the development of a precise concept. The fuzzy front end disapears when an organisation approves and begins formal development of the concept.

Although the fuzzy front end may not require expensive capital investment, it can consume 50 per cent of development time and it is where major commitments are typically made involving time, money and the product's nature, thus setting the course for the entire project and final end product. Consequently, this phase should be considered as an essential part of development rather than something that happens 'before development', and its cycle time should be included in the total new product development cycle time.

There has been much written in the NPD literature about the need to involve customers at an early stage in the process and to integrate them into the process in order to fully capture ideas (Cooper, 1999; von Hippel, 1986; Brown and Eisenhardt, 1995; 1998; Thomke, 2003). Despite this, customer involvement in NPD has been limited and largely passive in most industries (Weyland and Cole, 1997). There are many reasons for this limited utilisation of consumers in NPD and some have touched on above, but perhaps the most limiting factor is the disconnection between customers and producers.

Nowadays, technology enables an innovative way of involving and integrating customers to the product development process. In this context, it is here that new technologies, most notably in the form of 'toolkits', offer considerable scope for improving connection between consumers and producers. Franke and Piller's (2004)

Table 12.4 **Customer roles in NPD**

Customer role	NPD phase	Key issues/managerial challenges
Customer as resource	Ideation	Appropriateness of customer as a source of innovation Selection of customer innovator Need for varied customer incentives Infrastructure for capturing customer knowledge Differential role of existing (current) and potential (future) customers
Customer as co-creator	Design and development	Involvement in a wide range of design and development tasks Nature of the NPD context: industrial/consumer products Tighter coupling with internal NPD teams Managing the attendant project uncertainty
	Product testing	Enhancing customers' product/technology knowledge Time-bound activity Ensuring customer diversity
Customer as user	Product support	Ongoing activity Infrastructure to support customer–customer interactions

Source: Adapted from Nambisan, S. (2002) Designing virtual customer environments for new product development: Toward a theory, *Academy of Management Review*, Vol. 27, No. 3, 395.

study analysed the value created by so-called 'toolkits for user innovation and design'. This was a method of integrating customers into new product development and design. The so-called toolkits allow customers to create their own product, which in turn is produced by the manufacturer. An example of a toolkit in its simplest form is the development of personalised products through uploading digital family photographs via the internet and having these printed on to products such as clothing or cups, etc., thereby allowing consumers to create personalised individual products for themselves. User toolkits for innovation are specific to given product or service types and to a specified production system. Within those general constraints, they give users real freedom to innovate, allowing them to develop their custom product via iterative trial and error (von Hippel, 2001; Franke and Piller, 2004).

Nambisan (2002) offers a theoretical lens through which to view these 'virtual customer environments'. He considers the underlying knowledge creation issues and the nature of the customer interactions to identify three roles: customer as resource; customer as co-creator and customer as user. These three distinct but related roles provide a useful classification with which to examine the process of NPD. This classification recognises the considerably different management challenges for the firm if it is to utilise the customer into the NPD process (*see* Table 12.4).

Time to market

Time to market (TTM) is the length of time it takes from a product being conceived to it reaching the market place. TTM is important in industries where products are outdated quickly. A common assumption is that TTM matters most for innovative products, but actually the first mover often has the luxury of time, while the clock is clearly running for the followers. TTM can vary widely between industries, say 15 years in aircraft and six months in food products. Yet, in many ways it is a firm's

TTM capability relative to its direct competitors that is far more important than the naked figure. While other industries may be much faster, they do not pose a direct threat – although one may be able to learn from them and adapt their techniques.

As usual there are some other factors that need to be considered when analysing a firm's TTM. For example, rather than reaching the market as soon as possible, delivering on schedule may be more important: to have the new product available for a trade show could be more valuable. Many managers argue that the shorter the project the less it will cost, so they attempt to use TTM as a means of cutting expenses. Unfortunately, a primary means of reducing TTM is to staff the project more heavily, so a faster project may actually be more expensive. Finally, as we have seen throughout this chapter, the need for change often appears midstream in a project. Consequently, the ability to make changes during product development without being too disruptive can be valuable. For example, one's goal could be to satisfy customers, which could be achieved by adjusting product requirements during development in response to customer feedback. Then TTM could be measured from the last change in requirements until the product is delivered. The pursuit of pure speed of TTM may also harm the business (Cooper and Edgett, 2008).

Agile NPD

Flexible product development is the ability to make changes to the product being developed or in how it is developed, even relatively late in the development process, without being too disruptive. Consequently, the later one can make changes, the more flexible the process is; and the less disruptive the change is, the greater the flexibility. Change can be expected in what the customer wants and how the customer might use the product, in how competitors might respond, and in the new technologies being applied in the product or in its manufacturing process. The more innovative a new product is, the more likely it is that the development team will have to make changes during development. In his book *Flexible Product Development* (2007) Preston Smith uses the software industry to show that having an agile NPD process enables the firm to adapt to changing markets. These days many industrial new product development (NPD) software projects apply agile methodologies, such as *Scrum, eXtreme Programming (XP)* and *Feature-Driven Development (FDD)*. Petri Kettunen from Siemens studied some of these systems and found that agility in embedded software product development can be further enhanced by following typical NPD principles (Kettunen, 2009).

Models of new product development

Among the burgeoning management literature on the subject it is possible to classify the numerous models into eight distinct categories:

1 departmental-stage models;
2 activity-stage models and concurrent engineering;
3 cross-functional models (teams);
4 decision-stage models;

5 conversion-process models;
6 response models;
7 network models and
8 outsourced (see Chapter 16).

Within this taxonomy decision-stage models and activity-stage models are the most commonly discussed and presented in textbooks. Figure 12.13 (later) is an example of an activity-stage model and Cooper's stage-gate model is an example of a decision stage model.

It is worthy of note that there are many companies, especially small specialist manufacturing companies, that continue to operate a craftsman-style approach to product development. This has been the traditional method of product manufacture for the past 500 years. For example, in every part of Europe there are joinery companies manufacturing products to the specific requirements of the user. Many of these products will be single, one-off products manufactured to dimensions given on a drawing. All the activities, including the creation of drawings, collection of raw materials, manufacture and delivery, may be undertaken by one person. Today, when we are surrounded by technology that is sometimes difficult to use never mind understand, it is possible to forget that the traditional approach to product development is still prevalent. Many activities, moreover, remain the same as they have always been.

Departmental-stage models

Departmental-stage models represent the early form of NPD models. These can be shown to be based around the linear model of innovation, where each department is responsible for certain tasks. They are usually represented in the following way. R&D provides the interesting technical ideas; the engineering department will then take the ideas and develop possible prototypes; the manufacturing department will explore possible ways to produce a viable product capable of mass manufacture; the marketing department will then be brought in to plan and conduct the launch. Such models are also referred to as 'over-the-wall' models, so called because departments would carry out their tasks before throwing the project over the wall to the next department (*see* Figure 12.11).

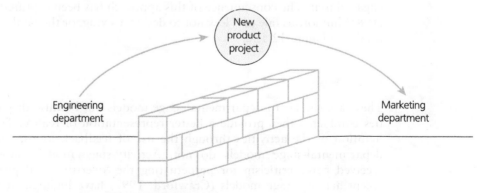

Figure 12.11 **Over-the-wall model**

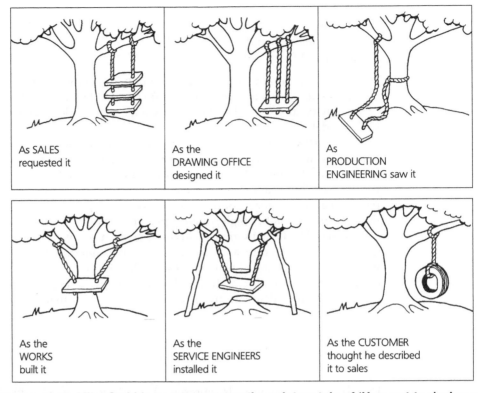

Figure 12.12 Mike Smith's secret weapon: the salutary tale of 'How not to design a swing, or the perils of poor coordination'

Source: C. Lorenz (1990) *The Design Dimension*, Blackwell Publishing Ltd, Oxford.

It is now widely accepted that this insular departmental view of the process hinders the development of new products. The process is usually characterised by a great deal of reworking and consultation between functions. In addition, market research provides continual inputs to the process. Furthermore, control of the project changes on a departmental basis depending on which department is currently engaged in it. The consequence of this approach has been captured by Mike Smith's (1981) humorous tale of 'How not to design a swing, or the perils of poor coordination' (*see* Figure 12.12).

Activity-stage models and concurrent engineering

These are similar to departmental-stage models but because they emphasise activities conducted they provide a better representation of reality. They also facilitate iteration of the activities through the use of feedback loops, something that the departmental-stage models do not. Activity-stage models, however, have also received fierce criticism for perpetuating the 'over-the-wall' phenomenon. More recent activity-stage models (Crawford, 1997) have highlighted the simultaneous nature of the activities within the NPD process, hence emphasising the need for a

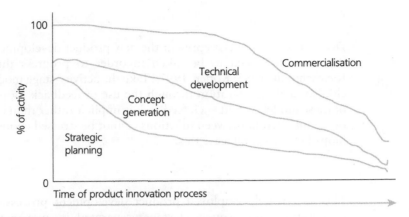

Figure 12.13 An activity-stage model

Source: From *New Products Management*, 5th edn (Crawford, C.M. 1997), © The McMcGraw-Hill Companies, Inc.

cross-functional approach. Figure 12.13 shows an activity-stage model where the activities occur at the same time but vary in their intensity.

In the late 1980s, in an attempt to address some of these problems, many manufacturing companies adopted a concurrent engineering or simultaneous engineering approach. The term was first coined by the Institute for the Defense Analyses (IDA) in 1986 (IDA, 1986) to explain the systematic method of concurrently designing both the product and its downstream production and support processes. The idea is to focus attention on the project as a whole rather than the individual stages, primarily by involving all functions from the outset of the project. This requires a major change in philosophy from functional orientation to project orientation. Furthermore, technology-intensive businesses with very specialist knowledge inputs are more difficult to manage. Such an approach introduces the need for project teams.

Cross-functional models (teams)

Common problems that occur within the product development process revolve around communications between different departments. This problem, specifically with regard to the marketing and the R&D departments, is explored more fully in Chapter 16. In addition, projects would frequently be passed back and forth between functions. Moreover, at each interface the project would undergo increased changes, hence lengthening the product development process. The cross-functional teams (CFT) approach removes many of these limitations by having a dedicated project team representing people from a variety of functions. The use of cross-functional teams requires a fundamental modification to an organisation's structure. In particular, it places emphasis on the use of project management and interdisciplinary teams.

Decision-stage models

Decision-stage models represent the new product development process as a series of decisions that need to be taken in order to progress the project (Cooper and Kleinschmidt, 1993; Kotler, 1997). Like the activity-stage models, many of these models also facilitate iteration through the use of feedback loops. However, a criticism of these models is that such feedback is implicit rather than explicit. The importance of the interaction between functions cannot be stressed enough – the use of feedback loops helps to emphasise this.

Stage-gate process

This is a widely employed product development process that divides the effort into distinct time-sequenced stages separated by management decision gates. It has been popularised by Robert Cooper's research in this area (Cooper, 1999; www.prod-dev.com/stage-gate). Multifunctional teams must successfully complete a prescribed set of related cross-functional tasks in each stage prior to obtaining management approval to proceed to the next stage of product development. The framework of the stage-gate process includes work-flow and decision-flow paths and defines the supporting systems and practices necessary to ensure the ongoing smooth operation of the process.

As with any prescribed approach the stage-gate process suffers from a number of limitations:

- The process is sequential and can be slow.
- The whole process is focused on end gates rather than on the customer.
- Product concepts can be stopped or frozen too early.
- The high level of uncertainty that accompanies discontinuous new products makes the stage-gate process unsuitable for these products.
- At each stage within the process a low level of knowledge held by the gatekeeper can lead to poor judgements being made on the project.

Conversion-process models

As the name suggests, conversion-process models view new product development as numerous inputs into a 'black box' where they are converted into an output (Schon, 1967). For example, the inputs could be customer requirements, technical ideas and manufacturing capability and the output would be the product. The concept of a variety of information inputs leading to a new product is difficult to criticise, but the lack of detail elsewhere is the biggest limitation of such models.

Response models

Response models are based on the work of Becker and Whistler (1967) who used a behaviourist approach to analyse change. In particular, these models focus on the individual's or organisation's response to a new project proposal or new idea. This approach has revealed additional factors that influence the decision to accept or reject new product proposals, especially at the screening stage.

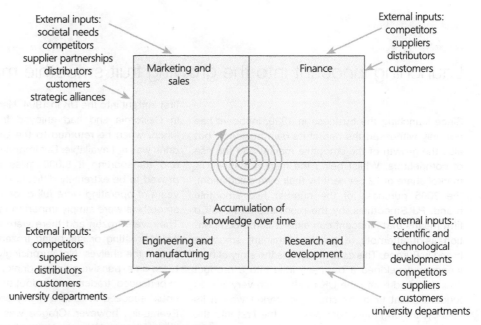

External inputs:
societal needs
competitors
supplier partnerships
distributors
customers
strategic alliances

External inputs:
competitors
suppliers
distributors
customers

Marketing and sales

Finance

Accumulation of knowledge over time

Engineering and manufacturing

Research and development

External inputs:
competitors
suppliers
distributors
customers
university departments

External inputs:
scientific and
technological
developments
competitors
suppliers
customers
university departments

Figure 12.14 **A network model of NPD**

Network models

This final classification of new product development models represents the most recent thinking on the subject. The case studies in Chapters 7 and 10 highlight the process of accumulation of knowledge from a variety of different inputs, such as marketing, R&D and manufacturing. This knowledge is built up gradually over time as the project progresses from initial idea (technical breakthrough or market opportunity) through development. It is this process that forms the basis of the network models (these models are explored more fully in Nonaka and Takeuchi, 1995).

Essentially, network models emphasise the external linkages coupled with the internal activities that have been shown to contribute to successful product development. There is substantial evidence to suggest that external linkages can facilitate additional knowledge flows into the organisation, thereby enhancing the product development process. These models suggest that NPD should be viewed as a knowledge-accumulation process that requires inputs from a wide variety of sources. The model in Figure 12.14 helps to highlight the accumulation of knowledge over time. This may be thought of as a snowball gaining in size as it rolls down a snow-covered mountain.

Pause for thought

Linear models are simple and hence dominate NPD, but they do not reflect reality.

Launching innocent into the growing fruit smoothie market

Introduction

Since launching the business in 1999, innocent has not only witnessed the rise of its own business, but also the growth of the smoothie market and the rise of competitors. Whilst being the market leader (UK market share of 72 per cent by their own calculation), the 2005 purchase of the number two smoothie brand, PJ Smoothies, by the multinational PepsiCo firm means that innocent can expect fierce competition as it attempts to be the dominant smoothie brand in Europe. This case study tells the story of how innocent developed a business idea into a product and launched it into the UK market with very limited funds. At that time the smoothie market was in its infancy, although innocent was not the first into the market and could not benefit from any early entrant advantages. None the less, the launch of the product coincided with the rapid growth of the market, especially in the form of own-label smoothies from Sainsbury, Tesco and M&S.

The fruit smoothies market

Fruit smoothies are a fruit-based beverage (usually 100 per cent crushed fruit and very little else). According to the advertisements they are nutritious and versatile, and are an excellent way of grabbing a quick meal. Smoothies have been popular in health-conscious California for many decades. They are generally low in fat and calories and make an excellent drink and/ or snack especially at lunchtime. innocent is now the brand leader in the UK smoothie market, generating revenue of £80 million annually. Pete & Johnny's – the first UK smoothie company – has annual sales of £13 million while private-label brands make up around one-third of the market. innocent's timing has been lucky or astute. As concern grows over rising levels of obesity in Europe, consumers are paying more attention to what they eat and drink and multinational food and beverage companies are trying to tap into changing consumer tastes by selling healthier products. Californians had been consuming fruit smoothies for a number of years before the concept was exported to the UK. It is Harry Cragoe, founder of PJ Smoothies, who is generally regarded as the first entrant into the UK in 1994. Harry had been living in California and had enjoyed fruit smoothies for lunch; when he returned to the UK he realised this drink was not available. But importing a fresh product and transporting it 8,000 miles across the world proved to be extremely difficult. Indeed, the first few years of operating were full of problems. Initially the smoothies were simply imported in large containers. They were frozen and there were problems of them not defrosting or still being frozen when they were put on the shelves. Not surprisingly the product was twice as expensive as other drinks at the time. Many experienced traders were doubtful such a product could succeed in such a highly competitive market. Eventually, however, Cragoe was able to establish production in Newark, Nottinghamshire, which has solved many of the initial logistical problems.

The success of the PJ Smoothie business is remarkable and unusual in that very little money has been spent on marketing and market research. This is even more remarkable for a fast moving consumer good. Cragoe is a critic of traditional market research, arguing that 'I've never spent a penny on market research because you end up looking at it too religiously. The growth we have experienced is purely from word of mouth. People have tasted the products and told their friends. We also tried to get away from bad labelling, deciding instead to use just pictures of apples and oranges. We have always tried to be fun, relevant and interesting with our packaging.' Cragoe insists that tasting the product is the best way to experience whether it is good or bad and this has led to even more growth. He believes that 99 per cent of people like the taste and pass on the message.

Source: Innocent Ltd

innocent and developing a new product concept

Hot on the heels of PJ Smoothies was innocent smoothies. In 2005 innocent drinks was the fastest growing food and drinks company in the UK; it was launched in 1999, and the company has grown into the No. 1 smoothie brand in the UK with 240 staff and an £80 million turnover. It has gone from making three recipes of smoothie to seventeen different drinks. Through constant innovation and refusal to compromise, innocent continues to make an un-rivalled range of totally natural fruit drinks that taste good and have health benefits. But the road to success was far from simple.

The beverage market is fiercely competitive, dominated by global players such as Coca-Cola and Pepsi. The range of beverages available is also vast, from bottled water to carbonated drinks in all flavours. The fruit smoothie product being launched was perishable, with a very short shelf life, and with a price tag at almost £2 a bottle it was four times that of other beverages on the shelf. Achieving success was not going to be easy.

The beginnings of the business idea stretch back many years and is the result of a friendship started at university. Richard Reed, Adam Balon and Jon Wright left university and went into the obligatory milk-round professions – one into advertising, two into management consultancy. Four years later, they were still talking about their business ideas, although they still had no product. One idea they all liked and enjoyed was fruit smoothies. They all enjoyed a fruit smoothie for lunch and all had enjoyed making them at home with fresh soft fruit and an electric blender. At the time there were very few smoothies on the shelf. In 1998, during their spare time from work and sometimes during their time at work the three friends began planning their business idea of fruit smoothies. During this time they continued trying out recipes on friends and developing their business plan. At the end of that time they spent £500 on fruit, turned it into smoothies and tested their drinks on visitors to the Jazz on the Green festival in London. Their much-recounted scenario goes like this:

We put up a big sign saying, 'Do you think we should give up our jobs to make these smoothies?' and put out a bin saying 'YES' and a bin saying

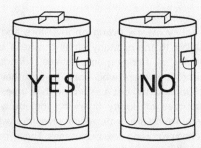

Figure 12.15 innocent's own form of concept testing

'NO' and asked people to put the empty bottle in the right bin (see Figure 12.15). At the end of the weekend the 'YES' bin was full so we went in the next day and resigned.

(innocentdrinks.co.uk)

But the launch of the business took much longer than they had realised; first, there was the problem of funds. How should the entrepreneurs raise money? The options were as follows.

Raising money

When it comes to financing a business, there are two basic types of funding: debt and equity. Loans are debt financing; you borrow money and must pay it back, with interest, within a certain timeframe. With equity funding, you raise money by selling a portion of your ownership in the company. This is the traditional route for people wishing to fund a start-up business, with friends and family probably the most common form of debt financiers; others are: banks, finance companies, credit unions, credit card companies and private corporations. Taking out a business loan allows the owners to remain in control of the company and not answer to investors. Getting a loan is also usually faster than searching out investors. Professional investors review thousands of investment opportunities each year, and only invest in a small fraction. Another benefit of debt financing is that as a firm repays its debts so it builds creditworthiness. This makes the business more attractive to lenders in the future.

Overall, debt financing is typically cheaper than equity financing because the firm only pays interest and fees, and retains full ownership of the company.

Equity financing

Selling equity means taking on investors and being accountable to them. Many small business owners raise equity by bringing in relatives, friends, colleagues or customers who hope to see their businesses succeed and get a return on their investment. Other sources of equity financing include venture capitalists, which are professional investors willing to take risks on promising new businesses. These investors include individuals with substantial net worth, corporations and financial institutions (this is the group highlighted in the BBC television programme *Dragons' Den*). Most investors do not expect an immediate return on their investment, but they would expect the business to be profitable in three to seven years. Equity investors can be passive or active. Passive investors are willing to offer capital but will play little or no part in running the company, while active investors expect to be heavily involved in the company's operations. Personality conflicts can arise in either arrangement. Equity financing is not cheap: investors are entitled to a share of the business's profits indefinitely. Conversely, small business owners who may have difficulty securing a traditional loan or are comfortable sharing control of their business with partners may find equity financing a mutually beneficial arrangement.

Venture capital is a widely used phrase that few people properly understand. It typically refers to investment funds or partnerships (and, increasingly, venture capital divisions within large corporations) that focus on investing in new, promising start-up and emerging companies. Venture capitalists (VCs) have invested in some of today's most famous corporate names, including Apple, Genentech, Intel and Compaq. Typically, the investment is in company stock – the venture capitalist gets an ownership interest for the money invested. Beyond supplying the company with money, the VC also provides assistance and expertise with business planning – bringing industry knowledge, experience in growing businesses and expertise in taking the company public some day. Entrepreneurs should be wary, venture capitalists' primary motive is to make a lot of money on their intended investment. Furthermore, most venture capitalists are interested only in businesses that can grow very big. So, if you're a small grocery store, you should seek funds elsewhere.

Fortunately, the founders of innocent benefited from very good educations and had many business contacts from over four years working in advertising and management consultancy; hence it was not long before they were in touch with venture capitalists. Eventually Maurice Pinto, a wealthy American businessman, invested £250,000 and became the fourth shareholder in the group, retaining a 20 per cent stake. The money provided salaries for the three entrepreneurs, office space, cash to buy production capacity at bottling plants, promotional material and labelling for the bottles.

Product development and growing the business

While on the surface this new business venture may seem slightly unusual, and the three founders would probably very much like to think that business is unique, the development of their fruit smoothie product follows the well-documented process from concept to commercialisation (*see* Figure 12.9).

Generation of new product concepts

The three founders of innocent had been exploring and planning starting their own business ever since they met at university. They had even tried a few crazy ideas, including a gadget that would prevent baths from overflowing. It was the fruit smoothie concept, however, that seemed to appeal to the three founders the most; this is probably largely due to the fact that they were developing a new product for people like them: young urban professionals who wanted a healthy lunchtime drink to go with their sandwich. In many large cities across Europe and the US lunch for most is a sandwich. And when buying your sandwich most people usually buy a drink to wash it down. Also, the UK Government Health Department was promoting the benefits of eating more fruit and vegetables. This was a publicity campaign that innocent could use to its advantage.

Idea screening

Having a new product concept is a long way from a commercially successful new product. Moreover, this was not a completely new product; fruit smoothies had been on the market for several years, hence, innocent was entering an established market, albeit a relatively new one. Their challenge was to become more successful than the existing players. To do this they believed their product had to be different. They were able to achieve this through clever and very different forms of promotion. In many ways they were developing the whole fruit smoothie market, without realising it at the time.

The main purpose of screening ideas is to select those that will be successful and drop those that will not – herein lies the difficulty. Trying to identify which ideas are going to be successful and which are not is extremely difficult. Screening product ideas is essentially an evaluation process. It occurs at every stage of the new product development process and involves such questions as:

1 Do we have the necessary commercial knowledge and experience?
2 Do we have the technical know-how to develop the idea further?
3 Would such a product be suitable for our business?
4 Are we sure there will be sufficient demand?

From here more detailed evaluation checklists can be drawn up, such as the one in Table 12.5.

Concept testing

innocent had already proved to themselves – with their unusual form of product testing using bins – that their target market liked the product. None the less, starting a company from scratch is daunting. There's little room for error so the product has to be pitched in exactly the right way. Given that this was a crowded

Table 12.5 Simple evaluation checklist

	Evaluation criteria
1	Technical abilities
2	Competitive rationale
3	Patentability
4	Stability of the market
5	Integration and synergy
6	Market: growth and competition
7	Channel fit
8	Manufacturing
9	Financial
10	Longer term strategic fit

market, innocent drinks realised early on that the product had to stand out on the shelf. Packaging is a critical issue, especially in FMCG markets. innocent decided to develop something different. A friend of the three founders was hired to look after branding. Once again a great deal of emphasis was placed on the fact that the three founders belonged to the target market and decisions were made based on their own thoughts and ideas, despite a lack of branding experience. Indeed, innocent confessed in interviews with the press that 'our user testing was done on people we knew. We'd email our friends with packaging designs.' None the less, the company has always sought advice and expertise from external experts; for example, Turner Duckworth designed the original bottle shape. innocent also used an agency for an advertising campaign in Ireland.

Design has played a big role in the product's success, from the logo and shape of the bottles to the delivery vans. Careful consideration of design and packaging has contributed to the success of the business. The brand was totally unknown so innocent had to rely on people being intrigued enough to try the product. It is not a cheap drink, so it had to appeal to the consumer and it had to stand out and look like something you would want to pick up. Finally, like all beverage producers, innocent relied on the taste to be sufficiently good to ensure a repeat purchase.

Prototype development

Given that the three founders were the target market – young (they were all in their mid-twenties), urban office workers (they all worked in central London), affluent (they all had very well paid jobs) – identifying what would appeal was simply a question of asking themselves: What do we like? They wanted to emphasise the purity and naturalness of the product, which is made completely from fresh fruit. This is a key point because most fruit drinks are made from concentrated juice with water – and perhaps sweeteners, colours and preservatives – added. innocent wanted to offer pure fruit juice. This had significant manufacturing implications and problems, as they later discovered. They also wanted a bottle that would sit easily in the hand for the 'grab-a-sandwich' crowd and they wanted to introduce an element of fun. Lacking any kind of knowledge about the design process or how to go about finding and developing the right image, the company was forced to use external experts and keep things simple. According to innocent the logo, which resembles an apple with a halo, or a person with a halo depending on how you look at it, was sketched on a serviette in felt-tip pen.

The creation of a brand image is crucial here, and especially so for products in FMCG markets. For all new entrants into an existing market the aim is to try to get existing users to change to your brand of fruit smoothie and to try to attract new buyers who currently purchase bottled water or Coca-Cola, for example. The brand image developed and carefully nurtured by innocent is one based on fun, and an almost hippie approach to life. This is reflected in the packaging, promotion and logo used for the product.

Another interesting point is that due to the high raw material costs and high production costs, initially the product offered was relatively expensive – three or four times as much as lunchtime beverage alternatives.

Market testing

Fruit is sourced from all over the world, and regular sampling is conducted at innocent's test kitchen to ensure that only the most flavoursome varieties are used in the drinks. Recipes created in the kitchen at their London offices are tested on people in surrounding office buildings. Once approved, the drinks are manufactured by one of four independent manufacturers in the UK and sold in outlets across the UK and Europe. The smoothies, which appeal to consumers whom innocent describe as 'slightly more female, slightly more affluent, slightly younger', are priced at the high end of the fruit juice market, selling for £1.79 to £1.99 in 'on the go' plastic bottles, and for £3.29 to £3.49 in larger take-home cartons. innocent has also recently launched a childrens' range, retailing at 99p.

Launch and promotion

Having developed their idea, the three founders then ran into numerous other operational difficulties that meant the launch of the product took much longer than expected. They encountered barriers, including various experts who told them their idea would not work. In particular this was because the product's shelf life was too short. Arguments then ensued about whether or not to include preservatives or additives to lengthen its life. Ignoring most of the expert advice, innocent created a range of smoothies made from 100 per cent pure and fresh fruit. Careful quality controlled production methods and the latest packaging technology gave it the longest possible shelf life.

Their first foray into the market was very modest. Out to Lunch, the local sandwich shop round the corner from their office in Ladbroke Grove, agreed to stock a few of their drinks. They supplied 20 bottles and, when they checked later, found that the drinks had sold out. Indeed, most of their early sales were through local delicatessens and sandwich shops, but it was not long before Coffee Republic, also a young and growing business, agreed to stock innocent drinks in their eight or nine shops.

innocent has not spent large sums of money on television, press or radio promotion. Emphasis is placed on packaging design and retailers who stock and shelf the product. Advertising copy tends to be witty and straightforward, as does other communications material. The relationship with retailers has been built up through regular communication, including a newsletter, which combines product information and fun stories. Each communication is intended to reinforce the unique brand image innocent has built for itself. The copy on the labelling is intended to break down the barriers between manufacturer and customer, using humour. For example, the 'this water' labels have a section called fruit corner, which gives the fruit a personality while also explaining why it's good for you. See the following example about the apple:

> Apples have a long history. God put them in his garden so that Adam and Eve would have something to talk about on that awkward first date. But it all went tragically wrong; indeed, the reason why you and I feel sinful thoughts is because of that pesky apple. But apples have done a lot to improve their public image since then. William Tell did some tricks with one a few hundred years ago, and there was the one that fell out of a tree and hit Archimedes on the head, prompting him to discover fire later that day. Marvellous.

> (innocentdrinks.co.uk)

Future growth

Growth for many businesses can cause problems and sometimes cause a firm to fail; usually this is because it overstretches to expand, borrows money and then runs into cash flow problems. innocent was careful not to fall into this well-known trap despite its dramatic growth. innocent adopted a cautious approach with the national multiples such as Tesco and Sainsbury, despite the lure of multi-million-pound orders. To begin with innocent would only supply a few of the multiples stores and as sales grew and revenue came in so the production would be increased. This is a much slower approach to growth and can sometimes allow competitors to enter the market or allow the multiples themselves to develop own-label versions. None the less, innocent adopted the prudent approach, which seems to have paid off.

innocent now employs 240 people and has slowly expanded along the line of industrial units rented by the company. innocent recorded turnover of £80 million in 2006 and is growing at an annual rate of 50 per cent to 60 per cent. innocent now supplies most of the major supermarkets and this year became Britain's leading brand of smoothie, selling, they calculate, about 72 per cent of the 50 million downed annually by British drinkers. If imitation is the sincerest form of flattery then innocent's founders should feel very pleased. The refrigerated shelves of the nation's supermarkets are filled with own-label versions of some of the company's best sellers such as its yogurt, vanilla bean and honey 'thickie'. But this could present a serious challenge to the firm. innocent would not be the first manufacturer to lose out to own-label multiples like Sainsbury, Tesco and Asda.

There would also seem to be many opportunities for future growth. innocent are still aware that while the business has grown extremely fast there are still plenty of people who have not yet tasted innocent drinks. innocent is continuing to extend its product line with new flavours of smoothies and a new product launched in 2003 called Juicy Water, whose packaging was designed by Coley Porter Bell. innocent's main market is still the UK and Ireland, which accounts for 90 per cent of its sales, but its smoothies are also sold in The Netherlands, Belgium, Luxembourg and France. It eventually plans to expand within and beyond Europe. 'We have the trademark registered in every country that we think it can become business relevant.' These include the US, Australia, New Zealand, China, India and countries in South America.

Like any growing business, maintaining innocent's internal culture as the company expands is going to

be a challenge. Much will depend on the rate of growth and whether the company will be able to control this growth. Clearly, employing the right people as the business expands, both in the UK and overseas, will be one of the significant challenges.

Many analysts argue that innocent is one of a new breed of virtual food and drink companies. Such companies develop the brand and outsource production. There's a division of labour between the owner of the brand and the manufacturer. Other such firms include: Green & Black's, the organic chocolate company; Duchy Originals, which sells organic foods; and Gu Chocolate Puds. These smaller food companies have found there is demand for products made with natural or organic ingredients and low in fats, sugars and salts. While larger food companies have been altering product ingredients to try to address consumer concerns, smaller companies have been quicker at creating products that meet specific demands. The success of these companies in identifying changes in consumer tastes has made them attractive acquisition targets; for example, in May 2005 Green & Black's was bought by Cadbury Schweppes for £20 million.

PepsiCo enters the smoothie market

In 2005 the maker of Pepsi dramatically entered the UK smoothie market with the purchase of the British smoothie and fruit juice brand PJ Smoothies. PepsiCo UK did not reveal the price it paid for the business, based in Newark, Nottinghamshire. PJ, launched in 1994, founded the British smoothie market and has become its leading brand. PepsiCo said PJ Smoothies is the only major brand that produces its own 100 per cent fruit smoothies.

Between 1998 and 2004, PJ spent £4 million developing the brand. It remained the top smoothie brand in terms of volume, with most of its sales in Britain. PJ was launched in the Irish Republic in 2003.

PepsiCo UK said it would maintain PJ's operational structure and manufacturing would continue at Newark. It said the move would give it a significant presence in the rapidly growing premium juice market. PepsiCo said PJ, which now has a 19 per cent market share, would complement its existing drinks brands Tropicana and Copella.

Pete & Johnny Smoothies have recently undertaken a major rebranding programme, with a new logo that

→

Table 12.6 **Smoothies brands (market value and market share)**

	2007 £m	% share	2008 £m	% share	2009 £m	% share	2007–09 % point different
Innocent	150	71	120	71	100	80	−33
PJs*	25	12	10	6	na	na	na
Tropicana Smoothies	8	4	15	9	3	2	−63
Ella's Kitchen	1.5	1	2.2	1	2.5	2	67
Others	4	2	5	3	4	3	–
Own-labels	22	10	18	10	16	12	−28
Total	**210**	**100**	**170**	**100**	**125**	**100**	**−40**

*brand discontinued in late 2008.

Source: Mintel Group 2011 Smoothies, UK, 2010, Market share.

is stronger, more modern and presents a clearer image. The PJ's rebranding is designed to maximise shelf impact and re-emphasise the company logo, which now incorporates different fruit for different blends. The reverse of the label carries humorous copy and cartoons, illustrating Pete & Johnny's adventures over the past ten years. In addition, PJ's is introducing a groundbreaking 500ml smoothie bottle in response to consumer demand. The market shares for smoothies is shown in Table 12.6.

The global recession has blown a cold wind through the UK smoothies market. During the recession people have understandably tried to cut their costs. The high-priced fruit smoothies have consequently suffered. In addition people have tended to abandon new products for ones they know and trust. For example, in 2010 Pepsi, Robinsons squash and the childrens' drink Fruit Shoot were among Britvic's best-selling brands. According to some analysts the UK smoothies market has fallen by 30 per cent in value. More worrying is that premium high street brands such as Waitrose and M&S have introduced own label competing products. The future for innocent looks more difficult now than at any time in the past five years.

Conclusions

innocent's turnover has increased from £35 million in 2004 to £80 million in 2006 and in 2005 the company overtook P&J Smoothies as brand leader. The success of innocent is remarkable partly because this is such a competitive market in which some of the world's largest brands operate and partly because this success has been achieved unconventionally

with minimal use of traditional advertising and promotional techniques. The development and launch of their business and new product in particular follows a conventional approach from concept to market, but innocent has used some very different approaches along the way. According to innocent there are some important factors that have contributed to its success. These are:

1 Keeping your potential customer's tastes, lifestyle and personality clearly in view.
2 Keeping designs simple and practical and concentrating on the quality of the product can be the key to standing out in an overcrowded market.
3 The brand image has to consistently reflect the product and the company's values.
4 Getting the product, packaging and marketing design right before diversifying and expanding will help establish the product.
5 How should innocent respond to falling sales and market share?

The founders of innocent perhaps project an image of being hippies who have emerged from a travelling caravan to start a drinks business and who are now investing all the profits into Third World social programmes. However, these friends had a privileged upbringing (one of them attending Winchester College, one of the world's most expensive private schools), gained even more knowledge from four years at university and then gained a further four years of practical experience working for large corporate city firms in London advising others on how to run a business. Although the promotional material might suggest a 'devil may care' attitude to life, the three were involved in meticulous planning of their business idea. For example, even when they had decided on their business idea and began planning it, they adopted a cautious approach by negotiating two months' leave from their employers as opposed to simply leaving employment.

Turning to another company and a similar scenario, but this time with ice cream, two self-confessed hippies built an ice cream brand in the 1980s on their socially conscious image – Ben & Jerry's 'all natural' ice cream – and then sold to the conglomerate Unilever for $326 million. While innocent are sticking to their values of doing something they can be proud of, whilst keeping an eye on the commercial side of things too, we can see from Ben & Jerry's example that there is always the potential for a 'hippie' brand to be sold for a huge amount of money.

Source: AC Nielsen Scantrack Total Market, 4 weeks to WE 30 October 2004; Cummings, L. (2005) Just an Innocent business?, BBC News Online: Business, 23 August; Wiggins, J. (2005) An Innocent making its way in the big bad world of health, FT.com, 22 August; Wiggins, J. (2009) Tried and trusted brands give smoothies and bottled water a hard time, FT.com, 15 July.

Questions

1 innocent are very clear about the image it wishes to project to the public. This is one based on being different, fun-loving and having a care-free approach to life. This hippie-style image has helped the brand become acceptable to the young urban professionals at which it is aimed. But beneath the surface of this image there is evidence of a business that could be characterised as single-minded, profit driven and very business orientated. Where is the evidence of the latter?

2 The success of the business is partly based on extremely good communications with retailers. How is this achieved?

3 What type of financing did innocent secure? Does it matter?

4 Would you sell the company to Coca-Cola for £400 million? As one of the shareholders you could pocket tens of millions of pounds. If not, why not?

5 innocent benefited from a key advantage: what was this and explain how it helped in the product development process.

6 How is innocent 'virtual' and how is this different from traditional food and drink manufacturers? What advantages and disadvantages does this provide?

7 Use CIM (Figure 1.9) to illustrate the innovation process.

Chapter summary

This chapter has considered the relationship between new products and prosperity and shown that new product development is one of the most common forms of organic growth strategies. The range of NPD strategies is wide indeed and can range from packaging alterations to new technological research. The chapter stressed the importance of viewing a product as a multi-dimensional concept.

The later part of the chapter focused on the various models of NPD that have emerged over the past 50 years. All of these have strengths and weaknesses. By their very nature, models attempt to capture and portray a complex notion and in so doing often oversimplify elements. This is the central argument of critics of the linear model of NPD, that it is too simplistic and does not provide for any feedback or concurrent activities. More recent models such as network models try to emphasise the importance of the external linkages in the NPD process.

Discussion questions

1 Explain why the process of new product development is frequently represented as a linear process and why this does not reflect reality.

2 Explain why screening should be viewed as a continual rather than a one-off activity.

3 Discuss how the various groups of NPD models have contributed to our understanding of the subject of NPD.

4 To what extent has BMW repositioned the Mini?

5 Examine the concept of a multi-dimensional product; how is it possible to create a new product by modifying the price dimension?

6 The software industry seems to have a very flexbile NPD process enabling changes to be made to the product at any time. Consider whether this approach could be applicable for a car production line or mobile phone handset products.

7 Explain why time to market may be less important than a flexible NPD process.

8 Discuss the strengths of network models of NPD.

Key words and phrases

New product lines *429*

Line additions *429*

Cost reductions *430*

Repositionings *430*

Line extensions *431*

New-to-the-world products *432*

Departmental-stage models *437*

Activity-stage models and concurrent engineering *437*

Cross-functional models (teams) *437*

Decision-stage models *437*

Conversion-process models *438*

Response models *438*

Network models *438*

References

Abernathy, W.L. and Utterback, J. (1978) 'Patterns of industrial innovation', in Tushman, M.L. and Moore, W.L. (eds) *Readings in Management of Innovation*, HarperCollins, New York, 97–108.

Allen, T.J. (1969) Communication networks in R&D laboratories, *R&D Management*, Vol. 1, 14–21.

Allen, T.J. (1977) *Managing the Flow of Technology*, MIT Press, Cambridge, MA.

Ambler, T. and Styles, C. (1997) Brand development vs new product development: Towards a process model of extension decisions, *Journal of Product and Brand Management*, Vol. 6, No. 1, 13–26.

Ancona, D.G. and Caldwell, D.F. (1992) Bridging the boundary: external processes and performance in organisational teams, *Administrative Science Quarterly*, Vol. 37, 634–65.

Ansoff, I. (1965) *Corporate Strategy*, Penguin, Harmondsworth.

Ansoff, I. (1968) *Toward a Strategy of the Theory of the Firm*, McGraw-Hill, New York.

Becker, S. and Whistler, T.I. (1967) The innovative organisation: a selective view of current theory and research, *Journal of Business*, Vol. 40, No. 4, 462–69.

Bhat, S. and Reddy, S.K. (1998) Symbolic and functional positioning of brands, *Journal of Consumer Marketing*, Vol. 15, No. 1, 32–43.

Bingham, F.G. and Raffield, B.T. (1995) *Business Marketing Management*, South Western Publishing, Cincinnati, OH.

Booz, Allen & Hamilton (1982) *New Product Management for the 1980s*, Booz, Allen & Hamilton, New York.

Brown, J.S. and Eisenhardt, K.M. (1998) *Competing on the Edge – Strategy as Structured Chaos*, Harvard Business School, Boston, M.A.

Brown, S.L. and Eisenhardt, K.M. (1995) Product development: past research, present findings and future directions, *Academy of Management Review*, Vol. 20, No. 2, 343–78.

Clark, K. and Fujimoto, T. (1991) *Product Development Performance*, Harvard Business School Press, Boston, MA.

Cooper, R.G. (1999) From experience: the invisible success factors in product innovation, *Journal of Product Innovation Management*, Vol. 16, No. 2, 115–33.

Cooper R.G. and Edgett, S.J. (2008) Maximizing productivity in product innovation, *Research Technology Management*, March.

Cooper, R.G. and Kleinschmidt, E.J. (1993) Major new products: what distinguishes the winners in the chemical industry?, *Journal of Product Innovation Management*, Vol. 10, No. 2, 90–111.

Corrocher, N. and Zirulia, L. (2010) Demand and innovation in services: The case of mobile communications, *Research Policy*, Vol. 39, No. 7, 945–55.

Craig, A. and Hart, S. (1992) Where to now in new product development?, *European Journal of Marketing*, Vol. 26, 11.

Dolan, R.J. (1993) *Managing the New Product Development Process*, Addison-Wesley, Reading, MA.

Dougherty, D. (1990) Understanding new markets for new products, *Strategic Management Journal*, Vol. 11, 59–78.

Doyle, P. (1994) *Marketing Management and Strategy*, Prentice-Hall, Englewood Cliffs, NJ, 159–65.

Finger, S. and Dixon, J.R. (1989a) A review of research in mechanical engineering design, part I: Descriptive, prescriptive, and computer-based models of design processes, *Research in Engineering Design*, Vol. 1, No. 1, 51–68.

Finger, S. and Dixon, J.R. (1989b) A review of research in mechanical engineering design, part II: Representations, analysis, and design for the life cycle, *Research in Engineering Design*, Vol. 1, No. 2, 121–37.

Franke, N. and Piller, F. (2004) Value creation by toolkits for user innovation and design: The case of the watch market, *Journal of Product Innovation Management*, Vol. 21, No. 6, 401–16.

Green, P.E. and Srinivasan, V. (1990) Conjoint analysis in marketing: New developments with implications for research and practice, *Journal of Marketing*, Vol. 54, No. 4, 3–19.

Hart, S. (1993) Dimensions of success in new product development: an exploratory investigation, *Journal of Marketing Management*, Vol. 9, No. 9, 23–41.

IDA (1986) *The Role of Concurrent Engineering in Weapons Systems Acquisition*, report R–338, IDA Washington, DC.

Imai, K., Ikujiro, N. and Takeuchi, H. (1985) 'Managing the new product development process: how Japanese companies learn and unlearn', in Hayes, R.H., Clark, K. and Lorenz C. (eds) *The Uneasy Alliance: Managing the Productivity–Technology Dilemma*, Harvard Business School Press, Boston, MA, 337–75.

Johne, F.A. and Snelson, P.A. (1988) The role of marketing specialists in product development, Proceedings of the 21st Annual Conference of the Marketing Education Group, Huddersfield, Vol. 3, 176–91.

Johnson, G. and Scholes, K. (1997) *Exploring Corporate Strategy*, 4th edn, Prentice Hall, Hemel Hempstead.

Johnson, S.C. and Jones, C. (1957) How to organise for new products, *Harvard Business Review*, May–June, Vol. 35, 49–62.

Kettunen, P. (2009) Adopting key lessons from agile manufacturing to agile software product development – A comparative study, *Technovation*, Vol. 29, Nos 6–7, 408–22.

Kim, J. and Wilemon, D. (2002) Focusing the fuzzy front end in new product development, *R&D Management*, Vol. 32, No. 4, 269–79.

Koen, P., Ajamian, G., Burkart, R., Clamen, A., Davidson, J., Ámore, R.D., Elkins, C., Herald, K., Incorvia, M., Johnson, A., Karol, R., Seibert, R., Slavejkov, A. and Wagner, K. (2001) Providing clarity and a common language to the 'fuzzy front end', *Research Technology Management*, March–April, 46–55.

Kotler, P. (1997) *Marketing Management*, Prentice-Hall, Englewood Cliffs, NJ.

Krishnan, V. and Ulrich, K.T. (2001) Product development decisions: A review of the literature, *Management Science*, Vol. 47, No. 1, 1–21.

Mahajan, V.E. and Wind, J. (1992) New product models – Practice, shortcomings and desired improvements, *Journal of Product Innovation Management*, Vol. 9(June), 128–39.

Myers, S. and Marquis, D.G. (1969) Successful industrial innovation: a study of factors underlying innovation and selected firms, National Science Foundation, NSF 69–17, Washington.

Nambisan, S. (2002) Designing virtual customer environments for new product development: Toward a theory, *Academy of Management Review*, Vol. 27, No. 3, 392–413.

Nonaka, I. and Takeuchi, H. (1995) *The Knowledge Creating Company*, Oxford University Press, Oxford.

Park, J.-W., Kim, K.-H. and Kim, J. (2002) 'Acceptance of brand extensions: interactive influences of product category similarity, typicality of claimed benefits, and brand relationship quality', in Broniarczyk, S. and Nakamoto, K. (eds) *Advances in Consumer Research*, Vol. 29, Association for Consumer Research, Valdosta, GA.

Rogers, E. and Shoemaker, R. (1972) *Communications of Innovations*, Free Press, New York.

Rothwell, R., Freeman, C., Horlsey, A., Jervis, V.T.P., Robertson, A.B. and Townsend, J. (1974) SAPPHO updated: Project SAPPHO phase II, *Research Policy*, Vol. 3, 258–91.

Saren, M. (1984) A classification of review models of the intra-firm innovation process, *R&D Management*, Vol. 14, No. 1, 11–24.

Saunders, J. and Jobber, D. (1994) Product replacement: Strategies for simultaneous product deletion and launch, *Journal of Product Innovation Management*, Vol. 11, No. 5, 433–50.

Schon, D. (1967) Champions for radical new inventions, *Harvard Business Review*, March–April, 77–86.

Smith, P.G. (2007) *Flexible product development: building agility for changing markets*, John Wiley and Sons, New York.

Smith, M.R.H. (1981) Paper presented to the National Conference on Quality and Competitiveness, London, November, reported in *Financial Times*, 25 November.

Tauber, E.M. (1981) Brand franchise extension: new product benefits from existing brand names, *Business Horizons*, Vol. 24, No. 2, 36–41.

Thomas, R.J. (1993) *New Product Development*, John Wiley, New York.

Thomke, S.H. (2003) *Experimentation Matters: Unlocking the Potential of New Technologies for Innovation*, Harvard Business School Press, Boston, MA.

von Hippel, E. (1986) Lead users: a source of novel product concepts, *Management Science*, Vol. 32, No. 7, 791–805.

von Hippel, E. (2001) Perspective: User toolkits for innovation, *The Journal of Product Innovation Management*, 18, 247–57.

Weyland, R. and Cole, P. (1997) *Customer Connections*, Harvard Business School Press, Boston, MA.

Yakimov, R. and Beverland, M. (2004) Brand repositioning capabilities: Enablers of ongoing brand management, Australia and New Zealand Marketing Academy (ANZMAC) Conference, 27 November–1 December, University of Wellington, Victoria, NZ.

Zirger, B.J. and Maidique, M.A. (1990) A model of new product development: an empirical test, *Management Science*, Vol. 36, 876–88.

Further reading

For a more detailed review of the new product development literature, the following develop many of the issues raised in this chapter:

Barczak, G., Griffin, A. and Kahn, K.B. (2009) PERSPECTIVE: Trends and Drivers of Success in NPD Practices: Results of the 2003 PDMA Best Practices Study, *Journal of Product Innovation Management*, Vol. 26, No. 1, 3–23.

Belliveau, P., Griffin, A. and Somermeyer, S. (eds) (2002) *The PDMA ToolBook for New Product Development*, John Wiley & Sons, New York.

Biemans, W., Griffin, A. and Moenaert, R. (2007) Twenty Years of the Journal of Product Innovation Management: History, Participants, and Knowledge Stocks and Flows, *Journal of Product Innovation Management*, Vol. 24, 193–213.

Biemans, W., Griffin, A. and Moenaert, R. (2010) In Search of the Classics: A Study of the Impact of *JPIM* Papers from 1984 to 2003, *Journal of Product Innovation Management*, Vol. 27, 461–84.

Grindling, E. (2000) *The 3M Way to Innovation: Balancing people and profit*, Kodansha International, New York.

HSBC (2010) 100 Thoughts, HSBC, London.

Chapter 15
Market research and its influence on new product development

Introduction

The role and use of market research in the development of new products is commonly accepted and well understood. There are times, however, when market research results produce negative reactions to discontinuous new products (innovative products) that later become profitable for the innovating company. Famous examples such as the fax machine, the VCR and James Dyson's bagless vacuum cleaner are often cited to support this view. Despite this, companies continue to seek the views of consumers on their new product ideas. The debate about the use of market research and, more importantly, what type of research should be used in the development of new products is long-standing and controversial. This chapter will explore these and other related issues. It also provides a case study which shows how Dyson pursued 'unpopular' designs that later become the industry standard.

Chapter contents

Learning objectives

When you have completed this chapter you will be able to:

- understand the contribution market research can make to the new product development process;
- recognise the benefits and weaknesses of consumer new product testing;
- recognise the powerful influence of the installed base effect on new product introductions;
- understand the significance of discontinuous products; and
- recognise the role of switching costs in new product introductions.

Market research and new product development

Business students in particular are very familiar with the well-trodden paths of arguments about the need for market research. Indeed, they are warned of the dangers and pitfalls that lie ahead if firms fail to conduct sufficient market research. Compelling and potentially alarming stories are used to highlight the importance of market research. One of these is presented in Illustration 15.1.

Chapters 11 and 12 outlined the activities involved in the development of new products. In this chapter it is necessary to examine in more detail some of these activities and to identify areas of potential difficulty. Figure 12.9 outlined the key activities of the new product development process. Within the product concept generation stage, however, there is a significant amount of internal reviews and testing. Figure 15.1 expands this stage into a series of further activities. As can be seen from the diagram, it is extremely difficult to delineate between the activities of concept testing, prototype development and product testing. The activities are intimately related and interlinked. There is a considerable amount of iteration. Product concepts are developed into prototypes only to be quickly redeveloped following technical inputs from production or R&D. Similarly, early product prototypes may be changed almost on a daily basis as a wide variety of market inputs are received. This could include channel members who have particular requirements and early results from consumer tests may reveal a number of minor changes that can be made simply and quickly by prototype designers.

Yet, we also recognise that consumers frequently have difficulty articulating their needs. This has recently been confirmed by two CEOs. Steven Jobs, CEO of

Illustration 15.1

The traditional view of new product testing

FT

McDonald's recently admitted to making a big mistake with a new product. Several years ago it was considering launching the McPloughman's, a cheese and pickle salad sandwich. The McPloughman's was developed to compete with the UK's supermarket chains in the cold sandwich market. Unfortunately, had the company conducted market research it would have found that this product was not highly desirable. Indeed, their customers did not want the product and their staff were embarrassed to sell it. From now on, said the company, rather than relying on 'gut-feeling' that it knew what its customers wanted McDonald's intended to conduct rigorous fact-based market research.

Source: Pearson Education Ltd/Burke Triolo Productions/Brand X Pictures

Source: Financial Times, 28 October 1994. Reprinted with permission.

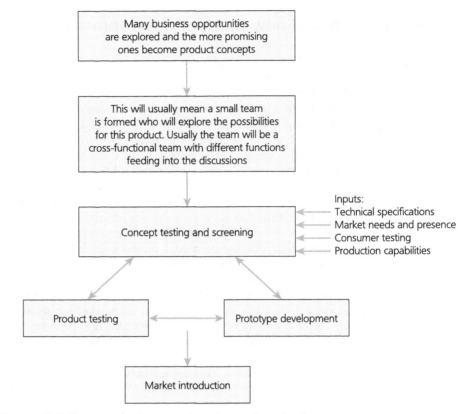

Figure 15.1 **New product concept and prototype testing**

Apple, in an interview with *Fortune* magazine (2008) said: 'Apple does no market research, and in fact just wants to "make great products".' And Bart Becht, CEO of Reckitt Benckiser, said in an interview with the *Sunday Times* (2008): 'Consumers are not very good at imagining what they might want to buy if it were available . . . consumers are not very innovative.' The issue here is clear. There are some firms who wish to lead the public with new products, for they believe that the public do not know what is possible and market research frequently reinforces this lack of knowledge.

The purpose of new product testing

The main objective here is to estimate the market's reaction to the new product under consideration, prior to potentially expensive production and promotional costs. To achieve this objective it is necessary to consider a number of other factors:

1 The market:
current buying patterns;
existing segments; and
customer's view of the products available.

2 Purchase intention:
  trial and repeat purchase;
  barriers to changing brands; and
  switching costs (more about this later).
3 Improvements to the new product:
  overall product concept; and
  features of the product concept.

All these factors are linked and are usually covered in consumer new product testing and referred to as *customer needs and preferences*. This, however, raises an important issue: the type of needs required would surely depend on the type of product under consideration and the consumer. King (1985) argues needs can be classified into three types:

- Basic needs are those that a customer would expect. For example, a customer would expect a new car to start every time.
- Articulated needs are those that a customer can readily express. For example, a customer may express a desire for additional features on a motor vehicle.
- Exciting needs are those that will surprise customers and are not being met by any provider at present. In the example here it may be finance packages enabling easy and quick purchase of a new car.

While this is helpful it is the so-called 'exciting needs' that all new product developers want to uncover. For success will surely come to those who are able to understand these needs and use them in the next generation of new products. This, however, is extremely difficult to capture. Some of the techniques and concepts used in consumer product testing are reviewed in the following sections.

Testing new products

Have you ever been stopped in a supermarket and asked for your opinion on a new food product? This is more than a diversion from the chore of shopping – you could be tasting the next big product. For example, all food manufacturers hope it will be their company that will develop the next 'Flora' or 'Sunny Delight' (two of the most successful new food products of the past ten years). In-store tasting is a serious business and millions of pounds are spent on this activity to create new foods that will tempt consumers. This is the accepted and well-known face of consumer research. Indeed, the food industry is one of the most prolific developers of new products and a heavy user of consumer research. Frequently the process involves enhancing an existing winner or repackaging tried and tested products. 'Flora' was one of many 'yellow spreads' but the brand has become so successful that it has been extended to other product lines including cheese.

Food manufacturers are continually seeking to add value to their products. This clearly enhances their profit margins, but competition in food retailing is fierce and retailers have been able to put pressure on manufacturers to keep prices down. Indeed, during 1999 and 2000 average food retail prices actually fell. Initially manufacturers pushed down their own costs in an attempt to improve margins, but when these could be reduced no further manufacturers turned to new product development to

Illustration 15.2

Robinsons Fruit Shoot

Fruit Shoot from Robinsons was launched in 2001 and is now a £72.7 million super brand (July 2006). It achieved value sales growth of 44 per cent from 2003–04. Its success has been attributed to the unique design and packaging of the drink. Prior to Fruit Shoot, most children's drinks were packaged in paper board cartons with straw. Fruit Shoot revolutionised the market by using a colourful resealable plastic bottle. In the UK, Fruit Shoot was bought by 41 per cent of all households with kids in 2005–06 and achieves 98 per cent awareness among children, according to Britvic. During 2003 and 2004 Fruit Shoot incorporated two new flavours and this redesign promises to maintain and continue the strong growth of the brand.

Source: www.Britvic.com (2004 and 2007).

enable them to add value and command a higher price. Frequently the success of the product lies in the packaging, as Illustration 15.2 shows.

Put crudely, to command a higher price a manufacturer of, say, baked beans will have to develop different forms of packaging, add curry, meat balls, etc., all of which will have been tested by the taste buds of consumers first. But if a product is not liked by consumers, should it always be dumped and labelled 'bad idea'? In the food industry a disliked new flavour crisp may indeed be a 'bad idea' and a potential flop if the product gets to market, but in other industries initial rejection by consumers may not be a good indication of future success. The Dyson case study at the end of this chapter is a good illustration of a successful product that was initially rejected by manufacturers, retailers and some consumers, yet it turned out to be a success. There are, of course, many other well-known cases such as the fax machine. Peter Drucker once observed that 'one can use market research only on what is already in the market'. He supported his point by saying that American companies failed to put the fax machine on the market 'because market research convinced them there was no demand for such a gadget'.

Techniques used in consumer testing of new products

The following is a brief guide to some of the research techniques used in consumer testing of new products. Some products and services go through all the stages listed, but few do or should go through all these. The techniques would have to be adapted to meet the specific requirements of the product or service under consideration.

Concept tests

Qualitative techniques, especially group discussions, are used to obtain target customer reactions to a new idea or product. Question areas would cover:

- understanding and believability in the product;
- ideas about what it would look like;
- ideas about how it would be used; and
- ideas about when and by whom it might be used.

This would help to reveal the most promising features of the new product, and groups to whom it might appeal. It might be argued that the assessment of *purchase intent* is the primary purpose of concept testing, so that products and services with poor potential can be removed. The most common way to assess purchase intention is to provide a description of the product or take the product to respondents and ask whether they:

- definitely would buy;
- probably would buy;
- might or might not buy;
- probably would not buy; or
- definitely would not buy.

Test centres

These are used for product testing when the product is too large, too expensive or too complicated to be taken to consumers for testing. One or more test centres will be set up and a representative sample of consumers brought to the test centre for exposure to the product and questioning about their reaction to it. See the development of the tooth whitening product in the case study at the end of Chapter 11.

Hall tests/mobile shops

These are commonly used for product testing or testing other aspects of the marketing mix such as advertising, price, packaging, etc. A representative sample of consumers is recruited, usually in a shopping centre, and brought to a conveniently located hall or a mobile caravan, which acts as a shop. Here they are exposed to the test material and asked questions about it.

Product-use tests

These are frequently used in business-to-business markets. A small group of potential customers are selected to use the product for a limited period of time. The manufacturer's technical people watch how these customers use the product. From this test the manufacturer learns about customer training and servicing requirements. Following the test the customer is asked detailed questions about the product including intent to purchase.

Trade shows

Such shows draw large numbers of buyers who view new products in a few days. The manufacturer can see how buyers react to various products on display. This technique is convenient and can deliver in-depth knowledge of the market because the buyers' views may differ considerably from those of the end-user consumers.

Monadic tests

The respondents are given only one (hence the name) product to try, and are asked their opinion of it. This is the normal situation in real life when a consumer tries a new product and draws on recent experience with the product they usually use, to judge the test product. The method is not very sensitive in comparing the test product with other products because of this.

Paired comparisons

A respondent is asked to try two or more products in pairs and asked, with each pair, to say which they prefer. This is less 'real' in terms of the way consumers normally use products, but does allow products to be deliberately tested against others.

In-home placement tests

These are used when an impression of how the product performs in normal use is required. The product(s) are placed with respondents who are asked to use the product in the normal way and complete a questionnaire about it. Products may be tested comparatively or sequentially.

Test panels

Representative panels are recruited and used for product testing. Test materials and questionnaires can be sent through the post, which cuts down the cost of conducting in-home placement tests. Business-to-business firms may also have test panels of customers or intermediaries with whom new product or service ideas or prototypes can be tested.

When market research has too much influence

It is argued by many from within the market research industry that only extensive consumer testing of new products can help to avoid large-scale losses such as those experienced by RCA with its Videodisc, Procter & Gamble with its Pringles and General Motors with its rotary engine (Barrett, 1996). Sceptics may point to the issue of vested interests in the industry, and that it is merely promoting itself. It is, however, widely accepted that most new products fail in the market because consumer needs and wants are not satisfied. Study results show that 80 per cent of newly introduced products fail to establish a market presence after two years (Barrett, 1996). Indeed, cases involving international high-profile companies are frequently cited to warn of the dangers of failing to utilise market research (e.g. Unilever's Persil Power and R.J. Reynold's smokeless cigarette).

Given the inherent risk and complexity, managers have asked for many years whether this could be reduced by market research. Not surprisingly, the marketing literature takes a market-driven view, which has extensive market research as its key driver. That is, find out what the customer would like and then produce it (the market-pull approach to innovation). The benefits of this approach to the new product development process have been widely articulated and are commonly understood (Cooper, 1990; Kotler, 1998). Partly because of its simplicity this view now dominates management thinking, but unfortunately this sometimes goes beyond the marketing department. The effect can be that major or so-called discontinuous innovations are rejected or accepted based on consumer research.

Advocates of market research argue that such activities ensure that companies are consumer oriented. In practice, this means that new products are more successful if they are designed to satisfy a perceived need rather than if they are designed simply to take advantage of a new technology (Ortt and Schoormans, 1993). The approach taken by many companies with regard to market research is that if sufficient research is undertaken the chances of failure are reduced (Barrett, 1996). Indeed, the danger that many companies wish to avoid is the development of products without any consideration of the market. Moreover, once a product has been carried through the early stages of development it is sometimes painful to raise questions about it once money has been spent. The problem then spirals out of control, taking the company with it. Illustration 15.3 highlights many of the difficulties facing firms introducing new products.

The issue of market research in the development of new products is controversial. The marketing literature has traditionally portrayed new product development as essentially a market/customer-led process, but paradoxically, many major market innovations appear in practice to be technologically driven, to arise from a technology seeking a market application rather than a market opportunity seeking a technology. This, of course, is the antithesis of the marketing concept, which is to start with trying to understand customer needs. The role of market research in new product development is most clearly questionable with major product innovations, where no market exists. First, if potential customers are unable adequately to understand the product, then market research can only provide negative answers (Brown, 1991). Second, consumers frequently have difficulty articulating their needs. Hamel and Prahalad (1994: 8) argue that customers lack foresight; they refer to Akio Morita, Sony's influential leader:

> *Our plan is to lead the public with new products rather than ask them what kind of products they want. The public does not know what is possible, but we do.*

This leads many scientists and technologists to view marketing departments with scepticism. Frequently they have seen their exciting new technology rejected due to market research findings produced by their marketing department. Market research specialists would argue that such problems could be overcome with the use

Illustration 15.3

Neuromarketing accesses subconscious views on products and brands

Last month, I surrendered my subconscious to analysis. A red swimming cap was stretched over my head, long grey wires stuck to my skull and my innermost thoughts fed into a computer as I nervously watched an advertisement for Volkswagen.

In turn, the computer told a team of researchers which scenes I paid attention to, what I responded to emotionally and what I would go away remembering.

It was a far cry from the marketing industry's traditional method of finding out what consumers think about their brands: asking them.

The problem is, when gathered in traditional focus groups, respondents can be swayed by those sitting next to them or by the presence of researchers. Alternatively, they may be unable to articulate their responses accurately. As a result, an increasing number of marketers now prefer to analyse the response of peoples' brainwaves to brands and advertisements by using the latest developments in neuroscience.

In recent months, these techniques have not just been applied to the marketing of finished products, but also to product development. 'It's about uncovering new undiscovered needs', says Martin Lindstrom, author of *Buyology*, who has been studying the development of neuromarketing since its inception seven years ago. 'A lot of manufacturers are struggling as it's easy to come up with ideas consumers don't feel they need.'

He cites the example of dishwasher tablets. Consumers are attracted to tablets embedded with a blue ball because, subconsciously, they believe

they clean better. However, when asked in the context of traditional marketing methods, they claim no preference about colour.

'The main reason why [traditional market research often] fails is that we look at things from a conscious point of view', says Mr Lindstrom. 'We ask: "Do you like the brand?" We ask the consumer to be incredibly rational and we know today from neuroscience that 85 per cent of the decisions we make are made by the unconscious part of brain.'

Neuromarketers believe their work will be especially useful for products consumers find hard to describe – particularly when they need to know consumers' reactions to smell, taste and touch.

According to Neurofocus, the global market leader in neurological testing, consumer goods companies are even creating their own in-house testing units that mock up supermarkets. They can use them to change everything from shelf positioning to point-of-sale advertisements with the flick of a switch and monitor the shopper's brain during the few seconds it takes to select a product.

But some advertisers fear this adherence to science could stamp out 'light bulb' ideas and destroy creativity in the industry.

Neurofocus argues that mind-reading actually helps sell original thinking to companies that would otherwise stick with tried-and-tested methods.

Source: Kuchler, H. (2010) Marketing industry turns to mind-reading, FT.com, April 11.

of 'benefits research'. The problem here is that the benefits may not be clearly understood, or even perceived as a benefit by respondents. King (1985: 2) sums up the research dilemma neatly:

> *Consumer research can tell you what people did and thought at one point in time: it can't tell you directly what they might do in a new set of circumstances.*

In Illustration 15.4, from GlaxoSmithKline, consumer healthcare highlights the difficulties of trying to understand consumer research.

Illustration 15.4

GlaxoSmithKline

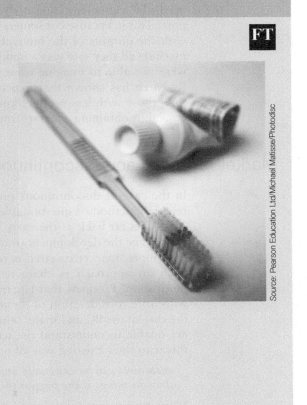

GSK have known for many years that consumers are fickle. Many years after the launch of its very successful Aquafresh striped toothpaste GlaxoSmithKline undertook consumer research to try to explore product development opportunities. Some of the findings were surprising. Consumers questioned the need or benefit of having stripes in the paste. Yet, in store trials, when given the opportunity to purchase a single colour paste consumers continued to purchase the striped toothpaste. A similar reaction was recorded when consumers were asked about flavouring of the toothpaste. Consumers suggested that they would prefer a wider variety of flavours such as strawberry or banana rather than mint, yet when other flavours were offered few consumers purchased them. The product manager emphasised the need to check consumer rhetoric with their actions.

Source: P. Trott and A. Lataste (2003) The role of consumer market research in new product decision-making: some preliminary findings from European firms, Entrepreneurship, Marketing and Innovation Conference, University of Karlsrühe, 8–9 September, conference proceedings.

Source: Pearson Education Ltd/Michael Matisse/Photodisc

Discontinuous new products

Major innovations are referred to as discontinuous new products when they differ from existing products in that field, sometimes creating entirely new markets and when they require buyers to change their behaviour patterns. For example, the personal computer and 3M's Post-it notes created entirely new markets and required consumers to change their behaviour. Such products usually require a period of learning on the part of the user. Indeed, sometimes the manufacturer has to explain and suggest to users how the product should and could be used. Rogers' (1995) study on the diffusion of innovations as a social process argues that it requires time for societies to learn and experiment with new products. This raises the problem of how to deal with consumers with limited prior knowledge and how to conduct market research on a totally new product or a major product innovation. The two major difficulties are:

1 the problem of selection of respondents; and
2 the problem of the understanding of the major innovation.

Confronted with a radically new technology, consumers may not understand what needs the technology can satisfy, as was the case with the fax machine or the Post-it note. This is because consumers are not able to link physical product characteristics with the outputs of the innovation. For example, when consumers first saw a fax machine all they saw was a bulky expensive machine that looked like a copier. They were not able to imagine using it, hence they were not receptive to the new idea. Research has shown that experts are better able to understand potential benefits than those with less product knowledge. The type of research technique selected is crucial in obtaining accurate and reliable data.

Market research and discontinuous new products

In the case of discontinuous product innovations, the use and validity of market research methods is questionable (von Hippel and Thomke, 1999; Elliot and Roach, 1991). As far back as the early 1970s Tauber (1974) argued that such approaches discourage the development of major innovations. It may be argued that less, rather than more, market research is required if major product innovations are required. Such an approach is characterised by the so-called technology-push model of innovation. Products that emerge from a technology-push approach are generated with little consideration of the market. Indeed, a market may not yet exist, as with the case of the PC and many other completely new products. Frequently, consumers are unable to understand the technology in question and view new products as a threat to their existing way of operating. Martin (1995: 122) argues that:

> customers can be extremely unimaginative . . . trying to get people to change the way they do things is the biggest obstacle facing many companies.

Many writers on this subject argue that potential consumers are not able to relate the physical aspects of a major innovative product with the consequences of owning and using it (Ortt and Schoormans, 1993). Others argue that while market research can help to fine-tune product concepts it is seldom the spur for an entirely new product concept. Consequently most conventional market research techniques deliver invalid results (Hamel and Prahalad, 1994).

More recently, new approaches are being recognised in the area of discontinuous product innovations. One technique adopts a process of probing and learning, where valuable experience is gained with every step taken and modifications are made to the product and the approach to the market based on that learning (Lynn et al., 1997). This is not trial and error but careful experimental design and exploration of the market often using the heritage of the organisation. This type of new product development is very different from traditional techniques and methods described in most marketing texts.

Circumstances when market research may hinder the development of discontinuous new products

Product developers and product testers tend to view the product offering in a classical layered view, where the product is assumed to have a core benefit and additional attributes and features are laid around it, hence layered view. Saren and

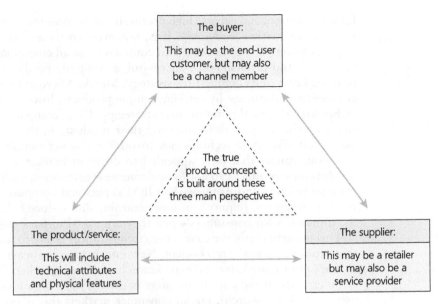

Figure 15.2 **The tripartite product concept**

Source: Adapted from M.A.J. Saren and N. Tzokas (1994) *Proceedings of the Annual Conference of the European Marketing Academy,* Maastricht.

Tzokas (1994) have argued that much of the problem is due to the way we view a product. They state that we often view it in isolation from:

- its context;
- the way it is used; and
- the role of the customer–supplier relationship.

This contributes to misleading views on new products. Figure 15.2 illustrates the tripartite product concept that captures the three views highlighted by Saren and Tzokas. The significance of this alternative view is that it highlights the reality of any product's situation. That is, product developers and product testers need to recognise that a product will be viewed differently by channel members than by end-users. For example, end-users will be concerned about how the product will perform, whereas channel members are more interested in how the product will *sell,* whether it will be easy to *stock and display* and, most important, whether it will be *profitable.* The Dyson case study at the end of this chapter illustrates the difficulties in trying to convince retailers to stock a new, slightly unusual product with which they are not familiar.

Technology-intensive products

Adopting a technology-push[1] approach to product innovations can allow a company to target and control premium market segments, establish its technology as the industry standard, build a favourable market reputation, determine the industry's

---

[1] The technology-push approach to NPD centres on trying to deliver the most effective technology available.

future evolution, and achieve high profits. It can become the centrepiece in a company's strategy for market leadership. It is, however, costly and risky. Such an approach requires a company to develop and commercialise an emerging technology in pursuit of growth and profits. To be successful, a company needs to ensure its technology is at the heart of its competitive strategy. Merck, Microsoft and Dyson have created competitive advantage by offering unique products, lower costs or both by making technology the focal point in their strategies. These companies have understood the role of technology in differentiating their products in the marketplace. They have used their respective technologies to offer a distinct bundle of products, services and price ranges that have appealed to different market segments. Such products revolutionise product categories or define new categories, such as Hewlett-Packard's laser-jet printers and Apple's (then IBM's) personal computer. These products shift market structures, require consumer learning and induce behaviour changes, hence the difficulties for consumers when they are asked to pass judgement.

This is particularly the case if the circumstances relate to an entirely new product that is unknown to the respondent. New information is always interpreted in the light of one's prior knowledge and experience. In industrial markets the level of information symmetry about the core technology is usually very high indeed (hence the limited use of market research), but in consumer markets this is not always the case. For example, industrial markets are characterised by:

- relatively few (information-rich) buyers;
- products often being customised and involving protracted negotiations regarding specifications;
- and, most importantly, the buyers usually being expert in the technology of the new product (i.e. high information symmetry about the core technology).

In situations of low information symmetry consumers have difficulty in understanding the core product and are unable to articulate their needs and any additional benefits sought. Conversely, in situations of high information symmetry consumers are readily able to understand the core product and hence are able to articulate their needs and a wide range of additional benefits sought, for example in tasting new food products.

Furthermore, discontinuous product innovations or radical product innovations frequently have to overcome the currently installed technology base – usually through displacement. This is known as the installed base effect. The installed base effect is the massive inertial effect of an existing technology or product that tends to preclude or severely slow the adoption of a superseding technology or product. This creates an artificial adoption barrier that can become insurmountable for some socially efficient and advantageous innovations. An example of this is the DVORAK keyboard, which has been shown to provide up to 40 per cent faster typing speeds. Yet the QWERTY keyboard remains the preference for most users because of its installed base, i.e. the widespread availability of keyboards that have the QWERTY configuration (Herbig *et al.*, 1995).

The idea of being shackled with an obsolete technology leads to the notion of switching costs. Switching is the one-time cost to the buyer who converts to the new product. Porter (1985) notes that switching costs may be a significant impediment to the adoption of a new consumer product. Buyer switching costs may arise as a result of prior commitments to a technology (a) and to a particular vendor (b) (Jackson, 1985). Computer software is an obvious example where problems of compatibility frequently arise. Similarly, buyers may have developed routines and procedures for dealing with a specific vendor that will need to be modified if a new relationship is established. The effect of both types of switching costs for a buyer is a disincentive to explore new vendors. There is a clear dilemma facing firms: market research may reveal genuine limitations with the new product but it may also produce negative feedback on a truly innovative product that may create a completely new market. The uncertainty centres on two key variables:

1 information symmetry about the core technology between producer and buyer; and
2 the installed base effect and switching costs.

Breaking with convention and winning new markets

There is evidence to suggest that many successful companies were successful because they were prepared to take the risky decision to ignore their customers' views and proceed with their new product ideas because they passionately believed that it would be successful. Subsequent success for these new products suggested that the firm's existing customers were unable to peer into the future, recognise that a different product or service would be desirable and articulate this to the firm. On reflection this seems a lot to ask of customers, and indeed is extremely difficult.

Between 1975 and 1995, 60 per cent of the companies in the *Fortune* 500 listing were replaced. Irrespective of their industry, new entrants either created new markets or recreated existing ones. Compaq overtook IBM to become the world's largest manufacturer of personal computers; Dyson overhauled Hoover's established position of market leader to become the new market leader in vacuum cleaners; Xerox lost out to Canon, which quickly became the bestseller in copiers; and there are many other examples. So why is it that established highly respected firms fail to recognise the future? In the cases already mentioned hindsight suggests that more resources should have been devoted to innovation, but that is not all. Established businesses that have been successful for many years also develop comfortable routines and become complacent. Hierarchies, systems, rulebooks and formulae work pretty well for controlling and improving the efficiency of repeated actions. They are hopeless for inventing, experimenting with and developing something that has never happened before (*see* 'The dilemma of innovation management', Chapter 3). Furthermore, a growing number of academics (Christensen, 1997; Hamel and Prahalad, 1994) argue that a particular problem exists because firms rely too heavily on market research and that some of the techniques reinforce the present and do not peer into the future. It is well known that market research results often produce negative reactions to discontinuous new products (innovative products) that later become profitable for the innovating company. Indeed, there are some famous examples such as the fax machine, the VCR and James Dyson's bagless vacuum cleaner. Despite this, companies continue to seek the views of consumers on their new product ideas. The debate about the use of market research in the development of new products is long-standing and controversial.

In his award-winning 'business book of the year'[2] Clayton Christensen (1997) investigated why well-run companies that were admired by many failed to stay on

---

[2] Christensen (1997) was awarded the *Financial Times* business book of the year award in 1999.

Closures for the wine industry: the customer does not know best

Consumers made it clear time and again that they did not want a screw-cap on their bottle of wine. They preferred the theatre of the cork and pop. Yet the international wine brands and retailers were determined to show customers that screw-cap was better: 75 per cent of wine sales in Australia and New Zealand are now screw-cap (see the case study at end the of Chapter 6).

top of their industry. His research showed that in the cases of well-managed firms such as Digital, IBM, Apple and Xerox, 'good management' (sic) was the most powerful reason why they failed to remain market leaders. It was precisely because these firms listened to their customers and provided more and better products of the sort they wanted that they lost their position of leadership. He argues that there are times when it is right not to listen to customers. Indeed, many companies share the same ideas about who their customers are and what products and services they want. The more that companies share this conventional wisdom about how they compete, the more they fight for incremental improvements in cost reductions and quality, and the more they avoid the discontinuous disruptive new products. Illustration 15.5 highlights the dangers of falling into this trap.

It is not surprising that many firms try to meet the needs of their customers. After all, successful companies have established themselves and built a successful business on providing the customer with what he or she wanted. IBM and Hoover, for example, became very good at serving their customers. But when a new, very different, technology came along these companies struggled. These large successful companies have been fighting known competitors for many years through careful planning and reducing costs. Suddenly they were faced with a completely different threat: new, smaller firms doing things differently and using unusual technologies. In IBM's case it was personal computers and in Hoover's case it has been bagless vacuum cleaners. Table 15.1 illustrates a wide range of products that were initially rejected by consumers, but went on to be successful.

If sufficient care is not exercised by managers, market research can be used to support conservative product development decision making. The previous sections have highlighted the difficulty faced by many managers in the field of new product development. In many crucial new product development decisions, the course of action that is most desirable over the long run is not the best course of action in the short term. This is the dilemma addressed in the debate about short-termism, that is, an emphasis on cutting costs and improving efficiencies in the immediate future, rather than on creativity and the development of innovative new product ideas for the long term. What is of concern is not the desire to cut costs but the apparent disregard of the implications and damage that such policies may bring about, and in particular the neglect of the company's ability to create new business opportunities for the future well-being of the company.

To return to a point made earlier by Akio Morita, Sony's influential leader. Morita argued that the public did not know what was possible and it was the firm that should lead the customer. This point is explored more fully by Hamel and Prahalad (1994: 108) who argue that firms need to go beyond customer-led ideas if

Table 15.1 Products that were initially rejected by consumers but went on to be successful

New product	Year	
Fax machines	1960s	Initially rejected by consumers who could not see any application for this product.
Microcomputers	1960s	Initially consumers could not foresee all the potential uses for microcomputers.
Benson & Hedges Gold cigarettes	1970s	Gallagher launched this product in the UK in 1978. Early consumer tests revealed indifferent support, yet the product was eventually a huge commercial success and brand leader in the UK.
Baileys Irish Cream Liqueur	1980s	Early consumer trials of this product suggested that it was not liked by consumers.
Dyson bagless vacuum cleaner	1990	Consumer research by retailers led them to believe consumers did not want a vacuum cleaner that displayed dirt collected in a transparent container. In fact consumers later preferred this design.
Chryslers PT Cruiser	1990s	Actually this product was not rejected, but Chrysler interpreted its consumer research as a niche product rather than a mass volume product. Hence, sales production could not match demand.
Screw-cap wine bottle closures	2000	Wine bottlers bowed to the demand of large retailers (buyers) to incorporate screw-caps. Consumers initially rejected screw-caps, but many now prefer it.

Source: A dirty business, *Guardian* 16/03/1999, copyright Guardian News & Media Ltd 2010.

they wish to be successful in the future. They are brutal in their criticism of customers' ability to peer into the future:

> *Customers are notoriously lacking in foresight. Ten or fifteen years ago, how many of us were asking for cellular telephones, fax machines and copiers at home, 24 hour discount brokerage accounts, multivalve automobile engines, video dial tone, etc.?*

Successful companies of the future will be those that are part of its creation. This means developing products that will be used in the future. Companies need to continually challenge existing products and markets. This can be achieved by pushing at the boundaries of current product concepts. Some firms have recognised this and are putting the most advanced technology they have available into the hands of the world's most sophisticated and demanding customers. IBM and Xerox have learnt through bitter experience what it is like to lose out to newcomers with new ideas and new technology. They know that today's customers may not be tomorrow's.

Using a simple two-by-two matrix (Figure 15.3) showing needs and customers, Hamel and Prahalad have shown that however well a company meets the articulated needs of current customers, it runs a great risk if it does not have a view of the needs customers cannot yet articulate: in other words the products of the future.

All this raises the problem of how to deal with consumers with limited prior knowledge and how to conduct market research on a totally new product or a major product innovation. In their research analysing successful cases of discontinuous product innovations, Lynn *et al.* (1997) argue that firms adopt a process of probing and learning. Valuable experience is gained with every step taken and modifications are made to the product and the approach to the market based on that learning.

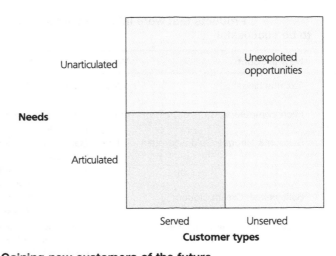

Figure 15.3 Gaining new customers of the future

Source: S. Hamel and C.K. Prahalad (1994) Competing for the future, *Harvard Business Review*, Vol. 72, No. 4, 122–8.

This is not trial and error, but careful experimental design and exploration of the market often using the experience and heritage of the organisation. This type of new product development is very different from traditional techniques and methods described in marketing texts.

Technology intensive products present similar difficulties. Nyström (1990) described high-tech markets as marketing dependent and technologically driven. Unfortunately, there is evidence that this linkage is not often recognised by organisations (Gupta *et al.*, 1985). High-tech markets are characterised as complex. In addition, they exist under rapidly changing technological conditions which lead to shorter life cycles and the need for rapid decisions. The importance of speed in high-tech markets is driven by increasing competition and the continually evolving expectations of customers. All of this is compounded by higher levels of risk for both the customer and the producer. Herein lies the problem: highly innovative products have an inherent high degree of uncertainty about exactly how an emerging technology may be formulated into a usable product and what the final product application will be. Market vision, or the ability to look into the future and picture products and services that will be successful, is a fundamental requirement for those firms wishing to engage in innovation but also very problematic (Van der Duin, 2006). It involves assessing one's own technological capability and present or future market needs and visioning a market offering that people will want to buy. While this may sound simple it lies at the heart of the innovation process and focuses attention on the need to examine not only the market but the way the new product offering is used or consumed.

When it may be correct to ignore your customers

Many industry analysts and business consultants are now arguing that the devotion to focus groups and market research has gone too far (Christensen, 1997; Martin, 1995; Francis, 1994). Indeed, the traditional new product development process of market research, segmentation, competitive analysis and forecasting, prior to passing the resultant information to the research and development (R&D) department, leads to commonality and bland new products. This is largely because the process constrains rather than facilitates innovative thinking and creativity. Furthermore, and more alarming, these techniques are well known and used by virtually all companies operating in consumer markets. In many of these markets the effect is an over-emphasis on minor product modifications and on competition that tends to focus on price. Indeed, critics of the market-orientated approach to new product development argue that the traditional marketing activities of branding, advertising and positioning, market research and consumer research act as an expensive obstacle course to product development rather than facilitating the development of new product ideas.

For many large multi-product companies it seems the use of market research is based upon accepted practice in addition to being an insurance policy. Many large companies are not short of new product ideas – the problem lies in deciding in which ones to invest substantial sums of money (Cooper, 2001; Liddle, 2004), and then justifying this decision to senior managers. Against this background one can see why market research is so frequently used without hesitation, as decisions can be justified and defended. Small companies in general, and small single-product companies in particular, are in a different situation. Very often new product ideas are scarce; hence, such companies frequently support ideas based upon their intuition and personal knowledge of the product.

The significance of discontinuous new products is often overlooked. Morone's (1993) study of successful US product innovations suggests that success was achieved through a combination of discontinuous product innovations and incremental improvements. Furthermore, in competitive, technology-intensive industries success is achieved with discontinuous product innovations through the creation of entirely new products and businesses, whereas product line extensions and incremental improvements are necessary for maintaining leadership (Lynn *et al.*, 1997). This, however, is only after leadership has been established through a discontinuous product innovation. This may appear to be at variance with accepted thinking that Japan secured success in the 1980s through copying and improving US and European technology. This argument is difficult to sustain on close examination of the evidence. The most successful Japanese firms have also been leaders in research and development. Furthermore, as Cohen and Levinthal (1990, 1994) have continually argued, access to technology is dependent on one's understanding of that technology.

Pause for thought

Ignoring your customers' views seems like a very high risk strategy, especially for an ambitious new manager; and if the product eventually fails, so might the career of the new manager!

Striking the balance between new technology and market research

Market research can provide a valuable contribution to the development of innovative products. The difficulties lie in the selection and implementation of research methods. It may be that market research has become a victim of its own success, that is, business and product managers now expect it to provide solutions to all difficult product management decisions. Practitioners need to view market research as a collection of techniques that can help to inform the decision process.

The development and adoption process for discontinuous or complex products is particularly difficult. The benefits to potential users may be difficult to identify and value, and usually because there are likely to be few substitute products available it is difficult for buyers to compare and contrast. Sometimes product developers have to lead buyers/consumers and show them the benefits, even educate them. This is where some marketing views suggest the process is no longer customer led or driven by the market, and they would argue that what is now occurring is a technology-push approach to product development. Day (1999) suggests that on closer examination there are a number of false dichotomies here:

- that you must either lead or follow customers;
- that you cannot stay close to both current and potential customers; and
- that technology-push cannot be balanced with market-pull.

It is true, as we have seen in this chapter, that customers respond most positively to what is familiar and comfortable and that customers view the high costs of new technology (including switching costs) in a largely negative way. Firms need to try to understand how customers will view innovations in the marketplace; this may include adoption influences such as consumption pattern, product capability and technological capability (Veryzer, 2003). Valid good management should be capable of selecting the appropriate market research techniques to avoid superficial consumer reactions. A thorough understanding of all aspects of the market and the needs of users should inform managers that it is possible to provide customers with what they want and lead them through education.

The argument about current markets and future markets is powerfully made by both Christensen (1997) and Hamel and Prahalad (1994). The suggestion here is that firms become myopic towards their current customers and fail to see the larger slowly changing market. The case of IBM in the 1980s is often given here. It surely is a responsibility of senior management to try to understand the wider and future environment of the firm. This may be very easy to record, but in practice it is extremely difficult to carry out. There are real dangers for all firms here. For example, discontinuous new technologies may require huge changes for firms, and one can see that for many the easy option is to hope the new technology fails and the firm can carry on as normal. Failure to change and adopt may result in more cases like IBM, Xerox, Hoover and many financial service firms that failed to respond to online banking. Once again it should be possible for a well-run company to fully exploit its current markets and develop and enter the markets of the future. For example, both Kodak and Fuji have exploited the massive changes in the photographic market with the introduction of digital photography.

Finally, the arguments about market-pull or technology-push never seem to go away. But readers of this book should now be clear that this is a stale argument. What is required is an understanding of innovation. While it is clear that in some industries the role of science and technology is far greater than in other industries, innovation requires inputs from both. It is true there are many firms in the pharmaceutical sector that argue that their approach to product development is to start with brilliant science and to look for ways of using it in new drugs; and that the role of marketing and sales is to develop sales of these products. While this approach may work for a few, even in this industry sector there are many firms that operate differently. Some of the most successful pharmaceutical firms including Glaxo-SmithKline, Pfizer and Merck work very closely with buyers and users to develop new drugs and to improve many existing ones. Indeed, the success of one of the world's bestselling drugs, Viagra, is surely testament to the benefits of working closely with the market.

Innovation in action

Self-service is growing in some industries. What other sectors can it be applied to?

MiNiBAR, in the heart of Amsterdam, is a self-service bar. When you arrive, a concierge gives you the key to your own fridge which is stocked with beer, wine, spirits and snacks. You and your friends help yourselves over the course of the evening, and settle up your account before leaving. The mini-bars are stocked from the back, making for easy restocking. It's simply extending the concept of the hotel mini-bar to the high street of course – but it's new and is bound to attract interest.

From the customer perspective, it's fun, convenient and there's no more queuing at the bar. From a business perspective it also means fewer staff members, and more customers can be accommodated because less space is taken up by the bar.

Source: HSBC (2010) 100 Thoughts, HSBC, London.

The challenge for senior management

Innovation is clearly a complex issue and sometimes it is a concept that sits uneasily in organisations. Indeed, some writers on the subject have argued that organisations are often the graveyard rather than the birthplace for many innovations. Applying pressure on product managers to seek high profits from quick volume sales rather than develop business opportunities for the future is a common mistake made by senior management. Similarly a heavy reliance on market research to minimise risk when developing new product ideas also contributes to an early grave for product ideas. The use of financial systems that minimise risk and avoid investment in more long-term projects is another common preference, which frequently emanates from senior management.

Correcting such ills will never be easy, but given the strategic importance of innovation it is a challenge senior management must take up. The adjustments which need to be made in order to encourage innovation in large companies may break some of the established rules of corporate life. They will require changes to internal systems and structures and the culture of the organisation. However, without such changes, potential innovations will continue to be squeezed out by the system, and thus rob the company of the most effective means of survival (Brown, 1991).

Dyson, Hoover and the bagless vacuum cleaner

This case study illustrates many of the obstacles and difficulties of launching a new product. The product in question used new technology that was initially rejected by existing manufacturers. It was priced at more than double that of existing products, but eventually captured more than 50 per cent of the UK vacuum cleaner market in less than four years.

Introduction

Conventional wisdom would surely suggest that Dyson Appliances Ltd would fail within a few months. After all, it appeared to be a small company with an eccentric manager at its helm, trying to sell an over-priced product of limited appeal in a very competitive market with less expensive, conventional, mass-market products made by respected manufacturers whose names were, quite literally, household words. The result was very different. The story of the Dyson bagless vacuum cleaner is not a classic tale of 'rags to riches'. The charismatic inventor James Dyson was afforded many privileges and opportunities not available to most. It is, none the less, a fascinating story and illustrates many of the difficulties and problems faced by small businesses and 'lone inventors'; and demonstrates the determination, hard work and sacrifices necessary in order to succeed. The cliché *against the odds*, which Dyson (1998) used as the title of his autobiography, is certainly appropriate and tells the story of the development and launch of the first bagless vacuum cleaner – the Dyson DC01.

This case raises several significant research questions in the field of innovation management. First, how and why did senior executives at leading appliance manufacturers across Europe, such as Electrolux, Bosch and Miele, decide not to utilise the technology offered to them by Dyson? Second, how and why did senior buyers for many retail chains across the United Kingdom fail to recognise the potential for the DC01? Third, technology transfer experts would point out that the Dyson vacuum cleaner is a classic case of technology transfer – a technology developed for one industry, i.e. dust extraction from sawmills, is applied to a different use in a new industry. Hence, it is technology transfer that needs to be championed

and supported further by governments. Fourth, as a mechanism for protecting intellectual property, it seems that patents depend on the depth of your pocket. That is, they are prohibitively expensive and are almost exclusively for the benefit of large multinational organisations. What can be done to help small businesses without such large pockets and unlimited financial resources? And finally, many commentators would argue Dyson was successful partly because he had some influential contacts that he had established – he was fortunate. But there may be a hundred failed Mr Dysons littering the business highways who did not have such contacts. How can governments try to facilitate inventors like Dyson and ensure that more innovations succeed (thereby developing the economic base of their country)?

Reaping the rewards from technological innovation

Since Dyson's entry into the domestic appliance market two of the largest world players in the vacuum cleaner market have responded to the challenge laid down by James Dyson's bagless vacuum cleaner, launched in the United Kingdom in 1993. Dyson now accounts for a third of all vacuum cleaner sales in the United Kingdom. In 1998 Dyson Appliances

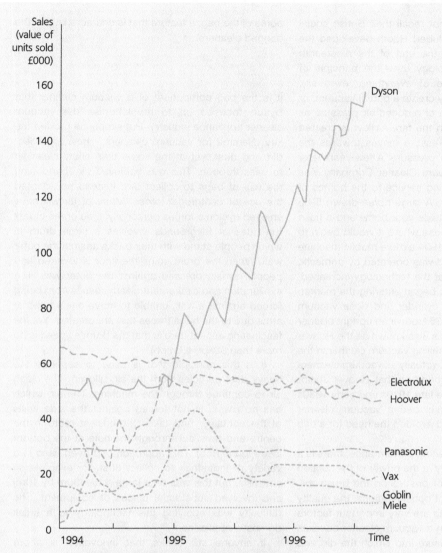

Figure 15.4 **The spectacular growth of Dyson**

sold nearly 1.4 million units worldwide. Revenues for the year were £190 million but, surprisingly, net income was £29 million – 15 per cent of sales (*see* Figure 15.4).

Background

Prior to the development of the bagless vacuum cleaner James Dyson had already demonstrated his prowess as a designer and businessman. He was responsible for the 'ballbarrow', a wheelbarrow that revolutionised that market by using a ball rather than a wheel. This was to provide the financial foundation for the development of the bagless vacuum cleaner. That particular experience taught James Dyson many lessons. One in particular is worth mentioning. The patents for the ballbarrow were owned by the company that James Dyson helped to set up. He eventually parted with this company but unfortunately lost all control of the patents as they belonged to the company and not to himself. Dyson was determined that any future patent would personally belong to him and not a company.

For those who may not recall their British social and economic history, Hubert Booth developed the first vacuum cleaner at the end of the nineteenth century. Vacuum technology uses the principle of a vacuum (the absence of everything, even air). Vacuum cleaners actually create a partial vacuum, or more accurately, an area of reduced air pressure as air moves outward within the fan. Airflow is created as air with normal air pressure moves towards the area with the reduced air pressure. A few years later in 1902 the British Vacuum Cleaner Company was offering a vacuum cleaning service to the homes of the affluent and wealthy. A large horse-drawn 5-hp engine would pull up outside your home and a hose would be fed into the house where it would begin to suck out all the dust. By 1904 a more mobile machine was available for use and was operated by domestic servants. As popularity of the technology increased, additional manufacturers began entering the market. Electrolux introduced a cylinder and hose vacuum cleaner in 1913 and in 1936 Hoover an upright cleaner with rotating brushes. This was known as the Hoover Junior and was the bestselling vacuum cleaner in the United Kingdom. Indeed, virtually all vacuum cleaners since this time are variations on that Hoover Junior design. That was until the late 1970s and early 1980s when James Dyson developed a vacuum cleaner using cyclonic forces and avoided the need for a bag to collect dust.

When it comes to cleaning performance, there is a tendency to look primarily at the power of the suction motor and the amount of bristles on the brush roll. While these are important considerations, the quality and size of the paper bag are very important factors as well. The paper bag in a vacuum cleaner consists of a special paper enclosure into which the dirt and air are directed as part of the filtering system. The paper used is specially processed to permit the air to pass through it while retaining as much of the dust and dirt as possible. The quality of the bag's filter media affects both its ability to retain the fine dust and allergens and its ability to allow air to flow easily through it. The size of the bag will also affect how easily the air flows. A good-quality paper bag is a very important vacuum cleaner component, which needs to be regularly replaced. The Dyson vacuum cleaner maintains its performance during the vacuuming process because it has no bag, hence there is no reduction in suction due to clogging of the pores of the bag, a feature that is characteristic of the bagged cleaners.

The development of a bagless vacuum cleaner

It is the bag component of a vacuum cleaner that Dyson focused on to revolutionise the vacuum cleaner appliance industry. Put simply he tackled the key dilemma for vacuum cleaners – how to collect dirt and dust, yet at the same time allow clean air to pass through. This was achieved by abandoning the use of bags to collect dirt. Instead he adapted the use of centrifugal forces. Many of us will have enjoyed cyclonic forces personally. One of the oldest fun rides at fairgrounds involves a large drum in which people stand with their backs against the outer wall. When the drum spins the floor is lowered and people remain pressed against the outer wall. The exhilaration and excitement clearly results from being forced against a wall, unable to move one's head or arms due to the huge forces that are created. Yet the fascinating aspect here is that the drum's speed is no more than 33kph (20mph).

It is this principle that is used to separate the heavy dust particles from the air, allowing the clean air to continue through the machine. The air, which has no mass, is not forced against the side walls of the container and takes the easiest route in the centre and thus out through the hole at the bottom (see Figure 15.5). This approach had been used in a variety of industries to collect dust, for example, in sawmills, but this was on a large scale (30m by 10m) and involved substantial pieces of equipment. The difficulty was applying this technology to a small domestic appliance.

If anyone still thinks that innovation is about waking up in the morning with a bright idea and shouting 'Eureka!' they should consider carefully James Dyson's difficult road to success. Between 1978 and 1982 he built over 1,000 prototype vacuum cleaners, spent over £2 million and experienced many years of sweat and headaches before eventually developing a successful prototype. But this was merely the start of an even longer project to get manufacturers to buy the licence to manufacture. Indeed, over 10 years later Dyson decided to mass produce the product for the UK market himself.

The story begins in 1978 with James Dyson at home with his young family helping with some of the

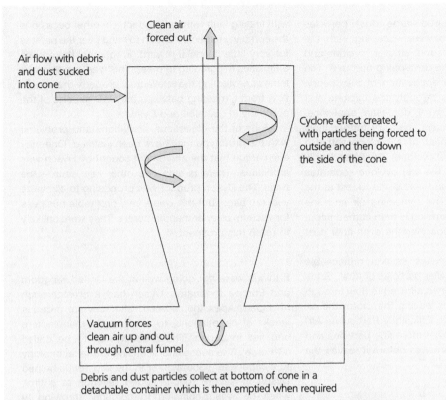

Clean air forced out

Air flow with debris and dust sucked into cone

Cyclone effect created, with particles being forced to outside and then down the side of the cone

Vacuum forces clean air up and out through central funnel

Debris and dust particles collect at bottom of cone in a detachable container which is then emptied when required

Figure 15.5 Basic operating principle of Dyson bagless vacuum cleaner

chores around the home. Like many families at the time, the Dysons owned a Hoover Junior upright vacuum cleaner. Dyson noticed that when a new bag is fitted to the vacuum cleaner it works well, but quickly loses much of its suction. He soon had the vacuum cleaner in pieces on his workbench and was amazed to realise that the standard vacuum cleaner technology relied on holes in the bag to allow clean air to pass through. As soon as these clogged up (which starts to occur immediately) suction begins to deteriorate. Moreover, he quickly discovered that all bagged vacuum cleaners operate on the same principle. How, then, can this limitation be overcome? The idea came to Dyson while he was investigating a problem at his ballbarrow factory. To improve toughness the product was powder-coated and then heated. This involved spraying the powder coating, which was messy. To overcome this problem an industrial vacuum cleaner was required. The suppliers of the powder coating informed Dyson that most of their larger customers use cyclones to collect the

powder. Such cyclones are also used in a variety of industrial settings such as sawmills to extract dust from the air. This information was the beginning of what turned out to be a 15-year project.

Cyclonic cleaning systems separate the dust particles from the airflow by spinning the air within a separation chamber. The Dyson system operates as follows.

Any dirt and air enters the nozzle near the floor and travels through the hose towards the separation chambers. It first enters the primary dirt-separation chamber where the larger dirt particles are deposited. From there the air with the remaining fine dirt and dust travels to the cyclonic chamber. Once in the cyclonic chamber, the spinning action separates most of the fine dirt and dust particles from the airflow. The spinning causes centrifugal force to act upon the dust particles, moving them outward while the air exits from the inner part of the chamber (*see* Figure 15.5).

The Dyson vacuum cleaner uses two cyclones and several filters to capture dirt and dust. While the first cyclonic chamber captured large dust particles some fine dust particles were escaping with the air. The answer was a second, smaller, cyclone and Dyson spent many months developing this idea. The key problem was in the application of the theory, that is, having dust pass through one cyclone and then another, all in a small domestic appliance. After months, and eventually years, of further trials and errors the development of a cyclone within a cyclone was born (the dual cyclone). As dirt and air is sucked into the machine the first cyclone separates the large dust particles and these come to rest at the bottom of the canister. The remaining air and fine dust (including cigarette smoke) is then carried into a second cyclone which separates the even finer dust particles from the air.

The technology also uses several replaceable filters to remove even smaller particles of dust. Since the air is quite clean, it is then allowed to flow through the motor to cool it. After leaving the motor the air is filtered by a HEPA (High Efficiency Particulate Air) exhaust filter to remove even more fine particles and carbon from the motor brushes before it leaves the vacuum cleaner.

In search of a manufacturer – 'don't let them get you down'

Thanks to experience gained with other products, most notably the ballbarrow, Dyson was able to ensure that patent applications were in place prior to negotiations. This is essential if you wish to ensure that large multinational companies are not going to steal your intellectual property. From Dyson's experience he would argue that they would probably try to steal it regardless of any protection one held.

Dyson was offering a licence to manufacturing companies that included exclusive rights to his patents. In return Dyson would receive a percentage of their profits from the sale of the manufactured product. Dyson was looking for a five- to ten-year licence with a royalty of 5 per cent of the wholesale price and £40,000 up front. In addition he was offering his help in the development of the product from its prototype form. Unfortunately Hoover, Electrolux, Goblin, Black and Decker, AEG, Vax and many others all declined. There were many different reasons given. Sometimes the companies appeared to be arrogant and dismissed Dyson as a 'loony crank'. What was surprising was that throughout, companies appeared to be obsessed with finding fault with the product. On other occasions the company expected Dyson to hand over the patents for very little financial reward. Frequently there were difficulties in agreeing to meet. This was due to problems of protecting the intellectual property that would flow from a meeting between the R&D experts of the company in question and Dyson.

Many of the objections, limitations and problems with the prototype may have been justified. One may even argue that the agreement sought by Dyson was ambitious. There is also one other key issue – the bags. The Dyson product was proposing to eliminate vacuum bags, but this was a very profitable business for vacuum cleaner manufacturers. They were unlikely to relish this prospect.

Breaking through in Japan

If things were not going well in the United Kingdom and Europe fortunately Dyson had a breakthrough in Japan. Apex Inc. agreed, after several arduous weeks of negotiations, to a licence to manufacture and sell in Japan. The product was to be called 'G-Force'. The successful licensing of the technology to a Japanese manufacturer in the late 1980s helped Dyson to secure much-needed revenue at a time when he was beginning to consider throwing in the towel. This small level of income also provided the encouragement he needed to start planning the establishment of manufacturing facilities in the United Kingdom. What is interesting about the licensing arrangement in question is that Dyson was uncertain that licensing revenues received reflect the true sales figures. As with all licensing and royalty agreements, there is a significant element of trust required. For example, authors trust their publishers that sales of their book will be accurately recorded and appropriate royalties paid. There is, however, the small matter of who establishes the level of sales. This, of course, is taken by the publisher who then pays the royalties to authors. This 'high-trust' relationship also operates with other licensing agreements where royalties are paid per item sold.

Entering the UK market and manufacturing in the United Kingdom

With a small amount of revenue starting to trickle in Dyson decided that it was time to start in Britain. The existing appliance manufacturers had expressed no interest, hence Dyson planned to manufacture the product in Britain by offering the product to existing contract manufacturers. Essentially Dyson decided to offer a series of contracts to two existing manufacturing companies, one to mould the component parts and another to assemble. For the existing moulding and assembly companies it was additional capacity. Unfortunately the companies selected by Dyson caused further problems. First, the quality of the completed product was not acceptable to Dyson. Second, the companies seemed to be squeezing Dyson's work in between existing long-standing contracts. In the end Dyson decided that he would prefer to manufacture and assemble the product himself. He purchased the moulds from the plastic moulding company and attempted to establish a factory in the United Kingdom, the rationale being that this would at least ensure that he was in control of his own destiny and would not have to rely on others. Further difficulties, however, were encountered by Dyson. First, he found that it is extremely difficult to borrow money – even with a proven successful product. Dyson explored the possibility of setting up a factory in an area where government development grants are available. For example, he tried South Wales but David Hunt, the then Welsh Office Minister, refused his application for a grant.

The project had now consumed 12 years of his life and had cost £2 million. Once again Dyson was forced to consider whether it was all worth it.

After months of negotiations Dyson's local bank manager agreed to lend him some more money and he was able to set up his manufacturing factory in Wiltshire. Soon Dyson was producing his own product in his own factory and the first Dyson bagless vacuum cleaner rolled off the production line in 1992.

Trying to sell to the retailers

Armed with a shiny new DC01 under his arm James Dyson began visiting the large UK white-goods retailers such as Currys, Dixons and Comet to arrange sales orders. Unfortunately Dyson was disappointed at their reaction. Quite simply, the retailers were not convinced that the UK consumer would be willing to pay possibly three times as much for a vacuum cleaner. Moreover, Dyson's bagless product was twice the price of the brand leader. The response was almost universal:

Consumers are very happy with this one – why should they pay twice as much for yours? And anyway, if your idea was any good Hoover or Electrolux would have thought of it years ago.

Eventually, several of the home catalogue companies agreed to feature the product. In addition, an electricity board shop in the Midlands also agreed to stock a few products. Initially, sales were slow but gradually they increased. Eventually John Lewis, the national department store, agreed to take the product. From here sales began to take off.

In terms of marketing and promoting the product what is interesting is that, to date, the company has spent virtually nothing on promotion. Dyson has always adopted a strong product orientation and has believed that if a product is good enough it should require very little promotion. It is this approach which Dyson adopted for the bagless vacuum cleaner. Despite the use of revolutionary technology Dyson decided against large advertising budgets and instead relied upon a few press releases and features in newspapers.

The competition responds

With Dyson beginning to challenge the once-comfortable dominant position of Electrolux and Hoover, both companies mounted a strong defence of their products' technology, claiming that their traditional vacuum cleaning technology was more effective than the Dyson. Much of the debate, usually via press advertisements, centred on cleaning effectiveness. Hoover and Electrolux were able to make some headline-grabbing claims, in particular, that their products had more suction power and, hence, were better. Certainly the traditional vacuum cleaner with a bag had an initial high level of suction power, but this was necessary because the bag soon clogged up, reducing the level of suction. There are two different ways of viewing cleaning effectiveness. The most common use has to do with the ability of a vacuum cleaner to pick up dirt from the surface being cleaned. The other is the ability of the filtering system to clean the air so that a minimum amount of dirt and allergens is recirculated back into the home. The variable that is significant in a vacuum cleaner, however, is the flow of air and is measured in cubic metres per minute (CMM). It is one of the most important aspects of vacuum cleaner performance. Airflow

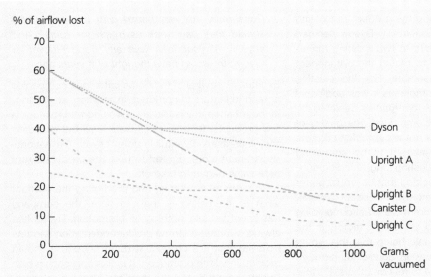

Figure 15.6 **Cleaning performance of five vacuum cleaners**

in a vacuum cleaner is inversely proportional to the total resistance within the system and directly proportional to the suction created by the suction motor.

Figure 15.6 depicts cleaning performance after vacuuming 1,000 grams of ASTM (American Society for Testing and Materials) Test Dirt. You will see that the Dyson machine maintains a steady airflow while other 'bagged' machines lose airflow.

Hoover's bagless vacuum cleaner

With sales and market share continuing to decline (*see* Table 15.2) Miele and Hoover attempted to fight Dyson in the vacuum cleaner market by developing similar bagless vacuum technologies. Hoover embarked on a technology transfer exercise to utilise technology first developed for the oil industry. The centrifugal force technology (similar to that used by Dyson) was used to separate gas or sand from crude oil. This technology has now been applied to Hoover's range of Triple Vortex vacuum cleaners in an attempt to compete with Dyson's own patented centrifugal force technology (www.Hoover.co.uk). Interestingly, Hoover's technology dispenses with the need for any filters. This may provide the advantage Hoover requires to re-establish itself as a key player in the vacuum cleaner market. Dyson, however, claimed that Hoover's technology copied its patents and sued Hoover for patent

Table 15.2 **With sales declining Miele and Hoover have attempted to take on Dyson in the vacuum cleaner market**

	Volume (%)	Value (%)
Dyson		
Total market	33.5	53.5
Upright	51.6	66.9
Cylinder	13.6	29.8
Hoover		
Total market	12.3	9.2
Upright	16.5	10.2
Cylinder	8.2	7.1
Miele		
Total market	2.1	2.6
Cylinder	6.1	10.4

Source: A dirty business, *Guardian*, 16 March 1999.

infringement in March 2000, eventually winning around £3 million in damages.

Dyson has had several legal battles with his competitors over patent infringement and advertising standards. In January 2000 the Advertising Standards Association (ASA) ruled in favour of Dyson regarding an advertisement from Electrolux that claimed its vacuum cleaner was the most powerful. The ASA ruled that power of the motor was no indication of vacuum cleaner effectiveness (*Sunday Times*, 2000).

Hitting the big time

In 2002 Dyson entered the US market. In 2004 sales reached almost 1 million units. This contributed to a surge in profits at Dyson, which were £102.9 million in 2005, more than double 2003's figure. Sales efforts have continued and in 2006 Dyson was the brand leader in the United States. This has been achieved with no intellectual property protection in the United States. Unusually Dyson decided to enter the US market without any patent protection. He relied on the brand's strength that had been built and developed over the previous 10 years. Sales in 2006 were 1.5 million units. Dyson revealed that success in the United States was partly down to a very successful $30 million ad campaign. This was a very different strategy to that used in the UK and Europe.

More recently Dyson Appliances has been enjoying continued and improved success in one of the fiercest markets of all – Japan. Indeed, in 2006 Dyson overtook Toshiba to become the third biggest vacuum brand in Japan. This success is due to the Dyson DC12, a small digital machine designed especially for Japanese consumers. For Dyson Appliances Ltd success continues largely due to success in overseas markets. In Japan, the hand-held DC12 was the biggest selling carpet cleaner last year, outdoing such Japanese brands as Sharp and Sanyo. This helped push profits in 2006 past the £100 million barrier for the first time. The group's annual report reveals that the inventor awarded himself a £30 million dividend on top of his £29 million salary following a 9 per cent rise in annual sales and a 19 per cent pre-tax profits boost, to £115 million. Profits have almost trebled in four years, when the group made pre-tax profits of £43 million. This is largely because of success in the United States and Japan. Turnover has rocketed from £2.4 million in 1993 to £515 million. Its exports have increased three-fold in the past three years, now accounting for 80 per cent of turnover (*see* Figure 15.7).

Conclusions

James Dyson certainly believes it was worth it in the end. But during the 15-year period there were probably many occasions when he felt like giving up or more likely would have sold out for a few hundred thousand pounds. The period 1980–92 was very difficult, not just for himself but also for his family,

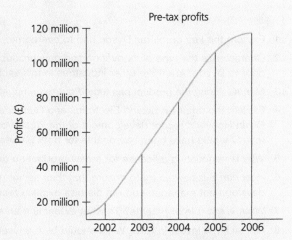

Figure 15.7 **Dyson's pre-tax profits (2002–06)**

and enormous pressures were placed on them. Fortunately they survived; arguably someone without the background, resources and contacts would have failed. Many people have great ideas but only a few achieve success. Very often it is due to the determination of the individual involved; sometimes events seem to conspire against even the best efforts of the individual.

Dyson invests heavily in R&D and believes that this is the key to success. Not all firms support this view. The level of investment in R&D varies considerably. The high value he places on creativity sets Dyson apart from other firms and helps to explain his insistence on maintaining what in Britain are considered insanely large annual investments in research and development. Nearly 17 per cent of revenues regularly goes to supporting the company's R&D efforts, a figure some ten times greater than the average in the United Kingdom. As a result of these ongoing research expenditures, a company that started with just one product now offers more than a dozen – all either upright or canister vacuum cleaners, each a more refined and technologically advanced model than its predecessors.

Reference: Dyson, J. (1998) *Against the Odds*, Orion Books, London; *Sunday Times* (2000) Dyson bags ruling on Electrolux, Business Section, 24 January, 1; Wallop, H. (2006) Dyson cleans up with £31m payday, *Daily Telegraph*, 1 November, Business Section, 4.

Questions

1 Explore the key problems Dyson had to overcome.

2 Characterise the type of innovation and new product development in the mature vacuum cleaner market prior to Dyson. Are there other industries in this situation?

3 Manufacturing the product has turned out to be hugely profitable, yet this was not the original plan; why not?

4 Explain the rationale behind Electrolux and Hoover's decision not to purchase the licence from Dyson. Given Hoover's recent development of the *Triple Vortex* how do you assess this decision? What level of royalty would have been reasonable for both parties – that is, Dyson and Hoover?

5 Why is negotiating a licence for a new product so difficult?

6 How can businesses try to ensure that their senior managers (both buyers and new business development managers) do not dismiss exciting technology and with it potentially profitable business?

7 What is the role of patents? To what extent is it an effective system for protecting intellectual property?

8 Not all firms invest in R&D. What should be the level of expenditure on R&D for a firm?

9 Explain the very different market entry strategy used for the United States?

Note: This case has been written as a basis for class discussion rather than to illustrate effective or ineffective managerial or administrative behaviour. It has been prepared from a variety of published sources, as indicated, and from observations.

Chapter summary

This chapter has shown that great care must be exercised in market research, for there are times when market research results produce negative reactions to discontinuous new products (innovative products) that later become profitable for the innovating company. Like any activity that contributes to new product development, it has strengths and weaknesses. Many of these weaknesses are highlighted when the new product is discontinuous. Finally, some new products have particularly difficult problems to overcome if they are to be successful, like high switching costs. If these are recognised in advance, however, it is possible to overcome even these significant challenges.

Discussion questions

1 Explain why consumer market testing might not always be beneficial.

2 We are told that many new products fail, but is this because many firms are impatient? Discuss whether firms should allow more time for their product to be adopted and whether they would end up with a successful product.

3 Explain why discontinuous new products present a different challenge.

4 Show why the more radical the innovation, the greater the pertinence of qualitative market research techniques (e.g. customer visits and focus groups).

5 Examine whether there do exist innovations, typically radical, where market research of almost any kind is premature, not cost-justified or of limited value.

6 Discuss the advantages of the tripartite product concept in developing new products.

7 Discuss the dilemma faced by all firms of trying to listen to customers' needs and wants and yet also trying to develop new products for those customers that they do not yet serve.

8 Explain why some writers argue that organisations are the graveyard of product innovations rather than the birthplace.

Key words and phrases

Market research *524*	**Tripartite product concept** *534*
Concept testing *528*	**Installed base effect** *535*
Discontinuous new products *532*	**Switching costs** *535*

References

Barrett, P. (1996) The good and bad die young, *Marketing*, 11 July, 16.

Brown, R. (1991) Managing the S curves of innovation, *Journal of Marketing Management*, Vol. 7, No. 2, 189–202.

Christensen, C.M. (1997) *The Innovator's Dilemma: When New Technologies Cause Great Firms to Fail*, HBS Press, Cambridge, MA.

Cohen, W.M. and Levinthal, D.A. (1990) A new perspective on learning and innovation, *Administrative Science Quarterly*, Vol 35, No. 1, 128–52.

Cohen, W.M. and Levinthal, D.A. (1994) Fortune favours the prepared firm, *Management Science*, Vol. 40, No. 3, 227–51.

Cooper, R.G. (1990) New products: What distinguishes the winners, *Research and Technology Management*, November–December, 27–31.

Cooper, R.G. (2001) *Winning at New Products*, 3rd edn, Perseus Publishing, Cambridge, MA.

Day, G.S. (1999) *The Market Driven Organisation*, The Free Press, New York.

Elkind, P. (2008) The trouble with Steve Jobs, *Fortune*, 5–8, 5 March.

Elliot, K. and Roach, D. (1991) Are consumers evaluating your products the way you think and hope they are?, *Journal of Consumer Marketing*, Vol. 8, No. 1, 5–14.

Fortune (2008) Steven Jobs, Apple, 3 March.

Francis, J. (1994) Rethinking NPD: giving full rein to the innovator, *Marketing*, 26 May, 6.

Guardian (1999) A dirty business, 16 March, 22.

Gupta, A.K., Ray, S.P. and Wilemon, D.L. (1985) R & D and Marketing Dialogue in High-Tech Firms, *Industrial Marketing Management*, Vol. 14, 289–300.

Hamel, G. and Prahalad, C.K. (1994) *Competing for the future*, Harvard Business Review, Vol. 72, No. 4, 122–8.

Herbig, P., Howard, C. and Kramer, H. (1995) The installed base effect: implications for the management of innovation, *Journal of Marketing Management*, Vol. 11, No. 4, 387–401.

Jackson, B.B. (1985) *Winning and Keeping Industrial Customers*, Lexington Books, Lexington, MA.

King, S. (1985) Has marketing failed or was it never really tried?, *Journal of Marketing Management*, Vol. 1, 1–19.

Kotler, P. (1998) *Marketing Management*, Prentice Hall, London.

Laurance, B. (2008) Reckitt Benckiser cleans up with research to boost global sales, *Sunday Times*, Business p. 3, 17 February.

Liddle, D. (2004) R&D Project Selection at Danahar, MBA Dissertation, University of Portsmouth.

Lynn, G.S., Morone, J.G. and Paulson, A.S. (1997) 'Marketing and discontinuous innovation: The probe and learn process', in Tushman, M.L. and Anderson, P. (eds) *Managing Strategic Innovation and Change, a Collection of Readings*, Oxford University Press, New York, 353–75.

Martin, J. (1995) Ignore your customer, *Fortune*, Vol. 8, No. 1, 121–25.

Morone, J. (1993) *Winning in High-tech Markets*, Harvard Business School Press, Cambridge, MA.

Nyström, H. (1990) *Technological and market innovation: strategies for product and company development*, Wiley, Chichester.

Ortt, R.J. and Schoormans, P.L. (1993) Consumer research in the development process of a major innovation, *Journal of the Market Research Society*, Vol. 35, No. 4, 375–89.

Porter, M.E. (1985) *Competitive Advantage*, Harvard Business School Press, Cambridge, MA.

Rogers, E. (1995) *The Diffusion of Innovation*, The Free Press, New York.

Saren, M.A.J. and Tzokas, N. (1994) *Proceedings of the Annual Conference of the European Marketing Academy*, Maastricht.

Sunday Times (2008) 17 February.

Tauber, E.M. (1974) Predictive validity in consumer research, *Journal of Advertising Research*, Vol. 15, No. 5, 59–64.

Van der Duin, P.A. (2006) *Qualitative futures research for innovation*, Eburon Academic Publishers, Delft, The Netherlands.

Veryzer, R. (2003) 'Marketing and the development of innovative products', in Shavinina, L. (ed.), *The International Handbook on Innovation*, Elsevier, Oxford.

von Hippel, E. and Thomke, S. (1999) Creating breakthroughs at 3M, *Harvard Business Review*, Vol. 77, No. 5, 47–57.

Further reading

For a more detailed review of the role of market research in new product development, the following develop many of the issues raised in this chapter:

Hamel, G. and Prahalad, C.K. (1994) Competing for the future, *Harvard Business Review*, Vol. 72, No. 4, 122–8.

HSBC (2010) 100 Thoughts, HSBC, London.

Hutlink, E.J., Hart, S., Henery, R.S.J. and Griffin, A. (2000) Launch decisions and new product success: an empirical comparison of consumer and industrial products, *Journal of Product Innovation Management*, Vol. 17, No. 1, 5–23.

Kumar, N., Scheer, L. and Kotler, P. (2000) From market driven to market driving, *European Management Journal*, Vol. 18, No. 2, 129–41.

Swink, M. (2000) Technological innovativeness as a moderator of new product design integration and top management support, *Journal of Product Innovation Management*, Vol. 17, No. 1, 208–20.

Section 9

Retailers, Manufacturers and Consumers

Chapter 12

Creating and managing brands and brand equity

IN THIS CHAPTER, WE WILL ADDRESS THE FOLLOWING QUESTIONS:

1 What do we understand by branding?

2 What are the key strategic brand management decisions?

3 How do we create and manage brand equity?

4 How do we manage service brands?

A strong brand aims to command intense customer loyalty. The most successful brands in the world are worth billions to companies. Zara, the Spanish fashion retailer brand, is valued at €3.34 billion. IKEA, the Swedish furniture brand, is another successful European brand, valued at €6.5 billion. How marketers create and manage brands is of the utmost importance. More than one-third of the world's powerful brands are European.

One of the master marketers at creating brands is Procter & Gamble.[1]

Procter & Gamble successfully markets nearly 300 brands in 160 countries by managing the totality of the marketing mix variables and focusing on the brand image of quality and innovation, aligned to excellent brand management and extension strategies.

Source: Courtesy of Procter & Gamble UK.

Strategic brand management

Brand management uses the choice, design and implementation of marketing mix activities to build, measure and manage the brand value.[37] **Strategic brand management** is the long-term effort of consciously providing an offering with an identity that is understood on all levels. This means both internally and externally and includes customers, employees, suppliers and resellers. It is the sustained effort by the company to encourage people to see its brand in the light in which it portrays it.

Strategic brand management can dramatically increase corporate success according to a study by Booz Allen Hamilton, which noted that 80 per cent of European companies that are managed with a strong brand focus have operating profits twice as high as the sector average.[38] The stock values for companies reflect a belief that strong brands result in better earnings and profit performance for companies, which, in turn, create greater value for shareholders.[39] See the marketing insight box on next page.

An important issue is to have a brand vision that offers a clear and consistent message about the value of the brand. A brand vision involves recognising the inherent potential of a brand, which is based in part on its customer brand equity – the value of the brand to the company. The brand value is only realised if the right marketing processes, programmes and activities are put in place.

There must be clear value propositions from the consumer perspective. The long-term brand vision is operationalised through both long- and short-term marketing endeavours.

Marketing insight

Europe's brand-oriented companies almost twice as successful

Brand-oriented companies enjoy a high public profile and consumer confidence. Both are painstakingly developed over time as a result of high-quality and innovative products and services, and often resource-intensive communication. Brands created in this way then generate more added value and often constitute the most valuable asset of the company. The consumer confidence that has been built up is extremely important for brand-oriented companies and constitutes a strategic element to competition.

Strategic brand management can dramatically increase corporate success, according to a study by Booz Allen Hamilton and branding experts Wolff Olins. The Booz Allen Hamilton–Wolff Olins study is based on interviews with leading marketing and sales executives at Europe's top 500 companies.

Some 90 per cent of the companies surveyed are convinced that brand orientation is a key factor in their success – a twofold increase compared to five years

ago. 'However, only 18 per cent of companies currently place brand management at the heart of their activities and have a clear understanding of the brand across the entire organisation,' said Booz Allen Vice President, Gregor Harter. 'This small group of companies is proving to be exceptionally successful.'

The study places companies into one of three categories:

1 Brand agnostic companies: management assumes that branding only makes a modest contribution to corporate success, focusing instead on factors such as costs and optimising processes.

2 Emerging brand companies: on the threshold of full-brand orientation. These companies recognise the growing importance of brand's contribution to value and have already begun to embed it into their corporate strategy.

3 Brand guided companies: already rigorously implementing brand management to achieve corporate success. The study revealed a clear correlation among brand-guided companies, the application of sophisticated marketing techniques, and corporate success.

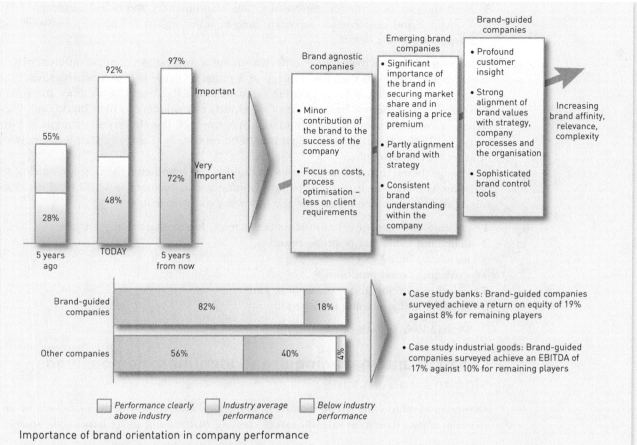

Importance of brand orientation in company performance

*According to the statements of the interviewees

Source: Booz Allen Wolff Olins, European Survey Among Marketing and Sales Officers, 8/2004. In Harter, G., Koster, A. and Peterson, M. (2005) *Managing Brands for Value Creation*, Booz & Co., p. 2, Exhibit 1, Exhibit 2.

Companies with a strong brand orientation more frequently measure the key ratios that enable them to manage their marketing performance. For example, 45 per cent regularly calculate their share of their customers' total spend, compared to 24 per cent of the other companies surveyed; 64 per cent of brand-guided companies regularly examine whether their brand position allows any degree of price flexibility, compared to only 20 per cent of brand agnostic or emerging brand companies.

The study also revealed another common trait shared by brand guided companies. Brand management is handled at the strategic management level of the organisation and is closely tied to developing strategy and managing the organisation.

Sources: German Brand Association (2009) European Commission Consultation Follow-up to the Green Paper on Consumer Collective Redress: www.c.europa.eu/consumers/redress_cons/responses/CP_GBA_en.pdf; Gregor Harter, Alex Koster, Dr Michael Peterson and Michael Stomberg, *Managing Brands for Value Creation* (2005).

Marketers must provide a clear sense of direction for each employee within the company to appreciate how their role affects brand values. The four core activities are:

1 Ensure identification of the brand with customers and an association of the brand in customers' minds with a specific product or service class or customer need.
2 Firmly establish the brand meaning in the minds of customers (by strategically linking a host of tangible and intangible brand associations).

3 Elicit the proper customer responses to this brand identity and brand meaning.
4 Convert brand response to create an intense, active loyalty relationship between the customer and the brand.

Different marketing activities have different strengths and can accomplish different objectives. Marketers should therefore engage in a range of marketing mix activities, each of which plays a specific role in building or maintaining the brand. Sometimes marketers don't understand the real importance of all aspects of marketing to their brand until they change a crucial element of the brand and over time see the effects. An example is Burberry, the British luxury brand, which had to be repositioned skilfully after it lost control of aspects of its marketing.

Strategic brand management focuses on building the brand after the positioning choices (Chapter 11) have been made. It is the planning and implementing of a brand management programme which consists of the following six main features:

1 creating and managing brand identities: names, logos, slogans and images;
2 managing individual or house brands;
3 managing brand extensions;
4 managing brand portfolios;
5 brand reinforcing and revitalisation; and
6 growing and sustaining brand equity.

We will look at each of these in turn.

Creating and managing brand identities: names, logos, slogans and images

As more and more firms realise that the brand names associated with their products or services are among their most valuable assets, creating, maintaining and enhancing the strength

Burberry

Burberry found, to its cost, that how the consumer views a company and its products can change. The familiar check pattern, synonymous throughout the world as the Burberry brand of luxury and elitism, began to be worn by more and more people, by C-grade celebrities and even at football matches. The distinctive beige check, once only associated with A-listers, had become the uniform of a rather different social group within the United Kingdom called 'chavs'. 'Chav' is a mainly derogatory slang term for a person fixated on low-quality or counterfeit goods and is often associated with anti-social behaviour. Burberry's appeal to 'chav' fashion sense is a sociological example of prole drift, where an up-market product begins to be consumed *en masse* by a lower socioeconomic group. Burberry argued that the brand's popular association with 'chav' fashion sense was linked to counterfeit versions of the clothing.

Burberry had to react fast to the damage to its brand image. From a product perspective it removed the checked pattern from all but 10 per cent of its product range and discontinued sales of baseball caps from its product line. Burberry also cracked down on fake/counterfeit goods, which allowed what it considered to be the wrong sort of people to look as if they were wearing the brand. It took legal action against high-profile infringements of the brand and invested heavily in protecting against counterfeit. Burberry also changed its supply network, and again became available only in upmarket shops, reflecting its brand image.[40]

The 'chav' phenomenon in Britain damaged the Burberry brand while the image above profiles the brand image that Burberry would like to present.
Source: Image courtesy of The Advertising Archives

of those brands has become a marketing management imperative.[41] There are three main challenges to creating and managing brand identities:

1 The initial choices need to be made for the brand elements or identities making up the brand. These include the brand names, logos, symbols, characters, slogans, accompanying music, websites, product or service design and features, packaging, and so on.

2 All accompanying marketing activities must support the brand. The Juicy Couture label is one of the fastest-growing fashion labels, whose edgy, contemporary sportswear and accessories have a strong lifestyle appeal to women, men and children. Positioned as a luxury, the brand maintains its exclusive image by limiting distribution, designing cutting-edge fashion and using a somewhat risqué name linked to a rebellious attitude.[42]

3 Other associations need to be transferred indirectly to the brand by linking it to other entities (people, places or things) called secondary brand associations. The brand name Credit Suisse, used as a symbol of reliability in commercial banking, leverages the perceived view of the country as reliable in banking and helps to communicate the positioning of the brand.

Secondary branding

Many brands create brand equity by linking the brand to secondary brand associations. For example, when Nokia introduced a mini laptop it was referred as the Nokia 3G Booklet, thereby creating an association, as consumers are already aware of Nokia mobile phones. Associations can also be made to countries or other geographical regions: for example, Audi's slogan 'Vorsprung durch Technik' solidified its association with Germany – renowned for excellent engineering – and has become one of the best-known slogans in advertising. Brands can be associated with channels of distribution (through channel strategy), as well as to other brands (through ingredient or co-branding), characters (through licensing), spokespeople (through endorsements), sporting or cultural events (through sponsorship), or some other third-party sources (through awards or reviews). Figure 12.2 shows the range of secondary sources of brand knowledge.

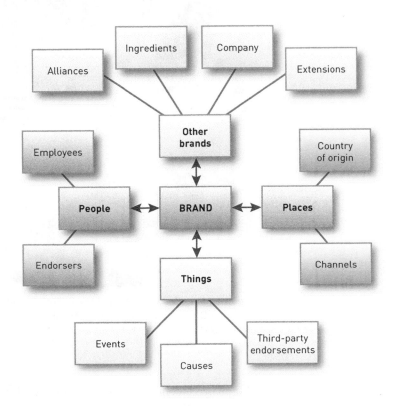

Figure 12.2 Secondary sources of brand knowledge

Choosing brand elements

Brand elements are those trademarkable devices that identify and differentiate the brand. They are often the most tangible representation of the brand. Most strong brands employ multiple brand elements. Nike has the distinctive 'swoosh' logo, the empowering 'Just Do It' slogan, and the 'Nike' name based on the Greek winged goddess of victory. Marketers should choose brand elements to build as much brand equity as possible. The test is how consumers would think or feel about the product or service if the brand elements were all they knew. For example, based on the name alone, what might consumers expect from RightGuard deodorant or the Michelin man cartoon character.

Criteria for choosing brand names

There are six main criteria for choosing brand names, listed below. The first three – memorable, meaningful and likeable – are 'brand building'. The latter three – transferable, adaptable and protectable – are 'defensive' and deal with how to leverage and preserve the equity in a brand element in the face of challenges.

In general, brand names should be short and simple, easy to spell and pronounce, pronounceable in only one way and one language, and easy to recognise and remember. Many, such as BBC, Orange and Mastercard, follow the criteria below, while some very successful names do not. Examples are Birkenstock, Adidas and Stella Artois.

1 **Memorable**. How easily is the brand element recalled and recognised? Short names such as Virgin, Sky, Dove and Zara are memorable brand names.
2 **Meaningful**. Is the brand name credible and suggestive of the product or service? Does it suggest something about a product ingredient or service quality, or the type of person who might use the brand? Consider the inherent meaning in names such as Crisp 'n Dry, Head and Shoulders, Fast Fit Exhausts, RightGuard deodorant, Sure Underarm Protection, Energeriser Batteries and Lean Cuisine low-calorie foods.
3 **Likeable**. How aesthetically appealing is the brand name? Is it likeable visually, verbally and in other ways? A recent trend is playful names like Flickr photo sharing. Concrete brand names such as Mr Muscle, Little Chef, and Shake and Vac are likeable names. Many characters associated with brands are also inherently likeable. Think of Snuggle the Fabric Softener Bear or 'The Snuggle Bear'.[43]
4 **Transferable**. Can the brand element be used to introduce new products or services in the same or different categories? Does it add to brand equity across geographic boundaries and market segments? Though American, Amazon was smart enough not to use an American word so that the brand could be used across the globe. Amazon is the name of the world's largest river and the name suggest the wide variety of goods that can be shipped and is an important descriptor of the diverse range of products the company now sells.
5 **Adaptable**. How adaptable and updatable is the brand name? Take Zara – the brand name is adaptable and timeless across their markets.
6 **Protectable**. How legally protectable is the brand name? Names that become synonymous with product or service categories can be difficult to manage. Brand names such as Kleenex, Hoover, Sellotape, Google, Xerox and Bandaid have all become known as the general title for the product or sevice. You hear people saying 'Did you google that or do you have a bandaid?

See the marketing memo for more discussion of brand names.

Brand elements can play a number of brand-building roles.[44] Brand elements should be easy to recognise and recall, and inherently descriptive and persuasive. The likeability and appeal of brand elements may also play a critical role in awareness and associations, leading to high brand equity.[45] The Snap, Crackle and Pop characters from Kellogg's reinforce the sense of magic and fun for breakfast cereals. The three elf brothers made their debut in 1933 but have since had several makeovers and still maintain their popularity with children all over the world. Bird's Eye also developed an image that remains relevant today – Captain Bird's Eye still sails the Bird's Eye ship. Many UK-based insurance companies have used symbols of strength (the Rock of Gibraltar for Prudential and the stag for Hartford), security (the eagle of Eagle Star), and agility and strength (the horse for Lloyds Bank).

Marketing memo

Brand names

Brand names come in many styles.

- Acronym: a name made of initials, e.g. BP, UPS and IBM.
- Descriptive: names that describe a product benefit or function, Whole Foods, Volkswagen and Airbus.
- Alliteration and rhyme: names that are fun to say and stick in the mind, Planters Peanuts and Dunkin' Donuts.
- Evocative: names that evoke a relevant vivid image, e.g. Amazon and Crest.
- Neologisms: completely made-up words, e.g. Wii and Kodak.

- Foreign word: adoption of a word from another language, e.g. Volvo and Samsung.
- Founders' names: using the names of real people and founder's name, e.g. Henkel and Adidas. Alfa Romeo combines an acronym from Anonima Lombarda Fabbrica Automobili and an owner's name, as Romeo was added when Nicola Romeo bought ALFA in 1915.
- Geography: many brands are named after regions and landmarks, e.g. Cisco Systems, named after San Francisco, where the company is based.

Source: Merriam Associates (2009) Styles and types of company and product names, http://merriamassociates.com/2009/02/styles-and-types-of-company-and-product-names/.

Brand slogans

Brand slogans or tag lines are an extremely efficient means to build and manage brands and are eternally focused. Slogans are part of a persuasive appeal that is intended to convey something good or to remind consumers of a brand's attributes.[46] Brands are attributed humanlike personality traits with whom consumers develop emotional attachments and share commitments. Therefore the **brand slogans** or tag lines can function as useful 'hooks' or 'handles' to help consumers grasp what the brand is and what makes it special – summarising and translating the intent of the total marketing programme. Think of the inherent brand meaning in slogans such as Kit Kat – 'Have a break – have a Kit Kat'; L'Oréal – 'Because you're worth it'; Carlsberg – 'Probably the best lager in the world' or their more recent –'That calls for a Carlsberg'; Boot's – 'Trust Boots', Gillette – 'The best a man can get'; Burger King – 'Have it your way'.

These slogans can be used globally with greater or lesser success. A great example is the 'Snap, Crackle and Pop' slogan, which has been translated across Europe:[47]

- English: 'Snap! Crackle! Pop!'
- French: 'Cric! Crac! Croc!'
- Spanish: 'Pim! Pum! Pam!'
- German: 'Knisper! Knasper! Knusper!'
- Swedish: 'Piff! Paff! Puff!'
- Finnish: 'Riks! Raks! Poks!'
- Dutch: 'Pif! Paf! Pof!'

In a German survey of 1,000 consumers aged 14–49, some slogans did not work so well. When asked to translate 12 popular advertising slogans, almost two-thirds did not properly understand the slogans. For example, Adidas's 'Impossible is nothing' was translated as 'An imposing nothing' and 'Welcome to the Becks experience' was translated as 'Welcome to the Becks experiment'.[48]

The Snap, Crackle and Pop slogan has been translated into many European languages.
Source: Courtesy of the Kellogg Group

Brand mantras

To support the intent of brand positioning and the way firms would like consumers to think about the brand, it is often useful to define a brand mantra which is an internal focus for the brand.[49] A **brand mantra** is an articulation of the heart and soul of the brand and is closely related to other branding concepts like 'brand essence' and 'core brand promise.' Brand mantras are short, three- to five-word phrases that capture the irrefutable essence or spirit of the brand positioning. Their purpose is to ensure that all employees within the organisation and all external marketing partners understand what the brand fundamentally represents with consumers, so they can adjust their actions accordingly. BMW (Bavarian Motor Works) has been known as the 'ultimate driving machine' for over 50 years. This successful mantra applies to all its products, including cars, motorcycles and sport utility vehicles. BMW's communication strategy and brand equity comes with its message about speed, driving and handling.

Brand mantras are powerful devices. They can provide guidance about what products to introduce under the brand, what ad campaigns to run, and where and how to sell the brand. Their influence, however, can extend beyond these tactical concerns. Brand mantras may even guide the most seemingly unrelated or mundane decisions, such as the look of a reception area or the way phones are answered. In effect, they create a mental filter to screen out brand-inappropriate marketing activities or actions of any type that may have a negative bearing on customers' impressions of a brand.

Brand mantras must economically communicate what the brand is and what it is *not*. What makes for a good brand mantra? A high-profile and successful examples is Nike, which shows the power, range and utility of a well-designed brand mantra.

Nike

Nike has a rich set of associations with consumers, based on its innovative product designs, its sponsorships of top athletes, its award-winning advertising, its competitive drive and its irreverent attitude. Internally, Nike marketers adopted the three-word brand mantra, 'authentic athletic performance' to guide their efforts. Thus, in Nike's eyes, its entire marketing programme – its products and how they are sold – must reflect those key brand values. Over the years, Nike has expanded its brand meaning from 'running shoes' to 'athletic shoes' to 'athletic shoes and clothing' to 'all things associated with athletics (including equipment)'. Each step of the way, however, it has been guided by its 'authentic athletic performance' brand mantra. For example, as Nike rolled out its successful clothing line, one important hurdle for the products was that they could be made innovative enough through material, cut or design to truly benefit top athletes. At the same time, the company has been careful to avoid using the Nike name to brand products that do not fit with the brand mantra (like casual 'brown' shoes).

Brand mantras are designed with internal purposes in mind. A brand slogan is an external translation that attempts creatively to engage consumers. Although Nike's internal mantra was 'authentic athletic performance', its external slogan was 'Just do it'. Here are the three key criteria for a brand mantra.

1 **Communicate**. A good brand mantra should define the category (or categories) of business for the brand and set the brand boundaries. It should also clarify what is unique about the brand.
2 **Simplify**. An effective brand mantra should be memorable. For that, it should be short, crisp and vivid in meaning.
3 **Inspire**. Ideally, the brand mantra should also stake out ground that is personally meaningful and relevant to as many employees as possible.

Brand mantras are typically designed to capture the brand's points-of-difference: that is, what is unique about the brand. Other aspects of the brand positioning – especially the brand's points-of-parity – may also be important and may need to be reinforced in other ways.

For brands facing rapid growth, it is helpful to define the product, service or benefit space in which the brand would like to compete, as Nike did with 'athletic performance' and Disney does with 'family entertainment.' Words that describe the nature of the product or service, or the type of experiences or benefits the brand provides, can be critical to identifying appropriate categories into which to extend. For brands in more stable categories where extensions into more distinct categories are less likely to occur, the brand mantra may focus more exclusively on points-of-difference.

Brand mantras derive their power and usefulness from their collective meaning. Other brands may be strong on one, or perhaps even a few, of the brand associations making up the brand mantra. But for the brand mantra to be effective, no other brand should singularly excel on all dimensions. Part of the key to both Nike's and Disney's success is that for years no competitor could really deliver on the combined promise suggested by their brand mantras.

Brand narratives and storytelling

Rather than outlining specific attributes or benefits, some marketing experts describe positioning a brand as telling a narrative or story.[50]

Randall Ringer and Michael Thibodeau see *narrative branding* as based on deep metaphors that connect to people's memories, associations and stories.[51] They identify five elements of narrative branding: (1) the brand story in terms of words and metaphors; (2) the consumer journey in terms of how consumers engage with the brand over time and touchpoints where they come into contact with it; (3) the visual language or expression for the brand; (4) the manner in which the narrative is expressed experientially in terms of how the brand engages the senses; and (5) the role/relationship the brand plays in the lives of consumers. Based on literary convention and brand experience, they also offer the following framework for a brand story:

- **Setting**: the time, place and context.
- **Cast**: the brand as a character, including its role in the life of the audience, its relationships and responsibilities, and its history or creation myth.
- **Narrative Arc**: the way the narrative logic unfolds over time, including actions, desired experiences, defining events and the moment of epiphany.
- **Language**: the authenticating voice, metaphors, symbols, themes and leitmotifs.

Patrick Hanlon developed the related concept of 'primal branding', which views brands as complex belief systems. According to Hanlon, diverse brands such as Google, Mini Cooper, Starbucks, Apple, UPS and Aveda all have a 'primal code' or DNA that resonates with their customers and generates their passion and fervour. He outlines seven assets that make up this belief system or primal code: a creation story, creed, icon, rituals, sacred words, a way of dealing with non-believers, and a good leader.[52]

Managing individual or house brands

A branding strategy decision is how to develop a brand name for a product or service category. A brand name should provide a positive contribution to brand equity: for example, it should convey certain value associations or responses. Based on its name alone, a consumer might expect ColorStay lipsticks to be long-lasting and Sunkist Orange Juice to be a healthy, natural orange juice full of vitamin C.

Four general strategies are often used:

1 **Individual names**. The British/Dutch company Unilever has many individually named brands within its company, including many familiar brands such as Hellmann's, Knorr, Bird's Eye, Surf, Dove, Pond's and Calvin Klein fragrances. L'Oréal, the French

cosmetics company, also has many brands including Maybelline New York, the Garnier brand and – more recently – The Body Shop. A major advantage of an individual names strategy is that the company does not tie its reputation to the individual product or service. If a product or service fails or appears to have a brand image contrary to the company's, the other products or service are not damaged. Companies often use different brand names for different quality lines within the same product or service class. Lufthansa owns most of GermanWings but does not share a name with the low-cost airline, in part to protect the brand equity of its Lufthansa brand.

2 **Blanket corporate, family or house names.** Many companies use their corporate, family or house brand across their range of products or services.[53] Development costs are lower with blanket brand names because there is no need to run a 'name' search or spend heavily on advertising to create recognition. An example is Tata – the Indian company probably most famous for the Tata car. It uses the Tata family name across its diverse product categories, such as salt, tea, coffee, cars, and steel. Sales of a new product or service are likely to be strong if the family corporate or house name is good.

3 **Separate family or house names for all products and services.** Inditex, a company most people have probably never heard of, uses separate brand names for its retail shops, from the very familiar Zara and Massimo Dutti to the less familiar Pull & Bear, Stradivarius and Bershka. These are all very different brand names targeted at different segments with various levels of success. If a company produces quite different products, one blanket name is often not desirable. Louis Vuitton and Moët Hennessy manage a whole portfolio of luxury brands under different brand names. They range from wines and spirits (Krug, Belvedere vodka) to jewellery (TAG Heuer, Chaumet) to fashion labels (Marc Jacobs, Donna Karan) and perfume (Gerlain, Parfums Givenchy).

4 **Corporate name combined with individual product names.** Kellogg's combines corporate and individual names in Kellogg's Rice Krispies, Kellogg's Bran Flakes and Kellogg's Corn Flakes, as do Honda, Sony and HP for their products. The company name legitimises, and the individual name individualises, the product or service.

Individual names and blanket family names are sometimes referred to as a 'house of brands' and a 'branded house' respectively, and they represent two ends of a brand relationship continuum. Separate family names come in between the two, and corporate-plus-individual names combine them. Companies rarely adopt a pure example of any of the four strategies.[54]

Two key components of virtually any branding strategy are brand extensions and brand portfolios.

Managing brand extensions

Most new products or services are in fact line extensions – typically 80–90 per cent of new products and services introduced in any one year are brand extensions. Examples include Mars extending its brand to ice cream, Caterpillar to shoes and watches, Michelin to a restaurant guide, Adidas to an aftershave and Apple computers to the iPod music player. Mattel, the owner of the Barbie brand, has had many marketing struggles to extend the Barbie brand from a doll to other products that its customer base will use after they have grown out of playing with their Barbie doll. Mattel has launched a range of Barbie-inspired teenage clothing and also Barbie make-up for teenagers, which it markets through the MAC make-up company. Brand extensions are popular in the industrial market too. Dyson innovated in the vacuum cleaning area with a new improved Dyson cleaner and then moved to hand dryers with the new improved Dyson Airblade hand dryer.

Deciding how to brand new services or products is critical and involves three main choices:

1 The company can develop new brand elements for the new product or service.
2 It can apply some of its existing brand elements.
3 It can use a combination of new and existing brand elements.

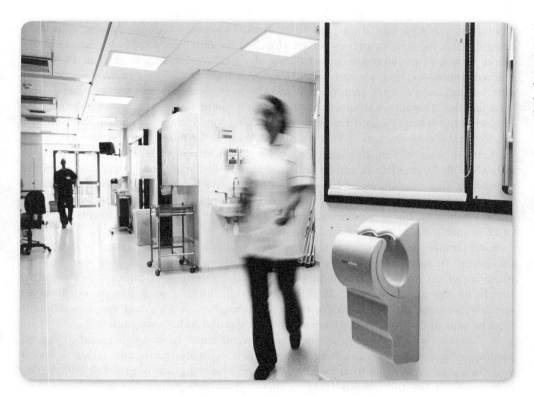

The Dyson hand dryer is a brand extension from the Dyson vacuum cleaner, which in itself was a revolution in vacuuming.
Source: Courtesy of Dyson.

The existing brand is the parent of the brand extension. If the parent brand is already associated with multiple products through brand extensions, it can also be called a **family brand**. The Lucozade brand is now a family brand for the following sports products: Lucozade Sport, Lucozade Hydro Active and Lucozade Sport Nutrition.

Brand extensions fall into two general categories.[55] In a **line extension**, the parent brand covers a new product or service within a product or service category it currently serves, such as with new flavours, forms, colours, ingredients and package sizes. The French food company Danone has introduced several types of Danone yogurt line extension over the years. These include Fruit on the Bottom, All Natural Flavours, and Fruit Blends.

Magnum

Magnum, the Swiss ice cream brand which is now owned by the British/Dutch Unilever company, is marketed as part of the Heartbrand line of products in most countries. The original 1990 Magnum Classic consisted of a thick bar of vanilla ice cream on a stick, covered with white or dark chocolate, with a weight of 86 grams (120 ml). In 1994 the company also started selling Magnum ice cream cones, and in 2002 an ice cream sandwich along with its Magnum Mint, Double Chocolate and other flavours. Also in 2002 Magnum branched into frozen yogurt with its raspberry fruit swirl covered in milk chocolate. Late 2002 saw the launch of 'Magnum Intense' and the limited edition '7 Deadly Sins' series of ice creams. The line extension 'Moments' was introduced in 2003 – these were bite-size ice cream treats with caramel, chocolate or hazelnut centres, followed later in the year by 'mini', 'crunchy' (with almonds) and 'light'. This was followed by another limited edition range in 2005, in which each flavour was named after one of the senses: Magnum Aroma, Magnum Touch, Magnum Sound, Magnum Taste and Magnum Vision. In 2008 Magnum brought out a new variant in the United Kingdom – Mayan Mystica. In 2009 it introduced Magnum Mini Moments and in 2011 Magnum ice cream was launched in the USA and Canada with six varieties: Double Caramel, Double Chocolate, Classic, Almond, White and Dark.

In a **category extension**, the parent brand is used to enter a different product or service category from the one it currently serves. Honda is the fifth largest car manufacturer in the world as well as the largest engine-maker in the world, producing more than 14 million internal combustion engines each year. Honda has used its company name to cover such different products as cars, motorcycles, snowblowers, lawnmowers, marine engines and snowmobiles. This allows Honda to advertise that it can fit 'six Hondas in a two-car garage'. English entrepreneur Richard Branson has used his Virgin brand to enter many different product and service markets, from the airline industry to the music business and soft drinks markets, all with varying degrees of success. His latest project is in the space aviation industry with Virgin Galactic: this will be the world's first spaceline, giving customers the groundbreaking opportunity of being one of the world's first non-professional astronauts.

A **brand line** consists of all products or service – original as well as line and category extensions – sold under a particular brand. A **brand mix** (or brand assortment) is the set of all available brand lines from a company.

Some companies produce **branded variants**, which are specific brand lines supplied exclusively to specific retailers or distribution channels. They result from the pressure retailers put on manufacturers to provide distinctive offerings. A camera company may supply its low-end cameras to large retailers while limiting its higher-priced items to speciality camera shops. Valentino, the Italian designer, designs and supplies different lines of suits and jackets to department stores compared to his own outlets.[56]

A **licensed product or service** is one whose brand name has been licensed to others. Marketers have seized on licensing to push their company name and image across a wide range of products – from bedding to shoes – making licensing a €30 billion plus business.[57] TinTin, the familiar French cartoon character's image, has been licensed to companies manufacturing a range of products from clocks to keyrings. The Harry Potter brand has had phenomenal success with licensing with the books and films spawning eight video games and more than 400 additional Harry Potter products, including an iPod. The Harry Potter brand has been estimated to be worth as much as €15 billion. Hallmark obtained the Harry Potter licence to design Harry Potter greeting cards, wrapping paper and partyware, while Warner Bros own the licence for Harry Potter clothing, ornaments and sweets.

Marketers must judge each potential brand extension by how effectively it leverages existing brand equity from the parent brand, as well as how effectively it contributes to the parent brand's equity.[58] Crest White Strips leveraged the strong reputation of Crest and dental care to provide reassurance in the teeth-whitening arena, while also reinforcing its dental authority image. The most important consideration with extensions is that there should be a 'fit' in the mind of the consumer, based on common attributes, usage situations or user types.

Figure 12.3 lists a number of academic research findings on brand extensions.[59]

One benefit of a successful extension is that it may also serve as the basis for subsequent extensions.[60]

Advantages of brand extensions

As the costs of establishing a new brand name are so high, it is understandable that brand extensions are so popular. Extensions can avoid the difficulty – and expense – of coming up with a new name. They also allow for many efficiencies across all the marketing mix variables, including distribution, inventory, communications, packaging and labelling. Similar or identical packages and labels can result in lower production costs for extensions and, if coordinated properly, more prominence in the retail store via a 'billboard' effect. For example, Bird's Eye offers a variety of frozen foods with similar packaging that increases their visibility when they are stocked together in the freezer. With a portfolio of brand variants within a product category, consumers who need a change – because of boredom, satiation or whatever – can switch to a different product type without having to leave the brand family.

Academics have studied brand extensions closely. Here is a summary of some of their key research findings.

- Successful brand extensions occur when the parent brand is seen as having favourable associations and there is a perception of fit between the parent brand and the extension product.
- There are many bases of fit: product-related attributes and benefits, as well as non-product-related attributes and benefits related to common usage situations or user types.
- Depending on consumer knowledge of the categories, perceptions of fit may be based on technical or manufacturing commonalities or more surface considerations such as necessary or situational complementarity.
- High-quality brands stretch farther than average-quality brands, although both types of brand have boundaries.
- A brand that is seen as prototypical of a product category can be difficult to extend outside the category.
- Concrete attribute associations tend to be more difficult to extend than abstract benefit associations.
- Consumers may transfer associations that are positive in the original product class but become negative in the extension context.
- Consumers may infer negative associations about an extension, perhaps even based on other inferred positive associations.
- It can be difficult to extend into a product class that is seen as easy to make.
- A successful extension can not only contribute to the parent brand image but also enable a brand to be extended even farther.
- An unsuccessful extension hurts the parent brand only when there is a strong basis of fit between the two.
- An unsuccessful extension does not prevent a firm from 'backtracking' and introducing a more similar extension.
- Vertical extensions can be difficult and often require subbranding strategies.
- The most effective advertising strategy for an extension emphasises information about the extension (rather than reminders about the parent brand).

Figure 12.3 Research insights on brand extensions
Source: From K. L. Keller (2008) *Strategic Brand Management*, 3rd edn, Upper Saddle River, NJ: Prentice Hall. Copyright © 2008. Reproduced by permission of Pearson Education, Inc., Upper Saddle River, NJ.

Using brand extensions can ensure positive expectations, as extensions can reduce risk.[61] It may also be easier to convince retailers to stock and promote a brand extension because of increased customer demand. From a marketing communications perspective, an introductory campaign for an extension does not have to create awareness of both the brand *and* the new product or service, but can concentrate instead on the new product or service itself.[62]

Business-to-business companies can use brand extensions as a powerful way to enter consumer markets, as Michelin and Goodyear, both companies with strong brand names discovered.

Disadvantages of brand extensions

On the downside, line extensions may cause the brand name to be less strongly identified with any one product.[65] Ries and Trout call this the 'line-extension trap'.[66] By linking its brand to mainstream food products such as mashed potatoes, powdered milk, soups and beverages, Cadbury ran the risk of losing its more specific meaning as a chocolate brand.[67] **Brand dilution** occurs when consumers no longer associate a brand with a specific or highly similar products or service and start thinking less of the brand.

Michelin and Goodyear

Both French in origin, Michelin and Goodyear were known primarily for their rubber tyres, but have launched a number of brand extensions over the years.[63] Michelin's brand extensions have mainly been in the car accessories area – from inflation and pressure monitoring goods to car floor mats. So far its brand extensions fall into three categories: (1) car and cycle-related products; (2) footwear, clothing, accessories and equipment for work, sports and leisure; and (3) personal accessories – gifts and collectables. Its sports and leisure category now has the potential to overtake the car accessories line.

Like Michelin, Goodyear has a category of products closely aligned to the car industry – such as jack stands and car repair tools – but it, too, has branched out into consumer areas. The company is marketing its own line of cleaning wipes for windows and upholstery, mechanics' gloves and garden hose nozzles, among other products. Interestingly, Goodyear and Adidas partnered to create a series of driving shoes, prominently featuring the Goodyear 'Wingfoot' mark.[64] This was a brand extension for both companies.

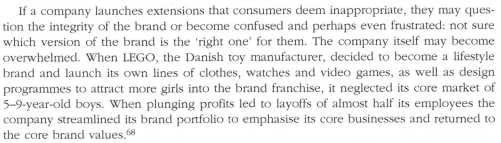

If a company launches extensions that consumers deem inappropriate, they may question the integrity of the brand or become confused and perhaps even frustrated: not sure which version of the brand is the 'right one' for them. The company itself may become overwhelmed. When LEGO, the Danish toy manufacturer, decided to become a lifestyle brand and launch its own lines of clothes, watches and video games, as well as design programmes to attract more girls into the brand franchise, it neglected its core market of 5–9-year-old boys. When plunging profits led to layoffs of almost half its employees the company streamlined its brand portfolio to emphasise its core businesses and returned to the core brand values.[68]

The worst possible scenario is for an extension not only to fail, but also to harm the parent brand image in the process. Fortunately, such events are rare. 'Marketing failures', where insufficient consumers were attracted to a brand, are typically much less damaging than 'product or service failures', where the brand fundamentally fails to live up to its promise. New products such as Virgin Cola, Levi's Tailored Classic suits, Fruit of the Loom washing powder, Bic Perfume, Capital Radio restaurant and Pond's toothpaste failed because consumers found them inappropriate extensions for the brand.[69] Even then, product or service failures dilute brand equity only when the extension is seen as very similar to the parent brand.

Virgin

The Virgin brand, which revolves around an authentic and people-orientated brand image, has hundreds of brand extensions – Virgin consists of more than 400 companies around the world. At one stage the brand extension potential of Virgin was widely debated as Virgin entered a range of industries with brand extensions from aeroplanes to trains, from record stores to mobile phones. The UK newspaper, the *Observer* explored a fictitious future world – entitled 'The Virgin Life' – which Virgin controlled if the brand extensions did not stop. 'Every morning you can wake up to Virgin Radio, put on Virgin clothes and make-up, drive to work in a car bought with money transferred from your Virgin bank account' and so on, the article also citing the Virgin gym, Virgin cinema and Virgin hotels.

Virgin has had many successes but also some brand extension failures. Virgin Coke was one such failure and may have been a brand extension too far for the Virgin Group.[70] According to Matt Haig in his book *Brand Failures*, Virgin Cola failed because it did not show the competitor's weakness. In addition, distribution is key in the soft drinks industry and Virgin struggled in this area. Some brand extensions could be seen as brand ego trips and have been costly failures for the group, but others have really engaged with customer needs and brand values, such as Virgin Airways.

Brand switching

Even if sales of a brand extension are high and meet targets, the revenue may be coming from consumers switching to the extension from existing parent-brand offerings – in effect, *cannibalising* the parent brand. Intra-brand shifts in sales may not be a disadvantage if they are a form of *pre-emptive cannibalisation*. In other words, consumers might have switched to a competing brand instead of the line extension if the extension had not been introduced.

One easily overlooked disadvantage of brand extensions is that the company forgoes the chance to create a new brand with its own unique image and equity. Consider the advantages to Disney of having introduced more adult-oriented Touchstone films; to Levi's of creating casual Dockers pants; and to Black and Decker of introducing high-end Dewalt power tools.

Managing brand portfolios

The **brand portfolio** is the set of all brands and brand lines that a particular company offers for sale in a particular category or market segment. Marketers often need multiple brands in order to pursue multiple target markets.

Armani

Armani has set out to create a product line differentiated by style, luxury, customisation and price to compete in three distinct price tiers. In the most expensive, Tier I, it sells Giorgio Armani and Giorgio Armani Privé, which are custom-made runway couture products that sell for thousands of pounds/euro. In the more moderately priced Tier II, it offers Emporio Armani, young and modern, as well as the informal A|X Armani. In the lower-priced Tier III, the company sells the more youthful and street-savvy translation of Armani style, Armani Exchange, at retail locations in cities and shopping centres.

Armani's line of luxury clothing is differentiated to appeal to three distinct price tiers, each with different styles and levels of luxury, using the brand names Giorgio Armani, Emporio Armani, A|X Armani and Armani Exchange.
Source: Daniele La Monaca/Reuters/Corbis

The hallmark of an optimal brand portfolio is the ability of each brand in it to maximise equity in combination with all the other brands. If a company can only increase profits by dropping brands, a portfolio is too big; if it can increase profits by *adding* brands, it is not big enough. The basic principle in designing a brand portfolio is to *maximise market coverage*, so that no potential customers are being ignored, but to *minimise brand overlap*, so company brands are not competing for customer approval. Each brand should be clearly differentiated and appealing to a sizeable enough market segment to justify its marketing and production costs.[71]

Brands can also play a number of specific roles as part of a brand portfolio.

Flankers

Flanker or 'fighter' brands are positioned with respect to competitors' brands so that more important (and more profitable) *flagship brands* can retain their desired positioning. Procter & Gamble markets Luvs nappies in a way that flanks its more popular and premium Pampers. Marketers walk a fine line in designing fighter brands, which must not be so attractive that they take sales away from their higher-priced comparison brands.

Cash cows

Some brands may be kept around despite dwindling sales because they still manage to hold on to enough customers and maintain their profitability with virtually no marketing support. Companies can effectively 'milk' these 'cash cow' brands by capitalising on their reservoir of existing brand equity. For example, despite the fact that technological advances have moved much of its market to the newer Mach III brand of razors, Gillette still sells the older Trac II, Atra and Sensor brands. Withdrawing them may not necessarily move customers to another Gillette brand, so it is more profitable for Gillette to keep them in its brand portfolio for razor blades.

Low-end entry level

The role of a relatively low-priced brand in the portfolio may often be to attract customers to the brand franchise. Retailers like to feature these 'traffic builders' because they are able to 'trade up' customers to a higher-priced brand. For example, BMW introduced a 1-series car in part as a means of bringing new customers into the brand franchise, with the hope of later 'moving them up' to higher-priced models.

High-end prestige

The role of a relatively high-priced brand is often to add prestige and credibility to the entire portfolio. Mobile phone companies such as Nokia always have a high-end model in their range. Most Nokia customers will not buy this product but will buy its mid-range, flagship model. Nonetheless, it is often the case that it is the high-end model which attracts the consumers' attention.

Brand reinforcing and revitalisation

As a company's major enduring asset, a brand needs to be carefully managed so that its value does not depreciate.[72]

Brand reinforcement

Marketing reinforces brand equity by marketing actions that consistently convey the meaning of the brand to the consumers with the brand representing the core benefits it supplies and what needs it satisfies. It also conveys what makes the brand superior and what strong favourable and unique brand association should exist in the mind of the consumer. The most important consideration is consistency of support in terms of both the amount and the nature of that support.[73]

Brand equity is reinforced by marketing actions that consistently convey the meaning of the brand in terms of:

- What products and service the brand represents, what core benefits it supplies and what needs it satisfies. Nivea, one of Europe's strongest brands, has expanded its scope from a skin cream brand to a skin care and personal care brand through carefully designed and implemented brand extensions, reinforcing the Nivea brand promise of 'mild', 'gentle' and 'caring' in a broader arena.
- How the brand provides them with the service or products they need and what value added is created.[74] Ryanair has become the largest airline in Europe by focusing on its core brand value – providing cheap airline travel to over 70 million passengers annually,[75] who prefer low cost to high service.

Apple

Apple is the story of a brand that has been managed well throughout its lifespan, which started on April Fool's Day 1976. This €77 billion company has some of the world's best and most innovative consumer products and 82 per cent of the hard drive music market. The company's ability to delight consumers in a bland world of technological equipment and software makes it easy to see why it impacts on so many and across so many segments. From the student who loves their iPod, to the executives who worship their Mac, Apple has brought emotion to their brand and created a brand image and experience that endures and makes us 'Think Differently'.

Apple, Inc. is a master at building a strong brand that resonates with customers across generations and national boundaries. It achieves incredible brand loyalty largely by delivering on its mission, as defined by former CEO Steve Jobs: 'To create great things that change people's lives.' The company has created an army of Apple evangelists, not just because it produces great products that reflect consumer needs, but also because everything it does and all its communcations reflect its brand values. Apple's innovative products combine superior design, functionality and style, and many cite the wildly successful iPod music player as a prime example. Apple has 150 retail stores worldwide to fuel excitement for the brand. The rationale behind the move to retail is that the more people can see and touch Apple products, see what Apple can do for them, the more likely Apple is to increase its market share.

One or even two 'revolutionary' products alone won't keep you at the top of the list of the most successful companies in the world. A major key to Apple's continued success is its ability to keep pushing the boundaries of innovation. Key lessons from Apple are:

- **Don't just focus on building beautiful products.** Build beautiful business models, new ways to create, deliver and capture value. The iPod and iPhone would not have had nearly as much impact if they had not been matched with iTunes and the App Store respectively.

- **Think in terms of platforms and pipelines.** Competitors that chase Apple's latest release find themselves behind when six months later Apple introduces its latest and greatest offering.

- **Take a portfolio approach.** While Apple has been on a phenomenal run, not everything it has introduced has been a success. For example, Apple TV has not had the 'revolutionary' impact that Jobs predicted upon its launch in 2007. But the success of the Apple iPhone and iPad created hype, interest and demand. The sales topped over 125 million iPhones by mid-2011 with Apple set to launch a new phone later in the year, showing how it continually innovates into its brand identity to maintain the image of an innovative company in tune with customer needs.[76]

Reinforcing brand image requires innovation and relevance throughout the marketing programme. The brand must always be moving forward – but moving forward in the right direction, with new and compelling offerings and ways to market them.

Brands that failed to move forwards – such as Benetton and Kodak – find that their market leadership dwindles or even disappears.

Brand revitalisation

Changes in consumer tastes and preferences, the emergence of new competitors or new technology, or any new development in the marketing environment can affect the fortunes of a brand. In virtually every product or service category, once-prominent and admired brands – such as Little Chef, Alitalia and British Airways – have fallen on hard times, struggled with their brand image or even disappeared.[77] A number of brands have managed to make impressive comebacks in recent years, as marketers have breathed new life into them. Volkswagen, Dr Scholl's and Birkenstock are brands that have been revitalised, becoming popular once again but in a different market. For example, Birkenstock – the German sandal – was predominantly used by the medical profession but moved into everyday comfort shoes within the environmentally friendly target market.

Often the first thing to do in revitalising a brand is to understand what the sources of brand equity are to begin with. Are positive associations losing their strength or uniqueness? Have negative associations become linked to the brand? Then it has to be decided whether to retain the same positioning or create a new one and, if so, which new one. Sometimes the marketing programme or marketing mix activities are the source of the problem, because they fail to deliver on the brand promise. In other cases, however, the old positioning is just no longer viable and a 'reinvention' strategy is necessary. Lucozade completely overhauled its brand image to become an energy drink powerhouse.

Brand reinforcement and brand revitalisation strategies

At some point, failure to fortify the brand will diminish brand awareness and weaken brand image. Without these sources of brand equity, the brand itself may not continue to

Lucozade

The European energy drink market continues to grow with Germany and the UK accounting for the largest market share. Energy drinks account for £1 in every £5 spent on soft drinks in the United Kingdom. One of the main players, Lucozade is only in this market due to a successful rebranding or revitalisation of the brand that saw the company move from a child-oriented, health-related tonic to an energy sports drink. The original Lucozade, first manufactured in 1927, was available throughout the United Kingdom for use in hospitals. In 1983, a rebranding of Lucozade into an energy drink started moving the slogan from 'Lucozade aids recovery' to 'Lucozade replaces lost energy', with an advertising campaign featuring the world and Olympic champion decathlete Daley Thompson. The effect of the rebranding was dramatic: the value of UK sales of the drink tripled to almost €95 million. During the 1990s it tapped into the sports market and introduced Lucozade Sport, which is the market leader in sports drinks. Lucozade uses leading sports teams and personalities to keep the sports brand value in front of the consumer. Lucozade is the official drink of the FA and FA Premier League and also sponsors the England Rugby Football Union, the Irish Football Team, the London Marathon, Michael Owen, Steven Gerrard, Damien Duff and Jonny Wilkinson. The brand message is 'Lucozade Sport keeps top athletes going 33% longer', accompanied by the powerful slogan 'Hunger has a thirst'.

These two campaigns show how the Lucozade brand was repositioned from a tonic for sick children to an energy drink for athletes.
Source: Images courtesy of The Advertising Archives

yield valuable benefits. With a fading brand, the depth of brand awareness is often not as much of a problem as the breadth – that is, the consumer has too narrow a view of the brand. Although changing brand awareness is probably the easiest means of creating new sources of brand equity, we often need to create a new marketing mix programme to improve the strength, favourability and uniqueness of brand associations. The challenge in all these efforts to modify the brand image is not to destroy the equity that already exists. *Reinforcing brands* involves ensuring innovation in product design, manufacturing and merchandising, and ensuring relevance in user and usage imagery. *Brand revitalisation*, on the other hand, requires either that lost sources of brand equity are recaptured, or that new sources of brand equity are identified and established. Figure 12.4 summarises the main features of brand revitalisation and brand reinforcment strategies.[78]

Growing, sustaining and managing brand equity

Brand equity is the added value endowed on products and services. It may be reflected in the way consumers think, feel and act with respect to the brand, as well as in the prices, market share and profitability the brand commands.[79]

Brands play a major role in enhancing the financial value of companies, and thus the ability to value them or understand their brand value or equity is critical. To companies, brands represent enormously valuable pieces of legal property that can influence consumer behaviour, be bought and sold, and provide the security of sustained future revenues. Companies have paid large sums of money for brands in mergers and acquisitions, often justifying the price premium on the basis of the extra profits to be extracted and sustained from the brands, as well as the tremendous difficulty and expense of creating similar brands from scratch. Although only founded in 1998, Google is one of the most

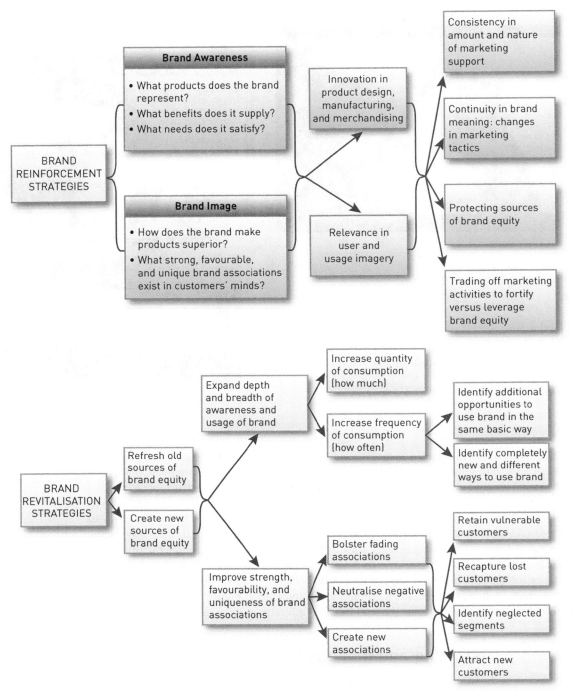

Figure 12.4 Brand reinforcement and brand revitalisation strategies

Source: Keller, Kevin, *Strategic Brand Management*, © 2008. Printed and electronically reproduced by permission of Pearson Education, Inc., Upper Saddle River, NJ.

recognised and valuable brand in the world, valued at €11.51 billion.[80] A strong brand is a valuable asset, as can be seen from Table 12.1, which highlights brand values for the top five brands in Europe.[81]

As Rita Clifton, the author of *Brands and Branding* and the chairperson of Interbrand UK, puts it: 'Well-managed brands have extraordinary economic value and are the most effective and efficient creators of sustainable wealth.'[82] Malcolm Forbes described them as

Table 12.1 The top five European brands

Ranking 2010 (2009)	Brand	Industry	Country of ownership	Brand value (€ m)	(% change)
1(1)	Nokia	Telecommunications	Finland	25,331	−28.1
2(2)	Vodafone	Telcom	U.K.	25,318	6.4
3(4)	Louis Vuitton	Luxury	France	17,186	−10.0
4(3)	Mercedes-Benz	Automotive	Germany	16,940	−12.6
5(5)	BMW	Automotive	Germany	15,267	−9.5

Source: Adapted from Interbrand.com (2011)

'the best marketable investment a company can make'.[83] Brand value is typically over half the total company market capitalisation and so the importance of the brand to the company is clear. Brand value is increasingly included on balance sheets in countries such as the United Kingdom, Hong Kong and Australia. A recent PricewaterhouseCoopers report revealed that 74 per cent of the average purchase prices of acquired companies was made up of intangible assets and goodwill – what is called **brand value**.[84]

Brand valuation

Marketers should distinguish brand equity from brand valuation, which is the job of estimating the total financial value of the brand. The **brand value chain** is a structured approach to assessing the sources and outcomes of brand equity and the manner in which marketing activities create brand value – see the marketing insight box.

For brand equity to perform a useful strategic function and guide marketing decisions, marketers need to understand fully: (1) the sources of brand equity and how they affect outcomes of interest; (2) how these sources and outcomes change, if at all, over time. Brand audits are important for the former; brand tracking for the latter.

A **brand audit** is a consumer-focused procedure to assess the health of the brand, uncover its sources of brand equity and suggest ways to improve and leverage its equity. Conducting brand audits on a regular basis, such as annually, allows marketers to keep their fingers on the pulse of their brands so they can manage them more proactively and responsively. Brand audits are particularly useful background information for marketing managers as they set up their marketing plans and select marketing mix variables, and when they are considering making changes.

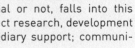

Marketing insight

The brand value chain

The brand value chain is a structured approach to assessing the sources and outcomes of brand equity and the manner in which marketing activities create brand value (see Figure 12.5). It is based on several premises.

First, the brand value creation process is assumed to begin when the firm invests in a marketing programme targeting actual or potential customers. Any marketing

programme investment that can be attributed to brand value development, intentional or not, falls into this category – for example, product research, development and design; trade or intermediary support; communications and pricing decisions.

Next, customers' mindsets are assumed to change as a result of the marketing programme. The question is how. This change, in turn, is assumed to affect the way the brand performs in the marketplace through the collective impact of individual customers deciding how

much to purchase and when, how much they will pay, and so on. Finally, the investment community considers market performance and other factors such as replacement cost and purchase price in acquisitions to arrive at an assessment of shareholder value in general and the value of a brand in particular.

The model also assumes that a number of linking factors intervene between these stages and determine the extent to which value created at one stage transfers to the next stage. Three sets of multipliers moderate the transfer between the marketing programme and the subsequent three value stages – the programme multiplier, the customer multiplier and the market multiplier.

The *programme multiplier* determines the marketing programme's ability to affect the customer mindset and is a function of the quality of the programme investment. The *customer multiplier* determines the extent to which value created in the minds of customers affects market performance. This result depends on contextual factors external to the customer.

Three such factors are:

1   Competitive superiority: how effective the quantity and quality of the marketing investment of other competing brands are.

2   Channel and other intermediary support: how much brand reinforcement and selling effort various marketing partners are putting forth.

3   Customer size and profile: how many and what types of customer, profitable or not, are attracted to the brand.

The *market multiplier* determines the extent to which the value shown by the market performance of a brand is manifested in shareholder value. It depends, in part, on the actions of financial analysts and investors.

Sources: K. Keller (2009) Brand planning, a Shoulders of Giants publication, http://marksherrington.com/downloads/Brand%20Planning%20eArticle.pdf; K. Keller (2008) *Strategic Brand Management*, New York: Pearson; K. L. Keller and D. Lehmann (2003) How do brands create value?, *Marketing Management*, May–June, 27–31. See also M. J. Epstein and R. A. Westbrook (2001) Linking actions to profits in strategic decision making, *MIT Sloan Management Review*, Spring, 39–49; and R. K. Srivastava, T. A. Shervani and L. Fahey (1998) Market-based assets and shareholder value, *Journal of Marketing*, 62(1), January, 2–18.

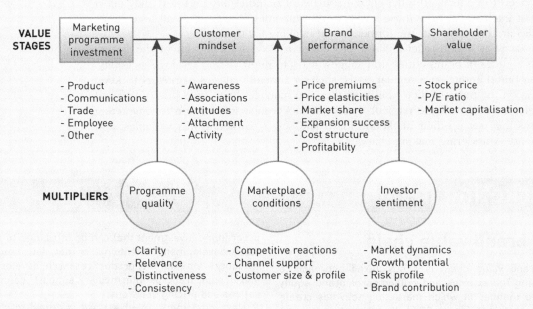

Figure 12.5 The brand value chain
Source: K. L. Keller (2008) *Strategic Brand Management*, Pearson International Edition, New Jersey; K. L. Keller and D. Lehmann (2003) How do brands create value?, *Marketing Management*, May–June, 27–31. See also M. J. Epstein and R. A. Westbrook (2001) Linking actions to profits in strategic decision making, *MIT Sloan Management Review*, Spring, 39–49; and R. K. Srivastava, T. A. Shervani and L. Fahey (1998) Market-based assets and shareholder value, *Journal of Marketing*, 62(1), January, 2–18. K. Keller (2009) Brand Planning, A Shoulders of Giants Publication, http://marksherrington.com/downloads/Brand%20Planning%20eArticle.pdf

Brand tracking studies collect quantitative data from consumers on a routine basis over time to provide marketers with consistent, baseline information about how their brands and marketing programmes are performing on key dimensions. Tracking studies are a means of understanding where, how much, and in what ways brand value is being created, to facilitate day-to-day decision making.

Managing brand equity and brand performance

Marketing managers need a model to link brand equity and brand performance.[85] There are four major stages, as outlined in Figure 12.6.

1 What companies/marketing managers do. The full marketing programme and other aspects of the company operations must be managed from both quantitative (factors such as amount of marketing expenditure) and qualitative (clarity and consistency of the marketing programme) perspectives.

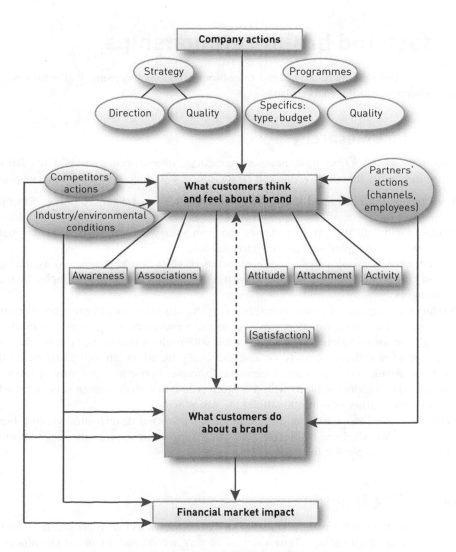

Figure 12.6 A systems model of brand antecedents and consequences
Source: K. L. Keller and D. R. Lehmann (2006) Brand and branding: research findings and future priorities, *Marketing Science*, 25(6), 740–59. Copyright © 2006 The Institute for Operations Research and the Management Sciences (INFORMS).

2   **What customers think and feel**. Individual customer characteristics as well as competition and other aspects of the environment will influence how customers feel. What they think and feel is not under the sole control of the company. Personal experience and the experience of others will both affect what a customer thinks of a brand.

3   **What customers do**. The main payoff is when the customer buys the product or service and so affects revenue, share and other metrics commonly used to judge brand success. Of course, other things that customers do (especially word of mouth) impact on the future development of the brand.

4   **How financial markets react**. Most brands are judged by how they perform financially internally and also in relation to stock prices and market capitalisation (the value of the company if it was sold). This is called the bottom line and is what the chief executive will ask of marketing – that the brand provides a return to the company.[86]

Product and brand relationships

Each market offering can be compared to competitive ones to ensure that a firm is performing effectively in the marketplace.

The product hierarchy

The hierarchy stretches from basic needs to particular value attributes and benefits that satisfy those needs. Six hierarchy levels can be identified, using life insurance as an example:

1   **Need family**: the core need that underlies the existence of a family policy. Example: security.

2   **Product family**: all the product classes that can satisfy a core need with reasonable effectiveness. Example: savings and income.

3   **Product class**: a group of products within the product family recognised as having a certain functional coherence; Also known as a product category. Example: financial instruments.

4   **Product line**: a group of products within a product class that are closely related because they perform a similar function, are sold to the same customer groups, are marketed through the same outlets or channels, or fall within given price ranges. A product line may consist of different brands, or a single family brand, or an individual brand that has been developed from a line extension. Example: house and property insurance.

5   **Product type**: a group of items within a product line that share one of several possible forms of the market offering. Example: life insurance.

6   **Item** (also called *stock keeping unit* or *product variant*): a distinct unit within a brand or product line distinguishable by size, price, appearance or some other attribute. Example: renewable life insurance.

Product-line length

Company objectives influence product-line length. One objective is to create a line to induce customers to trade up. Thus General Motors would like to move customers up from its entry market Chevrolet to an Opel or Vauxhall. A different objective is to create a line that facilitates cross-selling: Hewlett-Packard sells printers as well as computers. Still another objective is to create a product line that protects against economic cycles; Electrolux offers white goods such as refrigerators, dishwashers and vacuum cleaners under different brand names in the discount, middle-market and niche segments.[33] Companies seeking high market share and market growth will generally carry longer lines. Companies that emphasise high profitability will carry shorter lines consisting of carefully chosen items.

Product lines tend to lengthen over time. Excess manufacturing capacity puts pressure on firms to develop new items. The sales force and distributors also pressure the company for a more complete portfolio of market offerings to satisfy customers. However, as items are added, costs rise: design and engineering costs, inventory-carrying costs, manufacturing-changeover costs, order-processing costs, transportation costs and new item promotional costs. Eventually, someone calls a halt: top management may stop development because of insufficient funds or manufacturing capacity. The controller may call for a study of money-losing items. A pattern of market offering/product-line growth followed by massive pruning may repeat itself many times. Increasingly, consumers are growing weary of dense market offering/product lines, overextended brands and feature-laden market offerings (see the marketing insight box).

A company lengthens its product line in two ways: line stretching and line filling.

Line stretching

Every company's product line covers a certain part of the total possible range. For example, Mercedes and Porsche cars are located in the upper price niche segment of the car market. Line stretching occurs when a company lengthens its line beyond its current range. The company can stretch its line down market, up market, or both ways.

Marketing insight

When less is more

Although many customers find the notion of having more choices appealing, the reality is that customers can sometimes be overwhelmed by the choices involved. With thousands of new products introduced each year, customers find it harder and harder to navigate shop aisles successfully. Although customers with well-defined preferences may benefit from more differentiated offers with specific benefits to better suit their needs, too much choice may be a source of frustration, confusion and regret for other customers. Product proliferation has another disadvantage. Exposing the customer to constant offer changes and introductions may nudge them into reconsidering their choices, resulting in their switching to a competitor as a result.

Also, not all the new choices may be winners anyway, as Nestlé found out with its KitKat bars, among the best-selling confectionery bars in the United Kingdom since they were invented there in the 1930s. To increase sales in 2004, the company rolled out a vast array of new flavours. The summer saw the launch of strawberries and cream, passion fruit and mango, and red berry versions; with winter came Christmas pudding, tiramisu (with real wine and mascarpone), and low-carbohydrate versions. The new flavours were a disaster – the tastes were too sweet and unusual for many – and even worse,

some consumers could not find the classic KitKat bars among all the new varieties. An ill-timed switch from the classic slogan, 'Have a break, have a KitKat', didn't help, and sales dropped 18 per cent as a result. The new flavours were then discontinued.

Perceptive marketers are also realising that it is not just the lines that are confusing customers – many items are just too complicated for the average consumer. Royal Philips Electronics learned its lesson when the company asked 100 top managers to take various Philips electronic products home one weekend and see whether they could make them work. The number of executives who returned frustrated and angry spoke volumes about the challenges the ordinary consumer faced.

Sources: D. Ball (2006) Flavor experiment for KitKat leaves Nestlé with a bad taste, *Wall Street Journal*, 6 July; B. Schwartz (2004) *The Paradox of Choice: Why More Is Less*, New York: HarperCollins Ecco; F. Endt (2004) It is rocket science, *Newsweek*, 18 October, E8; A. Chernev (2003) When more is less and less is more: the role of ideal point availability and assortment in choice, *Journal of Consumer Research*, 30 September, 170–83; S. S. Iyengar and M. R. Lepper (2000) When choice is demotivating: can one desire too much of a good thing?, *Journal of Personality and Social Psychology*, 79(6), 995–1006; R. Dhar (1997) Consumer preference for a no-choice option, *Journal of Consumer Research*, 27 September, 233–48.

Down-market stretch A company positioned in the middle market may want to introduce a lower-priced line for any of three reasons:

1 The company may notice strong growth opportunities as mass retailers such as Carrefour, Tesco and others attract a growing number of shoppers who want lower-priced goods.
2 The company may wish to tie up lower-end competitors that might otherwise try to move up market. If the company has been attacked by a low-end competitor, it often decides to counterattack by entering the low end of the market.
3 The company may find that the middle market is stagnating or declining.

A company faces a number of naming choices in deciding to move a brand down market:

- Use the parent brand name on all its offerings. Sony has used its name on products in a variety of price tiers.
- Introduce lower-priced offerings using a sub-brand name, such as General Motors's Chevrolet models in Europe.
- Introduce the lower-priced offerings under a different name, as VW did with Seat and Skoda. This strategy is expensive to implement, and consumers may not accept a new brand that lacks the equity of the parent brand name.

Moving down market carries risks. Kodak introduced Kodak Funtime film to counter lower-priced brands, but it did not price it low enough to match the lower-priced film. It also found some of its regular customers buying Funtime, so it was cannibalising its core brand. Kodak withdrew the product and may also have lost some of its quality image in the process. On the other hand, Mercedes successfully introduced its C-class cars without injuring its ability to sell other top-priced Mercedes cars. In these cases, consumers may have been better able to compartmentalise the different brand offerings and understand and rationalise functional differences between offerings in higher and lower price tiers.

Up-market stretch Companies may wish to enter the high end of the market to achieve more growth, either to realise higher margins or simply to position themselves as full-line manufacturers. Many markets have spawned surprising upmarket segments: Starbucks in coffee, Mövenpick in ice cream, and Danone's Evian in bottled water. However, other companies have included their own name in moving up market, as is evidenced by supermarket premium lines.

Two-way stretch Companies serving the middle market might decide to stretch their line in both directions. Pet food companies have stretched up and down to create a portfolio to offer varieties in the entry, middle and niche market segments.

Holiday Inn

Holiday Inn Worldwide has also performed a two-way stretch of its hotel product line. The hotel chain segmented its domestic hotels into five separate chains to tap into five different benefit segments – the upscale Crowne Plaza, the traditional Holiday Inn, the budget Holiday Inn Express, and the business-oriented Holiday Inn Select and Holiday Inn Suites & Rooms. Different branded chains received different marketing programmes and emphasis. Holiday Inn Express has been advertised with a humorous advertising campaign. By basing the development of these brands on distinct consumer targets with unique needs, Holiday Inn is able to insure against overlap between brands.

The relative position of a brand and its competitor context will also affect consumer acceptance. Research has shown that a high-end model of a low-end brand is favoured over a low-end model of a high-end brand, even when information about competing categories is made available.[34]

Line filling

A firm can also lengthen its product line by adding more items within the present range. There are several motives for *line filling*: reaching for incremental profits, trying to satisfy dealers who complain about lost sales because of missing items in the line, trying to utilise excess capacity, trying to be the leading full-line company, and trying to plug holes to keep out competitors.

Line filling is overdone if it results in self-cannibalisation and customer confusion. The company needs to differentiate each item in the consumer's mind with a *just-noticeable difference*. The company should also check that the proposed product meets a market need.

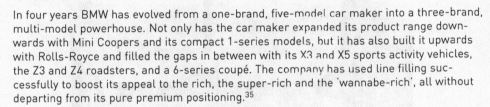

BMW AG

In four years BMW has evolved from a one-brand, five-model car maker into a three-brand, multi-model powerhouse. Not only has the car maker expanded its product range downwards with Mini Coopers and its compact 1-series models, but it has also built it upwards with Rolls-Royce and filled the gaps in between with its X3 and X5 sports activity vehicles, the Z3 and Z4 roadsters, and a 6-series coupé. The company has used line filling successfully to boost its appeal to the rich, the super-rich and the 'wannabe-rich', all without departing from its pure premium positioning.[35]

Line modernisation, featuring and pruning

Product lines need to be modernised. The issue is whether to overhaul the line piecemeal or all at once. A piecemeal approach allows the company to see how customers and dealers take to the new style. It is also less draining on the company's cash flow, but it allows competitors to see changes and to start redesigning their own lines.

In rapidly changing markets, modernisation is continuous. Companies plan improvements to encourage customer migration to higher-valued, higher-priced items. Microprocessor companies such as Intel and AMD, and software companies such as Microsoft and Sage, continually introduce more advanced versions of their products. A major issue is *timing* improvements so they do not appear too early (damaging sales of the current line) or too late (after the competition has established a strong reputation for more advanced equipment).

Firms must periodically review the line for products that are depressing profits.[36] The weak items can be identified through sales and cost analysis. One study found that for a big Dutch retailer, a major assortment reduction led to a short-term drop in category sales, caused mainly by fewer category purchases by former buyers, but it also attracted new category buyers at the same time. These new buyers partially offset the sales losses among former buyers of the delisted items.[37]

In 1999, Unilever announced its 'Path to Growth' programme designed to get the most value from its brand portfolio by eliminating three-quarters of its 1,600 distinct brands by 2003.[38] More than 90 per cent of its profits came from just 400 brands, prompting Unilever co-chairman Niall FitzGerald to liken the brand reduction to weeding a garden, so 'the light and air get into the blooms which are likely to grow the best'. The company retained global brands such as Lipton, as well as regional brands and 'local jewels' such as Persil, the leading detergent in the United Kingdom.

Multibrand companies all over the world are attempting to optimise their brand portfolios. In many cases, this has led to a greater focus on core brand growth and to concentrating energy and resources on the biggest and most established brands.

Pruning slow-selling brands from product lines often benefits the brands that are left, such as Unilever's global bestsellers including Lipton worldwide and Persil in the United Kingdom. Source: Martin Meissner/AP Wide World Photos.

VW

VW has four different brands to manage in its European portfolio. Initially, Audi and Seat had a sporty image and VW and Skoda had a family-car image. Audi and VW were in a higher price-quality tier than their respective counterparts. Skoda and Seat, with their basic spartan interiors and utilitarian engine performance, were clearly differentiated. With the goal of reducing costs, streamlining parts/systems designs and eliminating redundancies, Volkswagen upgraded the Seat and Skoda brands. Once viewed as below-par products by European consumers, Skoda and Seat have captured market share with attractive interiors, a full array of safety systems and reliable power-trains borrowed from Volkswagen. The danger, of course, is that by borrowing from its upper-echelon Audi and Volkswagen products, Volkswagen may have diluted their cachet. Frugal European car buyers may convince themselves that a Seat or Skoda is almost identical to a VW, but it is several thousand euro cheaper.[39]

Section 10

Working with
Case Studies

A Step-by-Step Approach

2.1 RATIONALE

In order to understand each step of the approach the whole process is described in this chapter in outline. In addition, suggestions for learning to use the approach are discussed. Before doing this, however, it might be worth describing where this approach originated. Most papers and books on complex problem solving describe a similar approach. The basic ideas in different combinations have been around for a long time. The approach is often described as the rational problem-solving approach. However, two important adaptations have been made.

Firstly, an attempt has been made to develop the approach into a set of practical guidelines. This wasn't an easy task. It may be that in the process some ideas have been distorted: that isn't too important. If the guidelines are relevant and practical, then that justifies what has been done. Secondly, the approach has been specifically tailored to the case method. Complex problems differ in all sorts of ways. By concentrating on the kinds of problems that arise in case studies, a more specific and therefore useful approach is possible.

It has been argued that people don't actually solve problems in this way. There are limits to human information-processing capacity, especially when the data are 'soft', which lead to short cuts, heuristics and sub-optimal or even unsatisfactory outcomes. Rational problem solving is beyond our capabilities. I have a great deal of sympathy with this view. How I suggest you cope with this problem is set out in section 2.3.

2.2 THE SEVEN STEPS

1. *Understanding the situation*
   The basic meat of a case study is information. In the first step you must become familiar with this information and begin to work on

it. The goal is to build a descriptive, almost certainly qualitative, model of the situation. The information should be organized to help you understand it and help you locate it easily later on. The information contained in the case also needs evaluation. Not all of the information is valid, precise, or relevant. Vital pieces are missing. You will need to extrapolate from what is given if you are to make any decisions at all.

2. *Diagnosing problem areas*

A problem is defined as the difference between what is (or will be) and what we would like the situation to be. In this step you will be attempting to uncover these differences in the case situation. You already know what is happening in the organization. What is or will be wrong with it? This is not altogether an easy task. Sometimes problems are simply symptoms of more fundamental problems. Sometimes problems are caused by a number of factors. Sometimes basic problems can lead to any number of symptoms. In this step you will be attempting to unravel these relationships. You will state the problems as precisely as you can and will relate them to each other. Not all problems are equally important. As your last task in this step, you will have to decide which problem (or problems) gets priority and why.

3. *Generating alternative solutions*

This is a creative step. You need to understand, however, the nature of alternative solutions before you begin to use a variety of methods to think them up. This process could produce an enormous number of alternatives. There must therefore be some process of ranking the alternatives. Major strategic alternatives must be examined first. When a decision has been reached concerning them, it then makes sense to examine tactical alternatives. This may involve cycling through steps 4, 5 and 6 a number of times.

4. *Predicting outcomes*

The first stage in choosing among alternatives is to predict what would happen if a particular solution were put into action. Two particular warnings are important here. The first is to be sure to predict most of the possible important outcomes. It may be that a particular solution solves one problem only at the expense of creating another. Secondly, predicting is a difficult and uncertain business. Not all outcomes are equally likely to occur. You should be aware of the techniques which attempt to cope with the risk and uncertainty associated with a particular action.

5. *Evaluating alternatives*

   In this stage you will choose among the alternatives. This starts with the listing of pros and cons for each. In a series of stages these may be elaborated, qualified, and quantified to allow direct comparisons to be made. The choice is then made.

6. *Rounding out the analysis*

   Step 6 forms a bridge between the case analysis and communication of its results. It involves making a decision about how many times you wish to cycle through stages 4 to 6 or, in other words, how much detail you wish to include. Events may not always turn out as you hope. A way of coping with this is contingency planning. It helps to add breadth as well as depth to your solution.

7. *Communicating the results*

   Your task does not end with a successfully completed case analysis. You must be prepared to undertake quite a bit more work planning how to communicate it. Chapters 12 and 13 cover oral and written communication using a traditional communication framework. Suffice it to say that there are more factors to take into account when designing a case presentation than most students realize.

2.3 USING THIS APPROACH

At this point it seems a useful idea to give some general advice on how to use this approach even before you fully understand it. One important psychological point to start with: it takes more time to read about the approach than to apply it, so don't be discouraged by the amount of material facing you. Once you have grasped the main points, the detail will fall into place.

My position on learning complex skills is that they can only be acquired incrementally. You have to start from what you can do now and improve bit by bit. Thus I would not advocate that the reader attempt to 'learn' the approach, in detail and in total, as set out below. I suggest it can be used in two ways. Firstly, as a bank of separate ideas and concepts upon which to draw. Secondly, as an overall, rather general, framework to give shape to case analysis. Most important of all is to experiment and try out the ideas. If they do not work for you abandon them, but not the quest for the skills that they seek to provide. Start by reading Chapters 3 to 11 fairly quickly to get an overall appreciation of the ideas being presented. Try to grasp the essentials rather than worry about the details. You may not be ready for this degree of complexity yet. To help you, at the end of each chapter or pair of chapters there is a section called 'Guide to use'. This section discusses which procedures are more fundamental and which may be regarded as optional, at least in the early stages of learning the case method.

Choose a short case and try out the procedures described. In each chapter read the 'Guide to use' first and decide which procedures you think will be most useful at your next stage of development. Compare your results with the examples given in the text to make sure you can apply the ideas correctly. As your case experience increases try out the optional procedures. You should find that they help you to continue improving your skills.

While you are still a beginner, you may find that you have to cycle back to earlier steps in the process because you missed a problem or failed to see a particularly attractive solution. Don't worry too much about this. However, you should beware of missing out steps if you are using the approach as a framework only. This is a 'building up from the foundations' approach. You may find that your finished work does not stand up to criticism if you have not laid the groundwork well. You may also notice that different cases will make varying demands on different steps of the process. This is only to be expected. In recognizing this you are beginning to develop as a case analyst.

In the long term, the aim must be to develop your own approach. It is important to emphasize that the approach described here is not meant to be a mechanical set of procedures to be followed *ad nauseam*. It is meant to bridge the gap between the complete novice and the skilled practitioner. Your own personal case work style might incorporate elements from this approach or it may be completely different. The objective of this book is simply to get you over the initial learning hurdles so that you can develop in your own way.

Appendix I

Starbucks: Delivering Customer Service

9-504-016

REV: JULY 10, 2006

YOUNGME MOON

JOHN QUELCH

Starbucks: Delivering Customer Service

In late 2002, Christine Day, Starbucks' senior vice president of administration in North America, sat in the seventh-floor conference room of Starbucks' Seattle headquarters and reached for her second cup of toffee-nut latte. The handcrafted beverage—a buttery, toffee-nut flavored espresso concoction topped with whipped cream and toffee sprinkles—had become a regular afternoon indulgence for Day ever since its introduction earlier that year.

As she waited for her colleagues to join her, Day reflected on the company's recent performance. While other retailers were still reeling from the post-9/11 recession, Starbucks was enjoying its 11th consecutive year of 5% or higher comparable store sales growth, prompting its founder and chairman, Howard Schultz, to declare: "I think we've demonstrated that we are close to a recession-proof product."[1]

Day, however, was not feeling nearly as sanguine, in part because Starbucks' most recent market research had revealed some unexpected findings. "We've always taken great pride in our retail service," said Day, "but according to the data, we're not always meeting our customers' expectations in the area of customer satisfaction."

As a result of these concerns, Day and her associates had come up with a plan to invest an additional $40 million annually in the company's 4,500 stores, which would allow each store to add the equivalent of 20 hours of labor a week. "The idea is to improve speed-of-service and thereby increase customer satisfaction," said Day.

In two days, Day was due to make a final recommendation to both Schultz and Orin Smith, Starbucks' CEO, about whether the company should move forward with the plan. "The investment is the EPS [earnings per share] equivalent of almost seven cents a share," said Day. In preparation for her meeting with Schultz and Smith, Day had asked one of her associates to help her think through the implications of the plan. Day noted, "The real question is, do we believe what our customers are telling us about what constitutes 'excellent' customer service? And if we deliver it, what will the impact be on our sales and profitability?"

---

[1] Jake Batsell, "A Grande Decade for Starbucks," *The Seattle Times*, June 26, 2002.

Company Background

The story of how Howard Schultz managed to transform a commodity into an upscale cultural phenomenon has become the stuff of legends. In 1971, three coffee fanatics—Gerald Baldwin, Gordon Bowker, and Ziev Siegl—opened a small coffee shop in Seattle's Pike Place Market. The shop specialized in selling whole arabica beans to a niche market of coffee purists.

In 1982, Schultz joined the Starbucks marketing team; shortly thereafter, he traveled to Italy, where he became fascinated with Milan's coffee culture, in particular, the role the neighborhood espresso bars played in Italians' everyday social lives. Upon his return, the inspired Schultz convinced the company to set up an espresso bar in the corner of its only downtown Seattle shop. As Schultz explained, the bar became the prototype for his long-term vision:

> The idea was to create a chain of coffeehouses that would become America's "third place." At the time, most Americans had two places in their lives—home and work. But I believed that people needed another place, a place where they could go to relax and enjoy others, or just be by themselves. I envisioned a place that would be separate from home or work, a place that would mean different things to different people.

A few years later, Schultz got his chance when Starbucks' founders agreed to sell him the company. As soon as Schultz took over, he immediately began opening new stores. The stores sold whole beans and premium-priced coffee beverages by the cup and catered primarily to affluent, well-educated, white-collar patrons (skewed female) between the ages of 25 and 44. By 1992, the company had 140 such stores in the Northwest and Chicago and was successfully competing against other small-scale coffee chains such as Gloria Jean's Coffee Bean and Barnie's Coffee & Tea.

That same year, Schultz decided to take the company public. As he recalled, many Wall Street types were dubious about the idea: "They'd say, 'You mean, you're going to sell coffee for a dollar in a paper cup, with Italian names that no one in America can say? At a time in America when no one's drinking coffee? And I can get coffee at the local coffee shop or doughnut shop for 50 cents? Are you kidding me?'"[2]

Ignoring the skeptics, Schultz forged ahead with the public offering, raising $25 million in the process. The proceeds allowed Starbucks to open more stores across the nation.

By 2002, Schultz had unequivocally established Starbucks as the dominant specialty-coffee brand in North America. Sales had climbed at a compound annual growth rate (CAGR) of 40% since the company had gone public, and net earnings had risen at a CAGR of 50%. The company was now serving 20 million unique customers in well over 5,000 stores around the globe and was opening on average three new stores a day. (See **Exhibits 1–3** for company financials and store growth over time.)

What made Starbucks' success even more impressive was that the company had spent almost nothing on advertising to achieve it. North American marketing primarily consisted of point-of-sale materials and local-store marketing and was far less than the industry average. (Most fast-food chains had marketing budgets in the 3%–6% range.)

For his part, Schultz remained as chairman and chief global strategist in control of the company, handing over day-to-day operations in 2002 to CEO Orin Smith, a Harvard MBA (1967) who had joined the company in 1990.

---

[2] Batsell.

The Starbucks Value Proposition

Starbucks' brand strategy was best captured by its "live coffee" mantra, a phrase that reflected the importance the company attached to keeping the national coffee culture alive. From a retail perspective, this meant creating an "experience" around the consumption of coffee, an experience that people could weave into the fabric of their everyday lives.

There were three components to this experiential branding strategy. The first component was the coffee itself. Starbucks prided itself on offering what it believed to be the highest-quality coffee in the world, sourced from the Africa, Central and South America, and Asia-Pacific regions. To enforce its exacting coffee standards, Starbucks controlled as much of the supply chain as possible—it worked directly with growers in various countries of origin to purchase green coffee beans, it oversaw the custom-roasting process for the company's various blends and single-origin coffees, and it controlled distribution to retail stores around the world.

The second brand component was service, or what the company sometimes referred to as "customer intimacy." "Our goal is to create an uplifting experience every time you walk through our door," explained Jim Alling, Starbucks' senior vice president of North American retail. "Our most loyal customers visit us as often as 18 times a month, so it could be something as simple as recognizing you and knowing your drink or customizing your drink just the way you like it."

The third brand component was atmosphere. "People come for the coffee," explained Day, "but the ambience is what makes them want to stay." For that reason, most Starbucks had seating areas to encourage lounging and layouts that were designed to provide an upscale yet inviting environment for those who wanted to linger. "What we have built has universal appeal," remarked Schultz. "It's based on the human spirit, it's based on a sense of community, the need for people to come together."[3]

Channels of Distribution

Almost all of Starbucks' locations in North America were company-operated stores located in high-traffic, high-visibility settings such as retail centers, office buildings, and university campuses.[4] In addition to selling whole-bean coffees, these stores sold rich-brewed coffees, Italian-style espresso drinks, cold-blended beverages, and premium teas. Product mixes tended to vary depending on a store's size and location, but most stores offered a variety of pastries, sodas, and juices, along with coffee-related accessories and equipment, music CDs, games, and seasonal novelty items. (About 500 stores even carried a selection of sandwiches and salads.)

Beverages accounted for the largest percentage of sales in these stores (77%); this represented a change from 10 years earlier, when about half of store revenues had come from sales of whole-bean coffees. (See **Exhibit 4** for retail sales mix by product type; see **Exhibit 5** for a typical menu board and price list.)

Starbucks also sold coffee products through non-company-operated retail channels; these so-called "Specialty Operations" accounted for 15% of net revenues. About 27% of these revenues came from North American food-service accounts, that is, sales of whole-bean and ground coffees to hotels, airlines, restaurants, and the like. Another 18% came from domestic retail store licenses that, in

---

[3] Batsell.

[4] Starbucks had recently begun experimenting with drive-throughs. Less than 10% of its stores had drive-throughs, but in these stores, the drive-throughs accounted for 50% of all business.

North America, were only granted when there was no other way to achieve access to desirable retail space (e.g., in airports).

The remaining 55% of specialty revenues came from a variety of sources, including international licensed stores, grocery stores and warehouse clubs (Kraft Foods handled marketing and distribution for Starbucks in this channel), and online and mail-order sales. Starbucks also had a joint venture with Pepsi-Cola to distribute bottled Frappuccino beverages in North America, as well as a partnership with Dreyer's Grand Ice Cream to develop and distribute a line of premium ice creams.

Day explained the company's broad distribution strategy:

Our philosophy is pretty straightforward—we want to reach customers where they work, travel, shop, and dine. In order to do this, we sometimes have to establish relationships with third parties that share our values and commitment to quality. This is a particularly effective way to reach newcomers with our brand. It's a lot less intimidating to buy Starbucks at a grocery store than it is to walk into one of our coffeehouses for the first time. In fact, about 40% of our new coffeehouse customers have already tried the Starbucks brand before they walk through our doors. Even something like ice cream has become an important trial vehicle for us.

Starbucks Partners

All Starbucks employees were called "partners." The company employed 60,000 partners worldwide, about 50,000 in North America. Most were hourly-wage employees (called *baristas*) who worked in Starbucks retail stores. Alling remarked, "From day one, Howard has made clear his belief that partner satisfaction leads to customer satisfaction. This belief is part of Howard's DNA, and because it's been pounded into each and every one of us, it's become part of our DNA too."

The company had a generous policy of giving health insurance and stock options to even the most entry-level partners, most of whom were between the ages of 17 and 23. Partly as a result of this, Starbucks' partner satisfaction rate consistently hovered in the 80% to 90% range, well above the industry norm,[5] and the company had recently been ranked 47th in the *Fortune* magazine list of best places to work, quite an accomplishment for a company with so many hourly-wage workers.

In addition, Starbucks had one of the lowest employee turnover rates in the industry—just 70%, compared with fast-food industry averages as high as 300%. The rate was even lower for managers, and as Alling noted, the company was always looking for ways to bring turnover down further: "Whenever we have a problem store, we almost always find either an inexperienced store manager or inexperienced baristas. Manager stability is key—it not only decreases partner turnover, but it also enables the store to do a much better job of recognizing regular customers and providing personalized service. So our goal is to make the position a lifetime job."

To this end, the company encouraged promotion from within its own ranks. About 70% of the company's store managers were ex-baristas, and about 60% of its district managers were ex-store managers. In fact, upon being hired, all senior executives had to train and succeed as baristas before being allowed to assume their positions in corporate headquarters.

---

[5] Industrywide, employee satisfaction rates tended to be in the 50% to 60% range. Source: Starbucks, 2000.

Delivering on Service

When a partner was hired to work in one of Starbucks' North American retail stores, he or she had to undergo two types of training. The first type focused on "hard skills" such as learning how to use the cash register and learning how to mix drinks. Most Starbucks beverages were handcrafted, and to ensure product quality, there was a prespecified process associated with each drink. Making an espresso beverage, for example, required seven specific steps.

The other type of training focused on "soft skills." Alling explained:

> In our training manual, we explicitly teach partners to connect with customers—to enthusiastically welcome them to the store, to establish eye contact, to smile, and to try to remember their names and orders if they're regulars. We also encourage partners to create conversations with customers using questions that require more than a yes or no answer. So for example, "I noticed you were looking at the menu board—what types of beverages do you typically enjoy?" is a good question for a partner to ask.

Starbucks' "Just Say Yes" policy empowered partners to provide the best service possible, even if it required going beyond company rules. "This means that if a customer spills a drink and asks for a refill, we'll give it to him," said Day. "Or if a customer doesn't have cash and wants to pay with a check (which we aren't supposed to accept), then we'll give her a sample drink for free. The last thing we want to do is win the argument and lose the customer."

Most barista turnover occurred within the first 90 days of employment; if a barista lasted beyond that, there was a high probability that he or she would stay for three years or more. "Our training ends up being a self-selection process," Alling said. Indeed, the ability to balance hard and soft skills required a particular type of person, and Alling believed the challenges had only grown over time:

> Back in the days when we sold mostly beans, every customer who walked in the door was a coffee connoisseur, and it was easy for baristas to engage in chitchat while ringing up a bag. Those days are long gone. Today, almost every customer orders a handcrafted beverage. If the line is stretching out the door and everyone's clamoring for their coffee fix, it's not that easy to strike up a conversation with a customer.

The complexity of the barista's job had also increased over time; making a *venti tazoberry and crème*, for instance, required 10 different steps. "It used to be that a barista could make every variation of drink we offered in half a day," Day observed. "Nowadays, given our product proliferation, it would take 16 days of eight-hour shifts. There are literally hundreds of combinations of drinks in our portfolio."

This job complexity was compounded by the fact that almost half of Starbucks' customers customized their drinks. According to Day, this created a tension between product quality and customer focus for Starbucks:

> On the one hand, we train baristas to make beverages to our preestablished quality standards—this means enforcing a consistent process that baristas can master. On the other hand, if a customer comes in and wants it their way—extra vanilla, for instance—what should we do? Our heaviest users are always the most demanding. Of course, every time we customize, we slow down the service for everyone else. We also put a lot of strain on our baristas, who are already dealing with an extraordinary number of sophisticated drinks.

One obvious solution to the problem was to hire more baristas to share the workload; however, the company had been extremely reluctant to do this in recent years, particularly given the economic downturn. Labor was already the company's largest expense item in North America (see **Exhibit 3**), and Starbucks stores tended to be located in urban areas with high wage rates. Instead, the company had focused on increasing barista efficiency by removing all non-value-added tasks, simplifying the beverage production process, and tinkering with the facility design to eliminate bottlenecks.

In addition, the company had recently begun installing automated espresso machines in its North American cafés. The *verismo* machines, which decreased the number of steps required to make an espresso beverage, reduced waste, improved consistency, and had generated an overwhelmingly positive customer and barista response.

Measuring Service Performance

Starbucks tracked service performance using a variety of metrics, including monthly status reports and self-reported checklists. The company's most prominent measurement tool was a mystery shopper program called the "Customer Snapshot." Under this program, every store was visited by an anonymous mystery shopper three times a quarter. Upon completing the visit, the shopper would rate the store on four "Basic Service" criteria:

- **Service**—Did the register partner verbally greet the customer? Did the barista and register partner make eye contact with the customer? Say thank you?

- **Cleanliness**—Was the store clean? The counters? The tables? The restrooms?

- **Product quality**—Was the order filled accurately? Was the temperature of the drink within range? Was the beverage properly presented?

- **Speed of service**—How long did the customer have to wait? The company's goal was to serve a customer within three minutes, from back-of-the-line to drink-in-hand. This benchmark was based on market research which indicated that the three-minute standard was a key component in how current Starbucks customers defined "excellent service."

In addition to Basic Service, stores were also rated on "Legendary Service," which was defined as "behavior that created a memorable experience for a customer, that inspired a customer to return often and tell a friend." Legendary Service scores were based on secret shopper observations of service attributes such as partners initiating conversations with customers, partners recognizing customers by name or drink order, and partners being responsive to service problems.

During 2002, the company's Customer Snapshot scores had increased across all stores (see **Exhibit 7**), leading Day to comment, "The Snapshot is not a perfect measurement tool, but we believe it does a good job of measuring trends over the course of a quarter. In order for a store to do well on the Snapshot, it needs to have sustainable processes in place that create a well-established pattern of doing things right so that it gets 'caught' doing things right."

Competition

In the United States, Starbucks competed against a variety of small-scale specialty coffee chains, most of which were regionally concentrated. Each tried to differentiate itself from Starbucks in a different way. For example, Minneapolis-based Caribou Coffee, which operated more than 200 stores in nine states, differentiated itself on store environment. Rather than offer an upscale, pseudo-European atmosphere, its strategy was to simulate the look and feel of an Alaskan lodge, with knotty-pine cabinetry, fireplaces, and soft seating. Another example was California-based Peet's Coffee & Tea, which operated about 70 stores in five states. More than 60% of Peet's revenues came from the sale of whole beans. Peet's strategy was to build a super-premium brand by offering the freshest coffee on the market. One of the ways it delivered on this promise was by "roasting to order," that is, by hand roasting small batches of coffee at its California plant and making sure that all of its coffee shipped within 24 hours of roasting.

Starbucks also competed against thousands of independent specialty coffee shops. Some of these independent coffee shops offered a wide range of food and beverages, including beer, wine, and liquor; others offered satellite televisions or Internet-connected computers. Still others differentiated themselves by delivering highly personalized service to an eclectic clientele.

Finally, Starbucks competed against donut and bagel chains such as Dunkin Donuts, which operated over 3,700 stores in 38 states. Dunkin Donuts attributed half of its sales to coffee and in recent years had begun offering flavored coffee and noncoffee alternatives, such as Dunkaccino (a coffee and chocolate combination available with various toppings) and Vanilla Chai (a combination of tea, vanilla, honey, and spices).

Caffeinating the World

The company's overall objective was to establish Starbucks as the "most recognized and respected brand in the world."[6] This ambitious goal required an aggressive growth strategy, and in 2002, the two biggest drivers of company growth were retail expansion and product innovation.

Retail Expansion

Starbucks already owned close to one-third of America's coffee bars, more than its next five biggest competitors combined. (By comparison, the U.S.'s second-largest player, Diedrich Coffee, operated fewer than 400 stores.) However, the company had plans to open 525 company-operated and 225 licensed North American stores in 2003, and Schultz believed that there was no reason North America could not eventually expand to at least 10,000 stores. As he put it, "These are still the early days of the company's growth."[7]

The company's optimistic growth plans were based on a number of considerations:

- First, coffee consumption was on the rise in the United States, following years of decline. More than 109 million people (about half of the U.S. population) now drank coffee every day, and an additional 52 million drank it on occasion. The market's biggest growth appeared to be among drinkers of specialty coffee,[8] and it was estimated that about one-third of all U.S. coffee consumption took place outside of the home, in places such as offices, restaurants, and coffee shops. (See **Exhibit 6**.)

---

[6] Starbucks 2002 Annual Report.

[7] Dina ElBoghdady, "Pouring It On: The Starbucks Strategy? Locations, Locations, Locations," *The Washington Post*, August 25, 2002.

[8] National Coffee Association.

- Second, there were still eight states in the United States without a single company-operated Starbucks; in fact, the company was only in 150 of the roughly 300 metropolitan statistical areas in the nation.

- Third, the company believed it was far from reaching saturation levels in many existing markets. In the Southeast, for example, there was only one store for every 110,000 people (compared with one store for every 20,000 people in the Pacific Northwest). More generally, only seven states had more than 100 Starbucks locations.

Starbucks' strategy for expanding its retail business was to open stores in new markets while geographically clustering stores in existing markets. Although the latter often resulted in significant cannibalization, the company believed that this was more than offset by the total incremental sales associated with the increased store concentration. As Schultz readily conceded, "We self-cannibalize at least a third of our stores every day."[9]

When it came to selecting new retail sites, the company considered a number of criteria, including the extent to which the demographics of the area matched the profile of the typical Starbucks drinker, the level of coffee consumption in the area, the nature and intensity of competition in the local market, and the availability of attractive real estate. Once a decision was made to move forward with a site, the company was capable of designing, permitting, constructing, and opening a new store within 16 weeks. A new store typically averaged about $610,000 in sales during its first year; same-store sales (comps) were strongest in the first three years and then continued to comp positively, consistent with the company average.

Starbucks' international expansion plans were equally ambitious. Starbucks already operated over 300 company-owned stores in the United Kingdom, Australia, and Thailand, in addition to about 900 licensed stores in various countries in Asia, Europe, the Middle East, Africa, and Latin America. (Its largest international market was Japan, with close to 400 stores.) The company's goal was to ultimately have 15,000 international stores.

Product Innovation

The second big driver of company growth was product innovation. Internally, this was considered one of the most significant factors in comparable store sales growth, particularly since Starbucks' prices had remained relatively stable in recent years. New products were launched on a regular basis; for example, Starbucks introduced at least one new hot beverage every holiday season.

The new product development process generally operated on a 12- to 18-month cycle, during which the internal research and development (R&D) team tinkered with product formulations, ran focus groups, and conducted in-store experiments and market tests. Aside from consumer acceptance, whether a product made it to market depended on a number of factors, including the extent to which the drink fit into the "ergonomic flow" of operations and the speed with which the beverage could be handcrafted. Most importantly, the success of a new beverage depended on partner acceptance. "We've learned that no matter how great a drink it is, if our partners aren't excited about it, it won't sell," said Alling.

In recent years, the company's most successful innovation had been the 1995 introduction of a coffee and non-coffee-based line of Frappuccino beverages, which had driven same-store sales primarily by boosting traffic during nonpeak hours. The bottled version of the beverage (distributed

---

[9] ElBoghdady.

by PepsiCo) had become a $400 million[10] franchise; it had managed to capture 90% of the ready-to-drink coffee category, in large part due to its appeal to non-coffee-drinking 20-somethings.

Service Innovation

In terms of nonproduct innovation, Starbucks' stored-value card (SVC) had been launched in November 2001. This prepaid, swipeable smart card—which Schultz referred to as "the most significant product introduction since Frappuccino"[11]—could be used to pay for transactions in any company-operated store in North America. Early indications of the SVC's appeal were very positive: After less than one year on the market, about 6 million cards had been issued, and initial activations and reloads had already reached $160 million in sales. In surveys, the company had learned that cardholders tended to visit Starbucks twice as often as cash customers and tended to experience reduced transaction times.

Day remarked, "We've found that a lot of the cards are being given away as gifts, and many of those gift recipients are being introduced to our brand for the first time. Not to mention the fact that the cards allow us to collect all kinds of customer-transaction data, data that we haven't even begun to do anything with yet."

The company's latest service innovation was its T-Mobile HotSpot wireless Internet service, introduced in August 2002. The service offered high-speed access to the Internet in selected Starbucks stores in the United States and Europe, starting at $49.99 a month.

Starbucks' Market Research: Trouble Brewing?

Interestingly, although Starbucks was considered one of the world's most effective marketing organizations, it lacked a strategic marketing group. In fact, the company had no chief marketing officer, and its marketing department functioned as three separate groups—a market research group that gathered and analyzed market data requested by the various business units, a category group that developed new products and managed the menu and margins, and a marketing group that developed the quarterly promotional plans.

This organizational structure forced all of Starbucks' senior executives to assume marketing-related responsibilities. As Day pointed out, "Marketing is everywhere at Starbucks—it just doesn't necessarily show up in a line item called 'marketing.' Everyone has to get involved in a collaborative marketing effort." However, the organizational structure also meant that market- and customer-related trends could sometimes be overlooked. "We tend to be great at measuring things, at collecting market data," Day noted, "but we are not very disciplined when it comes to using this data to drive decision making." She continued:

> This is exactly what started to happen a few years ago. We had evidence coming in from market research that contradicted some of the fundamental assumptions we had about our brand and our customers. The problem was that this evidence was all over the place—no one was really looking at the "big picture." As a result, it took awhile before we started to take notice.

---

[10] Refers to sales at retail. Actual revenue contribution was much lower due to the joint-venture structure.

[11] Stanley Holmes, "Starbucks' Card Smarts," *BusinessWeek*, March 18, 2002.

Starbucks' Brand Meaning

Once the team did take notice, it discovered several things. First, despite Starbucks' overwhelming presence and convenience, there was very little image or product differentiation between Starbucks and the smaller coffee chains (other than Starbucks' ubiquity) in the minds of specialty coffeehouse customers. There *was* significant differentiation, however, between Starbucks and the independent specialty coffeehouses (see **Table A** below).

Table A   Qualitative Brand Meaning: Independents vs. Starbucks

---

Independents:
- Social and inclusive
- Diverse and intellectual
- Artsy and funky
- Liberal and free-spirited
- Lingering encouraged
- Particularly appealing to younger coffeehouse customers
- Somewhat intimidating to older, more mainstream coffeehouse customers

Starbucks:
- Everywhere—the trend
- Good coffee on the run
- Place to meet and move on
- Convenience oriented; on the way to work
- Accessible and consistent

Source: Starbucks, based on qualitative interviews with specialty-coffeehouse customers.

More generally, the market research team discovered that Starbucks' brand image had some rough edges. The number of respondents who strongly agreed with the statement "Starbucks cares primarily about making money" was up from 53% in 2000 to 61% in 2001, while the number of respondents who strongly agreed with the statement "Starbucks cares primarily about building more stores" was up from 48% to 55%. Day noted, "It's become apparent that we need to ask ourselves, 'Are we focusing on the right things? Are we clearly communicating our value and values to our customers, instead of just our growth plans?'" (see **Table B** below).

Table B   The Top Five Attributes Consumers Associate with the Starbucks Brand

---

- Known for specialty/gourmet coffee (54% strongly agree)
- Widely available (43% strongly agree)
- Corporate (42% strongly agree)
- Trendy (41% strongly agree)
- Always feel welcome at Starbucks (39% strongly agree)

Source: Starbucks, based on 2002 survey.

The Changing Customer

The market research team also discovered that Starbucks' customer base was evolving. Starbucks' newer customers tended to be younger, less well-educated, and in a lower income bracket than Starbucks' more established customers. In addition, they visited the stores less frequently and had very different perceptions of the Starbucks brand compared to more established customers (see **Exhibit 8**).

Furthermore, the team learned that Starbucks' historical customer profile—the affluent, well-educated, white-collar female between the ages of 24 and 44—had expanded. For example, about half of the stores in southern California had large numbers of Hispanic customers. In Florida, the company had stores that catered primarily to Cuban-Americans.

Customer Behavior

With respect to customer behavior, the market research team discovered that, regardless of the market—urban versus rural, new versus established—customers tended to use the stores the same way. The team also learned that, although the company's most frequent customers averaged 18 visits a month, the typical customer visited just five times a month (see **Figure A** below).

Figure A   Customer Visit Frequency

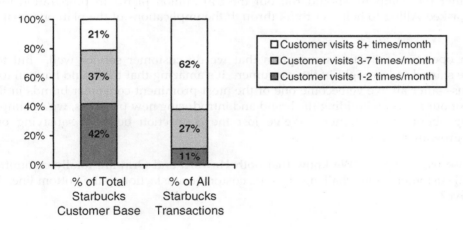

Source: Starbucks, 2002.

Measuring and Driving Customer Satisfaction

Finally, the team discovered that, despite its high Customer Snapshot scores, Starbucks was not meeting expectations in terms of customer satisfaction. The satisfaction scores were considered critical because the team also had evidence of a direct link between satisfaction level and customer loyalty (see **Exhibit 9** for customer satisfaction data).

While customer satisfaction was driven by a number of different factors (see **Exhibit 10**), Day believed that the customer satisfaction gap could primarily be attributed to a *service gap* between Starbucks scores on key attributes and customer expectations. When Starbucks had polled its customers to determine what it could do to make them feel more like valued customers, "improvements to service"—in particular, speed-of-service—had been mentioned most frequently (see **Exhibit 11** for more information).

Rediscovering the Starbucks Customer

Responding to the market research findings posed a difficult management challenge. The most controversial proposal was the one on the table before Day—it involved relaxing the labor-hour controls in the stores to add an additional 20 hours of labor, per week, per store, at a cost of an extra $40 million per year. Not surprisingly, the plan was being met with significant internal resistance. "Our CFO is understandably concerned about the potential impact on our bottom line," said Day. "Each $6 million in profit contribution translates into a penny a share. But my argument is that if we move away from seeing labor as an expense to seeing it as a customer-oriented investment, we'll see a positive return." She continued:

> We need to bring service time down to the three-minute level in all of our stores, regardless of the time of day. If we do this, we'll not only increase customer satisfaction and build stronger long-term relationships with our customers, we'll also improve our customer throughput. The goal is to move each store closer to the $20,000 level in terms of weekly sales, and I think that this plan will help us get there.

In two days, Day was scheduled to make a final recommendation to Howard Schultz and Orin Smith about whether the company should roll out the $40 million plan. In preparation for this meeting, Day had asked Alling to help her think through the implications of the plan one final time. She mused:

> We've been operating with the assumption that we do customer service well. But the reality is, we've started to lose sight of the consumer. It's amazing that this could happen to a company like us—after all, we've become one of the most prominent consumer brands in the world. For all of our focus on building the brand and introducing new products, we've simply stopped talking about the customer. We've lost the connection between satisfying our customers and growing the business.

Alling's response was simple: "We know that both Howard and Orin are totally committed to satisfying our retail customers. Our challenge is to tie customer satisfaction to the bottom line. What evidence do we have?"

Exhibit 1   Starbucks' Financials, FY 1998 to FY 2002 ($ in millions)

	FY 1998	FY 1999	FY 2000	FY 2001	FY 2002
Revenue					
Co-Owned North American	1,076.8	1,375.0	1,734.9	2,086.4	2,583.8
Co-Owned Int'l (UK, Thailand, Australia)	25.8	48.4	88.7	143.2	209.1
Total Company-Operated Retail	1,102.6	1,423.4	1,823.6	2,229.6	2,792.9
Specialty Operations	206.1	263.4	354.0	419.4	496.0
Net Revenues	**1,308.7**	**1,686.8**	**2,177.6**	**2,649.0**	**3,288.9**
Cost of Goods Sold	578.5	747.6	961.9	1,112.8	1,350.0
Gross Profit	**730.2**	**939.2**	**1,215.7**	**1,536.2**	**1,938.9**
Joint-Venture Income[a]	1.0	3.2	20.3	28.6	35.8
Expenses:					
Store Operating Expense	418.5	543.6	704.9	875.5	1,121.1
Other Operating Expense	44.5	54.6	78.4	93.3	127.2
Depreciation & Amortization Expense	72.5	97.8	130.2	163.5	205.6
General & Admin Expense	77.6	89.7	110.2	151.4	202.1
Operating Expenses	**613.1**	**785.7**	**1,023.8**	**1,283.7**	**1,656.0**
Operating Profit	**109.2**	**156.7**	**212.3**	**281.1**	**310.0**
Net Income	**68.4**	**101.7**	**94.5**	**181.2**	**215.1**
% Change in Monthly Comparable Store Sales[b]					
North America	5%	6%	9%	5%	7%
Consolidated	5%	6%	9%	5%	6%

Source: Adapted from company reports and Lehman Brothers, November 5, 2002.

[a]Includes income from various joint ventures, including Starbucks' partnership with the Pepsi-Cola Company to develop and distribute Frappuccino and with Dreyer's Grand Ice Cream to develop and distribute premium ice creams.

[b]Includes only company-operated stores open 13 months or longer.

Exhibit 2   Starbucks' Store Growth

	FY 1998	FY 1999	FY 2000	FY 2001	FY 2002
Total North America	**1,755**	**2,217**	**2,976**	**3,780**	**4,574**
Company-Operated	1,622	2,038	2,446	2,971	3,496
Licensed Stores[a]	133	179	530	809	1,078
Total International	**131**	**281**	**525**	**929**	**1,312**
Company-Operated	66	97	173	295	384
Licensed Stores	65	184	352	634	928
Total Stores	**1,886**	**2,498**	**3,501**	**4,709**	**5,886**

Source: Company reports.

[a]Includes kiosks located in grocery stores, bookstores, hotels, airports, and so on.

Exhibit 3   Additional Data, North American Company-Operated Stores (FY2002)

	Average
Average hourly rate with shift supervisors and hourly partners	$ 9.00
Total labor hours per week, average store	360
Average weekly store volume	$15,400
Average ticket	$ 3.85
Average daily customer count, per store	570

Source: Company reports.

Exhibit 4   Product Mix, North American Company-Operated Stores (FY2002)

	Percent of Sales
Retail Product Mix	
Coffee Beverages	77%
Food Items	13%
Whole-Bean Coffees	6%
Equipment & Accessories	4%

Source: Company reports.

Exhibit 5   Typical Menu Board and Price List for North American Company-Owned Store

Espresso Traditions	Tall	Grande	Venti
Classic Favorites			
Toffee Nut Latte	2.95	3.50	3.80
Vanilla Latte	2.85	3.40	3.70
Caffe Latte	2.55	3.10	3.40
Cappuccino	2.55	3.10	3.40
Caramel Macchiato	2.80	3.40	3.65
White Chocolate Mocha	3.20	3.75	4.00
Caffe Mocha	2.75	3.30	3.55
Caffe Americano	1.75	2.05	2.40

Espresso	Solo		Doppio
Espresso	1.45		1.75

Extras		
Additional Espresso Shot		.55
Add flavored syrup		.30
Organic milk & soy available upon request		

Frappuccino	Tall	Grande	Venti
Ice Blended Beverages			
Coffee	2.65	3.15	3.65
Mocha	2.90	3.40	3.90
Caramel Frappuccino	3.15	3.65	4.15
Mocha Coconut	3.15	3.65	4.15
(limited offering)			

Crème Frappuccino	Tall	Grande	Venti
Ice Blended Crème			
Toffee Nut Crème	3.15	3.65	4.15
Vanilla Crème	2.65	3.15	3.65
Coconut Crème	3.15	3.65	4.15

Tazo Tea Frappuccino	Tall	Grande	Venti
Ice Blended Teas			
Tazo Citrus	2.90	3.40	3.90
Tazoberry	2.90	3.40	3.90
Tazo Chai Crème	3.15	3.65	4.15

Brewed Coffee	Tall	Grande	Venti
Coffee of the Day	1.40	1.60	1.70
Decaf of the Day	1.40	1.60	1.70

Cold Beverages	Tall	Grande	Venti
Iced Caffe Latte	2.55	3.10	3.50
Iced Caramel Macchiato	2.80	3.40	3.80
Iced Caffe Americano	1.75	2.05	3.40

Coffee Alternatives	Tall	Grande	Venti
Toffee Nut Crème	2.45	2.70	2.95
Vanilla Crème	2.20	2.45	2.70
Caramel Apple Cider	2.45	2.70	2.95
Hot Chocolate	2.20	2.45	2.70
Tazo Hot Tea	1.15	1.65	1.65
Tazo Chai	2.70	3.10	3.35

Whole Beans: Bold	½ lb	1 lb
Our most intriguing and exotic coffees		
Gold Coast Blend	5.70	10.95
French Roast	5.20	9.95
Sumatra	5.30	10.15
Decaf Sumatra	5.60	10.65
Ethiopia Sidame	5.20	9.95
Arabian Mocha Sanani	8.30	15.95
Kenya	5.30	10.15
Italian Roast	5.20	9.95
Sulawesi	6.10	11.65

Whole Beans: Smooth	½ lb	1 lb
Richer, more flavorful coffees		
Espresso Roast	5.20	9.95
Decaf Espresso Roast	5.60	10.65
Yukon Blend	5.20	9.95
Café Verona	5.20	9.95
Guatemala Antigua	5.30	10.15
Arabian Mocha Java	6.30	11.95
Decaf Mocha Java/SWP	6.50	12.45

Whole Beans: Mild	½ lb	1 lb
The perfect introduction to Starbucks coffees		
Breakfast Blend	5.20	9.95
Lightnote Blend	5.20	9.95
Decaf Lightnote Blend	5.60	10.65
Colombia Narino	5.50	10.45
House Blend	5.20	9.95
Decaf House Blend	5.60	10.65
Fair Trade Coffee	5.95	11.45

Source: Starbucks location: Harvard Square, Cambridge, Massachusetts, February 2003.

Exhibit 6   Total U.S. Retail Coffee Market (includes both in-home and out-of-home consumption)

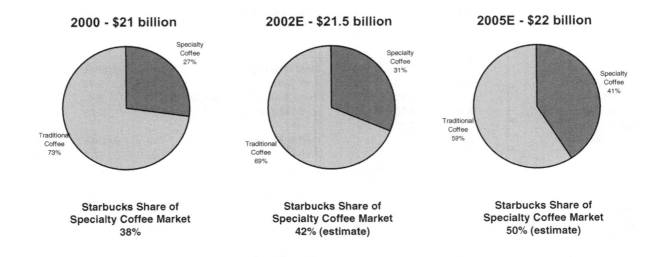

2000 - $21 billion	2002E - $21.5 billion	2005E - $22 billion
Specialty Coffee 27% / Traditional Coffee 73%	Specialty Coffee 31% / Traditional Coffee 69%	Specialty Coffee 41% / Traditional Coffee 59%
Starbucks Share of Specialty Coffee Market 38%	**Starbucks Share of Specialty Coffee Market 42% (estimate)**	**Starbucks Share of Specialty Coffee Market 50% (estimate)**

Other estimates[a] for the U.S. retail coffee market in 2002:

- In the home, specialty coffee[b] was estimated to be a $3.2 billion business, of which Starbucks was estimated to have a 4% share.

- In the food-service channel, specialty coffee was estimated to be a $5 billion business, of which Starbucks was estimated to have a 5% share.

- In grocery stores, Starbucks was estimated to have a 7.3% share in the ground-coffee category and a 21.7% share in the whole-beans category.

- It was estimated that over the next several years, the overall retail market would grow less than 1% per annum, but growth in the specialty-coffee category would be strong, with compound annual growth rate (CAGR) of 9% to 10%.

- Starbucks' U.S. business was projected to grow at a CAGR of approximately 20% top-line revenue growth.

Source: Adapted from company reports and Lehman Brothers, November 5, 2002.

[a]The value of the retail coffee market was difficult to estimate given the highly fragmented and loosely monitored nature of the market (i.e., specialty coffeehouses, restaurants, delis, kiosks, street carts, grocery and convenience stores, vending machines, etc.).

[b]Specialty coffee includes espresso, cappuccino, latte, café mocha, iced/ice-blended coffee, gourmet coffee (premium whole bean or ground), and blended coffee.

Exhibit 7 Customer Snapshot Scores (North American stores)

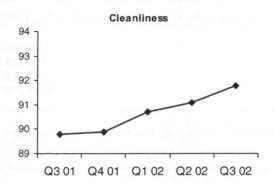

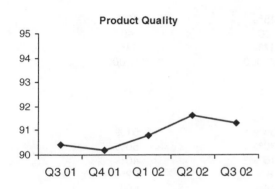

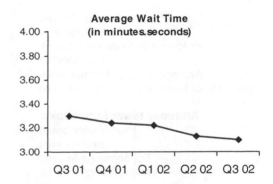

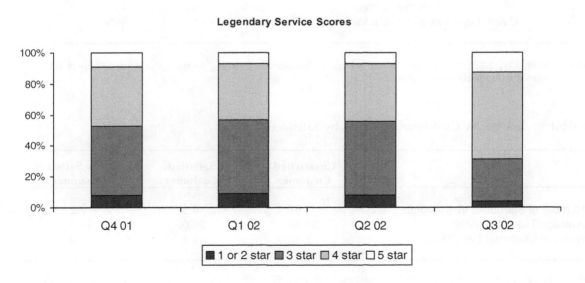

Source: Company information.

Exhibit 8   Starbucks' Customer Retention Information

% of Starbucks' customers who first started visiting Starbucks . . .	
In the past year	27%
1–2 years ago	20%
2–5 years ago	30%
5 or more years ago	23%

Source: Starbucks, 2002. Based on a sample of Starbucks' 2002 customer base.

	New Customers (first visited in past year)	Established Customers (first visited 5+ years ago)
Percent female	45%	49%
Average Age	36	40
Percent with College Degree +	37%	63%
Average income	$65,000	$81,000
Average # cups of coffee/week (includes at home and away from home)	15	19
Attitudes toward Starbucks:		
High-quality brand	34%	51%
Brand I trust	30%	50%
For someone like me	15%	40%
Worth paying more for	8%	32%
Known for specialty coffee	44%	60%
Known as the coffee expert	31%	45%
Best-tasting coffee	20%	31%
Highest-quality coffee	26%	41%
Overall opinion of Starbucks	**25%**	**44%**

Source: Starbucks, 2002. "Attitudes toward Starbucks" measured according to the percent of customers who agreed with the above statements.

Exhibit 9   Starbucks' Customer Behavior, by Satisfaction Level

	Unsatisfied Customer	Satisfied Customer	Highly Satisfied Customer
Number of Starbucks Visits/Month	3.9	4.3	7.2
Average Ticket Size/Visit	$3.88	$4.06	$4.42
Average Customer Life (Years)	1.1	4.4	8.3

Source: Self-reported customer activity from Starbucks survey, 2002.

Exhibit 10   Importance Rankings of Key Attributes in Creating Customer Satisfaction

To be read: *83% of Starbucks' customers rate a clean store as being highly important (90+ on a 100-point scale) in creating customer satisfaction.*

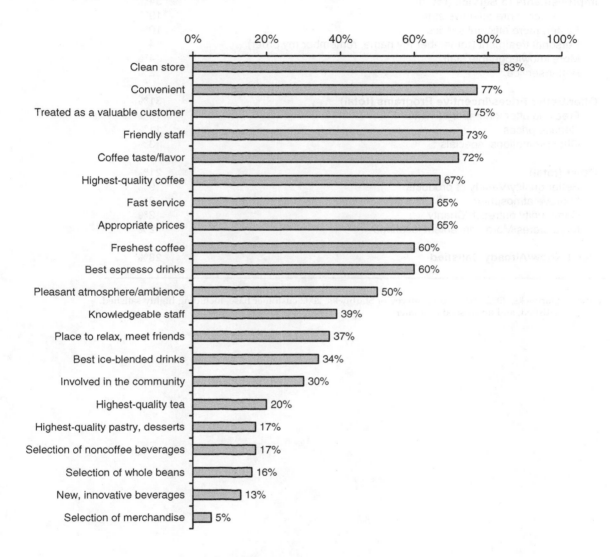

Source: Self-reported customer activity from Starbucks survey, 2002.

Exhibit 11 Factors Driving "Valued Customer" Perceptions

How could Starbucks make you feel more like a valued customer?	% Responses
Improvements to Service (total)	**34%**
Friendlier, more attentive staff	19%
Faster, more efficient service	10%
Personal treatment (remember my name, remember my order)	4%
More knowledgeable staff	4%
Better service	2%
Offer Better Prices/Incentive Programs (total)	**31%**
Free cup after x number of visits	19%
Reduce prices	11%
Offer promotions, specials	3%
Other (total)	**21%**
Better quality/Variety of products	9%
Improve atmosphere	8%
Community outreach/Charity	2%
More stores/More convenient locations	2%
Don't Know/Already Satisfied	**28%**

Source: Starbucks, 2002. Based on a survey of Starbucks' 2002 customer base, including highly satisfied, satisfied, and unsatisfied customers.

Appendix 2

A Classical Linear
Perspective
of New Product
Development

Chapter 15

Introducing new market offerings

IN THIS CHAPTER, WE WILL ADDRESS THE FOLLOWING QUESTIONS:

1 What challenges does a company face in developing new customer-perceived value (CPV) offerings (products and services)?

2 What organisational structures and processes do managers use to develop new market offerings?

3 What are the main stages in developing new market offerings?

4 What is the best way to manage the process of developing new market offerings?

5 What factors affect the rate of diffusion and consumer adoption of newly launched market offerings?

Dyson knows the value of innovation and new-product development. The company's engineers are continuously seeking to innovate and see the establishment of the new design and engineering school in 2010 as a major part of the Dyson mission.

Source: Rex Features.

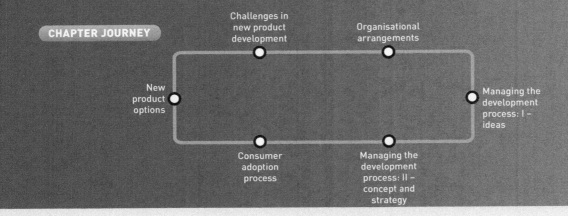

CHAPTER JOURNEY

Challenges in
new product
development

Organisational
arrangements

New
product
options

Managing the
development
process: I –
ideas

Consumer
adoption
process

Managing the
development
process: II –
concept and
strategy

Firms all over the world are challenged by the need in highly competitive buyers' markets to innovate new products. The term 'product' in this chapter, following the argument in Chapter 14, refers to a market offering that is a package of tangible (product) and intangible (service) attributes and benefits. Marketers play a key role in the development of new market offerings by identifying and evaluating new ideas and working with R & D personnel and other functional areas in every stage of development. Companies need to grow their revenue over time by developing new market offerings (products) and by expanding into new markets. New product development shapes the company's future. Improved or replacement products can maintain or build sales; new-to-the-world products can transform industries and companies and change lives. However, the low success rate of new products and services points to the many challenges involved. More and more companies are doing more than just talking about innovation. They are fundamentally changing the way they develop their new CPV market offerings.

Look how Sir James Dyson has and is approaching this all-important task.

To encourage and to improve the speed of development of new product innovations Sir James Dyson, who invented the 'bagless' vacuum cleaner, remains keen to encourage design and engineering education and training, despite having his plans for a school turned down when the UK government rejected his funding bid in 2008. The main Dyson website carries an invitation for young would-be engineers to spend some time with the company and learn what they do.

The dual cyclone 'bagless' cleaner took five years to develop and it was a further two years before Sir James managed to obtain financial backing in Japan. Using income from the Japanese licence, he began to manufacture a new model under his own name in the United Kingdom in 1993. The new concept and colourful design of his cleaners resulted in much popular acclaim and his 'bagless' vacuum cleaners now have 46 per cent of the UK market. In addition to the cleaners, Sir James has a number of other inventions carrying his name, including the Sea Truck, the award-winning Ballbarrow, as well as the Trolleyball, a trolley that makes it easier to launch boats, and the less successful Wheelboat, which can travel at speeds of up to 64 km/h on both land and water. To revive falling sales in the vacuum cleaner business in 2005, Sir James incorporated his Dyson Ball™ technology into a new version of the Dyson vacuum cleaner principle to create the more manoeuvrable

DC25 model. This offers the tried and trusted benefits from Root Cyclone™ technology and is easy to operate as it has no wheels and can pivot easily round awkward corners as it cleans.

However, Dyson has suffered several setbacks on its way to becoming an iconic company. Sir James advises companies to 'Enjoy failure and learn from it. You can never learn from success.' The most notable was the early failure of the company's venture into the washing machine market. After making heavy losses, the company pulled out of the market but it has recently announced a determination to re-enter it. Sir James hopes that his enthusiastic support of the need to train new designers and engineers will do much to reclaim some of the lost appeal following the company's decision for economic reasons to move its manufacturing base from the United Kingdom to Malaysia.[1]

New market offering options

The following sections review several ways in which companies innovate as they strive to achieve an evolving portfolio of new market offerings. Is there one best way to manage this process that involves specific managers and executives? Or perhaps the creation of new products is really about a coordinated effort involving everyone within the company as well as key organisations in the company's value chain.

The celebrated guru Peter Drucker believed that a continual determination to develop new products was a crucial matter for all organisations.

> **If the prime purpose is to create a customer, the business has two – and only two – functions: marketing and innovation. Marketing and innovation produce results. Everything else is a cost.[2]**

Make or buy?

A company can add new products through acquisition or by innovative development. The acquisition route can take three forms. The company can buy other companies, it can acquire patents from other companies, or it can buy a licence or franchise from another company.

However, firms can make only so many acqusitions successfully. At some point, there becomes a pressing need for *organic growth* – the development of new products from within the company. New products can evolve in its own organisation or it can contract with independent researchers or specialist agencies to develop specific new products or provide new technology. Many firms have engaged consultants to provide fresh insights and different points of view.[3]

Types of new product

New products range from completely new items that create an entirely new market at one end, to minor improvements or revisions of existing products at the other. Most new product development activity is devoted to the improvement of existing products. At Sony, over 80 per cent of such activity is modifying and improving existing products. Some of the most successful new consumer products in recent years have been brand extensions.

In many categories, it is becoming increasingly difficult to identify high-potential products that will transform a market. However, continuous innovation to improve customer satisfaction can force competitors to retaliate.[4] Continually launching new products as brand extensions into related offering categories can also broaden the brand meaning. Nike started as a running-shoe manufacturer but now competes in the sports market with all types of athletic shoes, clothing and equipment. Armstrong World Industries moved from selling floor coverings to selling finishes for ceilings and to total interior surface decoration. Product innovation and effective marketing programmes have allowed these firms to expand their 'market footprint'. (See also Chapters 12 and 13.)

Comparatively few new products are truly innovative and so really new. These incur the greatest cost and risk because they are new to both the company and the marketplace.[5] Radical innovations can strain the company's profit performance in the short term, but their successful addition to a company's portfolio of products can create a greater sustainable competitive advantage than existing conventional products. Companies typically must create a strong R & D and marketing partnership to achieve radical innovations.[6] Few reliable techniques exist for estimating demand for these innovations. Focus groups will provide some perspectives on customer interest and need, but marketers may need to use a 'probe and learn' approach based on observation and feedback of early users' experiences and other suitable means.[7]

Many high-tech firms strive for radical innovation.[8] High-tech covers a wide range of industries – telecommunications, computers, consumer electronics, biotech and software. High-tech marketers face a number of challenges in launching their products: high technological uncertainty; high market uncertainty; high competitive volatility; high investment costs; short product life cycles; and difficulty in finding funding sources for risky projects.[9]

Challenges in new product development

New product introductions have accelerated in recent years. In many industries, such as retailing, consumer goods, electronics and cars, among others, the time it takes to introduce new products has been halved.[10] Luxury leather-goods maker Louis Vuitton implemented a new factory format dubbed Pégase so that it could ship fresh collections to its boutiques every six weeks – more than twice as frequently as in the past – offering customers a choice of more new 'looks'.[11]

The innovation imperative

In strong buyers' markets many products fall into decline – as a result of technological developments, severe competition, changing market and societal factors, and customer purchase experiences – making innovation a necessity. Highly innovative firms are able to identify and quickly seize new market opportunities. In a Special Report published by *BusinessWeek*, featuring the top 50 most innovative companies in the world, just four (Nokia at 9; Volkswagen at 18; BMW at 20 and Vodafone at 25) were based in Europe[12] (see Table 15.1). Innovative firms, such as Vodafone, which has a special business unit solely devoted to increasing innovation, creates a positive attitude towards innovation and risk taking, streamlines the innovation process, practises teamwork and allows its people to experiment and even fail. Overall 14 out of the top 50 innovative companies were based in Europe.

Table 15.1 The world's top 50 most innovative companies

2009 rank	2008 rank	Company	HQ country	HQ continent	Stock returns 2005–8 *(in %)	Revenue growth 2005–8 **(%)	Margin growth 2005–8 ***(in %)	Known for its most innovative (%)
1	1	Apple	USA	North America	5.9	30.4	15.8	Product (47%)
2	2	Google	USA	North America	–9.5	52.6	–8.2	Customer experience (26%)
3	3	Toyota Motor	Japan	Asia	–20.7	4.2	–35.9	Process (35%)
4	5	Microsoft	USA	North America	–8	13.5	–1.3	Process (26%)
5	7	Nintendo	Japan	Asia	36.7	61.1	20.6	Product (48%)
6	12	IBM	USA	North America	2.3	4.4	14.3	Process (31%)
7	15	Hewlett-Packard	USA	North America	9.1	10.9	31.6	Process (39%)
8	13	Research In Motion	Canada	North America	24.6	74.1	11.2	Product (53%)
9	10	Nokia	Finland	Europe	–8.3	14	–10.3	Product (38%)
10	23	Wal-Mart Stores	USA	North America	8	9.1	–2.1	Process (49%)
11	11	Amazon.com	USA	North America	2.8	31.2	–4.8	Customer experience (41%)
12	8	Procter & Gamble	USA	North America	4.5	11.7	2.4	Process (27%)
13	6	Tata Group	India	Asia	Private	Private	Private	Product (44%)
14	9	Sony	Japan	Asia	–25.8	3.1	–41.1	Product (40%)
15	19	Reliance Industries	India	Asia	22.6	28.5	11.9	Business model (35%)
16	26	Samsung Electronics	South Korea	Asia	–10.8	10.5	–1.5	Product (41%)
17	4	General Electric	USA	North America	–19.7	10.1	–12.2	Process (36%)
18	NR	Volkswagen	Germany	Europe	–14.4	7.1	33.6	Customer experience (38%)
19	30	McDonald's	USA	North America	25.8	7.2	9.5	Customer experience (55%)
20	14	BMW	Germany	Europe	–14.8	6.9	–14.6	Customer experience (37%)
21	17	Walt Disney	USA	North America	–0.2	6.4	17.2	Customer experience (68%)
22	16	Honda Motor	Japan	Asia	–15.4	4.8	–14.6	Product (47%)
23	27	AT&T	USA	North America	9.9	41.5	9.7	Product (33%)
24	NR	Coca-Cola	USA	North America	6.8	11.4	0.1	Customer experience (38%)
25	47	Vodafone	Britain	Europe	8.6	10.2	NA	Product (25%)
26	NR	Infosys	India	Asia	–8.1	32.4	2	Process (40%)
27	NR	LG Electronics	South Korea	Asia	–5	9.6	17	Product (46%)
28	NR	Telefónica	Spain	Europe	12.2	17	–2	Business model (40%)
29	31	Daimler	Germany	Europe	–11.9	1.5	39	Product (40%)
30	34	Verizon Communications	USA	North America	10.4	11.9	–1	Customer experience (38%)
31	NR	Ford Motor	USA	North America	–32.6	–3.3	NA	Product (36%)
32	35	Cisco Systems	USA	North America	–1.6	14.3	–8	Process (27%)
33	48	Intel	USA	North America	–14.3	–1.1	–8	Process (35%)
34	28	Virgin Group	Britain	Europe	Private	Private	Private	Customer experience (45%)
35	NR	ArcelorMittal	Luxembourg	Europe	–6.7	64.4	–18	Business model (63%)

Table 15.1 (*Continued*)

2009 rank	2008 rank	Company	HQ country	HQ continent	Stock returns 2005–8 *(in %)	Revenue growth 2005–8 **(%)	Margin growth 2005–8 ***(in %)	Known for its most innovative (%)
36	40	HSBC Holdings	Britain	Europe	–6.1	20.3	–18	Process (32%)
37	42	ExxonMobil	USA	North America	14.5	8.8	2	Process (47%)
38	NR	Nestlé	Switzerland	Europe	4.3	6.5	–14	Product (47%)
39	NR	Iberdrola	Spain	Europe	7.5	54	–14	Customer experience (40%)
40	25	Facebook	USA	North America	Private	Private	Private	Customer experience (51%)
41	22	3M	USA	North America	–7.2	6.1	–3	Product (44%)
42	NR	Banco Santander	Spain	Europe	–9.3	11.8	2	Business model (37%)
43	45	Nike	USA	North America	7.1	11.5	–4	Customer experience and Product (36% each)
44	NR	Johnson & Johnson	USA	North America	2.4	8.1	1	Customer experience (42%)
45	49	Southwest Airlines	USA	North America	–19.2	13.3	–25	Customer experience (45%)
46	NR	Lenovo	China	Asia	–14.2	6.6	4	Business model (35%)
47	NR	JPMorgan Chase	USA	North America	–4.4	–2.6	NA	Process (62%)
48	NR	Fiat	Italy	Europe	–13.5	8.5	2	Product (30%)
49	24	Target	USA	North America	–13.5	8.1	2	Customer experience (60%)
50	NR	Royal Dutch Shell	Netherlands	Europe	4.7	14.3	–8	Process (45%)

Notes: Analysis and data provided in collaboration with the innovation practice of the Boston Consulting Group and BCG-ValueScience. Reuters and Compustat were used for financial and industry data and Bloomberg for total shareholder returns. *Stock returns are annualised, 31 Dec. 2005 to 31 Dec. 2008, and account for price appreciation and dividends. **Revenue and operating margin growth are annualised based on 2005–8 fiscal years. Margin growth is earnings before interest and taxes as a percentage of revenues reported in most recent statements or filings. Where possible, quarterly and semiannual data were used to bring performance for pre-June year-ends closer to December 2008. Financial figures were calculated in local currency. ***Calculating three-year compound annual growth rate for operating margins was not possible when either figure was negative. NR: Not Rated.
Source: The World's Fifty Most Innovative Companies (2009), Special Report, BusinessWeek, 9 May. Used with permission of Bloomberg L.P. Copyright © 2012. All rights reserved.

W. L. Gore

W. L. Gore, best known for its durable Gore-Tex outdoor fabric, has innovated breakthrough new products in a number of diverse areas – guitar strings, dental floss, medical devices and fuel cells. It has adopted several principles to guide its new product development. First, it works with potential customers. Its thoracic graft, designed to combat heart disease, was developed in close collaboration with physicians. Second, it lets employees choose projects and appoints few of its actual product leaders and teams. Gore likes to nurture 'passionate champions' who convince others a project is worth their time and commitment. The development of the fuel cell rallied over 100 of the company's 6,000 research associates. Third, Gore gives employees 'dabble' time. All research associates spend 10 per cent of their work hours developing their own ideas. Promising ideas are pushed forward and judged according to a 'Real, Win, Worth' exercise: Is the opportunity real? Can we win? Can we make money? Fourth, it knows when to let go. Sometimes dead ends in one area can spark an innovation in another. Elixir acoustic guitar strings were a result of a failed venture into bike cables. Even successful ventures may need to move on. Glide shred-resistant dental floss was sold to Procter & Gamble because Gore-Tex knew that retailers would want to deal with a company selling a whole family of health care products.[13]

Table 15.2 Kodak CEO Antonio Perez's seven notions of innovation

---

1   See the future through the eyes of your customer.

2   Intellectual property and brand power are key assets.

3   Use digital technology to create tools for customers.

4   Build a championship team, not a group of champions.

5   Innovation is a state of mind.

6   Speed is critical, so push your organisation.

7   Partner up if you're not the best in something.

Source: Based on S. Hamm and W. C. Symonds (2006) Mistakes made on the road to innovation, *BusinessWeek IN Inside Innovation*, November, 27–31.

Companies that fail to develop new products put themselves at risk. Their existing products are vulnerable to changing customer needs and tastes, new technologies, shortened product life cycles and increased domestic and foreign competition. New technologies are especially threatening. Kodak has worked hard to develop a new business model and product-development processes that work well in a digital photography world. Its new goal is to do for photos what Apple does for music by helping people to organise and manage their personal libraries of images. Table 15.2 displays the company's philosophy of innovation and transformation.

New product success

Most established companies focus on *incremental innovation*. Incremental innovation can allow companies to enter new markets by adapting existing market offerings for new customers, use variations on a core product to stay one step ahead of the market, and create interim solutions for industry-wide problems.[14]

Newer companies create *disruptive technologies* that are cheaper and more likely to challenge the competitive space. Established companies can be slow to react or to invest in these disruptive technologies because they threaten their existing business. As a result they may find themselves facing formidable new competitors, and many fail.[15] To avoid this trap, firms must carefully monitor the preferences of both customers and potential customers to discover new viable market opportunities.[16]

What else can a company do to develop successful new products? In a study of US industrial products, the new products specialist agency Cooper & Kleinschmidt found that the main success factor was a unique, superior product. Another key factor is a well-defined product concept. The company carefully defines and assesses the target market, product requirements and benefits before proceeding. Other success factors are technological and marketing synergy, quality of execution in all stages, and market attractiveness.

The study also found that products designed solely for the domestic market tend to show a high failure rate, low market share and low growth. On the other hand, products designed for foreign markets achieved significantly better profits. Yet few of the new products in their study were designed specifically for export markets. A study of small and medium-sized firms in Finland, Germany, Japan, South Korea and South Africa found that committed management leadership resulted in significant success in foreign markets. The implication is that companies should adopt an international focus in designing and developing new products.[17]

New product failure

New product development can be risky. New products continue to fail at a disturbing rate. Recent studies put the rate as high as 50 per cent and potentially as high as 95 per cent in

Table 15.3 Causes of new product failure

1 Market/marketing failure
   • Small size of the potential market
   • No clear product differentiation
   • Poor positioning
   • Misunderstanding of customer needs
2 Financial failure
   • Low return on investment
3 Timing failure
   • Late in the market
   • 'Too early' – market not yet developed
4 Technical failure
   • Product did not work
   • Bad design
5 Organisational failure
   • Poor fit with the organisation's culture
   • Lack of organisational support
6 Environmental failure
   • Government regulations
   • Macroeconomic factors

Source: D. Jain (2001) Managing new-product development for strategic competitive advantage, in D. Iacobucci (ed.), *Kellogg on Marketing*, New York: Wiley, Table 6.1, p. 131. Reproduced with permission.

the United States and 90 per cent in Europe.[18] Failure can result for many reasons: ignored or misinterpreted market research; overestimates of market size; high development costs; poor design; incorrect positioning, ineffective advertising or wrong pricing; insufficient distribution support; and competitors that retaliate fiercely. Some additional factors hindering new product development are:

• **Shortage of important ideas in certain areas.** There may be few ways left to improve some basic market (such as steel or detergents).
• **Fragmented markets.** Companies must aim their new products at smaller market segments, and this can mean lower sales and profits for each product.
• **Social and governmental constraints.** New products must satisfy consumer safety and environmental concerns.
• **Cost of development.** A company must typically generate many ideas to find just one worthy of development and often faces high R & D, manufacturing and marketing costs.
• **Capital shortages.** Some companies with good ideas cannot raise the funds needed to research and launch them.
• **Shorter required development time.** Companies must learn how to compress development time by using new techniques, strategic partners, early concept tests and advanced marketing planning.
• **Shorter product life cycles.** When a new product is successful, rivals are quick to copy it. Sony used to enjoy a three-year lead on its new products. Now Matsushita will copy the product within six months, barely leaving time for Sony to recoup its investment.
• **Hostile reception by the media.** Coca-Cola successfully launched a new brand of mineral water in the United States called Dasani but failed to gain any success in the United Kingdom and was forced to withdraw the product from all distribution outlets. The media criticised Dasani as being 'rebottled tap water' following the broadcast of an episode

of the UK TV hit comedy programme *Only Fools and Horses*, which featured the lead character filling bottles from tap water and branding the product as 'Peckham Springs'.

Failure comes with the task, and truly innovative firms accept it as part of what is required to be successful (see the chapter-opening vignette). Many web companies are the result of failed business ventures and experience numerous failed initiatives as they evolve their products and services.

Initial failure is not always the end of the road for an idea. Recognising that 90 per cent of experimental drugs fail, ethical pharmaceutical companies have established a corporate culture that looks at failure as an inevitable part of discovery, and its scientists are encouraged to look for new uses for compounds that fail at any stage in a human clinical trial.[19]

Organisational arrangements

(See also Chapters 3 and 21.)

Many companies use *customer-driven engineering* to design new market offerings. This strategy attaches high importance to incorporating customer value preferences in the final design.

Xerox

Xerox traditionally developed new products as many firms did in the past: come up with an idea, develop a prototype, and get some consumer feedback. When Xerox researchers first came up with the idea for a dual-engine commercial printer, it decided to first go straight to the consumer to collect feedback before even developing any prototypes. Lucky it did. Although the Xerox team thought customers would want a second engine for special purposes, the fact that the second engine would be a back-up if the main engine failed turned out to be the biggest draw. In introducing the dual-engine Nuvera 288 Digital Perfecting System in April 2007, 'customer-led innovation' was cited as a critical driver. Xerox now believes in **brainstorming**, or 'dreaming with the customer', by combining company experts who know technology with customers who know the problem areas and what the most valuable product features can be. In addition, scientists and engineers are encouraged to meet face to face with customers, in some cases working on-site for a few weeks to see how customers interact with products.[20]

Xerox's popular new dual-engine printer was a response to customers' feedback on the value of a commercial printer with a back-up engine.

Source: Courtesy of the Xerox Corporation.

Unilever

Unilever champions innovation to widen consumer choice and thus give it a consistent competitive edge. Unilever's R & D test kitchen in the Netherlands is one of its centres of culinary expertise. Its chefs create ideas for new products, recipes and product demonstrations for its Foodsolutions professional catering business, as well as providing culinary training for employees. The company aims to provide consumers with choice in terms of product varieties, such as low-fat and low-sugar versions of its ice creams, and low-fat versions of its margarines. Unilever also invests in developing new products with added health and nutrition benefits.

The work is led by the Unilever Food and Health Research Institute, which employs around 450 scientific staff and collaborates with external experts on product innovation and enhancement. The Institute is part of the company's wider commitment to research and development across both its Foods and Home and Personal Care categories. Around 6,000 Unilever scientists and product developers work on the discovery and development of new ingredients and processes for products that provide proven benefits in nutrition, hygiene and personal care for consumers while minimising environmental impacts. In 2007, Unilever invested €868 million in R & D, equivalent to 2.2 per cent of sales.

Here are some examples of recent innovations.

Knorr Vie – increasing fruit and vegetable intake

People the world over do not eat enough fruit and vegetables. The World Health Organization and the UN Food and Agriculture Organization recommend a minimum intake of 400 g/day, but the average is only 100 g/day in developing countries and around 300 g/day in the western world. In 2005 Unilever launched Knorr Vie in Europe, a smoothie-style shot made from concentrated vegetable and fruit juices without any additives. In a 100 ml bottle, it provides half the recommended daily intake of fruit and vegetables. Sales of Knorr Vie fruit and vegetable shots continue to grow, increasing by 67 per cent with around 162 million bottles sold in Europe in 2007.

Ice cream – a choice

Unilever invests around €50 million in ice cream R & D each year, and 40 per cent of this is now devoted to opportunities in the fast-growing health and wellness sector. Ice cream is primarily about pleasure and indulgence, but eaten sensibly it can form part of a nutritionally balanced diet. The company provides a broad range of options, with light, low-fat and no-sugar-added versions. Many brands, such as Cornetto and Magnum, are available in snack size, too, to help with calorie control. Moo is a range of children's ice creams based on the goodness of milk, with each ice cream containing as much calcium as in 100 ml of milk. Since 2006, most of Unilever's ice creams have been labelled with the values for eight nutrients, including energy, protein, fat and sugars.

After successful test marketing in Belgium and Ireland in 2006, Frusì, Unilever's frozen yogurt brand, has been rolled out in France, Italy, the United Kingdom and the Netherlands. Frusì contains 110 calories or less per 100 ml pot and just 2.4 g of fat. Each pot also provides 50 per cent of the recommended daily allowance of vitamin C. The Solero range of products is made with fruit juice and fruit pieces and has a maximum of 99 kilo calories per product.

The company has also developed non-dairy alternatives for ice cream, such as Carte d'Or, Soy and Ades ice creams.

Source: Paul Aresu/PunchStock.

Becel/Flora pro-activ – improving heart health

According to the World Health Organization, heart disease is the principal cause of premature death worldwide. Reducing cholesterol is key to minimising the risks of heart disease. Since 2003 the company has worked in partnership with the World Heart Federation and national groups to promote heart health. Becel/Flora's Love your Heart campaign focuses on raising awareness and has distributed 4.5 million heart health leaflets to consumers and health professionals. It also offers free cholesterol testing, for example in Greece, where 25,000 people have been tested. Becel/Flora pro-activ was originally launched as a spread to help people reduce cholesterol levels – it is proven to lower blood cholesterol levels by 10–15 per cent. The healthy heart foods market is growing fast and the pro-activ range has been extended to include milk drinks and yogurt products. Between 2003 and 2005 sales of pro-activ grew by 40 per cent and it now reaches over 13 million households.

Source: Adapted from Unilever website: www.unilever.com/ourvalues/environment-society/ sustainabledevelopment-report/nutrition-hygiene-wellbeing/nutrition/innovation.asp?print=true. Reproduced with kind permission of Unilever PLC and group companies.

New product development requires senior management to define business domains, product categories and specific criteria for success. Most importantly, they need to be willing to devote significant financial and management support over the medium to long term. For example, Siemens VAI, one of the largest metallurgical firms in the world, took 12 years to develop COREX, a direct reduction technology for iron production that cuts costs and improves the production environment.

Budgeting for new product development

Senior management also need to decide how much to budget for new product development. R & D outcomes are so uncertain that it is difficult to use normal investment criteria. Some companies solve this problem by financing as many projects as possible, hoping to achieve a few winners. Other companies apply a conventional percentage-of-sales figure or spend what the competition spends. Still other companies decide how many successful new products they need and work backwards to estimate the required investment. In either case, new product development is an expensive activity as several ideas need to be generated and screened for their potential in order to identify one strong runner.

Success rates vary. Inventor Sir James Dyson claims he made 5,127 prototypes of his bagless, transparent vacuum cleaner before finally achieving success. However, he does not regret his failures: 'If you want to discover something that other people haven't, you need to do things the wrong way . . . watching why that fails can take you on a completely different path.' Toshiba had great expectations of leading the way when it launched its cutting-edge, high-definition TV in 2007 but by early 2008 that had been comprehensively outsold by the Sony-developed Blu-ray system.[21]

Organising new product development

Companies handle the organisational aspect of new product development in several ways. Many assign responsibility for new ideas to *product managers*. However, product managers are often so busy managing existing lines that they give little thought to new projects other than line extensions.[22] They also lack the specific skills and knowledge needed to develop and critique potential new products. Some companies have a *high-level management committee* charged with reviewing and approving proposals. Large companies often establish a new product development department headed by an executive who has direct access to top management. The department's major responsibilities include generating and screening new ideas, working with the R & D department, and carrying out field testing and final marketing.

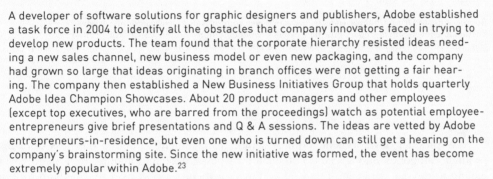

Adobe Systems, Inc.

A developer of software solutions for graphic designers and publishers, Adobe established a task force in 2004 to identify all the obstacles that company innovators faced in trying to develop new products. The team found that the corporate hierarchy resisted ideas needing a new sales channel, new business model or even new packaging, and the company had grown so large that ideas originating in branch offices were not getting a fair hearing. The company then established a New Business Initiatives Group that holds quarterly Adobe Idea Champion Showcases. About 20 product managers and other employees (except top executives, who are barred from the proceedings) watch as potential employee-entrepreneurs give brief presentations and Q & A sessions. The ideas are vetted by Adobe entrepreneurs-in-residence, but even one who is turned down can still get a hearing on the company's brainstorming site. Since the new initiative was formed, the event has become extremely popular within Adobe.[23]

Some companies assign new product development work to **venture teams**, cross-functional groups charged with developing a specific product or business. These 'intrapreneurs' are relieved of their other duties and given a budget, time frame and 'skunkworks' setting. (*Skunkworks* are informal workplaces, sometimes garages, where intrapreneurial teams attempt to develop new products.)

Cross-functional teams can collaborate and use concurrent new offering development to push new offerings to market.[24] Concurrent product development resembles a football match, with team members passing the new market offering back and forth as they head towards the goal.

Many top companies use the *stage-gate system* to manage the innovation process.[25] The system enables companies to strike a considered balance between entrepreneurial creativity and business acumen. They divide the process into stages, at the end of each being a gate or checkpoint. The project leader, working with a cross-functional team, must bring a set of known deliverables to each gate before the project can pass to the next stage. To move from the business plan stage into offering development requires a convincing market research study of consumer needs and interests, a competitive analysis and a technical appraisal. Senior managers review the criteria at each gate to make one of four decisions: *go, kill, hold* or *recycle*. Stage-gate systems make the innovation process visible to all involved and clarify the project leader's and team's responsibilities at each stage.[26]

The stages in the new product development process are shown in Figure 15.1. Many firms have parallel sets of projects working through the process, each at a different stage. Think of the process as a *funnel*: a large number of initial new product ideas and concepts are winnowed down to a few high-potential products that are ultimately launched. However, the process is not always linear. Many firms use a *spiral development process* that recognises the value of returning to an earlier stage to make improvements before moving forward.[27]

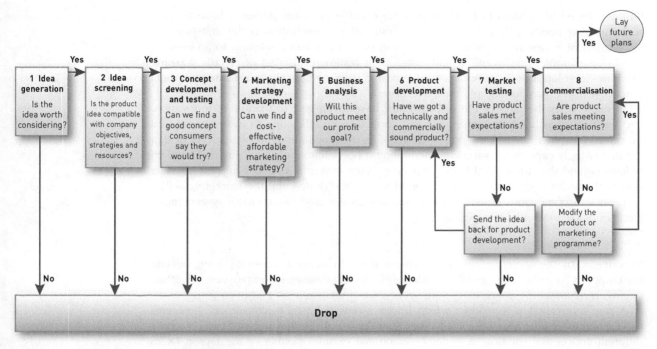

Figure 15.1 The new product development decision process

Managing the development process I: ideas

Process stages

Introducing a new product to the marketplace requires a firm to manage three process activities:

To learn more about the extension of Richard's Branson's Virgin umbrella brand into Virgin Media, set up as rival to Rupert Murdoch's BSkyB, visit www.pearsoned.co.uk/marketingmanagementeurope.

1 managing idea generation and screening;
2 managing activities as selected ideas develop from concepts to strategy, paying particular attention to concept development and timing, marketing strategy development and business analysis;
3 managing the introduction of the new product to the marketplace with particular reference to product development, market testing and commercialisation.

Idea generation

The new product development process starts with the search for ideas. Some marketing experts believe the greatest opportunities and best advantages with new products are found by uncovering the best possible set of unmet customer needs or technological innovations.[28]

Inventions and innovations

The term 'invention' traditionally refers to turning money into ideas; innovation is turning ideas into money. There is a fine line between these two essential new product activities. Patent offices provide a testimony to the creative activity of individuals. Some are just interesting ideas that inventors have patented. Inventions that are taken up by businesses and developed from ideas to products that are capable of being marketed have to meet real customer needs if they are to become innovations. Innovation is the first practical application of a new mode of thought that can generate a better solution to an existing need (for example, the invention and subsequent commercialisation of electric washing machines revolutionised domestic clothes washing) or completely transform traditional practices (in the way mobile phones have done).

In many ways the days of the mad inventor have given way to the age of innovation, and existing ideas are being improved and applied more efficiently to meet known and perceived customer needs. New presentations of existing technology through clever design are increasingly capturing customers' attention and becoming 'must-have' items. The technology behind the Apple iPod is not that new. What makes it a successful new product is how the technology is packaged – in other words, the design and the marketing skills.

Ideas can come from interacting with various groups and using creativity-generating techniques (see the marketing memo).

Interacting with others

Encouraged by the *open innovation* movement, many firms are increasingly going outside the company to gather sources of new ideas,[29] including customers, employees, scientists, engineers, channel members, marketing agencies, top management and even competitors.

A true innovation is a product which brings a new solution to consumers' problems by offering more customer-perceived value than the usual solution or by offering a totally different conceptual solution. A better conventional vacuum cleaner or the Dyson DC25 roller ball model? The Dyson engineers are seeking to make the company's vacuum machines smaller and easier to handle while keeping and if possible improving on their performance. The Gallup Organisation has produced a series of audits or Innobarometers to assist the EU civil service and politicians to audit the degree of innovation evident within the EU member states. The Innobarometer 2009 researched 'the experience of European managers in innovative activities'. It sought to discover the degree of 'innovative readiness in Europe'.

Marketing memo

Ten ways to find great new product ideas

1 Run informal sessions where groups of customers meet with company engineers and designers to discuss problems and needs and brainstorm potential solutions.

2 Allow time off – scouting time – for technical people to discuss their own pet projects.

3 Make a customer brainstorming session a standard feature of plant tours.

4 Survey your customers: find out what they like and dislike in your and your competitors' products.

5 Encourage spontaneous ideas and hold idea-generating away-day meetings with key customers.

6 Use iterative rounds: a group of customers in one room, focusing on identifying problems; and a group of technical people in the next room, listening and brainstorming solutions. Immediately test proposed solutions with the group of customers.

7 Set up a keyword search that routinely scans trade publications in multiple countries for new offering announcements.

8 Treat trade shows as intelligence missions, where you view all that is new in your industry under one roof.

9 Have your technical and marketing people visit your suppliers' labs and spend time with their technical people – find out what's new.

10 Set up an ideas workshop, and make it open and easily accessed. Allow employees to review the ideas and add constructively to them.

Source: Adapted from R. Cooper (1998) *Product Leadership: Creating and Launching Superior New Products*, New York: Basic Books. Copyright © 1998 Robert G. Cooper. Reprinted by permission of Basic Books, a member of the Perseus Books Group.

The research showed that only 10 per cent of the EU-15 companies surveyed were deemed to be 'highly innovative' with over half of their turnover being generated by new products and services. Twice this percentage were found to be 'non-innovator' companies. A country-by-country comparison reveals Portugal, the United Kingdom and Spain as having the highest proportion of innovative companies, while Belgium, Greece and France have the most non-innovator companies.

The latest 2009 Innobarometer survey focused on innovation spending. Table 15.4 presents some summary data showing how some of the long-standing members of the EU have altered their expenditure on innovation as a result of the economic downturn. Based on the Summary Innovation Index, the EU member states fall into the following four groupings:

- **Group 1**: Denmark, Finland, Germany and Sweden all show a performance above that of the EU-27. These countries are the *innovation leaders*.
- **Group 2**: Austria, Belgium, Cyprus, Estonia, France, Ireland, Luxembourg, Netherlands, Slovenia and the UK all show a performance close to that of the EU-27. These countries are *innovation followers*.
- **Group 3**: The performance of the Czech Republic, Greece, Hungary, Italy, Malta, Poland, Slovakia and Spain is below that of the EU-27. These countries are *moderate innovators*.
- **Group 4**: The performance of Bulgaria, Latvia, Lithuania and Romania is well below that of the EU-27. These countries are classified as *catching-up countries*.

Customer needs and wants are the logical place to start the search for new ideas. One-to-one interviews and focus group discussions can explore needs and reactions. Griffin and Hauser suggest that conducting 10–20 in-depth experiential interviews per market segment often uncovers the vast majority of customer needs.[30] But many additional approaches can be profitable (see the marketing memo on p. 624).

The traditional company-centric approach to innovation is giving way to a world in which companies co-create products with customers.[31] Companies are increasingly turning to 'crowd sourcing' to generate new ideas and to create consumer-generated marketing campaigns. Crowd sourcing means inviting the internet community to help create content or software, often with prize money or a celebratory moment involved. This strategy has helped create new offerings and companies such as Wikipedia and Google's popular video website YouTube.

Regular users of a product can be a good source of input when they innovate without the consent or even the knowledge of the companies that produce them. Mountain bikes developed as a result of young people taking their bicycles up to the top of a mountain and riding down. When the bicycles broke, the young riders began building more durable machines and adding such things as motorcycle brakes, improved suspension and accessories. The young cyclists, not the companies, developed these innovations. Some companies, particularly those that want to appeal to young consumers, bring the lead users into their product design process.[32]

Technical companies can learn a great deal by studying customers who make the most advanced use of the company's products and who recognise the need for improvements before other customers do. Employees throughout the company can be a source of ideas for improving production, and development of new products and services. Toyota claims its employees submit 2 million ideas annually (about 35 suggestions per employee), over 85 per cent of which are implemented. Many firms, such as Kodak and Oticon, the Danish hearing aid company, give monetary, holiday or other recognition awards to employees who submit the best ideas. Nokia inducts engineers with at least ten patents into its 'Club 10', recognising them each year in a formal awards ceremony hosted by the company's CEO.[33]

A company can motivate its employees to submit new ideas to an *idea manager* whose name and phone number are widely circulated or by means of the traditional *suggestion box*. Internal brainstorming sessions also can be quite effective – if they are conducted correctly. The marketing memo on p. 625 provides some brainstorming guidelines.

Marketing insight

Reckitt Benckiser's connect-and-develop approach to innovation

Since its creation in 1999 through the merger of the UK's Reckitt & Colman and Benckiser of Germany, although listed on the Netherlands' stock exchange, profits almost doubled by 2004 and the share price has more than doubled since the start of the millennium. In 2006 revenues of €6.5 billion were achieved together with profits of €910 million. The company has achieved this by fostering an innovative approach which has developed several new products that customers never knew they needed. So where do these ideas come from? According to the company's chief executive during this period, Bart Becht:

> Consumers will generally not come up with the next innovation. So we try to have ideas that

target consumers in specific areas. Then we screen them. We go through literally thousands of ideas every quarter. Then we ask consumers about the ideas.

This relentless quest to find and exploit new market offering/product ideas generated over 35 per cent of the company's sales between 2004 and 2007. To ensure that consumers know about these ideas Reckitt Benckiser spends over 12 per cent of its entire revenue on media and significantly more when other aspects of marketing are included such as education programmes, marketing to professionals and PR. The company aims to double its sales by 2012 and double its profit margins to more than 30 per cent.

The key word, never omitted from any Reckitt Benckiser presentation, is 'powerbrands'. In February 2008 there were 18 such brands – the best known in Britain being Veet hair remover, Dettol, Nurofen, Strepsils, Calgon, Vanish, Woolite, Cillit Bang, Harpic, Finish, AirWick, Lemsip and Gaviscon.

An important contributor to the company's success has been its development of a strong innovative culture across all of its branded offerings. The company seeks to generate 40 per cent of its revenues from market offerings/products launched in the previous three years. Its culture values swift decision making, innovation and a focus on financial results. Managers' pay is closely linked to individual performance and – to foster teamwork – to that of their colleagues.

Cillit Bang is a good example of well-known technology that has been given a new set of clothes and a clever slogan which most people remember.

Two of Reckitt Benckiser brands that are markedly imaginative: Cillit Bang '. . . and the dirt is gone!' and 'Dettol kills all known germs stone dead!'

Source: Courtesy of Reckitt Benckiser Group plc.

Sources: M. Urry (2008) Reckitt's strongly flavoured essence, *Financial Times*, 21 January; Cleaning up, *The Economist*, 14 February 2008; B. Laurence (2008) Reckitt Benckiser cleans up with research to boost global sales, *Sunday Times*, 17 February.

Table 15.4 Innovation in Europe: expenditure on innovation, 2006–8

Country	% decreased	% increased	No change
Belgium	9.3	40.2	50.5
Denmark	10.4	35.3	54.4
Germany	5.3	43.1	51.6
Greece	15.0	45.7	39.2
Spain	11.1	28.8	60.0
France	7.0	35.3	57.7
Ireland	14.9	30.8	54.3
Italy	13.4	35.8	50.8
Luxembourg	6.6	31.6	61.8
Netherlands	8.7	35.5	55.7
Austria	5.8	40.8	53.4
Portugal	14.0	37.2	48.8
Finland	6.4	42.7	50.9
Sweden	5.8	54.2	40.0
United Kingdom	9.6	32.9	57.5
EU-15	9.6	38.0	52.4

Source: Adapted from Flash EB No. 267 – 2009 Innobarometer.

Companies can find good ideas by researching the market offerings of competitors and other companies. They can find out what customers like and dislike about competitors' products. They can buy their competitors' products, take them apart, and build better ones. Company sales representatives and intermediaries are a particularly good source of ideas. These groups have first-hand exposure to customers and are often the first to learn about competitive developments.

Marketing memo

Seven ways to draw new ideas from your customers

1 Observe how your customers are using your products.

2 Ask your customers about their problems with your products.

3 Ask your customers about their dream goods. Ask your customers what they want your product to do, even if the ideal sounds impossible.

4 Use a customer advisory board to comment on your company's ideas.

5 Use websites for new ideas. Companies can use specialised search engines to find blogs and postings relevant to their businesses.

6 Form a brand community of enthusiasts who discuss your offerings. Sony engaged in collaborative dialogues with consumers to codevelop Sony's PlayStation 2. LEGO draws on children and influential adult enthusiasts for feedback on new product concepts in the early stages of development.

7 Encourage or challenge your customers to change or improve your products. BMW posted a toolkit on its website to let customers develop ideas using telematics and in-car online services.

Source: From an unpublished paper, P. Kotler (2007) Drawing new ideas from your customers.

Marketing memo

How to run a successful creative problem-solving session

Group creative problem-solving (CPS) sessions have much to recommend them, but also some drawbacks. If carried out incorrectly, they can frustrate and antagonise participants; if carried out correctly, however, they can create insights, ideas and solutions that would have been impossible without everyone's participation. To ensure success, experts recommend the following guidelines:

1   There should be a trained facilitator to guide the session.

2   Participants must feel that they can express themselves freely.

3   Participants must see themselves as collaborators working towards a common goal.

4   Rules need to be set up and followed, so conversations do not stray.

5   Participants must be given proper background preparation and materials so that they can get into the task quickly.

6   Individual sessions before and after the CPS workshop can be useful to think and learn about the topic ahead of time as well as to reflect afterwards on what happened.

7   CPS sessions must lead to a clear plan of action and implementation, so the ideas that materialise can provide tangible value.

8   CPS sessions can do more than just generate ideas – they can help build teams and leave participants better informed and energised.

Source: Based on L. Tischler (2007) Be creative: you have 30 seconds, *Fast Company*, May, 47–50.

Top management can be another major source of ideas. Some company leaders, such as the former CEO of Intel, take personal responsibility for technological innovation in their companies. Ideas can come from inventors, patent lawyers, university and commercial laboratories, industrial consultants, advertising agencies, marketing research firms and industrial publications. However, although ideas can flow from many sources, their chances of receiving serious attention often depend on whether the company has a formal screening system and new offering responsibility.

Table 15.5 summarises data from the 2009 Innovator report on actions taken by companies to integrate activities in support of innovation by the EU-15 countries.

Creativity techniques

The following list presents a sample of techniques for stimulating creativity in individuals and groups.[34]

- **Attribute listing**. List the attributes of an object, such as a screwdriver. Then modify each attribute, such as replacing the wooden handle with plastic, providing torque power, adding different screw heads, and so on.
- **Forced relationships**. List several ideas and consider each in relation to each other one. In designing new office furniture, for example, consider a desk, bookcase and filing cabinet as separate ideas. Then imagine a desk with a built-in bookcase or a desk with built-in files or a bookcase with built-in files.
- **Morphological analysis**. Start with a problem, such as 'getting something from one place to another via a powered vehicle'. Now think of dimensions, such as the type of platform (cart, chair, sling, bed), the medium (air, water, oil, rails), and the power source (compressed air, electric motor, magnetic fields). By listing every possible combination, many new solutions can be generated.
- **Reverse assumption analysis**. List all the normal assumptions about an entity and then reverse them. Instead of assuming that a restaurant has menus, charges for and serves food, reverse each assumption. The new restaurant may decide to serve only what the chef bought that morning and cooked; it may provide some food and charge only for how long the person sits at the table; or it may design an exotic atmosphere and rent out the space to people who bring their own food and beverages.

'I've got a great idea!'

'It won't work here.'

'We've tried it before.'

'This isn't the right time.'

'It can't be done.'

'It's not the way
we do things.'

'We've done all
right without it.'

'It will cost too much.'

'Let's discuss it at
our next meeting.'

Figure 15.2 Forces
fighting new ideas

Source: Jerold Panas,
Young & Partners.
Reproduced with
permission.

Table 15.5 Integration activities in support of innovation in the EU-15

Country	Knowledge management systems	Internal mechanisms for employees to submit innovative ideas	Staff rotations or secondments between different functions	Creation of cross-functional or cross-departmental teams on innovation projects
Belgium	34.9	45.6	40.2	35.2
Denmark	34.7	43.9	51.1	45.1
Germany	24.7	52.3	28.7	44.8
Greece	48.4	42.8	38.0	28.4
Spain	47.1	53.6	51.5	45.0
France	37.8	49.1	39.6	22.8
Ireland	41.3	45.7	45.5	51.9
Italy	24.0	38.2	48.4	26.8
Luxembourg	44.8	55.9	52.2	33.6
Netherlands	32.8	39.3	29.6	33.8
Austria	31.5	53.7	42.7	45.8
Portugal	48.5	43.6	51.6	36.2
Finland	55.4	40.7	53.4	45.6
Sweden	30.9	50.5	47.0	29.3
United Kingdom	40.2	35.2	34.2	37.9

Source: Adapted from Flash EB No. 267 – 2009 Innobarometer.

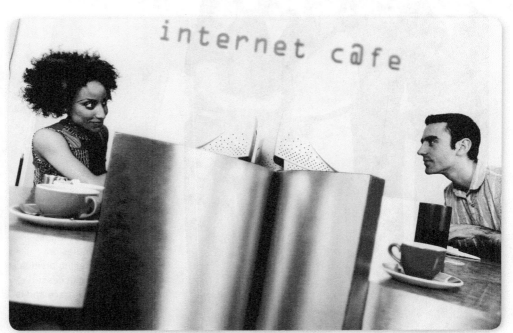

A cyber café: cafeteria + internet
Source: image 100/Corbis.

- **New contexts**. Take familiar processes, such as people-helping services, and put them into a new context. Imagine helping dogs and cats instead of people with day-care service, stress reduction, psychotherapy, animal funerals, and so on. As another example, instead of sending hotel guests to the front desk to check in, greet them at kerb side and use a wireless device to register them.
- **Mind mapping**. Start with a thought, such as a car, write it on a piece of paper, then think of the next thought that comes up (say Mercedes); link it to car, then think of the next association (Germany); and do this with all associations that come up with each new word. Perhaps a whole new idea will materialise.

Increasingly, offering ideas arise from *lateral marketing* that combines two value concepts or ideas to create a new offering. Here are some successful examples:

- petrol station shops = petrol stations + food
- cyber cafés = cafeteria + internet
- cereal bars = cereal + snacking
- Kinder Surprise = confectionery + toy
- Sony Walkman = audio + portable.

Idea screening

In screening ideas the company must avoid two types of error. A *DROP-error* occurs when the company dismisses a good idea. It is extremely easy to find fault with other people's ideas (see Figure 15.2). Some companies shudder when they look back at ideas they dismissed or breathe sighs of relief when they realise how close they came to dropping what eventually became a huge success. This was the case with the hit television show *Friends*.

Friends

An idea that did not get off the storyboard was the pilot for *Friends*, one of the longest-running hit comedies on television. Dismissing an idea that later proves successful is a marketer's nightmare and is called a DROP error.
Source: Warner Brothers TV/ Bright/Crane Pro/The Kobal Collection/Chris Haston.

The US NBC situation comedy *Friends* enjoyed a ten-year run from 1994 to 2004 as a perennial ratings powerhouse. But the show almost did not see the light of day. According to an internal NBC research report, the pilot episode was described as 'not very entertaining, clever or original' and was given a failing grade, scoring 41 out of 100. Ironically, the pilot for an earlier hit sit-com, *Seinfeld,* was also rated 'weak', although the pilot for the medical drama *ER* scored a healthy 91. Courtney Cox's Monica was the *Friends* character who scored best with test audiences, but characters portrayed by Lisa Kudrow and Matthew Perry were deemed to have marginal appeal, and the Rachel, Ross and Joey characters scored even lower. Adults 35 and over in the sample found the characters as a whole 'smug, superficial and self-absorbed'.[35]

Friends was a substantial success in the United Kingdom but another US comedy import, *Pushing Daisies*, while a success in the United States, obtained poor viewing figures elsewhere.

A *GO-error* occurs when the company permits a poor idea to move into development and commercialisation. An *absolute product failure* loses money; its sales do not cover variable costs. A *partial product failure* loses money, but its sales cover all its variable costs and some of its fixed costs. A *relative product failure* yields a profit lower than the company's target rate of return.

The purpose of screening is to drop poor ideas as early as possible. The rationale is that development costs rise substantially with each successive development stage. Most companies require ideas to be described on a standard form for a review. The description states the idea, the target market and the competition, and roughly estimates market size, product price, development time and costs, manufacturing costs and rate of return.

The executive committee then reviews each idea against a set of criteria. Does the product meet a need? Would it offer superior in-use value? Can it be distinctively advertised? Does the company have the necessary know-how and capital? Will the new product deliver the expected sales volume, sales growth and profit? Consumer input may be necessary to tap into marketplace realities.[36]

Management can rate the surviving ideas using a weighted-index method such as that in Table 15.6. The first column lists factors required for successful product launches, and the second column assigns importance weights. The third column scores the product idea on a scale from 0 to 1.0, with 1.0 the highest score. The final step multiplies each factor's importance by the product score to obtain an overall rating. In this example, the product idea scores 0.69, which places it in the 'good idea' level. The purpose of this basic rating device is to promote systematic evaluation and discussion. It is not supposed to make the decision for management.

Table 15.6 Product–idea rating device

Product success requirements	Relative weight (a)	Product score (b)	Product rating (c) = (a) × (b)
Unique or superior product	0.40	0.8	0.32
High performance-to-cost ratio	0.30	0.6	0.18
High marketing euro support	0.20	0.7	0.14
Lack of strong competition	0.10	0.5	0.05
Total	1.00		0.69[a]

[a]Rating scale: .00–.30 poor; .31–.60 fair; .61–.80 good. Minimum acceptance rate: .61

As the idea moves through development, the company will constantly need to revise its estimate of the product's overall probability of success, using the following formula:

Overall probability of success	=	Probability of technical completion	×	Probability of commercialisation given technical completion	×	Probability of economic success given commercialisation

For example, if the three probabilities are estimated as 0.50, 0.65 and 0.74, respectively, the overall probability of success is 0.24. The company must then judge whether this probability is high enough to warrant continued development.

Managing the development process II: concept to strategy

Attractive ideas must be refined into testable product concepts. An *idea* is a possible product that the company might introduce to the market. A *product concept* is a statement of the idea expressed in customer-perceived value terms.

Concept development and testing

Concept development

This can be illustrated by considering concept development as follows: a large food-processing company has the idea of producing a powder to add to milk to increase its nutritional value and taste. This is a product *idea*, but customers do not buy such ideas; they buy product *concepts*.

A product idea can be turned into several concepts. The first question is: who will use this product? The powder can be targeted at infants, children, teenagers, young or middle-aged adults or older adults. Second, what primary benefit should this product provide? Taste, nutrition, refreshment, energy? Third, when will people consume this drink? Breakfast, mid-morning, lunch, mid-afternoon, dinner, late evening? By answering these questions, a company can form several concepts:

- **Concept 1**: an instant breakfast drink for adults who want a quick, nutritious breakfast without preparation.
- **Concept 2**: a tasty snack for children to drink as a midday refreshment.
- **Concept 3**: a health supplement for older adults to drink in the late evening before they go to bed.

Each concept represents a *category concept* that defines the product's competition. An instant breakfast drink would compete against bacon and eggs, breakfast cereals, coffee and pastry, and other breakfast alternatives. A tasty snack drink would compete against soft drinks, fruit juices, sports drinks and other thirst quenchers.

Suppose the instant-breakfast-drink concept looks best. The next task is to show where this powdered product would stand in relationship to other breakfast products. *Perceptual maps* are a visual way to display consumer perceptions and preferences (see Chapter 10). They provide quantitative portrayals of market situations and how consumers see different market products, services and brands. By overlaying consumer preferences with brand perceptions, marketers can reveal 'holes' or 'openings' that suggest unmet customer needs.

Figure 15.3(a) uses the two dimensions of cost and preparation time to create a *product-positioning map* for the breakfast drink. An instant breakfast drink offers low cost and

(a) Product-positioning map (breakfast market)

(b) Brand-positioning map (instant breakfast market)

Figure 15.3 Product and brand positioning

quick preparation. Its nearest competitor is cold cereal or breakfast bars; its most distant competitor is bacon and eggs. These contrasts can help communicate and promote the concept to the market.

Next, the product concept becomes a *brand concept* (see Chapters 12 and 13). Figure 15.3(b) is a *brand-positioning map*, a perceptual map showing the current positions of three existing brands of instant breakfast drinks (A–C), as seen by consumers. It can also be useful to overlay consumer preferences on to the map in terms of their current or desired preferences. Figure 15.3(b) also shows that there are four segments of consumers (1–4) whose preferences are clustered around the points displayed on the map.

The brand-positioning map helps the company to decide how much to charge and how calorific to make its drink. Three segments (1–3) are well served by existing brands (A–C). The company would not want to position itself next to one of those existing brands, unless that brand is weak or inferior or market demand was high enough to be shared. As it turns out, the new brand would be distinctive in the medium-price, medium-calorie market or in the high-price, high-calorie market. There is also a segment of consumers (4) clustered fairly near the medium-price, medium-calorie market, suggesting that it may offer the greatest opportunity.

Concept testing

Concept testing involves presenting the product idea concept, symbolically or physically, to target consumers and getting their reactions. The more the tested concepts resemble the final market offering or experience, the more dependable concept testing is. Concept testing of prototypes can help avoid costly mistakes and can be especially challenging with radically different, innovative products.[37] In the past, creating physical prototypes was costly and time consuming, but today firms can use *rapid prototyping* to design products on a computer, and then produce outline models to show potential customers for their reactions. Companies are also using *virtual reality* to test product concepts. Virtual reality programmes use computers and sensory devices (such as gloves or goggles) to simulate real-time experiences.

Concept testing presents customers with a version of the product concept that they can experience. In the case of Concept 1 in the milk example, the expanded concept might look like this:

> **The market product idea is a powdered mixture added to milk to make an instant breakfast that gives the person all the day's needed nutrition along with good taste and high convenience. The product comes in three flavours (chocolate, vanilla and strawberry) and individual packets, six to a box, at €5 a box.**

After receiving this information, researchers measure the new product dimensions by asking customers to respond to the following types of question:

1 **Communicability and believability**. Are the CPV benefits clear and believable? If the scores are low, the concept must be refined or revised.
2 **Need level**. Does the proposed product solve a problem or fill a need? The stronger the need, the higher the expected customer and consumer interest.
3 **Gap level**. Do any other products currently meet this need and are they satisfactory? The greater the gap, the higher the expected customer interest. Marketers can multiply the need level by the gap level to produce a *need-gap score*. A high score means the customer sees the proposed product as filling a strong need not satisfied by available alternatives.
4 **Customer-perceived value**. Is the potential benefit of the proposed product (using the term product to mean a market offering that is a mix of tangible and intangible benefits) acceptable? The higher the value, the higher is the expected customer and consumer interest.

5   **Purchase intention**. Would the respondents (definitely, probably, probably not, definitely not) buy the product? Customers who answered the first three questions positively should answer 'Definitely' here.

6   **User targets, purchase occasions, purchasing frequency**. Who would use this product, when and how often?

Respondents' answers indicate whether the concept has a strong customer and consumer appeal, what rival market products it competes against, and which customers are the best targets. The need-gap levels and purchase-intention levels can be checked against norms for the market category to see whether the concept appears to be a winner, a long shot or a loser.

Conjoint analysis

This is a scaling technique method for deriving the use benefit values that consumers attach to varying levels of a product's CPV value attributes. It is also called trade-off analysis as it models the relative customer-perceived value of competing products and throws light on how customers decide what CPV value attributes (quality or transaction) can be offset. The technique has become one of the most popular concept development and testing tools. With conjoint analysis, respondents see and rank different hypothetical products formed by combining varying combinations of CPV attributes. Management can then identify the most appealing product's CPV attributes and its estimated market share and profit.

Suppose the new product marketer is considering five CPV attribute benefit design elements:

1   three package designs (A, B, C – see Figure 15.4);
2   three brands (Euro 1, Euro 2 and Euro 3);
3   three retail prices (€1.20, €1.40 and €1.60);
4   a possible seal of approval such as *Good Housekeeping* magazine in the United Kingdom (yes, no); and
5   a possible money-back guarantee (yes, no).

Although the researcher can form 108 possible product concepts (3 × 3 × 3 × 2 × 2), it would be too much to ask customers to rank 108 concepts. A sample of, say, 18 contracting product concepts is feasible, and customers would rank them from the most to the least preferred.

The marketer can then use a statistical software program to discover the customer's preferred utility functions for each of the five attributes (see Figure 15.5). Utility ranges between 0 and 1; the higher the utility, the stronger the consumer's preference for that level of the attribute. Looking at packaging, it is clear that package B is the most favoured, followed by C and then A, which has hardly any perceived utility. The preferred brands are Bissell, K2R and Glory, in that order. The consumer's utility varies inversely with price. A *Good Housekeeping* seal is preferred, but it does not add that much utility and may not be worth the effort to obtain it. A money-back guarantee is strongly preferred.

The consumer's most desired market offering is package design B, brand name Bissell, priced at €1, with a *Good Housekeeping* seal and a money-back guarantee. It is also possible to determine the relative importance of each attribute to this consumer – the difference between the highest and lowest utility level for that attribute. The greater the difference, the more important the attribute. Clearly this consumer sees price and package design as the most important attributes, followed by money-back guarantee, brand name and a *Good Housekeeping* seal.

CPV preference data from a sufficient sample of target consumers help the company to estimate the market share any specific offer is likely to achieve, given any assumptions about competitive responses. Still, the organisation may not launch the market offering

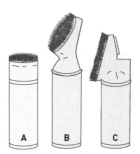

Figure 15.4 Vacuum cleaner samples for conjoint analysis

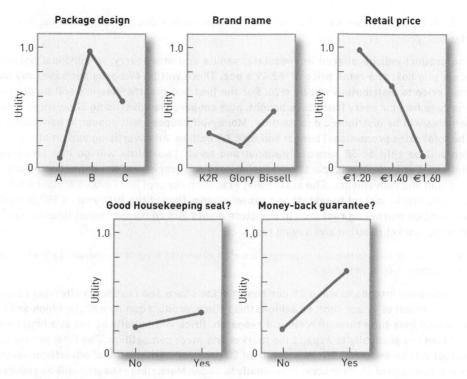

Figure 15.5 Utility functions based on conjoint analysis

that promises to gain the greatest market share, because of cost considerations. The most customer-appealing product (in CPV terms) is not always the most profitable one to bring to market.

Under some conditions, researchers will collect the data without a full-profile description of each product, by presenting two factors at a time. For example, respondents may see a table with three price levels and three package types and indicate which of the nine combinations they would like most, second best and so on. A further table consists of trade-offs between two other variables. The trade-off approach may be easier to use when there are many variables and possible offers. However, it is less realistic in that respondents are focusing on only two variables at a time. Adaptive conjoint analysis (ACA) is a 'hybrid' data collection technique that combines self-explicated importance ratings with pair-wise trade-off tasks.[38]

Marketing strategy development

Following a successful concept test, the firm will develop a preliminary three-part strategy plan for introducing the new product offering to the market. The first part describes the target market's size, structure and behaviour; the planned positioning; and the sales, market share and profit goals sought in the first few years:

> The target market for the instant breakfast drink is families with children who are receptive to a new, convenient, nutritious and inexpensive form of breakfast. The company's brand will be positioned at the higher-price, higher-quality end of the instant breakfast drink category. The company will initially aim to sell 500,000 cases or 10 per cent of the market, with a loss in the first year not exceeding €1.5 million. The second year will aim for 700,000 cases or 14 per cent of the market, with a planned profit of €2.2 million.

The second part outlines the planned price, distribution strategy and marketing budget for the first year:

> The product will be offered in chocolate, vanilla and strawberry in individual packets of six to a box, at a retail price of €2.49 a box. There will be 48 boxes per case, and the case price to distributors will be €24. For the first two months, dealers will be offered one case free for every four cases bought, plus cooperative advertising allowances. Free samples will be distributed door to door. Money-off coupons will appear in newspapers. The total sales promotional budget will be €2.9 million. An advertising budget of €6 million will be split 50:50 between national and local. Two-thirds will go into television and one-third into newspapers. Advertising copy will emphasise the benefit concepts of nutrition and convenience. The advertising execution concept will revolve around a small boy who drinks instant breakfast and grows strong. During the first year, €100,000 will be spent on marketing research to buy store audits and consumer-panel information to monitor market reaction and buying rates.

The third part of the marketing strategy plan describes the long-run sales and profit goals and marketing mix strategy over time:

> The company intends to win a 25 per cent market share and realise an after-tax return on investment of 12 per cent. To achieve this return, product quality will start high and be improved over time through technical research. Price will initially be set at a high level and lowered gradually to expand the market and meet competition. The total promotion budget will be boosted each year by about 20 per cent, with the initial advertising–sales promotion split of 65:35 evolving eventually to 50:50. Marketing research will be reduced to €60,000 per year after the first year.

Business analysis

After management develops the product concept and marketing strategy, it can evaluate the business attractiveness of the proposal. Management needs to prepare sales, cost and profit projections to determine whether they satisfy company objectives. If they do, the concept can move to the development stage. As new information comes in, the business analysis will undergo revision and expansion.

Estimating total sales

Total estimated sales are the sum of estimated first-time sales, replacement sales and repeat sales. Sales estimation methods depend on whether the product is purchased once (such as an engagement ring or retirement home), infrequently or often. For one-time products, sales rise at the beginning, peak, and approach zero as the number of potential buyers is exhausted (see Figure 15.6(a)). If new buyers keep entering the market, the curve will not go down to zero.

Infrequently purchased products – such as cars, toasters and industrial equipment – exhibit replacement cycles dictated by physical wear or obsolescence associated with changing styles, features and performance. Sales forecasting for this category calls for estimating first-time sales and replacement sales separately (see Figure 15.6(b)).

Frequently purchased products, such as consumer and industrial non-durables, have product life cycle sales resembling Figure 15.6(c). The number of first-time buyers initially increases and then decreases as fewer buyers are left (assuming a fixed population). Repeat purchases occur soon, providing the product satisfies some buyers. The sales curve eventually falls to a plateau representing a level of steady repeat-purchase volume; by this time, the product market offering is no longer a new product.

In estimating sales, the manager's first task is to estimate first-time purchases of the new product in each period. To estimate replacement sales, management researches the

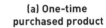
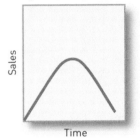

(a) One-time purchased product

(b) Infrequently purchased product

(c) Frequently purchased product

Figure 15.6 Product life cycle sales for three types of product

products' *survival-age distribution* – that is, the number of units that fail in year 1, 2, 3, and so on. The low end of the distribution indicates when the first replacement sales will take place. Replacement sales can be difficult to estimate before the product is in use; some manufacturers therefore base the decision to launch a new offering solely on the estimate of first-time sales.

For a frequently purchased new product, the seller estimates repeat sales as well as first-time sales. A high rate of repeat purchasing means customers are satisfied; sales are likely to stay high even after all first-time purchases take place. The seller should note the percentage of repeat purchases in each repeat-purchase class: those who rebuy once, twice, three times and so on. Some products and brands are bought a few times and then dropped.[39]

Estimating costs and profits

Costs are estimated by the R & D, manufacturing, marketing and finance departments. Table 15.7 illustrates a five-year projection of sales, costs and profits for a company marketing an instant breakfast drink.

Row 1 shows projected sales revenue over the five-year period. The company expects to sell €11,889,000 (approximately 500,000 cases at €24 per case) in the first year. Behind this projection is a set of assumptions about the rate of market growth, the company's market share and the ex-factory price. *Row 2* shows the cost of goods sold, which hovers around 33 per cent of sales revenue. This cost is calculated by estimating the average cost of labour, ingredients and packaging per case. *Row 3* shows the expected gross margin, the difference between sales revenue and cost of goods sold.

Row 4 shows anticipated development costs of €3.5 million, including product development costs, marketing research costs and manufacturing development costs. *Row 5* shows the estimated marketing costs over the five-year period to cover advertising, sales promotion and marketing research, and an amount allocated for sales force coverage and marketing administration. *Row 6* shows the allocated overhead to this new product to cover its share of the cost of executive salaries, heat, light and so on.

Row 7, the gross contribution, is gross margin minus the preceding three costs. *Row 8*, supplementary contribution, lists any change in income from other company products caused by the new product introduction. *Dragalong income* is additional income to them, and *cannibalised income* is reduced income. Table 15.7 assumes no

Table 15.7 Projected five-year cash-flow statement (in €000)

	Year 0	Year 1	Year 2	Year 3	Year 4	Year 5
1 Sales revenue	0	11,889	15,381	19,654	28,253	32,491
2 Cost of goods sold	0	3,981	5,150	6,581	9,461	10,880
3 Gross margin	0	7,908	10,231	13,073	18,792	21,611
4 Development costs	−3,500	0	0	0	0	0
5 Marketing costs	0	8,000	6,460	8,255	11,866	13,646
6 Allocated overhead	0	1,189	1,538	1,965	2,825	3,249
7 Gross contribution	−3,500	−1,281	2,233	2,853	4,101	4,716
8 Supplementary contribution	0	0	0	0	0	0
9 Net contribution	−3,500	−1,281	2,233	2,853	4,101	4,716
10 Discounted contribution (15%)	−3,500	−1,113	1,691	1,877	2,343	2,346
11 Cumulative discounted cash flow	−3,500	−4,613	−2,922	−1,045	1,298	3,644

supplementary contributions. *Row 9* shows net contribution, which in this case is the same as gross contribution. *Row 10* shows discounted contribution – that is, the present value of each future contribution discounted at 15 per cent per annum. For example, the company will not receive €4,716,000 until the fifth year. This amount is worth only €2,345,000 today if the company can earn 15 per cent on its money through other investments.[40]

Finally, *row 11* shows the cumulative discounted cash flow, the accumulation of the annual contributions in row 10. Two things are of central interest. The first is the maximum investment exposure, the highest loss the project can create. The company will be in a maximum loss position of €4,613,000 in year 1. The second is the payback period, the time when the company recovers all its investment, including the built-in return of 15 per cent. The payback period here is about three and a half years. Management must decide whether to risk a maximum investment loss of €4.6 million and a possible payback period of three and a half years.

Companies use other financial measures to evaluate the merit of a new product proposal. The simplest is breakeven analysis, which estimates how many units the company must sell (or how many years it will take) to break even with the given price and cost structure. If management believes sales could easily reach the break-even number, it is likely to develop the new offering.

A more complex method of estimating profit is risk analysis. Here three estimates are obtained (optimistic, pessimistic and most likely) for each uncertain variable affecting profitability, under an assumed marketing environment and marketing strategy for the planning period. The computer simulates possible outcomes and computes a distribution showing the range of possible rates of return and their probabilities.

Managing the development process III: development to commercialisation

Up to now, the new market offering has existed only as a description of an idea, a drawing or a prototype. The next step represents a jump in investment that dwarfs the costs incurred so far. The company will determine whether the new idea can translate into a technically and commercially feasible CPV market offering. If not, the accumulated project cost will be lost, except for any useful information gained in the process.

Product and market development

The job of translating target customer requirements into a working prototype is helped by a set of methods known as *quality function deployment* (QFD). The methodology takes the list of desired *customer attributes* (CAs) generated by market research and turns them into a list of *engineering attributes* (EEs) that engineers can use. For example, customers of a proposed truck may want a certain acceleration rate (CA). Engineers can turn this into the required horsepower and other engineering equivalents (EEs). The methodology measures the trade-offs and costs of meeting customer requirements. A major contribution of QFD is improved communication between marketers, engineers and manufacturing people.[41]

Physical prototypes

The R & D department will develop one or more versions of the core offer product concept. Its goal is to develop a prototype that embodies the key customer-perceived (CPV) attributes and benefits described in the product concept statement. The prototype must perform safely under normal use and conditions and be produced within budgeted manufacturing costs. In the past, developing and manufacturing a successful prototype could take days, weeks, months or even years. The web now permits more rapid prototyping and more flexible development processes.[42] Sophisticated virtual-reality technology is also speeding up the process. By designing and testing product designs through simulation, for example, companies can achieve the flexibility to respond to new information and resolve uncertainties by exploring alternatives.

Boeing

Boeing designed its 777 aircraft on a totally digital basis. Engineers, designers and more than 500 suppliers designed the aircraft on a special computer network without ever making a blueprint on paper. Project partners were connected by an extranet enabling them to communicate, share ideas and work on the design at a distance. A computer-generated 'human' could climb inside the three-dimensional design on-screen to show how difficult maintenance access would be for a live mechanic. Such computer modelling allowed engineers to spot design errors that otherwise would have remained undiscovered until a person began to work on a physical prototype. Avoiding the time and cost of building physical prototypes reduced development time, wastage and rework by 60–90 per cent.[43]

Scientists must not only design the new product's functional characteristics, but also communicate its psychological aspects and brand image through physical cues. How will consumers react to different colours, sizes and weights? Marketers need to supply design and development staff with information about what CPV attributes consumers seek and how consumers judge whether these attributes are present.

Customer tests

When the prototypes are ready, they must be put through rigorous functional tests and customer tests before they enter the marketplace. *Alpha testing* is testing the proposed new product within the firm to see how it performs in different applications. After refining the prototype, the company moves to *beta testing* with customers.[44] Consumer testing can take several forms, from bringing potential customers into a laboratory to giving them samples to use in their homes. Procter & Gamble has on-site labs such as a nappy-testing centre where dozens of mothers bring their babies to be studied. In-home placement tests are common for products ranging from ice cream flavours to new appliances.

How are customer preferences measured? The *rank-order* method asks the consumer to rank the options. The *paired-comparison* method presents pairs of options and asks the consumer which one is preferred in each pair. The *monadic-rating* method asks the consumer to rate each product on a scale so marketers can derive the individual's preference order and levels.

Market testing

After management is satisfied with functional and psychological performance, the new product is ready to be branded, packaged and market tested. In an authentic setting, marketers can learn how large the market is and see how consumers and dealers react to handling, using and repurchasing the new product.

Not all companies undertake market testing but many believe it can yield valuable information about buyers, dealers, marketing programme effectiveness and market potential. The main issues are: how much market testing should be done, and what kind(s)?

The amount of market testing is influenced by the investment cost and risk on the one hand, and the time pressure and research cost on the other. High-investment–high-risk new products, where the chance of failure is high, must be market tested; the cost of the market tests will be an insignificant percentage of total project cost. High-risk products – those that create really new product categories (first instant breakfast drink) or have novel features (first gum-strengthening toothpaste) – warrant more market testing than modified new products (another toothpaste brand).

The amount of market testing may be severely reduced if the company is under great time pressure because the season is just starting, or because competitors are about to launch their brands. The company may prefer the risk of a new product failure to the risk of losing distribution or market penetration on a highly successful product.

Consumer goods market testing

Consumer new product tests seek to estimate four variables: *trial*, *first repeat*, *adoption* and *purchase frequency*. The company hopes to find all these variables at high levels. Many consumers may try the new product but few rebuy it; or it might achieve high permanent adoption but low purchase frequency (e.g. gourmet frozen foods).

Here are four major methods of consumer goods market testing, from least to most costly.

Sales-wave research In sales-wave research, consumers who initially try the new product at no cost are reoffered it, or a competitor's product, at slightly reduced prices. The offer may be made as many as five times (sales waves), while the company notes how many customers selected that product again and their reported level of satisfaction. Sales-wave research can also expose consumers to one or more advertising concepts to measure the impact of that advertising on repeat purchase.

Sales-wave research can be implemented quickly and conducted with a fair amount of security. It can be carried out without final packaging and advertising. However, it does not indicate trial rates that the new product would achieve with different sales promotion incentives, as the consumers are pre-selected to try the product. Nor does it indicate the brand's power to gain distribution and a favourable shelf position.

Simulated test marketing Simulated test marketing calls for finding 30–40 qualified shoppers and questioning them about brand familiarity and preferences in a specific product category. These consumers attend a brief screening of both well-known and new TV commercials or print advertisements. One advertisement promotes the new product but is not singled out for attention. Consumers receive a small amount of money and are invited into a store where they may buy any items. The company notes how many consumers buy the new product brand and competing brands. This provides a measure of the advertisement's relative effectiveness against competing advertisements in stimulating customer trials. Consumers are asked the reasons for their purchases or non-purchases. Those who did not buy the new product are given a free sample. Some weeks later, they are interviewed by phone to determine product attitudes, usage, satisfaction and repurchase intention, and are offered an opportunity to repurchase the new product.

This method gives fairly accurate results on advertising effectiveness and trial rates (and repeat rates if extended) in a much shorter time and at a fraction of the cost of using real test markets. The results are incorporated into new product forecasting models to project ultimate sales levels. Marketing research firms have reported surprisingly accurate predictions of sales levels of new market offerings/products that are subsequently launched in the market.[45] In a world where media and channels have become highly fragmented, however, it will become increasingly hard for simulated test marketing to truly simulate market conditions with only traditional approaches.

Controlled test marketing In controlled test marketing, a research firm manages a panel of stores that will carry new products for a fee. The company with the new product specifies the number of stores and geographic locations it wants to test. The research firm delivers the new product to the participating stores and controls shelf position; number of facings, displays and point-of-purchase promotions; and pricing. Electronic scanners measure sales at checkout. The company can also evaluate the impact of local advertising and promotions.

Controlled test marketing allows the company to test the impact of in-store factors and limited advertising on buying behaviour. A sample of consumers can be interviewed later to give their impressions of the new product. The company does not have to use its own sales force, give trade allowances or 'buy' distribution. However, controlled test marketing provides no information on how to persuade the trade to carry the new product. This technique also exposes the product and its features to competitors' scrutiny.

Test markets The ultimate way to test a new consumer product is to put it into full-scale test markets. The company chooses a few representative cities, and the sales force tries to persuade the trade to carry the new product and give it good shelf exposure. The company puts on a full advertising and promotion campaign similar to the one it would use in national marketing. Test marketing also measures the impact of alternative marketing plans by varying the marketing programme in different cities and or/regions: a full-scale test can cost over €1 million, depending on the number of test areas, the test duration, and the amount of data the company wants to collect.

Management faces several decisions:

- **How many test sites?** Most tests use two to six sites. The greater the possible loss, the greater the number of contending marketing strategies, the greater the regional differences and the greater the chance of test-market interference by competitors, the more sites management should test.
- **Which sites?** Each company must develop selection criteria such as having good media coverage, cooperative chain stores and average competitive activity. How representative the site is of other markets must also be considered.
- **Length of test?** Market tests last anywhere from a few months to a year. The longer the average repurchase period, the longer the test period.
- **What information to collect?** Warehouse shipment data will show gross stock buying but will not indicate weekly sales at the retail level. Store audits will show retail sales and competitors' market shares but will not reveal buyer characteristics. Consumer panels will indicate which people are buying which brands and their loyalty and switching rates. Buyer surveys will yield in-depth information about consumer attitudes, usage and satisfaction.
- **What action to take?** If the test markets show high trial and repurchase rates, the marketer should launch the new product nationally; if a high trial rate and low repurchase rate, redesign or drop the new product; if a low trial rate and high repurchase rate, develop marketing communications to convince more people to try it. If trial and repurchase rates are both low, abandon the new product. Many managers find it difficult to kill a project that created much effort and attention even if they should, resulting in an unfortunate (and typically unsuccessful and expensive) escalation of commitment.[46]

In spite of its benefits, many companies today do not do any test marketing and rely on faster and more economical testing methods. Absolut vodka and Colgate-Palmolive often launch a new product in a set of small 'lead countries' and keep rolling it out if it proves successful.

Business-product market testing

New business products (market offerings) can also benefit from market testing. Expensive industrial new products and new technologies will normally undergo alpha testing (within the company) and beta testing (with outside customers). During beta testing, the company's technical people observe how test customers use the new product, a practice that often exposes unanticipated problems of safety and servicing, and alerts the company to customer training and service support requirements. The company can also observe how much CPV the equipment adds to the customer's operation as a clue to subsequent pricing.

The company will ask test customers to express their purchase intention and other reactions after the test. Companies must interpret beta test results carefully because only a small number of test customers are used, they are not randomly drawn, and tests are somewhat customised to each site. Another risk is that test customers who are unimpressed with the new product may leak unfavourable reports about it.

A second common test method for business new products is to introduce them at trade shows. The company can observe how much interest buyers show in the new product, how they react to various CPV attributes and benefits, and how many express purchase intentions or place orders.

New industrial products can be tested in distributor and dealer display rooms, where they may stand next to the manufacturer's other products and possibly competitors' products. This method yields preference and pricing information in the product's normal selling atmosphere. The disadvantages are that customers might want to place early orders that cannot be fulfilled, and those customers who come in might not represent the target market.

Industrial manufacturers come close to using full test marketing when they give a limited supply of the new product to the sales force to sell in a limited number of areas that receive sales promotion support and printed catalogue sheets.

Commercialisation and new product launch

If the company goes ahead with commercialisation, it will face its largest costs to date.[47] It will need to contract for manufacture or build or rent a full-scale manufacturing facility. Another major cost is marketing. To introduce a major new consumer packaged product into the national market can cost from €25 million to as much as €100 million in advertising, promotion and other marketing communications in the first year. In the introduction of new food products, marketing expenditures typically represent 57 per cent of sales during the first year. Most new product campaigns rely on a sequenced mix of marketing communication tools.

When (timing)

In commercialising a new product, market-entry timing is critical. Suppose a company has almost completed the development work on its new product and learns that a competitor is nearing the end of *its* development work. The company faces three choices:

1 **First entry.** The first firm entering a market usually enjoys the 'first mover advantages' of locking up key distributors and customers and gaining leadership. But if the new product is rushed to market before it is ready, the first entry can backfire.
2 **Parallel entry.** The firm might time its entry to coincide with the competitor's entry. The market may pay more attention when two companies are advertising the new products.[48]
3 **Late entry.** The firm might delay its launch until after the competitor has entered. The competitor will have borne the cost of educating the market, and its new product may reveal faults the late entrant can avoid. The late entrant can also learn the size of the market.

The timing decision requires additional considerations.[49] If a new product replaces an older product, the company might delay the introduction until the old product's stock is drawn down. If the product is seasonal, it might be delayed until the right season arrives; often a new product waits for a 'killer application' to occur. Complicating new product launches, many companies are encountering competitive 'design-arounds' – rivals are imitating inventions but making their own versions just different enough to avoid patent infringement and the need to pay royalties.

Where (geographic strategy)

The company must decide whether to launch the new product in a single locality, a region, several regions, the national market or the international market. Most will develop a planned market roll-out over time. Company size is an important factor here. Small companies will select an attractive site area and put on a blitz campaign, entering other sites one at a time. Large companies will introduce their new product into a whole region and then move to the next region or country. Companies with national distribution networks, such as car companies, will launch their new models in the national market.

Most companies design new products to sell primarily in the domestic market. If the product does well, the company considers exporting to neighbouring countries or the world market, redesigning if necessary. In choosing roll-out markets, the major criteria are: market potential; the company's local reputation; the cost of setting up the supply channels; the cost of communication media; the influence of the area on other areas; and the strength of competition.

With the web connecting near and distant parts of the globe, competition is more likely to cross national borders. Companies are increasingly rolling out new products simultaneously across the globe, rather than nationally or even regionally. However, masterminding a global launch poses challenges, and a sequential roll-out across countries may still be the best option.[50]

To whom (target-market prospects)

Within the roll-out markets, the company must adopt a customer relationship approach and target its initial distribution and marketing communications to appeal to the best prospect groups. The company will have profiled these, and ideally they should be early adopters, heavy users and opinion leaders who can be reached at low cost.[51] Few groups have all these characteristics. The company should rate the various prospect groups on these characteristics and target the best group. The aim is to generate strong sales as soon as possible to attract further prospects.

How (introductory market strategy)

The company must develop an action plan for introducing the new product. Because new product launches often take longer and cost more money than expected, many potentially successful offerings suffer from underfunding. It is important to allocate sufficient time and resource as the new product gains a foothold in the marketplace.[52]

A master of new product introductions, Apple Computers staged a massive marketing blitz in 1998 to launch the iMac, its re-entry into the computer PC business after a hiatus of 14 years. Five years later, Apple struck gold again with the launch of the iPod. The company continues to set a fast pace and in the spring of 2010 launched its iPad which is a design leader as well as a technological first that can provide entertainment and business-related features.

To coordinate the many activities involved in launching a new product, management can use network-planning techniques such as critical path scheduling. This calls for developing a master chart showing the simultaneous and sequential activities that must take place to launch the product. By estimating how much time each activity takes, the planners estimate completion time for the entire project. Any delay in any activity on the critical path – the shortest route to completion – will cause the project to become overdue.[53]

Breakthrough marketing

Apple iPad

Hundreds of people gathered on 1 March 2011 at Apple's flagship store in London to be among the first to buy the company's latest new offering – the iPad – following a delayed launch caused by unexpected high demand in the USA.

Financial Times technology reporter Jonathan Fildes, who went along to the Apple store, said it was besieged with hundreds of people, the police were on hand to keep people in order, and every time a new owner of an iPad emerged they won a cheer from the crowd. He said there was a 'carnival' atmosphere outside the store aided by the appearance of the world's tallest married couple, Wilco van-Kleef and Keisha Bolton, who turned up to promote the Guinness World Records iPad app. Long-standing Apple fan Stephen Fry also turned up to buy a 3G version of the iPad.

Despite the success of the iPad's launch in the USA, some have criticised it for being a closed system that limited what people could do with the books, magazines, music and video they enjoy. The BBC's technology correspondent Rory Cellan-Jones commented that 'magazine editors were enthusing about the possibility of glossy interactive editions which will convince premium advertisers to keep spending'. The tablet-device is also starting to see competition from other devices such as the Dell Streak and the established Archos media tablets. Similar devices that run Google's Android operating system were launched in the final three months of 2010. Two versions of the iPad are available and prices start at £429 including VAT. One model only uses wi-fi to connect to the net and the other can use both wi-fi and 3G mobile technology. The iPad went on sale in continental Europe on 28 May. In the UK mobile phone providers Vodafone, Orange, O2 and 3 revealed details of the price plans for the 3G version which requires a separate micro-Sim card in order to connect to the internet. The 3G version requires owners to buy airtime to use the gadget while out and about.

The iPad is essentially an emotional luxury product – a purchase that is not really needed, as many of the things the iPad offers can be done on other gadgets such as phones and laptops. Most of the people in the world do not interact with content, they just consume it, and the iPad is a great device for consuming content but not great for creating it. In an attempt to retain its lead in the market with the iPad in the face of emerging competition, Apple launched its iPad 2 in March 2011. The new device features front- and back-facing cameras and a gyroscope, and is dramatically faster with a A5 dual-core processor. It is 33 per cent thinner at 8.8 mm – slimmer than the iPhone 4. It also fell in weight from 1.5 pounds to 1.3 pounds.

Source: BBC, 28 February 2010; *Financial Times*, 2 March 2011 (Tim Bradshaw, Chris Nuttall and Shannon Bond).

The campaign for the Apple iPad was a masterful new product introduction that helped it quickly achieve a dominant market share.
Source: Chris Batson/Alamy.

The consumer adoption process

Adoption is an individual's decision to become a regular user of a product. The *consumer adoption process* is followed by the *consumer loyalty process*, which is the concern of the established producer. Years ago, new product marketers used a *mass market approach* to launch products, which had two main drawbacks: it called for heavy marketing expenditures, and it wasted many exposures. These drawbacks led to a second approach, *heavy-user target marketing*. This approach makes sense, provided that heavy users are identifiable and are early adopters. However, even within the heavy-user group, many heavy users are loyal to existing brands. New product marketers now aim at early adopters and use the theory of innovation diffusion and customer adoption to identify them. Mozilla launched its new Firefox 3 Web browser in the United Kingdom in the summer of 2008 and hopes to build on its encouraging market share in Europe with its new software that is claimed to be more user friendly and adaptable than Microsoft's Internet Explorer's web browser.

Stages in the adoption process

An **innovation** is any good, service or idea that someone *perceives* as new, no matter how long its history. Innovations take time to spread. Rogers defines the **innovation diffusion process** as 'the spread of a new idea from its source of invention or creation to its ultimate users or adopters'.[54] The consumer adoption process tracks the steps an individual takes from first hearing about an innovation to its final adoption.[55]

Adopters of new products move through five stages:

1 **Awareness**. The consumer becomes aware of the innovation but lacks information about it.
2 **Interest**. The consumer is stimulated to seek information about the innovation.
3 **Evaluation**. The consumer considers whether to try the innovation.
4 **Trial**. The consumer tries the innovation to improve his or her estimate of its value.
5 **Adoption**. The consumer decides to make full and regular use of the innovation.

The new product marketer should facilitate movement through these stages. A portable electric dishwasher manufacturer might discover that many customers are stuck in the interest stage; they do not buy because of their uncertainty and the large investment cost.[56] But these same customers would be willing to use an electric dishwasher on a trial basis for a small monthly fee. The manufacturer should consider offering a trial-use plan with an option to buy.

Factors influencing the adoption process

Marketers recognise the following characteristics of the adoption process: differences in individual readiness to try new products; the effect of personal influence; differing rates of adoption; and differences in organisations' readiness to try new products. Some researchers are focusing on use-diffusion processes as a complement to adoption process models, to see how consumers actually use new products.[57]

Readiness to try new products and personal influence

Rogers[58] defines a person's level of innovativeness as 'the degree to which an individual is relatively earlier in adopting new ideas than the other members of his social system'. In each product area, there are pioneers and early adopters. Some people are the first to adopt new clothing fashions or new appliances; some doctors are the first to prescribe new medicines; some farmers are the first to adopt new farming methods.[59] People fall

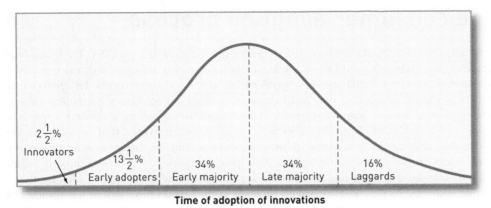

Time of adoption of innovations

Figure 15.7 Adopter categorisation on the basis of relative time of adoption of innovations
Source: Adapted with the permission of Free Press, a Division of Simon & Schuster, Inc., from *Diffusion of Innovations*, Third Edition by Everett M. Rogers. Copyright © 1962, 1971, 1983 by The Free Press. All rights reserved.

into the adopter categories shown in Figure 15.7. After a slow start, an increasing number of people adopt the innovation, the number reaches a peak, and then it diminishes as fewer non-adopters remain. The five adopter groups differ in their value orientations and their motives for adopting or resisting the new product.[60]

- **Innovators**: technology enthusiasts; they are venturesome and enjoy tinkering with new products and mastering their intricacies. In return for low prices, they are happy to conduct alpha and beta testing and report on early weaknesses.
- **Early adopters**: opinion leaders who carefully search for new technologies that might give them a dramatic competitive advantage. They are less price sensitive and willing to adopt the product if given personalised solutions and good service support.
- **Early majority**: deliberate pragmatists who adopt the new technology when its benefits are proven and a lot of adoption has already taken place. They make up the mainstream market.
- **Late majority**: sceptical conservatives who are risk averse, technology shy and price sensitive.
- **Laggards**: tradition bound and resist the innovation until they find that the status quo is no longer defensible.

Each group must be approached with a different type of marketing if the firm wants to move its innovation through the stages of the full product life cycle.[61]

Personal influence is the effect one person has on another's attitude or purchase probability. Its significance is greater in some situations and for some individuals than others, and it is more important in the evaluation stage than the other stages. It has more influence on late adopters than early adopters and is more important in risky situations.

Companies often target innovators and early adopters with product introductions. For Vespa scooters, the Italian company Piaggio has hired models to go around cafés and clubs to publicise the new scooters.[62]

Characteristics of the innovation

Some products are an instant success (rollerblades), whereas others take a long time to gain acceptance (diesel engine cars).[63] Five characteristics influence the rate of adoption of an innovation. These are considered in relation to personal video recorders (PVRs) for home use.

The first characteristic is *relative advantage* – the degree to which the innovation appears superior to existing products. The greater the perceived relative advantage of using a PVR, say for easily recording favourite shows, pausing live TV or skipping commercials, the more quickly it will be adopted. The second is *compatibility* – the degree to which the innovation matches the values and experiences of the individuals. PVRs, for example, are highly compatible with the preferences of avid television watchers. Third is *complexity* – the degree to which the innovation is difficult to understand or use. PVRs are somewhat complex and will therefore take a slightly longer time to penetrate into home use. Fourth is *divisibility* – the degree to which the innovation can be tried on a limited basis. This provides a sizeable challenge for PVRs – sampling can only occur in a retail store or perhaps a friend's house. Fifth is *communicability* – the degree to which the benefits of use are observable or describable to others. The fact that PVRs have some clear advantages can help create interest and curiosity.

Other characteristics that influence the rate of adoption include cost, risk and uncertainty; scientific credibility and social approval. The new product marketer must research all these factors and give the key ones maximum attention in designing the new product and marketing programme.

Organisations' readiness to adopt innovations

The creator of a new teaching method would want to identify innovative schools. The producer of a new piece of medical equipment would want to identify innovative hospitals. Adoption is associated with variables in the organisation's environment (community progressiveness, community income), the organisation itself (size, profits, pressure to change) and the administrators (education level, age, sophistication). Other forces come into play in trying to get a product adopted into organisations that receive the bulk of their funding from the government, such as state schools and hospitals in the United Kingdom. A controversial or innovative new product offering can be seriously damaged by negative public opinion.

SUMMARY

1 Once a company has segmented the market, chosen its target customer groups and identified their needs, and determined its desired market positioning, it is ready to develop and launch appropriate new market offerings. Marketing should participate with other departments in every stage of the development of new value offerings.

2 Successful new product/market offering development requires the company to establish an effective organisation for managing the process. Traditionally, companies have chosen to use product managers, new product managers, new product committees, new product departments or new product venture teams. Increasingly, companies are adopting cross-functional teams, connecting to individuals and organisations outside the company, and developing multiple market offerings as they accept that the right CPV requires the coordinated effort of all internal and external parties.

3 Eight stages take place in the new product/ market offering development process: idea generation, screening, concept development and testing, marketing strategy development, business analysis, product/offer development, market testing and commercialisation. At each stage, the company must determine whether the idea should be dropped or moved to the next stage.

4 The consumer adoption process is the process by which customers learn about new market offerings, try them, and adopt or reject them. Today many marketers are targeting heavy users and early adopters of new products, because both groups can be reached by specific media and tend to be opinion leaders. The consumer adoption process is influenced by many factors beyond the marketer's control, including consumers' and organisations' willingness to try new market offerings.

APPLICATIONS

Marketing debate

Whom should you target with new products? Some new product experts maintain that getting close to customers through intensive research is the only way to develop successful new products. Other experts disagree and maintain that customers cannot possibly provide useful feedback on what they don't know and cannot provide insights that will lead to breakthrough products.

Take a position: Consumer research is critical to new product development *versus* Consumer research may not be all that helpful in new product development.

Marketing discussion

Think about the last new product you bought. How do you think its success will be affected by the five characteristics of an innovation: relative advantage, compatibility, complexity, divisibility and communicability?

REFERENCES

[1]James Dyson (2002) Business whirlwind, *BBC Business News*, 5 February; P. Marsh (2006) Dyson keeps its wash day hopes alive, *Financial Times*, 27 June; Sir James Dyson and family (2008) *Sunday Times* online, 27 April.

[2]For some scholarly reviews, see P. Drucker (2001) *The Essential Drucker*, Oxford: Butterworth-Heinemann; E. Dahan and J. R. Hauser (2002) Product development: managing a dispersed process, in B. Weitz and R. Wensley (eds), *Handbook of Marketing*, London: Sage, 179–222.

[3]P. Cameron (2007) Innovation and new product development: Sky1 – a mini case study, *Marketing Review*, 7(4), 313–23; S. J. Carson (2007) When to give up control of outsourced new product development, *Journal of Marketing*, January, 71(1), 49–66.

[4]Don't laugh at gilded butterflies, *The Economist*, 24 April 2004, 71. For some academic discussion of the effects of new product introduction on markets, see H. J. Van Heerde, C. F. Mela and P. Manchanda (2004) The dynamic effect of innovation on market structure, *Journal of Marketing Research*, 41 (May), 166–83.

[5]S. Min, M. U. Kalwani and W. T. Robinson (2006) Market pioneer and early follower survival risks: a contingency of new versus incrementally new-product markets, *Journal of Marketing*, 70 (January), 15–33; C. P. Moreau, A. B. Markman and D. R. Lehmann (2001) What is it? Category flexibility and consumers' response to really new products, *Journal of Consumer Research*, 27 (March), 489–98; M. Zhao, S. Hoeffler and D. W. Dahl (2009) The role of imagination-focused visualization on new product evaluation, *Journal of Marketing Research (JMR)*, 46(I) 1, 46–55.

[6]S. Wuyts, S. Dutta and S. Stremersch (2004) Portfolios of interfirm agreements in technology-intensive markets: consequences for innovation and profitability, *Journal of Marketing*, 68 (April), 88–100; H. Perks, K. Kahn and C. Zhang (2009) An empirical evaluation of R & D–marketing NPD integration in Chinese firms: the Guanxi effect, *Journal of Product Innovation Management*, 26(6), 640–51.

[7]C. Hui-Chun (2010) Linkage community based innovation and speed to market: the mediating role of new product development

process, *International Journal of Organizational Innovation*, 2(4), 49–60.

[8]A. Sood and G. J. Tellis (2005) Technological evolution and radical innovation, *Journal of Marketing*, 69 (July), 152–68; P. N. Golder, R. Shacham and D. Mitra (2009) Innovations' origins: when, by whom, and how are radical innovations developed?, *Marketing Science*, 28(1), 166–79; V. Story, S. Hart and L. O'Malley (2009) Relational resources and competences for radical product innovation, *Journal of Marketing Management*, 25(6), 461–81.

[9]See S. E. Reid and U. de Brentani (2010) Market vision and market visioning competence: impact on early performance for radically new, high-tech products, *Journal of Product Innovation Management*, 27(4), 500–18.

[10]M. R. Murray and D. Wilemon (2010) The impact of changing markets and competition on the NPD speed/market success relationship, *International Journal of Innovation Management*, 14(5), 841–70; M. R. Millson and D. Wilemon (2010) The impact of changing markets and competition on the NPD speed/market success relationship, *International Journal of Innovation Management*, 14(5), 841–70.

[11]C. Passariello (2006) Brand new bag: Louis Vuitton tries modern methods on factory lines, *Wall Street Journal*, 9 October.

[12]The world's fifty most innovative companies (2007) Special Report, *BusinessWeek*, 9 May.

[13]B. Weiners (2004) Gore-Tex tackles the great indoors, *Business 2.0*, April, 32; A. Harrington (2003) Who's afraid of a new product?, *Fortune*, 10 November, 189–92; W. L. Gore & Associates, *The Times* online, 11 March.

[14]D. G. McKendrick and J. B. Wade (2010) Frequent incremental change, organizational size, and mortality in high-technology competition, *Industrial & Corporate Change*, 19(3), 613–39.

[15]D. Lange, S. Boivie and A. D. Henderson (2009) The parenting paradox: how multibusiness diversifiers endorse disruptive technologies while their corporate children struggle. *Academy of Management Journal*, 52(1), 179–98.

[16]T-J. Chang, W. C. Chen, L. Wen-Chiang, L. Z. Lin and J. S-K. Chiu (2010) The impact of market orientation on customer knowledge development and NPD success, *International Journal of Innovation and Technology Management*, 7(4), 303–27.

[17]S. Salomo, E. J. Keinschmidt, J. Elko and U. de Brentani (2010) Managing new product development teams in a globally dispersed NPD program, *Journal of Product Innovation Management*, 27(7), 955–71; U. de Brentani, E. J. Kleinschmidt and S. Salomo (2010) Success in global new product development: impact of strategy and the behavioral environment of the firm, *Journal of Product Innovation Management*, 27(2), 143–60.

[18]S. Ogama and F. T. Pillar (2006) Reducing the risks of new-product development, *MIT Sloan Management Review*, Winter, 65–71; J. Hlavacek, C. Maxwell and J. Williams, Jr (2009) Learn from new product failures, *Research Technology Management*, 52(4), 31–9.

[19]T. N. Burton (2004) By learning from failures Lilly keeps drug pipelines full, *Wall Street Journal*, 21 April.

[20]N. Byrnes (2007) Xerox's new design team customers, *BusinessWeek*, 7 May, 71.

[21]D. Sabbagh (2008) Blu-ray delivers fatal sting to rival in battle of high definition DVD, *The Times*, 19 February.

[22]B. S. Blichfeldt (2005) On the development of brand and line extensions, *Journal of Brand Management*, 12(3), 177–90; A.E. Akgün, H. Keskin and J. C. Byrne (2010) Procedural justice climate in new product development teams: antecedents and consequences, *Journal of Product Innovation Management*, 27(7), 1096–111.

[23]D. Sacks, C. Salter, A. Deutschmann and S. Kirsner (2007) Innovation scouts, *Fast Company*, May, 90.

[24]H. Ernst, W. D. and C. Rübsaamen (2010) Sales, marketing, and research-and-development cooperation across new product development stages: implications for success, *Journal of Marketing*, 74(5), 80–92; R. Bunduchi (2009) Implementing best practices to support creativity in NPD cross-functional teams, *International Journal of Innovation Management*, 13(4), 537–54; C. Nakata and S. Im (2010) Spurring cross-functional integration for higher new product performance: a group effectiveness perspective, *Journal of Product Innovation Management*, 27(4), 554–71; G. Gemser and M. A. A. M. Leenders, Managing cross-functional cooperation for new product development success, *Long Range Planning*, 44(1), 26–41.

[25]J. Grönlund, D. Sjödin and F. J. Rönnberg (2010) Open innovation and the stage-gate process: a revised model for new product development, *California Management Review*, 52(3), 106–31.

[26]K. van Oorschot, K. Sengupta, H. Akkermans and L. van Wassenhove (2010) Get fat fast: surviving stage-gate® in NPD, *Journal of Product Innovation Management*, 27(6), 828–39.

[27]An alternative approach to the funnel process advocates 'rocketing'. See D. Nichols, *Return on Ideas*, Chichester: John Wiley & Sons.

[28]J. Hauser, G. J. Tellis and A. Griffin (2006) Research on innovation: a review and agenda for Marketing Science, *Marketing Science*, 25 (November–December), 687–717.

[29]H. Chesbrough (2006) *Open Business Models: How to Thrive in the New Innovation Landscape*, Boston, MA: Harvard University Press; E. Von Hipple (2005) *Democratizing Innovation*, Cambridge, MA: MIT Press; B. Helm (2005) Inside a white-hot idea factory, *BusinessWeek*, 15 January, 72–1; C. K. Prahalad and V. Ramaswamy (2004) *The Future of Competition: Co-creating Unique Value with Customers*, Boston, MA: Harvard University Press.

[30]A. J. Griffin and J. Hauser (1993) The voice of the customer, *Marketing Science*, Winter, 1–27.

[31]P. C. Hoenbein and R. F. Cammarano (2006) Customers at work, *Marketing Management*, January–February, 26–31.

[32]P. Seybold (2007) Customer-controlled innovation: collaboration with customers is transforming product-development strategies and unlocking new ways for companies to innovate, *Optimize*, 6(2), 26.

[33]*BusinessWeek* (2007) op. cit.

[34]D. W. Dahl and P. Moreau (2002) The influence and value of analogical thinking during new-product ideation, *Journal of Marketing Research*, 39 (February), 47–60; M. Goodman (1995) *Creative Management*, Hemel Hempstead: Prentice Hall International.

[35]See www.smokinggun.com.

[36]O. Toubia and L. Flores (2007) Adaptive idea screening using consumers, *Marketing Science*, 26 (May–June), 342–60.

[37]Hoeffler (2003) op. cit.; Dahl and Moreau (2002) op. cit.; J. Sharan, J. Kamel and M. Jamil (2007) A multibrand concept-testing methodology for new product strategy, *Journal of Product Management*, 24(1), 34–51.

[38]For additional information see D. Bakken and C. L. Frazier (2006) Conjoint analysis: understanding consumer decision making, in R. Grover and M. Vriens (eds), *The Handbook of Marketing Research*, Thousand Oaks, CA: Sage; V. T. Rao and J. R. Hauser (2004) Conjoint analysis, related modeling and application, in Y. Wind and P. E. Green (eds), *Market Research and Modeling: Progress and Prospects – A Tribute to Paul Green*, New York: Springer, 141–68.

[39]P. N. Golder and G. J. Tellis (1997) Will it ever fly? Modeling the takeoff of really new durables, *Marketing Science*, 16(3), 256–70.

[40]The present value (V) of a future sum (I) to be received t years from today and discounted at the interest rate (r) is given by $V = I_t/(1 + r)^t$. Thus €4,716,000/(1.15)^5 = €2,345,000.

[41]See L. R. Guinta and N. C. Praizler (1993) *The QFD Book: The Team Approach to Solving Problems and Satisfying Customers through Quality Function Deployment*, New York: AMACOM.

[42]Peters (1997) *The Circle of Innovation*, New York: Alfred A. Knopf; K. Zheng Zhou, Y. Chi Kin and D. K. Tse (2005) The effects of strategic orientations on technology and market-based breakthrough innovations, *Journal of Marketing*, 2, 42–60.

[43]M. Iansiti and A. MacCormack (1997) Developing products on internet time, *Harvard Business Review*, September–October, 108–17.

[44]Peters (1997) op. cit., 96.

[45]K. J. Clancy, P. C. Krieg and M. M. Wolf (2005) *Marketing New Products Successfully: Using Simulated Test Marketing Methodology*, New York: Lexington Books.

[46]E. Biyalogorski, W. Boulding and R. Staelin (2006) Stuck in the past: why managers persist with new-product failures, *Journal of Marketing*, 70 (April), 108–21.

[47]R. Chandy, B. Hopstaken, O. Narasimhan and J. Prabhu (2006) From invention to innovation: conversion in product development, *Journal of Marketing Research*, 43 (August), 404–508.

[48]R. Prins and P. C. Verhoef (2007) Marketing communication drivers of adoption timing of a new e-service among existing customers, *Journal of Marketing*, 71 (April), 169–83.

[49]For further discussion, see Y. Wu, S. Balasubramanian and V. Mahajan (2004) When is a pre-announced new product likely to be

delayed?, *Journal of Marketing*, 68 (April), 104–13; R. Srinivasan, G. L. Lilien and A. Rangaswamy (2004) First in first out? The effects of network externalities on pioneer survival, *Journal of Marketing*, 68 (January), 41–58; B. L. Bayus, S. Jain and A. Rao (2001) Consequences: an analysis of truth or vaporware and new-product announcements, *Journal of Marketing Research*, February, 3–13.

[50]K. Gielens and J.-B. E. M. Steenkamp (2007) Drivers of consumer acceptance of new packaged goods: an investigation across products and countries, *International Journal of Research in Marketing*, 97–111.

[51]P. Kotler and G. Zaltman (1976) Targeting prospects for a new product, *Journal of Advertising Research*, February, 7–20; E. Gummesson (1998) Implementation requires a relationship marketing paradigm, *Journal of the Academy of Marketing Science*, 26(3), 242–9.

[52]M. Leslie and C. A. Holloway (2006) The sales learning curve, *Harvard Business Review*, July–August, 114–23.

[53]For details, see K. G. Lockyer (1984) *Critical Path Analysis and Other Project Network Techniques*, London: Pitman. Also see A. Rangasway and G. L. Lilien (1997) Software tools for new product development, *Journal of Marketing Research*, February, 177–84.

[54]The following discussion is based on E. M. Rogers (1962) *Diffusion of Innovations*, New York: Free Press. Also see the 3rd edn published in 1973.

[55]C. P. Moreau, D. R. Lehmann and A. B. Markman (2001) Entrenched knowledge structures and consumer response to new products, *Journal of Marketing Research*, 38 (February), 14–29.

[56]J. T. Gourville (2006) Eager sellers and stony buyers, *Harvard Business Review*, June, 99–106.

[57]C.-F. Shih and A. Ventkatesh (2004) Beyond adoption: development and application of a use-diffusion model, *Journal of Marketing*, 68 (January), 59–72.

[58]E. M. Rogers (1962) *Diffusion of Innovations*, New York: Free Press, 1962; see also his 3rd edn published in 1983.

[59]M. Hertzenstein, S. S. Posavac and J. J. Brakuz (2007) Adoption of new and really new products: the effects of self regulation systems and risk salience, *Journal of Marketing Research*, 44 (May), 251–60; C. Van den Bulte and Y. V. Joshi (2007) New-product diffusion with influentials and imitators, *Marketing Science*, 26 (May–June), 400–21; Hoeffler (2003) op. cit.

[60]Rogers (1962) op. cit. 192; G. A. Moore (1999) *Crossing the Chasm: Marketing and Selling High-Tech Products to Mainstream Customers*, New York: HarperBusiness.

[61]A. Parasuraman and C. L. Colby (2001) *Techno-ready Marketing*, New York: Free Press; Mohr (2001) op. cit.

[62]M. M. Hall, Selling by stealth, *Business Life*, November, 51–55.

[63]B. Kamrad, S. S. Lele, A. Siddique and R. J. Thomas (2005) Innovation diffusion uncertainty, advertising and pricing policies, *European Journal of Operational Research*, 164(3), 829–50; G. B. Voss, M. Montoya-Weiss and Z. G. Voss (2006) Aligning innovation with market characteristics in the non-profit professional theatre industry, *Journal of Marketing Research*, 43(2), 296–302; M. J. Brand and E. K. R. E. Hurzingh (2008) Into the drivers of innovation adoption: what is the impact of the current level of adoption?, *European Journal of Innovation Management*, 11(1), 5–21; A. Murray and D. Demick (2006) Wine retailing in Ireland: the diffusion of innovation, *International Journal of Wine Marketing*, 18(3); G. Yaleinkaya (2008) A culture-based approach to understanding the adoption and diffusion of new products across countries, *International Marketing Review*, 25(2), 202–14.